The *Essay Connection*

The Essay Connection

READINGS FOR WRITERS

Seventh Edition

Lynn Z. Bloom
The University of Connecticut

Houghton Mifflin Company
Boston   New York

Executive Editor: Suzanne Phelps Weir
Senior Development Editor: Sarah Helyar Smith
Associate Project Editor: Lindsay Frost
Editorial Assistant: Teresa Huang
Senior Production/Design Coordinator: Carol Merrigan
Senior Manufacturing Coordinator: Jane Spelman

Text, Photo, and Cartoon Credits appear on pages 625–30, which constitute a
continuation of the copyright page.

Printed in the U.S.A.

Library of Congress Catalog Card Number: 2002116638

ISBN: 0-618-33591-9

23456789-QF-07 06 05 04 03

Contents

   > "I spend a great deal of my time thinking about the power of language —the way it can evoke an emotion, a visual image, a complex idea, or a simple truth. Language is the tool of my trade. And I use them all—all the Englishes I grew up with."

   > "Close reading," for the sighted as well as the blind, "is a task of discovery, recovery, uncovering, detection, dissection—struggle. Sometimes close reading is even painful."

   > "I learned from the age of two or three that any room in our house, at any time of day, was there to read in, or to be read to."

   > "The essayist . . . can . . . be any sort of person, according to his mood or his subject matter—philosopher, scold, jester, raconteur, confidant, pundit, devil's advocate, enthusiast."

   > "As our baby grows more into her own life, so I recover mine, but it is an ambiguous blessing. With one hand I drag the pen across the page and with the other, the other hand, I cannot let go of hers."

   > "For the survivor, writing is not a profession, but an occupation, a duty. Camus calls it 'an honor.' . . . Not to transmit an experience is to betray it. . . . [I write] to help the dead vanquish death."

❈ *Student writings.*

Part II   Determining Ideas in a Sequence   117

Part V Controversy in Context: *Implications of World Terrorism and World Peace* AN ARGUMENT CASEBOOK   523

RABIN: *"There is one universal message which can embrace the entire world . . . the message of the Sanctity of Life."*

ARAFAT: *"Peace . . . is an absolute human asset that allows an individual to freely develop his individuality unbound by any regional, religious or ethnic fetters."*

MANDELA: *"We shall, together, rejoice in a common victory over racism, apartheid and white minority rule."*

DE KLERK: *"The coming election . . . will not be about apartheid or armed struggle. It will be about future peace and stability, about progress and prosperity, about nation-building."*

"'To live the full life . . . one must have the courage to bear the responsibility of the needs of others . . . one must want to bear this responsibility.'"

"Who can predict what other great scientific conquests and developments these [Mayan] people could have achieved, if they had not been conquered in blood and fire, and subjected to an ethnocide that affected nearly 50 million people in the course of 500 years."

"Peace . . . starts with each one of us. When we have inner peace, we can be at peace with those around us. When our community is in a state of peace, it can share that peace with neighbouring communities. . . ."

"We are honoured, in the name of all women, that women have been honoured especially for their part in leading a non-violent movement for a just and peaceful society. Compassion is more important than intellect, in calling forth the love that the work of peace needs. . . ."

Topical Table of Contents

❀ *Student writings.*

3 Families/Heritage

8 Human and Civil Rights

9 Society and Community

10 Turning Points/Watershed Experiences

Preface: Transforming a Textbook for a Transformed World

Like the symbolic bridge on the cover of this book, *The Essay Connection* attempts to span the distance between reading and writing and bring the two activities closer together. To read, to write is to be human, to find the voice, the power, and the authority to communicate. As we become immersed in a new century, the importance of communication—clear, elegant, to the point—has never been more important.

During the spring and summer of 2001 I had been revising *The Essay Connection* to prepare for the seventh edition, the one you are now reading. Textbooks tend to get larger over time; editors retain readers' favorite high-calorie essays even as they add new ones that explore innovative ideas and bring the book up to date. Eventually the book becomes unwieldy, so I decided to put this version on a diet. Rather than eliminate essays here and there that would destroy the integrity of each chapter's focus, I decided to remove the two essay clusters of literary criticism.

Then came September 11, 2001, the attack on the Pentagon and the collapse of the twin towers of the World Trade Center—and the world changed. I quickly realized that in this new millennium, a collection of readings intended to stimulate students' reasoned discussion and critical thinking and writing had to respond to this cataclysmic event. Elie Wiesel explains in "Why I Write" his reasons for witnessing the Holocaust in everything he writes: "Not to transmit an experience is to betray it. . . . [I write, he says,] to help the dead vanquish death." I could ask the student readers of *The Essay Connection* to do no less—not because of morbid reasons, or a sentimental desire to memorialize a past that will never come again, but as an ethical response to a world we did not ask for, but will nevertheless have to live in. So, in the twinkling of an eye, I reinstated the two last chapters—newly configured as a mini-casebook on "Controversy in Context: Implications of World Terrorism and World Peace." A balanced, ethical perspective on international terrorism that avoids polarizing "us vs. them" attitudes (the chapter "Terrorism") is complemented by a chapter on world peace, comprised of excerpts from Nobel Peace Prize speeches and brief biographies of the international spectrum of recipients, ranging from Jimmy Carter to Nelson Mandela and the 14th Dalai Lama. High moral principles can emerge even in times of trauma—often in response to the challenges of trauma itself. Their talks, like their works, offer beacons of faith, hope, and good will. If, as Franklin Roosevelt said, "the only thing we have to fear is fear itself," these chapters reinforce a value system that helps readers to lead lives governed by principles that bring out the best rather than the worst of our common humanity.

Writing," observes Toni Morrison, "is discovery; it's talking deep within myself." In *The Essay Connection* the voices in this conversation are many and varied—professional writers, experts in a variety of fields, and students with their own abilities and experiences, side by side. Their good writing is good reading in itself, provocative, elegant, engaging, sometimes incendiary. This writing is also a stimulus to critical thinking, ethical reflection, social and political analysis, humorous commentary—and decision-making, on how to live in the present and to make meaningful contributions to life in the newly uncertain future. These are among the many possibilities when students write essays of their own.

What's Familiar, What's New

The seventh edition of *The Essay Connection* incorporates a number of new features and new essays into the format and essays retained from the sixth edition.

Photographs

To reinforce—and enliven—the sense of what is both contemporary and timeless, the essays in this edition of *The Essay Connection* are now supplemented by forty-two photographs and two cartoons. These range from depictions of historical events (President Abraham Lincoln arriving at Gettysburg to deliver his address); to the timeless (the periodic table); to the contemporary (the precariously poised skeleton of the World Trade Center). Many of the photographs show people engaging in familiar activities—studying, reading, writing, fishing, working, learning, arguing, loving. Just as there is no one right way to read a text, for much of the meaning resides in the reader and in the context in which any given work is read, there is no single way to look at, to "read" a photograph. Thus these pictures can be interpreted literally, and metaphorically as well; the added layers of meaning are enriched by juxtaposition.

Readings

The Essay Connection includes eighty-three readings: lively, varied, timely, provocative—and of high literary quality. Here you will find forty-eight favorite essays, modern classics and contemporary works, and thirty-one new selections, including one poem, by a wide range of writers, discussed in later sections of this Preface. The first four chapters address aspects of the writing process—Speaking, Reading, Writing, and Revising. The next nine chapters are organized according to familiar rhetorical principles— Narration, Process Analysis, Cause and Effect, Description, Division and Classification, Definition, Comparison and Contrast, Deductive and Inductive Arguments, and Emotional and Ethical Appeals. The last two chapters, new to this edition, comprise an argument casebook on terrorism and peace.

Mini-Casebook: *Controversy in Context: Implications of World Terrorism and World Peace*

The most distinctive change in this edition is the addition of *Controversy in Context: Implications of World Terrorism and World Peace*. This contains fifteen core readings to help students find a foothold and a focus on the most significant issues of our still-young century: war—of a kind scarcely imaginable to most of us before September 11, 2001—and, as the antithesis of international terrorism, world peace. As is true of any earth-shaking event, we looked at our world one way before the attacks on the World Trade Center and the Pentagon, and afterward have come to see it another way— in fact, many other ways. Has the world changed? Or have we? Does our sojourn involve nation with (or against) nation; culture with (or against) culture; technology, economy, or ideology with (or against) its counterpart? What changes will terrorist attacks, and the infinite possibilities of future terrorism, specific or vague, make in the ways we live our lives, plan for our futures, look at our neighbors, our friends—and our enemies? What can we, as individuals and as a nation, do to balance the free and open nature of our hospitable society against needs for protection and security? How can we avoid suspicion and paranoia, dividing the world into "us" against "them," and nevertheless be on guard—but against what?

"We tell ourselves stories in order to live," says Joan Didion; these readings incorporate true stories by eyewitnesses and those more distant, and analyses from a wide range of literary, philosophical, historical, political, and economic perspectives. The readings on international terrorism by poet Seamus Heaney ("Horace and the Thunder"), artist Laurie Fendrich ("History Overcomes Stories"), historian Bernard Lewis ("What Went Wrong"), political scientist Mark Juergensmeyer (from *Terror in the Mind of God*), and economist David Carr ("The Futility of 'Homeland Defense'") provide a starting point from which students can begin to find their way through the tangle of evidence and interpretations—the messiness of life into which reflective writing can hope to bring some order.

It would be inappropriate to allow this book to end on the shrill note of sirens, falling planes, and terror in the skies, on the streets, in our hearts. In this Casebook section it is fitting to balance terrorism against tranquility, war against peace, national interests against global, humanitarian concerns. Consequently, the "World Peace" chapter consists of excerpts from Nobel

Peace Prize acceptance speeches by men and women of global distinction who form an international spectrum of the brave, the bold, the morally beautiful: Jimmy Carter (U.S.A.); Kofi Annan (Egypt); Yitzak Rabin (Israel) and Yasser Arafat (Palestine); Nelson Mandela and Frederik Willem de Klerk (South Africa); Aung San Suu Kyi (Mayanmar/Burma); Rigoberta Menchú (Maya); the 14th Dalai Lama (Tibet); Betty Williams (Northern Ireland); and the organization Doctors Without Borders. Goodness, selflessness, and adherence to high moral principles, as the lives and works of the Nobel Peace Prize winners reveal, can emerge even in times of trauma—often in response to the challenges of trauma itself. Their talks, like their works, are beacons of faith, hope, goodwill, and moral courage.

Familiar Essays

Forty-eight favorite essays have been retained from the previous edition, by authors such as Frederick Douglass, Stephen Jay Gould, Martin Luther King, Jr., Maxine Hong Kingston, Anne Lamott, Nancy Mairs, Richard Rodriguez, Scott Russell Sanders, Eudora Welty, E. B. White, and Elie Wiesel. Amy Tan's "Mother Tongue" opens the readings, a happy balance to the concluding discussions of terrorism and peace, which are themselves affirmations of the essential values of civilization, and of life itself. Although humorous works by authors such as David Foster Wallace, Garry Trudeau, and Judy Brady signal the book's upbeat tone, they do not diminish the seriousness of its essential concerns or its underlying ethical stance.

New Authors

Among the works new to this edition of *The Essay Connection* are those by Anne Fadiman, Atul Gawande, Seamus Heaney, Linda Hogan, Garrett Hongo, Stephen King, Georgina Kleege, Anna Quindlen, Oliver Sacks, Esmeralda Santiago, Deborah Tannen, David Foster Wallace—and the constellation of Nobel Peace Prize winners identified above. Representations of women, cultures, and writers who address issues of class, race, ethnicity, and disabilities have been maintained in this edition, as in its predecessor.

Student Authors

Ten essays are by students, although a total of twenty-three pieces of student work appear because an additional thirteen excerpts from student notebooks are combined in one selection. Although all the works were written when the students were enrolled in American universities, these students have come from places throughout the United States—from Connecticut to Pennsylvania to Minnesota to Colorado—and all over the world, from Jamaica to England to Pakistan to the People's Republic of China.

These distinguished student writings discuss a variety of compelling subjects: coming to terms with oneself; with one's parents—whether known

or unknown, living, or dead—with one's ethnic, political, or religious background—African-American, Asian, Chinese, Jewish, Muslim, Native American—and with one's social and economic class. The student writings also
deal with understanding the endangered: hospital patients in medical crisis,
family farms in economic distress, migrant workers, ethnic minorities in a
hostile climate. And there are topics provoking irreverence—learning to
drive, encountering bad cooking, detesting housework. All provide examples of excellent writing that other students should find meaningful as
models in form, technique, and substance. Moreover, the section on revising concludes with ten drafts of student Mary Ruffin's work—writing
process made visible—culminating in the stunning essay, "Mama's Smoke."

Whole Essays

To maintain the integrity of the authors' style and structure as well as their
arguments, most of these essays are printed in their entirety, averaging
three to eight pages; a number are chapters or self-contained sections of
books. Footnotes are the authors' own.

Varied Subjects, Varied Disciplines

The essays in this edition are drawn from many sources, mostly engaging
and distinguished contemporary writing on varied subjects, as indicated in
the Topical Table of Contents, with a leavening of classics by such authors
as Swift, Lincoln, and Darwin. The exception is the collection of excerpts
from the speeches of recent winners of the Nobel Peace Prize—the point
here is to emphasize the common elements of their values and work,
rather than to address the political conditions in their respective countries
and cultures that triggered their activism, imprisonment, or exile. *The Essay
Connection* includes, not surprisingly, the work of professional writers distinguished in a variety of genres: *essayists*—classical and newly-canonical
—Anne Fadiman, Linda Hogan, Scott Russell Sanders, and E. B. White; *crea-
tive non-fiction* writers Georgina Kleege, Anne Lamott, William Least Heat-
Moon, Nancy Mairs, and David Foster Wallace; *autobiographers* Frederick
Douglass, Garrett Hongo, Eric Liu, Richard Rodriguez, and Esmeralda
Santiago; *novelists* Louise Erdrich, Stephen King, Maxine Hong Kingston,
Amy Tan, and Eudora Welty; *journalists* Gelareh Asayesh, David Carr, Anna
Quindlen, and Charles M. Young; *satirist* Jonathan Swift; *playwright* Ntozake
Shange; and *composition scholars* Donald Murray and John Trimbur.
    Other fine essayists are specialists in other professions: *physicians* (Atul
Gawande, Spencer Nadler, Oliver Sacks, Abraham Verghese); *scientists and
science writers* (Natalie Angier, Isaac Asimov, Charles Darwin, Stephen Jay
Gould); *religious leaders* (the Dalai Lama, Martin Luther King, Jr.); *political
leaders* (Kofi Annan, Jimmy Carter, Frederik Willem de Klerk, Thomas Jefferson, Aung San Suu Kyi, Abraham Lincoln, Nelson Mandela, Yitzak Rabin);

political activists (Rigoberta Menchú, Betty Williams); *artist* (Laurie Fendrich); *political scientist* (Mark Juergensmeyer); *cartoonist* (Garry Trudeau); *linguist* (Deborah Tannen); *psychologist* (Howard Gardner); *economist* (Robert Reich); *computer scientist* (Paul De Palma); *sociologist* (Stephanie Coontz); *futuristic businessman* (Stewart Brand); and *literary critic* (Gilbert Highet).

Critical Thinking, Reading, and Writing

Many readings are clustered thematically to encourage dialogue and debate among authors, and among student readers and writers. For example, the chapter *Narration* emphasizes the significance of family, race, and class; and the development of new insight into people (including one-self) and places revisited as one comes into maturity. The chapter *Process Analysis* clusters essays on processes involved in science and technology, and includes two on processes reflecting racial and family heritage—harvesting and learning English as a second language. The chapter *Cause and Effect* has three essays on education as it pertains to both margin and mainstream; four also focus on confusion of causes with effects as they influence public policy—and private lives. The chapter *Division and Classification* extends the subject to totalitarian, democratic, and postcolonial societies; and to comparative differences between men and women. The chapter *Description* has two essays on unusual aspects of the natural environment and two describing common medical conditions—obesity and alcoholism—and their devastating effects on the afflicted and on their families. The chapter *Definition* deals with the nature, meaning, and representation of two iconic underclass figures: Judy Brady's *wife* in "I Want a Wife" and Nancy Mairs's *cripple*. In the chapter *Comparison and Contrast* an essay by Stephen Jay Gould on evolution refracts with Darwin's "Understanding Natural Selection" and Howard Gardner's "Who Owns Intelligence?" in the chapter *Definition*. The chapter *Appealing to Reason* debates civil rights and civil disobedience; and issues of social class and poverty, domestic and world-wide. The chapter *Appealing to Emotion and Ethics* features essays on power and oppression, winning and losing, life and death—of individuals, nations, teams, farms, and families

Blended Types

In difficulty the essays range from the easily accessible to the more complicated. They have been chosen to represent the common essay types indicated by the chapter divisions, from narration and definition through argumentation and analysis of contemporary social and political phenomena. Nevertheless, because these are real essays by real writers, who use whatever writing techniques suit their purpose, there are very few "pure" types. An essay of definition, such as Nancy Mairs's "On Being a Cripple," for instance, includes comparisons and contrasts, narrative, description, illustration and example. The entire essay, like many others in this book, could in fact be considered an argument for the author's point of view. Consequently, although the introduction to each essay and the study questions following it often encourage the reader to view the work through the lens of its designated category in the Table of Contents, the reader should be aware that the category represents only one segment of a broad spectrum of possible readings.

Conceptual Context of the Book

The Essay Connection is informed conceptually by extensive classroom testing of the essays and writing assignments included here. The book is likewise informed by contemporary scholarship in the dynamic fields of composition, literary and rhetorical theory, autobiography, creative non-fiction, and the teaching of writing. The language of *The Essay Connection* intentionally remains clear and reader-friendly.

Apparatus

The essays are placed in a context of materials designed to encourage reading, critical thinking, and good writing. The following materials reinforce *The Essay Connection*'s pervasive emphasis on the process(es) of writing.

- **Tables of Contents.** The main Table of Contents reflects the book's organization, by types of writing. The Topical Table of Contents offers an alternative organization by subject ("Science and Technology," "Society and Community," "Human and Civil Rights," "Turning Points/Watershed Experiences," etc.). This arrangement provides many alternative possibilities for discussion and writing.
- **Chapter introductions.** These have two purposes. They define the particular type of writing in the chapter and identify its purposes (descriptions, process analysis, etc.), uses, and typical forms. They also discuss the rhetorical strategies authors typically use in that type of writing (for instance, how to structure an argument to engage a hostile audience), illustrated with reference to essays in the chapter. For quick reference, these strategies are summarized in a checklist at the end of the introduction.
- **Biographical introductions to each author.** These capsule biographies are intended to transform the writers from names into real people. Casebook excepted, they focus on how and why the authors write (in general, and in particular) and how and for what audience they wrote the work that appears in *The Essay Connection*.
- **Study questions.** These follow most of the essays, and are intended to encourage thoughtful discussion and writing about Content, rhetorical Strategies/Structures, Language, and larger concerns. It should be

noted that whatever is said or implied about writing processes in Chapters 1–4, or in the study questions and suggestions for writing following most selections, may be adapted as the instructor or student chooses to accommodate either individual or collaborative writing. Likewise, any of the study questions or suggestions for writing may be augmented by consulting a variety of materials in print or on Web sites. They are too numerous and change too rapidly to be identified in connection with each subject, except some that address the global issues of international terrorism and peace in the chapters "Terrorism" and "World Peace."

- **Suggestions for Writing.** Each set of study questions ends with suggestions For Writing pertinent to a given work. Most chapters end with a longer list of Additional Topics for Writing that encourage dialogue and debate about essays related in theme, technique, or mode. Often these incorporate strategic suggestions, derived from extensive classroom testing, for writing particular papers and for avoiding potential pitfalls.
- **Glossary.** The Glossary (613–23) defines terms useful in discussing writing (analogy, argument, voice) with illustrations from the essays.

Acknowledgments

The Essay Connection has, in some ways, been in the making for the past forty years, and I am particularly indebted to the candid commentaries of multitudes of writing students over the years whose preferences and perplexities have so significantly influenced both the shape and emphasis of this volume, and the process-oriented style of teaching that it reflects. I am likewise grateful for the thoughtful suggestions of writing teachers throughout the country who have commented on earlier editions of *The Essay Connection:* Susan Ahern, Chris Anderson, Lois Avery, Lynn Dianne Beene, Judith L. Bleicher, Ruth Brown, Larry Carver, Roberta Clipper-Sethi, Pat Coldwell, Lou-Ann Crouther, Sara G. Cutting, Daryl Dance, Kathleen Danker, Sydney Darby, Charla Dawson, Charles R. Duke, Janet E. Eber, Mark Edelstein, Michael Emery, Julie Farrar, John Faulkner, David Fleming, J. Vail Foy, Tahita Fulkerson, Donald Gadow, Edgar Glenn, Howard Hamrick, Sandra Hanson, Joanne M. Haynes, Nan Johnson, Daniel Kasowitz, Robert Keane, Walter Klarner, Jane Knopf, Geraldine Lash, Kay Litten, Arline March, Jay K. Maurer, John M. McCluskey, Charles C. Nash, Alvin W. Past, Linda H. Peterson, Elaine Roberts, Susan Romano, Edna H. Shaw, Charles Smith, Louise Z. Smith, William E. Smith, Jeffrey Smitten, Bill Stiffler, Barbara Stout, Karen Sylte, Frank Thornton, Barbara Turnwall, Arthur Wagner, Tom Waldrep, Cheryl L. Ware, Rosemary Winslow, Margarett Ann Wolfe, Marie Woolf, Pauline Wheeler, and Richard Yarborough.

I am also indebted to the reviewers who contributed to the development of the seventh edition of *The Essay Connection:* Melissa Castino, Inver Hills Community College; Devan Cook, Boise State University; John Faulkner, Ohio University–Lancaster; Ray Foster, Scottsdale Community College; Sara McLaughlin, Texas Tech University; Lisa M. Stepanski, Emmanuel College; Frances A. Tolliver, University of Arkansas, Little Rock; and Rosemary Winslow, The Catholic University of America.

To Donald M. Murray who contributed an original text on revising, and Margaret Whitt who contributed student essays, I am particularly grateful. I also owe special thanks to the students who contributed to this volume not only their essays but comments on how they wrote them: Rosalind Bradley Coles, Ann Upperco Dolman, Art Greenwood, Jasmine Innerarity, Sumbul Khan, Amy Jo Keifer, Kristin King, Richard Loftus, Leslie S. Moore, Matt Nocton, Mary Ruffin, Stephen E. Ryan, Barbara Schofield, Jenny Spinner, Asiya S. Tschannerl, Betty J. Walker, Cheryl Watanabe, Tammy Weast, Jill Woolley, Susan Yoritomo, and Ning Yu.

Laird Bloom (yes, he is my son), a graduate of Massachusetts Institute of Technology, read much of the manuscript of early editions with uncommonly good critical understanding and the parodist's intolerance of the banal and the sentimental. Bard Bloom (yes, he too is my son), also an MIT grad, provided computer expertise. Their work has been later supplemented by the intelligence, ingenuity, wit, classroom experience, and technological sophistication of a series of superb research assistants: Kathrine Aydelott; Sarah Aguiar; Matthew Simpson; Laura Tharp; Ning Yu; and Valerie M. Smith, now at Quinnipiac University and co-author of the Instructor's Guide. Lori Corsini-Nelson cheerfully handled the paper flow. Houghton Mifflin editors Suzanne Phelps Weir, Becky Wong, and Sarah Helyar Smith, Lindsay Frost, Debbie Prato, Marcy Lunetta, and Deborah Karacozian have been enthusiastic supporters of the current edition; they have aided the production from start to finish with goodwill, good humor, and good sense.

When the first edition of *The Essay Connection* was in process, my sons were in high school. Over the intervening years they've earned doctorates (in biology and computer science), have married inspiring women, Sara (a U.S. attorney) and Vicki (a food scientist), and parented joyous children, Paul and Beth. An ever-active participant in the protracted process of making *The Essay Connection* more friendly to readers has been my writer-friendly husband, Martin Bloom, social psychologist, professor, world traveler, and fellow author. He has provided a retentive memory for titles and key words that I've called out from an adjacent lane during our early morning lap swims, homemade apple pies at bedtime, and all the comforts in between. My whole family keeps me cheerful; every day is a gift.

Lynn Z. Bloom

The *Essay* *Connection*

Part I

On Writing

Writers in Process—
Speaking and Reading

As the photograph on p. 1 implies, writing is a complicated process that involves reading (note the open book in the foreground) as well as putting words on the page—or computer screen. You will encounter essays in this book that, as E. B. White remarked, philosophize, scold, jest, tell stories, argue, or plead, among the many things they can do. You'll be able to read essays more easily and understand them better if you bear in mind as you read some of the following questions concerning the essay's author, intended audience, type, purposes, and rhetorical strategies, as well as your own responses as a reader.

Who Is the Author?

a. When did the author live? Where? Is the author's ethnic origin, gender, or regional background relevant to understanding this essay?

b. What is the author's educational background? Job experience? Do these or other significant life experiences make him or her an authority on the subject of the essay?

c. Does the author have political, religious, economic, cultural, or other biases that affect the essay's treatment of the subject? The author's credibility? The author's choice of language?

What Are the Context and Audience of the Essay?

a. When was the essay first published? Is it dated, or is it still relevant?

b. Where (in what magazine, professional journal, or book, if at all) was the essay first published?

c. For what audience was the essay originally intended? How much did the author expect the original readers to know about the subject? To what extent did the author expect the original readers to share his or her point of view? To resist that view?

d. Why would the original audience have read this essay?

e. What similarities and differences exist between the essay's original audience and the student audience now reading it?

f. What am I as a student reader expected to bring to my reading of this essay? My own or others' beliefs, values, past history, personal experience? Other reading? My own writing, previous or in an essay I will write in response to the essay(s) I am reading?

What Are the Purposes of the Essay?

a. Why did the author write the essay? To inform, describe, define, explain, argue, or for some other reason or combination of reasons?

b. Is the purpose explicitly stated anywhere in the essay? If so, where? Is this the thesis of the essay? Or is the thesis different?

c. If the purpose is not stated explicitly, how can I tell what the purpose is? Through examples? Emphasis? Tone? Other means?

d. Does the form of the essay suit the purpose? Would other forms have been more appropriate?

What Are the Strategies of the Essay?

a. What does the author do to make the essay interesting? Is he or she successful?

b. What organizational pattern (and subpatterns, if any) does the author use? How do these patterns fit the subject? The author's purpose?

c. What emphasis do the organization and proportioning provide to reinforce the author's purpose?

d. What evidence, arguments, and illustrations does the author employ to illustrate or demonstrate the thesis?

e. On what level of language (formal, informal, slangy) and in what tone (serious, satiric, sincere, etc.) does the author write?

f. Have I enjoyed the essay, or found it stimulating or otherwise provocative? Why or why not?

g. If I disagree with the author's thesis, or am not convinced by or attached to the author's evidence, illustrations, or use of language, am I nevertheless impelled to continue reading? If so, why? If not, why not?

The ways we read and write, and how we think about the ways we read and write, have been dramatically altered in the past thirty years. The New Critics, whose views dominated the teaching of reading and writing during the early and mid-twentieth century, promoted a sense of the text as a static, often enigmatic entity, whose sleeping secrets awaited a master critic or brilliant teacher to arrive, like Prince Charming on a white horse, and awaken their meaning. The numerous courses and textbooks encouraging students to read for experience, information, ideas, understanding, and appreciation reflect that view.

Yet contemporary literary theory encourages the sense of collaboration among author, text, and readers to make meaning. How we interpret any written material, whether a recipe, computer manual, love letter, or Martin Luther King, Jr.'s "Letter from Birmingham Jail" (445–61) depends, in part, on our prior knowledge of the subject, our opinion of the author, our experience with other works of the genre under consideration (what other recipes, or love letters, have we known?), and the context in which we're reading. We read Dr. King's "Letter" differently today than when he wrote it, jailed in Birmingham in 1963 for civil rights protests; liberals read it differently than conservatives; African-Americans may read it differently than whites, Southern or Northern. Where readers encounter a piece of writing greatly influences their interpretation, as well. Readers might read Dr. King's "Letter" as a document of news, history, social protest, argument, literary style—or some combination of these—depending on whether they encounter it in a newspaper of the time, in a history of the United States or of the civil rights movement, or in *The Essay Connection.*

A variety of critical theories reinforce the view that a work invites multiple readings, claiming that strong readers indeed bring powerful meanings to the texts they read. The selections in *The Essay Connection*, supplemented by photographs, open up a world of possibilities in interpreting not only what's on the written page, but also what is not on the page. What's there for the writer, as for the reader, is not just another story but an assemblage of stories, all that has occurred in one's life and thought, waiting to bleed through and into the paper on which these stories, in all their variations, will be told. Readers and writers alike are always in process, always in flux, no matter what their sources of inspiration or places to think.

There are many ways of learning to read, determined by age, culture, and physical and intellectual circumstances. Eudora Welty, Georgina Kleege, and Ning Yu wrote to explain the phenomenon of learning to read from dramatically different perspectives. Welty's "In Love with Books," from *One Writer's Beginnings* (22–26), explains part of her own background, showing how very young children can learn to love both reading and being read to. What child could fail to be inspired, as Welty was, by the enthusiasm of a mother who "read Dickens in the spirit in which she would have eloped with him"? What child could fail to respond to the inviting presence of "beautifully made, heavy books" with engaging pictures and stories, welcome initiations into the "knowledge of the word, into reading and spelling"? In "Up Close, In Touch" (12–22), a chapter from *Sight Unseen,* Georgina Kleege explains what it means to read and write with only peripheral vision that is 10 percent of normal sight. Denied the opportunity to learn braille as a child, due to social and medical prejudices against blindness, Kleege can read print only with a magnifying glass held close to her eyes or see a TV screen only with 100× magnification. Reading Braille, which she learned as an adult, becomes for her an enjoyable and lovely activity. The photograph on p. 19 reveals the grace and beauty of this activity.

Ning Yu's difficulties in learning English were cultural. "Red and Black, or One English Major's Beginning" (191–202), modeled consciously after Welty's essay, explains how Yu learned two different kinds of English in China during the repressive Cultural Revolution. (The photo on p. 195 captures the newfound literacy of a Chinese pupil.) As a middle school student, he and his peers were required to learn English versions of Maoist political slogans—a "series of meaningless, unutterable sounds." Yu's father, a professor of languages, had taught Yu the English alphabet and some English grammar before he was imprisoned for intellectual activities. Before his father was dragged off to prison for the fourth time, he gave Yu a copy of Jane Austen's *Pride and Prejudice* and an English-Chinese dictionary, instructing his son to translate the book. What could a youth reared in cultural isolation in communist China understand of Austen's ironic first sentence: "It is a truth universally acknowledged, that a single man in possession of good fortune, must be in want of a wife"?

When several (or more) readers share a background, common values, and a common language, they may be considered a *discourse community*. In "Mother Tongue" (6–12), Amy Tan explores how her writing reflects her Chinese-American discourse community. She understands, and uses, "all the Englishes I grew up with"—one for formal writing, another for intimate conversation with Chinese family members, and a combination of public and private languages for storytelling. Tan also understands, very well, the conventions of a professional American discourse community. When she speaks to her mother's bankers (¶s 10–12) or hospital personnel (¶ 14), she knows that her impeccable standard English will get the respect—and results—that prejudice denies to her mother's Chinese-accented English.

Thus, all the words, all the languages we speak, all the languages we understand (including the nonverbal communication of body language and social conventions) invariably influence how we write, for ourselves and those strangers who become friends—or antagonists—as they read our writing.

AMY TAN

Tan was born in Oakland, California, in 1952. Fascinated with language, she earned a B.A. in English (1973) and an M.A. in linguistics (1974) from San Jose State University. Her first jobs as a language development specialist working with disabled children and a freelance technical writer prepared her to write fiction. Her sensitivity to both languages spoken (conversation) and unspoken (behavior) was translated into the stories of complex relationships between Chinese-born mothers and their American-born daughters that comprise *The Joy Luck Club,* whose publication in 1989 brought her immediate fame, fortune, and critical esteem.

Tan followed this book with the equally successful *The Kitchen God's Wife* (1991), a novel modeled on her mother's traumatic life in China before she emigrated to the United States after World War II; *The Hundred Secret Senses* (1995); and *The Bonesetter's Daughter* (2001). Indeed, as Tan explains in the essay "Mother Tongue," originally published in *Threepenny Review* in 1990, her ideal reader became her mother, "because these were stories about mothers." Tan wrote "using all the Englishes [she] grew up with"—the "simple" English she used when speaking to her mother, the "broken" English her mother used when speaking to her, her "watered down" translation of her mother's Chinese, and her mother's "internal language": "her intent, her passion, her imagery, the rhythms of her speech and the nature of her thoughts." Her mother paid the book the ultimate compliment: "So easy to read." Hearing these multiple languages by reading the essay aloud weds the words and the music.

Mother Tongue

1   I am not a scholar of English or literature. I cannot give you much more than personal opinions on the English language and its variations in this country or others.

2   I am a writer. And by that definition, I am someone who has always loved language. I am fascinated by language in daily life. I spend a great deal of my time thinking about the power of language—the way it can evoke an emotion, a visual image, a complex idea, or a simple truth. Language is the tool of my trade. And I use them all—all the Englishes I grew up with.

3   Recently, I was made keenly aware of the different Englishes I do use. I was giving a talk to a large group of people, the same talk I had already given to half a dozen other groups. The nature of the talk was about my writing, my life, and my book, *The Joy Luck Club.* The talk was going along well enough, until I remembered one major difference that made the whole talk sound wrong. My mother was in the room. And it was perhaps the first time she had heard me give a lengthy speech, using

the kind of English I have never used with her. I was saying things like, "The intersection of memory upon imagination" and "There is an aspect of my fiction that relates to thus-and-thus"—a speech filled with carefully wrought grammatical phrases, burdened, it suddenly seemed to me, with nominalized forms, past perfect tenses, conditional phrases, all the forms of standard English that I had learned in school and through books, the forms of English I did not use at home with my mother.

Just last week, I was walking down the street with my mother, and I again found myself conscious of the English I was using, the English I do use with her. We were talking about the price of new and used furniture and I heard myself saying this: "Not waste money that way." My husband was with us as well, and he didn't notice any switch in my English. And then I realized why. It's because over the twenty years we've been together I've often used that same kind of English with him, and sometimes he even uses it with me. It has become our language of intimacy, a different sort of English that relates to family talk, the language I grew up with.

So you'll have some idea of what this family talk I heard sounds like, I'll quote what my mother said during a recent conversation which I videotaped and then transcribed. During this conversation, my mother was talking about a political gangster in Shanghai who had the same last name as her family's, Du, and how the gangster in his early years wanted to be adopted by her family, which was rich by comparison. Later, the gangster became more powerful, far richer than my mother's family, and one day showed up at my mother's wedding to pay his respects. Here's what she said in part:

"Du Yusong having business like fruit stand. Like off the street kind. He is Du like Du Zong—but not Tsung-ming Island people. The local people call putong, the river east side, he belong to that side local people. That man want to ask Du Zong father take him in like become own family. Du Zong father wasn't look down on him, but didn't take seriously, until that man big like become a mafia. Now important person, very hard to inviting him. Chinese way, came only to show respect, don't stay for dinner. Respect for making big celebration, he shows up. Mean give lots of respect. Chinese custom. Chinese social life that way. If too important won't have to stay too long. He come to my wedding. I didn't see, I heard it. I gone to boy's side, they have YMCA dinner. Chinese age I was nineteen."

You should know that my mother's expressive command of English belies how much she actually understands. She reads the *Forbes* report, listens to *Wall Street Week,* converses daily with her stockbroker, reads all of Shirley MacLaine's books with ease—all kinds of things I can't begin to understand. Yet some of my friends tell me they understand 50 percent of what my mother says. Some say they understand 80 to 90 percent. Some say they understand none of it, as if she were speaking pure Chinese. But to me, my mother's English is perfectly clear, perfectly natural. It's my mother tongue. Her language, as I hear it, is vivid, direct, full of observation and imagery. That was the language that helped shape the way I saw things, expressed things, made sense of the world.

8   Lately, I've been giving more thought to the kind of English my mother speaks. Like others, I have described it to people as "broken" or "fractured" English. But I wince when I say that. It has always bothered me that I can think of no way to describe it other than "broken," as if it were damaged and needed to be fixed, as if it lacked a certain wholeness and soundness. I've heard other terms used, "limited English," for example. But they seem just as bad, as if everything is limited, including people's perceptions of the limited English speaker.

9   I know this for a fact, because when I was growing up, my mother's "limited" English limited *my* perception of her. I was ashamed of her English. I believed that her English reflected the quality of what she had to say. That is, because she expressed them imperfectly her thoughts were imperfect. And I had plenty of empirical evidence to support me: the fact that people in department stores, at banks, and at restaurants did not take her seriously, did not give her good service, pretended not to understand her, or even acted as if they did not hear her.

10   My mother has long realized the limitations of her English as well. When I was fifteen, she used to have me call people on the phone to pretend I was she. In this guise, I was forced to ask for information or even to complain and yell at people who had been rude to her. One time it was a call to her stockbroker in New York. She had cashed out her small portfolio and it just happened we were going to go to New York the next week, our very first trip outside California. I had to get on the phone and say in an adolescent voice that was not very convincing, "This is Mrs. Tan."

11   And my mother was standing in the back whispering loudly, "Why he don't send me check, already two weeks late. So mad he lie to me, losing me money."

12   And then I said in perfect English, "Yes, I'm getting rather concerned. You had agreed to send the check two weeks ago, but it hasn't arrived."

13   Then she began to talk more loudly. "What he want, I come to New York tell him front of his boss, you cheating me?" And I was trying to calm her down, make her be quiet, while telling the stockbroker, "I can't tolerate any more excuses. If I don't receive the check immediately, I am going to have to speak to your manager when I'm in New York next week." And sure enough, the following week there we were in front of this astonished stockbroker, and I was sitting there red-faced and quiet, and my mother, the real Mrs. Tan, was shouting at his boss in her impeccable broken English.

14   We used a similar routine just five days ago, for a situation that was far less humorous. My mother had gone to the hospital for an appointment, to find out about a benign brain tumor a CAT scan had revealed a month ago. She said she had spoken very good English, her best English, no mistakes. Still, she said, the hospital did not apologize when they said

they had lost the CAT scan and she had come for nothing. She said they did not seem to have any sympathy when she told them she was anxious to know the exact diagnosis, since her husband and son had both died of brain tumors. She said they would not give her any more information until the next time and she would have to make another appointment for that. So she said she would not leave until the doctor called her daughter. She wouldn't budge. And when the doctor finally called her daughter, me, who spoke in perfect English—lo and behold—we had assurances the CAT scan would be found, promises that a conference call on Monday would be held, and apologies for any suffering my mother had gone through for a most regrettable mistake.

I think my mother's English almost had an effect on limiting my possibilities in life as well. Sociologists and linguists probably will tell you that a person's developing language skills are more influenced by peers. But I do think that the language spoken in the family, especially in immigrant families which are more insular, plays a large role in shaping the language of the child. And I believe that it affected my results on achievement tests, IQ tests, and the SAT. While my English skills were never judged as poor, compared to math, English could not be considered my strong suit. In grade school I did moderately well, getting perhaps B's, sometimes B-pluses, in English and scoring perhaps in the sixtieth or seventieth percentile on achievement tests. But those scores were not good enough to override the opinion that my true abilities lay in math and science, because in those areas I achieved A's and scored in the ninetieth percentile or higher. 15

This was understandable. Math is precise; there is only one correct answer. Whereas, for me at least, the answers on English tests were always a judgment call, a matter of opinion and personal experience. Those tests were constructed around items like fill-in-the-blank sentence completion, such as, "Even though Tom was _____, Mary thought he was _____." And the correct answer always seemed to be the most bland combinations of thoughts, for example "Even though Tom was shy, Mary thought he was charming," with the grammatical structure "even though" limiting the correct answer to some sort of semantic opposites, so you wouldn't get answers like, "Even though Tom was foolish, Mary thought he was ridiculous." Well, according to my mother, there were very few limitations as to what Tom could have been and what Mary might have thought of him. So I never did well on tests like that. 16

The same was true with word analogies, pairs of words in which you were supposed to find some sort of logical, semantic relationship—for example, "*Sunset* is to *nightfall* as _____ is to _____." And here you would be presented with a list of four possible pairs, one of which showed the same kind of relationship: *red* is to *spotlight*, *bus* is to *arrival*, *chills* is to *fever*, *yawn* is to *boring*. Well, I could never think that way. I knew what the tests were asking, but I could not block out of my mind the images already 17 created by the first pair, "*sunset* is to *nightfall*"—and I would see a burst of colors against a darkening sky, the moon rising, the lowering of a curtain of stars. And all the other pairs of words—red, bus, spotlight, boring—just threw up a mass of confusing images, making it impossible for me to sort out something as logical as saying: "A sunset precedes nightfall" is the same as "a chill precedes a fever." The only way I would have gotten that answer right would have been to imagine an associative situation, for example, my being disobedient and staying out past sunset, catching a chill at night, which turns into feverish pneumonia as punishment, which indeed did happen to me.

18   I have been thinking about all this lately, about my mother's English, about achievement tests. Because lately I've been asked as a writer, why there are not more Asian Americans represented in American literature. Why are there few Asian Americans enrolled in creative writing programs? Why do so many Chinese students go into engineering? Well, these are broad sociological questions I can't begin to answer. But I have noticed in surveys—in fact, just last week—that Asian students, as a whole, always do significantly better on math achievement tests than in English. And this makes me think that there are other Asian-American students whose English spoken in the home might also be described as "broken" or "limited." And perhaps they also have teachers who are steering them away from writing and into math and science, which is what happened to me.

19   Fortunately, I happen to be rebellious in nature and enjoy the challenge of disproving assumptions made about me. I became an English major my first year in college, after being enrolled as pre-med. I started writing nonfiction as a freelancer the week after I was told by my former boss that writing was my worst skill and I should hone my talents toward account management.

20   But it wasn't until 1985 that I finally began to write fiction. And at first I wrote using what I thought to be wittily crafted sentences, sentences that would finally prove I had mastery over the English language. Here's an example from the first draft of a story that later made its way into *The Joy Luck Club*, but without this line: "That was my mental quandary in its nascent state." A terrible line, which I can barely pronounce.

21   Fortunately, for reasons I won't get into today, I later decided I should envision a reader for the stories I would write. And the reader I decided upon was my mother, because these were stories about mothers. So with this reader in mind—and in fact she did read my early drafts—I began to write stories using all the Englishes I grew up with: the English I spoke to my mother, which for lack of a better term might be described as "simple"; the English she used with me, which for lack of a better term might be described as "broken"; my translation of her Chinese, which could certainly be described as "watered down"; and what I imagined to

be her translation of her Chinese if she could speak in perfect English, her internal language, and for that I sought to preserve the essence, but neither an English nor a Chinese structure. I wanted to capture what language ability tests can never reveal: her intent, her passion, her imagery, the rhythms of her speech and the nature of her thoughts.

Apart from what any critic had to say about my writing, I knew I had succeeded where it counted when my mother finished reading my book and gave me her verdict: "So easy to read."   22

Content

1. What connections does Tan make throughout the essay between speaking and writing? Why is it necessary for the writer to be "keenly aware of the different Englishes" she uses?
2. What is Tan's relationship with her mother? How can you tell?
3. What problems does Mrs. Tan experience as a result of not speaking standard English? Are her problems typical of other speakers of "limited" English?
4. Do you agree with Tan that "math is precise" but that English is "always a judgment call, a matter of opinion and personal experience" (¶ 16)? Why or why not? If English is so subjective, how is it possible to write anything that is clear, "so easy to read" (¶ 22)?

Strategies/Structures

5. Tan uses illustrative examples: a story told in her mother's speech (¶ 6), her mother's altercation with the stockbroker (¶s 10–13), her mother's encounter with rude and indifferent hospital workers who lost her CAT scan (¶ 14). What is the point of each example? Does Tan have to explain them? Why or why not?

Language

6. In what English has Tan written "Mother Tongue"? Why?
7. How do the "Englishes" that Tan and her mother use convey their characters, personalities, intelligence? In what ways are mother and daughter similar? Different?

For Writing

8. How many Englishes did you grow up with? Explain, either in speaking or in writing, to someone who doesn't know you very well, two of the different languages—whether these are variations of English or another language—that you use and identify the circumstances under which you use each of them—perhaps at home, in conversation with friends, or in writing papers. Consider such features as vocabulary (and amount of slang or specialized words), sentence length, and simplicity or complexity of what you're trying to say. How much can you count on your readers to understand without elaborate explanation on your part? Do you write papers for English classes in a different language than papers for some of your other courses?

9. If you are trying to communicate with someone whose native language or dialect is different from yours, how do you do it? To what extent did this communication depend on words? Other means (such as gestures, tone of voice)? As Tan does, tell the story of such an experience (to a reader who wasn't there) in order to explain the nature of your communication. If there were any misunderstandings, what were they? How did they occur, and how did you resolve (or attempt to resolve) them? What advice would you offer to help others in similar situations to communicate clearly?

10. Present to an audience of college-educated readers an argument for or against the necessity of speaking in standard English. Are there any exceptions to your position?

GEORGINA KLEEGE

Kleege, who was born in 1956, became legally blind at the age of eleven as a result of macular degeneration, which left her with only peripheral vision. Educated at Yale University (B.A. in English, 1979), she is a novelist (*Home for the Summer*, 1989), essayist, and translator of *Sitt Marie Rose,* by Lebanese writer Etel Adnan. Her work has appeared in publications ranging from *Redbook* to *The Yale Review* to the *Disability Studies Quarterly.*

In *Sight Unseen* (1999) Kleege offers a meditative, unsentimental account of visual impairment—both in her own view of the world and in the world's largely negative stereotyping of the blind as helpless objects of pity. In mainstream films, for instance, blind men perform the function usually assigned to women: "They exist to be looked at . . . all spectacle. The viewer contemplates the blind man on screen with both fascination and revulsion." Kleege's precise explanations of what it is like to function as a blind person in a sighted society (very well, thank you) are designed to dispel stereotypes and create an understanding of a disability both misunderstood and feared. For example, she explains her macular degeneration: "My blind spot always occupies the central region of my visual field. The wider the field, the larger the blind spot. When I look at my hand from arm's length, it vanishes. When I bring it closer to my face, only the fingertips are gone."

From this thoughtful, sometimes meditative perspective Kleege offers a new understanding of what it means to read—and to write—in "Up Close, In Touch," from a chapter of *Sight Unseen.* Here she explores the mechanisms—physical and intellectual—of coping with written texts with varying degrees of magnification and of reading efficiently—whether skimming junk mail or dwelling with delight on favorite literary passages. The simplest and most elegant of all is to read in braille, a thoroughly pleasurable skill Kleege didn't learn until she was middle-aged because of social and medical prejudices against blindness: "If I did not need braille," as an eleven-year old, "then my vision must not be 'that bad.'"

Up Close, In Touch

T here is pain above my right eye, between my eyebrow and the tear   1
duct. It is a dull, constant pain, an ache rather than a throb, not excruciating by any means. If I continue writing as I am, my nose skimming
the page, my eye peering through a heavy magnifying lens, the pain will
deepen and spread, migrating to my forehead and the other eye. My neck
and shoulders will start to ache too, since I am in a rather cramped position. But that pain is only muscular. I can relieve it by stretching and
shifting my posture.

The pain around my eye may be muscular too. Muscles squeeze the   2
lens tight for close focus. The standard remedy for this kind of eyestrain
is to look at a distant object. The muscles that compress the lens, making
it thick for reading and writing, will relax for distance vision. But when
I look up, the image through the window seems chaotic. There is a shifting scintillation of light and color. It is a windy day, and tree limbs shift
with each gust. Sunlight is reflecting off the smooth surface of leaves. On
top of this, there is the ever-present quivering motion that comes from
my marred central vision. But today my vision seems worse than usual.
For some reason my brain will not resolve what I see into anything meaningful. If I had not just been writing, my brain would be able to sort out
the different aspects of the image and perceive a comprehensible impression—not what a sighted person would see, naturally, but familiar
enough for me to say, "That's part of the tree. That's part of the neighbor's
house." But now, because (as I surmise) I've had my eyes clenched in
extreme close focus, they seem unable to shift back, so everything appears
blurry and indistinct. In fact, I have trouble seeing beyond the window itself. The verticals and horizontals of the frame and panes shimmy wildly.
Outside the window, the wind blows harder, and I feel a little seasick as
the motion increases.

But if I work at it, concentrating on a known, stable object—the white   3
trim along my neighbor's roofline—I can feel my focus shift. The chaos
resolves into recognizable (to me, anyway) shapes. I can distinguish different objects from one another, light from shadow, inside from outside.

But I don't always have the patience for this. I have another thought   4
and dive back toward the page, pressing my magnifying glasses up on
my nose. At first, the regularity of black marks on white paper is a relief
after the chaos outside. But after another sentence or two the pain is back.
This pain is familiar to me. I think that it is there most of the time when
I read, lurking in the background of consciousness. But it is certainly not
the worst pain I've ever known. And it's nothing compared with the de-
bilitating agony that migraine sufferers describe. In general, I can ignore
this pain. It occupies only as much attention as the mosquito bite on my
left ankle, or the patch of dry skin on my right elbow. A tear forms at the

corner of my right eye. I blink to spread it over the eyeball, and this is soothing. But I know that if I keep at this, the pain will get worse. There is a point of no return, beyond which the usual remedies of blinking or looking out the window will not help. Then, somewhere in my nervous system a switch is thrown, and the pain swells. At its worst, it will feel as if a rigid shaft pierces my head, twisting with the slightest movement. If I let the pain get to this point I will be dizzy when I stand up, almost nauseated. I may black out for a second—blackness will well up around me, swallowing me whole from the ground up. If I let it go that far, drugs will dull the pain but won't erase it. I will find it hard to focus, hard to look at light, hard to think of anything else. The pain will be with me for the rest of the day, perhaps even tomorrow.

5   There is urgency now. I should stop, or at least move to the computer since I can type without focusing. Or I could just close my eyes, but even then I feel the same tautness inside. Besides, I want to finish this thought, commit this idea to paper while it's still fresh. I bargain with the pain: I'll stop, I promise, just let me get to the end of the paragraph. Another minute, another sentence, one more word.

6   I bring this on myself. The damage to my maculas impairs my ability to perceive detail, such as the letters in the words I am writing. To read them at all I must bring my eye very close to the page. I augment the physical proximity with a magnifying lens. I used to use handheld magnifiers, but now I wear eyeglass frames with a magnifying lens mounted on the right side. The lens enlarges everything six times normal size. This magnification means that my blind spot, which obliterates whatever is directly before my eyes, affects a smaller portion of the enlarged word. So if I stare at the middle of a word (the *dd* in "middle," for instance) I can see the *m* at the beginning and the *e*, even the *le* at the end. It looks like *m——le*. As I move my eye to the right while my pen tip begins the next word, my blind spot erases the end of the word: *mid——*.

7   I use only my right eye when I read and wear no lens over the left. I used to wear a patch over that side of my glasses, but I discovered that I didn't need it. My left retina is more degenerated than my right, so as my pen travels across the page, everything to the left of it fades to blankness—my blind spot erases what I've just written. Occasionally my left eye still seems to think that it should be doing something. Sometimes there's an odd muscular twitch, or I feel my eye drift out of alignment, giving me double vision, ghost lines of writing veering off at crazy angles. If it gets bad, I hold the lid closed with a finger.

8   Of course, I don't have to write this way. When I type I don't have to focus my eyes on anything. And the computer allows me even more magnification. At the moment I'm typing at 36 point. This *L* is about half an inch tall. To read what I've just written, I still must get very close, about two inches from the screen, and to proofread it (to be sure there are two

e's in screen) I put on my glasses and move in closer, my nose brushing the screen. Now my blind spot effaces only parts of letters, everything below or above the median line.

I also own a closed-circuit TV reading device, which allows me even greater magnification. The machine has a tiny video camera pointing at a movable easel below. I put a book, a page of manuscript, a letter, or a form under the camera, and an image appears on a TV screen at eye level. I can magnify the text up to a hundred times original size, and reverse the image from positive to negative, so the print appears white and the background is black. This reduces glare, making reading more comfortable. I can also mask portions of the text, isolating one paragraph or one line at a time. Using the machine to write requires adjustments in eye-hand coordination since I must look up at the screen to see what my hand is writing below it. Still, the device is handy for filling out forms and computerized grade sheets. It allows me to use phone books and dictionaries. But I cannot use it to read for a long period of time. The flashing movement of words on the screen, caused by the sliding table the text lies on, sometimes leads to a sort of motion sickness, familiar to users of microfilm readers. A different kind of pain.

Oddly, even with all this magnification, I find it necessary to be very close to the text when I read. It feels unnatural to read from a distance. There are aids that would force me to back away from the text. I could, for instance, get a pair of eyeglasses with miniature telescopes mounted in the lenses. These would be set to allow me to stand at a podium and read a text without holding it up in front of my face. The problem would be that glasses set for that distance and that angle of vision would not work if I wanted to read a book while lying on the couch. The solution then would be several pairs of glasses, and for the time being I'm unconvinced that the advantages outweigh the inconvenience and expense.

The fact is, reading close is such an old habit I'm not sure that I can shake it this late in life, or even that I should. Contrary to popular belief, reading from a closer than average distance does not necessarily damage the eyes. Eyestrain won't make you nearsighted or farsighted; it may simply indicate to your eye doctor that you have developed one of these, or some other condition. Changes in the curvature of the cornea or the shape of the lens or the eyeball occur genetically or as a result of the body's aging process, not as a side effect of reading habits. Besides, the notion of a correct distance for reading is only a measure of what's average. If your visual activity measures 20/20, it means when you stand 20 feet from the eye chart, you can read what the average person reads from that distance. When George Snellen created his familiar eye chart in the middle of the nineteenth century, he chose twenty feet as the base unit for no better reason than it was the length of the typical classroom of his day. And perhaps the catchy ring of the phrase "20/20" was irresistible.

12   Thus, though my up-close reading posture deviates from convention, it probably won't make my eyesight any worse. So it shouldn't matter. Except for the pain. The reason reading becomes painful to me is that my eyes are focusing at the maximum for prolonged periods of time. The angle at which the light enters the eye tells the brain how far the object of interest is from the eyes, and the brain automatically adjusts the muscles that control the lenses to refract the light onto the retina. My lenses and the muscles that contract and relax them are more or less normal. They do what they're told, oblivious to the defect in the retinas behind them. With my head pressed close to the computer screen this way, the focusing muscles receive the instruction to focus as if for extremely close reading—the fine print at the bottom of a contract, the ingredients list on a medication label, the *OED*. The pain I feel is the same as a sighted person feels when reading a dictionary for a long time.

13   When I first heard the expression "close reading" as an English major in college, I felt a tremendous sense of affirmation. This was the Yale English department, where close reading was something like a religion, and hearing the phrase made me feel that I belonged. I always read close. I always read every word, every syllable, every letter. So the literary practice, to read every word, to dwell on them, to contemplate not only their meanings but connotations, resonances, and history, came very naturally to me. Close reading presupposes that the text is worth taking time over. Close reading is a task of discovery, recovery, uncovering, detection, dissection—struggle. Sometimes close reading is even painful. Since all print is fine print to me, I must always read it closely. Fine print is not only the part that gives you headaches but also the part that only the truly patient, diligent, and discerning reader can decipher. I felt physically well-suited, if not predestined, to be a close reader.

14   Around this time I met my husband, Nick. He recalls that the first time he saw me I was reading in the library. The book was in French, and he could tell (his vision is normal) that it was not a textbook but a recently published novel. It was my unusual posture that attracted his attention. My nose was scraping across the page, the covers of the book folded around my face. He thought, "If reading is that difficult, it must really matter to her." Was this love at first sight? Not exactly. But Nick's first glimpse of me revealed something fundamental about who I was. As an aspiring writer and student of literature, reading was not only the way I spent most of my time but the central activity of my life. Reading mattered more than anything. And he probably recognized a kinship, a shared passion, or at least our common education. As a graduate student in the same department he perhaps saw in me the physical embodiment of close reading.

15   But the literary scholar who can dwell for hours on a single passage can also skim junk mail, scan the box scores for a particular team, and speed-read a pile of student midterms. Competence in reading involves more than holding the text at a distance that does not lead to eyestrain.

Efficient reading means that the eyes move across and down the page in an orderly way, with a minimum of regressive or backward movements. The eye of a normally sighted, competent reader does not track along the line but moves in short jumps, or saccades, fixating briefly on small groups of characters before jumping to a new location. During the microsecond that the eye fixates on a single word or group of words, the brain processes the characters whose images fall on the center area of the retina, which is most sensitive to detail. At the same time, peripheral areas of the retina give a general preview of what's coming. Your peripheral vision can make broad, general distinctions about the size and shape of the words that follow the one in your central vision. You combine this general preview with your knowledge of the language you're reading, and the context of what you're reading, make an educated guess about what's next, and jump ahead. The most proficient readers can both process a large number of characters at each fixation and jump over a large number of characters with each saccade. And they rarely need to look back to verify what they've just read.

When I read, I keep my eyes staring straight ahead and move either the text or my head. Since I am always reading magnified text, my eye can process only about three characters at each fixation, while yours may process as many as a dozen at a time. And while my eye moves forward a character or two at a time, your eye may leapfrog fourteen or fifteen characters in a single saccade. Since I have next to no central vision, I rely on my peripheral vision to give me the general features of the letters and words. But the information is vague. The cells on the periphery are not sensitive to detail in the way cells at the center are. I can distinguish tall letters from short ones and straight lines from curves, but I lack the kind of cells that can definitively discern the orientation of these features relative to each other. An *a* could be an *o*, which could be a *c*, which could be an *e*. It's all too easy to confuse an *r* with a *t* or even an *f*. I regularly reverse or invert some letters—*b* and *d*, *p* and *q*. My tendency toward double vision makes minims multiply. I suspect every *n* might be an *m*, every *u* a *w*.

Thus, my problem with reading is not simply that my oversized blind spot erases every character as I look at it. I also lack the visual equipment to allow me to make definitive judgments. As I stare at a word, it changes. I move my gaze around each letter, and it seems to reconfigure before my eyes. In quick succession a series of alternatives present themselves. The word "road" could easily be "toad," which could be "tool." "Wood" could be "weed" or perhaps "ward," or even "word."

The only constant in my reading is the fickleness and instability of the text. I am plagued by uncertainty. As I progress through the sentence, each new word makes me question the ones before. I glance back. A word I thought I'd recognized has now changed. My brain says, "If that 'word' is actually 'wood,' then that 'tool' must actually be 'toad.'"

If I manage at all it is because I started my reading career fully sighted. Part of learning to read involves the ability to process incomplete information. For instance, you don't always need to see the whole word to recognize it. Typically, readers learn to aim their eyes at the beginnings of long words, and skip the endings. In English, grammatical information about verb tense or noun number generally occurs at the ends of words, and you can usually extrapolate this from the context. Similarly, if you're given a text in which only the top half of the letters is visible, you could still make out the words. Mask the upper half, and you'll have a tougher time. This is true because there are eight letters in our alphabet with stems or dots above the middle line, and only five with tails below it. We gamble on statistical probabilities. My brain, like yours, is programmed to make the most of minimal information.

20   Still, what I do is child's play compared to your fluency. I read so slowly, with such difficulty and inaccuracy, that I can hardly claim to read at all. Fortunately, there are other ways to read—books on tape, for instance, which I began to rely on in my early twenties, and braille, which I have learned in the past few years.

21   Like most of the truly important inventions in human history, the braille code is elegantly simple. The braille cell is made up of six raised dots, arranged like the six in dominos, two vertical columns of three. All the letters of the alphabet, plus special symbols for certain common words, consist of from one to all six of these dots. Each character is the right size to fit even a child's fingertip, so the reader moves the finger smoothly from left to right. The braille alphabet is easy to memorize, and it's hard to mistake one letter for another. . . .

22   When I learned all the letters of the alphabet I read this: "Congratulations! You have now mastered the entire braille alphabet." I was startled, then enthralled. I read it again. For the first time in decades I felt in absolute and stable contact with the text. This had nothing to do with the precarious guesswork I'd called reading since I lost my visual acuity. This was certain, unequivocal. I touched the words. Meaning flowed into my brain. Suddenly, my mind rushed ahead to imagine the thousands of texts I wanted to read and reread in this way. I moved on to study Braille II, the system of contractions and special signs that makes braille less cumbersome. I found the contractions so intuitive, so akin to the personal shorthands that people use taking notes, it hardly required memorization. Frequently, the initial letter or letters are used to stand for the whole word, so *p* stands for people, *ab* for about, and *imm* for immediate. Other contractions omit the vowels: *grt* means great, *rcv* means receive. Braille readers, like sighted readers, don't read every letter. This is not to say that reading braille is perfectly analogous to reading print. The finger does not saccade as the eye does, and it's necessary to stay in touch with the text. Still, proficient braille readers can skim text in much the way sighted readers do, reading only the first sentences of paragraphs or only the central three or four words of each line. As I read I found that context allowed

What dimensions does this photograph contribute to your understanding of what it means to be able to read? To the process of reading in Braille? What in the photograph makes this reading look graceful and easy? Does Kleege's explanation reinforce this impression?

me to speed up, my finger barely grazing articles, prepositions, and conjunctions. As soon as I could identify a word from the first few letters, my finger glided rapidly over the rest and on to the next word.

In the beginning, I found myself leaning close to the page, as I would with print. But soon I leaned back, way back, the book pushed away from me, my forearms stretched out comfortably on the table. This became a source of pleasure in itself, because reading had always been up-close and closed-in. When I read visually, my nose brushing the page, or aurally, a recorded voice in my ears, I am sometimes oppressed by claustrophobia. Now I felt refreshed by the space around me. I stretched out on the couch, the book on my lap. I leaned my head back. I closed my eyes. The muscles of my lips and tongue twitched, whispering. My progress was slow but steady. My brain did not backtrack as it would reading print. I recognized each letter or contraction, then it stood still, steadfast, unwavering. The frantic uncertainty of reading print was gone. And there was no pain. The anxiety that another word would be one too many, the nausea and dizziness creeping toward the surface of consciousness—none of this now. Occasionally my wrist cramped, and I learned that I was pressing too hard. My touch became lighter, more fleeting, and the pain went away. I was serene, floating. A tranquil faith sustained me letter by letter, word by word.

24   Why did I wait so long to learn this? If braille is such a pleasure, and if it seems to hold out the possibility that I can read fluently and without pain, why didn't I learn it sooner? After all, when I lost my visual acuity in the mid-sixties, the sight-enhancing technologies available today were not yet invented. And surely as a child of eleven I would have picked it up quickly. I was in school; braille could have been a part of my regular curriculum. Learning it as an adult, I often had to juggle to fit practice time into my schedule.

25   In fact, when I lost my sight, my mother made inquiries about braille instruction for me. We were told that I had too much sight. The inference was that only the totally blind could become proficient at braille. A person with any sight at all would be tempted to cheat, to read the pattern of raised dots visually rather than through touch. It was an odd thing to say, since many sighted people have learned braille, teachers and family members of blind children, for instance, not to mention sighted braille transcribers. In fact, though Louis Braille was blind, his writing system was a modification of a system designed by a sighted French artillery officer, Captain Charles Barbier de la Serre. Barbier's code was originally intended as a method of night writing so that officers at the front could write and read messages without signaling their location to the enemy by showing a light.

26   But I didn't know this then. As it turns out, I cannot see braille. When I stare at a page of braille it looks blank at first. I move my gaze around it and detect a few speckles of shadow. These seem to shiver and shake, to move and multiply. It takes a lot of magnification and a good deal of effort for me to make out any pattern there.

27   But at the time, no one so much as showed me a page of braille. My mother may have been too quick to accept that person's advice. Or perhaps she did not describe my condition adequately. She tended to shy away from the ugly words "blindness" and "macular degeneration" and use the more neutral "vision problem" instead. Like many parents of newly blind children, she was eager for good news. This made it easy to translate "cannot learn braille" into "does not need braille," which was reassuring. If I did not need braille then my vision must not be "that bad." And for my part, I accepted this misinformation without question. I was eleven. I didn't want to be blind. The only blind person I'd ever seen was a beggar in the subway. And I had faith that adults generally looked out for my best interests and that experts knew what they were talking about. Besides, they were only reinforcing my uncertainty about my new status as blind. How could I be blind if I still saw as much as I did? It made me feel ashamed for even asking. They seemed to be saying that asking for braille was like wanting a wheelchair for a skinned knee. I had sight, so I should use it to read print, because that's how sighted people do it. If it was difficult, I must simply try harder. If it hurt, it must be the kind of discomfort that leads to some ultimate good.

Content

1. If your vision is within the normal range, what do you take for granted about being able to read and write? In what ways does Kleege's explanation of how these processes work for people with very restricted sight illuminate your understanding of the activities of reading and writing?

2. Why does Kleege move back and forth between descriptions of sighted people's experiences with reading and her own experiences with reading by means of sight (including various magnification devices) and by touch? If reading through braille is so much easier than trying to see the text, why doesn't she use braille for everything?

3. Why didn't Kleege study braille as soon as she learned as a child that she had macular disease and was legally blind (¶s 20–27)?

Strategies/Structures

4. Kleege begins her essay with detailed descriptions of the pain that occurs when she tries to read (¶s 1–5), but she doesn't explain the reasons for the process until paragraph 6. What effect is such a delay likely to have on her audience?

5. Why does Kleege devote so much space, in such painstaking detail (¶s 1–9), to explaining the difficulties she has in reading visually? Since she has mastered a difficult process that her sighted readers don't need to use, of what interest and value is this information to these readers? Why does Kleege want sighted readers to follow her struggle?

6. Kleege's central question, "Why did I wait so long to learn this?," and her answer to that question do not begin to emerge until paragraph 20, three-quarters of the way through the essay (18). Why does she wait so long to explain this? What does she achieve by delaying this important question and answer?

Language

7. Explain the multiple meanings of the words in Kleege's title, "Up Close, In Touch." What is the complicated significance of the term "close reading" in paragraph 13, which Kleege defines as "a task of discovery, recovery, uncovering, detection, dissection—struggle" and "even painful."

8. Kleege and Nancy Mairs ("On Being a Cripple," 364–75) both write about their physical deficits and the challenges these present to their everyday functioning. What is the attitude of each toward these challenges? Do they regard these conditions as disabilities? How do they want their readers to react?

For Writing

9. Write an analysis of your own reading or writing process, as Kleege does in her early paragraphs. What sensations do you notice (physical, mental, emotional) and what types of effort do you exert during the act of reading or writing? What is automatic and what do you need to think about, either every time you read or write or when you're encountering something new? Identify the new phenomena or tasks that present problems for you to solve—perhaps issue by issue, such as

finding an engaging topic, deciding whether you have enough to say about it, or where to find more information. Where can you find solutions to or help with these problems? Discuss your paper or process with other students to determine whether your experiences are unusual or common, and compare possible solutions to the problems you raise.

10. Kleege describes the "tangle of prejudice and fear" with which sighted people react to her blindness. Why are people often prejudiced against and afraid of those with disabilities or significant deviance from the norm (see Nancy Mairs, "On Being a Cripple," 364–75, and Spencer Nadler, "Fat," 265–74)? After discussing with others how "Up Close, In Touch" works to dispel this prejudice, write your own response (individual or group) to this subject, using as illustrations your own experiences (of some loss, deficit, or inability to perform "normally") or that of someone you know. The essay does not have to be about blindness.

EUDORA WELTY

Welty's editor at the *New Yorker,* William Maxwell, sums up her reputation, "I can't think of any American writer more universally acknowledged to be a great writer. Everybody—every *cat*—knows that Eudora Welty is a great writer." Yet Welty, winner of a Pulitzer Prize for her novel *The Optimist's Daughter* (1972), the Gold Medal award of the National Institute of Arts and Letters, and a Presidential Medal of Freedom, among other honors, retains her lifelong modesty and sense of humor. Until her death in 2001, she wrote and gardened in her beloved home in Jackson, Mississippi, where she was born in 1909. She left town to attend college, transferring in 1927 from Mississippi State College for Women to the University of Wisconsin, where she earned a B.A. in 1929, followed by a year of graduate work in advertising at the Columbia University Graduate School of Business.

In the mid-1930s Welty traveled through "Depression-worn" Mississippi towns as a junior publicist for the Works Progress Administration. There she took the photographs that became the basis for *One Time, One Place: Mississippi in the Depression* (1971), but her record of small-town Mississippi life lingered in these "revelations of the instant. Like the flash of a camera, the record of a movement or an emotion is what fiction is, really" she says. She explains her career as a writer of short stories and fiction, including *A Curtain of Green* (1941), *The Wide Net* (1943), *Delta Wedding* (1946), *The Ponder Heart* (1952), and *Losing Battles* (1970) with a characteristically honest understatement, "I think I became a writer because I love stories. I never had any idea that I could be a professional writer. I'm now realizing, maybe the reason I first sent stories out to magazines was that I was too shy to show them to anybody I knew."

"In Love with Books" is from Welty's autobiography, *One Writer's Beginnings* (1983), which began as a series of three lectures at Harvard that memorably demonstrated the importance of "Listening," "Learning to See," and "Finding a Voice" in her development as a writer.

In Love with Books

I learned from the age of two or three that any room in our house, at any   1
time of day, was there to read in, or to be read to. My mother read to
me. She'd read to me in the big bedroom in the mornings, when we were
in her rocker together, which ticked in rhythm as we rocked, as though we
had a cricket accompanying the story. She'd read to me in the diningroom
on winter afternoons in front of the coal fire, with our cuckoo clock ending the story with "Cuckoo," and at night when I'd got in my own bed. I
must have given her no peace. Sometimes she read to me in the kitchen
while she sat churning, and the churning sobbed along with *any* story. It
was my ambition to have her read to me while *I* churned; once she
granted my wish, but she read off my story before I brought her butter.
She was an expressive reader. When she was reading "Puss in Boots," for
instance, it was impossible not to know that she distrusted *all* cats.

It had been startling and disappointing to me to find out that story   2
books had been written by *people,* that books were not natural wonders,
coming up of themselves like grass. Yet regardless of where they came
from, I cannot remember a time when I was not in love with them—with
the books themselves, cover and binding and the paper they were printed
on, with their smell and their weight and with their possession in my
arms, captured and carried off to myself. Still illiterate, I was ready for
them, committed to all the reading I could give them.

Neither of my parents had come from homes that could afford to   3
buy many books, but though it must have been something of a strain on
his salary, as the youngest officer in a young insurance company, my
father was all the while carefully selecting and ordering away for what he
and Mother thought we children should grow up with. They bought first
for the future.

Besides the bookcase in the livingroom, which was always called   4
"the library," there were the encyclopedia tables and dictionary stand
under windows in our diningroom. Here to help us grow up arguing
around the diningroom table were the Unabridged Webster, the Columbia
Encyclopedia, Compton's Pictured Encyclopedia, the Lincoln Library of
Information, and later the Book of Knowledge. And the year we moved
into our new house, there was room to celebrate it with the new 1925 edition of the Britannica, which my father, his face always deliberately
turned toward the future, was of course disposed to think better than any
previous edition.

In "the library," inside the mission-style bookcase with its three   5
diamond-latticed glass doors, with my father's Morris chair and the glass-
shaded lamp on its table beside it, were books I could soon begin on—and
I did, reading them all alike and as they came, straight down their rows,
top shelf to bottom. There was the set of Stoddard's lectures, in all its late

nineteenth-century vocabulary and vignettes of peasant life and quaint beliefs and customs, with matching halftone illustrations: Vesuvius erupting, Venice by moonlight, gypsies glimpsed by their campfires. I didn't know then the clue they were to my father's longing to see the rest of the world. I read straight through his other love-from-afar: the Victrola Book of the Opera, with opera after opera in synopsis, with portraits in costume of Melba, Caruso, Galli-Curci, and Geraldine Farrar, some of whose voices we could listen to on our Red Seal records.

6   My mother read secondarily for information; she sank as a hedonist into novels. She read Dickens in the spirit in which she would have eloped with him. The novels of her girlhood that had stayed on in her imagination, besides those of Dickens and Scott and Robert Louis Stevenson, were *Jane Eyre, Trilby, The Woman in White, Green Mansions, King Solomon's Mines.* Marie Corelli's name would crop up but I understood she had gone out of favor with my mother, who had only kept *Ardath* out of loyalty. In time she absorbed herself in Galsworthy, Edith Wharton, above all in Thomas Mann of the *Joseph* volumes.

7   *St. Elmo* was not in our house; I saw it often in other houses. This wildly popular Southern novel is where all the Edna Earles in our population started coming from. They're all named for the heroine, who succeeded in bringing a dissolute, sinning roué and atheist of a lover (St. Elmo) to his knees. My mother was able to forgo it. But she remembered the classic advice given to rose growers on how to water their bushes long enough: "Take a chair and *St. Elmo.*"

8   To both my parents I owe my early acquaintance with a beloved Mark Twain. There was a full set of Mark Twain and a short set of Ring Lardner in our bookcase, and those were the volumes that in time united us all, parents and children.

9   Reading everything that stood before me was how I came upon a worn old book without a back that had belonged to my father as a child. It was called *Sanford and Merton.* Is there anyone left who recognizes it, I wonder? It is the famous moral tale written by Thomas Day in the 1780s, but of him no mention is made on the title page of this book; here it is *Sanford and Merton in Words of One Syllable* by Mary Godolphin. Here are the rich boy and the poor boy and Mr. Barlow, their teacher and interlocutor, in long discourses alternating with dramatic scenes—danger and rescue allotted to the rich and the poor respectively. It may have only words of one syllable, but one of them is "quoth." It ends with not one but two morals, both engraved on rings: "Do what you ought, come what may," and "If we would be great, we must first learn to be good."

10   This book was lacking its front cover, the back held on by strips of pasted paper, now turned golden, in several layers, and the pages stained, flecked, and tattered around the edges; its garish illustrations had come unattached but were preserved, laid in. I had the feeling even in my heedless childhood that this was the only book my father as a little boy had had

of his own. He had held onto it, and might have gone to sleep on its cover-less face: he had lost his mother when he was seven. My father had never made any mention to his own children of the book, but he had brought it along with him from Ohio to our house and shelved it in our bookcase.

My mother had brought from West Virginia that set of Dickens; those 11 books looked sad, too—they had been through fire and water before I was born, she told me, and there they were, lined up—as I later realized, wait-ing for *me*.

I was presented, from as early as I can remember, with books of my 12 own, which appeared on my birthday and Christmas morning. Indeed, my parents could not give me books enough. They must have sacrificed to give me on my sixth or seventh birthday—it was after I became a reader for myself—the ten-volume set of Our Wonder World. These were beauti-fully made, heavy books I would lie down with on the floor in front of the diningroom hearth, and more often than the rest volume 5, *Every Child's Story Book,* was under my eyes. There were the fairy tales—Grimm, Andersen, the English, the French, "Ali Baba and the Forty Thieves"; and there was Aesop and Reynard the Fox; there were the myths and legends, Robin Hood, King Arthur, and St. George and the Dragon, even the history of Joan of Arc; a whack of *Pilgrim's Progress* and a long piece of *Gulliver.* They all carried their classic illustrations. I located myself in these pages and could go straight to the stories and pictures I loved; very often "The Yellow Dwarf" was first choice, with Walter Crane's Yellow Dwarf in full color making his terrifying appearance flanked by turkeys. Now that vol-ume is as worn and backless and hanging apart as my father's poor *Sanford and Merton.* The precious page with Edward Lear's "Jumblies" on it has been in danger of slipping out for all these years. One measure of my love for Our Wonder World was that for a long time I wondered if I would go through fire and water for it as my mother had done for Charles Dickens; and the only comfort was to think I could ask my mother to do it for me.

I believe I'm the only child I know of who grew up with this treas- 13 ure in the house. I used to ask others, "Did you have Our Wonder World?" I'd have to tell them the Book of Knowledge could not hold a candle to it.

I live in gratitude to my parents for initiating me—and as early as I 14 begged for it, without keeping me waiting—into knowledge of the word, into reading and spelling, by way of the alphabet. They taught it to me at home in time for me to begin to read before starting to school. I believe the alphabet is no longer considered an essential piece of equipment for trav-eling through life. In my day it was the keystone to knowledge. You learned the alphabet as you learned to count to ten, as you learned "Now I lay me" and the Lord's Prayer and your father's and mother's name and address and telephone number, all in case you were lost.

My love for the alphabet, which endures, grew out of reciting it but, 15 before that, out of seeing the letters on the page. In my own story books, before I could read them for myself, I fell in love with various winding, enchanted-looking initials drawn by Walter Crane at the heads of fairy tales. In "Once up a time," an "O" had a rabbit running it as a treadmill, his feet upon flowers. When the day came, years later, for me to see the Book of Kells, all the wizardry of letter, initial, and word swept over me a thousand times over, and the illumination, the gold, seemed a part of the world's beauty and holiness that had been there from the start.

Content

1. Most professional writers of quality have been in love with books since childhood. Why?
2. How can parents encourage their children to become avid readers? What are the benefits of this process?
3. What else does Welty's adoration of books as a child reveal about her as a person? What does her discussion of how she came to know and love books reveal about her parents?

Strategies/Structures

4. Throughout the essay Welty describes the context in which she encountered the books she loved; why are these contexts important?
5. Welty refers to several books that people don't read anymore, such as *St. Elmo* and *Sanford and Merton*—perhaps even *Pilgrim's Progress*. How can her readers understand what's she's talking about if they haven't read the books?

Language

6. Comment on Welty's rich, embellished language in the last paragraph. How does it fit the subject?

For Writing

7. If you love to read, write an essay for an audience of television viewers explaining the joys of reading, either in general or with reference to particular kinds of books or other materials. See also Kleege, "Up Close, In Touch" (12–22).
8. Describe your ideal collection of books, general or specialized, either as a child or as an adult. Let your readers see, as Welty does, why your favorites are so treasured.
9. See the suggestion for writing (#8) in connection with Kozol's essay, "The Human Cost of an Illiterate Society" (210–18).

The Essay, a Vision: Definition and Reasons for Writing

There are two sorts of essays in this book, essays of literary nonfiction (sometimes called *literature of fact,* or *creative nonfiction,* or *belletristic essays*) and articles. In essays of literary nonfiction, the writer's artistry is paramount, illuminated by, as Elizabeth Hardwick says, an "individual intelligence and sparkle. We consent to watch a mind at work, without agreement often, but only for pleasure." In this type of essay, writers are seeking self-expression as much as exploration of the topic. Fulfillment brings satisfaction, as the writer who brings her laptop on the picnic hears from her companion, who admires this writing in a natural setting: "Whoa! Move over, Thoreau" (p. 31). Essays of literary nonfiction, which some people claim are the only true essays, are short prose pieces that use many of the same techniques that fiction does. They can present characters in action, in dialogue (even in interior monologue), in context, and in costume. They can play with time, with language, with points of view, and with narrative persona. As professional essayist E. B. White claims in "The Essayist and the Essay" (30–32), an essayist "can pull on any sort of shirt, be any sort of person, according to his mood or his subject matter— philosopher, scold, jester, raconteur, confidant, pundit, devil's advocate, enthusiast." The writer may also be a witness to events small or cataclysmic, firsthand or through—for example—understanding historic documents and photographs, as the visitors to the Holocaust museum at the site of the Dachau concentration camp in Germany are doing in the photograph on p. 27.

According to this view, the essay, says Annie Dillard, herself an essayist, "can do everything a poem can do, and everything a short story can do—everything but fake it. The elements in any nonfiction should be true not only artistically, the connections must hold at base and must be veracious," for essayists claim and readers believe that what they're reading is the truth. As Dillard says, "There's a lot of truth out there to work with. The real world arguably exerts a greater fascination on people than any fictional one. . . . The essayist thinks about actual things. He can make sense of them analytically or artistically."

The Essay Connection includes many types of essays of literary nonfiction: *memoir* and *partial autobiography,* such as Scott Russell Sanders's "Under the Influence" (274–86); *character sketches,* among them Leslie S. Moore's "Framing My Father" (239–44); *descriptions of a place,* as in Linda Hogan's "Dwellings" (259–65), or of *an experience,* such as the excerpts from Zitkala-Sa's *The School Days of an Indian Girl* (218–26); *narratives of events,* including Frederick Douglass's account of how he stood up to his cruel overseer ("You have seen how a man was made a slave; you shall see how a slave was made a man.") (133–38); *interpretive reviews* that comment at length on a work or a performance, as in Gilbert Highet's "The Gettysburg Address" (486–91); and *social commentary,* such as Jonathan Kozol's "The Human Cost of an Illiterate Society" (210–18).

Articles, in contrast, claims critic William Gass, are more concerned with substance than with style, for charm and elegance "will interfere with the impression of seriousness" they wish to maintain. An article, Gass continues, "must appear complete and straightforward and footnoted and useful and certain," for the article "pretends that everything is clear, that its argument is unassailable, that there are no soggy patches, no illicit interferences." Articles, he says, are written by professionals whose personality is unobtrusive in academic prose that "sounds like writing written down" rather than spoken aloud.

Although Gass clearly prefers essays to articles, he is also exaggerating the case to make his point. Indeed, much of your writing in college will be articles in the language and conventions of the particular subjects you study—critical interpretations of literature, position papers in philosophy or political science, interpretive presentations of information in history, case histories in psychology or business or law, explanations of processes in computer science or auto mechanics. For instance in the course of explaining what's "Inside the Engine" (178–84), master mechanics Tom and Ray Magliozzi tell readers how and why motor oil keeps the engine humming smoothly. Dr. Martin Luther King, Jr., in "Letter from Birmingham Jail" (445–61) uses evidence from world religions, his own life experience and that of numerous other African-Americans, theology, history, and the law to make the case for civil disobedience. And in "Blaming the Family for Economic Decline" (226–31), Stephanie Coontz interprets American public policy as it affects the way the American public conceives of the relationship between family stability and economic status—a confusion, she contends, between cause and effect.

Gass's preference for essays notwithstanding, articles such as these do not have to be dry, dull, and devoid of a point of view. For instance, the science writings of Isaac Asimov (158–67), Atul Gawande (231–39), Natalie Angier (299–304), and Oliver Sacks (314–22) are known for their reader-friendly clarity as well as their absolute accuracy. And we can count on them to have a point of view—Angier invariably favors what is moderate and healthful. Even academic essays don't have to be deadly serious (or dull), plodding along under the weight of obscure jargon as all of these essays indicate.

Why a person writes often determines his or her point of view on a particular subject. George Orwell claims that people write for four main reasons: "sheer egoism," "esthetic enthusiasm," "historical impulse," and—his primary motive—"political purpose, the desire to push the world in a certain direction." Joan Didion, echoing Orwell, believes that writers are always pushing and nagging and tugging at their readers, saying *"listen to me, see it my way, change your mind."* In "Why I Write: Making No Become Yes" (38–43), Elie Wiesel interprets *"see it my way,"* as the role of the writer as witness. The survivor of imprisonment in several Nazi concentration camps, Wiesel explains, "I was duty-bound to give meaning to my survival, to justify each moment of my life. . . . Not to transmit an experience is to betray it." In this eloquent essay Wiesel, winner of the 1986 Nobel Peace Prize, demonstrates his continuing commitment to make survivors, the entire world, continually remember the meaning of the Holocaust: "Why do I write? To wrench those victims from oblivion. To help the dead vanquish death"—a purpose also served by the museum at the Dachau concentration camp (see photo p. 27).

If you wish, you can use the definitions of *essay* and *article* provided here. Or for simplicity's sake you can consider all the writings in this book to be *essays*. No matter what you call them, we hope you'll find them engaging, provocative, stimulating examples of minds at work, ideas at play, artistry in action.

E. B. WHITE

Born in peaceful Mount Vernon, New York, in 1899, White was editor of the Cornell *Daily Sun* during his senior year in college, 1920–1921. In 1927, he joined the staff of the year-old *New Yorker,* writing "Talk of the Town" and "Notes and Comments" columns. Over the next thirty years he also wrote an estimated thirty thousand witty rejoinders to "newsbreaks," mangled sentences and misprints that filled out *New Yorker* columns and appeared under headings that White invented, such as "Letters We Never Finished Reading." In 1957 the Whites moved permanently to Allen Cove, Maine, where White wrote until his death in 1985. His distinguished works include the essays collected in *One Man's Meat* (1944), *The Second Tree from the Corner* (1954), and *The Points of My Compass* (1962); landmark advice on how to write clear, plain prose, *The Elements of Style* (rev. 1973), with his Cornell professor, William Strunk; and three classic children's books, *Stuart Little* (1945), *Charlotte's Web* (1952), and *The Trumpet of the Swan* (1970).

In this essay White amplifies upon Samuel Johnson's definition of the familiar, personal essay as "an irregular, undigested piece" of writing. He underestimates the skill of essayists, including himself, in considering them self-consigned to "second-class citizenship" in comparison with novelists, poets, and playwrights. In fact, the essays in this book are skillful works of thought and art, carefully controlled in structure, substance, language, and tone. In many essays the writer appears as a character or persona in his or her own work, speaking in a distinctive voice and interpreting the subject from an equally individualist—some would say idiosyncratic—point of view, as White does here and in all of his essays.

The Essayist and the Essay[1]

1   The essayist is a self-liberated man, sustained by the childish belief that everything he thinks about, everything that happens to him, is of general interest. He is a fellow who thoroughly enjoys his work, just as people who take bird walks enjoy theirs. Each new excursion of the essayist, each new "attempt," differs from the last and takes him into new country. This delights him. Only a person who is congenitally self-centered has the effrontery and the stamina to write essays.

2   There are as many kinds of essays as there are human attitudes or poses, as many essay flavors as there are Howard Johnson ice creams. The essayist arises in the morning and, if he has work to do, selects his garb from an unusually extensive wardrobe: he can pull on any sort of shirt, be any sort of person, according to his mood or his subject matter—

---

[1] Title supplied.

"Whoa! Move over, Thoreau."

What does this cartoon convey about the power of writing? The value of writing in an inspiring setting? The importance of an appreciative audience? Is it essential to know Thoreau and his writing in order to understand this cartoon? Why or why not?

philosopher, scold, jester, raconteur, confidant, pundit, devil's advocate, enthusiast. I like the essay, have always liked it, and even as a child was at work, attempting to inflict my young thoughts and experiences on others by putting them on paper. I early broke into print in the pages of *St. Nicholas*. I tend still to fall back on the essay form (or lack of form) when an idea strikes me, but I am not fooled about the place of the essay in twentieth-century American letters—it stands a short distance down the line. The essayist, unlike the novelist, the poet, and the playwright, must be content in his self-imposed role of second-class citizen. A writer who has his sights trained on the Nobel Prize or other earthly triumphs had best write a novel, a poem, or a play and leave the essayist to ramble about, content with living a free life and enjoying the satisfactions of a somewhat undisciplined existence. (Dr. Johnson called the essay "an irregular, undigested piece"; this happy practitioner has no wish to quarrel with the good doctor's characterization.)

There is one thing the essayist cannot do, though—he cannot indulge himself in deceit or in concealment, for he will be found out in no time. Desmond MacCarthy, in his introductory remarks to the 1928 E. P. Dutton & Company edition of Montaigne, observes that Montaigne "had the gift of natural candour. . . ." It is the basic ingredient. And even the essayist's escape from discipline is only a partial escape: the essay, although a relaxed form, imposes its own disciplines, raises its own problems, and

3

these disciplines and problems soon become apparent and (we all hope) act as a deterrent to anyone wielding a pen merely because he entertains random thoughts or is in a happy or wandering mood.

4   I think some people find the essay the last resort of the egoist, a much too self-conscious and self-serving form for their taste; they feel that it is presumptuous of a writer to assume that his little excursions or his small observations will interest the reader. There is some justice in their complaint. I have always been aware that I am by nature self-absorbed and egoistical; to write of myself to the extent I have done indicates a too great attention to my own life, not enough to the lives of others. I have worn many shirts, and not all of them have been a good fit. But when I am discouraged or downcast I need only fling open the door of my closet, and there, hidden behind everything else, hangs the mantle of Michel de Montaigne, smelling slightly of camphor.

Content

1. How can the writer avoid the deceit or concealment that White says is impossible for an essayist, and nevertheless engage in any sort of pose he wants, as White claims in paragraph 2?
2. If you are familiar with some of the essays in this book, refer to them in commenting on White's assertion that essayists are "by nature self-absorbed and egoistical" (¶ 4).

Strategies/Structures

3. What kind of a person does White appear to be in this essay? Does he in fact seem to be "self-absorbed and egoistical"? Does he seem to be the sort of person who would write essays, as he defines them?

Language

4. White refers to essayists as self-imposed second-class citizens (¶ 2). Explain why you agree or disagree.
5. Is the essay "an irregular, undigested piece," as Dr. Samuel Johnson remarked, or expressive of "a ramble" through "a free life . . . of a somewhat undisciplined existence"?

For Writing

6. Like love, the essay may be a form that everyone recognizes but that is hard to define; like love, the essay may have as many definitions as there are practitioners. For readers and writers of essays, write a definition of the essay that is broad enough to encompass some of its characteristic types.
7. Explain how an essay is a work of revelation, concealment, and shaping (or manipulation) of facts. Use a specific essay, preferably one from *The Essay Connection,* to illustrate your analysis.

LOUISE ERDRICH

Erdrich, a poet and novelist, writes out of her heritage. She was born in 1954 in Little Falls, Minnesota, the daughter of a Chippewa nation mother and a German-American father who taught for the Bureau of Indian Affairs. Erdrich graduated from Dartmouth College in 1976, and earned an M.A. from Johns Hopkins University in 1979. Returning to Dartmouth as writer-in-residence, she collaborated with Michael Dorris, first director of Dartmouth's Native American studies department, on a prize-winning short story, "The World's Greatest Fisherman," which the couple later expanded as *Love Medicine* (1984, again expanded 1993). Erdrich subsequently published two other volumes of this prize-winning trilogy, *The Beet Queen* (1986) and *Tracks* (1988), and later *Antelope Wife* (1998) and *The Birchbark House* (1999).

Erdrich and Dorris married in 1981; they collaborated on Dorris's *A Yellow Raft in Blue Water* (1988)—about his adoption of a child with learning disabilities as a result of Fetal Alcohol Syndrome—and on other works. Their unusual collaborative process left confusion about who actually was the author, although the couple was very clear about how they worked. Whoever had the original idea for the book wrote the first draft and was identified as the author; the other person edited it and another draft was written; then they repeated the process five or six more times. Finally they read the entire work aloud, never allowing a single manuscript to leave their home without, as Dorris said, "consensus on every word."

The appearance of ideal collaboration, indeed of a blissful though complicated life, is sustained throughout *The Blue Jay's Dance: A Birth Year* (1995), of which "Leap Day, the Baby-sitter, Dream, and Walking" are sections. In Erdrich's book about the process of being, concurrently and inseparably, a mother and a writer, the baby is a composite of the couple's youngest three children whom Erdrich "cared for in a series of writing offices" in a household on a New Hampshire farm with three older adopted Native American children. "I am not . . . the best or worst mother," says Erdrich, "but a writer only, a woman constantly surprised." Of enormous surprise—and sorrow—to the couple's close friends as well as their reading public was Dorris's suicide in 1997.

Leap Day, the Baby-sitter, Dream, Walking

Leap Day

As I write this, my left hand rests lightly on baby's back. She's trying to sleep but doesn't want me to put her down. With two fingers, I stroke the hair above her aching ear. If I take the fingers away, she wakes, she wails, as if my hand served a medicinal purpose. My arm below the elbow feels enormous, throbs with blood, seems almost to hum with electricity. It's a toss-up which will first lose consciousness: my arm or her head. At her inoculation last week, our four-year-old shrieked in surprise at the sudden pain of the needle. Then, to take the hurt away, she put the sting against my bare arm, held our skin together. Her tears stopped. My flesh still had magic. I could absorb her pain by touch.

The Baby-sitter

2 As our baby grows more into her own life, so I recover mine, but it is an ambiguous blessing. With one hand I drag the pen across the page and with the other, the other hand, I cannot let go of hers. There comes a day when we're at odds. I look at her, she looks at me. I put her down in a playpen filled with toys but she wants me and me alone after five minutes. I take her from the playpen, hold her, but she's not a lap baby for long anymore and wants to move, move anywhere. Soon she is bumping, creeping, undulating, standing, making her way through the little house on a hazardous obstacle course of delight.

3   There is a time in a baby's life when parents practically live at a crouch. She wants to move no matter what, to engage with the world. She is not a sleeper, but naps in short drops and then is ready for the adventure of me. I've just begun a thought, I'm writing my way in, when she laughs herself awake and bolts up, expectant, her grin wide, her eyes wild and magnetic, and electricity of hope rising off her, a thrill of mirth.

4   Her smile is so touching, so alight. I put my head down on my desk and within the dark cave of my hands a shout gathers. I'm at the moment. I will turn to her and lay aside this story, but with loss. I will play with her but part of me won't be there. Conflict has entered our perfect circle in a new set of clothes, and I'm torn between wanting to be with her always and needing to be—through writing and through concentration—who I am.

5   How perfectly, how generously she fits into my arms, how comfortably I receive her. How unsurpassed and fine. She props herself up on a chair and roams it, standing and dragging herself around its edges, nearly pulling it over onto herself. She dives for the woodstove tongs. I lunge after her, remove them. She creeps for the light socker. I divert her. She tries eagerly to stuff carpet lint, shoelaces, marbles, cat foot, dustpan, bark, paper clip, fork, ancient noodle, the cat herself, gravel, shoe, mop board, book, toy into her mouth. I remove these things from her spit damp fists. She makes for me, won't let me hold her. Goes hell-bent for the bathroom where she once found a toilet pond. She goes after table legs with teeth, puts her hands under rockers, grabs, clutches, falls, screams, goes blue, comes up laughing in my arms.

6   When she's had enough and I can nurse her, when she's tense with eager hunger in my arms and then quieter, quieter, regrouping for her

next set of bold charges and forays, when at last I can hold her for a space of time, I finally talk. I finally tell her I need help.

The first half day with the baby-sitter is a misery. Jean is a kind and forth-   7
right woman licensed for day care in her home. A small mother with dark eyes and a sweet smile, a woman who had been caring for babies for many years, even Jean is surprised by how long our baby manages to cry. Scream. Wail. Fret. I know the water torture and I hope Jean can wait it out. One hour. Another half. Two. My breasts burn, blood pumps hard in my temples. I call. Behind Jean's voice our baby's roar, continual and harsh as the sea, breaks and falls, over and over.

I get into the car and pick baby up. The experiment is not repeated   8
for a short while—then, then, the change. A hard week of teething, the first sudden breakthrough in language, and we try again. Little by little, she looks forward to this new routine. It happens. One day a week, two, finally three, she grows more out of my life and into her own.

The hours stretch wide on the mornings I work alone. Time expands   9
in a blue haze. I am lighter, fuller, ballooning with stunned surprise. I constantly possess the feeling we usually have only momentarily, the where-was-I that causes us to slap at our foreheads. I'm trying to jostle out the thoughts. *Where was I? Where was I?* Of course, I know. I was in an am-biguous heaven, a paradise both difficult and temporary, the only kind on earth we know.

I ease into the day making noise, banging the tea kettle, rich in my   10
aloneness again. Outside, the hoarfrost glitters, chickadees flip through the air, the woods and branches of the trees are outlines with a fine bril-liance. I am ready now to finish this book of scraps, of jottings, of notes and devotions taken at another time, another era in our lives. The little cat reclaims my lap and curls possessively beneath my hands, as I begin. . . .

Dream

One day, one night, I'll dream a dream, perhaps like any other dream, ex-   11
cept that I won't know it is the last dream of my life.

I am keeping track for baby, waiting for her to dream something that she   12
can put into words. There are spaces on the baby calendar for the first tooth, the first smile, the first word, but nowhere to record the first dream. I leave space in the margins and wait. She has been dreaming all along, there is no question watching her face complex in sleep, her eyes moving under delicate, violet-pink, sunrise lids.

Grand elk moving underneath the grand sky. Tyrant blue jays. Cats   13
loping bannerlike across the fields. Moths fanning their pale wings against the light. Spiders. Brown recluse, marked like a violin. The beat-ing of a heart perhaps, moving in, moving out. My own voice—perhaps

she dreams my own voice as I dream hers—starting out of sleep, awake, certain that she's cried out.

14   For years now I have been dreaming the powerful anxiety dreams of all parents. Something is lost, something must be protected. A baby swims in an aquarium, a baby sleeps in a suitcase. The suitcase goes astray, the airline company will not return it. I spend all night arguing with people at a baggage claims desk. Parents endure exhausting nights searching drawers and running through corridors and town streets and emptying laundry baskets looking for their missing babies. Mine is hiding in a washing machine or behind a Corinthian column or out in the long grass, the endless grass. Mine is running toward the nameless sky.

15   Now, as I move into the pages of manuscripts, I fall asleep anxious but embark on no tiring searches through piles of bricks and trains stations. The dream junk and dream treasure, the excess bliss and paranoia, goes into the pages of books. I do not dream when I am writing.

Walking

16   To pull herself upright, to strain upward, to climb, has been baby's obsession for the past three months and now, on her first birthday, it is that urge I celebrate and fear. She has pulled herself erect by the strings of her sister's hair, by using my clothes, hands, earrings, by the edges and the rungs and the unstable handles of the world. She has yanked herself up, stepped, and it is clear from her grand excitement that walking is one of the most important things we ever do. It is raw power to go forward, to lunge, catching at important arms and hands, to take control of the body, tell it what to do, to leave behind the immobility of babyhood. With each step she swells, her breath goes ragged and her eyes darken in a shine of happiness. A glaze of physical joy covers her, moves through her, more intense than the banged forehead, bumped chin, the bruises and knocks and losses, even than the breathtaking falls and solid thumps, joy more powerful than good sense.

17   It would seem she has everything she could want—she is fed, she is carried, she is rocked, put to sleep. But no, *walking* is the thing, the consuming urge to seize control. She has to walk to gain entrance to the world. From now on, she will get from here to there more and more by her own effort. As she goes, she will notice worn grass, shops or snow or the shapes of trees. She will walk for reasons other than to get somewhere in particular. She'll walk to think or not to think, to leave the body, which is often the same as becoming at one with it. She will walk to ward off anger in its many forms. For pleasure, purpose, or to grieve. She'll walk until her feet hurt, her muscles tremble, until her eyes are numb with looking. She'll walk until her sense of balance is the one thing left and the rest of the world is balanced, too, and eventually, if we do the growing up right, she will walk away from us.

Content

1. How, if at all, is it possible to combine the demands of parenting a very young child with the demands of being a writer? What qualities are needed for performing each role? Are these demands at all compatible? If so, in what ways? If not, why not?

2. Would a father's answer to question 1 be any different than a mother's? Why or why not?

Strategies/Structures

3. "Leap Day" has one paragraph, "The Baby-sitter" has nine, "Dream" has five, and "Walking" has two. Is each section self-contained? Why or why not?

4. Although each section focuses on the topic of its title, each subsequent section gains in perspective and complexity from its predecessors. Explain how organization of prior sections enables the enrichment of succeeding sections. Should Erdrich have tried to make the sections equal in length?

5. Could the sections have been arranged in any other order? Why or why not?

Language

6. Writing about babies, small children, and other little things (tiny objects, small animals) often elicits sentimental (overly emotional) language from the writer, who expects the reader to respond with equal sentimentality. Is this desirable? Why or why not?

7. Does Erdrich treat her subject sentimentally (don't confuse *sentimentality* with *sentiment*)? If so, where, and with what effect? If not, why not? What are the effects of straightforward (though loving) writing on a potentially sentimental topic?

For Writing

8. It is clear that Erdrich loves her baby, and that she also loves writing: "As our baby grows more into her own life, so I recover mine, but it is an ambiguous blessing. With one hand I drag the pen across the page and with the other, the other hand, I cannot let go of hers" (¶ 2). How is it possible to devote appropriate time and thought to writing (or to any other compelling creative endeavor—say, that of playing an instrument or playing a sport) amidst life's other demands? Determine what's most important in your life and work out a plan to balance two or three competitive, perhaps conflicting, demands on your time, thought, and energy. (For a variety of perspectives, see the essays in Part I, and also Judy Brady's "I Want a Wife" [361–64].)

9. Erdrich says, "The dream junk and dream treasure, the excess bliss and paranoia, goes into the pages of books" (¶ 15). How can a writer, in particular, sort out the "dream junk" from the "dream treasure"? At what stage in your writing does this sorting occur—before or during the writing of a particular draft? What do you need to enable you to do your best work—of any kind? Make a list (with the most important items at the top) and explain the order of the list and why each item is necessary.

ELIE WIESEL

Wiesel, a survivor of the Holocaust, explains, "For me, literature abolishes the gap between [childhood and death]. . . . Auschwitz marks the decisive, ultimate turning point . . . of the human adventure. Nothing will ever again be as it was. Thousands and thousands of deaths weigh upon every word. How speak of redemption after Treblinka? and how speak of anything else?" As a survivor, he became a writer in order to become a witness: "I believed that, having survived by chance, I was duty-bound to give meaning to my survival, to justify each moment of my life. I knew the story had to be told. Not to transmit an experience is to betray it." Wiesel has developed a literary style that reflects the distilled experience of concentration camps, in which "a sentence is worth a page, a word is worth a sentence. The unspoken weighs heavier than the spoken. . . . Say only the essential— say only what no other would say . . . a style sharp, hard, strong, in a word, pared. Suppress the imagination. And feeling, and philosophy. Speak as a witness on the stand speaks. With no indulgence to others or oneself."

In May 1944, when he was fifteen, Wiesel was forcibly removed from his native town of Sighet, Hungary ("which no longer exists," he says, "except in the memory of those it expelled"), to the first of several concentration camps. Although six million Jews died in the camps, including members of his family, Wiesel was liberated from Buchenwald in April 1945 and sent to Paris, where he studied philosophy. For twenty years "of exploration and apprenticeship" he worked as a journalist for Jewish newspapers, but the turning point in his career as a writer came in 1954 when he met novelist François Mauriac, who urged him to speak on behalf of the children in concentration camps. This encouraged Wiesel (who has lived in New York since 1956) to write some forty books of fiction, nonfiction, poetry, and drama, starting in 1958 with *Night,* which opens, "In the beginning was faith, confidence, illusion." (The photograph on the Holocaust museum wall [p. 27] shows these in the process of being shattered as families were rounded up for deportation by the Gestapo.) He published his memoirs *All the Rivers Run to the Sea* in 1996, and *And the Sea Is Never Full* in 1999. Wiesel, true citizen of the world, received the Nobel Peace Prize in 1986 for his efforts epitomized in "Why I Write: Making No Become Yes," originally published in the *New York Times Book Review,* April 14, 1986.

Why I Write:
Making No Become Yes

1   Why do I write?
2   Perhaps in order not to go mad. Or, on the contrary, to touch the bottom of madness. Like Samuel Beckett, the survivor expresses himself "en désepoir de cause"—out of desperation.

Speaking of the solitude of the survivor, the great Yiddish and Hebrew poet and thinker Aaron Zeitlin addresses those—his father, his brother, his friends—who have died and left him: "You have abandoned me," he says to them. "You are together, without me. I am here. Alone. And I make words."

So do I, just like him. I also say words, write words, reluctantly.

There are easier occupations, far more pleasant ones. But for the survivor, writing is not a profession, but an occupation, a duty. Camus calls it "an honor." As he puts it: "I entered literature through worship." Other writers have said they did so through anger, through love. Speaking for myself, I would say—through silence.

It was by seeking, by probing silence that I began to discover the perils and power of the word. I never intended to be a philosopher, or a theologian. The only role I sought was that of witness. I believed that, having survived by chance, I was duty-bound to give meaning to my survival, to justify each moment of my life. I knew the story had to be told. Not to transmit an experience is to betray it. This is what Jewish tradition teaches us. But how to do this? "When Israel is in exile, so is the word," says the Zohar. The word has deserted the meaning it was intended to convey— impossible to make them coincide. The displacement, the shift, is irrevocable.

This was never more true than right after the upheaval. We all knew that we could never, never say what had to be said, that we could never express in words, coherent, intelligible words, our experience of madness on an absolute scale. The walk through flaming night, the silence before and after the selection, the monotonous praying of the condemned, the Kaddish of the dying, the fear and hunger of the sick, the shame and suffering, the haunted eyes, the demented stares. I thought that I would never be able to speak of them. All words seemed inadequate, worn, foolish, lifeless, whereas I wanted them to be searing.

Where was I to discover a fresh vocabulary, a primeval language? The language of night was not human, it was primitive, almost animal hoarse shouting, screams, muffled moaning, savage howling, the sound of beating. A brute strikes out wildly, a body falls. An officer raises his arm and a whole community walks toward a common grave. A soldier shrugs his shoulders, and a thousand families are torn apart, to be reunited only by death. This was the concentration camp language. It negated all other language and took its place. Rather than a link, it became a wall. Could it be surmounted? Could the reader be brought to the other side? I knew the answer was negative, and yet I knew that "no" had to become "yes." It was the last wish of the dead.

The fear of forgetting remains the main obsession of all those who have passed through the universe of the damned. The enemy counted on people's incredulity and forgetfulness. How could one foil this plot? And if memory grew hollow, empty of substance, what would happen to all we had accumulated along the way? Remember, said the father to his son, and the son to his friend. Gather the names, the faces, the tears. We had all taken an oath: "If, by some miracle, I emerge alive, I will devote my life to testifying on behalf of those whose shadow will fall on mine forever and ever."

10   That is why I write certain things rather than others—to remain faithful.

11   Of course, there are times of doubt for the survivor, times when one gives in to weakness, or longs for comfort. I hear a voice within me telling me to stop mourning the past. I too want to sing of love and of its magic. I too want to celebrate the sun, and the dawn that heralds the sun. I would like to shout, and shout loudly: "Listen, listen well! I too am capable of victory, do you hear? I too am open to laughter and joy! I want to stride, head high, my face unguarded, without having to point to the ashes over there on the horizon, without having to tamper with facts to hide their tragic ugliness. For a man born blind, God himself is blind, but look, I see, I am not blind." One feels like shouting this, but the shout changes to a murmur. One must make a choice; one must remain faithful. A big word, I know. Nevertheless, I use it, it suits me. Having written the things I have written, I feel I can afford no longer to play with words. If I say that the writer in me wants to remain loyal, it is because it is true. This sentiment moves all survivors; they owe nothing to anyone, but everything to the dead.

12   I owe them my roots and my memory. I am duty-bound to serve as their emissary, transmitting the history of their disappearance, even if it disturbs, even if it brings pain. Not to do so would be to betray them, and thus myself. And since I am incapable of communicating their cry by shouting, I simply look at them. I see them and I write.

13   While writing, I question them as I question myself. I believe I have said it before, elsewhere. I write to understand as much as to be understood. Will I succeed one day? Wherever one starts, one reaches darkness. God? He remains the God of darkness. Man? The source of darkness. The killers' derision, their victims' tears, the onlookers' indifference, their complicity and complacency—the divine role in all that I do not understand. A million children massacred—I shall never understand.

14   Jewish children—they haunt my writings. I see them again and again. I shall always see them. Hounded, humiliated, bent like the old men who surround them as though to protect them, unable to do so. They are thirsty, the children, and there is no one to give them water. They are hungry, but there is no one to give them a crust of bread. They are afraid, and there is no one to reassure them.

15   They walk in the middle of the road, like vagabonds. They are on the way to the station, and they will never return. In sealed cars, without air or food, they travel toward another world. They guess where they are going, they know it, and they keep silent. Tense, thoughtful, they listen to the wind, the call of death in the distance.

16   All these children, these old people, I see them. I never stop seeing them. I belong to them.

But they, to whom do they belong?   17

People tend to think that a murderer weakens when facing a child.   18
The child reawakens the killer's lost humanity. The killer can no longer
kill the child before him, the child inside him.

But with us it happened differently. Our Jewish children had no effect   19
upon the killers. Nor upon the world. Nor upon God.

I think of them, I think of their childhood. Their childhood is a small   20
Jewish town, and this town is no more. They frighten me; they reflect an
image of myself, one that I pursue and run from at the same time—the
image of a Jewish adolescent who knew no fear, except the fear of God,
whose faith was whole, comforting, and not marked by anxiety.

No, I do not understand. And if I write, it is to warn the reader that   21
he will not understand either. "You will not understand, you will never
understand," were the words heard everywhere during the reign of night.
I can only echo them. You, who never lived under a sky of blood, will
never know what it was like. Even if you read all the books ever written,
even if you listen to all the testimonies ever given, you will remain on this
side of the wall, you will view the agony and death of a people from afar,
through the screen of a memory that is not your own.

An admission of impotence and guilt? I do not know. All I know is   22
that Treblinka and Auschwitz cannot be told. And yet I have tried. God
knows I have tried.

Have I attempted too much or not enough? Among some twenty-five   23
volumes, only three or four penetrate the phantasmagoric realm of the
dead. In my other books, through my other books, I have tried to follow
other roads. For it is dangerous to linger among the dead, they hold on to
you and you run the risk of speaking only to them. And so I have forced
myself to turn away from them and study other periods, explore other des-
tinies and teach other tales—the Bible and the Talmud, Hasidism and its
fervor, the shtetl and its songs, Jerusalem and its echoes, the Russian Jews
and their anguish, their awakening, their courage. At times, it has seemed
to me that I was speaking of other things with the sole purpose of keeping
the essential—the personal experience—unspoken. At times I have wondered: And what if I was wrong? Perhaps I should not have heeded my
own advice and stayed in my own world with the dead.

But then, I have not forgotten the dead. They have their rightful place   24
even in the works about the Hasidic capitals Ruzhany and Korets, and
Jerusalem. Even in my biblical and Midrashic tales, I pursue their presence, mute and motionless. The presence of the dead then beckons in such
tangible ways that it affects even the most removed characters. Thus they
appear on Mount Moriah, where Abraham is about to sacrifice his son, a
burnt offering to their common God. They appear on Mount Nebo, where
Moses enters solitude and death. They appear in Hasidic and Talmudic
legends in which victims forever need defending against forces that would
crush them. Technically, so to speak, they are of course elsewhere, in time

and space, but on a deeper, truer plane, the dead are part of every story, of every scene.

25   "But what is the connection?" you will ask. Believe me, there is one. After Auschwitz everything brings us back to Auschwitz. When I speak of Abraham, Isaac and Jacob, when I invoke Rabbi Yohanan ben Zakkai and Rabbi Akiba, it is the better to understand them in the light of Auschwitz. As for the Maggid of Mezeritch and his disciples, it is in order to encounter the followers of their followers that I reconstruct their spellbound, spellbinding universe. I like to imagine them alive, exuberant, celebrating life and hope. Their happiness is as necessary to me as it was once to themselves.

26   And yet—how did they manage to keep their faith intact? How did they manage to sing as they went to meet the Angel of Death? I know Hasidim who never vacillated—I respect their strength. I know others who chose rebellion, protest, rage—I respect their courage. For there comes a time when only those who do not believe in God will not cry out to him in wrath and anguish.

27   Do not judge either group. Even the heroes perished as martyrs, even the martyrs died as heroes. Who would dare oppose knives to prayers? The faith of some matters as much as the strength of others. It is not ours to judge, it is only ours to tell the tale.

28   But where is one to begin? Whom is one to include? One meets a Hasid in all my novels. And a child. And an old man. And a beggar. And a madman. They are all part of my inner landscape. The reason why? Pursued and persecuted by the killers, I offer them shelter. The enemy wanted to create a society purged of their presence, and I have brought some of them back. The world denied them, repudiated them, so I let them live at least within the feverish dreams of my characters.

29   It is for them that I write, and yet the survivor may experience remorse. He has tried to bear witness; it was all in vain.

30   After the liberation, we had illusions. We were convinced that a new world would be built upon the ruins of Europe. A new civilization would see the light. No more wars, no more hate, no more intolerance, no fanaticism. And all this because the witnesses would speak. And speak they did, to no avail.

31   They will continue, for they cannot do otherwise. When man, in his grief, falls silent, Goethe says, then God gives him the strength to sing his sorrows. From that moment on, he may no longer choose not to sing, whether his song is heard or not. What matters is to struggle against silence with words, or through another form of silence. What matters is to gather a smile here and there, a tear here and there, a word here and there, and thus justify the faith placed in you, a long time ago, by so many victims.

32   Why do I write? To wrench those victims from oblivion. To help the dead vanquish death.

(Translated from the French by Rosette C. Lamont)

Content

1. Wiesel says, "The only role I sought [as a writer] was that of witness" (¶ 6). What does he mean by "witness"? Find examples of this role throughout the essay.

2. What does Wiesel mean by "not to transmit an experience is to betray it" (¶ 6)? What experience does his writing transmit? Why is this important to Wiesel? To humanity?

3. Does "Why I Write" fulfill Wiesel's commitment to "make no become yes" (¶ 8)? Explain.

Strategies/Structures

4. Identify some of Wiesel's major ethical appeals in this essay. Does he want to move his readers to action as well as to thought?

5. Why would Wiesel use paradoxes in an effort to explain and clarify? Explain the meaning of the following paradoxes:

   a. "No, I do not understand. And if I write, it is to warn the reader that he will not understand either" (¶ 21).
   b. I write "to help the dead vanquish death" (¶ 32).

6. For what audience does Wiesel want to explain "Why I Write"? What understanding of Judaism does Wiesel expect his readers to have? Of World War II? Of the operation of concentration camps? Why does he expect his reasons to matter to these readers, whether or not they have extensive knowledge of any of them?

Language

7. Does Wiesel's style here fulfill his goals of a style that is "sharp, hard, strong, pared"? Why is such a style appropriate to the subject?

8. Explain the meaning of "concentration camp language" (¶ 8). Why did it negate all other language and take its place (¶ 8)?

For Writing

9. Write an essay for someone who doesn't like to write comparing Elie Wiesel's and Amy Tan's reasons for writing as expressed in their essays "Why I Write" (38–43) and "Mother Tongue" (6–12).

10. Write an essay exploring for yourself how you know when you get ideas that are interesting or otherwise compelling enough to write about. If you're devoid of ideas, what are some ways you might go about getting some? In addition to the essays by White and Wiesel, consider the essays by Lamott, Least Heat-Moon, and Wallace, as well as the Writers' Notebooks in the chapter "Getting Started."

Getting Started

To expect some people to learn to write by showing them a published essay or book is like expecting novice bakers to learn to make a wedding cake from looking at the completed confection, resplendent with icing and decorations. Indeed, the completed product in each case offers a model of what the finished work of art should look like—in concept, organization, shape, and style. Careful examination of the text exposes the intricacies of the finished sentences, paragraphs, logic, illustrative examples, and nuances of style. The text likewise provides cues about the context (intellectual, political, aesthetic . . .) in which it originated, its purpose, and its intended audience. But no matter how hard you look, it's almost impossible to detect in a completed, professionally polished work much about the process by which it was composed—the numerous visions and revisions of ideas and expression; the effort, frustration, even exhilaration; whether the author was composing in bed (see the photo of Mark Twain above), at a desk, or at a computer terminal (see the photos on pp. 1 and 84). Blood, sweat, and tears don't belong on the printed page any more than they belong in the gymnast's flawless public performance on the balance beam. The audience doesn't want to agonize over the production but to enjoy the result.

Becoming a Writer

You've been training to become a writer all your life. Whether you want to become a professional writer or merely to write well enough to survive in college or on the job, your senses (particularly of sight and hearing) were functioning—even before you could interpret and understand in words the stimuli they conveyed. Indeed, the three sections of Eudora Welty's *One Writer's Beginnings* focus on the topics "Listening" (excerpted on 22–26), "Learning to See," and "Finding a Voice." Yet even in "Listening," which examines Welty's oral memories of songs sung, stories told, Welty is exploring the pleasures of sight, not only in learning to read, but in the pleasure of seeing the "winding, enchanted-looking initials drawn by Walter Crane at the heads of fairy tales." Welty's pleasure is in stark contrast to the ambivalent pleasure Georgina Kleege experiences in reading "up close" with only 10% eyesight, which produces "a dull, constant pain" above her right eye, that will "deepen and spread, migrating to my forehead and the other eye," and eventually to the neck and shoulders if she stays hunched over the beloved book or her writing in progress: "I bargain with the pain: I'll stop, I promise, just let me get to the end of the paragraph. Another minute, another sentence, one more word."

As you start to work, urges Stephen King in "A door . . . you are willing to shut" (49–52), find a private writing space, keeping people out and yourself in. "The closed door is your way of telling the world and yourself that you mean business; you have made a serious commitment to write. . . " King suggests you settle on a "daily writing goal" and get to work.

Getting started for many people is the most difficult part of writing. It's hard to begin if you don't know what to write about. In "Polaroids" (56–60) Anne Lamott illustrates a good way to find a subject, analogous to "watching a Polaroid develop. You can't," she says, "know exactly what the picture is going to look like until it has finished developing." Indeed, you're "not supposed to know" at the outset what you'll find when you begin to focus; the picture emerges as you immerse yourself in the subject and begin to identify themes, individuals, revealing details. And gradually the overall shape and structure appear. Aha!

Making "A List of Nothing in Particular" (52–56), as William Least Heat-Moon did when he drove his van through the "barren waste" of west Texas on a circuit of the country, can enable one to extract some meaning, some significance even out of a territory where "'there's nothing out there.'" Heat-Moon's list has an eclectic span, seemingly random until it snaps into focus, ranging from "mockingbird" to "jackrabbit (chewed on cactus)" to "wind (always)." Talking with others, making an "idea tree," brainstorming, reading, thinking—even dreaming or daydreaming—all of these can provide you with something to write about, if you remain receptive to the possibilities.

You may end up writing a piece—preferably short—composed entirely of lists, as David Foster Wallace does in "Lunchtime at the Illinois State Fair" (69–74). Even if you simply go somewhere and take notes on what you see, once you've organized them into categories that make logical or artistic sense, you've got the start—if not the finish—of a paper. As Wallace strolls the gauntlet of food booths, he appears to be taking cynical snapshot after snapshot of the ugly in quest of the inedible, a "grand mass of Midwest humanity, eating and shuffling and rubbing," as illustrated in the photo on p. 71.

Anne Fadiman's "Mail" (60–69) discusses writing of a different kind, in an engaging exploration of the phenomena associated with writing and receiving letters. In seventeenth-century London there was "mail service nearly every hour because there were no telephones." Until 1840, in England postage was paid by the recipient of the mail, rather than by the sender; when the sender assumed the cost, the mails expanded democratically. The 1990s saw the advent of e-mail, which embodied the motto of sixteenth-century correspondents: "Haste, haste, haste, for lyfe, for lyfe, haste!" She details the process of switching to e-mail, learning a new way of writing that replaces the old method of "folding the paper, sealing the envelope, looking up the address, licking the stamp. . . ." But the ease of writing and sending e-mail comes at a price. Are e-mails well written? While they are brief, they are "frequently devoid of capitalization, minimally punctuated, and creatively spelled." Unlike letters—preferably handwritten—in hard copy, e-mails do not fulfill a good letter's essential function—"to express the personality of its writer"—communicating instead by e-acronyms (BTDT, ROTFL) and "smileys" :-). Nevertheless, because e-mail correspondence is so rapid, it provides a way of getting started with ideas that may be developed in an amplified fashion later on.

Writers' Notebooks

Keeping a writer's diary or notebook, whether you do it with pencil, pen, typewriter, or word processor, can be a good way to get started—and even to keep going. Writing regularly—and better yet, at a regular time of the day or week—in a notebook or its equivalent, can give you a lot to think about while you're writing, and a lot to expand on later. You could keep an account of what you do every day (6:30–7:30, swimming laps, shower; 7:30–8:15, breakfast—toasted English muffin, orange juice, raspberry yogurt . . .), but if your life is routine, that might get monotonous.

The notebook entries included in this section were written in a variety of circumstances. "Selections from Student Writers' Notebooks" (74–83) met not only course requirements but were also obviously outlets for many types of expressions and explorations ranging from the meaning of education, race, and sexuality to the importance of family, music, an ordered environment, and writing.

A provocative and potentially useful writer's notebook might contain any or all of the following types of writing, and more:

- Reactions to one's reading: "I should pick up *Mansfield Park* again. Reading Austen or anyone that good reminds me of what I could be saying, and of the work that has to be put into it" (Loftus 75).
- Provocative quotations—invented, read, or overheard; appealing figures of speech; dialogue, dialect: "There are uncountable pork options: Paulie's Pork Out, the Pork Patio, Freshfried Pork Skins, the Pork Street Cafe. The Pork Street Cafe is a 'One Hundred Percent All-Pork Establishment,' says its loudspeaker. 'Ever last thing.' I'm praying this doesn't include the beverages" (Wallace 70).
- Lists—including sights, sounds, scents: "On one wall [of the living room] was a dart board with no darts and the wall behind pocked with holes. The lining had been torn from the bottom of a yellow Chippendale sofa and stuffing poked through. . . . On the carpet . . . was a bowl of milk with Cheerios floating" (K. King 79).
- Memorable details—of clothing, animals, objects, settings, phenomena, processes: "The camp seems loudest at night. A huge, dulled murmur flows up from the valleys with hacking, rattling coughs, unending moaning like mantras, mules braying, wails, and shrieks like a child stepped on a nail. Clank tap-tapping, metal pots clanking and wood chopping sounds but no sounds of laughter" (Ryan 81).
- Personal aspirations, fears, joy, anger: "My apartment is stark. I'm stark. I hate those irresponsible, indulgent feminine traits that are me, the real me. I want my masculine, minimal, logical, problem-solving self to dominate. I want that hard, durable exterior that is not unlike a wall. A cool marble wall that endures" (Yoritomo 77).
- Sketches of people, either intrinsically interesting or engaged in intriguing activities, whether novel or familiar: "A tall African American man with no front teeth . . . handed me a Polaroid someone had taken of him and his friends. . . His two friends in the picture had Down's syndrome. All three of them looked extremely pleased with themselves. I admired the picture and then handed it back to him. He stopped, so I stopped, too. He pointed to his own image. 'That,' he said, 'is one cool man'" (Lamott 58).
- Analyses of friendships, family relationships: "My parents are getting divorced. . . . We did not put up a [Christmas] tree. . . . This year [since dad was gone] mom said we could eat when we wanted. But we never did. I ate a beans n franks dinner [by myself]. My brother went to drink his gift certificate" (Weast 78).
- Commentary on notable events, current or past, national or more immediate: "In California thongs are still Nipper Flippers or Jap Slaps. . . . December seventh is the Ides of March. I'm asked how I can see, is my field of vision narrowed?" (Watanabe 81).

- Possibilities for adventure, exploration, conflict: "Today in class Dudley said he's 'tired of racial issues in class.' Well—if he's tired of them, how does he think I feel? For years I have been the only Black (or at most one of two or three) in class and I have had to deal with white negativism towards Blacks" (Coles 79).
- Jokes, anecdotes, and humorous situations, characters, comic mannerisms, punch lines, provocative settings: "two circling buzzards (not yet, boys)" (Least Heat-Moon 53).

You'll need to put enough explanatory details in your notebook to remind yourself three weeks—or three years—later what something meant when you wrote it down, as the notebook keepers here have done. As all of these notebook entries reveal, those of the student writers in particular, in a writer's notebook you can be most candid, most off guard, for there you're writing primarily for yourself. You're also writing for yourself when you're freewriting—writing rapidly, with or without a particular subject, without editing, while you're in the process of generating ideas. As you freewrite you can free-associate, thinking of connections among like and unlike things or ideas, exploring their implications. Anything goes into the notebook, but not everything stays in later drafts if you decide to turn some of your most focused discussion into an essay. If you get into the habit of writing regularly on paper, you may find that you're also hearing the "voices in your head" that professional writers often experience. As James Thurber explained to an interviewer, "I never quite know when I'm not writing. Sometimes my wife comes up to me at a party and says, 'Dammit, Thurber, stop writing.' Or my daughter will look up from the dinner table and ask, 'Is he sick?' 'No,' my wife says, 'he's writing something.'"

Playing around with words and ideas in a notebook or in your head can also lead to an entire essay: a narrative, character sketch, reminiscence, discussion of how to do it, an argument, review, or some other form suitable for an extended piece of writing. After several drafts (107–13), Mary Ruffin's evocative portrait of her mother, who died when Mary was thirteen, emerged from fragments in her writer's notebook to become the polished "Mama's Smoke" (113–15), sophisticated in concept and techniques.

No matter what you write about, rereading a notebook entry or a freewriting can provide some material to start with. Ask yourself, "What do I want to write about?" "What makes me particularly happy—or angry?" (Don't write about something that seems bland, like a cookie without sugar. If it doesn't appeal to you, it won't attract your readers either.) As you write you will almost automatically be using description, narration, comparison and contrast, and other rhetorical techniques to express yourself, even if you don't attach labels to them. Enjoy.

STEPHEN KING

"People want to be scared," says Stephen King (a.k.a. Richard Bachman and John Swithen), but "beneath its fangs and fright wig," horror fiction is quite conservative, for readers understand that "the evildoers will almost certainly be punished." He was born in Portland, Maine, in 1947, and after working as a janitor, mill hand, and laundry laborer, he graduated from the University of Maine (B.A., 1970) and taught high school English briefly while writing his enormously popular first novel, *Carrie* (1974). This inaugurated a career-long series of bestsellers, from *The Shining* (1977) to *Dreamcatcher* (2001), as well as short stories, film, and video scripts characterized by a mix of horror, fantasy, science fiction, and humor. In June 1999 he was hit by a car while taking his habitual walk along a Maine highway. During his long recuperation from serious injuries he wrote *On Writing: A Memoir of the Craft* (2000), in which "A door . . . you are willing to shut" appears.

"Once I start to work on a project," explains King, "I don't stop and I don't slow down. . . . I write every day, workaholic dweeb or not. That includes Christmas, the Fourth [of July], and my birthday." Not working, he says, "is the real work. When I'm writing, it's all the playground, and the worst three hours I ever spent there were still pretty damn good." The work starts, he says, by finding "a door . . . you are willing to shut," avoiding distractions such as telephones and video games. "Put your desk in the corner, and every time you sit down there to write, remind yourself of why it isn't in the middle of the room. Life isn't a support-system for art. It's the other way around."

"A door . . . you are willing to shut," *from* On Writing

Y ou can read anywhere, almost, but when it comes to writing, library   1
carrels, park benches, and rented flats should be courts of last resort—
Truman Capote said he did his best work in motel rooms, but he is an exception; most of us do our best in a place of our own. Until you get one, you'll find your new resolution to write a lot hard to take seriously.

Your writing room doesn't have to sport a Playboy Philosophy decor,   2
and you don't need an Early American rolltop desk in which to house your writing implements. I wrote my first two published novels, *Carrie* and *'Salem's Lot*, in the laundry room of a doublewide trailer, pounding away on my wife's portable Olivetti typewriter and balancing a child's desk on my thighs; John Cheever reputedly wrote in the basement of his Park Avenue apartment building, near the furnace. The space can be humble (probably *should* be, as I think I have already suggested), and it really needs only one thing: a door which you are willing to shut. The closed door is

your way of telling the world and yourself that you mean business; you have made a serious commitment to write and intend to walk the walk as well as talk the talk.

3   By the time you step into your new writing space and close the door, you should have settled on a daily writing goal. As with physical exercise, it would be best to set this goal low at first, to avoid discouragement. I suggest a thousand words a day, and because I'm feeling magnanimous, I'll also suggest that you can take one day a week off, at least to begin with. No more; you'll lose the urgency and immediacy of your story if you do. With that goal set, resolve to yourself that the door stays closed until that goal is met. Get busy putting those thousand words on paper or on a floppy disk. In an early interview (this was to promote *Carrie,* I think), a radio talk-show host asked me how I wrote. My reply—"One word at a time"—seemingly left him without a reply. I think he was trying to decide whether or not I was joking. I wasn't. In the end, it's always that simple. Whether it's a vignette of a single page or an epic trilogy like *The Lord of the Rings,* the work is always accomplished one word at a time. The door closes the rest of the world out; it also serves to close you in and keep you focused on the job at hand.

4   If possible, there should be no telephone in your writing room, certainly no TV or videogames for you to fool around with. If there's a window, draw the curtains or pull down the shades unless it looks out at a blank wall. For any writer, but for the beginning writer in particular, it's wise to eliminate every possible distraction. If you continue to write, you will begin to filter out these distractions naturally, but at the start it's best to try and take care of them before you write. I work to loud music—hard-rock stuff like AC/DC, Guns 'n Roses, and Metallica have always been particular favorites—but for me the music is just another way of shutting the door. It surrounds me, keeps the mundane world out. When you write, you want to get rid of the world, do you not? Of course you do. When you're writing, you're creating your own worlds.

5   I think we're actually talking about creative sleep. Like your bedroom, your writing room should be private, a place where you go to dream. Your schedule—in at about the same time every day, out when your thousand words are on paper or disk—exists in order to habituate yourself, to make yourself ready to dream just as you make yourself ready to sleep by going to bed at roughly the same time each night and following the same ritual as you go. In both writing and sleeping, we learn to be physically still at the same time we are encouraging our minds to unlock from the humdrum rational thinking of our daytime lives. And as your mind and body grow accustomed to a certain amount of sleep each night—six hours, seven, maybe the recommended eight—so can you train your waking mind to sleep creatively and work out the vividly imagined waking dreams which are successful works of fiction.

But you need the room, you need the door, and you need the de- ₆ termination to shut the door. You need a concrete goal, as well. The longer you keep to these basics, the easier the act of writing will become. Don't wait for the muse. As I've said, he's a hardheaded guy who's not susceptible to a lot of creative fluttering. This isn't the Ouija board or the spirit-world we're talking about here, but just another job like laying pipe or driving long-haul trucks. Your job is to make sure the muse knows where you're going to be every day from nine 'til noon or seven 'til three. If he does know, I assure you that sooner or later he'll start showing up, chomping his cigar and making his magic.

Content

1. Why are "the basics" King identifies—"the room," "the door," "the determi- nation to shut the door," and "a concrete goal"—so important for writing? In your own experience, is each of equal importance? Do you share King's preference for writing with the shades drawn to "loud music—hard-rock stuff"? What is your ideal writing environment? How can you or do you control it?

2. If you've read any of King's fiction or seen his movies, how does this knowl- edge affect your receptiveness to his advice on writing? Does King's advice pertain to other types of writing in addition to the mixture of horror, fantasy, sci-fi, and humor that characterizes most of his work?

3. What does King mean when he says, "The closed door is your way of telling the world and yourself that you mean business" (¶ 2)? Why is it important for begin- ning writers to make such a statement both to "the world" and to themselves? What does King mean by the term "creative sleep" (¶ 5)? How does "creative sleep" work?

Strategies/Structures

4. When King speaks to "you" throughout his essay, does it seem as if he is talking to you personally? Would the effectiveness of his advice (to you or to other readers) differ significantly had he written impersonally (say, in the third person) instead?

5. Advice givers often preach. And readers often resent being preached at. King delivers his advice very emphatically. Is he preaching? If he doesn't offend you, will you take his advice?

Language

6. King alludes to the muse of creativity—traditionally considered a beautiful woman playing alluring music—as a male, "chomping his cigar and making his magic" (¶ 6). Why does King choose such a macho muse instead of a more tra- ditional figure? How does this muse relate to King's writing—his subjects and his style?

7. "A door which you are willing to shut" (¶ 2) works on both the literal and metaphorical levels. Explain why this is a good way to get double mileage out of your language.

For Writing

8. Take King's advice and find a private writing space to which you can retreat daily. Make it your own by adapting the furniture and decoration (if possible), the temperature, ventilation, view (or no view), and sound (music? If so, what kind?) to your liking. Write one page (around 250 words) a day for a full week. As the week goes on, try changing some of the features in your environment (write at different times of the day or night, let people or pets in or keep them out, turn off the music or TV), stop answering the telephone, and see what effect each of these changes has on the quantity and quality of your writing.

9. Write an essay that advises beginners about "the basics" of some activity that you love and know how to do well. What do they have to know first? What builds next on that? Then what? What is the desired result? Where can they go astray? Try presenting this information in a step-by-step fashion, and then write at least one step as a narrative (King's method) to see which works better. Have a novice try out your directions to see whether they are clear and produce the intended outcome. If not, ask your reader to help you figure out what needs to be added. Then, revise your directions and try again.

WILLIAM LEAST HEAT-MOON

William Least Heat-Moon, as William Trogdon renamed himself to acknowledge his Osage Indian ancestry, was born in 1939 in Kansas City, Missouri. He earned four degrees from the University of Missouri–Columbia, including a B.A. in photojournalism (1978) and a Ph.D. in literature (1973). His books include *PrairyErth* (1991) and *River-Horse* (1992). On one cold day in February 1979, "a day of canceled expectations," Least Heat-Moon lost both his wife ("the Cherokee") and his part-time job teaching English at a Missouri college.

True to the American tradition, to escape he took to the road, the "blue highways"—back roads on the old road maps—in the van that would be home as he circled the United States clockwise "in search of places where change did not mean ruin and where time and men and deeds connected." His account of his trip, *Blue Highways* (1982), is an intimate exploration of America's small towns, "Remote, Oregon; Simplicity, Virginia; New Freedom, Pennsylvania; New Hope, Tennessee; Why, Arizona; Whynot, Mississippi; Igo, California (just down the road from Ono). . . ." Though he tried to lose himself as a stranger in a strange land, as he came to know and appreciate the country through its back roads and small towns, Least Heat-Moon came inevitably to know and come to terms with himself. "The mere listing of details meaningless in themselves, at once provides them with significance which one denies in vain," says novelist Steven Millhauser. "The beauty of irrelevance fades away, accident darkens into design." Consequently, traveling—moving along a linear route—lends itself to list making, a good way to impose design on happenstance, to remember where you're going, where you've been, whom you've met, what you've seen or done.

A List of Nothing in Particular

S traight as a chief's countenance, the road lay ahead, curves so long and
gradual as to be imperceptible except on the map. For nearly a hundred miles due west of Eldorado, not a single town. It was the Texas some
people see as barren waste when they cross it, the part they later describe
at the motel bar as "nothing." They say, "There's nothing out there."

Driving through the miles of nothing, I decided to test the hypothesis
and stopped somewhere in western Crockett County on the top of a broad
mesa, just off Texas 29. At a distance, the land looked so rocky and dry, a religious man could believe that the First Hand never got around to the creation in here. Still, somebody had decided to string barbed wire around it.

No plant grew higher than my head. For a while, I heard only miles
of wind against the Ghost; but after the ringing in my ears stopped, I heard
myself breathing, then a bird note, an answering call, another kind of bird-
song, and another: mockingbird, mourning dove, an enigma. I heard the
high zizz of flies the color of gray flannel and the deep buzz of a blue
bumblebee. I made a list of nothing in particular:

1. mockingbird
2. mourning dove
3. enigma bird (heard not saw)
4. gray flies
5. blue bumblebee
6. two circling buzzards (not yet, boys)
7. orange ants
8. black ants
9. orange-black ants (what's been going on?)
10. three species of spiders
11. opossum skull
12. jackrabbit (chewed on cactus)
13. deer (left scat)
14. coyote (left tracks)
15. small rodent (den full of seed hulls under rock)
16. snake (skin hooked on cactus spine)
17. prickly pear cactus (yellow blossoms)
18. hedgehog cactus (orange blossoms)
19. barrel cactus (red blossoms)
20. devil's pincushion (no blossoms)
21. catclaw (no better name)
22. two species of grass (neither green, both alive)
23. yellow flowers (blossoms smaller than peppercorns)
24. sage (indicates alkali-free soil)
25. mesquite (three-foot plants with eighty-foot roots to reach water that
    fell as rain two thousand years ago)

26. greasewood (oh, yes)
27. joint fir (steeped stems make Brigham Young tea)
28. earth
29. sky
30. wind (always)

That was all the nothing I could identify then, but had I waited until dark when the desert really comes to life, I could have done better. To say nothing is out here is incorrect; to say the desert is stingy with everything except space and light, stone and earth is closer to the truth.

4   I drove on. The low sun turned the mesa rimrock to silhouettes, angular and weird and unearthly; had someone said the far side of Saturn looked just like this, I would have believed him. The road dropped to the Pecos River, now dammed to such docility I couldn't imagine it formerly demarking the western edge of a rudimentary white civilization. Even the old wagonmen felt the unease of isolation when they crossed the Pecos, a small but once serious river that has had many names: Rio de las Vacas (River of Cows—perhaps a reference to bison), Rio Salado (Salty River), Rio Puerco (Dirty River).

5   West of the Pecos, a strangely truncated cone rose from the valley. In the oblique evening light, its silhouette looked like a Mayan temple, so perfect was its symmetry. I stopped again, started climbing, stirring a panic of lizards on the way up. From the top, the rubbled land below— veined with the highway and arroyos, topographical relief absorbed in the dusk—looked like a roadmap.

6   The desert, more than any other terrain, shows its age, shows time because so little vegetation covers the ancient erosions of wind and storm. What appears is tawny grit once stone and stone crumbling to grit. Everywhere rock, earth's oldest thing. Even desert creatures come from a time older than the woodland animals, and they, in answer to the arduousness, have retained prehistoric coverings of chitin and lapped scale and primitive defenses of spine and stinger, fang and poison, shell and claw.

7   The night, taking up the shadows and details, wiped the face of the desert into a simple, uncluttered blackness until there were only three things: land, wind, stars. I was there too, but my presence I felt more than saw. It was as if I had been reduced to mind, to an edge of consciousness. Men, ascetics, in all eras have gone into deserts to lose themselves—Jesus, Saint Anthony, Saint Basil, and numberless medicine men—maybe because such a losing happens almost as a matter of course here if you avail yourself. The Sioux once chanted, "All over the sky a sacred voice is calling."

8   Back to the highway, on with the headlamps, down Six Shooter Draw. In the darkness, deer, just shadows in the lights, began moving toward the desert willows in the wet bottoms. Stephen Vincent Benét:

> *When Daniel Boone goes by, at night,*
> *The phantom deer arise*

> *And all lost, wild America*
> *Is burning in their eyes.*

From the top of another high mesa: twelve miles west in the flat val-   9
ley floor, the lights of Fort Stockton blinked white, blue, red, and yellow
in the heat like a mirage. How is it that desert towns look so fine and big
at night? It must be that little is hidden. The glistening ahead could have
been a golden city of Cibola. But the reality of Fort Stockton was plywood
and concrete block and the plastic signs of Holiday Inn and Mobil Oil.

The desert had given me an appetite that would have made carrion   10
crow stuffed with saltbush taste good. I found a Mexican cafe of adobe,
with a whitewashed log ceiling, creekstone fireplace, and jukebox pumping
out mariachi music. It was like a bunk house. I ate burritos, chile rellenos,
and pinto beans, all ladled over with a fine, incendiary sauce the color of
sludge from an old steel drum. At the next table sat three big, round men:
an Indian wearing a silver headband, a Chicano in a droopy Pancho Villa
mustache, and a Negro in faded overalls. I thought what a litany of grievances that table could recite. But the more I looked, the more I believed they
were someone's vision of the West, maybe someone making ads for Levy's
bread, the ads that used to begin "You don't have to be Jewish."

Content

1. What details of the desert landscape does Least Heat-Moon use to describe
it? How clearly can you visualize this place? Although this desert can be precisely located on a highway map, do you need to know its exact location in order
to imagine it? What does it have in common with other deserts? Does it have any
particularly unique features?

2. Travel writer Paul Theroux says, "The journey, not the arrival, matters." Is that
true for Least Heat-Moon? Explain your answer.

Strategies/Structures

3. Least Heat-Moon structures this chapter from *Blue Highways* according to time
(daylight to night) and distance. How does the structure relate to the subject matter?

4. What is the effect of ending this trip through the desert with the image of
"three big, round men"—an Indian, a Chicano, and a black (¶ 10)? Does the reference to Levy's Jewish rye bread in the last sentence trivialize this example?

5. What kind of character does Least Heat-Moon play in his own narrative? Is
this character identical to the author who is writing the essay?

Language

6. Least Heat-Moon includes many place names. With what effect? Do you need
to read the essay with a map in hand?

7. Why are the parentheses in the list? Why do they appear beside some items
and not others?

For Writing

8. Make a list of "nothing in particular" that you observe in a place so familiar that you take its distinguishing features for granted: your yard, your refrigerator, your clothes closet, your desk, a supermarket or other store, a library, or any other ordinary place. Write down as many specific details as you can, in whatever order you see them. (Use parenthetical remarks, too, if you wish.) Then, organize them according to some logical or psychologically relevant pattern (such as closet to farthest away, most to least dominant impression, largest to smallest, whatever) and put them into a larger context. For instance, how does the closet or the refrigerator relate to the rest of your house? Does organizing the list stimulate you to include even more details? What can you do to keep your essay from sounding like a collection of miscellaneous trivia?

9. Write an essay about some portion of a trip you have taken, where you have been a stranger in a strange land. Characterize yourself as a traveler, possibly an outsider, with a particular relationship to the place you're in (enjoyment, curiosity, boredom, loneliness, fear, fatigue, a desire to move on, or any combination of emotions you want to acknowledge).

ANNE LAMOTT

Lamott, born in San Francisco in 1954, dropped out of Goucher College after two years to return to Marin County, California and write fiction. Although she published four novels in the 1980s, *Hard Laughter, Rosie, Joe Jones,* and *All New People,* her nonfiction has drawn the most attention—and affection—for its author. *Operating Instructions: A Journal of My Son's First Year* (1993) is an ironically witty account of her first months as a single parent at age thirty-six, including sleep deprivation, financial anxieties, speculations on what she will tell Sam when he asks about his absent father, and her appreciation of the friends and relatives whose involvement expands the definition of *family.*

But the book from which serious writers take comfort, as well as good advice, is *Bird by Bird: Instructions on Writing and Life* (1994), of which "Polaroids" is an early chapter. Her explanation of the book's title serves also as an explanation of the metaphorical connection between the process of pictures emerging in Polaroid photographs and the way controlling ideas gradually emerge from a writer's experience and come into focus with slow precision. She says,

> Thirty years ago my older brother, who was ten years old at the time, was trying to get a report on birds written that he'd had three months to write. [It] was due the next day. We were out at our family cabin in Bolinas, and he was at the kitchen table close to tears, surrounded by binder paper and pencils and unopened books on birds, immobilized by the hugeness of the task ahead. Then my father sat down beside

him, put his arm around my brother's shoulder, and said, "Bird by
bird, buddy. Just take it bird by bird."

Polaroids

Writing a first draft is very much like watching a Polaroid develop.   1
You can't—and, in fact, you're not supposed to—know exactly what
the picture is going to look like until it has finished developing. First you
just point at what has your attention and take the picture. In the last chapter, for instance, what had my attention were the contents of my lunch bag.
But as the picture developed, I found I had a really clear image of the boy
against the fence. Or maybe *your* Polaroid was supposed to be a picture of
that boy against the fence, and you didn't notice until the last minute that
a family was standing a few feet away from him. Now, maybe it's his family, or the family of one of the kids in his class, but at any rate these people
are going to be in the photograph, too. Then the film emerges from the
camera with a grayish green murkiness that gradually becomes clearer
and clearer, and finally your see the husband and wife holding their baby
with two children standing beside them. And at first it all seems very
sweet, but then the shadows begin to appear, and then you start to see the
animal tragedy, the baboons baring their teeth. And then you see a flash of
bright red flowers in the bottom left quadrant that you didn't even know
were in the picture when you took it, and these flowers evoke a time or a
memory that moves you mysteriously. And finally, as the portrait comes
into focus, you begin to notice all the props surrounding these people, and
you begin to understand how props define us and comfort us, and show
us what we value and what we need, and who we think we are.

You couldn't have had any way of knowing what this piece of work   2
would look like when you first started. You just knew that there was
something about these people that compelled you, and you stayed with
that something long enough for it to show you what it was about.

Watch this Polaroid develop: 3

Six or seven years ago I was asked to write an article on the Special   4
Olympics. I had been going to the local event for years, partly because a
couple of friends of mine compete. Also, I love sports, and I love to watch
athletes, special or otherwise. So I showed up this time with a great deal
of interest but no real sense of what the finished article might look like.

Things tend to go very, very slowly at the Special Olympics. It is not   5
like trying to cover the Preakness. Still, it has its own exhilaration, and I
cheered and took notes all morning.

The last track-and-field event before lunch was a twenty-five-yard   6
race run by some unusually handicapped runners and walkers, many of

whom seemed completely confused. They lumped and careened along, one man making a snail-slow break for the stands, one heading out toward the steps where the winners receive their medals; both of them were shepherded back. The race took just about forever. And here it was nearly noon and we were all so hungry. Finally, though, everyone crossed over the line, and those of us in the stands got up to go—when we noticed that way down the track, four or five yards from the starting line, was another runner.

7   She was a girl of about sixteen with a normal-looking face above a wracked and emaciated body. She was on metal crutches, and she was just plugging along, one tiny step after another, moving one crutch forward two or three inches, then moving a leg, then moving the other crutch two or three inches, then moving the other leg. It was just excruciating. Plus, I was starving to death. Inside I was going, Come on, come on, come on, swabbing at my forehead with anxiety, while she kept taking these two- or three-inch steps forward. What felt like four hours later, she crossed the finish line, and you could see that she was absolutely stoked, in a shy, girlish way.

8   A tall African American man with no front teeth fell into step with me as I left the bleachers to go look for some lunch. He tugged on the sleeve of my sweater, and I looked up at him, and he handed me a Polaroid someone had taken of him and his friends that day. "Look at us," he said. His speech was difficult to understand, thick and slow as a warped record. His two friends in the picture had Down's syndrome. All three of them looked extremely pleased with themselves. I admired the picture and then handed it back to him. He stopped, so I stopped, too. He pointed to his own image. "That," he said, "is one cool man."

9   And this was the image from which an article began forming, although I could not have told you exactly what the piece would end up being about. I just knew that something had started to emerge.

10   After lunch I wandered over to the auditorium, where it turned out a men's basketball game was in progress. The African American man with no front teeth was the star of the game. You could tell that he was because even though no one had made a basket yet, his teammates almost always passed him the ball. Even the people on the *other* team passed him the ball a lot. In lieu of any scoring, the men stampeded in slow motion up and down the court, dribbling the ball thunderously. I had never heard such a loud game. It was all sort of crazily beautiful. I imagined describing the game for my article and then for my students: the loudness, the joy. I kept replaying the scene of the girl on crutches making her way up the track to the finish line— and all of a sudden my article began to appear out of the grayish green murk. And I could see that it was about tragedy transformed over the years into joy. It was about the beauty of sheer effort. I could see it almost as clearly as I could the photograph of that one cool man and his two friends.

11   The auditorium bleachers were packed. Then a few minutes later, still with no score on the board, the tall black man dribbled slowly from one end of the court to the other, and heaved the ball up into the air, and

it dropped into the basket. The crowd roared, and all the men on both teams looked up wide-eyed at the hoop, as if it had just burst into flames.

You would have loved it, I tell my students. You would have felt like   12 you could write all day.

Content

1. In what ways is participating in the Special Olympics like finding one's way into writing about a particular topic? Is it possible to be both a spectator (appreciating what's going on, including the out-of-control parts, but sometimes getting frustrated by the slow pace [¶s 5–7]) and a participant concurrently?

2. What is Lamott's attitude toward the participants in the Special Olympics? How does she convey this? What clues does she give to indicate that she expects her readers to share her point of view? Would the families of Special Olympics participants have a similar point of view? Would the participants themselves?

3. In this essay about "the beauty of sheer effort" (¶ 10), intended as advice for beginning writers, why doesn't Lamott spend more time actually talking about writing?

Strategies/Structures

4. Why does Lamott use the relation of the gradual development of a Polaroid picture (¶s 1–3) as a metaphor for the process of writing? How does this relate to the actual Polaroid photograph (¶ 8) that appears in the essay? Why is the first paragraph so much longer than those that immediately follow it?

5. Only paragraph 10 is of comparable length to the opening paragraph. Why is it located where it is? In it, Lamott uses two scenes, an enactment of a basketball game in action and her replay of "the scene of the girl on crutches making her way . . . to the finish line." How do these scenes contribute to the author's "Aha!" moment, her sudden insight as the meaning of the essay snaps into place?

6. Lamott's technique is to present a collage of many snapshots to illustrate her point. Identify some of these snapshots and explain how they reinforce her concept of "Polaroids."

Language

7. Identify some of the ways in which Lamott conveys the slow pace of the Special Olympics and indicates her changing attitude toward this pace.

For Writing

8. Use an extended metaphor coupled with a series of illustrations to explain to newcomers how to perform a process (see Dolman's "Learning to Drive" [146–50] and the Magliozzis' "Inside the Engine" [178–84] for examples).

9. In many areas of academic research today, ethical questions are raised about who has the right to speak for whom. In "Polaroids," as in many other essays in this book (see those by Kozol [210–18], Coontz [226–31], and Barry [500–04]), the

author speaks on behalf of people who can't always speak articulately for themselves. With other classmates, compose a set of guidelines for a writer's ethical behavior in representing such people, and include your rationale for these guidelines.

ANNE FADIMAN

Fadiman was born (in 1953) to bookish parents, the noted writer and editor Clifton Fadiman and Annalee Fadiman, a writer. After graduating from Harvard (B.A., 1975), Fadiman worked as an editor and staff writer for *Life* magazine, then as a columnist for *Civilization*, the now-defunct magazine of the Library of Congress. Since 1998 she has been editor of the *American Scholar*, the national magazine of Phi Beta Kappa. Her first book, *The Spirit Catches You and You Fall Down: A Hmong Child, Her American Doctors, and the Collision of Two Cultures* (1997), won a National Book Critics Circle Award for general nonfiction. Her second book, *Ex Libris: Confessions of a Common Reader* (1998), is a collection of personal essays about reading. The opening essay, "Marrying Libraries," begins "A few months ago, my husband and I decided to mix our books together. We had known each other for ten years, lived together for six, been married for five. Our mismatched coffee mugs cohabited amicably; we wore each other's T-shirts and, in a pinch, socks; and our record collections had long ago miscegenated without incident. . . . We agreed that it made no sense for my *Billy Budd* to languish forty feet from his *Moby-Dick*, yet neither of us had lifted a finger to bring them together."

Much of the time Fadiman lives and writes in New York City, where she and her equally bookish husband, the writer George Howe Colt, had taken pride in their "retrograde status," not having "a car, a microwave, a Cuisinart," a cell phone, CD, cable TV, or a computer. Then came that fateful day in October 1998, as she explains in "Mail," when they succumbed to the need for the speed and convenience of e-mail, its motto "'Haste, haste, haste, for lyfe, for lyfe, haste!'" "Mail" is distinguished by the same good-humored love of life, literature, and esoteric lore (expressed with zestful understatement) that characterizes all of Fadiman's essays.

Mail

1   Some years ago, my parents lived at the top of a steep hill. My father kept a pair of binoculars on his desk with which, like a pirate captain hoisting his spyglass to scan the horizon for treasure ships, he periodically inspected the mailbox to see if the flag had been raised. When it finally went up, he trudged down the driveway and opened the extra-large black metal box, purchased by my mother in the same accommodating spirit with which some wives buy their husbands extra-large trousers. The day's

load—a mountain of letters and about twenty pounds of review books packed in Jiffy bags, a few of which had been pierced by their angular contents and were leaking what my father called "mouse dirt"—was always tightly wedged. But he was a persistent man, and after a brief show of resistance the mail would surrender, to be carried up the hill in a tight clinch and dumped onto a gigantic desk. Until that moment, my father's day had not truly begun.

His desk was made of steel, weighed more than a refrigerator, and 2 bristled with bookshelves and secret drawers and sliding panels and a niche for a cedar-lined humidor. (He believed that cigar-smoking and mail-reading were natural partners, like oysters and Muscadet.) I think of it as less a writing surface than a mail-sorting table. He hated Sundays and holidays because there was nothing new to spread on it. Vacations were taxing, the equivalent of forced relocations to places without food. His homecomings were always followed by day-long orgies of mail-opening—feast after famine—at the end of which all the letters were answered; all the bills were paid; the outgoing envelopes were affixed with stamps from a brass dispenser heavy enough to break your toe; the books and manuscripts were neatly stacked; and the empty Jiffy bags were stuffed into an extra-large copper wastebasket, cheering confirmation that the process of postal digestion was complete.

"One of my unfailing minor pleasures may seem dull to more ener- 3 getic souls: opening the mail," he once wrote.

> Living in an advanced industrial civilization is a kind of near- 4
> conquest over the unexpected. . . . Such efficiency is of course
> admirable. It does not, however, by its very nature afford scope
> to that perverse human trait, still not quite eliminated, which is
> pleased by the accidental. Thus to many tame citizens like me the
> morning mail functions as the voice of the unpredictable and keeps
> alive for a few minutes a day the keen sense of the unplanned and
> the unplannable. The letter opener is an instrument that has per-
> sisted from some antique land of chance and adventure into our
> ordered world of the perfectly calculated.

What chance and adventure might the day's haul contain? My brother 5 asked him, when he was in his nineties, what kind of mail he liked best. "In my youth," he replied, "a love letter. In middle age, a job offer. Today, a check." (That was false cynicism, I think. His favorite letters were from his friends.) Whatever the accidental pleasure, it could not please until it arrived. Why were deliveries so few and so late (he frequently grumbled), when, had he lived in central London in the late seventeenth century, he could have received his mail between ten and twelve times a day?

We get what we need. In 1680, London had mail service nearly every hour 6 because there were no telephones. If you wished to invite someone to tea in the afternoon, you could send him a letter in the morning and receive his reply before he showed up at your doorstep. Postage was one penny.

7   If you wished to send a letter to another town, however, delivery was less reliable and postage was gauged on a scale of staggering complexity. By the mid-1830s,

8   the postage on a single letter delivered within eight miles of the office where it was posted was . . . twopence, the lowest rate beyond that limit being fourpence. Beyond fifteen miles it became fivepence; after which it rose a penny at a time, but by irregular augmentation, to one shilling, the charge for three hundred miles. There was as a general rule an additional charge of a half penny on a letter crossing the Scotch border; while letters to or from Ireland had to bear, in addition, packet rates, and rates for crossing the bridges over the Conway and the Menai.

9   So wrote Rowland Hill, the greatest postal reformer in history, who in 1837 devised a scheme to reduce and standardize postal rates and to shift the burden of payment from the addressee to the sender.

10   Until a few years ago I had no idea that if you sent a letter out of town—and if you weren't a nobleman, a member of Parliament, or other VIP who had been granted the privilege of free postal franking—the postage was paid by the recipient. This dawned on me when I was reading a biography of Charles Lamb, whose employer, the East India House, allowed clerks to receive letters gratis until 1817: a substantial perk, sort of like being able to call your friends on your office's 800 number. (Lamb, who practiced stringent economies, also wrote much of his personal correspondence on company stationery. His most famous letter to Wordsworth, for instance—the one in which he refers to Coleridge as "an Archangel a little damaged"—is inscribed on a page whose heading reads "Please to state the Weights and Amounts of the following Lots.")

11   Sir Walter Scott liked to tell the story of how he had once had to pay "five pounds odd" in order to receive a package from a young New York lady he had never met: an atrocious play called *The Cherokee Lovers*, accompanied by a request to read it, correct it, write a prologue, and secure a producer. Two weeks later another large package arrived for which he was charged a similar amount. "Conceive my horror," he told his friend Lord Melville, "when out jumped the same identical tragedy of *The Cherokee Lovers*, with a second epistle from the authoress, stating that, as the winds had been boisterous, she feared the vessel entrusted with her former communication might have foundered, and therefore judged it prudent to forward a duplicate." Lord Melville doubtless found this tale hilarious, but Rowland Hill would have been appalled. He had grown up poor, and, as Christopher Browne notes in *Getting the Message,* his splendid history of the British postal system, "Hill had never forgotten his mother's anxiety when a letter with a high postal duty was delivered,

nor the time when she sent him out to sell a bag of clothes to raise 3s for a batch of letters."

Hill was a born Utilitarian who, at the age of twelve, had been so 12 frustrated by the irregularity of the bell at the school where his father was principal that he had instituted a precisely timed bell-ringing schedule. In 1837 he published a report called "Post Office Reform: Its Importance and Practicability." Why, he argued, should legions of accountants be employed to figure out the Byzantine postal charges? Why should Britain's extortionate postal rates persist when France's revenues had risen, thanks to higher mail volume, after its rates were lowered? Why should postmen waste precious time waiting for absent addressees to come home and pay up? A national Penny Post was the answer, with postage paid by the senders, "using a bit of paper . . . covered at the back with a glutinous wash, which the bringer might, by the application of a little moisture, attach to the back of the letter."

After much debate, Parliament passed a postal reform act in 1839. 13 On January 10, 1840, Hill wrote in his diary, "Penny Postage extended to the whole kingdom this day! . . . I guess that the number despatched tonight will not be less than 100,000, or more than three times what it was this day twelve-months. If less I shall be disappointed." On January 11 he wrote, "The number of letters despatched exceeded all expectation. It was 112,000, of which all but 13,000 or 14,000 were prepaid." In May, after experimentation to produce a canceling ink that could not be surreptitiously removed, the Post Office introduced the Penny Black, bearing a profile of Queen Victoria: the first postage stamp. The press, pondering the process of cancellation, fretted about the "untoward disfiguration of the royal person," but Victoria became an enthusiastic philatelist, and renounced the royal franking privilege for the pleasure of walking to the local post office from Balmoral Castle to stock up on stamps and gossip with the postmaster. When Rowland Hill—by that time, *Sir* Rowland Hill—retired as Post Office Secretary in 1864, *Punch* asked, "SHOULD ROWLAND HILL have a Statue? Certainly, if OLIVER CROMWELL should. For one is celebrated for cutting off the head of a bad King, and the other for sticking on the head of a good Queen."

The Penny Post, wrote Harriet Martineau, "will do more for the cir- 14 culation of ideas, for the fostering of domestic affections, for the humanizing of the mass generally, than any other single measure that our national wit can devise." It was incontrovertible proof, in an age that embraced progress on all fronts ("the means of locomotion and correspondence, every mechanical art, every manufacture, every thing that promotes the convenience of life," as Macaulay put it in a typical gush of national pride), that the British were the most civilized people on earth. Ancient Syrian runners, Chinese carrier pigeons, Persian post riders, Egyptian papyrus bearers, Greek *hemerodromes*, Hebrew dromedary riders, Roman equestrian relays, medieval monk-messengers, Catalan *troters*, international couriers of the House of Thurn and Taxis, American mail wagons—what could these all have been leading up to, like an ever-ascending staircase, but the Victorian postal system?

15   And yet (to raise a subversive question), might it be possible that, whatever the profit in efficiency, there may have been a literary cost associated with the conversion from payment by addressee to payment by sender? If you knew that your recipient would have to bear the cost of your letter, wouldn't courtesy motivate you to write an extra-good one? On the other hand, if you paid for it yourself, wouldn't you be more likely to feel you could get away with "Having a wonderful time, wish you were here"?

16   I used to think my father's attachment to the mail was strange. I now feel exactly the way he did. I live in an apartment building and, with or without binoculars, I cannot see my mailbox, one of thirteen dinky aluminum cells bolted to the lobby wall. The mail usually comes around four in the afternoon (proving that the postal staircase that reached its highest point with Rowland Hill has been descending ever since), which means that at around three, *just in case,* I'm likely to visit the lobby for the first of several reconnaissance missions. There's no flag, but over the years my fingers have become postally sensitive, and I can tell if the box is full by giving it the slightest of pats. If there's a hint of convexity—it's very subtle, nothing as obvious, let us say, as the bulge of a can that might harbor botulism—I whip out my key with the same excitement with which my father set forth down his driveway.

17   There the resemblance ends. The thrill of the treasure hunt is followed all too quickly by the glum realization that the box contains only four kinds of mail: (1) junk, (2) bills, (3) work, and (4) letters that I will read with enjoyment, place in a folder labeled "To Answer," leave there for a geologic interval, and feel guilty about. The longer they languish, the more I despair of my ability to live up to the escalating challenge of their response. It is a truism of epistolary psychology that, for example, a Christmas thank-you note written on December 26 can say any old thing, but if you wait until February, you are convinced that nothing less than *Middlemarch* will do.

18   In October of 1998 I finally gave in and signed up for e-mail. I had resisted for a long time. My husband and I were proud of our retrograde status. Not only did we lack a modem, but we didn't have a car, a microwave, a Cuisinart, an electric can opener, a cellular phone, a CD player, or cable television. It's hard to give up that sort of backward image; I worried that our friends wouldn't have enough to make fun of. I also worried that learning how to use e-mail would be like learning how to program our VCR, an unsuccessful project that had confirmed what excellent judgment we had shown in not purchasing a car, etc.

As millions of people had discovered before me, e-mail was fast.   19
Sixteenth-century correspondents used to write "Haste, haste, haste, for
lyfe, for lyfe, haste!" on their most urgent letters; my "server," a word that
conjured up a delicious sycophancy, treated *every* message as if someone's
life depended on it. Not only did it get there instantly, caromed in a series
of analog cyberpackets along the nodes of the Internet and reconverted to
digital form via its recipient's modem. (I do not understand a word of
what I just wrote, but that is immaterial. Could the average Victorian have
diagrammed the mail coach route from Swansea to Tunbridge Wells?)
More important, I *answered* e-mail fast—almost always on the day it arrived. No more guilt! I used to think I did not like to write letters. I now
realize that what I didn't like was folding the paper, sealing the envelope,
looking up the address, licking the stamp, getting in the elevator, crossing
the street, and dropping the letter in the postbox.

At first I made plenty of mistakes. I clicked on the wrong icons, my   20
attachments didn't stick, and, not having learned how to file addresses, I
sent an X rated message to my husband (I thought) at gcolt@aol.com instead of georgecolt@aol.com. I hope Gerald or Gertrude found it flattering. But the learning curve was as steep as my father's driveway, and
pretty soon I was batting out fifteen or twenty e-mails a day in the time it
had once taken me to avoid answering a single letter. My box was nearly
always full—no waiting, no binoculars, no convexity checks, no
tugging—and when it wasn't, the reason was not that the mail hadn't
arrived, it was that it hadn't been *sent.* I began to look forward every morning to the festive green arrow with which AT&T WorldNet welcomed me
into my father's "antique land of chance and adventure." Would I be
invited to purchase Viagra, lose thirty pounds, regrow my thinning hair,
obtain electronic spy software, get an EZ loan, retire in three years, or win
a Pentium III 500 MHz computer (presumably in order to receive such
messages even faster)? Or would I find a satisfying little clutch of friendly
notes whose responses could occupy me until I awoke sufficiently to
tackle something that required intelligence? As Hemingway wrote to Fitzgerald, describing the act of letter-writing: "Such a swell way to keep
from working and yet feel you've done something."

My computer, without visible distension, managed to store a flood   21
tide of mail that in nonvirtual form would have silted up my office to the
ceiling. This was admirable. And when I wished to commune with my
friend Charlie, who lives in Taipei, not only could I disregard the thirteen-
hour time difference, but I was billed the same amount as if I had dialed
his old telephone number on East 22nd Street. The German critic Bernhard
Siegert has observed that the breakthrough concept behind Rowland Hill's
Penny Post was "to think of all Great Britain as a single city, that is, no
longer to give a moment's thought to what had been dear to Western discourse on the nature of the letter from the beginning: the idea of distance."

E-mail is a modern Penny Post: the world is a single city with a single postal rate.

22   Alas, our Penny Post, like Hill's, comes at a price. If the transfer of postal charges from sender to recipient was the first great demotivator in the art of letter-writing, e-mail was the second. "It now seems a good bet," Adam Gopnik has written, "that in two hundred years people will be reading someone's collected e-mail the way we read Edmund Wilson's diaries or Pepys's letters." Maybe—but will what they read be any good? E-mails are brief. (One doesn't blather; an overlong message might induce carpal tunnel syndrome in the recipient from excessive pressure on the Down arrow.) They are also—at least the ones I receive—frequently devoid of capitalization, minimally punctuated, and creatively spelled. E-mail's greatest strength—speed—is also its Achilles' heel. In effect, it's always December 26; you are not expected to write *Middlemarch,* and therefore you don't.

23   In a letter to his friend William Unwin, written on August 6, 1780, William Cowper noted that "a Letter may be written upon any thing or Nothing." This observation is supported by the index of *The Faber Book of Letters, 1578–1939.* Let us examine some entries from the *d* section:

24   damnation, 87
      dances and entertainments, 33, 48, 59, 97, 111, 275
      dentistry, 220
      depressive illness, 81, 87
      Dictionary of the English Language, Johnson's, 61
      Diggers, 22
      dolphins, methods of cooking, 37

25   I have never received an e-mail on any of these topics. Instead, I am informed that Your browser is not Y2K-compliant. Your son left his Pokémon turtle under our sofa. Your column is 23 lines too long. Important pieces of news, but, as Lytton Strachey (one of the all-time great letter writers) pointed out, "No good letter was ever written to convey information, or to please its recipient: it may achieve both these results incidentally; but its fundamental purpose is to express the personality of its writer." *But wait!* you pipe up. *Someone just e-mailed me a joke!* So she did, but wasn't the personality of the sender slightly muffled by the fact that she forwarded it from an e-mail *she* received, and sent it to seventeen additional addressees?

26   I also take a dim, or perhaps a buffaloed, view of electronic slang. Perhaps I should view it as a linguistic milestone, as historic as the evolution of Cockney rhyming slang in the 1840s. But will the future generations who reopen our hard drives be stirred by the eloquence of the e-acronyms recommended by a Web site on "netiquette"?

27   BTDT   been there done that
      FC   fingers crossed

IITYWTMWYBMAD
             if I tell you what this means will you buy me a drink?
MTE   my thoughts exactly
ROTFL   rolling on the floor laughing
RTFM   read the f——— manual
TAH   take a hint
TTFN   ta-ta for now

Or by the "emoticons," otherwise known as "smileys"—punctuational 28
images, read sideways—that "help readers interpret the e-mail writer's
attitude and tone"?

     :-)   ha ha   29
     :-(boo hoo
     (-:   I am left-handed
     %-)   I have been staring at a green screen for 15 hours straight
     :-&   I am tongue-tied
     {:-) I wear a toupee
     :-[I am a vampire
     :-F   I am a bucktoothed vampire with one tooth missing
   = | :)= I am Abraham Lincoln

"We are of a different race from the Greeks, to whom beauty was 30
everything," wrote Thomas Carlyle, a Victorian progress-booster. "Our
glory and our beauty arise out of our inward strength, which makes us
victorious over material resistance." We have achieved a similar victory of
efficiency over beauty. I wouldn't give up e-mail if you paid me, but I'd
feel a pang of regret if the epistolary novels of the future were to revolve
around such messages as

Subject: R U Kidding?   31
From: Clarissa Harlowe <claha@virtue.com>
To: Robert Lovelace <lovelaceandlovegirlz@vice.com
hi bob, TAH. if u think i'm gonna run off w/ u, :-F, do u really
think i'm that kind of girl?? if you're looking 4 a trollop, CLICK
HERE NOW: *http://www.hotpix.html.* TTFN

I own a letter written by Robert Falcon Scott, the polar explorer, to G. T. 32
Temple, Esq., who helped procure the footgear for Scott's first Antarctic
expedition. The date is February 26, 1901. The envelope and octavo stationery have black borders because Queen Victoria had died in January.
The paper is yellowed, the handwriting is messy, and the stamp bears the
Queen's profile—and the denomination ONE PENNY. I bought the letter
many years ago because, unlike a Cuisinart, which would have cost about
the same, it was something I believed I could not live without. I could
never feel that way about an e-mail.

33   I also own my father's old wastebasket, which now holds my own empty Jiffy bags. Several times a day I use his stamp dispenser; it is tarnished and dinged, but still capable of unspooling its contents with a singular smoothness. And my file cabinets hold hundreds of his letters, the earliest written in his sixties in small, crabbed handwriting, the last in his nineties, after he lost much of his sight, penned with a Magic Marker in huge capital letters. I hope my children will find them someday, as Hart Crane once found his grandmother's love letters in the attic,

34
          pressed so long
     Into a corner of the roof
     That they are brown and soft,
     And liable to melt as snow.

Content

1. Fadiman's first three paragraphs are devoted to her father. Describe the tone of the first three paragraphs and then consider how the description of her father's habits, possessions, and preferences sets the stage for the remainder of her essay.

2. When Fadiman first discovers e-mail she refers to its positive aspects; what are these? What, in her view, are some of the negative aspects of e-mail? Why does she claim that tangible mail is superior to e-mail in the long run? Do you agree with her assessment?

3. Fadiman refers to a number of historical figures throughout her essay, ranging from Rowland Hill, "the greatest postal reformer in history" (¶ 9), to Harriet Martineau (¶ 14) and Thomas Carlyle (¶ 30). Does her use of historical figures contribute to your understanding of "Mail" even if you don't know precisely who these figures are?

Strategies/Structures

4. Fadiman begins her essay by comparing her father to "a pirate captain hoisting his spyglass to scan the horizon for treasure ships" (¶ 1). How does her use of this simile set the stage for what is to follow? How does her initial use of the term "treasure" compare with her later use of this term (¶ 17)?

5. Fadiman combines the story of her father's relationship to mail (¶s 1–3), the history of the English postal system (¶ 4–9), famous writers' comments about mail (¶s 10–14, 22, 23, 25), and her own personal story in relation to mail and to e-mail. How does such a combination of elements contribute to Fadiman's argument that surface mail is superior to e-mail?

6. Fadiman asks two questions in paragraph 20: "Would I be invited to purchase [a host of costly items and services]?" (in other words, invaded by a host of unwelcome ads) and "Would I find a satisfying little clutch of friendly notes . . . ?" Given the evidence concerning the "eloquence of the e-acronyms recommended by a Web site on 'netiquette'" that she provides (¶s 26–29), what answers does she expect from her reader? What answers does she get in comparison with those she'd like to receive (¶s 20–25)?

Language

7. What does Fadiman mean when she says "It is a truism of epistolary psychology that, for example, a Christmas thank-you note written on December 26 can say any old thing, but if you wait until February, you are convinced that nothing less than *Middlemarch* will do" (¶ 17)? If you don't catch the allusion to *Middlemarch* (to which she returns in ¶ 22), what in the context helps you to understand what Fadiman is referring to?

8. Is Fadiman being serious when she claims, "I used to think I did not like to write letters. I now realize that what I didn't like was folding the paper, sealing the envelope, looking up the address, licking the stamp, getting in the elevator, crossing the street, and dropping the letter in the postbox" (¶ 19)? How can you tell?

For Writing

9. Using a central metaphor or event such as Fadiman uses to describe her father's relationship with the mail, write an essay in which you describe an experience you look forward to each day, each week, or each month.

10. Compose both a letter and an e-mail to the same friend or family member. What differences do you note between the two? Which one is more fulfilling to write? Which, do you imagine, might be more satisfying to receive?

11. "Mail" was the only essay published in the United States in 2000 selected for reprint in two different collections of "Best" American essays of that year. Write an essay that argues for or against the merits of the judges' decision.

DAVID FOSTER WALLACE

David Foster Wallace was born in 1962 in Ithaca, New York. Shortly after he completed his formal education at Amherst (B.A., 1985) and the University of Arizona (M.F.A., 1987), his career-long string of prestigious literary awards began with a Whiting Writers' Award. He received a MacArthur Foundation "genius grant" in 1997. He has published novels *The Broom of the System* (1987) and *Infinite Jest* (1996); short stories in *Girl with Curious Hair* (1989); and nonfiction, including *Signifying Rappers: Rap and Race in the Urban Present* (1990) and analyses of contemporary culture in *A Supposedly Fun Thing I'll Never Do Again: Essays and Arguments* (1997). Wallace is to literature, says one critic, "what Robin Williams . . . is to live comedy: a creator so maniacally energetic and amused with himself that he often follows his riffs out into the stratosphere, where he orbits all alone."

"Lunchtime at the Illinois State Fair" appears as part of a freewheeling essay, "getting away from already pretty much being away from it all," one chapter of *A Supposedly Fun Thing*. Here Wallace, attending the Illinois State Fair in 1993 as a reporter "for a swanky East-Coast magazine," has kept a diary for ten days, including this list that intermingles a mishmash of "high-lipid foods" with the "rare grand mass of Midwest humanity,

eating and shuffling and rubbing" along in a "peripatetic feeding frenzy."
Reviewer Michiko Kakutani explains that this work is animated by the
author's "wonderfully exuberant prose, a zingy, elastic gift for metaphor
and imaginative sleight of hand, combined with a taste for amphetamine-
like stream-of-consciousness riffs"—characteristics calculated to electrify
readers of "Lunchtime" even if the menu appears gross and indigestible:
"bright-yellow popcorn that stinks of salt; onion rings big as leis; Poco
Penos Stuffed Jalapeño Peppers. . . ."

"Lunchtime at the Illinois State Fair"

1   08/13/1235h. Lunchtime. The Fairgrounds are a St. Vitus's dance of black-
top footpaths, the axons and dendrites of mass spectation, connecting
buildings and barns and corporate tents. Each path is flanked, pretty
much along its whole length, by booths hawking food. There are tall
Kaopectate-colored shacks that sell Illinois Dairy Council milkshakes for
an off-the-scale $2.50—though they're mindbendingly good milkshakes,
silky and so thick they don't even insult your intelligence with a straw or
spoon, giving you instead a kind of small plastic trowel. There are uncountable pork options: Paulie's Pork Out, the Pork Patio, Freshfried Pork
Skins, the Pork Street Cafe. The Pork Street Cafe is a "One Hundred Percent All-Pork Establishment," says its loudspeaker. "Ever last thing." I'm
praying this doesn't include the beverages. No way I'm eating any pork
after this morning's swine stress, anyway. And it's too hot even to think
about the Dessert Competitions. It's at least 95° in the shade here due
east of Livestock, and the breeze is shall we say fragrant. But food is getting bought and ingested at an incredible clip all up and down the path.
The booths are ubiquitous, and each one has a line in front of it. Everybody's packed in together, eating as they walk. A peripatetic feeding
frenzy. Native Companion is agitating for pork skins. Zipper or no, she's
"storvin,'" she says, "to *daith*." She likes to put on a parodic hick accent
whenever I utter a term like "peripatetic."

2   (You do not want details on what pork skins are.)

3   So along the path there are I.D.C. milkshakes (my lunch), Lemon
Shake-Ups, Ice Cold Melon Man booths, Citrus Push-Ups, and Hawaiian
Shaved Ice you can suck the syrup out of and then crunch the ice (my
dessert). But a lot of what's getting bought and gobbled is to my mind not
hot-weather food at all: bright-yellow popcorn that stinks of salt; onion
rings big as leis; Poco Penos Stuffed Jalapeño Peppers; Zorba's Gyros;
shiny fried chicken; Bert's Burritos—"BIG AS YOU'RE HEAD" (sic); hot
Italian beef; hot New York City Beef (?); Jojo's Quick Fried Donuts (the
only booth selling coffee, by the way); pizza by the shingle-sized slice and

*What are these people eating? What does the combination of food, condiments, food-holding
material, and context in which the food is eaten reveal about this dining experience?
To what extent can this be generalized to any and all fairs? In what ways do other
outdoor eating experiences (such as picnics, barbecues) resemble or differ from this?*

chitlins and Crab Rangoon and Polish sausage. (Rural Illinois' complete
lack of ethnic identity creates a kind of postmodern embarrassment of
riches—foods of every culture and creed become our own, quick-fried
and served on cardboard and consumed on foot.) There are towering
plates of "Curl Fries," which are pubic-hair-shaped and make people's
fingers shine in the sun. Cheez-Dip Hot Dogs. Pony Pups. Hot Fritters.
Philly Steak. Ribeye BBQ Corral. Joanie's Original ½-lb Burgers' booth's
sign says 2 CHOICES—RARE OR MOOIN.' I can't believe people eat this
kind of stuff in this kind of heat. The sky is cloudless and galvanized; the
sun fairly pulses. There's the green reek of fried tomatoes. (Midwesterners
say "tomāto.") The sound of myriad deep fryers forms a grisly sound-
carpet all up and down the gauntlet of booths. The Original 1-lb Butterfly
Pork Chop booth's sign says PORK: THE OTHER WHITE MEAT, the only
discernible armwave to the health-conscious so far. Non-natives note, it's
the Midwest: no nachos, no chili, no Evian, nothing Cajun.

But holy mackerel are there sweets: Fried Dough; Black Walnut Taffy;   4
Fiddlesticks; Hot Crackerjack. Caramel apples for a felonious $1.50. Angel's
Breath, known also as Dentist's Delight. Vanilla fudge that breaks a kind of
weird sweat the minute it leaves its booth's freezer. The crowd moves at one
slow pace, eating, dense-packed between the rows of booths. No ag-pros in
sight. The crowd's adults are either pale or with the pink tinge of new burn,

thin-haired and big-bellied in tight jeans, some downright fat and moving by sort of shifting their weight from side to side; boys minus shirts and girls in primary-colored halters; littler boys and girls in squads; parents with strollers; terribly pale academics in Bermudas and sandals; big women in curlers; lots of people carrying shopping bags; absurd floppy hats; almost all with '80s-fashion sunglasses—all seemingly eating, crowded together, twenty abreast, moving slowly, packed in, sweating, shoulders rubbing, the air deep-fried and spicy with antiperspirant and Coppertone, jowl to jowl. Picture Tokyo's rush-hour subway on an epic scale. It's a rare grand mass of Midwest humanity, eating and shuffling and rubbing, moving toward the Coliseum and Grandstand and Expo Building and the Livestock shows beyond. It's maybe significant that nobody looks like they're feeling oppressed or claustrophobic or bug-eyed at being airlessly hemmed in by the endless crowd we're all part of. Native Companion cusses and laughs when people step on her feet. Something East-Coast in me prickles at the bovine and herdlike quality of the crowd, though, i.e. us, hundreds of hands rising from paper tray to mouth as we jostle and press toward our respective attractions. From the air we'd look like some kind of Bataan March of docile consumption. (Native Companion laughs and says the batons aren't ever till the second day.) We're Jr.-Beef-Show-bound. You do not want to know what appalling combination of high-lipid foods N. Companion lunches on as we're borne by a living river toward prize-winning beef. The booths keep rolling past. There's Ace-High All-Butter Fudge. There are Rice-Krispie-squarish things called Krakkles. Angel Hair Cotton Candy. There are Funnel Cakes, viz. cake batter quick-fried to a tornadic spiral and rolled in sugared butter. Eric's Salt Water Taffy. Something called Zak's Fried Ice Cream. Another artery-clogger: Elephant Ears. An Elephant Ear is an album-sized expanse of oil-fried dough slathered with butter and cinnamon-sugar, sort of cinnamon toast from hell, really and truly shaped like an ear, surprisingly yummy, it turns out, but sickly soft, the texture of adipose flesh, and undeniably elephant-sized—no one's in line for Ears except the morbidly obese.

5   One food venue we fight across the current to check out special is a huge high-tech neonated stand: DIPPIN DOTS—*"Ice Cream Of The Future."* The countergirl sits on a tall stool shrouded in dry-ice steam and is at most thirteen years old, and my Press Credentials for the first time make someone's eyes widen, and we get free samples, little cups of what seems to be tiny little ice-cream pellets, fluorescent BB's that are kept, the countergirl swears to *God*, at 55° below 0—Oh *God* she doesn't *know* whether it's 0°C or 0°F; that wasn't in the DIPPIN DOTS training video. The pellets melt in your mouth, after a fashion. More like evaporate in your mouth. The taste is vivid, but the Dots' texture's weird, abstract. Futuristic. The stuff's intriguing but just too Jetsonian to really catch on. The countergirl spells her last name for us and wants to say Hey to someone named Jody in return for the samples.

Content

1. Wallace spent ten days attending the Illinois State Fair as a reporter for "a swanky East-Coast magazine." How does his intended readership influence what he includes and the attitude he takes toward his material, as signaled by the language in his opening paragraph, such as the "Kaopectate-colored shacks that sell Illinois Dairy Council milkshakes." What is Kaopectate? And why couldn't have Wallace just said "white"?

2. Why does Wallace describe the person who accompanies him to the fair as "Native Companion" (¶ 1)? Why does he capitalize the first letter of each word in this label? Why doesn't he just use his companion's name? What is a "peripatetic feeding frenzy" (¶ 1), and why does Native Companion "put on a parodic hick accent" whenever Wallace uses terms like "peripatetic"?

3. What is Wallace's attitude toward the "bovine and herdlike" (¶ 4) crowd he describes? Does he expect his readers to share his attitude—both toward the food and the crowd—even people who might have attended the Illinois State Fair? Is he making moral judgments of both, or either, when he refers to the "appalling combination of high-lipid foods N. Companion lunches on" or explains that Elephant Ears, another "artery-clogger" are fit only for "the morbidly obese" (¶ 4)?

Strategies/Structures

4. "Lunchtime at the Illinois State Fair" is composed of lists. What governs the composition of each list in paragraphs 1, 3, and 4? Were you aware of the lists as you read the essay? Why or why not?

5. Why does Wallace capitalize so many slogans, names of businesses and foods throughout the essay ("Poco Penos Stuffed Jalapeño Peppers, Bert's Burritos—BIG AS YOU'RE HEAD") (¶ 3)? Why does he quote incorrect punctuation and spelling, as in YOU'RE HEAD?

6. What is the effect of the parenthetical asides Wallace includes in paragraphs 2, 3, and 4?

Language

7. What is a "Bataan March of docile consumption" (¶ 4) and why is Native Companion's misunderstanding of "Bataan" as "baton" significant?

8. Wallace uses some fairly elevated language ("axons and dendrites," "peripatetic," "postmodern embarrassment of riches" in the midst of his description of the food available at the fair ("Fried Dough; Black Walnut Taffy; Fiddlesticks; Hot Crackerjack" (¶ 4). What are the effects of these marked contrasts in language?

For Writing

9. Wallace is describing "Lunchtime"; does his description make the readers of the "swanky East-Coast magazine" that sponsored his trip want to have lunch at the Illinois State Fair? Most of Wallace's readers, including yourself, have probably had experience with some of the foods Wallace identifies, and have perhaps attended a state fair, as well. How does your experience compare with Wallace's?

Write an extended paragraph about your own experience, listing comparable details but presenting them in language of your choice that reflects your own attitude toward the fair—particularly if you liked it. Or if you prefer, go to a supermarket and write a comparable paragraph or longer paper about the foods and people you observe there. Let the details you choose reveal your attitude toward your subject.

10.   Attend a public event as an observer rather than as a participant and keep notes. What sorts of things (sights, sounds, smells, etc.) strike you as worthy of noting? As humorous? Write a brief essay from your notes, composed largely of lists. Because the notes will probably reflect the order in which you experienced the event, you'll probably need to reorganize them—grouping them by topic as Wallace has done.

❄ Selections from Student Writers' Notebooks

RICHARD LOFTUS, JILL WOOLLEY, ART GREENWOOD, BARBARA SCHOFIELD, SUSAN YORITOMO, BETTY J. WALKER, TAMMY WEAST, KRISTIN KING, ROSALIND BRADLEY COLES, CHERYL WATANABE, STEPHEN E. RYAN

The students who kept these writers' notebooks in courses at the University of Connecticut, Virginia Commonwealth University, and the College of William and Mary in recent years majored in a variety of subjects: King, Loftus, Ryan, and Watanabe, English; Woolley, archaeology; Greenwood, general studies; Schofield, education; Yoritomo, filmmaking; Walker, human resource management; Weast, mass communications; Coles, biology and creative writing. All share a love of the sounds as well as the sense of words, all like to play around with the language; some read omnivorously while others focus on visual images. All bring creativity to their work, which ranges from assisting on archaeological digs to personnel administration to pharmacological laboratory research to editing publications for a hospital and for the Wolf Trap music foundation.

The selections from their notebooks reflect a range of interests and moods as varied as the writers. Reactions to keeping a notebook ("It's better to do it than to talk about it"), a satiric recipe ("Oh, Mom, was there ever a worse cook than you?"), self-analysis ("I could get by, looking good"), an attempt at self-improvement ("I've been trying to put cigarettes down for six years now"), explorations of sound ("HE'LL BANG EM AND HIS CYMBALS CRASH AND HISS"), analysis of an apartment style that mirrors the writer's personal style ("My apartment is stark. I'm stark"), a humorous tirade against housework ("I hate it"), the devastating impact of a divorce on a family's Christmas ("I ate a beans n franks dinner later. My brother went to drink his gift certificate"), reactions to being black in a white world (Coles), homosexual in a straight world (Loftus), Asian in America (Watanabe). And a joyous reaction to the writer's first publication—"and not in the Letters to the Editor column, either."

These entries offer just a hint of the infinite potential of writers' notebooks.

Richard Loftus

I read something in some book from some new author in some bookshop   1
somewhere to the effect that writer's block is "reading old fat novels instead of making new skinny ones." My secret is out.

• • •

I don't feel like writing now. I should pick up *Mansfield Park* again. Read-   2
ing Austen or anyone that good reminds me of what I could be saying, and of the work that has to be put into it. How often have I begun a jour-nal and stopped because two days later it didn't seem so good? I suppose I saved myself from some self-flagellation, but also from a record of growth. There are some people in the class who write often, and though their perceptions are no more acute or their difficulties in writing no less than my own, I feel that they're ahead. I must remember what Susan said to me, that "It's better to do it than talk about it." This is doing it, huh? This is getting it down on paper. Knowing that I have to keep this record is the best part.

• • •

Green Bean Surprise Casserole

1 can green beans, drained
1 can cream of mushroom soup
1 box cheez-bits

Layer ingredients—beans, then soup and cheez-bits—in greased casserole. Place casserole in preheated 350° oven. Bake forty-five minutes. Serve.

I'm telling you something I've never told anyone. Never, through the   3
long years of dinners made possible by the invention of the electric can opener and the publication of Peg Bracken's *The I Hate to Cook Cookbook.* Never, though the mention of meatloaf still conjures images of a dark, brick-like thing, ketchup glazed and gurgling angrily in a sea of orangish drippings in a pyrex baking dish. Never, even when her mantra spun in my brain like an old forty-five: "Some people live to eat, Richard (my name spoken with accusative gravity), *I* eat to live." Oh, Mom, was there ever a worse cook than you?

Jill Woolley

4 I don't want to be a scholar. I run on intuition. My pleasure is in creating.
. . . I hate collecting information and acting like I have something new and
exciting to say about any of it. I'm not an organizer. Maybe I'm not a syn-
thesizer. I'm all talent and no discipline. I can get away with some sweat
and inspiration. I can get by with bullshit because my bull is better than
85% of everybody else's hard work. But I know what's coming off the top
of my head. I know I'm a phony. At least that's how I feel. No substance.
I've disconnected my soul. I've sold myself out because I could get by,
looking good.

•   •   •

5 I meant to throw these boots away. I had them in a box for the Salvation
Army pick-up. Somehow they worked their way back on to my feet. It's
the same with so many things—boots, men, cigarettes—you try to get
them out of your life and they keep coming out on top.

6   I've been trying to put cigarettes down for six years now, on and off.
Still, day after day, I pay my [money] for a pack of poison. Why is it easier
to smoke than to not smoke? It certainly isn't easier to exercise than to not
exercise. It isn't easier to work hard than to not work hard. So why is it
easier to smoke?

7   I try all kinds of tricks. I count how many cigarettes I've smoked in
a day. I wait until dark to light up. I brush my teeth after every cigarette.
But these gimmicks soon fall away and again I'm chain smoking from the
time I get up until I retire.

8   I guess I'll keep trying though. Tomorrow, the boots go back on the
pile for the Salvation Army. It's a start.

Art Greenwood

9 I live in an apartment with two musicians. Stan is a black man with a
deep voice and a mild relaxed demeanor, who plays the drums. Meloni is
his complement, fair-skinned and youthful , she sings and she plays the
guitar. The are both rock musicians, perhaps, but their types of music are
very different. STANLEY—HE PLAYS HIS DRUMS, SOMETIMES, AND
HE BANGS EM, HE BANGS EM AND HE BANGS EM, HE'LL ROLL EM,
BACK AND FORTH AND BACK REAL QUICK WITH A BASE THUMP,
AND HE'LL BANG EM AND HE'LL BANG EM AND HIS CYMBALS
CRASH AND HISS WHILE HE BANGS EM AND THE BASE THUMPS.
And when he does this it's loud, and the place gets filled, and it feels
good, as if you were in your own heart while it was beating. Meloni's
music, though, is as different from his as she is, physically, from him. The
deep rhythm of his drums doesn't surface in the trickling stream of her
singsong. He puts you in your heart, but she leads you through your

head. When you listen to her it's like the breeze in the trees or butterflies in springtime: light, airy, and hopeful.

Barbara Schofield

Sitting in class I realized that I would never be more naked than when I shared my writing. It is painful; it is frightening, because you open your very soul to acceptance or rejection by your peers. All this attempt to communicate with others is complicated by each individual's understanding of language; we try to present ourselves to others with as much clarity and understanding as is possible for another human being to comprehend of another.

In my mind's eye, I see all my physical, and thus symbolically, mental scars and deformities, and I wonder. Do my classmates see the moles on my neck? Do they see the puffy rolls of my flesh, my stretch-marked belly reminiscent of three pregnancies? Do they see the eight inch long scars down the sides of each thigh that resemble railroad tracks? What about the broken blood vessel at the back of my left knee that came with the stress of the second hip surgery? Do they see the peculiar scar on the first digit of my right hand, a constant reminder of the day I sliced a piece of me off with the salami onto the deli scale? If they do, do they recognize these things for what they are, representations of someone's life? Do they accept all this? Do they reject it? And if they do, does it really matter? Have they not come naked to this class also, and aren't their scars just as visible? Of course they are, or so I tell myself, but it barely soothes me enough to honestly write about who I am, and how I came to be the way I am, today.

Susan Yoritomo

I want to be safe, so I'll hide in my apartment. I'm always hiding in my apartment. I love my apartment. I can see the sunset from one window and sunrise from another. And it's not really hiding, there's no one after me. It's isolation. It's windows and doors and walls and floors and ceilings, the physical barriers I cherish. I have plants. I wonder and worry and care for them, but it's very technical. There's no love. I like them because they soften the sterile interior of my apartment. As a friend said, they are the "bare minimum" in the way of plants. I have to agree. They are the pointy, blade-like plants which are called tropical but are reminiscent of the desert. Stark. My apartment is stark. I'm stark. I strive for starkness. I hate those irresponsible, indulgent feminine traits that are me, the real me. I want my masculine, minimal, logical, problem-solving self to dominate. I want that hard, durable exterior that is not unlike a wall. A cool marble wall that endures.

Betty J. Walker

13   HOUSEWORK—Housework—I hate it. I have tried for the past 20 years to learn to like it but to no avail. It is so boring. It is repetitive and stagnates the mind. Anyone can do it; it requires no real talent except the willingness to do the same thing over and over again.

14   Now take dusting . . . an exercise in sheer futility. You take a cloth and spray some type of polish on it. You move it around on the surface of the table or chair or whatever and pick up the dust on the rag. You move around the room dusting whatever level surface there is available that does not move. You move on from room to room. After a lapsed period of perhaps 20 minutes, you return to the room you dusted first. What do you find there . . . dust!

15   How about dishwashing and cooking. Those two things will drive you crazy. The cooking goes on forever and you no sooner get one meal completed then it is time to begin another. . . . Over the years I have developed a standard menu of things I can prepare that I don't burn or cause people to be poisoned. My family has learned that if it's Tuesday, it must be hamburgers. Or, if it's Friday, it must mean that we'll eat out. You see, I don't cook on Fridays. . . .

16   Lest you form the opinion that I am lazy, let me reassure you—I am. I will work all day at something I enjoy doing. Writing or sewing or creating something keeps me interested and busy and I am never bored. But the repetitive things drive me up the walls. The trouble with housework is that once you have it all done and the house is all clean and shining, six months later you have to do it all over again.

Tammy Weast

17   What makes Christmas Christmas? It is not the carols, the decorations, nor the cold weather. It is not even Santa Claus or turkey advertisements on TV. It must be something in the mind. That's it. Christmas is a state of mind.

18   My parents are getting divorced. This was the first Christmas my mom, brother, and I have spent without my dad. We did not put up a tree. I got the decorations out of the attic though. The first box I opened contained dad's stocking. Mom cried so I put it all away.

19   December 25th was weird. I did not get up until 11 A.M. The whole world had opened their presents while I slept. My brother gave me a leather briefcase. I gave him a $50 gift certificate from Darryl's restaurant. He goes there and drinks a lot lately.

20   Dinnertime has always been around 3 P.M. on holidays. That was because my dad liked to watch the football games. This year mom said we could eat when we wanted. But we never did. I ate a beans n franks dinner later. My brother went to drink his gift certificate.

I worked the day after Christmas. All the secretaries in my office had   21
new gold necklaces from men. They all cooed about what a wonderful
holiday they had had. I got nauseous because everyone was asking me,
"How was your holiday, Tammy?" or "What did Santa bring you?" or
"How long will you be eating turkey leftovers?"

I went home early. Mom and my brother were all early too. We each   22
seemed to have upset stomachs. It must have been something we didn't
eat. Or maybe it was just our state of mind.

Kristin King

They lived in a three-hundred-thousand-dollar house that looked like a sty.   23
I remember walking into the living room once and seeing the abuse. On one
wall was a dart board with no darts and the wall behind pocked with holes.
The lining had been torn from the bottom of a yellow Chippendale sofa and
stuffing poked through where the buttons had been ripped off. In front of
the sofa was a cherry table with a half-finished model spread out and a tube
of glue dripping. There were several high-backed chairs in the room, one
Windsor without an arm, another with a torn velvet cover. On the carpet in
front of the chair was a bowl of milk with Cheerios floating. An empty pop
bottle lay on the brick hearth. Someone had tossed a crumpled McDonald's
bag on the ashes of last winter's fires. A Steinway stretched underneath a
broad picture window. Water rings spoiled the finish and a tinker toy was
wedged between two keys. The piano bench, loaded with *Sports Illustrated*,
was pushed against the wall. A china bureau, filled with Wedgwood and
Lenox, stood in the corner next to the door. A lacrosse stick was propped
against one of its broken panes. A black woman in a blue housecoat was
attempting to compensate for the absence of a cat's litter box by pushing a
vacuum back and forth over the stained carpet.

Rosalind Bradley Coles

Today in class Dudley said he's "tired of racial issues in class." Well—if he's   24
tired of them, how does he think I feel? For years I have been the only Black
(or at most one of two or three) in class and I have had to deal with white
negativism towards Blacks. . . . Every time I've taken writing classes I've
had to deal with some white person who had to put a Black person in their
story— unfortunately the Black person is never a professional or middle
class person, but illiterate, poor, kitchen workers or country hicks or
rapists. Even Dudley in his first essay continuously used the word nigger
derogatorily (although that's the only way whites can use it). . . . In the same
week Grace had a sentence in her essay about a rural man who "knew the
difference between a nigger and a colored man." Buffy is writing a story
about two Blacks (with college degrees) who interact with a white lawyer.

She is trying to adopt a Black dialect for her characters that has rhythm. What she has produced are illiterate Blacks.

25   Sometimes I wonder if these stories are written simply because it was what the author wanted to tell, or if it is a personal attack against me (which really isn't fair to assume, but it has happened so often). It's easy for Dudley to be tired of racial issues when he's white and surrounded mostly by whites. But what about me? Dudley's tired of racial issues. Well, I'm tired of having to see only the negative side of my people portrayed by my peers.

Richard Loftus, again

26 Should I write about sex? Not to be sensational. That's purposeless. I don't think it would be wrong to write about sex, because sex is so personal a subject that to use it is akin to plowing up earth. In the wake of the plow you find things you would not have expected to find, fragments of bone, earthworms, snakes, an old boot, strange rocks, an old wristwatch. Talking about sex digs down and throws up old lies, new lies, guilt, excess, happy memories, all manner of self perceptions ranging from the most superficial to most basic. So sex becomes the catalyst towards some reaction.

27   I think I see my own sexuality—my homosexuality—as the thing that made me a better listener. Because it was at thirteen something un- pleasant to own up to. Can you imagine having to admit to yourself that you're black? Almost amusing, because I can remember little of my self- consciousness of that particular time, but it was definitely the experience of being the outsider, living through my friends' heterosexual fumblings, being the uninvolved sexless sage. Later, having come out, an experience that has now been appropriated by ostomites, alcoholics, barren parents and anorexics, I was learning the joys of rhetoric. Gay politics is nothing if not rich in rhetoric. The difference between homosexual and gay? Homo- sexual is what the *New York Times* calls you; gay is what you earn the right to call yourself.

28   It was always surprising to listen to others, if somehow they were aware of my sexuality, if, somehow, the subject came up. Listening to them as they revealed their positions, feigned acceptance, gushed too readily their acceptance, or guarded their words, or condemned—it seemed always to be an exercise in measuring and dissecting. They say this, they mean that. It made me even more careful to choose words that expressed my own individual sense and that told the truth. It also made me aware of how to lie, without *really* lying (hah!). Through listening, nuance is learned.

Cheryl Watanabe

29 After the homes were lost, the businesses destroyed, after the furniture was sold or stolen, after the fathers were taken away and the rights of the land-born children erased you come—to offer money and recognition.

Deeds not willing to be forgotten haunt you: Utah or California, horse stalls for hotels, manure for freshener, the death of our sons in Italy whose parents, buried deep in the desert, watered the brush with tears. But your offer comes too late. The children have grown, the night classes paid for, the businesses reestablished, and prominence regained. We have wealth enough to forgive with charity. Just put it in the textbooks, you never put it in the textbooks.

In California thongs are still Nipper Flippers or Jap Slaps. People imitate Japanese (or is it Chinese?) when I walk by. December seventh is the Ides of March. I'm asked how I can see, is my field of vision narrowed? Would I like to go to Japan? Only after I've seen Europe and Israel. Do I speak Japanese? No. How come? Do you, being fourth generation French, Polish, Greek, speak French, Polish, or Greek? "I was hoping you'd be Buddhist." "Say some Japanese for me." "Play for me, dance for me, sing for me, cook for me—I love rice." Prejudice is the spear of Ignorance. "You write English very well. Where are you going for vacation?" Back to California. "Have you ever been there?" Yes, I was born in San Mateo and raised in San Jose.

Stephen E. Ryan

Refugee Camp 2
Turk/Iraqi Border
Company A, 2nd Battalion, 10th Special Forces Group (Airborne)
April, 1991
Day 6

The camp seems loudest at night. A huge, dulled murmur flows up from the valleys with hacking, rattling coughs, unending moaning like mantras, mules braying, wails and shrieks like a child stepped on a nail. Clank tap-tapping, metal pots clanking and wood chopping sounds but no sounds of laughter. The footsteps and shifting of thousands make a pressure on the ear just below the level of a sound. And no strong wind whistles close distractions or carries the sound away. Rising to the hill in the middle of 85,000 Kurdish refugees, the sounds articulate our mission.

In the morning, A–10 jets fly across in a low, slow demonstration. The screaming whine of their turbofans demands acknowledgement of their habitual, matin visits. The men look up out of makeshift tents with squinted eyes in a fearful reflex drawn from the sound. They have been down south where the wells still burn. Former conscripts twice fleeing, they fled Coalition destruction and then fled Saddam's genocide. But they and we and the Iraqi division beneath the border know the jet's other sound; the harsh, ripping bellow of the main gun, the tank killer. Welcome, sweet, fearsome companion.

33   Under the wide, banking circles, the women walk the morning road carrying clutched bundles pressed close. The bundles are soft-wrapped like cocoons, the folds unlike the sharp creases in the strained faces of the mothers' dry, silent anguish carrying children to graves. Behind them, men carry angular, longer, wrapped burdens as the dust rises.

34   Above, a rhythmic, tympanic beat from the north begins the helos' arrivals. They approach the small landing pad at full power remonstrating loudly at their heavy loads in the thin, high altitude air. They settle in ungraceful bobs and tilts as wheels unevenly touch down and sag with rotor blade slowing, drooping, giving back their cargo's weight to the ground. Today's arrival of rations, medicine and plastic-bottled water is too late for some, desperate hope for many.

Betty J. Walker, again

35   GOOD NEWS. . . . When it first happened, I was so excited I wanted to just jump up and down and hug the world. I felt like a balloon being blown up and up and up until I was about ready to explode—a feeling of excitement and satisfaction, a pleased-with-myself feeling. I wanted to tell everyone, but at the same time I wanted to keep it as a delicious secret. . . . I am going to have something that I have written published in the newspaper, and not in the Letters to the Editor column, either.

Content

1. Compare your reading of diaries by people with well-known reputations with the way you read the student writers' notebooks. To what extent does external information, about the authors, their other work, or the conditions of their lives and writing, influence your reading of a particular diary segment—or other writing for that matter?

Strategies/Structures

2. What differences exist between writing an essay and keeping a diary or notebook, given that diary or notebook entries are short and written at daily or longer intervals, but are not necessarily self-contained or artistically complete?

Language

3. What clues in the language can tell readers whether the writer meant to keep the work private or meant for other people to read it?

For Writing

4. Keep a diary or writer's notebook, writing three to four times a week for fifteen minutes at a time. Use it as a place to jot down ideas for present or future writing. These may include:

a. Sketches of people you know well or whom you've recently met
b. Minidramas of people in action, discussion, or conflict
c. Reactions to news events or to your reading, other writing, media viewing, or internet messages
d. Thoughts you've had or decisions you're pondering
e. Colorful or otherwise memorable language—read, overheard, seen in ads, on menus, on packages or elsewhere
f. Events or issues that evoke a strong reaction from you, positive or negative—but not lukewarm
g. Anything else you want

Writing: Re-Vision and Revision

The pun is intentional. *Re-vision* and *revision* both mean, literally, "to see again." Revision is likewise implied by the photograph above, for what the writer begins in pen on notepad will be transferred to the waiting laptop before she leaves the shelter of the tree. The introduction to this book's first part, "On Writing," briefly identified some of the dramatic changes in the ways we currently think about reading and writing, our own and others' works (1–5).

The examples of revision by Donald Murray and student Mary Ruffin reveal the passionate commitment writers make to their work. Because they are fully invested in their writing, mind, heart, and spirit, they care enough about it to be willing to rewrite again and again and again until they get it right—in subject and substance, structure and style.

Of course, these examples are meant to inspire you, as well, to be willing "to see again." When you take a second, careful look at what you wrote as a freewriting or a first draft, chances are you'll decide to change it. If and when you do, you're approaching the process that most professional writers use—and your own work will be one step closer to professional. As playwright Neil Simon says, "Rewriting is when writing really gets to be fun. . . . In baseball you only get three swings and you're out. In rewriting, you get almost as many swings as you want and you know, sooner or later, you'll hit the ball."

Many people think that revision means correcting the spelling and punctuation of a first—and only—draft. Writers who care about their work know that such changes, though necessary, are editorial matters remote from the heart of real revising. For to revise is to rewrite. And rewrite, though not in the spirit that Calvin tells Hobbes in the cartoon (p. 96) that makes bad writing incomprehensible. Novelist Toni Morrison affirms, "The best part of all, the absolutely most delicious part, is finishing it and then doing it over. . . . I rewrite a lot, over and over again, so that it looks like I never did. I try to make it look like I never touched it, and that takes a lot of time and a lot of sweat."

When you rewrite, you're doing what computer language identifies as *add, delete, move* (reorganize), and *edit.* The concept of "draft" may have become elusive for people writing on a computer; one part of a given document may have been revised extensively, other parts may be in various stages of development, while others have yet to be written. For simplicity's sake, I'll use the term *draft* throughout *The Essay Connection* to refer to one particular version of a given essay (whether the writer considers it finished or not), as opposed to other versions of that same document. Even if you're only making a grocery list, you might add and subtract material, or change the organization. If your original list identified the items in the order they occurred to you, as lists often do, you could regroup them by categories of similar items, easier to shop for: produce, staples, meat, dairy products. You might provide specially detailed emphasis on the essentials, "a pound of Milagro super-hot green chilies," and "a half gallon of double chocolate extra fudge swirl ice cream."

Some writers compose essentially in their minds.* They work through their first drafts in their heads, over and over, before putting much—if anything—down on paper. As Joyce Carol Oates says, "If you are a writer, you locate yourself behind a wall of silence and no matter what you are doing, driving a car or walking or doing housework . . . you can still be writing." There's a lot of revising going on, but it's mostly mental. What appears on the paper the first time is what stays on the paper, with occasional minor changes. This writing process appears to work best with short pieces that can easily be held in the mind—a poem, a writing with a fixed and conventional format (such as a lab report), a short essay with a single central point, a narrative in which each point in the sequence reminds the writer of what comes next, logically, chronologically, psychologically. If you write

---

* Note: Some material on 84–87 is adapted from Lynn Z. Bloom, *Fact and Artifact: Writing Nonfiction*, 2nd ed. (Englewood Cliffs, N.J.: Blair Press [Prentice Hall], 1994), 51–53.

that way, then what we say about revising on paper should apply to your mental revising, as well.

Other writers use a first draft, and sometimes a second, and a third, and more, to enable themselves to think on paper. Novelist E. M. Forster observed, "How do I know what I think until I see what I say?" How you wrote the first draft may provide cues about what will need special attention when you revise. If you use a first draft to generate ideas, in revising you'll want to prune and shape to arrive at a precise subject and focus and an organization that reinforces your emphasis, as Mary Ruffin did between the ninth draft and final version of "Mama's Smoke" (112–15). Or your first draft may be a sketch, little more than an outline in paragraph form, just to get down the basic ideas. In revising you'd aim to flesh out this bare-bones discussion by elaborating on these essential points, supplying illustrations, or consulting references that you didn't want to look up the first time around. On the other hand, you may typically write a great deal more than you need, just to be sure of capturing random and stray ideas that may prove useful. Your revising of such an ample draft might consist in part of deleting irrelevant ideas and redundant illustrations.

In *Write to Learn* (Fort Worth, Tex.: Harcourt, 1993), Donald Murray suggests a three-stage revising process that you might find helpful in general, whether or not you've settled on your own particular style of revising:

1. A quick first reading "to make sure that there is a single dominant meaning" and enough information to support that meaning.
2. A second quick reading, only slightly slower than the first, to focus on the overall structure and pace.
3. A third reading, "slow, careful, line-by-line editing of the text . . . here the reader cuts, adds, and reorders, paragraph by paragraph, sentence by sentence, word by word" (*Write to Learn*, 167).

First you look at the forest, then at the shape and pattern of the individual trees, then close up, at the branches and leaves. Although this may sound slow and cumbersome, if you try it, you'll find that it's actually faster and easier than trying to catch everything in one laborious reading, alternating between panoramic views and close-ups.

John Trimble, in *Writing with Style* (Englewood Cliffs, N.J.: Prentice Hall, 1975), offers a number of suggestions for writing in a very readable style that work equally well for first drafts as well as for revision. Trimble's cardinal principles are these: (1) Write as if your reader is a "companionable friend" who appreciates straightforwardness and has a sense of humor. (2) Write as if you were "talking to that friend," but had enough time to express your thoughts in a concise and interesting manner. He also suggests that if you've written three long sentences in a row, make the fourth sentence short. Even very short. Use contractions. Reinforce abstract discussions with "graphic illustrations, analogies, apt quotations, and concrete details." To achieve continuity, he advises, make sure each sentence is connected with those preceding and following it. And, most important, "Read your prose aloud. *Always* read your prose aloud. If it sounds as if it's come out of a machine or a social scientist's report . . . spare your reader and rewrite it" (82).

Two pieces in this section illustrate the dramatic effects of re-vision, re-seeing, reconfiguring one's subject. Garry Trudeau's "The Draft: My Story/My Story: The Holes" (98–101) illustrates how Trudeau's decision to finally tell the truth about how and why he did not serve in the army during the Vietnam War made him re-examine the evidence and his motives. This radical reappraisal led him to question what he had for years assured himself was honorable and lawful behavior and to replace "spin-doctoring" with something closer to the truth. In contrast, Maxine Hong Kingston's "On Discovery" (101–03) makes a metaphor literal. Here she shows how a man's perspective on the world becomes utterly transformed when Tang Ao, a traditional Chinese male, is obliged to live and act as a woman. John Trimbur's "Guidelines for Collaborating in Groups" (103–07) illustrates the enrichment that a variety of perspectives can bring to the writing process when several people are involved, such as a group leader, mediator, notetaker, critic, timekeeper. The photograph on p. 106, three generations of males fishing and transmitting knowledge, serves as a metaphor for the way a good collaboration can work.

Ernest Hemingway has said that he "rewrote the ending of *A Farewell to Arms*, the last page of it, thirty-nine times before I was satisfied"—which means a great deal of rewriting, even if you don't think he kept exact count.

"Was there some technical problem?" asked an interviewer. "What had you stumped?"

"Getting the words right," said Hemingway.

That is the essence of revision.

STRATEGIES FOR REVISING

1. Does my draft have a *thesis*, a focal point? Does the thesis cover the entire essay, and convey my attitude toward the subject?
2. Does my draft contain sufficient *information, evidence* to support that meaning? Is the writing developed sufficiently, or do I need to provide additional information, steps in an argument, illustrations, or analysis of what I've already said?
3. Who is my intended *audience*? Will they understand what I've said? Do I need to supply any background information? Will I meet my readers as friends, antagonists, or on neutral ground? How will this relationship determine what I say, the order in which I say it, and the language I use?
4. Do the *form* and *structure* of my writing suit the subject? (For instance, would a commentary on fast-food restaurants be more effective in an essay or description, comparison and contrast, analysis, some combination of the three—or as a narrative or satire?) Does the *proportioning* reinforce my emphasis (in other words, do the most important points get the most space)? Or do I need to expand some aspects and condense others?
5. Is the writing recognizably mine in *style, voice,* and *point of view*? Is the body of my prose like that of an experienced runner: tight and taut, vigorous, self-contained, and supple? Do I like what I've said? If not, am I willing to change it?

DONALD M. MURRAY

Murray was a successful writer long before he began teaching others to write. Born in Boston in 1924, he was educated at the University of New Hampshire (B.A., 1948) and Boston University. He wrote editorials for the *Boston Herald*, 1948–1954, for which he won a Pulitzer Prize in 1954; in retirement, he now writes "Reflections," an award-winning column for the *Boston Globe*. During his quarter-century of teaching at the University of New Hampshire, Murray wrote numerous essays, volumes of short stories, poetry, and a novel, *The Man Who Had Everything* (1964). *A Writer Teaches Writing* (1964, rev. 1985), an explanation of how people really write (as opposed to how the rule books say they should), has been highly influential in persuading writing teachers to encourage their students to focus on the process of writing, rather than on the finished product. His recent books include *The Craft of Revision* (1997) and *My Twice-Lived Life* (2001), a memoir.

Revision, in Murray's view, is central to the writing process: "Good writing is essentially rewriting." Murray offers a straightforward account of just how writers move through the process of revising, by making changes—in content, in form and in proportion, and finally in voice and word choice—that will substantially improve their work, even though "the words on a page are never finished." The history of this essay illustrates his points. Murray completely rewrote the essay twice before it was first published in *The Writer* in 1973. Then, for an anthology, Murray "re-edited, re-revised, re-read, re-re-edited" it again. A draft of the first twelve paragraphs of the "re-edited, revised" version, with numerous changes is reprinted below. As you examine both versions, note that many changes appear in the final ("re-re-edited") version that are not in the "revised" draft.

THE MAKER'S EYE: REVISING YOUR OWN
MANUSCRIPTS* by DONALD M. MURRAY

When ~~the beginning writer~~ *students* complete~~s~~ ~~his~~ *a* first draft, ~~he~~ *they* ~~usually reads it through to correct typographical errors and~~ consider~~s~~ *-- and their teachers too often agree.* the job of writing done, When ~~the~~ professional writer~~s~~ complete~~s~~ ~~his~~ *the* first draft, ~~he~~ *they* usually feel~~s~~ ~~he is~~ *they are* at the start of the writing process. ~~Now that he has~~ *when* a draft, *(is completed, the job of* ~~he can begin~~ writing *can begin.* [1]

That difference in attitude is the difference between amateur and professional, inexperience and experience, journeyman and craftsman. Peter F. Dru~~g~~*c*ker, the prolific business writer, for example, calls his first draft "the zero draft" -after that he can start cou*n*rting. Most ~~productive~~ writers share the feeling ~~that~~ the first draft*,* *all* and ~~most of those~~ which follow *are* ~~is an~~ opportunit*ies* to discover what they have to say and how they can best say it. [2]

~~Detachment and caring~~

To produce a progression of drafts, each of which says more and says it better, the writer has to develop a special *kind of* reading skill. In school we are taught to ~~read~~ *decode* what ~~is~~ *appears* on the page*,* *as finished writing.* ~~We try to comprehend what the author has said,~~ ~~what he meant and what are the implications of his words.~~ [3]

Writers, however, face a different category of possibility and responsibility. To them, the words are never finished on the page. Each can be changed, rearranged, set off a chain reaction of confusion or clarified meaning. This is a different kind of reading, possibly more difficult and certainly more exciting. [4]

* A different version of this article was published in *The Writer,* October 1973.

5   ~~The~~ writer*s* ~~of such drafts~~ must [learn to] [^]be ~~his~~ [their] own best enemy.
[Writers] ~~He~~ must accept the criticism of others, ~~--especially teachers--~~ and be suspicious of
it; ~~he~~ [they] must accept the praise of others, ~~--especially teachers--~~ and be even more
suspicious of it. ~~He~~ [Writers] cannot depend on others. ~~He~~ [They] must
detach ~~himself~~ [themselves] from ~~his~~ [their] own page*s* so that ~~he~~ [they] can apply both
~~his~~ [their] caring and ~~his~~ [their] craft to ~~his~~ [their] own work.

6   Detachment is not easy. Science fiction writer Ray
Bradbury supposedly puts each manuscript away for a year and
then rereads it as a stranger. Not many writers can afford
the time to do this. We must read when our judgment may be
at its worst, when we are close to the euphoric moment of
creation. The writer "should be critical of everything that
seems to him most delightful in his style," advises novelist
Nancy Hale. "He should excise what he most admires, because
he wouldn't thus admire it if he weren't . . . in a sense
protecting it from criticism."

7   ~~The writer must learn to protect himself from his own~~
~~ego, when it takes the form of uncritical pride or~~
~~uncritical self-destruction.~~ [¶] ~~As~~ poet John Ciardi points
out, ". . . the last act of the writing must be to become
one's own reader. It is, I suppose, a schizophrenic
process, to begin passionately and to end critically, to
begin hot and to end cold; and, more important, to be
passion-hot and critic-cold at the same time."
[unproductive]
~~Just as dangerous as the protective writer is the~~
~~despairing one, who thinks everything he does is terrible,~~
~~dreadful, awful. If he is to publish, he must save what is~~
~~effective on his page while he cuts away what doesn't work.~~
~~The writer must hear and respect his own voice.~~

Remember ~~how each~~ *how the* craftsmen you have seen--the carpenter [9]
~~eyeing the level~~ *looking at the lie* of a shelf, the mechanic listening to the

motor--takes the instinctive step back. This is what ~~the~~
writer~~s~~ *have to* ~~has to~~ do when ~~he~~ *they* read~~s~~ *their* ~~his~~ own work. "The writer

must survey his work critically, coolly, and as though he

were a stranger to it," says children's book writer Eleanor

Estes. "He must be willing to prune, expertly and hard-

heartedly. At the end of each revision, a manuscript may

look like a battered old hive, worked over, torn apart,

pinned together, added to, deleted from, words changed and

words changed back. Yet the book must maintain its

original freshness and spontaneity."

¶ We are aware of ~~the~~ writers who think everything they have written is literature but a more ~~serious~~ frequent and serious problem is ~~the are writers is~~ who are ~~overly~~ overly critical of each page, tears up each page and never completes a draft. The ~~cut~~ writer must cut what is bad to ~~save~~ reveal what is good. [8]

~~It is far easier for most beginning writers to understand the need for rereading and rewriting than it is to understand how to go about it. The publishing writer doesn't necessarily break down the various stages of rewriting and editing, he just goes ahead and does it~~ [10]
¶ ~~one of our most~~ *in the English-speaking world,* . . . . . .
prolific ~~fiction~~ writers, (Anthony Burgess,) says, "I might
revise a page twenty times." Short story and children's
writer Roald Dahl states, "By the time I'm nearing the end
of a story, the first part will have been reread and altered
and corrected at least 150 times. . . . Good writing is
essentially rewriting. I am positive of this."

11   There is nothing ~~virtuous in~~ *itself about* the rewriting process *isn't virtuous*. It is simply an essential condition of life for most writers. There are *a few* writers who do very little rewriting, mostly because they have the capacity and experience to create and review a large number of invisible drafts in their minds before they get to the page. And ~~many~~ *some* writers ~~perform~~ *who slowly produce finished pages, performing* all ~~of~~ the tasks of revision simultaneously, page by page, rather than draft by draft. But it is still possible to break down the process of rereading one's own work into the sequence most published writers follow *most of the time.* ~~as he studies his own page.~~

~~Seven elements~~

12   Many writers ~~at first just~~ scan their manuscript, reading as quickly as possible ~~for~~ *to catch the larger* problems of subject and form. ~~In this way, they stand back~~ *They take the craftsman's step back* from the more ~~technical~~ *superficial* details of language so they can spot ~~any weaknesses in content or in organization.~~ *the larger problems in writing.* ~~When the writer reads his manuscript, he is usually looking for~~ *Then as they reread — and reread and ~~the reader~~ reread — they move in closer in a logical sequence which usually ~~must~~ involves* seven elements.

13   The first is subject. ~~As a writer~~ ~~Do you have anything to say? If~~ *Sometimes writers are lucky, they* ~~you are lucky, you will find~~ *Writers look first to discover if they have* ~~that~~ indeed ~~you do~~ *that they* have something to *say* *said* ~~perhaps a little more than you expected.~~ ~~If the subject is not clear, or if it is not yet limited or defined enough~~ *writers know they can't write anything* ~~for you to handle, don't go on.~~ *nothing,* ~~What you have to say is~~ *SAVE* ~~always more important than how you say it.~~

Novelist Elizabeth Janeway says, "I think there's a nice cooking word ~~which~~ that explains a little of what happens while (the manuscript is) standing. It clarifies, like a consommé perhaps."

The Maker's Eye: Revising Your Own Manuscripts

When students complete a first draft, they consider the job of writing 1 done—and their teachers too often agree. When professional writers complete the first draft, they usually feel they are at the start of the writing process. When a draft is completed, the job of writing can begin.

That difference in attitude is the difference between amateur and 2 professional, inexperience and experience, journeyman and craftsman. Peter F. Drucker, the prolific business writer, calls his first draft "the zero draft"—after that he can start counting. Most writers share the feeling the first draft, and all which follow, are opportunities to discover what they have to say and how they can best say it.

To produce a progression of drafts, each of which says more and says 3 it more clearly, the writer has to develop a special kind of reading skill. In school we are taught to decode what appears on the page as finished writing. Writers, however, face a different category of possibility and responsibility when they read their own drafts. To them the words on the page are never finished. Each can be changed and rearranged, can set off a chain reaction of confusion or clarified meaning. This is a different kind of reading which is possibly more difficult and certainly more exciting.

Writers must learn to be their own best enemy. They must accept the 4 criticism of others and be suspicious of it; they must accept the praise of others and be even more suspicious of it. Writers cannot depend on others. They must detach themselves from their own pages so that they can apply both their caring and their craft to their own work.

Such detachment is not easy. Science fiction writer Ray Bradbury 5 supposedly puts each manuscript away for a year to the day and then rereads it as a stranger. Not many writers have the discipline or the time to do this. We must read when our judgment may be at its worst, when we are close to the euphoric moment of creation.

Then the writer, counsels novelist Nancy Hale, "should be critical of 6 everything that seems to him most delightful in his style. He should excise what he most admires, because he wouldn't thus admire it if he weren't . . . in a sense protecting it from criticism." John Ciardi, the poet, adds, "The last act of the writing must be to become one's own reader. It is, I suppose, a schizophrenic process, to begin passionately and to end critically, to begin hot and to end cold; and, more important, to be passion-hot and critic-cold at the same time."

Most people think that the principal problem is that writers are too 7 proud of what they have written. Actually, a greater problem for most professional writers is one shared by the majority of students. They are overly critical, think everything is dreadful, tear up page after page, never complete a draft, see the task as hopeless.

8   The writer must learn to read critically but constructively, to cut what is bad, to reveal what is good. Eleanor Estes, the children's book author, explains: "The writer must survey his work critically, coolly, as though he were a stranger to it. He must be willing to prune, expertly and hard-heartedly. At the end of each revision, a manuscript may look . . . worked over, torn apart, pinned together, added to, deleted from, words changed and words changed back. Yet the book must maintain its original fresh-ness and spontaneity."

9   Most readers underestimate the amount of rewriting it usually takes to produce spontaneous reading. This is a great disadvantage to the student writer, who sees only a finished product and never watches the craftsman who takes the necessary step back, studies the work carefully, returns to the task, steps back, returns, steps back, again and again. Anthony Burgess, one of the most prolific writers in the English-speaking world, admits, "I might revise a page twenty times." Roald Dahl, the popular children's writer, states, "By the time I'm nearing the end of a story, the first part will have been reread and altered and corrected at least 150 times. . . . Good writing is essentially rewriting. I am positive of this."

10   Rewriting isn't virtuous. It isn't something that ought to be done. It is simply something that most writers find they have to do to discover what they have to say and how to say it. It is a condition of the writer's life.

11   There are, however, a few writers who do little formal rewriting, pri-marily because they have the capacity and experience to create and review a large number of invisible drafts in their minds before they approach the page. And some writers slowly produce finished pages, performing all the tasks of revision simultaneously, page by page, rather than draft by draft. But it is still possible to see the sequence followed by most writers most of the time in rereading their own work.

12   Most writers scan their drafts first, reading as quickly as possible to catch the larger problems of subject and form, then move in closer and closer as they read and write, reread and rewrite.

13   The first thing writers look for in their drafts is *information.* They know that a good piece of writing is built from specific, accurate, and interesting information. The writer must have an abundance of information from which to construct a readable piece of writing.

14   Next writers look for *meaning* in the information. The specifics must build to a pattern of significance. Each piece of specific information must carry the reader toward meaning.

15   Writers reading their own drafts are aware of *audience.* They put themselves in the reader's situation and make sure that they deliver infor-mation which a reader wants to know or needs to know in a manner which is easily digested. Writers try to be sure that they anticipate and answer the questions a critical reader will ask when reading the piece of writing.

16   Writers make sure that the *form* is appropriate to the subject and the audience. Form, or genre, is the vehicle which carries meaning to the

reader, but form cannot be selected until the writer has adequate information to discover its significance and an audience which needs or wants that meaning.

Once writers are sure the form is appropriate, they must then look at   17
the *structure,* the order of what they have written. Good writing is built on a solid framework of logic, argument, narrative, or motivation which runs through the entire piece of writing and holds it together. This is the time when many writers find it most effective to outline as a way of visualizing the hidden spine by which the piece of writing is supported.

The element on which writers may spend a majority of their time is   18
development. Each section of a piece of writing must be adequately developed. It must give readers enough information so that they are satisfied. How much information is enough? That's as difficult as asking how much garlic belongs in a salad. It must be done to taste, but most beginning writers underdevelop, underestimating the reader's hunger for information.

As writers solve development problems, they often have to consider   19
questions of *dimension.* There must be a pleasing and effective proportion among all the parts of the piece of writing. There is a continual process of subtracting and adding to keep the piece of writing in balance.

Finally, writers have to listen to their own voices. *Voice* is the force   20
which drives a piece of writing forward. It is an expression of the writer's authority and concern. It is what is between the words on the page, what glues the piece of writing together. A good piece of writing is always marked by a consistent, individual voice.

As writers read and reread, write and rewrite, they move closer and   21
closer to the page until they are doing line-by-line editing. Writers read their own pages with infinite care. Each sentence, each line, each clause, each phrase, each word, each mark of punctuation, each section of white space between the type has to contribute to the clarification of meaning.

Slowly the writer moves from word to word, looking through lan-   22
guage to see the subject. As a word is changed, cut, or added, as a construction is rearranged, all the words used before that moment and all those that follow that moment must be considered and reconsidered

Writers often read aloud at this stage of the editing process, mut-   23
tering or whispering to themselves, calling on the ear's experience with language. Does this sound right—or that? Writers edit, shifting back and forth from eye to page to ear to page. I find I must do this careful editing in short runs, no more than fifteen to twenty minutes at a stretch, or I become too kind with myself. I begin to see what I hope is on the page, not what actually is on the page.

This sounds tedious if you haven't done it, but actually it is fun. Mak-   24
ing something right is immensely satisfying, for writers begin to learn what they are writing about by writing. Language leads them to meaning, and there is the joy of discovery, of understanding, of making meaning clear as the writer employs the technical skills of language.

"I used to hate writing assignments, but now I enjoy them," Calvin observes. "With a little practice, writing can be an intimidating and impenetrable fog." Are readers meant to take him seriously? How can you tell? Judging from the authors in this book, particularly the pieces on writing, what is the ideal style—or range of styles—of writing for college essays?

25   Words have double meanings, even triple and quadruple meanings. Each word has its own potential for connotation and denotation. And when writers rub one word against the other, they are often rewarded with a sudden insight, an unexpected clarification.

26   The maker's eye moves back and forth from word to phrase to sentence to paragraph to sentence to phrase to word. The maker's eye sees the need for variety and balance, for a firmer structure, for a more appropriate form. It peers into the interior of the paragraph, looking for coherence, unity, and emphasis, which make meaning clear.

27   I learned something about this process when my first bifocals were prescribed. I had ordered a larger section of the reading portion of the glass because of my work, but even so, I could not contain my eyes with this new limit of vision. And I still find myself taking off my glasses and bending my nose towards the page, for my eyes unconsciously flick back and forth across the page, back to another page, forward to still another, as I try to see each evolving line in relation to every other line.

28   When does this process end? Most writers agree with the great Russian writer Tolstoy, who said, "I scarcely ever reread my published writings, if by chance I come across a page, it always strikes me: all this must be rewritten; this is how I should have written it."

29   The maker's eye is never satisfied, for each word has the potential to ignite the new meaning. This article has been twice written all the way through the writing process, and it was published four years ago. Now it is to be republished in a book. The editors made a few small suggestions, and then I read it with my maker's eye. Now it has been re-edited, re-revised, re-read, re-re-edited, for each piece of writing to the writer is full of potential and alternatives.

30   A piece of writing is never finished. It is delivered to a deadline, torn out of the typewriter on demand, sent off with a sense of accomplishment

and shame and pride and frustration. If only there were a couple more days, time for just another run at it, perhaps then. . . .

Content

1. Why does Murray say that when a first "draft is completed, the job of writing can begin" (¶ 1)? If you thought before you read the essay that one draft was enough, has Murray's essay convinced you otherwise?

2. How does Murray explain John Ciardi's analysis of the "schizophrenic process" of becoming one's own reader, "to be passion-hot and critic-cold at the same time" (¶ 6)? Why does he consider it so important for writers to be both?

3. What are writers looking for when they revise? How can writers be sure that their "maker's eye" has in revision an accurate perception of the "need for variety and balance, for a firmer structure, for a more appropriate form. . . . for coherence, unity, and emphasis" (¶ 26)? How do you, as a writer, know whether your writing is good or not?

Strategies/Structures

4. Many of Murray's revisions are for greater conciseness. For example, the first sentence of paragraph 11 initially read, "There is nothing virtuous in the rewriting process." Murray then revised it to "The rewriting process isn't virtuous." The published version says, "Rewriting isn't virtuous." What are the effects of these successive changes? And of other comparable changes?

5. Compare and contrast the deleted paragraph 8 of the original version and the rewritten paragraphs 8 and 9 of the typescript with paragraphs 7 and 8 in the printed version. Why did Murray delete the original paragraph 8? Which ideas did he salvage? Why did he delete the first two sentences of the original paragraph 9? Are the longer paragraphs of the printed version preferable to the shorter paragraphs of the original?

Language

6. In many places in the revision typescript (see ¶s 1, 5) Murray has changed masculine pronouns (he, his) to the plural (they, their). What is the effect of these changes? What occurred in America between 1973, when the essay was first written, and 1980, when it was again revised, to affect this usage?

7. In the typescript Murray has added references to students and teachers which were not in the original published version. For whom was the original version intended? What do the additions reveal about the intended readers of the revision?

For Writing

8. Prepare a checklist of the points Murray says that writers look for in revising a manuscript: information, meaning, audience, form, structure, development, dimension, voice (¶s 13–20). Add others appropriate to your writing, and use the checklist as a guide in revising your own papers.

GARRY TRUDEAU

Trudeau, born in New York City in 1948, launched his comic strip, *Doonesbury*, in 1969 when he was twenty-one, a year before he graduated from Yale. The strip was an instant hit; the characters of Zonker, Boopsie, Lacey, Duke, and Joanie Caucus have become as familiar to the American public as the characters in *Peanuts,* though they operate in a different register. Known for its consistent satire of contemporary events, politics, personalities, and lifestyles, the strip is also critical of the economically privileged class in which Trudeau grew up. Indeed, many newspapers print the strip on their editorial pages rather than with the rest of the comics; in 1975 he won a Pulitzer Prize for editorial cartooning. "Satire is an ungentlemanly art," says Trudeau. "It's lacking in balance. It's unfair." The cartoonist and his family, wife Jane Pauley and three children, live an exceptionally well-balanced, decidedly low-key life in Manhattan.

Trudeau scans the news for ideas, keeping them in files and note-books. He writes and draws in pencil, so he can easily erase and rewrite. Then—following a common practice among cartoonists—he faxes the strips to an inker, who redraws the strip in ink with exact fidelity to the original. In "The Draft: My Story/My Story: The Holes" Trudeau offers two versions of how and why he received a draft deferment in 1970. For more than twenty years he told the honorable, public version of the story (¶s 1–6), but in 1992 he decided to come clean and provide alternative interpretations of all the facts relevant to the decision (¶s 7–18). The *New York Times* published Trudeau's explanation in September 1992 as an op-ed article at a time when Bill Clinton, then running for his first term as president, was being called on to explain why he did not serve in the military during the Vietnam War even though he, like Trudeau, was eligible for the draft.

The Draft: My Story

1   In 1966, the Selective Service granted me a 2-S student deferment, which remained in effect until I graduated from college in 1970. One night in December 1969, I learned from the radio that I had received the number 27 in the draft lottery. I returned to my dorm room where for the next two hours I received a series of highly emotional phone calls from concerned family members and friends.

2   In January, I wrote my draft board and requested a deferment on grounds of national security, citing my involvement with a magazine for the "international community" in Washington. I asked for an interview with my draft board, for which occasion I received a memorable haircut. At the same time, I made inquiries at my local National Guard unit, where I received assurances of an opening.

In March, 1970, I reported for my draft physical. Confronted with a 3
written exam, I did what I had been trained to do my entire life—my best. I
do not recall why. During the physical exam, I did not try to fake a disquali-
fying affliction for one reason alone—and this I distinctly remember—it
would have been wrong.

Later, in examining my options, I ruled out applying for conscientious- 4
objector status because I was able to imagine scenarios in which I would be
capable of taking life, and I assumed that my draft board would be able to
imagine those scenarios, too.

In June 1970, I was reclassified as 1-A. Returning home, I accepted 5
my physician father's advice to have an X-ray at our local hospital. The
X-ray revealed evidence of a past ulcer. At the urging of my lawyer, I sent
the film to a doctor in New Hampshire, and in August 1970, just days before I had been ordered to report for induction, I was granted a permanent
medical deferment.

This account was prepared without benefit of consultation of exist- 6
ing records.

My Story: The Holes

My story of the draft, recounted in unvarying language for more than 20 7
years, was initially conceived for two purposes—first, to fulfill the autobiographical requirements of the examined life, and, secondly, to grant
myself permission to move on, secure in my assessment that I had acted
honorably and lawfully.

Had I, in fact? After writing the above, I talked to family members, 8
examined the record of my draft correspondence and revisited memories
that were called forth in the process.

Here is some of what I learned: 9

1. I did receive a student deferment in 1966. But it lasted only until 10
June 1967, when it had to be renewed.

2. No family member or friend recalls telephoning me the night of the 11
lottery. Did I imagine their concern? Possibly, since I also now remember
going out that evening for a few beers.

3. I applied for an occupational deferment, not a "national security" 12
deferment. Did I really believe that editing a glorified tourist magazine was
grounds for legitimate exemption? No one can say, since I never actually
appeared before the board in 1970. The memorable haircut never happened.

4. I applied to the Guard in May, not in January. I also apparently 13
applied to two different Army Reserve units, where I was placed on the
waiting list.

5. I now recall why I tried to do well in the written exam. I reasoned 14
that a good score might earn me a desk job. And while I did indeed feel

that to fake an injury was wrong, it should be added I was also pretty sure I couldn't pull it off.

15   6. Another reason I did not apply for C.O. status, I now recall, was the amount of paperwork. I felt it prohibitive.

16   7. I was reclassified 1-A on July 22, not in June. While my X-ray did indeed show evidence of an ulcer, I have discovered that my father wrote the cover letter to the radiologist's report. In it, he noted a three-year history of gastric distress. I only recall one such year. Was my father spin-doctoring?

17   8. Lastly, in order to qualify for a New Hampshire physician's exam (reportedly the most lenient in the country), one was required to reside in that state, which I didn't. I must have known a resident who was willing to lend me his address.

18   If I ever run for public office, I'm sure I'll hear from him.

Content

1. Trudeau provides two different interpretations of how and why he secured a draft deferment during the Vietnam War. Which is the most credible? Why?

2. Readers generally trust the author of nonfiction writing unless there are cues that the work is satiric or in other ways patently false. Are such cues present in either version of Trudeau's story?

3. Why did Trudeau wait twenty-one years to tell the second version of this story?

Strategies/Structures

4. When we think of revision we often think of changing individual words or sentence structures, adding or deleting material, or reorganizing larger sections of the work. Rarely do we consider telling a completely different story, as Trudeau does here. What elements, major and minor, does he revise? With what effects?

5. Why does Trudeau let the positive interpretation precede the negative one? In general, what is the effect on the reader or hearer of encountering something first? Second? Or later?

Language

6. What is the attitude of Trudeau the author to Trudeau the character in each version of the story? What clues in the tone and language support your interpretation?

For Writing

7. Write a paper in which you tell two or more versions of a story, using the same information in each but interpreting it very differently. Write as if you expect your readers to believe each version. To aid your thinking, consider Akira Kurosawa's film *Rashōmon*, which tells four different accounts of the same sexual infidelity, Trudeau's draft story, or multiple accounts of an event in your own life

as you might present the information to your parents, your best friend, a teacher, an audience of fellow students, the people where you work. . . . The possibilities are infinite.

8. Have you ever done something that you later told about in ways calculated, as Trudeau says, to reassure yourself—and others—that you "acted honorably and lawfully"? When you examined the evidence still later, could you find equally plausible, alternative interpretations much less favorable to yourself? Did these result from different ways of looking at the facts or from discovering different facts altogether? If so, write a paper presenting two (or even more) alternative versions, and explain why—as Trudeau does—these differ so much from one another.

MAXINE HONG KINGSTON

Kingston's autobiographical writings are haunted by questions of gender and identity and belonging; what relation has she and the others she writes about to China, to other family members, to America, how much to herself alone? And what belongs to her? Kingston was born in Stockton, California, in 1940, the eldest American-born child of recent Chinese immigrants. At home she learned Chinese, her only language until she started first grade (which caused her to score "zero" on her first I.Q. test, in English), and Chinese customs from stories exchanged in her parents' laundry. She graduated from the University of California at Berkeley in 1962, married actor Earll Kingston, had a son, and taught school in Hawaii before returning to Berkeley. She publishes poetry, stories, and essays in national magazines, but is best known for her autobiography, *The Woman Warrior: Memoirs of a Girlhood Among Ghosts* (1975), winner of the National Book Critics Circle Award for nonfiction, and *China Men* (1980), winner of the American Book Award. Her novel, *Tripmaster Monkey: His Fake Book,* was published in 1989. Since 1990 she has been a Chancellor's Distinguished Professor at the University of California, Berkeley.

China Men focuses primarily on the meaning of immigration, cultural displacement, and cultural assimilation for Chinese men who emigrated to America, the "Gold Mountain" of Chinese legend. Its opening section, "On Discovery," is a parable in which a traditional Chinese man arrives by accident in the Land of Women, where he is forced into looking and behaving like a woman through the painful processes of having his ears pierced, his foot bones broken and bound, his eyebrows plucked and face made up—much to his embarrassment and shame. This metaphorical definition of a Chinese woman implies an equation: Chinese women are to Chinese men as Chinese men are to Americans. And this equation defines China men (note the connotation of fragility) in America. Metaphors and parables are useful devices for making meaning—explaining, discovering, or inventing new significance.

On Discovery

1   Once upon a time, a man, named Tang Ao, looking for the Gold Mountain, crossed an ocean, and came upon the Land of Women. The women immediately captured him, not on guard against ladies. When they asked Tang Ao to come along, he followed; if he had had male companions, he would've winked over his shoulder.

2   "We have to prepare you to meet the queen," the women said. They locked him in a canopied apartment equipped with pots of makeup, mirrors, and a woman's clothes. "Let us help you off with your armor and boots," said the women. They slipped his coat off his shoulders, pulled it down his arms, and shackled his wrists behind him. The women who kneeled to take off his shoes chained his ankles together.

3   A door opened, and he expected to meet his match, but it was only two old women with sewing boxes in their hands. "The less you struggle, the less it'll hurt," one said, squinting a bright eye as she threaded her needle. Two captors sat on him while another held his head. He felt an old woman's dry fingers trace his ear; the long nail on her little finger scraped his neck. "What are you doing?" he asked. "Sewing your lips together," she joked, blackening needles in a candle flame. The ones who sat on him bounced with laughter. But the old women did not sew his lips together. They pulled his earlobes taut and jabbed a needle through each of them. They had to poke and probe before puncturing the layers of skin correctly, the hole in the front of the lobe in line with the one in back, the layers of skin sliding about so. They worked the needle through—a last jerk for the needle's wide eye ("needle's nose" in Chinese). They strung his raw flesh with silk threads; he could feel the fibers.

4   The women who sat on him turned to direct their attention to his feet. They bent his toes so far backward that his arched foot cracked. The old ladies squeezed each foot and broke many tiny bones along the sides. They gathered his toes, toes over and under one another like a knot of ginger root. Tang Ao wept with pain. As they wound the bandages tight and tighter around his feet, the women sang footbinding songs to distract him: "Use aloe for binding feet and not for scholars."

5   During the months of a season, they fed him on women's food: the tea was thick with white chrysanthemums and stirred the cool female winds inside his body; chicken wings made his hair shine; vinegar soup improved his womb. They drew the loops of thread through the scabs that grew daily over the holes in his earlobes. One day they inserted gold hoops. Every night they unbound his feet, but his veins had shrunk, and the blood pumping through them hurt so much, he begged to have his feet re-wrapped tight. They forced him to wash his used bandages, which were embroidered with flowers and smelled of rot and cheese. He hung the bandages up to dry, streamers that dropped and draped wall to wall. He felt embarrassed; the wrappings were like underwear, and they were his.

One day his attendants changed his gold hoops to jade studs and 6 strapped his feet to shoes that curved like bridges. They plucked out each hair on his face, powdered him white, painted his eyebrows like a moth's wings, painted his cheeks and lips red. He served a meal at the queen's court. His hips swayed and his shoulders swiveled because of his shaped feet. "She's pretty, don't you agree?" the diners said, smacking their lips at his dainty feet as he bent to put dishes before them.

In the Women's Land there are no taxes and no wars. Some scholars 7 say that the country was discovered during the reign of Empress Wu (A.D. 694–705), and some earlier than that, A.D. 441, and it was in North America.

JOHN TRIMBUR

Trimbur, born in San Francisco in 1946, grew up in Modesto, California, in the San Joaquin Valley and earned a B.A. in history at Stanford, followed by a Ph.D. in English at the State University of New York at Buffalo (1982). He currently directs the Technical, Scientific, and Professional Communication Program at Worcester Polytechnic Institute, where he is Distinguished Professor of Humanities. His professional papers and books focus on writing theory and cultural studies of literacy, as is clear in the co-edited, prize-winning *The Politics of Writing Instruction* (1993). "Guidelines for Collaborating in Groups" appears in his recent textbook, *The Call to Write* (2nd ed., 2002).

Trimbur explains his divergent views on writing alone and on collaborative writing, which he calls "co-writing." "I like to do both," he says, "in part because they're different. Co-writing gives me a lot of energy and accountability. There's less anxiety because you can pass a text back and forth, building and changing it along the way, believing that your team is eventually going to get it into a shape that everyone can live with." In contrast, he says, when I'm writing by myself I sometimes wonder "whether what I'm saying makes any sense or holds together in a public way. I keep wondering whether I'm adequate to the task, whereas in co-writing I'm confident we'll eventually get it right."

Guidelines for Collaborating in Groups

Any group of people working together on a project will face certain is- 1 sues, and a group collaborating on a writing project is no exception. The following guidelines are meant to keep a group running smoothly and to forestall some common problems.

Recognize that Group Members Need to Get Acquainted and that Groups Take Time to Form

2   People entering new groups sometimes make snap judgments without getting to know the other people or giving the group time to form and develop. Initial impressions are rarely reliable indicators of how a group will be. Like individuals, groups have life histories, and one of the most awkward and difficult moments is getting started. Group members may be nervous, defensive, or overly assertive. It takes some time for people to get to know one another and to develop a sense of connectedness to the group.

Clarify Group Purposes and Individual Roles

3   Much of people's initial discomfort and anxiety has to do with their uncertainty about what the purpose of the group is and what their role in the group will be. Group members need to define their collective task and develop a plan to do it. This way, members will know what to expect and how the group will operate.

Recognize that Members Bring Different Styles to the Group

4   . . . Individual styles of composing can vary considerably. The same is true of individuals' styles of working in groups. For example, individuals differ in the way they approach problems. Some people like to spend a lot of time formulating problems, exploring the complexities, contradictions, and nuances of a situation. Others want to define problems quickly and then spend their time figuring out how to solve them. By the same token people have different styles of interacting in groups. Some people like to develop their ideas by talking, while others prefer to decide what they think before speaking. So successful groups learn to incorporate the strengths of all these styles, making sure that even the most reticent members participate.

Recognize that You May Not Play the Same Role in Every Group

5   In some instances you may be the group leader, but in other instances the role you'll need to play is that of the mediator, helping members negotiate their differences, or the critic, questioning the others' ideas, or the timekeeper, prompting the group to stick to deadlines. You may play different roles in the same group from meeting to meeting or even within a meeting. For a group to be successful, members must be willing and able to respond flexibly to the work at hand.

Monitor Group Progress and Reassess Goals and Procedures

It's helpful to step back periodically to take stock of what has been accom- 6
plished and what remains to be done. Groups also need to look at their own
internal workings, to see if the procedures they have set up are effective
and if everyone is participating.

Quickly Address Problems in Group Dynamics

Problems arise in group work. Some members may dominate and talk too 7
much. Others may withdraw and not contribute. Still others may fail to
carry out assigned tasks. If a group avoids confronting these problems,
the problems will only get worse. Remember, the point of raising a problem is not to blame individuals but to promote an understanding about
what's expected of each person and what the group can do to encourage
everyone's participation.

Encourage Differences of Opinion

One of the things that makes groups productive is the different perspec- 8
tives individual members bring to group work. In fact, groups of like-
minded people who share basic assumptions are often not as creative as
groups where there are differences among members. At the same time,
group members may feel that there are ideas or feelings they can't bring
up in the group because to do so would threaten group harmony. This
feeling is understandable. Sometimes it's difficult to take a position that
diverges from what other members of the group think and believe. But
groups are not forms of social organization to enforce conformity; they are
working bodies that need to consider all the available options and points
of view. For this reason, groups need to encourage the discussion of differences and to look at conflicting viewpoints. . . .

Division of Labor or Integrated Team?

Some groups approach collaborative projects by developing a division of 9
labor that assigns particular tasks to group members who complete them
individually and then bring the results back to the group. This has been
the traditional model for collaborative work in business, industry, and
government. It is an efficient method of work, especially when groups are
composed of highly skilled members. Its limitations are that weak group
members can affect the quality of the overall work and that group members may lose sight of the overall project because they are so caught up in
their own specialized work.

What is the relationship among the people fishing here? In what ways are they collaborating? If not all participants can be expected to contribute equally in all circumstances, what should determine the extent and nature of the contribution of each? How can the principles underlying their collaborative behavior apply to other collaborative activities, including writing? If there are disagreements among the participants, on what grounds should they be resolved?

10   More recently, groups have begun to explore an integrated approach in which group members all work together through each stage of the project. An integrated-team approach involves members more fully in the work and helps them maintain an overall view of the project's goals and progress. But it also takes more time—time must be devoted to meetings and, often, to developing good working relations among members.

11   These two models of group work are not mutually exclusive. In fact many groups function along integrated-team lines when they are planning and reviewing work, but also farm out particular tasks to individuals or subgroups. So you need to discuss and develop some basic guidelines on group functioning.

Content

1. Why has Trimbur arranged the principles for collaborating in groups in the order in which they appear here?

2. In what ways can these principles be adapted to the interests and abilities of the group at hand? To what sorts of activities in addition to writing might these principles apply?

3. Discuss—preferably with a group—how Trimbur's principles might apply to writing a particular document, for instance, a report or other presentation of information.

For Writing

4. Form a group, draw up some principles of collaboration, and follow your group's guidelines to write a collaborative document. Then revise the principles to reflect your experience of collaborative writing and revise the document.

MARY RUFFIN

Ruffin was born in Richmond, Virginia, in 1964. She earned a B.A. in English and philosophy from Virginia Commonwealth University in 1984 and an M.A. in 1986. Her mother, an artist and aspiring writer, died when Ruffin was thirteen. As a college student, Ruffin attempted for several years in her writing to come to terms with the meaning of her mother's life and death. The nine notebook entries that follow show the genesis and evolution of "Mama's Smoke" over a two-month period. They include one freewriting (#1), three drafts of a poem (#2, 3, 7), a playful free association of words (#6), and the completed poem (#8)—with which she was "never happy." In retrospect, she found the poem's first draft "far better than [its] final draft . . . because the VOICE IS REAL! I killed it."

The three preliminary prose versions (#4, 5, 9) developed from the original freewriting. The ninth and tenth (final) versions both included the same topics and most of the same language. However, at her classmates' suggestions during group discussion, Ruffin decided to revise the paper so that the opening paragraphs reinforced the theme of the title and the ultimate message of the essay. Note that Ruffin tried dramatically different modes of writing—poetry, free association, and prose—in the process of discovering the version that best suited her and her subject.

"Mama's Smoke," the resulting combination of epitaph, eulogy, and portrait, is a tribute to the continuing complexity of their relationship. Ruffin's characterization of her mother epitomizes her own complicated narrative technique and illustrates the poetic aspects of her prose: "She is something like a sequel to herself, elliptical and confusing, out of context. She speaks in fragments, interrupting in the middle of my own sentences, giving to others the illusion that I have spoken her words. But the others don't know her, don't know her words from mine. The illusion is mine." As the smoke through which Ruffin imagines her mother swirls and eddies, the image of her mother emerges with precision, the different aspects of her activities and of her relationship with her daughter coalescing through the catalyst of love.

❄ Writer's Notebook Entries: The Evolution of "Mama's Smoke"

2/23　#1
Freewriting

A freewrite is all I can do again because the page is glaring, more ominous even than its traditional blank stare.

The poetry won't come. I've killed it with the spearhead of desire to be Outstanding English Major.

The prose won't come because it can't break out of the stillborn poetry.

The academics won't come because they're forced into the name-dropping realm of pretension. . . . Plus, I hate traditional white male southern writers. With those accents that sound like my mother but aren't my mother at all. . . .

There must be a starting point somewhere—a thread to grasp.

Can't do it all. Must at least reach out to the part that reaches back.

Mama.

2/24　#2
Writer's Notebook, first poem draft

Mama had fierce green eyes and black hair
I know from the black and white pictures
forty years old and more
and the salt and pepper I remember
and the tired hazel that I be inherited
for she could have been my grandma.

Jet black hair so thick the sheen
Matched the fierceness of green eyes
That were my Mama I know cause I've
heard tell and see the faded black and
white pictures stuffed in the cookie tin
she had for twenty some odd years
and I've kept for ten, and the memory
of the permed salt and pepper I played

in dangling my feet in mid air hung
over the chair back and the tired
hazel nestled in the hooded lids,
I inherited her eyes but without
the green snap

2/25 #3
Writer's Notebook, second poem draft

Rites

Back
~~when~~

~~Back~~ When
It was cool to smoke, she did, and was
I imagine, of course not able to remember,
the picture of glamourousness. It was
In the days before that surgeon general
Determined the hazardousness
~~immediately~~   is now as immediate as
that ~~to rings in my ears in unison~~
with "once upon a time", ~~steeped in~~ possessing

reared!
The familiarity of ~~what raised~~ that with which
Unfiltered   we were ~~raised~~. ~~Or reared,~~ She was never without
Camels in   An ivory holder I've heard tell
and seen the legendary
   a flash
~~the~~ flash of her ^ fierce green eyes
~~in the wrinkled~~ rusted   ~~yellowed~~
yellowing and wrinkled in the cookie tin of black and
snapshots
white ~~photos~~ she hung onto for
twenty some odd years, and I now
for ten.   difficult
The lid is ~~not easy~~ to pry open.
~~She passed on a spark to me, hazel~~
~~eyes~~   miraculously
The spark ~~somehow~~ passed on,
miscellaneous barely discernible in my hazel,
mediated by ~~gray chromosomes~~ and the bloodshot
~~itcha~~ of Menthol Virginia Slim Ultra Lights
~~itches, smolders and goes cold.~~ incessant.
Itches ~~a dry itch, beyond my years.~~

2/27   #4
Writer's Notebook, first prose draft

She was a smoker, but that began in the days when it was cool to smoke. Long before that surgeon general determined the hazardousness of the habit, and the behaviorists blasted it as an infantile fixation, she was glamorous. It was unfiltered Camels in the beginning, though by the time I was around she had gone to Merits, clunky with thick filters wrapped in blotchy brown.

My mother was an artist. She used to paint, in a turquoise studio smock, portraits of everyone she knew. Though I don't remember her ever painting herself—that is except for the red polish on her toenails. Her fingernails stayed natural yellow, she said because of the turpentine, but I think nicotine contributed to the hue. I've heard that when she was young she was never without her ivory cigarette holder. She readily admitted to her vanity.

later, 2/27
Writer's Notebook, first prose draft, second installment (excerpt)

She comes to me in the middle of the night, or rather I come to her, chase her even, through strange landscapes and insidescapes. Sometimes she is an old crone, witch-like, her black hair full of salt and her green eyes bloodshot knifeslits. . . .

3/3/85   #5
Writer's Notebook, second prose draft

She can surface without warning, anytime, anyplace. Sometimes she comes and goes so quickly that I hardly notice her presence. The other day, for instance, I stood in the kitchen staring at the can of Crisco and a tattered, encrusted cookbook page. Spoon in hand, I wondered blankly for a moment how to measure solid shortening. When the idea of displacement struck me and I filled the cup half full with water, I thought it was the ghost of a physics text. By the time I realized that it had been her, she was long gone and I had to shake my head. That's the way it happens frequently.

She never answers to her name—she almost seems to run away when she comes to mind. She is called Peggy, the only nickname for Margaret she could ever tolerate. She told me once that was why I had such a simple name, something virtually unalterable, to have forever. I resemble Peggy slightly, but just like the futility of calling her, when I look for the resemblance in the mirror it isn't there—It's those other times, catching an unexpected glimpse of my reflection out of the corner of my eye, that she suddenly appears.

3/10   #6
Writer's Notebook, "playing" (free association)

Dragons

Cookie tin——shining armor——rusty knight
Desert——fire——camels——dragons
Green dragons
Slain dragons & fair maidens
Dark fair maidens——unfair damsels
Once upon atime hazardousness——dragon
Dragon——take a "drag on" a cigarette
Smoke——cool smoke——hot smoke——smoke breath
Dragon's lair——womb——cave
cookies & stories——yellowing green
eyes & hazel bloodshot
Grendel's mother
Damsel in distress
Legend——spark of the divine
Glamourousness——amourousness—— clamourousness
Reptiles——evolution——snake——fake——fang
Red nails——red lips——glamour is dark——beauty light
Medieval—— Middle Ages——
Middle age——
The Tale——the monomyth——hero's journey
Separation——Initiation——Return
Smoke——illusion
Birthrite——legacy——heir——air——smoke
Glamour as aloof passion——cool hotness- —
artifice——surface image— -imagination
hard— -glamour = armor—— -defense mechanism
Smoking as oral fixation
Smoking as magic
Fairy tales— -scales——fear in fairy tails—— wicked
stepmother- =poison

3/17   #7
Writer's Notebook, third poem draft (excerpt)

Rites

Back when it was cool to smoke, she did, and was
I imagine, of course not able to remember, the picture
of glamourousness. It was in the days before the surgeon
general determined the dreadful gnawing
hazardousness that is now as immediate as

once-upon-a-time, possessing the familiarity
of that with which we were reared. . . .

3/28/85   #8
Writer's Notebook, final poem

Once Upon a Time

Back when it was cool to smoke, she did, and was
I imagine, of course not able to remember, the picture
of glamourousness.
Chains of unfiltered Camels, never without the ivory
holder between blood-red nails, I've heard tell
and seen the legendary flash of her fierce green
eyes yellowing and wrinkled in the rusted
cookie tin filled to brimming with brittle
undated black and white snapshots she hung onto
for twenty-some-odd years, and I still keep.

It is difficult to pry open the lid.

Once I caught her in the mirror, her tears
a simple bewilderment to me then,
turning more complex. Now
I catch her only on the edges
of my own reflection. Her spark in my hazel,
barely discernable, bloodshot
itches, runs, waters, burns
incessant.

4/2   #9
Writer's Notebook, third prose draft
(excerpt of entire essay)

Mama's Smoke

"Not 'plain'! Pure and ageless, incorruptible! That's what your name
is. I always hated mine with a passion! When people called me 'Margaret'
I felt squeamish. And 'Maggie'—ugh—a literal punch in the stomach! But
it's awkward to go through life with a nickname. It makes you feel always
like you're not quite ever really yourself. I didn't want that for you."

Peggy wanted only the best for me, the best being an abstraction she
pondered incessantly. When I was little, I would sit on the ancient wobbly
wooden stool in the corner of the kitchen, rocking and squeaking, listening to her. I liked that spot because it was right over the heat duct in the
winter, and caught the breeze from the screen door in the utility room in

the summer. Evenings, I asked her all kinds of questions—never afraid to broach any subject—and her answers usually took off miraculously, soaring.

Sometimes I just listened to the rhythm of her plastic-soled slippers....

4/23   Mama's Smoke #10
final prose version (whole essay, revised and completed)

Mama's Smoke

I never thought I would smoke. With her it was different—she started way back when it was cool to smoke—had been the very picture of glamour. But that was before the surgeon general determined the hazardousness that is as immediate in the origins of my consciousness as once-upon-a-time. 1

Myths are absorbing. I've been told of the chains of unfiltered Camels she used to smoke, never without the legendary ivory holder between fingers with blood-red nails. By the time I was around she had switched to Merits. 2

Peggy thrived on craving. She wanted only the best for me, the best being an abstraction she pondered incessantly. When I was little I would sit on the ancient wobbly wooden stool in the corner of the kitchen, rocking and squeaking, listening to her. I liked the spot because it was right over the heat duct in the winter, and caught the breeze through the screen door in the utility room in the summer. Evenings, I asked her all kinds of questions—never afraid to broach any subject—and her answers usually took off miraculously, soaring. 3

"Not 'plain'! Pure and ageless, incorruptible! That's what your name is. That's why I gave it to you. I always hated mine with a passion! When people called me 'Margaret' I felt squeamish. And 'Maggie'—ugh—a literal punch in the stomach! But it's awkward to go through life with a nickname. It makes you feel always like you're not quite ever really yourself. I didn't want that for you." 4

If I didn't understand the songs she sang, I knew the syllables by heart. Sometimes I would just listen to the rhythm of her plastic-soled slippers. I creaked my stool in time as her slippers slid on the red and white tiles, moving from one end of the long counter to the other and back, to the sink, ice box, sink again, stove, counter. There was a regularity to the irregularity that soothed me. 5

As I draw deeply on my menthol Virginia Slims Light, looking through the yellowing black and white snapshots in the rusty old cookie tin she held onto for twenty-some-odd years, I wonder what happened to make me start smoking. The lid is difficult to open. Inside there are faces, one face altered over and over, with fierce green eyes flashing, despite the brittle fadedness of the images. My hazel eyes have the spark, but only enough of a spark to torment me, to always make me seem not quite all 6 me. Peggy stays away when I look at the pictures of her—maybe she doesn't identify with them anymore herself. She certainly used to.

7   But she also used to answer me when I called, and she no longer does that either. Often deep in my sleep I glimpse her and chase her through strange insidescapes, but she always refuses to recognize me. Once recently she consented to meet me in an abandoned ice rink. When I skated in late, she simply stared down my apologies. Suddenly busying herself with an old movie projector, her back to me, she became a flailing chaos of limbs in the darkness of the rink. I gave in to the oppression of futility and seated myself behind her. At first the picture jumped and lurched on the screen, out of focus, broke once, and then smoothed out. Peggy danced a vaudeville set in our old kitchen, twirling whisks and spatulas to the soundtrack of "Clementine." When the lights came on she had disappeared, and I was alone shivering, with the distorted tune ringing in my ears.

8   Usually she surfaces so briefly and unobtrusively that I'm not sure she has been there until after she's gone. Sometimes she appears an old haggard crone, the salt in her hair so thick that the pepper looks like dirt streaks washing away. Other times she is vital, younger than I am, the sheen of her black hair almost blinding. In the buttered daylight of my kitchen, as I stand blankly staring at the can of Crisco and the Pyrex measuring cup, I guess it is the sudden memory of a physics lesson that makes me think of using water to measure the solid substance. Displacement. Only later, as I gently knead the biscuit dough, careful not to bruise it, I realize that she has been there. Her smirk of disgust at the soybean powder in the open cabinet gave her away—she couldn't resist a mild "eee-gad" under her breath.

9   Peggy is steeped in colloquialism, figures of speech that barely escape the shallows of cliché. She wrote a novel once, some kind of sequel to *Gone with the Wind* and now she comes to me at the typewriter sometimes, though rarely at the notebook stage, and whispers more criticism than commentary. She burned it, burned it in a fit of rage. Justified, for they wouldn't make her known. One attempt, one refusal. The only grace is to make a clean break.

10   She is something like a sequel to herself, elliptical and confusing, out of context. She speaks in fragments, interrupting in the middle of my own sentences, giving to others the illusion that I have spoken her words. But that's not exactly accurate either. The others don't know her, don't know her words from mine. The illusion is mine.

11   The hiss of the word "fixatif" on a spray can evokes a frustrated whimper of reminiscence. The bite of turpentine and linseed oil draws her. She is a painter of portraits and has rendered a likeness of almost everyone she is close to at one time or another, I believe, with the exception of herself. When I pick up a piece of charcoal she jumps in and jerks my hand, refusing to let me catch an image clearly. I have forsaken our art

and she will not let me be forgiven so easily. But when I settle back and contemplate my own regrets, she relents. I feel her take her dry brush in hand and trace my features, a delicious tickle I revered as a child.

The legacy of paint stains on her pale turquoise smock, like the rhythm of the shuffle of her slippers on the floor, is her highest art. She denies it, of course, as obstinately as she refuses to appear when I look for her in the mirror. But she proves it as she shows up at those moments when I catch my reflection unexpectedly out of the corner of my eye. 12

The conversations we have now in black coffee cups and clouds of smoke are the closest we come to shared sustenance. They are always late, the times when it's most conspicuous to be awake. We plan the colors for the drapes and the throw pillows to furnish some future studio. The studio gradually takes shape, perfect, and then shatters in a coughing fit. I hear her in another room, hacking, fading, and then she's gone. 13

Just as she never stays, she never stays away for long. She was beautiful in her day and she still preens, still believes underneath in the ultimate importance of surfaces. 14

At parties, her old acquaintances appear as her friends. They ask me if I'm in art school and the flinching negative reply is overridden by their awe at my study of "philosophy." 15

"So like her! Right down to the hair and eyes, though not quite so dark, not quite so green. But underneath, Peggy *was* a philosopher, she was, so wise. . . ." 16

And Peggy surfaces and "eec-gads" so loudly in my ear that the friends' politenesses go under and my own return politenesses are just-not-quite-right. I sip my wine and kick Peggy in the shin. The acquaintances wander off whispering, "Almost the spitting image, except not nearly so . . . *genuine*. . . . This new generation. . . ." 17

Later, Peggy and I have pillow fights. The pillows are wet. The stains in the morning are on my face in the angry mirror. My eyes are hazel, murky. Peggy's eyes are clear, stinging green. When the lids began to droop, right before they closed for good, she cried bitterly in the mirror. Then I felt simple bewilderment, turning more complex. She still will not understand that her spattered smock is finer than the portraits. We light up. We cough out our truce. 18

For Writing

These various drafts of notebook, poetry, freewriting, and prose demonstrate the evolution of Mary Ruffin's "Mama's Smoke." You can compare and analyze these for evidence of development of character, style, narrative persona, changes in organization, incorporation of poetic language into the prose versions, and control over tone and relationship between the mother and daughter. You might also want to try to write a poem as a preliminary draft of a prose paper. Just play around with words, ideas, images, and sounds until they coalesce.

Part II

Determining Ideas in a Sequence

Narration

Narration, telling a story, is a particularly attractive mode of writing. Ours is a storytelling culture. It is as old as Indian legends, Br'er Rabbit, Grimm's fairy tales, and the stories of Edgar Allan Poe. It is as new as speakers' warm-up jokes ("A funny thing happened on my way to . . .") and anecdotal leads to otherwise impersonal news stories. Narration can be as profound as the story of a life, the chronicle of a discovery, the history of a nation, or the account of one single, intense moment. Don DeLillo begins a brief story.

> Ash was spattering the windows, Karen was half dressed, grabbing the kids and trying to put on some clothes and talking with her husband and scooping things to take out to the corridor, and they looked at her, twin girls, as if she had fourteen heads.
>
> They stayed in the corridor for a while, thinking there might be secondary explosions. They waited, and began to feel safer, and went back to the apartment.
>
> At the next impact, Marc knew in the sheerest second before the shock wave broadsided their building that it was a second plane, impossible, striking the second tower. Their building was two blocks away, and he'd thought the first crash was an accident.

This excerpt from DeLillo's essay "In the Ruins of the Future" (*Harper's,* December 2001, p. 33) contains the major elements of a narrative.

1. *Characters:* Karen, Marc (whom we later learn is DeLillo's nephew), their twin daughters, and unidentified antagonists who are crashing planes into the World Trade Center
2. *Setting:* an apartment two blocks away from the World Trade Center
3. *Conflict:* terrorists vs. New York's peaceful civilian population
4. *Plot*—beginning to unfold: Will this family survive? Will more attacks occur? What will be the consequences?
5. *Motives:* although the attackers' are murky, the victims' motives are clear—safety for themselves and their children
6. *Point of view:* a third-person account by an omniscient narrator who understands what the characters are thinking

It is unnecessary to specify the date, indelibly engraved on the minds of the readers as well as the participants. Only *dialogue* is missing; actions and eloquent silence say what is necessary. All these features make the incident or any vivid narrative a particularly easy form of writing for readers to remember. As this narration reveals, a narrative does *not* necessarily have to be a personal essay.

Narratives can be whole novels, stories, essays, or segments of other types of writings. They can be as long and complicated as Charles Dickens's novels or an account of the Watergate break-in, trial, and aftermath. Or they can be as short and to the point as the following narrative by student Myrna Greenfield, complete in a single paragraph:

> now every dream i'd ever dreamed about college roommates said they are your best friends and the two of you fall in love with two men who are best friends and you get married after college to the best friends and you move to minneapolis or new rochelle and live next door and you have kids who grow up to be best friends with your best friend's kids. but kim was coolish and i was warmish and kim loved beethoven and i loved beatles and kim was neat and i was sloppy and kim was quiet and i was noisy as all hell broke loose. so much for the dream.

Myrna, as an author writing in the first person, has efficiently (although with unconventional punctuation) narrated two stories. The first, structured by a unified chronological progression, relates the myth of a college woman's stereotyped life history. The second, emphasizing variations on the theme of incompatibility, tells the story of the actual relationship between the author and her roommate. There are two main characters in the first story: Myrna's idealized version of herself and Kim. The two characters in the second story are the actual roommates. Each story has a setting: college and the suburbs in the first; college in the second. Each story covers a period of time—the entire life span in the first; the recent past in the second. The second sentence negates the first and leads to the short, punchy emotional climax, "so much for the dream."

A narrative need not be fictional, as the above examples and the essays in this section indicate. When you're writing a narrative based on real people, actual incidents, you shape the material to emphasize the *point of view, sequence of action* (a chase, an exploration), a *theme* (greed, pleasure), a *particular relationship between characters* (love, antagonism), or the *personalities of the people involved* (vigorous, passive). This shaping— supplying information or other specific details where necessary, deleting trivial or irrelevant material—is essential in transforming skeletal diary entries into three-dimensional configurations.

A narrative can *exist for its own sake*. As sixteenth-century poet and courtier Sir Philip Sidney observed, such writing can attract "children from play and old men from the chimney corner." Though Ann Upperco Dolman's comic tale of "Learning to Drive" (146–50) typifies the experiences of thousands of new teenage drivers, it won't improve anyone's learning curve—but everyone who has ever survived driving lessons will enjoy it. (The student driver depicted on p. 148 seems much happier than Dolman.) Through a narrative you can also *illustrate or explore a personality or an idea*. In the classic "Once More to the Lake" (122–28), E. B. White uses his own experiences on a timeless summer vacation to explore the continuity of generations of parents and children, embedding short narrative vignettes into the overarching narrative structure. The photographs of people fishing on pp. 106 and 117 tell two different stories, perhaps more, despite their common elements.

In "The Inheritance of Tools" (139–46) Scott Russell Sanders uses a comparable narrative technique to interpret the character of his father. As Sanders's essay becomes a tribute to his father, and to the extended family of which his father was a member, Sanders describes his legacy, the carpenters' tools ("the hammer [that] had belonged to him, and to his father before him") and the knowledge of how to use them, transmitted through years of patient teaching and an insistence on high-quality work, "making sure before I drove the first nail that every line was square and true." This type of description consists of stories embedded within stories: How Sanders's father taught him to use the hammer (¶s 6, 9), the saw (¶s 10, 12), the square (¶s 14–16). Still more stories incorporate the current use to which Sanders puts this knowledge (he's building a bedroom in the basement), the incident of the gerbil escaping behind the new bedroom wall (¶s 17, 22), learning of his father's death (¶s 26, 28)—all embedded in the matrix of the stories of four generations of the Sanders family.

If you wish to write a personal narrative you can *present a whole or partial biography or autobiography,* as does Frederick Douglass in "Resurrection" (133–38), an excerpt from his *Life and Times* that recounts a single narrative incident in the life of a slave. Here Douglass tells the story of how he defied—in a two-hour fistfight—a Simon Legree–like overseer who had determined to break his spirit through repeated beatings. This, explains Douglass, was "the turning-point in my career as a slave. . . . It recalled the departed self-confidence, and inspired me again with a determination to be free. . . . It was a glorious resurrection, from the tomb of slavery, to the heaven of freedom." The photograph on p. 135 corroborates Douglass's story with a story of its own.

Through narration you can *impart information* or *an account of historical events,* either from an impartial or—more likely—an engaged eyewitness point of view, as Zitkala-Sa does in excerpts from *The School Days of an Indian Girl* (218–26). Through narration you can, as Zitkala-Sa also does, *present a powerful argument, overt or implicit.* Lynda Barry's "The Sanctuary of School" (500–04) also uses the example of herself (and her brother— "children with the sound turned off") to present the implied argument that for neglected youngsters public schools are a lifeline and should be funded at a level that reflects their vital importance. Fables, parables, and other *morality* or *cautionary tales* are as old as Aesop, as familiar as the Old and New Testaments, as contemporary as Anne Fadiman's "Under Water" (128–32), a cautionary tale whose sunny beginning belies its complex moral undertow, which the narrator does not fully acknowledge until the passage of slow time for reflection, twenty-seven years after she was eighteen and "wanted to hurry through life as fast as I could." Although Fadiman focuses on telling the story and what it means to her, she expects the readers to apply to their own lives the moral understanding gained from reading about her experience of pleasure transformed, over time, to shame. The photograph on p. 129 captures the event, but does it convey the spirit and tone of Fadiman's essay?

To write a narrative you can ask, What do I want to demonstrate? Through what characters, performing what actions or thinking what thoughts? In what setting and time frame? From what point of view do I want to tell the tale? Do I want to use a first-person involved narrator who may also be a character in the story, as are the narrators of all the essays in this section? Or a third-person narrator, either on the scene or depending on the reports of other people, as in the account of terrorism quoted on page 118? An easy way to remember these questions is to ask yourself

1. *Who* participated?
2. *What* happened?
3. *Why* did this event/these phenomena happen?
4. *When* did it (or they) happen?
5. *Where* did it (or they) happen?
6. *How* did it (or they) happen? Under what circumstances?

Narratives have as many purposes, as many plots, as many characters as there are people to write them. You have but to examine your life, your thoughts, your experiences, to find an unwritten library of narratives yet to tell. Therein lie a thousand tales. Or a thousand and one. . . .

STRATEGIES FOR WRITING— NARRATION

1. You'll need to consider, "What is the purpose of my narrative?" Am I telling the tale for its own sake, or using it to make a larger point?
2. For what audience am I writing this? What will they have experienced or be able to understand, and what will I need to explain? How do I want my audience to react?
3. What is the focus, the conflict of my narrative? How will it begin? Gain momentum and develop to a climax? End? What emphasis will I give each part, or separate scenes or incidents within each part?
4. Will I write from a first- or third-person point of view? Will I be a major character in my narrative? As a participant or as an observer? Or both, if my present self is observing my past self?
5. What is my attitude toward my material? What tone do I want to use? Will it be consistent throughout, or will it change during the course of events?

E. B. WHITE

"Once More to the Lake," a narrative of father and son, timeless generations in the eternal Maine countryside, conveys significant intangibles (love—parental and filial; the importance of nature; the inevitability of growth, change, and death) through memorably specific details. White leads us to the lake itself ("cool and motionless"), down the path to yesteryear, where the continuity of generations intermingles past, present, and future until they become almost indistinguishable: "The years were a mirage and there had been no years. . . ." Everywhere White's son, thoroughly identified with his father, does the same things White had done at the same lake as a boy—putting about in the same boat, catching the same bass, drinking the same soda pop, enjoying the same ritualistic swim after the same summer thunderstorm (see also Scott Russell Sanders's "The Inheritance of Tools," 139–46). The mood of "peace and goodness and jollity" that White recreates indelibly shifts, however, as the cosmic chill of the last sentence reminds us of the inevitable passing of generations. (For a biographical sketch of E. B. White, see page 30.)

Once More to the Lake

1   One summer, along about 1904, my father rented a camp on a lake in Maine and took us all there for the month of August. We all got ringworm from some kittens and had to rub Pond's Extract on our arms and legs night and morning, and my father rolled over in a canoe with all his clothes on; but outside of that the vacation was a success and from then on none of us ever thought there was any place in the world like that lake in Maine. We returned summer after summer—always on August 1st for one month. I have since become a salt-water man, but sometimes in summer there are days when the restlessness of the tides and the fearful cold of the sea water and the incessant wind which blows across the afternoon and into the evening make me wish for the placidity of a lake in the woods. A few weeks ago this feeling got so strong I bought myself a couple of bass hooks and a spinner and returned to the lake where we used to go, for a week's fishing and to revisit old haunts.

2   I took along my son, who had never had any fresh water up his nose and who had seen lily pads only from train windows. On the journey over to the lake I began to wonder what it would be like. I wondered how time would have marred this unique, this holy spot—the coves and streams, the hills that the sun set behind, the camps and the paths behind the camps. I was sure the tarred road would have found it out and I wondered in what other ways it would be desolated. It is strange how much you can remember about places like that once you allow your mind to return into

the grooves which lead back. You remember one thing, and that suddenly reminds you of another thing. I guess I remembered clearest of all the early mornings, when the lake was cool and motionless, remembered how the bedroom smelled of the lumber it was made of and of the wet woods whose scent entered through the screen. The partitions in the camp were thin and did not extend clear to the top of the rooms, and as I was always the first up I would dress softly so as not to wake the others, and sneak out into the sweet outdoors and start out in the canoe, keeping close along the shore in the long shadows of the pines. I remembered being very careful never to rub my paddle against the gunwale for fear of disturbing the still-ness of the cathedral.

The lake had never been what you would call a wild lake. There were cottages sprinkled around the shores, and it was in farming country although the shores of the lake were quite heavily wooded. Some of the cottages were owned by nearby farmers, and you would live at the shore and eat your meals at the farmhouse. That's what our family did. But although it wasn't wild, it was a fairly large and undisturbed lake and there were places in it which, to a child at least, seemed infinitely remote and primeval.   3

I was right about the tar: it led to within half a mile of the shore. But when I got back there, with my boy, and we settled into a camp near a farmhouse and into the kind of summertime I had known, I could tell that it was going to be pretty much the same as it had been before—I knew it, lying in bed the first morning, smelling the bedroom, and hearing the boy sneak quietly out and go off along the shore in a boat. I began to sustain the illusion that he was I, and therefore by simple transposition, that I was my father. This sensation persisted, kept cropping up all the time we were there. It was not an entirely new feeling, but in this setting it grew much stronger. I seemed to be living a dual existence. I would be in the middle of some simple act, I would be picking up a bait box or laying down a table fork, or I would be saying something, and suddenly it would be not I but my father who was saying the words or making the gesture. It gave me a creepy sensation.   4

We went fishing the first morning. I felt the same damp moss cover-ing the worms in the bait can, and saw the dragonfly alight on the tip of my rod as it hovered a few inches from the surface of the water. It was the arrival of this fly that convinced me beyond any doubt that everything was as it always had been, that the years were a mirage and there had been no years. The small waves were the same, chucking the rowboat under the chin as we fished at anchor, and the boat was the same boat, the same color green and the ribs broken in the same places, and under the floor-boards the same fresh-water leavings and debris—the dead helgramite, the wisps of moss, the rusty discarded fishhook, the dried blood from yester-day's catch. We stared silently at the tips of our rods, at the dragonflies that came and went. I lowered the tip of mine into the water, tentatively,   5 pensively dislodging the fly, which darted two feet away, poised, darted two feet back, and came to a rest again a little farther up the rod. There had been no years between the ducking of this dragonfly and the other one—the one that was part of memory. I looked at the boy, who was silently watching his fly, and it was my hands that held his rod, my eyes watching. I felt dizzy and didn't know which rod I was at the end of.

6   We caught two bass, hauling them in briskly as though they were mackerel, pulling them over the side of the boat in a businesslike manner without any landing net, and stunning them with a blow on the back of the head. When we got back for a swim before lunch, the lake was exactly where we had left it, the same number of inches from the dock, and there was only the merest suggestion of a breeze. This seemed an utterly enchanted sea, this lake you could leave to its own devices for a few hours and come back to, and find that it had not stirred, this constant and trustworthy body of water. In the shallows, the dark, watersoaked sticks and twigs, smooth and old, were undulating in clusters on the bottom against the clean ribbed sand, and the track of the mussel was plain. A school of minnows swam by, each minnow with its small individual shadow, doubling the attendance, so clear and sharp in the sunlight. Some of the other campers were in swimming, along the shore, one of them with a cake of soap, and the water felt thin and clear and unsubstantial. Over the years there had been this person with the cake of soap, this cultist, and here he was. There had been no years.

7   Up to the farmhouse to dinner through the teeming, dusty field, the road under our sneakers was only a two-track road. The middle track was missing, the one with the marks of the hooves and the splotches of dried, flaky manure. There had always been three tracks to choose from in choosing which track to walk in; now the choice was narrowed down to two. For a moment I missed terribly the middle alternative. But the way led past the tennis court, and something about the way it lay there in the sun reassured me; the tape had loosened along the backline, the alleys were green with plantains and other weeds, and the net (installed in June and removed in September) sagged in the dry noon, and the whole place steamed with midday heat and hunger and emptiness. There was a choice of pie for dessert, and one was blueberry and one was apple, and the waitresses were the same country girls, there having been no passage of time, only the illusion of it as in a dropped curtain—the waitresses were still fifteen; their hair had been washed, that was the only difference—they had been to the movies and seen the pretty girls with the clean hair.

8   Summertime, oh summertime, pattern of life indelible, the fade-proof lake, the wood unshatterable, the pasture with the sweetfern and the juniper forever and ever, summer without end; this was the background, and the life along the shore was the design, the cottages with their innocent and tranquil design, their tiny docks with the flagpole and the American flag floating against the white clouds in the blue sky, the little paths over

the roots of the trees leading from camp to camp and the paths leading back to the outhouses and the can of lime for sprinkling, and at the souvenir counters at the store the miniature birchbark canoes and the post cards that showed things looking a little better than they looked. This was the American family at play, escaping the city heat, wondering whether the newcomers in the camp at the head of the cove were "common" or "nice," wondering whether it was true that the people who drove up for Sunday dinner at the farmhouse were turned away because there wasn't enough chicken.

It seemed to me, as I kept remembering all this, that those times and 9 those summers had been infinitely precious and worth saving. There had been jollity and peace and goodness. The arriving (at the beginning of August) had been so big a business in itself, at the railway station the farm wagon drawn up, the first smell of the pine-laden air, the first glimpse of the smiling farmer, and the great importance of the trunks and your father's enormous authority in such matters, and the feel of the wagon under you for the long ten-mile haul, and at the top of the last long hill catching the first view of the lake after eleven months of not seeing this cherished body of water. The shouts and cries of the other campers when they saw you, and the trunks to be unpacked, to give up their rich burden. (Arriving was less exciting nowadays, when you sneaked up in your car and parked it under a tree near the camp and took out the bags and in five minutes it was all over, no fuss, no loud wonderful fuss about trunks.)

Peace and goodness and jollity. The only thing that was wrong now, 10 really, was the sound of the place, an unfamiliar nervous sound of the outboard motors. This was the note that jarred, the one thing that would sometimes break the illusion and set the years moving. In those other summertimes all motors were inboard; and when they were at a little distance, the noise they made was a sedative, an ingredient of summer sleep. They were one-cylinder and two-cylinder engines, and some were make-and-break and some were jump-spark, but they all made a sleepy sound across the lake. The one-lungers throbbed and fluttered, and the twin-cylinder ones purred and purred, and that was a quiet sound too. But now the campers all had outboards. In the daytime, in the hot mornings, these motors made a petulant, irritable sound; at night, in the still evening when the afterglow lit the water, they whined about one's ears like mosquitoes. My boy loved our rented outboard, and his great desire was to achieve singlehanded mastery over it, and authority, and he soon learned the trick of choking it a little (but not too much), and the adjustment of the needle valve. Watching him I would remember the things you could do with the old one-cylinder engine with the heavy flywheel, how you could have it eating out of your hand if you got really close to it spiritually. Motor boats in those days didn't have clutches, and you would make a landing by shutting off the motor at the proper time and coasting in with a dead rudder. But there was a way of reversing them, if you learned the trick, by cutting the switch and putting it on again exactly on the final dying revolution of the flywheel, so that it would kick back against compression and begin reversing. Approaching a dock in a strong following breeze, it was difficult to slow up sufficiently by the ordinary coasting method, and if a boy felt he had complete mastery over his motor, he was tempted to keep it running beyond its time and then reverse it a few feet from the dock. It took a cool nerve, because if you threw the switch a twentieth of a second too soon you would catch the flywheel when it still had speed enough to go up past center, and the boat would leap ahead, charging bull-fashion at the dock.

11   We had a good week at the camp. The bass were biting well and the sun shone endlessly, day after day. We would be tired at night and lie down in the accumulated heat of the little bedrooms after the long hot day and the breeze would stir almost imperceptibly outside and the smell of the swamp drift in through the rusty screens. Sleep would come easily and in the morning the red squirrel would be on the roof, tapping out his gay routine. I kept remembering everything, lying in bed in the mornings— the small steamboat that had a long rounded stern like the lip of a Ubangi, and how quietly she ran on the moonlight sails, when the older boys played their mandolins and the girls sang and we ate doughnuts dipped in sugar, and how sweet the music was on the water in the shining night, and what it had felt like to think about girls then. After breakfast we would go up to the store and the things were in the same place—the minnows in a bottle, the plugs and spinners, disarranged and pawed over by the youngsters from the boys' camp, the Fig Newtons and the Beeman's gum. Outside, the road was tarred and cars stood in front of the store. Inside, all was just as it had always been, except there was more Coca-Cola and not so much Moxie and root beer and birch beer and sarsaparilla. We would walk out with a bottle of pop apiece and sometimes the pop would backfire up our noses and hurt. We explored the streams, quietly, where the turtles slid off the sunny logs and dug their way into the soft bottom; and we lay on the town wharf and fed worms to the tame bass. Everywhere we went I had trouble making out which was I, the one walking at my side, the one walking in my pants.

12   One afternoon while we were there at that lake a thunderstorm came up. It was like the revival of an old melodrama that I had seen long ago with childish awe. The second-act climax of the drama of the electrical disturbance over a lake in America had not changed in any important respect. This was the big scene, still the big scene. The whole thing was so familiar, the first feeling of oppression and heat and a general air around camp of not wanting to go very far away. In midafternoon (it was all the same) a curious darkening of the sky, and a lull in everything that had made life tick; and then the way the boats suddenly swung the other way at their moorings with the coming of a breeze out of the new quarter, and the premonitory rumble. Then the kettle drum, then the snare, then the

bass drum and cymbals, then crackling light against the dark, and the gods grinning and licking their chops in the hills. Afterward the calm, the rain steadily rustling in the calm lake, the return of light and hope and spirits, and the campers running out in joy and relief to go swimming in the rain, their bright cries perpetuating the deathless joke about how they were getting simply drenched, and the children screaming with delight at the new sensation of bathing in the rain, and the joke about getting drenched linking the generations in a strong indestructible chain. And the comedian who waded in carrying an umbrella.

When the others went swimming my son said he was going in too. He   13 pulled his dripping trunks from the line where they had hung all through the shower, and wrung them out. Languidly, and with no thought of going in, I watching him, his hard little body, skinny and bare, saw him wince slightly as he pulled up around his vitals the small, soggy, icy garment. As he buckled the swollen belt suddenly my groin felt the chill of death.

Content

1. Characterize White's son. Why is he referred to as "my son" and "the boy" but never by name?
2. How do the ways in which the boy and his father relate to the lake environment emphasize their personal relationship? In which ways are these similar to the relationship between the narrator and his father, the boy's grandfather? Are there any significant differences, stated or implied?
3. White emphasizes the "peace and goodness and jollity" of the summers at the lake. What incidents and details reinforce this emphasis? Why, then, does White end with "As he buckled the swollen belt suddenly my groin felt the chill of death" (¶ 13)?

Strategies/Structures

4. Many narratives proceed chronologically from the beginning to the end of the time period they cover, relating the events of that period in the sequence in which they occurred. Instead, White organizes this narrative topically. What are the major topics? Why do they come in the order they do, concluding with the thunderstorm and its aftermath?
5. What are the effects of White's frequent repetition of phrases ("there had been no years") and words ("same")? What details or incidents does he use to illustrate the cycle of time?

Language

6. What language contributes to the relaxed mood of this essay? In what ways does the mood fit the subject?
7. Beginning writers are often advised when writing description to be sparing of adjectives and adverbs—to put the weight on nouns and verbs instead. Does White do this? Consistently? Pick a paragraph and analyze it to illustrate your answer.

For Writing

8. Tell the story of your experiences in a particular place—school building, restaurant, vacation spot, hometown, place visited—that emphasizes the influence of the place on your experiences and on your understanding of them. Identify what makes it memorable, but do not describe it in the picture-pretty manner of a travel brochure.

9. Write a narrative in which you focus on a significant relationship between yourself at a particular age and another member of your family of a different generation, either older or younger. If you emphasize its specific features you will probably capture some of its common or universal elements as well.

ANNE FADIMAN

(For biographical information see page 60.) "Under Water" tells a very different story from White's "Once More to the Lake." Fadiman narrates the account of a happy summer wilderness expedition that turned into a tragedy. Although both stories focus on natural bodies of water, White's lake in Maine is tame and tranquil in contrast to the Green River, deceptively treacherous at flood stage. Both begin with the assumption of pleasure on the water, although only White's tale bears this out. There are some similarities between the two accounts: Both incorporate precise details to evoke a powerful sense of place and its effect on the people present, and both recount a young person's summer experiences recollected years later from the perspective of a mature narrator, wiser and—in both instances— somehow sadder. Yet White presents a picture of contentment, his own and his son's, while Fadiman is full of regret prompted by her inability not only to rescue her fellow student but by her unworthy—though thoroughly human—thoughts during the futile rescue and ever since: "I find myself wanting to backferry, to hover midstream, suspended. I might then avoid many things: harsh words, foolish decisions, moments of inattention, regrets that wash over me, like water."

Under Water

1   When I was eighteen, I was a student on a month-long wilderness program in western Wyoming. On the third day, we went canoeing on the Green River, a tributary of the Colorado that begins in the glaciers of the Wind River Range and flows south across the sagebrush plains. Swollen by warm-weather runoff from an unusually deep snowpack, the Green was higher and swifter that month—June of 1972—than it had been in forty years. A river at flood stage can have strange currents. There is

What has happened in this picture? What is about to happen? With what consequences? How does Fadiman's story in "Under Water" influence the ways you "read" this picture? Would you "read" it differently if you saw it as an ad for a wilderness travel company? An adventure film?

not enough room in the channel for the water to move downstream in an orderly way, so it collides with itself and forms whirlpools and boils and souse holes. Our instructors decided to stick to their itinerary nevertheless, but they put in at a relatively easy section of the Green, one that the flood had merely upgraded, in the international system of white-water classification, from Class I to Class II. There are six levels of difficulty, and Class II was not an unreasonable challenge for novice paddlers.

The Green River did not seem dangerous to me. It seemed magnificently unobstructed. Impediments to progress—the rocks and stranded trees that under normal conditions would protrude above the surface—were mostly submerged. The river carried our aluminum canoe high and lightly, like a child on a broad pair of shoulders. We could rest our paddles on the gunwales and let the water do our work. The sun was bright and hot. Every few minutes, I dipped my bandanna in the river, draped it over my head, and let an ounce or two of melted glacier run down my neck.

I was in the bow of the third canoe. We rounded a bend and saw, fifty feet ahead, a standing wave in the wake of a large black boulder. The students in the lead canoe were backferrying, slipping crabwise across the current by angling their boat diagonally and stroking backward. Backferrying allows paddlers to hover midstream and carefully plan their course instead of surrendering to the water's pace. But if they lean upstream—a natural inclination, for few people choose to lean toward the difficulties that lie ahead—the current can overflow the lowered gunwale and flip the boat. And that is what happened to the lead canoe.

4   I wasn't worried when I saw it go over. Knowing that we might capsize in the fast water, our instructors had arranged to have our gear trucked to our next campsite. The packs were all safe. The water was little more than waist-deep, and the paddlers were both wearing life jackets. They would be fine. One was already scrambling onto the right-hand bank.

5   But where was the second paddler? Gary, a local boy from Rawlins, a year or two younger than I, seemed to be hung up on something. He was standing at a strange angle in the middle of the river, just downstream from the boulder. Gary was the only student on the course who had not brought sneakers, and one of his mountaineering boots had become wedged between two rocks. The other canoes would come around the bend in a moment, and the instructors would pluck him out.

6   But they didn't come. The second canoe pulled over to the bank and ours followed. Thirty seconds passed, maybe a minute. Then we saw the standing wave bend Gary's body forward at the waist, push his face underwater, stretch his arms in front of him, and slip his orange life jacket off his shoulders. The life jacket lingered for a moment at his wrists before it floated downstream, its long white straps twisting in the current. His shirtless torso was pale and undulating, and it changed shape as hills and valleys of water flowed over him, altering the curve of the liquid lens through which we watched him. I thought, He looks like the flayed skin of St. Bartholomew in the Sistine Chapel. As soon as I had the thought, I knew that it was dishonorable. To think about anything outside the moment, outside Gary, was a crime of inattention. I swallowed a small, sour piece of self-knowledge: I was the sort of person who, instead of weeping or shouting or praying during a crisis, thought about something from a textbook (H. W. Janson's *History of Art,* page 360).

7   Once the flayed man had come, I could not stop the stream of images: Gary looked like a piece of seaweed, Gary looked like a waving handkerchief, Gary looked like a hula dancer. Each simile was a way to avoid thinking about what Gary was, a drowning boy. To remember these things is dishonorable, too, for I have long since forgotten Gary's last name and the color of his hair and the sound of his voice.

8   I do not remember a single word that anyone said. Somehow, we got into one of the canoes, all five of us, and tried to ferry the twenty feet or so to the middle of the river. The current was so strong, and we were so incompetent, that we never got close. Then we tried it on foot, linking arms to form a chain. The water was so cold that it stung. And it was noisy—not the roar and crash of white water but a groan, a terrible bass grumble, from

the stones that were rolling and leaping down the riverbed. When we got close to Gary, we couldn't see him; all we could see was the reflection of the sky. A couple of times, groping blindly, one of us touched him, but he was as slippery as soap. Then our knees buckled and our elbows unlocked, and we rolled downstream, like the stones. The river's rocky load, moving invisibly beneath its smooth surface, pounded and scraped us. Eventually, the current heaved us, blue-lipped and panting, onto the bank. In that other world above the water, the only sounds were the buzzing of bees and flies. Our wet sneakers kicked up red dust. The air smelled of sage and rabbitbrush and sunbaked earth.

We tried again and again, back and forth between the worlds. Wet, dry, cold, hot, turbulent, still.   9

At first, I assumed that we would save him. He would lie on the bank and the sun would warm him while we administered mouth-to-mouth resuscitation. If we couldn't get him out, we would hold him upright in the river; and maybe he could still breathe. But the Green River was flowing at nearly three thousand cubic feet—about ninety tons—per second. At that rate, water can wrap a canoe around a boulder like tinfoil. Water can uproot a tree. Water can squeeze the air out of a boy's lungs, undo knots, drag off a life jacket, lever a boot so tightly into the riverbed that even if we had had ropes—the ropes that were in the packs that were in the trucks—we could never have budged him.   10

We kept going in, not because we had any hope of rescuing Gary after the first ten minutes, but because we had to save face. It would have been humiliating if the instructors came around the bend and found us sitting in the sagebrush, a docile row of five with no hypothermia and no skinned knees. Eventually, they did come. The boats had been delayed because one had nearly capsized, and the instructors had made the other students stop and practice backferrying until they learned not to lean upstream. Even though Gary had already drowned, the instructors did all the same things we had done, more competently but no more effectively, because they, too, would have been humiliated if they hadn't skinned their knees. Men in wet suits, belayed with ropes, pried the body out the next morning.   11

When I was eighteen, I wanted to hurry through life as fast as I could. Twenty-seven years have passed, and my life now seems too fast. I find myself wanting to backferry, to hover midstream, suspended. I might then avoid many things: harsh words, foolish decisions, moments of inattention, regrets that wash over me, like water.   12

Content

1. What is Anne Fadiman's purpose in writing this essay? Is she telling a tale for its own sake or is she using it to make a larger point? Could this be interpreted as a morality play? A cautionary tale? Explain your answer.

2. From what point of view does Anne Fadiman narrate the events that take place in "Under Water"? How does this point of view help to shape the narrative? In what ways does Fadiman as author prepare her readers to interpret Fadiman as a character in this tale? How does she want the readers to react to the circumstances she describes and to the others on this trip, including the instructors?

3. Anne Fadiman's statement "The Green River did not seem dangerous to me. It seemed magnificently unobstructed. Impediments to progress—the rocks and stranded trees that under normal conditions would protrude above the surface— were mostly submerged" (¶ 2) is obviously meant to be read literally. Why can we also say it possesses another level of meaning that transcends the literal? What is this figurative meaning and how does it influence Fadiman's final paragraph?

Strategies/Structures

4. Fadiman's tale unfolds chronologically, although she speaks in the present, merely remembering the past. How and why does she foreshadow the events that will occur? At what point in the story is a reader likely to become aware of the inevitable outcome toward which the narrative is moving? Why not simply begin with the drowning of the young man?

5. Does Fadiman's tale contain all the major components of a narrative: characters, conflict, motives, plot, setting, point of view, and dialogue? Find examples from the text to illustrate which features are there. Since "Under Water" looks and reads like a short story, how do you know it's true?

Language

6. Why does Fadiman declare early on that "Class II was not an unreasonable challenge for novice paddlers" (¶ 1)?

7. Fadiman uses some extremely vivid description—for example, "Then we saw the standing wave bend Gary's body forward at the waist, push his face underwater, stretch his arms in front of him, and slip his orange life jacket off his shoulders" (¶ 6). What effect is such graphic representation likely to have on her readers?

For Writing

8. Write a narrative essay describing an incident you either witnessed or participated in that involved a serious error of judgment. This can be anything from a car accident to rejecting, insulting, discriminating against, or otherwise mistreating someone, to a mock fight that turned serious and ugly. Then revise that essay so it is told from a different point of view. This should be a story with a moral point that is made indirectly, and it should provide implicit judgments of the major characters.

9. Write a true story in which the setting, preferably a natural one, plays a major role in relation to the human participants. This role may be benign or malevolent, active or passive, but it should be important (as it is in "Under Water" and "Once More to the Lake"), and the humans should be constantly aware of this role. Because you will need to pay close attention to the specific details of the setting, it should be a place you either know well or can revisit.

FREDERICK DOUGLASS

Douglass (1817–1895) was born a slave in Talbot County, Maryland. Unlike many slaves, he learned to read, and the power of this accomplishment coupled with an iron physique and the will to match, enabled him to escape to New York in 1838. For the next twenty-five years he toured the country as a powerful spokesperson for the abolitionist movement, serving as an adviser to Harriet Beecher Stowe, author of *Uncle Tom's Cabin,* and to President Lincoln, among others. After the war he campaigned for civil rights for African-Americans and women. In 1890 his political significance was acknowledged in his appointment as minister to Haiti.

Slave narratives, written or dictated by the hundreds in the nineteenth century, provided memorable accounts of the physical, geographical, and psychological movement from captivity to freedom. Douglass's autobiography, an abolitionist document like many other slave narratives, is exceptional in its forthright language and absence of stereotyping of either white or black people; his people are multidimensional. Crisis points, and the insights and opportunities they provide, are natural topics for personal narratives (see also Richard Rodriguez's "None of This Is Fair" [322–27]). This episode, taken from the first version (of four) of *The Narrative of the Life of Frederick Douglass, an American Slave* (1845), explains the incident that was "the turning point in my career as a slave," for it enabled him to make the transformation from slave to independent human being.

Resurrection

I have already intimated that my condition was much worse, during the first six months of my stay at Mr. Covey's, than in the last six. The circumstances leading to the change in Mr Covey's course toward me form an epoch in my humble history. You have seen how a man was made a slave; you shall see how a slave was made a man. On one of the hottest days of the month of August, 1833, Bill Smith, William Hughes, a slave named Eli, and myself, were engaged in fanning wheat. Hughes was clearing the fanned wheat from before the fan. Eli was turning, Smith was feeding, and I was carrying wheat to the fan. The work was simple, requiring strength rather than intellect; yet, to one entirely unused to such work, it came very hard. About three o'clock of that day, I broke down; my strength failed me; I was seized with a violent aching of the head, attended with extreme dizziness; I trembled in every limb. Finding what was coming, I nerved myself up, feeling it would never do to stop work. I stood as long as I could stagger to the hopper with grain. When I could stand no longer, I fell, and felt as if held down by an immense weight. The fan of course stopped; every one had his own work to do; and no one could do the work of the other, and have his own go on at the same time.

2   Mr. Covey was at the house, about one hundred yards from the treading-yard where we were fanning. On hearing the fan stop, he left immediately, and came to the spot where we were. He hastily inquired what the matter was. Bill answered that I was sick, and there was no one to bring wheat to the fan. I had by this time crawled away under the side of the post and rail-fence by which the yard was enclosed, hoping to find relief by getting out of the sun. He then asked where I was. He was told by one of the hands. He came to the spot, and, after looking at me awhile, asked me what was the matter. I told him as well as I could, for I scarce had strength to speak. He then gave me a savage kick in the side, and told me to get up. I tried to do so, but fell back in the attempt. He gave me another kick, and again told me to rise. I again tried, and succeeded in gaining my feet; but, stooping to get the tub with which I was feeding the fan, I again staggered and fell. While down in this situation, Mr. Covey took up the hickory slat with which Hughes had been striking off the half-bushel measure, and with it gave me a heavy blow upon the head, making a large wound, and the blood ran freely; and with this again told me to get up. I made no effort to comply, having now made up my mind to let him do his worst. In a short time after receiving this blow, my head grew better. Mr. Covey had now left me to my fate. At this moment I resolved, for the first time, to go to my master, enter a complaint, and ask his protection. In order to do this, I must that afternoon walk seven miles; and this, under the circumstances, was truly a severe undertaking. I was exceedingly feeble; made so as much by the kicks and blows which I received, as by the severe fit of sickness to which I had been subjected. I, however, watched my chance, while Covey was looking in an opposite direction, and started for St. Michael's: I succeeded in getting a considerable distance on my way to the woods, when Covey discovered me, and called after me to come back, threatening what he would do if I did not come. I disregarded both his calls and his threats, and made my way to the woods as fast as my feeble state would allow; and thinking I might be overhauled by him if I kept to the road, I walked through the woods, keeping far enough from the road to avoid detection, and near enough to prevent losing my way. I had not gone far before my little strength again failed me. I could go no farther. I fell down, and lay for a considerable time. The blood was yet oozing from the wound on my head. For a time I thought I should bleed to death; and think now that I should have done so, but that the blood so matted my hair as to stop the wound. After lying there about three quarters of an hour, I nerved myself up again, and started on my way, through bogs and briers, barefooted and bareheaded, tearing my feet sometimes at nearly every step; and after a journey of about seven miles, occupying some five hours to perform it, I arrived at master's store. I then presented an appearance enough to affect

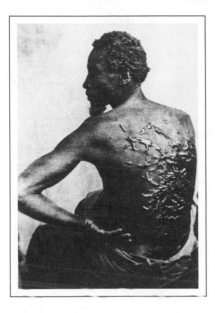

any but a heart of iron. From the crown of my head to my feet, I was covered with blood. My hair was all clotted with dust and blood; my shirt was stiff with blood. My legs and feet were torn in sundry places with briers and thorns, and were also covered in blood. I suppose I looked like a man who had escaped a den of wild beasts, and barely escaped them. In this state I appeared before my master, humbly entreating him to interpose his authority for my protection. I told him all the circumstances as well as I could, and it seemed, as I spoke, at times to affect him. He would then walk the floor, and seek to justify Covey by saying he expected I deserved it. He asked me what I wanted. I told him, to let me get a new home; that as sure as I lived with Mr. Covey again, I should live with but to die with him; that Covey would surely kill me; he was in a fair way for it. Master Thomas ridiculed the idea that there was any danger of Mr. Covey's killing me, and said that he knew Mr. Covey, that he was a good man, and that he could not think of taking me from him; that, should he do so, he would lose the whole year's wages; that I belonged to Mr. Covey for one year, and that I must go back to him, come what might; and that I must not trouble him with any more stories, or that he would himself *get hold of me*. After threatening me thus, he gave me a very large dose of salts, telling me that I might remain in St. Michael's that night, (it being quite late,) but that I must be off back to Mr. Covey's early in the morning; and that if I did not, he would *get hold of me*, which meant that he would whip me. I remained all night, and, according to his orders, I started off to Covey's in the morning, (Saturday morning,) wearied in body and broken in spirit. I got no supper that night, or breakfast that morning. I reached Covey's about nine o'clock; and just as I was getting over the fence that divided Mrs. Kemp's fields from ours, out ran Covey with his cowskin, to give me another whipping. Before he could reach me, I succeeded in getting to the corn-field; and as the corn was very high, it afforded me the means of hiding. He seemed very angry, and searched for me a long time. My behavior was altogether unaccountable. He finally gave up the chase, thinking, I suppose, that I must come home for something to eat; he would give himself no further trouble in looking for me. I spent that day mostly in the woods, having the alternative before me—to go home and be whipped to death, or stay in the woods and be starved to death. That night, I fell in with Sandy Jenkins, a slave with whom I was somewhat acquainted. Sandy had a free wife who lived about four miles from Mr. Covey's; and it being Saturday, he was on his way to see her. I told him my circumstances, and he very kindly invited me to go home with him. I went home with him, and talked this whole matter over, and got his advice as to what course it was best for me to pursue. I found Sandy an old adviser. He told me, with great solemnity, I must go back to Covey; but that before I went, I must go with him into another part of the woods, where there was a certain *root*, which, if I would take some of it with me, carrying it *always on my right side,* would render it impossible for Mr. Covey, or any other white man, to whip me. He said he had carried it for years; and since he had done so, he had never received a blow, and never expected to while he carried it. I at first rejected the idea, that the simple carrying of a root in my pocket would have any such effect as he had said, and was not disposed to take it; but Sandy impressed the necessity with much earnestness, telling me it could do no harm, if it did no good. To please him, I at length took the root, and, according to his direction, carried it upon my right side. This was Sunday morning. I immediately started for home; and upon entering the yard gate, out came Mr. Covey on his way to meeting. He spoke to me very kindly, bade me drive the pigs from a lot near by, and passed on towards the church. Now, this singular conduct of Mr. Covey really made me begin to think that there was something in the *root* which Sandy had given me; and had it been on any other day than Sunday, I could have attributed the conduct to no other cause than the influence of that root; and as it was, I was half inclined to think the *root* to be something more than I at first had taken it to be. All went well till Monday morning. On this morning, the virtue of the *root* was fully tested. Long before daylight, I was called to go and rub, curry, and feed, the horses. I obeyed, and was glad to obey. But whilst thus engaged, whilst in the act of throwing down some blades from the loft, Mr. Covey entered the stable with a long rope; and just as I was half out of the loft, he caught hold of my legs, and was about tying me. As soon as I found what he was up to, I gave a sudden spring, and as I did so, he holding to my legs, I was brought sprawling on the stable floor. Mr.

Covey seemed now to think he had me, and could do what he pleased; but at this moment—from whence came the spirit I don't know—I resolved to fight; and, suiting my action to the resolution, I seized Covey hard by the throat; and as I did so, I rose. He held on to me, and I to him. My resistance was so entirely unexpected, that Covey seemed taken all aback. He trembled like a leaf. This gave me assurance, and I held him uneasy, causing the blood to run where I touched him with the ends of my fingers. Mr. Covey soon called out to Hughes for help. Hughes came, and while Covey held me, attempted to tie my right hand. While he was in the act of doing so, I watched my chance, and gave him a heavy kick close under the ribs. This kick fairly sickened Hughes, so that he left me in the hands of Mr. Covey. This kick had the effect of not only weakening Hughes, but Covey also. When he saw Hughes bending over with pain, his courage quailed. He asked me if I meant to persist in my resistance. I told him I did, come what might; that he had used me like a brute for six months, and that I was determined to be used so no longer. With that, he strove to drag me to a stick that was lying just out of the stable door. He meant to knock me down. But just as he was leaning over to get the stick, I seized him with both hands by his collar, and brought him by a sudden snatch to the ground. By this time, Bill came. Covey called upon him for assistance. Bill wanted to know what he could do. Covey said, "Take hold of him, take hold of him!" Bill said his master hired him out to work, and not to help whip me; so he left Covey and myself to fight our own battle out. We were at it for nearly two hours. Covey at length let me go, puffing and blowing at a great rate, saying that if I had not resisted, he would not have whipped me half so much. The truth was, that he had not whipped me at all. I considered him as getting entirely the worst end of the bargain; for he had drawn no blood from me, but I had from him. The whole six months afterwards, that I spent with Mr. Covey, he never laid the weight of his finger upon me in anger. He would occasionally say, he didn't want to get hold of me again. "No," thought I, "you need not; for you will come off worse than you did before."

This battle with Mr. Covey was the turning-point in my career as a slave. It rekindled the few expiring embers of freedom, and revived within me a sense of my own manhood. It recalled the departed self-confidence, and inspired me again with a determination to be free. The gratification afforded by the triumph was a full compensation for whatever else might follow, even death itself. He only can understand the deep satisfaction which I experienced, who has himself repelled by force the bloody arm of slavery. I felt as I never felt before. It was a glorious resurrection, from the tomb of slavery, to the heaven of freedom. My long-crushed spirit rose, cowardice departed, bold defiance took its place; and I now resolved that, however long I might remain a slave in form, the day had passed forever when I could be a slave in fact. I did not hesitate to let it be known of me, that the white man who expected to succeed in whipping, must also succeed in killing me.

Content

1. Twelve years after he successfully defied Mr. Covey, Douglass identified this incident as "the turning-point in my career as a slave" (¶ 3). Why? Would Douglass have been able to recognize its significance at the time or only in retrospect?
2. What, if anything, does Douglass expect his audience—mostly white Northerners—to do about slavery, as a consequence of having read his narrative?

Strategies/Structures

3. Douglass's account begins with Friday afternoon and ends with Monday morning, but some events receive considerable emphasis while others are scarcely mentioned. Which ones does he focus on? Why?
4. Why is paragraph 2 so long? Should it have been divided into shorter units, or is the longer unit preferable? Justify your answer.
5. Douglass provides considerable details about his appearance after his first beating by Covey (¶ 2), but scarcely any about the appearance of either Covey or Master Thomas. Why?
6. Would slave owners have been likely to read Douglass's autobiography? Why or why not? Would Douglass's emphasis have been likely to change for an audience of Northern post–Civil War blacks? Southern antebellum whites?

Language

7. How sophisticated is Douglass's level of diction? Is it appropriate for the narrative he tells? How is this related to his self-characterization?
8. Why does Douglass explain his changed self-image as a "resurrection, from the tomb of slavery, to the heaven of freedom"?

For Writing

9. Write a narrative in which you recount and explain the significance of an event in which you participated that provided you with an important change of status in the eyes of others. (See Rodriguez's "None of This Is Fair," 322–27, and Yu's "Red and Black," 191–202.) Provide enough specific details so readers unfamiliar with either you or the situation can experience it as you did. Be sure to depict the personalities of the central characters; their physical appearance may not be nearly as significant.
10. Write a narrative intended to inspire your readers in which you recount an incident expressing the difficulties of a minority or oppressed person or group. (See essays by Rodriguez and Yu mentioned in the previous question.) You can also try to move your readers to take action concerning the problem. Try to move them by example rather than through preaching or an excess of emotion. Understatement is usually more appealing than overstatement.

SCOTT RUSSELL SANDERS

Sanders (born 1945) grew up in Ohio, earned a Ph.D. in English from Cambridge University in 1971, and has taught ever since at Indiana University. His twenty-five books include fiction, science fiction, a biography of Audubon, and several books of personal essays. The essay collections, including *In Limestone Country* (1985), *Staying Put* (1993), *Writing from the Center* (1995), and *Hunting for Hope* (1998), focus on living and writing in the Midwest. "My writing . . . is bound together by a web of questions," which he continues to ask in personal essays dealing with "the ways in which human beings come to terms with the practical problems of living on a small planet, in nature . . . in marriages and families and towns. . . ."

The elegiac "The Inheritance of Tools" appeared in the award-winning *The Paradise of Bombs* (1987), a collection of personal essays mainly about the American culture of violence. This essay reveals Sanders's concerns, as a writer and as a son, husband, and father, with the inheritance of skills and values through the generations.

In this essay, narration is explanation, as it is in a companion piece, "Skill" (*Georgia Review* 1998). Sanders shows how tools become not just extensions of the hand and brain, but of the human heart, as the knowledge of how to use and care for them is transmitted from grandfather to father to son to grandchildren—a girl as well as a boy. The ways in which people use tools, and think about tools and care for them, reflect their values and personalities; "each hammer and level and saw is wrapped in a cloud of knowing."

The Inheritance of Tools

A t just about the hour when my father died, soon after dawn one February morning when ice coated the windows like cataracts, I banged my thumb with a hammer. Naturally I swore at the hammer, the reckless thing, and in the moment of swearing I thought of what my father would say: "If you'd try hitting the nail it would go in a whole lot faster. Don't you know your thumb's not as hard as that hammer?" We both were doing carpentry that day, but far apart. He was building cupboards at my brother's place in Oklahoma; I was at home in Indiana, putting up a wall in the basement to make a bedroom for my daughter. By the time my mother called with news of his death—the long distance wires whittling her voice until it seemed too thin to bear the weight of what she had to say—my thumb was swollen. A week or so later a white scar in the shape of a crescent moon began to show above the cuticle and month by month it rose across the pink sky of my thumbnail. It took the better part of a year for the scar to disappear, and every time I noticed it I thought of my father.

2   The hammer had belonged to him, and to his father before him. The three of us have used it to build houses and barns and chicken coops, to upholster chairs and crack walnuts, to make doll furniture and bookshelves and jewelry boxes. The head is scratched and pockmarked, like an old plowshare that has been working rocky fields, and it gives off the sort of dull sheen you see on fast creek water in the shade. It is a finishing hammer, about the weight of a bread loaf, too light, really, for framing walls, too heavy for cabinet work, with a curved claw for pulling nails, a rounded head for pounding, a fluted neck for looks, and a hickory handle for strength.

3   The present handle is my third one, bought from a lumberyard in Tennessee, down the road from where my brother and I were helping my father build his retirement house. I broke the previous one by trying to pull sixteen-penny nails out of floor joists—a foolish thing to do with a finishing hammer, as my father pointed out. "You ever hear of a crow-bar?" he said. No telling how many handles he and my grandfather had gone through before me. My grandfather used to cut down hickory trees on his farm, saw them into slabs, cure the planks in his hayloft, and carve handles with a drawknife. The grain in hickory is crooked and knotty, and therefore tough, hard to split, like the grain in the two men who owned this hammer before me.

4   After proposing marriage to a neighbor girl, my grandfather used this hammer to build a house for his bride on a stretch of river bottom in northern Mississippi. The lumber for the place, like the hickory for the handle, was cut on his own land. By the day of the wedding he had not quite finished the house, and so right after the ceremony he took his wife home and put her to work. My grandmother had worn her Sunday dress for the wedding, with a fringe of lace tacked on around the hem in honor of the occasion. She removed this lace and folded it away before going out to help my grandfather nail siding on the house. "There she was in her good dress," he told me some fifty-odd years after that wedding day, "holding up them long pieces of clapboard while I hammered, and together we got the place covered up before dark." As the family grew to four, six, eight, and eventually thirteen, my grandfather used this hammer to enlarge his house room by room, like a chambered nautilus expanding its shell.

5   By and by the hammer was passed along to my father. One day he was up on the roof of our pony barn nailing shingles with it, when I stepped out the kitchen door to call him for supper. Before I could yell, something about the sight of him straddling the spine of that roof and swinging the hammer caught my eye and made me hold my tongue. I was five or six years old, and the world's commonplaces were still news to me. He would pull a nail from the pouch at his waist, bring the hammer down, and a moment later the *thunk* of the blow would reach my ears. And that is what had stopped me in my tracks and stilled my tongue, that momentary gap between seeing and hearing the blow. Instead of yelling from the kitchen door, I ran to the barn and climbed two rungs up the

ladder—as far as I was allowed to go—and spoke quietly to my father. On our walk to the house he explained that sound takes time to make its way through air. Suddenly the world seemed larger, the air more dense, if sound could be held back like any ordinary traveler.

By the time I started using this hammer, at about the age when I dis- 6 covered the speed of sound, it already contained houses and mysteries for me. The smooth handle was one my grandfather had made. In those days I needed both hands to swing it. My father would start a nail in a scrap of wood, and I would pound away until I bent it over.

"Looks like you got ahold of some of those rubber nails," he would 7 tell me. "Here, let me see if I can find you some stiff ones." And he would rummage in a drawer until he came up with a fistful of more cooperative nails. "Look at the head," he would tell me. "Don't look at your hands, don't look at the hammer. Just look at the head of that nail and pretty soon you'll learn to hit it square."

Pretty soon I did learn. While he worked in the garage cutting dove- 8 tail joints for a drawer or skinning a deer or tuning an engine, I would hammer nails. I made innocent blocks of wood look like porcupines. He did not talk much in the midst of his tools, but he kept up a nearly cease-less humming, slipping in and out of a dozen tunes in an afternoon, often running back over the same stretch of melody again and again, as if searching for a way out. When the humming did cease, I knew he was faced with a task requiring great delicacy or concentration, and I took care not to distract him.

He kept scraps of wood in a cardboard box—the ends of two-by- 9 fours, slabs of shelving and plywood, odd pieces of molding—and every-thing in it was fair game. I nailed scraps together to fashion what I called boats or houses, but the results usually bore only faint resemblance to the visions I carried in my head. I would hold up these constructions to show my father, and he would turn them over in his hands admiringly, specu-lating about what they might be. My cobbled-together guitars might have been alien spaceships, my barns might have been models of Aztec temples, each wooden contraption might have been anything but what I had set out to make.

Now and again I would feel the need to have a chunk of wood 10 shaped or shortened before I riddled it with nails, and I would clamp it in a vise and scrape at it with a handsaw. My father would let me lacerate the board until my arm gave out, and then he would wrap his hand around mine and help me finish the cut, showing me how to use my thumb to guide the blade, how to pull back on the saw to keep it from binding, how to let my shoulder do the work.

"Don't force it," he would say, "just drag it easy and give the teeth a 11 chance to bite."

As the saw teeth bit down, the wood released its smell, each kind 12 with its own fragrance, oak or walnut or cherry or pine—usually pine because it was the softest, easiest for a child to work. No matter how weathered and gray the board, no matter how warped and cracked, inside there was this smell waiting, as of something freshly baked. I gathered every smidgen of sawdust and stored it away in coffee cans, which I kept in a drawer of the workbench. When I did not feel like hammering nails, I would dump my sawdust on the concrete floor of the garage and land-scape it into highways and farms and towns, running miniature cars and trucks along miniature roads. Looming as huge as a colossus, my father worked over and around me, now and again bending down to inspect my work, careful not to trample my creations. It was a landscape that smelled dizzyingly of wood. Even after a bath my skin would carry the smell, and so would my father's hair, when he lifted me for a bedtime hug.

13   I tell these things not only from memory but also from recent observation, because my own son now turns blocks of wood into nailed porcupines, dumps cans full of sawdust at my feet and sculpts highways on the floor. He learns how to swing a hammer from the elbow instead of the wrist, how to lay his thumb beside the blade to guide a saw, how to tap a chisel with a wooden mallet, how to mark a hole with an awl before starting a drill bit. My daughter did the same before him, and even now, on the brink of teenage aloofness, she will occasionally drag out my box of wood scraps and carpenter something. So I have seen my apprenticeship to wood and tools reenacted in each of my children, as my father saw his own appren-ticeship renewed in me.

14   The saw I use belonged to him, as did my level and both of my squares, and all four tools had belonged to his father. The blade of the saw is the bluish color of gun barrels, and the maple handle, dark from the sweat of hands, is inscribed with curving leaf designs. The level is a shaft of walnut two feet long, edged with brass and pierced by three round windows in which air bubbles float in oil-filled tubes of glass. The middle window serves for testing if a surface is horizontal, the others for testing if a surface is plumb or vertical. My grandfather used to carry this level on the gun rack behind the seat in his pickup, and when I rode with him I would turn around to watch the bubbles dance. The larger of the two squares is called a framing square, a flat steel elbow, so beat up and tar-nished you can barely make out the rows of numbers that show how to figure the cuts on rafters. The smaller one is called a try square, for mark-ing right angles, with a blued steel blade for the shank and a brass-faced block of cherry for the head.

15   I was taught early on that a saw is not to be used apart from a square: "If you're going to cut a piece of wood," my father insisted, "you owe it to the tree to cut it straight."

16   Long before studying geometry, I learned there is a mystical virtue in right angles. There is an unspoken morality in seeking the level and the plumb. A house will stand, a table will bear weight, the sides of a box will

hold together, only if the joints are square and the members upright. When the bubble is lined up between two marks etched in the glass tube of a level, you have aligned yourself with the forces that hold the universe together. When you miter the corners of a picture frame each angle must be exactly forty-five degrees, as they are in the perfect triangles of Pythagoras, not a degree more or less. Otherwise the frame will hang crookedly, as if ashamed of itself and of its maker. No matter if the joints you are cutting do not show. Even if you are butting two pieces of wood together inside a cabinet, where no one except a wrecking crew will ever see them, you must take pains to ensure that the ends are square and the studs are plumb.

I took pains over the wall I was building on the day my father died. 17 Not long after that wall was finished—paneled with tongue-and-groove boards of yellow pine, the nail holes filled with putty and the wood all stained and sealed—I came close to wrecking it one afternoon when my daughter ran howling up the stairs to announce that her gerbils had escaped from their cage and were hiding in my brand new wall. She could hear them scratching and squeaking behind her bed. Impossible! I said. How on earth could they get inside my drum-tight wall? Through the heating vent, she answered. I went downstairs, pressed my ear to the honey-colored wood, and heard the *scritch scritch* of tiny feet.

"What can we do?" my daughter wailed. "They'll starve to death, 18 they'll die of thirst, they'll suffocate."

"Hold on," I soothed. "I'll think of something." 19

While I thought and she fretted, the radio on her bedside table de- 20 livered us the headlines: Several thousand people had died in a city in India from a poisonous cloud that had leaked overnight from a chemical plant. A nuclear-powered submarine had been launched. Rioting continued in South Africa. An airplane had been hijacked in the Mediterranean. Authorities calculated that several thousand homeless people slept on the streets within sight of the Washington Monument. I felt my usual helplessness in the face of all these calamities. But here was my daughter, weeping because her gerbils were holed up in a wall. This calamity I could handle.

"Don't worry," I told her. "We'll set food and water by the heating 21 vent and lure them out. And if that doesn't do the trick, I'll tear the wall apart until we find them."

She stopped crying and gazed at me. "You'd really tear it apart? Just 22 for my gerbils? The *wall*?" Astonishment slowed her down only for a second, however, before she ran to the workbench and began tugging at drawers, saying, "Let's see, what'll we need? Crowbar. Hammer. Chisels. I hope we don't have to use them—but just in case."

We didn't need the wrecking tools. I never had to assault my hand- 23 some wall, because the gerbils eventually came out to nibble at a dish of popcorn. But for several hours I studied the tongue-and-groove skin I had nailed up on the day of my father's death, considering where to begin prying. There were no gaps in that wall, no crooked joints.

24   I had botched a great many pieces of wood before I mastered the right angle with a saw, botched even more before I learned to miter a joint. The knowledge of these things resides in my hands and eyes and the web-work of muscles, not in the tools. There are machines for sale—powered miter boxes and radial-arm saws, for instance—that will enable any casual soul to cut proper angles in boards. The skill is invested in the gadget in-stead of the person who uses it, and this is what distinguishes a machine from a tool. If I had to earn my keep by making furniture or building houses, I suppose I would buy powered saws and pneumatic nailers; the need for speed would drive me to it. But since I carpenter only for my own pleasure or to help neighbors or to remake the house around the ears of my family, I stick with hand tools. Most of the ones I own were given to me by my father, who also taught me how to wield them. The tools in my workbench are a double inheritance, for each hammer and level and saw is wrapped in a cloud of knowing.

25   All of these tools are a pleasure to look at and to hold. Merchants would never paste NEW NEW NEW! signs on them in stores. Their designs are old because they work, because they serve their purpose well. Like folk songs and aphorisms and the grainy bits of language, these tools have been pared down to essentials. I look at my claw hammer, the distil-lation of a hundred generations of carpenters, and consider that it holds up well beside those other classics—Greek vases, Gregorian chants, *Don Quixote*, barbed fish hooks, candles, spoons. Knowledge of hammering stretches back to the earliest humans who squatted beside fires, chipping flints. Anthropologists have a lovely name for those unworked rocks that served as the earliest hammers. "Dawn stones," they are called. Their only qualification for the work, aside from hardness, is that they fit the hand. Our ancestors used them for grinding corn, tapping awls, smashing bones. From dawn stones to this claw hammer is a great leap in time, but no great distance in design or imagination.

26   On that iced-over February morning when I smashed my thumb with the hammer, I was down in the basement framing the wall that my daugh-ter's gerbils would later hide in. I was thinking of my father, as I always did whenever I built anything, thinking how he would have gone about the work, hearing in memory what he would have said about the wisdom of hitting the nail instead of my thumb. I had the studs and plates nailed together all square and trim, and was lifting the wall into place when the phone rang upstairs. My wife answered, and in a moment she came to the basement door and called down softly to me. The stillness in her voice made me drop the framed wall and hurry upstairs. She told me my father was dead. Then I heard the details over the phone from my mother. Build-ing a set of cupboards for my brother in Oklahoma, he had knocked off work early the previous afternoon because of cramps in his stomach.

Early this morning, on his way into the kitchen of my brother's trailer, maybe going for a glass of water, so early that no one else was awake, he slumped down on the linoleum and his heart quit.

For several hours I paced around inside my house, upstairs and 27 down, in and out of every room, looking for the right door to open and knowing there was no such door. My wife and children followed me and wrapped me in arms and backed away again, circling and staring as if I were on fire. Where was the door, the door, the door? I kept wondering. My smashed thumb turned purple and throbbed, making me furious. I wanted to cut it off and rush outside and scrape away at the snow and hack a hole in the frozen earth and bury the shameful thing.

I went down into the basement, opened a drawer in my workbench, 28 and stared at the ranks of chisels and knives. Oiled and sharp, as my father would have kept them, they gleamed at me like teeth. I took up a clasp knife, pried out the longest blade, and tested the edge on the hair of my forearm. A tuft came away cleanly, and I saw my father testing the sharpness of tools on his own skin, the blades of axes and knives and gouges and hoes, saw the red hair shaved off in patches from his arms and the backs of his hands. "That will cut bear," he would say. He never cut a bear with his blades, now my blades, but he cut deer, dirt, wood. I closed the knife and put it away. Then I took up the hammer and went back to work on my daughter's wall, snugging the bottom plate against a chalk line on the floor, shimming the top plate against the joists overhead, plumbing the studs with my level, making sure before I drove the first nail that every line was square and true.

Content

1. Sanders characterizes his father, and grandfather, and himself by showing how they used tools and transmitted this knowledge to their children. What characteristics do they have in common? Why does he omit any differences they might have, focusing on their similarities?

2. Sanders distinguishes between a machine and a tool, saying "The skill is invested in the gadget instead of the person who uses it" (¶ 24). Why does he favor tools over machines? Do you agree with his definition? With his preference?

Strategies/Structures

3. What is the point of this essay? Why does Sanders begin and end with the relation between banging his thumb with a hammer and his father's death?

4. Why does Sanders include the vignette of his daughter and her gerbils, which escaped inside the "drum-tight wall" he had just built (¶s 17–23)? Would he really have wrecked the wall to get the gerbils out?

5. For what audience is Sanders writing? Does it matter whether or not his readers know how to use tools?

Language

6. Sanders occasionally quotes his father's advice (¶s 7, 11, 15). What do these quotations reveal about his father?

7. Show, through specific examples, how Sanders's language fits his subject, tools, and the people who use them. Consider phrases such as "ice coated the windows like cataracts" (¶ 1) and "making sure before I drove the first nail that every line was square and true" (¶ 28).

For Writing

8. Sanders defines the "inheritance" of tools as, "So I have seen my apprenticeship to wood and tools re-enacted in each of my children, as my father saw his own apprenticeship renewed in me." (¶ 13). Tell the story of your own apprenticeship with a tool or collection of tools (kitchen utensils, art supplies, a sewing machine, computer, skis, or other equipment). The explanation of your increasing skill in learning to use it should be intertwined with your relationship with the person who taught you how to use it (not necessarily a family member) and the manner of the teaching—and of the learning. How many generations of teachers and learners does your inheritance involve? If you have taught others how to use it, incorporate this as well.

9. Sanders's father is the central figure in two essays in *The Essay Connection,* "The Inheritance of Tools" and "Under the Influence" (274–86). Each uses a series of stories, narratives, to characterize this significant figure in Sanders's life, yet the father of "Inheritance" is a very different character from the father in "Under the Influence." Write an essay in which you compare and contrast Sanders's portraits of his father to show the different ways of presenting the same person. Or—for an audience who doesn't know your subject—write a portrait of someone you know well, or of a public figure you know a great deal about. Use stories to present two or more significant—perhaps contradictory—sides of the same person.

ANN UPPERCO DOLMAN

Ann Upperco Dolman (born 1960) grew up in Arlington, Virginia, and majored in religion at the College of William and Mary (B.A., 1982). She then worked in Chicago as a textbook editor, and after marriage and a move to Wilson, North Carolina, as communications manager for the local Chamber of Commerce, where she wrote all the time—brochures, a newsletter, "even speeches." In 1996 she earned a master's degree in library science from the University of North Carolina.

Dolman had been a highly anxious writer, procrastinating for long periods of time and then spending miserable, long hours trying to grind out a paper in time to meet a deadline. However, in writing "Learning to Drive" for an undergraduate composition course, she explains, "I wrote it at one sitting, then revised it. I think this method of sitting down and writing something and then going back to revise is what enabled me to get over my fear of writing." She says, "I had originally intended to write a series of comic vignettes on the individual driving styles of each member of my family. But the more I thought about it, the more comfortable I felt with the idea of poking fun at myself instead. . . . Writing this essay was almost fun."

Dolman has captured a common set of experiences participated in by a set of familiar figures, comical to contemplate from the safe distance of time, however painful the traumas of a new driver may have been when they occurred. The tense, skittish novice driver is counterpointed against the patient teacher, her reassuring father, with the nervous figure of her mother hovering uneasily in the background.

❄ *Learning to Drive*

G reater love hath no man for his children than to teach them how to drive. As soon as I turned 15 years and 8 months—the requisite age for obtaining a learner's permit my father took me around our neighborhood to let me get a feel for the huge Chevrolet we own. The quiet, tree-shaded, narrow streets of the neighborhood witnessed the blunders of yet another new driver: too-wide (or too-narrow) turns; sudden screeching halts (those power brakes take some getting used to); defoliation of low-hanging trees by the radio antenna or the car too close to the curb; driving on the wrong side of the street to avoid the parked cars on the right side.

Through it all my father murmured words of advice and encouragement, drawing on a seemingly bottomless well of patience which I never before knew he possessed. One day while driving on the highway, I drifted dangerously close to a car in the lane to my right, almost scraping the shiny chrome strip right off its side. Dad looked nonchalantly into the terrified face of the other driver—a mere six inches away—then turned back to me and said, "You might want to steer to the left a bit; you're just a little close on this side." A mile further down the road, Dad chuckled and said, "I think you gave that poor lady a scare—her eyes were as big as golfballs!" Here was he, not only unperturbed, but actually amused by the whole incident while I watched my whole life pass before my eyes.

Not long after this incident I had another near miss, this time while intentionally changing lanes. I still was not accustomed to using the rearview mirror, so Dad had told me to glance over my shoulder to make sure all was clear. Being right-handed, I automatically looked over my right shoulder, and not seeing anything, proceeded to veer left. Not until I almost plowed into another car did I realize that when turning left, I needed to glance over my left shoulder to avoid causing a wreck. Despite the danger, Dad stuck it out, continuing to give me tips to improve my driving.

What is the relationship between the two people in this picture? Why is learning to drive an experience—and process—so often filled with tension? Does this photograph reinforce or undercut the stereotype of the common experience? At what stage of the process might this photograph have been taken? To what extent does it reflect your own experience of learning to drive?

4   Confident now of my driving prowess, I cajoled my parents into letting me drive every chance I got. Dad usually sat up front with me, to the relief of Mom, an uneasy driver herself whose nerves were still recovering from my brother's driving apprenticeship two years earlier. This arrangement suited me perfectly; Mom's behavior in the front seat tended to make me a trifle nervous. Gripping the dashboard as if it would fall off if she let go, and frequently pressing to the floor the nonexistent brake on her side of the car, Mom would periodically utter spine-chilling gasps at the slightest provocation—none of which increased my newly-won confidence behind the wheel. Whether Dad never suffered from such a case of jitters or whether he merely hid it better, I'm not sure. But whatever the reasons, he managed to remain calm, at least outwardly, when riding with me.

5   When I had mastered (in a manner of speaking) the skill of driving our full-size, power-steering, power-brake tank, Dad proceeded to show me the secrets of operating the small, standard-shift rattle-trap-of-a-Pinto which adorned the curb in front of our house. Had I known at the time the humiliation and tribulation I'd have to endure at the wheel of that car, I'm not sure I would have embarked as willingly on the adventure. But Dad, glutton for punishment that he is, knew what was in store; as

he buckled his seat belt he braced both feet against the floor and said, "Okay, let's give it a try." For at least an hour, I lurched up and down our driveway, trying to get a feel for "slipping the clutch." (Poor Dad didn't realize I hardly even knew which was the clutch, much less what "slipping" it entailed.) After one particularly violent jolt that almost sent us through the garage door, Dad decided to let me try taking the car around the block. Ostensibly, he wanted me to practice driving in all four gears, though I really think he was more concerned about the fate of the garage door than anything else.

Once out on the street (after a bristly encounter with the forsythia 6 bush which unfortunately stood at the end of the driveway), I embarrassed myself completely. To keep from stalling, I'd rev the engine while I tried to slip the clutch. I couldn't even pretend to be a racing driver; the car didn't have the decency to sound like a high-powered race car, it just roared like an outraged lion with a thorn in its paw. Feeling conspicuous about making all this noise, I let the clutch out too soon, which either stalled the car, or, worse still, made it jerk down the street like a bucking bronco. The poor car looked like a seesaw with the front end first taking a nose dive while the rear end flew up, then leaping into the air as the rear end came back down. Jolting around the block with tires screeching and rubber burning, I provided my neighbors with the best free entertainment they'd seen in a long time, since the days when my brother was learning how to drive that beastly little car.

With this display of ineptitude, I tumbled from the pedestal of spe- 7 cial privilege which a driver's permit had given me; once again the kids too young to drive regarded me as simply the klutz I was. Good ol' Dad stuck by me through the ignominy of it all, assuring me that everybody who learned to drive a stick-shift underwent the same ordeal. It still amazes me that with all that lurching around, he was willing to go with me again.

Now that I have several years' experience behind me, I actually enjoy 8 driving—especially driving a stick-shift. I'll often take to the road to relax, emptying my mind by concentrating on the mechanics of driving. Had it not been for Dad's patient, calm perseverance, I might still be the public menace today that I was three years ago. As for Dad, he lucked out—I'm the last kid in the family.

Content

1. This essay combines the telling of a story with the explanation of a process. Which is dominant? How do you know?

2. Could one learn how to drive—or how not to drive—from reading this essay? If not, what is its point?

3. What is the point of the last paragraph? What impact does the fact that not only did Dolman learn to drive but to enjoy it have on the rest of the essay?

Strategies/Structures

4. How can you tell that Dolman is writing from the perspective of someone who has mastered the skill of driving, rather than from the viewpoint of a learner? What effect does this have on the tone of the essay?

5. Much of Dolman's humor is visual. What comic scenes does she create and how does she help readers to see them? Why should close escapes from accidents provoke laughter instead of terrified relief?

Language

6. What does Dolman's terminology reveal about her intended readers? Are they experienced drivers? Novices? Unable to drive at all?

7. Find some instances where Dolman uses overstated language, understated language, and slang to enhance the humor. What is the effect of the occasional direct quotation of Mr. Upperco's comments (¶s 2, 5)?

For Writing

8. Write an essay in which you explain the process by which you learned or are still learning to do something fairly complicated. You can write it either (1) to explain to your readers how to do the same thing or (2) to entertain your readers by showing, as Dolman does, the amusing pitfalls of the learning process.

9. Write a narrative essay in which you at your present age and level of maturity are narrating an incident in which you at a younger age and a different level of maturity are one of the principal characters. See Sanders, "Under the Influence" (274–86), Zitkala-Sa, excerpts from *The School Days of an Indian Girl* (218–26), and White, "Once More to the Lake" (122–28). You may use this dual characterization and split point of view as the basis for humor, though the essay could also be serious.

Additional Topics for Writing
Narration   (For strategies for writing narration, see 121)

1. Write two versions of the earliest experience you can remember that involved some fright, danger, discovery, or excitement. Write the first version as the experience appeared to you at the time it happened. Then, write another version interpreting how the experience appears to you now.

2. Write a narrative of an experience you had that taught you a difficult lesson (see Fadiman, "Under Water," 128–32; and Ning Yu, "Red and Black, or One English Major's Beginning," 191–202). You can either make explicit the point of the lesson, or imply it through your reactions to the experience.

3. Sometimes a meaningful incident or significant relationship with someone can help us to mature, easily or painfully, as Douglass explains in "Resurrection" (133–38). Tell the story of such an incident or relationship in your own life or in the life of someone you know well.

4. Have you ever witnessed an event important to history, sports, science, or some other field of endeavor? If so, tell the story either as an eyewitness, or from the point of view of someone looking back on it and more aware now of its true meaning.

5. If you have ever been to a place that is particularly significant to you, narrate an incident to show its significance through specified details. (See White, "Once More to the Lake," 122–28; Fadiman, "Under Water," 128–32; and Ischannerl, "One Remembers Most What One Loves," 287–92.)

6. Have you ever worshipped someone as a hero or heroine, or modeled yourself after someone? Or been treated as someone's particular favorite (or nemesis)? Tell the story of this special relationship you have (or had) with a parent or grandparent, brother or sister, friend or antagonist, spouse, employer, teacher. Through narrating one or two typical incidents to convey its essence, show why this relationship has been beneficial or harmful to you. (See White, "Once More to the Lake," 122–28; Douglass, "Resurrection," 133–38; Ruffin, "Mama's Smoke," 107–15; or Barry, "The Sanctuary of School," 500–04.) Control your language carefully to control the mood and tone.

7. If you have had a "watershed experience"—made an important discovery, survived a major traumatic event, such as an automobile accident, a natural disaster, a flood, or a family breakup; met a person who has changed your life—that has changed your life or your thinking about life significantly, narrate the experience and analyze its effects, short- or long-term. You will need to explain enough of what you were like beforehand so readers can recognize the effects of the experience. (See Douglass, "Resurrection," 133–38, or Fendrich, "History Overcomes Stories," 529–32.)

8. Explain what it's like to be a typical student or employee (on an assembly line, in a restaurant or store, or elsewhere) through an account of "A Day in the Life of . . . ." If you find that life to be boring or demeaning, your narrative might be an implied protest or an argument for change.

9. Write a fairy tale or fable, a story with a moral. Make it suitable for children (but don't talk down to them) or for people of your own age.

10. Write a pseudo-diary, an imaginary account of how you would lead a day in your life if all your wishes were fulfilled—or if all your worst fears were realized.

11. Imagine that you're telling a major news event of the day (or of your lifetime) to someone fifty years from now. What details will you have to include and explain to make sure your reader understands it?

12. Through using your own experiences or those of someone you know well, write an essay showing the truth or falsity of an adage about human nature, such as

  a. Quitters never win. Or do they?
  b. Try hard and you'll succeed. Or will you?
  c. It doesn't matter whether you win or lose, it's how you play the game.
  d. Absence makes the heart grow fonder—or, Out of sight out of mind.

Process Analysis

Analysis involves dividing something into its component parts and explaining what they are, on the assumption that it is easier to consider and to understand the subject in smaller segments than in a large, complicated whole (see the chapter "Division and Classification," [295–98]). To analyze the human body, you could divide it into systems—skeletal, circulatory, respiratory, digestive, neurological—before identifying and defining the components of each. Of the digestive system, for instance, you would discuss the mouth, pharynx, esophagus, stomach, and large and small intestines.

You can analyze a process in the same way, focusing on *how* rather than *what*. A *directive process analysis* identifies the steps in how to make or do something: how to sail a catamaran; how to get to Kuala Lumpur; how to make brownies; how to collaborate in a writing group "to keep a group running smoothly and to forestall some common problems," as John Trimbur advises in "Guidelines for Collaborating in Groups" (103–07).

An *informative process analysis* can identify the stages by which something is created or formed, or how something is done. In "Those Crazy Ideas" (158–67), Isaac Asimov analyzes two "styles" of scientific investigation by comparing and contrasting the ways in which Charles Darwin (see also 342–48) and Alfred Russel Wallace arrived "independently and simultaneously" at the theory of evolution. A process analysis can also explain how something functions or works, as Tom and Ray Magliozzi do in "Inside the Engine" (178–84): "Overfilling [your car oil] is just as bad as underfilling. . . . If you're a quart and a half . . . overfilled, you could have so much oil in the crankcase that the spinning crankshaft is going to hit the oil and turn it into suds. It's impossible for the pump to pump suds, so you'll ruin the motor. It's kind of like a front-loading washing machine that goes berserk and spills suds all over the floor when you put too much detergent in." Or a process analysis can explain the meanings and implications of a concept, system, or mechanism as the basis for a philosophy that incorporates the process in question. Thus in the process of explaining the medical processes involved in a "Code Blue" alert (376–80), Jasmine Innerarity offers not only a philosophy of lifesaving, but a philosophy of life.

A process analysis can incorporate an explanation and appreciation of a way of life, as implied in the photograph of the Mennonite carpenter (p. 153), taken in 1999, but in many respects timeless. Ntozake Shange does this in "What Is It We Really Harvestin' Here?" (184–91). Shange explains how to grow potatoes, mustard greens, and watermelon, and how to cook "Mama's rice"; in the process, she offers a joyous interpretation not only of "'colored' cuisine," but of the people who cultivate, prepare, and eat this nourishment for the soul as well as the body. An analysis can also incorporate a critique of a process, sometimes as a way to advocate an alternative, as Scott Russell Sanders does in showing the deleterious effects of alcoholism on alcoholics' families in "Under the Influence" (274–86). Matt Nocton's "Harvest of Gold, Harvest of Shame" (515–21) provides both an overt explanation of a process—how tobacco is harvested—and an implied critique of the exploitation of the migrant workers who do the backbreaking labor. Each worker must "must tie [a burlap sack] around his waist as a source of protection against the dirt and rocks that he will be dragging himself through for the next eight hours."

A process analysis can also embed a critique of the process it discusses. "http://www.when_is_enough_enough?.com" (168–78) is computer science professor Paul De Palma's criticism of "the persistent misidentification of the computing sciences with microcomputer gadgetry," as represented by the detritus of obsolete computers in the photograph on p. 172. His essay explains the process not of how computers work, but of how society in general and colleges and universities in particular promote "computer literacy" in the mistaken belief that technical facility with the machines increases the users' ability to think. The primary beneficiary of this training is not the students, he claims, but the computer industry that profits from both the sales and the users' skills—a commercial process masquerading as an intellectual one. De Palma is writing for a dual audience: general readers familiar enough with computers to understand the irony of his comment, "To write a report on a machine with a Pentium II processor, sixty-four megabytes of memory, and an eight-gigabyte hard disk is like leasing the space shuttle to fly from New York to Boston to catch a Celtics game." And although his essay was published in the nonspecialized but highbrow *American Scholar,* the magazine of Phi Beta Kappa, his critique of the computer industry is also meant for decision makers in Silicon Valley, a group he understands very well from having worked there himself for a decade.

The following suggestions for writing an essay of process analysis are in themselves—you guessed it—a process analysis.

To write about a process, for whatever audience, you first have to *make sure you understand it yourself.* If it's a process you can perform, such as parallel parking or hitting a good tennis forehand, try it out before you begin to write, and note the steps and possible variations from start to finish.

Early on you'll need to *identify the purpose or function of the process and its likely outcome:* "How to lose twenty pounds in ten weeks." Then the steps or stages in the process occur in a given sequence; it's helpful to *list them in their logical or natural order* and to *provide time markers* so your readers will know what comes first, second, and thereafter. "First have a physical exam. Next: work out a sensible diet, under medical supervision. Then. . . ."

If the process involves many simultaneous operations, for clarity you may need to *classify all aspects of the process and discuss each one separately,* as you might in explaining the photograph of what the Chinese boy is doing in order to learn to read and write his native language (p. 195). For instance, since playing the violin requires bowing with the right hand and fingering with the left, it makes sense to consider each by itself. After you've done this, however, be sure to *indicate how all of the separate elements of the process fit together.* To play the violin successfully the right hand has to know what the left hand is doing. If the process you're discussing is cyclic or circular—as in the life cycle of a plant, or the water cycle, involving evaporation, condensation, and precipitation—start with whatever seems to you most logical or most familiar to your readers.

If you're using specialized or technical language, *define your terms* unless you're writing for an audience of experts. You'll also need to *identify specialized equipment* and *be explicit about whatever techniques and measurements your readers need to know.* For example, an essay on how to throw a pot would need to tell a reader who had never potted what the proper consistency of the clay should be before one begins to wedge it, or how to tell when all the air bubbles have been wedged out. But how complicated should an explanation be? The more your reader knows about your subject, the more sophisticated your analysis can be, with less emphasis, if any, on the basics. How thin can the pot's walls be without collapsing? Does the type of clay (white, red, with or without grog) make any difference? The reverse is true if you're writing for novices—keep it simple to start with.

If subprocesses are involved in the larger process, you can either *explain these where they would logically come in the sequence,* or *consider them in footnotes or an appendix.* You don't want to sidetrack your reader from the main thrust. For instance, if you were to explain the process of Prank Day, an annual ritual at Cal Tech, you might begin with the time by which all seniors have to be out of their residence halls for the day, 8 a.m. You might then follow a typical prank from beginning to end: the selection of a senior's parked car to disassemble; the transportation of its parts to the victim's dorm room; the reassembling of the vehicle; the victim's consternation when he encounters it in his room with the motor running. If the focus is on the process of playing the prank, you probably wouldn't want to give directions on how to disassemble and reassemble the car; to do so would require a hefty manual. But you might want to supplement your discussion with helpful hints on how to pay (or avoid paying) for the damage.

After you've finished your essay, if it explains how to perform a process, ask a friend, preferably one who's unfamiliar with the subject, to try it out. (Even people who know how to tie shoelaces can get all tangled up in murky directions.) She can tell you what's unclear, what needs to be explained more fully—and even point out where you're belaboring the obvious.

Your paper may be an informative analysis of a process, as is Spencer Nadler's "Fat" (265–74), which includes nontechnical accounts of the reasons for morbid obesity (when a person weighs more than one hundred pounds over normal), the process of bariatric surgery to shrink an obese patient's stomach, and brief analysis of the consequences of the operation, its advantages and disadvantages. Ask your reader to tell you how well she understands what you've said. If, by the end, she's still asking you what the fundamental concept is, you'll know you've got to run the paper through your typewriter or computer once again.

Process analysis can serve as a vehicle for explaining personal relationships. For example, an analysis of the sequential process of performing some activity can serve as the framework for explaining a complicated relationship among the people involved in performing the same process or an analogous one. In such essays the relationship among the participants or the character of the person performing the process is more important than the process itself; whether or not the explanation is sufficient to enable the readers to actually perform the process is beside the point.

Scott Russell Sanders's "The Inheritance of Tools" (139–46) is typical of such writing. Although his father is showing Sanders, as a young child, how to pound nails and to saw, the information is not sufficient in the text, even for such a simple process, to provide clear directions of how to do it. The real point of Sanders's commentary is not instructions in how to use tools, but in the relationship between the tender father and his admiring son. In contrast, even though Ntozake Shange's "What Is It We Really Harvestin' Here?" is not intended as a cookbook, her freewheeling recipes offer enough directions on how to prepare the food.

Writing parodies of processes, particularly those that are complicated, mysterious, or done badly—may be the ideal revenge of the novice
learner (see Ann Upperco Dolman's "Learning to Drive" [146–50]) or the
person obsessed with or defeated by a process. Parodies such as these
may include a critique of the process, a satire of the novice or victim (often
the author), or both.

STRATEGIES FOR WRITING— PROCESS ANALYSIS

1. Is the purpose of my essay to provide directions—a step-by-step explanation of
   how to do or make something? Or is the essay's purpose informative—to explain how something happens or works? Do I know my subject well enough to
   explain it clearly and accurately?
2. If I'm providing directions, how much does my audience already know about
   performing the process? Should I start with definitions of basic terms ("sauté,"
   "dado") and explanations of subprocesses, or can I focus on the main process
   at hand? Should I simplify the process for a naive audience, or are my readers
   sophisticated enough to understand its complexities? Likewise, if I'm providing an informative explanation, where will I start? How complicated will my
   explanation become? The assumed expertise of my audience will help determine my answers.
3. Have I presented the process in logical or chronological sequence (first, second,
   third . . .)? Have I furnished an overview so that my readers will have the outcome (or desired results) and major aspects of the process in mind before they
   immerse themselves in the particulars of the individual steps?
4. Does my language fit both the subject, however general or technical, and the
   audience? Do I use technical terms when necessary? Which of these do I need
   to define or explain for my intended readers?
5. What tone will I use in my essay? A serious or matter-of-fact tone will indicate
   that I'm treating my subject "straight." An ironic, exaggerated, or understated
   tone will indicate that I'm treating it humorously.

ISAAC ASIMOV

Asimov (1920–1992) said that his talent lay in his ability to "read a dozen dull books and make one interesting book out of them." He amplified, "I'm on fire to explain, and happiest when it's something reasonably intricate which I can make clear step by step." From these motives, Asimov wrote nearly five hundred books, averaging one every six weeks for over thirty-five years. Although Asimov held a doctorate in chemistry from Columbia University (1948), his subjects ranged from astronomy, biology, biochemistry, mathematics, and physics, to history, literature, the Bible, limericks, and a two-volume autobiography. Nevertheless, he is probably best known for his science fiction—stories and novels; "Nightfall" has been called "the best science fiction work of all time." In 1973 he won both the Hugo and Nebula Awards.

Even before the advent of word processors, Asimov wrote ninety words a minute, up to twelve hours a day, a superhuman pace. His demanding schedule allowed two—and only two—drafts of everything, the first on a typewriter, and in his final years, the second on a computer. He said, "But I have a completely unadorned style. I aim to be accurate and clear—whether for an audience of sci-fi fans or general readers, including children." Asimov has been praised for being "encyclopedic, witty, with a gift for colorful and illuminating examples and explanations"—qualities apparent in "Those Crazy Ideas." There he explains the creative processes by which two scientists, Charles Darwin and Alfred Russel Wallace, arrived independently at the theory of evolution. Then he analyzes how they worked to illustrate the common characteristics of the creative process, a combination of education, intelligence, intuition, courage—and luck.

Those Crazy Ideas

1   Time and time again I have been asked (and I'm sure others who have, in their time, written science fiction have been asked too): "Where do you get your crazy ideas?"

2   Over the years, my answers have sunk from flattered confusion to a shrug and a feeble smile. Actually, I don't really know, and the lack of knowledge doesn't really worry me, either, as long as the ideas keep coming.

3   But then some time ago, a consultant firm in Boston, engaged in a sophisticated space-age project for the government, got in touch with me.

4   What they needed, it seemed, to bring their project to a successful conclusion were novel suggestions, startling new principles, conceptual breakthroughs. To put it into the nutshell of a well-turned phrase, they needed "crazy ideas."

5   Unfortunately, they didn't know how to go about getting crazy ideas, but some among them had read my science fiction, so they looked me up

in the phone book and called me to ask (in essence), "Dr. Asimov, where do you get your crazy ideas?"

Alas, I still didn't know, but as speculation is my profession, I am perfectly willing to think about the matter and share my thoughts with you. 6

The question before the house, then, is: How does one go about creating or inventing or dreaming up or stumbling over a new and revolutionary scientific principle? 7

For instance—to take a deliberately chosen example—how did Darwin come to think of evolution? 8

To begin with, in 1831, when Charles Darwin was twenty-two, he joined the crew of a ship called the *Beagle*. This ship was making a five-year voyage about the world to explore various coast lines and to increase man's geographical knowledge. Darwin went along as ship's naturalist, to study the forms of life in far-off places. 9

This he did extensively and well, and upon the return of the *Beagle* Darwin wrote a book about his experiences (published in 1840) which made him famous. In the course of this voyage, numerous observations led him to the conclusion that species of living creatures changed and developed slowly with time; that new species descended from old. This, in itself, was not a new idea. Ancient Greeks had had glimmerings of evolutionary notions. Many scientists before Darwin, including Darwin's own grandfather, had theories of evolution. 10

The trouble, however, was that no scientist could evolve an explanation for the *why* of evolution. A French naturalist, Jean Baptiste de Lamarck, had suggested in the early 1800s that it came about by a kind of conscious effort or inner drive. A tree-grazing animal, attempting to reach leaves, stretched its neck over the years and transmitted a longer neck to its descendants. The process was repeated with each generation until a giraffe in full glory was formed. 11

The only trouble was that acquired characteristics are not inherited and this was easily proved. The Lamarckian explanation did not carry conviction. 12

Charles Darwin, however, had nothing better to suggest after several years of thinking about the problem. 13

But in 1798, eleven years before Darwin's birth, an English clergyman named Thomas Robert Malthus had written a book entitled *An Essay on the Principle of Population*. In this book Malthus suggested that the human population always increased faster than the food supply and that the population had to be cut down by either starvation, disease, or war; that these evils were therefore unavoidable. 14

In 1838 Darwin, still puzzling over the problem of the development of species, read Malthus's book. It is hackneyed to say "in a flash" but that, apparently, is how it happened. In a flash, it was clear to Darwin. Not only human beings increased faster than the food supply; all species of living things did. In every case, the surplus population had to be cut down by 15 starvation, by predators, or by disease. Now no two members of any species are exactly alike; each has slight individual variations from the norm. Accepting this fact, which part of the population was cut down?

16   Why—and this was Darwin's breakthrough—those members of the species who were less efficient in the race for food, less adept at fighting off or escaping from predators, less equipped to resist disease, went down.

17   The survivors, generation after generation, were better adapted, on the average, to their environment. The slow changes toward a better fit with the environment accumulated until a new (and more adapted) species had replaced the old. Darwin thus postulated the reason for evolution as being the action of *natural selection.* In fact, the full title of his book is *On the Origin of Species by Means of Natural Selection, or the Preservation of Favoured Races in the Struggle for Life.* We just call it *The Origin of Species* and miss the full flavor of what it was he did.

18   It was in 1838 that Darwin received this flash and in 1844 that he began writing his book, but he worked on for fourteen years gathering evidence to back up his thesis. He was a methodical perfectionist and no amount of evidence seemed to satisfy him. He always wanted more. His friends read his preliminary manuscripts and urged him to publish. In particular, Charles Lyell (whose book *Principles of Geology,* published in 1830–1833, first convinced scientists of the great age of the earth and thus first showed there was *time* for the slow progress of evolution to take place) warned Darwin that someone would beat him to the punch.

19   While Darwin was working, another and younger English naturalist, Alfred Russel Wallace, was traveling in distant lands. He too found copious evidence to show that evolution took place and he too wanted to find a reason. He did not know that Darwin had already solved the problem.

20   He spent three years puzzling, and then in 1858, he too came across Malthus's book and read it. I am embarrassed to have to become hackneyed again, but in a flash he saw the answer. Unlike Darwin, however, he did not settle down to fourteen years of gathering and arranging evidence.

21   Instead, he grabbed pen and paper and at once wrote up his theory. He finished this in two days.

22   Naturally, he didn't want to rush into print without having his notions checked by competent colleagues, so he decided to send it to some well-known naturalist. To whom? Why, to Charles Darwin. To whom else?

23   I have often tried to picture Darwin's feeling as he read Wallace's essay which, he afterward stated, expressed matters in almost his own words. He wrote to Lyell that he had been forestalled "with a vengeance."

24   Darwin might easily have retained full credit. He was well-known and there were many witnesses to the fact that he had been working on his project for a decade and a half. Darwin, however, was a man of the highest integrity. He made no attempt to suppress Wallace. On the contrary, he passed on the essay to others and arranged to have it published along with a similar essay of his own. The year after, Darwin published his book.

Now the reason I chose this case was that here we have two men   25
making one of the greatest discoveries in the history of science independently and simultaneously and under precisely the same stimulus. Does
that mean *anyone* could have worked out the theory of natural selection if
they had but made a sea voyage and combined that with reading Malthus?

Well, let's see. Here's where the speculation starts.   26

To begin with, both Darwin and Wallace were thoroughly grounded   27
in natural history. Each had accumulated a vast collection of facts in the field
in which they were to make their breakthrough. Surely this is significant.

Now every man in his lifetime collects facts, individual pieces of   28
data, items of information. Let's call these "bits" (as they do, I think, in
information theory). The "bits" can be of all varieties: personal memories,
girls' phone numbers, baseball players' batting averages, yesterday's
weather, the atomic weights of the chemical elements.

Naturally, different men gather different numbers of different varie-   29
ties of "bits." A person who has collected a larger number than usual of
those varieties that are held to be particularly difficult to obtain—say, those
involving the sciences and the liberal arts—is considered "educated."

There are two broad ways in which the "bits" can be accumulated.   30
The more common way, nowadays, is to find people who already possess
many "bits" and have them transfer those "bits" to your mind in good order
and in predigested fashion. Our schools specialize in this transfer of "bits"
and those of us who take advantage of them receive a "formal education."

The less common way is to collect "bits" with a minimum amount of   31
live help. They can be obtained from books or out of personal experience.
In that case you are "self-educated." (It often happens that "self-educated"
is confused with "uneducated." This is an error to be avoided.)

In actual practice, scientific breakthroughs have been initiated by   32
those who were formally educated, as for instance by Nicolaus Copernicus,
and by those who were self-educated, as for instance by Michael Faraday.

To be sure, the structure of science has grown more complex over the   33
years and the absorption of the necessary number of "bits" has become
more and more difficult without the guidance of someone who has already
absorbed them. The self-educated genius is therefore becoming rarer,
though he has still not vanished.

However, without drawing any distinction according to the manner   34
in which "bits" have been accumulated, let's set up the first criterion for
scientific creativity:

1) The creative person must possess as many "bits" of information   35
as possible; i.e., he must be educated.

Of course, the accumulation of "bits" is not enough in itself. We have   36
probably all met people who are intensely educated, but who manage to
be abysmally stupid, nevertheless. They have the "bits," but the "bits" just
lie there.

But what is there one can do with "bits"?   37

38   Well, one can combine them into groups of two or more. Everyone does that; it is the principle of the string on the finger. You tell yourself to remember *a* (to buy bread) when you observe *b* (the string). You enforce a combination that will not let you forget *a* because *b* is so noticeable.

39   That, of course, is a conscious and artificial combination of "bits." It is my feeling that every mind is, more or less unconsciously, continually making all sorts of combinations and permutations of "bits," probably at random.

40   Some minds do this with greater facility than others; some minds have greater capacity for dredging the combinations out of the unconscious and becoming consciously aware of them. This results in "new ideas," in "novel outlooks."

41   The ability to combine "bits" with facility and to grow consciously aware of the new combinations is, I would like to suggest, the measure of what we call "intelligence." In this view, it is quite possible to be educated and yet not intelligent.

42   Obviously, the creative scientist must not only have his "bits" on hand but he must be able to combine them readily and more or less consciously. Darwin not only observed data, he also made deductions— clever and far-reaching deductions—from what he observed. That is, he combined the "bits" in interesting ways and drew important conclusions.

43   So the second criterion of creativity is:

44   2) The creative person must be able to combine "bits" with facility and recognize the combinations he has formed; i.e., he must be intelligent.

45   Even forming and recognizing new combinations is insufficient in itself. Some combinations are important and some are trivial. How do you tell which are which? There is no question but that a person who cannot tell them apart must labor under a terrible disadvantage. As he plods after each possible new idea, he loses time and his life passes uselessly.

46   There is also no question but that there are people who somehow have the gift of seeing the consequences "in a flash" as Darwin and Wallace did; of feeling what the end must be without consciously going through every step of the reasoning. This, I suggest, is the measure of what we call "intuition."

47   Intuition plays more of a role in some branches of scientific knowledge than others. Mathematics, for instance, is a deductive science in which, once certain basic principles are learned, a large number of items of information become "obvious" as merely consequences of those principles. Most of us, to be sure, lack the intuitive powers to see the "obvious."

48   To the truly intuitive mind, however, the combination of the few necessary "bits" is at once extraordinarily rich in consequences. Without too much trouble they see them all, including some that have not been seen by their predecessors.[1]

---

[1] The Swiss mathematician, Leonhard Euler, said that to the true mathematician, it is at once obvious that $e^{\pi i} = -1$.

It is perhaps for this reason that mathematics and mathematical 49
physics has seen repeated cases of first-rank breakthroughs by youngsters. Evariste Galois evolved group theory at twenty-one. Isaac Newton
worked out calculus at twenty-three. Albert Einstein presented the theory
of relativity at twenty-six, and so on.

In those branches of science which are more inductive and require 50
larger numbers of "bits" to begin with, the average age of the scientists at
the time of the breakthrough is greater. Darwin was twenty-nine at the
time of his flash, Wallace was thirty-five.

But in any science, however inductive, intuition is necessary for crea- 51
tivity. So:

3) The creative person must be able to see, with as little delay as pos- 52
sible, the consequences of the new combinations of "bits" which he has
formed; i.e., he must be intuitive.

But now let's look at this business of combining "bits" in a little more 53
detail. "Bits" are at varying distances from each other. The more closely
related two "bits" are, the more apt one is to be reminded of one by the
other and to make the combination. Consequently, a new idea that arises
from such a combination is made quickly. It is a "natural consequence" of
an older idea, a "corollary." It "obviously follows."

The combination of less related "bits" results in a more startling 54
idea; if for no other reason than that it takes longer for such a combination
to be made, so that the new idea is therefore less "obvious." For a scientific breakthrough of the first rank, there must be a combination of "bits"
so widely spaced that the random chance of the combination being made
is small indeed. (Otherwise, it will be made quickly and be considered but
a corollary of some previous idea which will then be considered the
"breakthrough.")

But then, it can easily happen that two "bits" sufficiently widely 55
spaced to make a breakthrough by their combination are not present in
the same mind. Neither Darwin nor Wallace, for all their education, intelligence, and intuition, possessed the key "bits" necessary to work out the
theory of evolution by natural selection. Those "bits" were lying in
Malthus's book, and both Darwin and Wallace had to find them there.

To do this, however, they had to read, understand, and appreciate 56
the book. In short, they had to be ready to incorporate other people's
"bits" and treat them with all the ease with which they treated their own.

It would hamper creativity, in other words, to emphasize intensity 57
of education at the expense of broadness. It is bad enough to limit the nature of the "bits" to the point where the necessary two would not be in the
same mind. It would be fatal to mold a mind to the point where it was
incapable of accepting "foreign bits."

I think we ought to revise the first criterion of creativity, then, to read: 58

1) The creative person must possess as many "bits" as possible, falling 59
into as wide a variety of types as possible; i.e., he must be broadly educated.

60   As the total amount of "bits" to be accumulated increases with the advance of science, it is becoming more and more difficult to gather enough "bits" in a wide enough area. Therefore, the practice of "brain-busting" is coming into popularity; the notion of collecting thinkers into groups and hoping that they will cross-fertilize one another into startling new breakthroughs.

61   Under what circumstances could this conceivably work? (After all, anything that will stimulate creativity is of first importance to humanity.)

62   Well, to begin with, a group of people will have more "bits" on hand than any member of the group singly since each man is likely to have some "bits" the others do not possess.

63   However, the increase in "bits" is not in direct proportion to the number of men, because there is bound to be considerable overlapping. As the group increases, the smaller and smaller addition of completely new "bits" introduced by each additional member is quickly outweighed by the added tensions involved in greater numbers; the longer wait to speak, the greater likelihood of being interrupted, and so on. It is my (intuitive) guess that five is as large a number as one can stand in such a conference.

64   Now of the three criteria mentioned so far, I feel (intuitively) that intuition is the least common. It is more likely that none of the group will be intuitive than that none will be intelligent or none educated. If no individual in the group is intuitive, the group as a whole will not be intuitive. You cannot add non-intuition and form intuition.

65   If one of the group is intuitive, he is almost certain to be intelligent and educated as well, or he would not have been asked to join the group in the first place. In short, for a brain-busting group to be creative, it must be quite small and it must possess at least one creative individual. But in that case, does that one individual need the group? Well, I'll get back to that later.

66   Why did Darwin work fourteen years gathering evidence for a theory he himself must have been convinced was correct from the beginning? Why did Wallace send his manuscript to Darwin first instead of offering it for publication at once?

67   To me it seems that they must have realized that any new idea is met by resistance from the general population who, after all, are not creative. The more radical the new idea, the greater the dislike and distrust it arouses. The dislike and distrust aroused by a first-class breakthrough are so great that the author must be prepared for unpleasant consequences (sometimes for expulsion from the respect of the scientific community; sometimes, in some societies, for death).

68   Darwin was trying to gather enough evidence to protect himself by convincing others through a sheer flood of reasoning. Wallace wanted to have Darwin on his side before proceeding.

69   It takes courage to announce the results of your creativity. The greater the creativity, the greater the necessary courage in much more than direct

proportion. After all, consider that the more profound the breakthrough, the more solidified the previous opinions; the more "against reason" the new discovery seems, the more against cherished authority.

Usually a man who possesses enough courage to be a scientific genius   70
seems odd. After all, a man who has sufficient courage or irreverence to fly in the face of reason or authority must be odd, if you define "odd" as "being not like most people." And if he is courageous and irreverent in such a colossally big thing, he will certainly be courageous and irreverent in many small things so that being odd in one way, he is apt to be odd in others. In short, he will seem to the non-creative, conforming people about him to be a "crackpot."

So we have the fourth criterion: 71

4) The creative person must possess courage (and to the general   72
public may, in consequence, seem a crackpot).

As it happens, it is the crackpottery that is most often most noticeable   73
about the creative individual. The eccentric and absent-minded professor is a stock character in fiction; and the phrase "mad scientist" is almost a cliché.

(And be it noted that I am never asked where I get my interesting or   74
effective or clever or fascinating ideas. I am invariably asked where I get my *crazy* ideas.)

Of course, it does not follow that because the creative individual is   75
usually a crackpot, that any crackpot is automatically an unrecognized genius. The chances are low indeed, and failure to recognize that the proposition cannot be so reversed is the cause of a great deal of trouble.

Then, since I believe that combinations of "bits" take place quite at   76
random in the unconscious mind, it follows that it is quite possible that a person may possess all four of the criteria I have mentioned in super-abundance and yet may never happen to make the necessary combination. After all, suppose Darwin had never read Malthus. Would he ever have thought of natural selection? What made him pick up the copy? What if someone had come in at the crucial time and interrupted him?

So there is a fifth criterion which I am at a loss to phrase in any other   77
way than this:

5) A creative person must be lucky.   78

To summarize: 79

A creative person must be 1) broadly educated, 2) intelligent, 3) intui-   80
tive, 4) courageous, and 5) lucky.

How, then, does one go about encouraging scientific creativity? For   81
now, more than ever before in man's history, we must; and the need will grow constantly in the future.

Only, it seems to me, by increasing the incidence of the various cri-   82
teria among the general population.

Of the five criteria, number 5 (luck) is out of our hands. We can only   83
hope; although we must also remember Louis Pasteur's famous statement

that "Luck favors the prepared mind." Presumably, if we have enough of the four other criteria, we shall find enough of number five as well.

84   Criterion 1 (broad education) is in the hands of our school system. Many educators are working hard to find ways of increasing the quality of education among the public. They should be encouraged to continue doing so.

85   Criterion 2 (intelligence) and 3 (intuition) are inborn and their incidence cannot be increased in the ordinary way. However, they can be more efficiently recognized and utilized. I would like to see methods devised for spotting the intelligent and intuitive (particularly the latter) early in life and treating them with special care. This, too, educators are concerned with.

86   To me, though, it seems that it is criterion 4 (courage) that receives the least concern, and it is just the one we may most easily be able to handle. Perhaps it is difficult to make a person more courageous than he is, but that is not necessary. It would be equally effective to make it sufficient to be less courageous; to adopt an attitude that creativity is a permissible activity.

87   Does this mean changing society or changing human nature? I don't think so. I think there are ways of achieving the end that do not involve massive change of anything, and it is here that brainbusting has its greatest chance of significance.

88   Suppose we have a group of five that includes one creative individual. Let's ask again what that individual can receive from the non-creative four.

89   The answer to me, seems to be just this: Permission!

90   They must permit him to create. They must tell him to go ahead and be a crackpot.[2]

91   How is this permission to be granted? Can four essentially non-creative people find it within themselves to grant such permission? Can the one creative person find it within himself to accept it?

92   I don't know. Here, it seems to me, is where we need experimentation and perhaps a kind of creative breakthrough about creativity. Once we learn enough about the whole matter, who knows—I may even find out where I get those crazy ideas.

Content

1. How does Asimov define "crazy ideas"? Is he using "crazy idea" as a synonym for a "new and revolutionary scientific principle"? How would Asimov (or you) distinguish between a "crazy idea" and a "crackpot" idea? Or the insane notion of a "mad scientist"?

---

[2] AUTHOR'S NOTE: Always with the provision, of course, that the crackpot creation that results survives the test of hard inspection. Though many of the products of genius seem crackpot at first, very few of the creations that seem crackpot turn out, after all, to be products of genius.

2. Compare and contrast the creative processes by which Charles Darwin and Alfred Russel Wallace arrived independently at the theory of evolution.

3. How appropriate is it for Asimov to generalize about scientific creativity on the basis of two examples from a particular field?

4. Identify the five qualities Asimov says are necessary for the creative process to operate. Has he covered all the essentials? To what extent must the "climate be right" for the creative process to function effectively? What becomes of "crazy ideas" too advanced for their time?

Strategies/Structures

5. Show how Asimov's essay is an example of inductive reasoning—beginning with evidence, assessing that evidence, and drawing conclusions from it.

6. Although Asimov identifies the fifth quality in a successful creative process as luck (¶ 78), he doesn't define it, says it's "out of our hands" (¶ 83), and blithely assures us that "if we have enough of the four other criteria" we'll find enough luck as well (¶ 83). Is Asimov irresponsible here?

Language

7. Asimov uses a conversational tone and vocabulary, as well as two extended narrative examples (of Darwin and Wallace). Would you expect to find such literary techniques in scientific writing? If so, for what kind of audience? (Compare Darwin, "Understanding Natural Selection" [342–48] and Gould, "Evolution as Fact and Theory" [401–10].)

8. Asimov always identifies the scientists to whom he is referring when he first introduces them (Lamarck, ¶ 11; Malthus, ¶ 14; Lyell, ¶ 18). What does this practice reveal about the amount of scientific knowledge Asimov expects his readers to have?

For Writing

9. What does it take to be successful? Identify and define the essential criteria (four or five items) for an outstanding performance in one of the fields or roles below. Illustrate your definition with a detailed example or two from the lives of successful people in that field or role, perhaps people you know:

   a. Parent or grandparent
   b. Medicine (doctor, nurse, social worker, medical researcher)
   c. Politics, military, and the law (police or military officer, lawyer, elected official, bureaucrat, judge)
   d. Athletics (player of team or individual sports, coach)
   e. Education (student, teacher, or administrator)
   f. The fine arts (painter, sculptor, musician, writer)
   g. Business (self-made man or woman, salesperson, manager, executive, accountant, broker)
   h. Another profession or occupation of your choice.

PAUL DE PALMA

Paul De Palma (born 1947) studied English at the University of California at Berkeley (M.A., 1975) and was working on his doctorate in the same field, "contemplating a life not of ease but of almost certain underemployment," when he changed careers and went to work in Silicon Valley. A decade later he earned an M.S. in computer science from Temple University (1990), which allowed Gonzaga University to "turn me loose on students without a completed doctorate" as a professor of computer science, where he presently focuses on the social implications of computing and artificial intelligence. He explains his writing process: "My writing almost always begins with a run. This self-imposed isolation induces contentment and sometimes even euphoria. Both are under-appreciated aspects of clear thinking. When I get to my desk, I play with the list of points I cooked up while running, until my argument begins to sound convincing. The introduction is the hardest part. I usually start far afield, often with a story that leads me gradually to a topic sentence. When it works well, the rest is like a dream. By putting words on paper, I discover what I want to say. . . . I revise many, many, many times, reading whole sections aloud so that I can hear the cadence." His work in progress includes *Dim Sum for the Mind,* a collection of essays about computing.

"*http://www.when_is_enough_enough?.com,*" first published in *The American Scholar* (1999), offers a witty analysis and critique of the mythology that accompanies the ever-increasing spread of computers and computer applications in schools, business, and everyday life. "Prosperity follows computing" is the myth, whose realities De Palma investigates, coming to the controversial conclusion that "the skill imparted [through computer science courses] is at best trivial. . . ." This training, supported largely by educational institutions at public expense, "benefits the computer industry," rather than individuals, and should be vastly curtailed.

http://www.when_is_ enough_enough?.com

1   In the misty past, before Bill Gates joined the company of the world's richest men, before the mass-marketed personal computer, before the metaphor of an information superhighway had been worn down to a cliché, I heard Roger Schank interviewed on National Public Radio. Then a computer science professor at Yale, Schank was already well known in artificial intelligence circles. Because those circles did not include me, a new programmer at Sperry Univac, I hadn't heard of him. Though I've forgotten the details of the conversation, I have never forgotten Schank's insistence that most people do not need to own computers.

That view, of course, has not prevailed. Either we own a personal computer and fret about upgrades, or we are scheming to own one and fret about the technical marvel yet to come that will render our purchase obsolete. Well, there are worse ways to spend money, I suppose. For all I know, even Schank owns a personal computer. They're fiendishly clever machines, after all, and they've helped keep the wolf from my door for a long time. 2

It is not the personal computer itself that I object to. What reasonable person would voluntarily go back to a typewriter? The mischief is not in the computer itself, but in the ideology that surrounds it. If we hope to employ computers for tasks more interesting than word processing, we must devote some attention to how they are actually being used, and beyond that, to the remarkable grip that the idol of computing continues to exert. 3

A distressing aspect of the media attention paid to the glories of technology is the persistent misidentification of the computing sciences with microcomputer gadgetry. This manifests itself in many ways. Once my seatmate on a plane learns that I am a computer science professor, I'm expected to chat about the glories of the new DVD-ROM as opposed to the older CD-ROM drives; or about that home shopping channel for the computer literate, the World Wide Web; or about one of the thousand other dreary topics that fill *PC Magazine* and your daily paper, and that by and large represent computing to most Americans. On a somewhat more pernicious level, we in computer science must contend with the phenomenon of prospective employers who ask for expertise in this or that proprietary product. This has had the effect of skewing our mission in the eyes of students majoring in our field. I recently saw a student résumé that listed skill with Harvard Graphics but neglected to mention course work in data communications. Another recent graduate in computer science insisted that the ability to write WordPerfect macros belonged on her résumé. 4

This is a sorry state. How we got there deserves some consideration. 5

A few words of self-disclosure may be in order. What I have to say may strike some as churlish ingratitude to an industry that has provided me with a life of comparative ease for nearly two decades. The fact is that my career as a computer scientist was foisted upon me. When I discovered computers, I was working on a doctorate in English at Berkeley and contemplating a life not of ease but of almost certain underemployment. The computer industry found me one morning on its doorstep, wrapped me in its generous embrace, and has cared for me ever since. I am paid well to puzzle out the charming intricacies of computer programs with bright, attentive students, all happy in the knowledge that their skills will be avidly sought out the day after graduation. I can go to sleep confident that were tenure to be abolished tomorrow, the industry would welcome me back like a prodigal son. 6

Yet for all its largesse, I fear the computer industry has never had my full loyalty. Neither did English studies, for that matter, but this probably says more about those drawn to the study of texts than about me. 7

My memories of the time I spent in the company of the "best which has been thought and said" are hazy, perhaps because the study of literature is not so much a discipline as an attitude. The attitude that dominated all others when I was a student, that sustained my forays into the Western Americana of the Bancroft Collection, is that there is no text so dreary, so impoverished, so bereft of ideas that it does not cry out to be examined—deconstructed, as a graduate student a few years my junior might have said. But the text I now propose to examine, impelled, as it were, by early imprinting in the English department, goes beyond words on a page.

8   From an article here and a TV program there, from a thousand conversations on commuter trains and over lunch and dinner, from the desperate scrambling of local politicians after software companies, the notion that prosperity follows computing, like the rain that was once thought to follow the settler's plow, has become a fully formed mythology.

9   In his perceptive little book *Technopoly,* Neil Postman argues that all disciplines ought to be taught as if they were history. That way, students "can begin to understand, as they now do not, that knowledge is not a fixed thing but a stage in human development, with a past and a future." I wish I'd said that first. If all knowledge has a past—and computer technology is surely a special kind of knowledge—then all knowledge is contingent. The technical landscape is not an engineering necessity. It might be other than it is. Our prospective majors might come to us, as new mathematics or physics majors come to their professors, because of an especially inspiring high school teacher, because of a flair for symbol manipulation, or even because of a (dare I use the word?) curiosity about what constitutes the discipline and its objects of study—not simply because they like gadgets and there's a ton of money to be made in computing.

10   The misidentification of computer science with microcomputer gadgetry is a symptom of a problem that goes far beyond academe. Extraordinary assertions are being made about computers in general and microcomputers in particular. These assertions translate into claims on the American purse—either directly, or indirectly through the tax system. Every dollar our school districts spend on microcomputers is a dollar not spent reducing class size, buying books for the library, reinstating art programs, hiring school counselors, and so on. In fact, every dollar that each of us spends outfitting ourselves with the year's biggest, fastest microcomputer is a dollar we might have put away for retirement, saved for our children's education, spent touring the splendors of the American West, or even chosen not to earn. In the spirit of Neil Postman, then, I'd like to speculate about how the mythology of prosperity through computing has come to be and, in the process, suggest that like the Wizard of Oz, it may be less miraculous than it looks.

11   The place to begin is the spectacular spread of microcomputers themselves. By 1993 nearly a quarter of American households owned at least

one. Four years later, the *Wall Street Journal* put this figure at over 40 percent. For a home appliance that costs at least $1,000, probably closer to $2,000, this represents a substantial outlay. The home market, as it turns out, is the smaller part of the story by far. The Census Bureau tells us that in 1995, the last year for which data are available, Americans spent almost $48 billion on small computers for their homes and businesses. This figure excludes software, peripherals, and services purchased after the new machines were installed.

The title of an article in the *Economist*—"Personal Computers: The 12
End of Good Times?"—hints at the extraordinary world we are trying to understand. In it we learn that annual growth in the home computer market slowed from 40 percent in 1994 to between 15 percent and 20 percent in 1995. By the fall of 1998, market analysts were predicting 16 percent growth in the industry as a whole for the current year. Those of us involved in other sectors of the economy can only look on in astonishment. When a 20 percent, or even 16 percent, growth rate—well over five times that of the economy as a whole—is "the end of good times," we know we're in the presence of an industry whose expectations and promises have left the earth's gravitational pull.

To put some flesh on these numbers, let's try a thought experiment. 13
The computer on my desk is about 16 inches by 17 inches. The Census Bureau tells us that the microcomputer industry delivered over 18 million machines in 1994, the year when, according to the *Economist*, good times ended. Of these, perhaps a third went to the home market, the balance to business. At the 40 percent growth rate in the home market cited for that year and the more modest 16 percent growth rate for the business market, the boys in Redmond and Silicon Valley will have covered the United States' 3,679,192 square miles with discarded microcomputers well before my daughter, who is now thirteen, begins to collect Social Security.

Fabulous as they seem, these figures come from only part of the in- 14
dustry. Microcomputers do not define computing, despite their spectacular entry on the scene. The standard story goes like this: There was once a lumbering blue dinosaur called IBM that dominated the computer industry. In due course, smaller, more agile, and immensely more clever mammals appeared on the scene. The most agile and clever of these was Microsoft, which proceeded to expand its ecological niche and, in so doing, drove the feeble-minded IBM to the brink of extinction.

The business history in this story is as faulty as its paleontology. IBM 15
may be lumbering and blue, but in 1997 its sales were nearly $78 billion. Compare that with Microsoft's $9 billion. The real story is not in the sales volumes of the two companies but in their profit margins. In 1997 IBM's was 7.7 percent, while Microsoft's was a spectacular 28.7 percent. This almost mythical earning capability is expressed best in *Forbes*'s annual list of very rich Americans. We don't hear much about IBM billionaires these days, but Microsoft fortunes are conspicuous in the *Forbes* list, with Bill

Read this picture literally; what do you see? Then try a figurative reading. Might this symbolize the transient state of computers generally? What determines a computer's obsolescence?

Gates's $51 billion, Paul Allen's $21 billion, and Steven Ballmer's $10.7 billion. These fortunes were accumulated in less than twenty years from manufacturing a product that requires no materials beyond the inexpensive medium it is stored on—not so different from a pickle producer, whose only cost, after the first jar comes off the line, is the jar itself. It's a tale of alchemical transmutation if ever there was one. Is it really a surprise that most people don't know that IBM is still a very successful company or that computer science does not begin and end with Windows 98?

16   This joyous account of fortunes waiting to be made in the microcomputer industry has a dark side. Just as Satan is the strongest character in *Paradise Lost,* as C. S. Lewis observed, so is popular fascination with computers due as much to the dark side as to the light. Despite generally good economic news for the past few years, Americans seem gloomy about their prospects. Our brave new world, paved over with networked computers from sea to shining sea, may well be one in which we are mostly unemployed or have experienced a serious decline in living standards. Computers, if not always at the center of the problem, are popularly thought to have been a major contributing factor.

17   Look at the substantial decline in manufacturing as a segment of the workforce in the United States. Between 1970 and 1996 (the last year for

which data are available), the number of Americans employed increased by about 50 million. During this same period, the number of manufacturing jobs declined by about 200,000. The culprit here is often thought to be computer technology, through assembly line robots or through U.S.-owned (or U.S.-contracted) manufacturing facilities in developing countries. Asia and Latin America, of course, would have less appeal to American corporations without worldwide data communications networks.

This analysis of the decline in manufacturing employment is perhaps   18
more appealing than true. I will return to the relationship between computers and productivity. For now it's enough to observe that most people believe there is such a relationship. So if the money to be made in the computer industry is not sufficient inducement to vote for the next school bond issue that would outfit every classroom in your city with networked computers, then the poverty your children will certainly face without such a network should do the trick. With those staggering Microsoft fortunes in the background and the threat of corporate retrenchment in the foreground, I suppose I'm naive to expect the strangers I chat with on planes to know that the computing sciences are more like mathematics and the physical sciences than like desktop publishing—or, for that matter, like the rush to the Klondike goldfields.

The emergence of the microcomputer as a consumer item in the past   19
decade and a half has prompted a flood of articles in the educational literature promoting what has come to be called "computer literacy." In its most basic sense, this term appears to refer to something like a passing familiarity with microcomputers and their commercial applications, rather like the ability to drive a car and know when to get the oil changed. Sadly, the proponents of computer literacy have won the high ground by virtue of the term itself. Who would argue with literacy? It is, after all, one of the more complex human achievements. Not only is literacy a shorthand measure of a country's economic development, but as the rhetorician Walter J. Ong has long argued, once a culture becomes generally literate, its modes of conceptualization are radically altered. Literacy—like motherhood and apple pie in the America of my youth—is unassailable.

But what about the transformative nature of literacy? I am fully   20
aware that similar claims have been made about computers—namely, that computers, like writing, will alter our modes of conceptualization. Maybe so, but not just by running Microsoft Office. I've developed a rule of thumb about claims of this sort: If the subject matter is computers and the tense of the claim is future (and, therefore, its truth-value cannot be ascertained), look at the subtext. Is the claimant a salesman in disguise? To recognize the nonsense in the claim that computers will transform the way we think, we need only indulge in some honest self-examination. I would give up my word processor with great reluctance. This doesn't mean that my neuronal structure is somehow fundamentally different from what it was when I was writing essays similar to this one on my manual Smith Corona. It does

mean that the computer industry is a smidgen richer because of my contribution. It also means, as was recently pointed out to me, that it is a good bit easier to run on at great length on a computer than on a typewriter.

21   Not surprisingly, the number of articles addressing computer literacy in the educational literature has kept pace with microcomputer developments. ERIC is a database of titles published in education journals. When I searched ERIC using the keywords *computer literacy* and *computer literate,* I found 97 articles for the years 1966–1981, or an average of about 6 per year. The decade from 1982 to 1991 produced 2,703 hits, or about 270 per year. At first glance the production of articles since 1991 shows welcome signs of dropping off. But the Internet has come to the rescue of both the microcomputer industry and its prognosticators. When I add the terms "Internet," "World Wide Web," and "information superhighway" to the mix (subtracting for duplicates), the total rises to an astonishing 4,680 articles from 1992 through the first half of 1998. This works out to about 720 articles per year. The bulk of the recent articles, of course, are full of blather about the so-called information superhighway and how all those school districts that cannot give every child access to it will be condemning the next generation to lives of poverty and ignorance.

22   Since computer literacy advocates are eloquent on the benefits of computers in our schools (and equally eloquent on the grim fate that awaits those students not so blessed), a brief look at how microcomputers are actually used in primary and secondary schools is in order. Microcomputers are now a solid presence in American education. The U.S. Census Bureau put the number at nearly 7 million in 1997, or just over 7 students per machine, compared with 11 students per machine in 1994 and 63 per machine a decade earlier. Picture a classroom richly endowed with computers. Several students are bent over a machine, eyes aglow with the discoveries unfolding on the screen. Perhaps there is a kindly teacher in the portrait, pointing to some complex relationship that the computer has helped the budding physicists, social scientists, or software engineers to uncover. If this is the way you imagine primary and secondary school students using computers, you are dead wrong. Several important studies have concluded that primary and secondary school students spend more time mastering the intricacies of word processing than they do using computers for the kinds of tasks that we have in mind when we vote for a bond issue.

23   Programming, in fact, was the one area that school computer coordinators saw decline over previous years. I would be the first to acknowledge that programming does not define computer science. This simple fact is what makes the endless discussion of programming languages in computer science circles so tedious. Nevertheless, if computer science does not begin and end with programming, neither will it give up its secrets to those who cannot program. I greet the news that high school students do not program our millions of microcomputers as an English professor might greet the news that the school library is terrific but the kids don't read.

Here is a puzzle worth more than a moment's thought. There is an inverse relationship between the availability of microcomputers to primary and secondary school students and the chance that those students will do something substantial with them. I am not saying that the relationship is causal, but the association is there. Draw your own conclusions. . . .

Given the several thousand articles on computer literacy and the 24 emerging inverse relationship between productivity growth and computer expenditures, it seems reasonable to ask just who does benefit from the computer literacy movement—and who pays for it. The commonsense answer is, Students benefit. Well, common sense is right, but, as usual, only partially so. Students, of course, are served by learning how to use microcomputers. But the main beneficiaries are the major producers of hardware and software. The situation is really quite extraordinary. Schools and colleges across the country are offering academic credit to students who master the basics of sophisticated consumer products. Granted that it is more difficult to master Microsoft Office than it is to learn to use a VCR or a toaster oven, the difference is one of degree, not of kind.

The obvious question is why the computer industry itself does not 25 train its customers. The answer is that it doesn't have to. Schools, at great public expense, provide this service to the computer industry free of charge. Not only do the educational institutions provide the trainers and the setting for the training, they actually purchase the products on which the students are to be trained from the corporations that are the primary beneficiaries of that training. The story is an old but generally unrecognized one in the United States: the costs are socialized, while the benefits are privatized.

I have described a bleak landscape in this essay. Let me summarize my 26 observations:

Schools and universities purchase products from the computer in- 27 dustry to offer training that benefits the computer industry.

These purchases are both publicly subsidized through tax support 28 and paid for by students (and their parents) themselves.

The skill imparted is at best trivial and does not require faculty with 29 advanced degrees in computer science—degrees acquired by and large through public, not computer industry, support.

As the number of microcomputers in our schools has grown, the 30 chance that something interesting might be done with them has decreased.

The stunning complexity of microcomputer hardware and software 31 has had the disastrous effect of transforming every English professor, every secretary, every engineer, every manager into a computer systems technician.

For all the public subsidies involved in the computer literacy move- 32 ment, the evidence that microcomputers have made good on their central promise—increased productivity— is, at the very least, open to question.

33   If my argument is at least partially correct, we should begin to re-think computing. The microcomputer industry has been with us for a decade and a half. We have poured staggering sums down its insatiable maw. It is time to face an unpleasant fact: the so-called microcomputer revolution has cost much more than it has returned. One problem is that microcomputers are vastly more complex than the tasks ordinarily asked of them. To write a report on a machine with a Pentium II processor, sixty-four megabytes of memory, and an eight-gigabyte hard disk is like leasing the space shuttle to fly from New York to Boston to catch a Celtics game. Though there are those who wouldn't hesitate to do such a thing if they could afford it (or get it subsidized, which is more to the point), we follow their lead at great peril. The computer industry itself is beginning to recognize the foolishness of placing such computing power on every office worker's desk. Oracle, the world's premier manufacturer of data-base management systems; Sun Microsystems, a maker of powerful and highly respected engineering workstations; and IBM itself are arguing that a substantially scaled-down network computer, costing under $1,000, would serve corporate users better than the monsters necessary to run Microsoft's products.

34   Please don't misunderstand. This is not a neo-Luddite plea to toss computers out the window. I am, after all, a computer science professor, and I am certainly not ready (as the militias in my part of the country put it) to get off the grid. Further, the social benefits of computing—from telecommunications to business transactions to medicine to science—are well known. This essay is simply a plea to think reasonably about these machines, to recognize the hucksterism in the hysterical cries for computer literacy, to steel ourselves against the urge to keep throwing money at Redmond and Silicon Valley.

35   Putting microcomputers in their place will also have a salutary effect on my discipline. We in computer science could then begin to claim that our field—like mathematics, like English literature, like philosophy—is a marvelous human creation whose study is its own reward. To study computer science calls for concentration, discipline, even some amount of deferred gratification, but it requires neither Windows 98, nor a four-hundred-megahertz Pentium II processor, nor a graphical Web browser. Though I am tempted, I will not go so far as to say that the introductory study of computer science requires no computing equipment at all (though Alan Turing did do some pretty impressive work without a microcomputer budget). We do seem, however, to have confused the violin with the concerto, the pencil with the theorem, and the dancer with the dance.

36   I am afraid that we in computing have made a Faustian bargain. In exchange for riches, we are condemned to a lifetime of conversations about the World Wide Web. An eternity in hell with Dr. Faustus, suffering the torments of demons, would be an afternoon in the park by comparison.

Content

1. To what "mischief" is De Palma referring when he writes, "The mischief is not in the computer itself, but in the ideology that surrounds it" (¶ 3)? What is "ideology" and what does it have to do with the use of computers?

2. De Palma claims that the "notion that prosperity follows computing" is the result of "a fully formed mythology" (¶ 8). What series of interlocking processes does he identify as contributing to this mythology?

3. Why does De Palma claim that writing "a report on a machine with a Pentium II processor, sixty-four megabytes of memory, and an eight-gigabyte hard disk is like leasing the space shuttle to fly from New York to Boston to catch a Celtics game" (¶ 33)? This comparison embeds an ethic of process, a goodness of fit between the process and the product; explain.

Strategies/Structures

4. De Palma's essay is divided into six sections (of which four are included in this excerpt), each section contributing to his discussion of how we got into what he calls "a sorry state" (¶ 5). Identify the specific topic (or variation on the main topic) each section is concerned with, and consider the effect their order has on De Palma's audience. Would a different order of presentation have been equally as effective?

5. Why does De Palma wait until paragraphs 27–32 to sum up his complex argument? Why not start with a summary in paragraph 1 and work from there?

Language

6. What does De Palma mean by "It's a tale of alchemical transmutation if ever there was one" in relation to the vast accumulation of wealth by some Microsoft entrepreneurs (¶ 15)? What is "alchemical transmutation" and why does De Palma use such a metaphor to explain the process underlying this accumulation of wealth? This essay was published in 1999. Would the steep decline of many Internet startups and even established companies since then require a different metaphor, or does "alchemy" still fit?

7. Consider the level of language in De Palma's essay. Is it highly technical? Formal, informal, or academic? Does it vary according to sections? Is it accessible to the average reader who is not a computer expert? What does he do, in illustrations as well as in examples, to make the essay reader friendly?

For Writing

8. Write an essay that considers the way you and selected family members or friends use computers. What are your most frequent uses? How much time do you spend on the computer (including online) in an average day or week? Do you consider computers essential to your own life and work? How would your life and work change if you didn't have access either to a computer or the Internet? What is the simplest, cheapest computer that could do the work you need it to do? How does this compare with the capability of the machine(s) you actually use?

9. De Palma's essay implies an ethic of process, a goodness of fit between the process and the product or result(s). Using his essay as a model for a critique of an ideology surrounding an entire industry or combination of processes, write an essay on an ethic on the goodness (or badness) of fit between some kind of process and its product or result. For example, learning to play a sport or a musical instrument or to write at the level of a professional superstar may exceed the abilities of most people, who could nevertheless learn to perform well enough to enjoy amateur participation. What's the best ratio of effort spent to accomplishment? Is there an absolute standard, or does this require adaptation to each person's desires and abilities?

10. De Palma's essay was first published in *American Scholar* in 1999, and it reflects the state of the current technology from the beginnings of "the spectacular spread of microcomputers themselves" (in 1993) to the introduction of Windows 98 (¶s 11–15). Work in a group to prepare a report in which each member addresses an issue and its subissues embedded in one paragraph of De Palma's summary, paragraphs 27–32, such as whether microcomputers have really improved productivity (¶ 32). De Palma identifies some possible solutions in paragraph 33 (simpler, cheaper computers). Or each member of the group could select a particular aspect of the same topic and write a position paper on it that addressed the other members' concerns as well.

Because computer technology changes so rapidly, to write appropriately about any of these issues you will need to bring the information in this essay up to date by investigating recent developments in microcomputer technology and capability that bear on your topic. Consider whether this new information reinforces or refutes De Palma's concerns. (*Hint:* What you have read in this book is an excerpt; for the entire essay consult the *American Scholar,* Winter 1999, or the reprint in *Best American Science and Nature Writing, 2000,* ed., David Quammen.)

TOM AND RAY MAGLIOZZI

Tom (born 1938) and Ray (born 1947) Magliozzi were born in East Cambridge, Massachusetts, and educated at the Massachusetts Institute of Technology. Tom worked in marketing; Ray was a VISTA volunteer, and taught junior high school. In 1973 the brothers opened the Good News garage in Cambridge, which Ray continues to operate while Tom teaches business at Suffolk University. Three years later their career as Click and Clack, the Tappet Brothers, began with a local call-in radio show on car repair, "Car Talk," which has become a favorite on National Public Radio since 1987.

Speaking, as one commentator has observed, "pure Bostonese that sounds a lot like a truck running over vowels," and with considerable humor, including unrestrained (some say "maniacal") laughter at their own jokes, the brothers dispense realistic, easy-to-understand advice about how cars work and what to do when they don't, both on the radio and in *Car Talk* (1991), in which the following explanation of "Inside the Engine" appears.

Inside the Engine

A customer of ours had an old Thunderbird that he used to drive back   1
and forth to New York to see a girlfriend every other weekend. And
every time he made the trip he'd be in the shop the following Monday
needing to get something fixed because the car was such a hopeless piece
of trash. One Monday he failed to show up and Tom said, "Gee, that's
kind of unusual." I said jokingly, "Maybe he blew the car up."

Well, what happened was that he was on the Merritt Parkway in   2
Connecticut when he noticed that he had to keep the gas pedal all the way
to the floor just to go 30 m.p.h., with this big V-8 engine, and he figured
something was awry.

So he pulled into one of those filling stations where they sell gaso-   3
line and chocolate-chip cookies and milk. And he asked the attendant to
look at the engine and, of course, the guy said, "I can't help you. All I
know is cookies and milk." But the guy agreed to look anyway since our
friend was really desperate. His girlfriend was waiting for him and he
needed to know if he was going to make it. Anyway, the guy threw open
the hood and jumped back in terror. The engine was glowing red. Somewhere along the line, probably around Hartford, he must have lost all of
his motor oil. The engine kept getting hotter and hotter, but like a lot of
other things in the car that didn't work, neither did his oil pressure warning light. As a result, the engine got so heated up that it fused itself together. All the pistons melted, and the cylinder heads deformed, and the
pistons fused to the cylinder walls, and the bearings welded themselves
to the crankshaft—oh, it was a terrible sight! When he tried to restart the
engine, he just heard a *click, click, click* since the whole thing was seized up
tighter than a drum.

That's what can happen in a case of extreme engine neglect. Most of   4
us wouldn't do that, or at least wouldn't do it knowingly. Our friend didn't
do it knowingly either, but he learned a valuable lesson. He learned that
his girlfriend wouldn't come and get him if his car broke down. Even if
he offered her cookies and milk.

The oil is critical to keeping things running since it not only acts as a lu-   5
bricant, but it also helps to keep the engine cool. What happens is that the
oil pump sucks the oil out of what's called the sump (or the crankcase or
the oil pan), and it pushes that oil, under pressure, up to all of the parts
that need lubrication.

The way the oil works is that it acts as a cushion. The molecules of   6
oil actually separate the moving metal parts from one another so that they
don't directly touch; the crankshaft *journals,* or the hard parts of the crankshaft, never touch the soft connecting-rod *bearings* because there's a film
of oil between them, forced in there under pressure. From the pump.

7   It's pretty high pressure too. When the engine is running at highway speed, the oil, at 50 or 60 pounds or more per square inch (or about 4 bars, if you're of the metric persuasion—but let's leave religion out of this), is coursing through the veins of the engine and keeping all these parts at safe, albeit microscopic, distances from each other.

8   But if there's a lot of dirt in the oil, the dirt particles get embedded in these metal surfaces and gradually the dirt acts as an abrasive and wears away these metal surfaces. And pretty soon the engine is junk.

9   It's also important that the motor oil be present in sufficient quantity. In nontechnical terms, that means there's got to be enough of it in there. If you have too little oil in your engine, there's not going to be enough of it to go around, and it will get very hot, because four quarts will be doing the work of five, and so forth. When that happens, the oil gets overheated and begins to burn up at a greater than normal rate. Pretty soon, instead of having four quarts, you have three and a half quarts, then three quarts doing the work of five. And then, next thing you know, you're down to two quarts and your engine is glowing red, just like that guy driving to New York, and it's chocolate-chip cookie time.

10   In order to avoid this, some cars have gauges and some have warning lights; some people call them "idiot lights." Actually, we prefer to reverse it and call them "idiot gauges." I think gauges are bad. When you drive a car—maybe I'm weird about this—I think it's a good idea to look at the road most of the time. And you can't look at the road if you're busy looking at a bunch of gauges. It's the same objection we have to these stupid radios today that have so damn many buttons and slides and digital scanners and so forth that you need a copilot to change stations. Remember when you just turned a knob?

11   Not that gauges are bad in and of themselves. I think if you have your choice, what you want is idiot lights—or what we call "genius lights"—and gauges too. It's nice to have a gauge that you can kind of keep an eye on for an overview of what's going on. For example, if you know that your engine typically runs at 215 degrees and on this particular day, which is not abnormally hot, it's running at 220 or 225, you might suspect that something is wrong and get it looked at before your radiator boils over.

12   On the other hand, if that gauge was the only thing you had to rely on and you didn't have a light to alert you when something was going wrong, then you'd look at the thing all the time, especially if your engine had melted on you once. In that case, why don't you take the bus? Because you're not going to be a very good driver, spending most of your time looking at the gauges.

13   Incidentally, if that oil warning light ever comes on, shut the engine off! We don't mean that you should shut it off in rush-hour traffic when you're in the passing lane. Use all necessary caution and get the thing over to the

breakdown lane. But don't think you can limp to the next exit, because you can't. Spend the money to get towed and you may save the engine.

It's a little-known fact that the oil light does *not* signify whether or not you have oil in the engine. The oil warning light is really monitoring the oil *pressure.* Of course, if you have no oil, you'll have no oil pressure, so the light will be on. But it's also possible to have plenty of oil and an oil pump that's not working for one reason or another. In this event, a new pump would fix the problem, but if you were to drive the car (saying, "It must be a bad light, I just checked the oil!") you'd melt the motor.   14

So if the oil warning light comes on, even if you just had an oil change and the oil is right up to the full mark on the dipstick and is nice and clean—don't drive the car!   15

Here's another piece of useful info. When you turn the key to the "on" position, all the little warning lights *should light up:* the temperature light, the oil light, whatever other lights you may have. Because that is the *test mode* for these lights. If those lights *don't* light up when you turn the key to the "on" position (just before you turn it all the way to start the car), does that mean you're out of oil? No. It means that something is wrong with the warning light itself. If the light doesn't work then, it's not going to work at all. Like when you need it, for example.   16

One more thing about oil: overfilling is just as bad as underfilling. Can you really have too much of a good thing? you ask. Yes. If you're half a quart or even a quart overfilled, it's not a big deal, and I wouldn't be afraid to drive the car under those circumstances. But if you're a quart and a half or two quarts or more overfilled, you could have so much oil in the crankcase that the spinning crankshaft is going to hit the oil and turn it into suds. It's impossible for the pump to pump suds, so you'll ruin the motor. It's kind of like a front-loading washing machine that goes berserk and spills suds all over the floor when you put too much detergent in. That's what happens to your motor oil when you overfill it.   17

With all this talk about things that can go wrong, let's not forget that modern engines are pretty incredible. People always say, "You know, the cars of yesteryear were wonderful. They built cars rough and tough and durable in those days."   18

Horsefeathers.   19

The cars of yesteryear were nicer to look at because they were very individualistic. They were all different, and some were even beautiful. In fact, when I was a kid, you could tell the year, make, and model of a car from a hundred paces just by looking at the taillights or the grille.   20

Nowadays, they all look the same. They're like jellybeans on wheels. You can't tell one from the other. But the truth is, they've never made engines as good as they make them today. Think of the abuse they take!   21

None of the cars of yesteryear was capable of going 60 or 70 miles per hour all day long and taking it for 100,000 miles.

22   Engines of today—and by today I mean from the late '60s on up—are far superior. What makes them superior is not only the design and the metallurgy, but the lubricants. The oil they had thirty years ago was lousy compared to what we have today. There are magic additives and detergents and long-chain polymers and what-have-you that make them able to hold dirt in suspension and to neutralize acids and to lubricate better than oils of the old days.

23   There aren't too many things that will go wrong, because the engines are made so well and the tolerances are closer. And aside from doing stupid things like running out of oil or failing to heed the warning lights or overfilling the thing, you shouldn't worry.

24   But here's one word of caution about cars that have timing belts: Lots of cars these days are made with overhead camshafts. The camshaft, which opens the valves, is turned by a gear and gets its power from the crankshaft. Many cars today use a notched rubber *timing belt* to connect the two shafts instead of a chain because it's cheaper and easy to change. And here's the caveat: *if you don't change it and the belt breaks, it can mean swift ruin to the engine.* The pistons can hit the valves and you'll have bent valves and possibly broken pistons.

25   So you can do many hundreds of dollars' worth of damage by failing to heed the manufacturer's warning about changing the timing belt in a timely manner. No pun intended. For most cars, the timing belt replacement is somewhere between $100 and $200. It's not a big deal.

26   I might add that there are many cars that have rubber timing belts that will *not* cause damage to the engine when they break. But even if you have one of those cars, make sure that you get the belt changed, at the very least, when the manufacturer suggests it. If there's no specific recommendation and you have a car with a rubber belt, we would recommend that you change it at 60,000 miles. Because even if you don't do damage to the motor when the belt breaks, you're still going to be stuck somewhere, maybe somewhere unpleasant. Maybe even Cleveland! So you want to make sure that you don't fall into that situation.

27   Many engines that have rubber timing belts also use the belt to drive the water pump. On these, don't forget to change the water pump when you change the timing belt, because the leading cause of premature belt failure is that the water pump seizes. So if you have a timing belt that drives the water pump, get the water pump out of there at the same time. You don't want to put a belt in and then have the water pump go a month later, because it'll break the new belt and wreck the engine.

28   The best way to protect all the other pieces that you can't get to without spending a lot of money is through frequent oil changes. The manufacturers

recommend oil changes somewhere between seven and ten thousand miles, depending upon the car. We've always recommended that you change your oil at 3,000 miles. We realize for some people that's a bit of an inconvenience, but look at it as cheap insurance. And change the filter every time too.

And last but not least, I want to repeat this because it's important: 29 Make sure your warning lights work. The oil pressure and engine temperature warning lights are your engine's lifeline. Check them every day. You should make it as routine as checking to see if your zipper's up. You guys should do it at the same time.

What you do is, you get into the car, check to see that your zipper's 30 up, and then turn the key on and check to see if your oil pressure and temperature warning lights come on.

I don't know what women do. 31

Content

1. Are you convinced that the Magliozzi brothers know their subject? Does their explanation of how a car engine works contain sufficient information for you to trust their authority? Why or why not?

2. What assumptions do the authors make about their readers' technical knowledge? Why do they provide basic information (such as how oil works in an engine, ¶s 5–9)? How are they able to do this without either offending their readers' intelligence or boring them?

3. Why do the Magliozzi brothers make a point of dispelling myths about "the cars of yesteryear" in comparison with the "engines of today" (¶s 18–22)?

Strategies/Structures

4. Why do the authors begin their explanation of a process with a story—in this case, a cautionary tale of the guy whose beat-up old Thunderbird had a meltdown on the Merritt Parkway?

5. When writing about science and technology, why is it important to define fundamental terms, even terms readers have heard—and used—many times, such as *motor oil* (¶s 5–9), *gauges* (or *idiot gauges*, ¶s 10–12), and *oil warning light* (¶s 13–15)?

6. What part do cookies and milk play in this story? Does the author's use of humor reinforce or undermine the authority of their explanations? Does their humor help you to understand how an engine works?

Language

7. Typical of science writers, the authors use a number of analogies to explain how oil keeps an engine in good working order ("cushion," ¶ 6; "veins," ¶ 7; "front-loading washing machine" and "suds," ¶ 17). If these analogies help you to understand the subject, explain why they do. If they don't help, why don't they?

8. The authors give commands, such as "Don't drive the car!" when the oil warning light is on (¶ 15), and "Make sure your warning lights work" (¶ 29). Why can they expect readers to react to such commands without being offended?

9. There are two authors. Sometimes they refer to themselves in the plural ("A customer of ours," ¶ 1); but most of the time they use the singular pronoun "I" (¶s 11, 20, and throughout). With what effect? What's the effect of addressing their readers as "you")?

For Writing

10. Write an essay for a nonspecialized audience explaining how a tool, mechanical object, or more abstract process (about which you know a great deal) works and how to get maximum performance from it. Possible topics include: a racing bicycle, a particular exercise machine, a power tool, a kitchen implement, a spread sheet, a particular computer program, management of a particular small business, an election campaign.

11. Authors in the physical or social sciences customarily work in teams, reporting on their collaborative research. In the spirit of this model, collaborate with another equally knowledgeable person or team to explain a technical process for a specialized audience in the same field.

NTOZAKE SHANGE

In 1971, the year after she graduated from Barnard with a B.A. in American Studies, Paulette Williams, daughter of a noted St. Louis surgeon and a social worker, adopted the Zulu name Ntozake Shange (en-toh-ZAH-kee SHAHN-gay), Ntozake meaning "she who comes with her own things" and Shange, "who walks like a lion." "As a feminist I thought it was ridiculous to be named after a boy," she says. Within three years of earning an M.A. from the University of Southern California (1973), her first and most memorable play had been produced, *for colored girls who have considered suicide/when the rainbow is enuf.* It received an Obie award for the best play of 1977 and Tony and Grammy award nominations, and it established Shange as a writer as well as a dancer and an actress who performed in her own work.

Shange's works include over a dozen other plays and dramatic adaptations, ranging from *Boogie Woogie Landscapes* (1978) to an Obie award-winning adaptation of Bertolt Brecht's *Mother Courage and Her Children* (1981). She has written four novels including *Liliane: Resurrection of the Daughter* (1994), seven volumes of poetry, of which *Nappy Edges* (1978) is the best known, and numerous short stories and essays. "What Is It We Really Harvestin' Here?" published in *Creative Nonfiction* in 1998, is characteristic of Shange's free-flowing form and fast-paced conversational style, simultaneously lyrical, comical, and satiric. In the process of explaining how to grow sweet potatoes, mustard greens, and watermelon, Shange incorporates African-American history, social commentary, autobiography, and recipes—American studies with attitude.

What Is It We Really Harvestin' Here?

We got a sayin', "The blacker the berry, the sweeter the juice," which is usually meant as a compliment. To my mind, it also refers to the delectable treats we as a people harvested for our owners and for our own selves all these many years, slave or free. In fact, we knew something about the land, sensuality, rhythm and ourselves that has continued to elude our captors—puttin' aside all our treasures in the basement of the British Museum, or the Met, for that matter. What am I talkin' about? A different approach to the force of gravity, to our bodies, and what we produce: a reverence for the efforts of the group and the intimate couple. Harvest time and Christmas were prime occasions for courtin'. A famine, a drought, a flood or Lent do not serve as inspiration for couplin', you see.

The Juba, a dance of courtin' known in slave quarters of North America and the Caribbean, is a phenomenon that stayed with us through the jitterbug, the wobble, the butterfly, as a means of courtin' that's apparently very colored, and very "African." In fact we still have it and we've never been so "integrated"—the *Soul Train* dancers aren't all black anymore, but the dynamic certainly is. A visitor to Cuba in Lynne Fauley Emery's "Dance Horizon Book" described the Juba as a series of challenges.

> A woman advances and commencing a slow dance, made up of shuffling of the feet and various contortions of the body, thus challenges a rival from among the men. One of these, bolder than the rest, after a while steps out, and the two then strive which shall tire the other; the woman performing many feats which the man attempts to rival, often excelling them, amid the shouts of the rest. A woman will sometimes drive two or three successive beaux from the ring, yielding her place at length to some impatient belle.

John Henry went up against a locomotive, but decades before we simply were up against ourselves and the elements. And so we are performers in the fields, in the kitchens, by kilns, and for one another. Sterling Stuckey points out, in "Slave Culture," however, that by 1794 "it was illegal to allow slaves to dance and drink on the premises . . . without the written consent of their owners," the exceptions being Christmas and the burials, which are communal experiences. And what shall we plant and harvest, so that we might "Hab big times duh fus hahves, and duh fus ting wut growed we take tuh duh church so as ebrybody could hab a pieces ub it. We pray over it and shout. Wen we hab a dance, we use tuh shout in a rinig. We ain't have wutyuh call a propuh dance tuday."

Say we've gone about our owners' business. Planted and harvested his crop of sugar cane, remembering that the "ratio of slaves/sugar was ten times that of slaves/tobacco and slaves/cotton." That to plant a sugar crop we have to dig a pit 3 feet square and a few inches deep into which one young plant is set. Then, of course, the thing has to grow. A mature sugar-cane plant is 3–9 feet tall. That's got to be cut at exactly the right point. Then we've got to crush it, boil it, refine it, from thick black syrup to fine white sugar, to make sure, as they say in Virginia, that we "got the niggah out." Now it's time to tend to our own gardens. Let's grow some sweet potatoes to "keep the niggah alive."

Sweet Potatoes

5 *Like everything else, we have to start with something. Now we need a small piece of potato with at least one of those scraggly roots hanging about for this native Central American tuber. This vegetable will stand more heat than almost any other grown in the United States. It does not take to cool weather, and any kind of frost early or seasonal will kill the leaves, and if your soil gets cold the tubers themselves will not look very good. Get your soil ready at least two weeks before planting, weeding, turning, and generally disrupting the congealed and solid mass we refer to as dirt, so that your hands and the tubers may move easily through the soil, as will water and other nutrients.*

6   *Once the soil is free of winter, two weeks after the last frost, plant the potato slips in 6–12 inch ridges, 3–4.5 feet apart. Separate the plants by 9–12 inches. If we space the plants more than that, our tubers may be grand, but way too big to make good use of in the kitchen. We should harvest our sweet potatoes when the tubers are not quite ripe, but of good size, or we can wait until the vines turn yellow. Don't handle our potatoes too roughly, which could lead to bruising and decay. If a frost comes upon us unexpectedly, take those potatoes out the ground right away. Our potatoes will show marked improvement during storage, which allows the starch in them to turn to sugar. Nevertheless let them lie out in the open for 2 to 3 hours to fully dry. Then move them to a moist and warm storage space. The growing time for our crop'll vary from 95 to 125 days.*

7   *The easiest thing to do with a sweet potato is to bake it. In its skin. I coat the thing with olive oil, or butter in a pinch. Wrap it in some aluminum foil, set it in the oven at 400 degrees. Wait till I hear sizzling, anywhere from 45 minutes to an hour after, in a very hot oven. I can eat it with my supper at that point or I can let it cool off for later. (One of the sexiest dates I ever went on was to the movies to see "El Mariachi." My date brought along chilled baked sweet potatoes and ginger beer. Much nicer than canola-sprayed "buttered" popcorn with too syrupy Coca-Cola, wouldn't you say?)*

Mustard Greens

8 *No, they are not the same as collards. We could say they, with their frilly edges and sinuous shapes, have more character, are more flirtatious, than collards. This green can be planted in the spring or the fall, so long as the soil is workable (not cold).*

It's not a hot weather plant, preferring short days and temperate climates. We can use the same techniques for mustard greens that we use for lettuce. Sowing the seeds in rows 12–18 inches apart, seedlings 4–8 inches apart. These plants should get lots of fertilizer to end up tender, lots of water, too. They should be harvested before they are fully mature. Now, you've got to be alert, because mustard greens grow fast, 25–40 days from the time you set them in the soil to harvest. When it comes time to reap what you've sown, gather the outer leaves when they are 3–4 inches long, tender enough; let the inner leaves then develop more or wait till it's hot and harvest the whole plant.

Now we cook the mustard greens just like the collards, or we don't have to 9 *cook it at all. This vegetable is fine in salads or on sandwiches and soups. If you shy away from pungent tastes, mix these greens with some collards, kale, or beet greens. That should take some of the kick out of them. I still like my peppers and vinegar, though. If we go back, pre-Columbus, the Caribs did, too. According to Spanish travelers, the Caribs, who fancied vegetables, added strong peppers called aji-aji to just about everything. We can still find aji-aji on some sauces from Spanish-speaking countries if we read the labels carefully. Like "La Morena." So appropriate.*

Watermelon

The watermelon is an integral part of our actual life as much as it is a feature of our 10 *stereotypical lives in the movies, posters, racial jokes, toys, and early American portraits of the "happy darky." We could just as easily been eatin' watermelon in D. W. Griffith's "Birth of a Nation" as chicken legs. The implications are the same. Like the watermelon, we were a throwback of "African" pre-history, which isn't too off, since Lucy, the oldest Homo sapiens currently known is from Africa, too.*

But I remember being instructed not to order watermelon in restaurants or 11 *to eat watermelon in any public places because it makes white people think poorly of us. They already did that, so I don't see what the watermelon was going to precipitate. Europeans brought watermelon with them from Africa anyway. In Massachusetts by 1629 it was recorded as "abounding." In my rebelliousness as a child, I got so angry about the status of the watermelon, I tried to grow some in the flower box on our front porch in Missouri. My harvest was minimal to say the least.*

Here's how you can really grow you some watermelon. They like summer 12 *heat, particularly sultry, damp nights. If we can grow watermelons, we can grow ourselves almost any other kind of melon. The treatment is the same. Now, these need some space, if we're looking for a refrigerator-sized melon or one ranging from 25–30 pounds. Let them have a foot between plants in between rows 4–6 feet apart. They need a lot of fertilizer, especially if the soil is heavy and doesn't drain well. When the runners (vines) are a foot to a foot-and-a-half long, fertilize again about 8 inches from the plant itself. Put some more fertilizer when the first melons appear. Watermelons come in different varieties, but I'm telling you about the red kind. I have no primal response to a golden or blanched fleshed melon. Once your melons set on the vines and start to really take up some space, be sure not to forget to water the vines during the ripening process.*

13   *When is your watermelon ripe? You can't tell by thumping it nor by the curly tail at the point where the melon is still on the vine. The best way to know if your melon is ready is by looking at the bottom. The center turns from a light yellow to deep amber. Your melon'll have a powdery or mushy tasteless sorta taste if you let it ripen too long.*

14   *Surely you've seen enough pictures or been to enough picnics to know how to eat a watermelon, so I won't insult you with that information. However, there is a fractious continuing debate about whether to sprinkle sugar or salt on your watermelon slice. I am not going to take sides in this matter.*

15   Some of us were carried to the New World specifically because we knew 'bout certain crops, know 'bout the groomin' and harvestin' of rice, for instance.

> Plantation owners were perfectly aware of the superiority . . . of African slaves from rice country. Littlefield (journalist) writes that "as early as 1700 ships from Carolina were reported in the Gambia River." . . . In a letter dated 1756, Henry Laurens, a Charleston merchant, wrote, "The slaves from the River Gambia are prefer'd to all others with us save the Gold Coast." The previous year he had written: "Gold Coast or Gambias are best; next to them the Windward Coast are prefer'd to Angolas."

16   These bits of information throw an entirely different, more dignified light on "colored" cuisine, for me. Particularly since I was raised on rice and my mother's people on both sides are indefatigable Carolinians, South, to be exact, South Carolinians. To some, our "phrenologically immature brains" didn't have consequence until our mastery of the cultivation of "cargo," "patna," "joponica," and finally Carolina rice, "small-grained, rather long and wiry, and remarkably white" was transferred to the books and records of our owners. Nevertheless, our penchant for rice was not dampened by its relationship to our bondage. Whether through force or will, we held on to our rice-eatin' heritage. I repeat, I was raised on rice. If I was Joe Williams, insteada singin' "Every day, every day, I sing the blues," I'd be sayin', "Oh, every day, almost any kinda way, I get my rice."

17   My poor mother, Eloise, Ellie, for short, made the mistake of marrying a man who was raised by a woman from Canada. So every day, he wanted a potato, some kinda potato, mashed, boiled, baked, scalloped, fried, just a potato. Yet my mother was raising a sixth generation of Carolinians, which meant we had to eat some kinda rice. Thus, Ellie was busy fixing potato for one and rice for all the rest every day, until I finally learnt how to do one or the other and gave her a break. I asked Ellie Williams how her mother, Viola, went about preparing the rice for her "chirren"— a Low-country linguistic lapse referring to off-spring like me. Anyway, this is what Mama said.

Mama's Rice

"We'd buy some rice in a brown paper bag (this is in The Bronx). Soak it in a bit 18
of water. Rinse it off and cook it the same way we do now." "How is that, Ma?"
I asked. "Well, you boil a certain amount of water. Let it boil good. Add your rice
and let it boil till tender. Stirring every so often because you want the water to
evaporate. You lift your pot. You can tell if your rice is okay because there's no
water there. Then you fluff it with a fork. You want every kind, extra, extra, what
you call it. No ordinary olive oil will do.

"Heat this up. Just a little bit of it. You don't want no greasy rice, do you? 19
Heat this until, oh, it is so hot that the smoke is coming quick. Throw in 3–4 cloves
garlic, maybe 1 cup chopped onion too, I forgot. Let that sizzle and soften with ½
cup each cilantro, pimiento, and everything. But don't let this get burned, no. So
add your 4 cups water and 2 cups rice. Turn up the heat some more till there's a
great boiling of rice, water, seasonings. The whole thing. Then leave it alone for a
while with the cover on so all the rice cooks even. Now, when you check and see
there's only a small bit of water left in the bottom of the pot, stir it all up. Turn the
heat up again and wait. When there's no water left at all, at all. Just watch the
steam coming up. Of course you should have a good pegau *by now, but the whole*
pot of your rice should be delicioso, ready even for my table. If you do as I say."

For North Americans, a pot with burnt rice on the bottom is a scary con- 20
cept. But all over the Caribbean, it's a different story entirely. In order to
avoid making *asopao*—a rice moist and heavy with the sofrito or tomato-
achiote mixture, almost like a thick soup where the rice becomes one mass
instead of standing, each grain on its own—it is necessary to let the rice
on the bottom of the pot get a crustlike bottom, assuring that all moisture
has evaporated. My poor North American mother, Ellie, chastises me frequently for "ruining" good rice with all this spice. Then I remind her that
outside North America we Africans were left to cook in ways that reminded us of our mother's cooking, not Jane Austen's characters. The rice
tastes different, too. But sometimes I cheat and simply use Goya's Sazon—
after all, I'm a modern woman. I shouldn't say that too loudly, though
Mathilde can hear all the way from her front porch any blasphemous
notion I have about good cooking. No, it is her good cooking that I am to
learn. I think it is more than appropriate that we know something about
some of the crops that led to most of us African descendants of the Dias-
pora, being here, to eat anything at all.

But rather than end on a sour note, I am thinking of my classes with 21
the great Brazilian dancer, choreographer and teacher Mercedes Baptista
at the now legendary Clark Center. We learned a harvest dance, for there
are many, but the movements of this celebratory ritual were lyrical and
delicate, far from the tortured recounts of EuroAmericans to our "jiga-
boo" gatherings; no gyrations, repetitive shuffling that held no interest.
Indeed, the simple movement of the arms, which we worked on for days

until we got it, resembled a tropical port-à-bras worthy of any ballerina. Our hip movements, ever so subtle, with four switches to the left, then four to the right, all the while turning and covering space. The head leaning in the direction of the hips, the arms moving against it, till the next hip demanded counterpoint.

22   A healthy respect for the land, for what we produce for the blessing of a harvest begot dances of communal joy. On New Year's Eve in the late fifties, we danced the Madison; today it's a burning rendition of "The Electric Slide." Eighty-years-olds jammin' with toddlers after the weddin' toast. No, we haven't changed so much.

Content

1. What's the point of Shange's title? What *is* it "we really harvestin' "?
2. Shange gives directions on how to grow, prepare, and eat several foods—sweet potatoes, mustard greens, watermelon—and how to cook "Mama's Rice." Like many other directions written by experts, these seem easy to follow and the results seem assured. Why are most directions written so simply and positively?
3. "What Is It We Really Harvestin' Here?" was published in *Creative Nonfiction,* a publication usually read by creative writers, not in a home or cooking magazine. Why might this piece appeal to readers who are writers? Or to any readers who don't garden? Or cook? Or eat much " 'colored' cusine"?

Strategies/Structures

4. Shange's planting instructions are presented in a matrix of African-American political and social history (¶s 1–4), family history (¶s 16–17), and autobiography (¶s 20–22). How do these elements make the reading different from the usual instructions on how to perform a process, such as following a recipe or planting a garden?

Language

5. Whom does Shange include in *we?* Is the *we* of the title and "We got a sayin' " (¶ 1, sentence 1), the same as the *we* of "*we* as a people" (¶ 1, sentence 2)? The same as the *we* of "And so we are performers in the fields" (¶ 3, sentence 2)? Why does it matter, to writer and readers, who *we* are?
6. In this essay that is largely written in standard English, what are the effects of using dialect spelling (as in *chirren* [¶ 7]), or omitting the -*g* at the end of *ing* words, as in *puttin'* (¶ 1)? Why does Shange quote entire sentences in dialect: "Wen we hab a dance . . ." (¶ 3)?
7. Why does Shange use dialect much more extensively in the first four paragraphs of the essay than later on? What happens when she inserts a conversational spelling into an otherwise fairly formal sentence: "Yet my mother was raising a sixth generation of Carolinians, which meant we had to eat some kinda rice? (¶ 17, sentence 3)?
8. How does Shange's style suit her subject?

For Writing

9. If you're a competent cook, write out a favorite recipe so others less experienced than you can prepare it. Identify unusual ingredients, the major steps to follow, and also any subprocesses that need to be done to prepare the dish. Have someone read (better yet, try out) your recipe. What questions do they ask? Incorporate the information from your answers into the recipe as you revise it.

10. Explain how to do or make something that's integral to your cultural background(s) (such as how to interpret or perform a particular religious ritual, celebrate a particular holiday, do a particular dance step, play a particular game, perform a specific athletic activity, engage in a flirtation or courtship). Embed your instructions, as Shange does, in a matrix of cultural, family, or personal history—tell some true stories to provide a context for the instructions that will help to explain why certain things are done in a certain way, as well as how.

NING YU

Ning Yu was born in 1955 in Beijing, People's Republic of China, and came to the United States in 1986 for graduate study. He earned a Ph.D. in English from the University of Connecticut in 1993 and is now a professor of English and Chinese literature at Western Washington University.

Ning Yu recounts some of the significant events of his youth in the following prizewinning essay, "Red and Black, or One English Major's Beginning." When he was in fourth grade, his school was closed down as a consequence of the "Great Proletarian Cultural Revolution," which overturned the existing social order. The intellectual class (the "blacks," in Yu's classification scheme) to which Yu's family belonged because his father was a professor of Chinese language and literature, were replaced on their jobs by members of the People's Liberation Army, "the reds," whose status—as we can see from Ning Yu's teachers—was determined by their political loyalty rather than their academic training.

So Ning Yu learned one kind of English at school, the rote memorization of political slogans: "Long live Chairman Mao! Down with the Soviet Neo-Czarists!" He explains that because the Cultural Revolution stifled originality of language, as of thought, "the Cultural Revolution was rightly called the decade of clichés, when people couldn't say what they really wanted to say and therefore used trite phrases to say what they didn't want to say." "Consequently," he says, "I used the clichés deliberately to create a realistic atmosphere for my story, and also ironically to attack the decade of clichés."

Ning Yu learned another kind of English, the rich, imaginative language of high-culture literature, from his father. On the verge of his fourth imprisonment as an intellectual (and therefore by definition subversive), Dr. Yu taught his teenage son the alphabet, some rules for pronunciation, spelling, and grammar, and how to use a dictionary. As he went to prison, he gave Yu a copy of Jane Austen's *Pride and Prejudice* and an old English-Chinese dictionary and told him to translate the novel—which Ning Yu "struggled through from cover to cover" during the nineteen months of his father's incarceration. Ning Yu's essay makes clear the relations among politics, social class, and education under the Maoist regime.

❋ *Red and Black, or One English Major's Beginning*

1   I have always told my friends that my first English teacher was my father. That is the truth, but not the whole truth. It was a freezing morning more than twenty years ago, we, some fifty-odd boys and girls, were shivering in a poorly heated classroom when the door was pushed open and in came a gust of wind and Comrade Chang Hong-gen, our young teacher. Wrapped in an elegant army overcoat, Comrade Chang strode in front of the blackboard and began to address us in outrageous gibberish. His gestures, his facial expressions, and his loud voice unmistakably communicated that he was lecturing us as a People's Liberation Army captain would address his soldiers before a battle—in revolutionary war movies, that is. Of course we didn't understand a word of the speech until he translated it into Chinese later:

> Comrades, red-guards, and revolutionary pupils:
>
> The Great Revolutionary Teacher Marx teaches us: "A foreign language is an important weapon in the struggle of human life." Our Great Leader, Great Teacher, Great Supreme-Commander, and Great Helmsman, Chairman Mao, has also taught us that it is not too difficult to learn a foreign language. "Nothing in the world is too difficult if you are willing to tackle it with the same spirit in which we conquered this mountain."
>
> Now, as you know, the Soviet Social Imperialists and the U.S. Imperialists have agreed on a venomous scheme to enslave China. For years the U.S. Imperialists have brought war and disaster to Vietnam; and you must have heard that the Soviet troops invaded our Jewel Island in Heilongjiang Province last month. Their evil purpose is obvious—to invade China, the Soviets from the north and the Americans from the south through Vietnam.
>
> We are not afraid of them, because we have the leadership of Chairman Mao, the invincible Mao Zedong Thought, and seven hundred million people. But we need to be prepared. As intellectual youth, you must not only prepare to sacrifice your lives for the Party and the Motherland, but also learn to stir up our people's patriotic zeal and to shatter the morale of the enemy troops. To

encourage our own people, you must study Chairman Mao's works very hard and learn your lessons well with your teacher of Chinese; to crush the enemy, you must learn your English lessons well with me.

Then Comrade Chang paused, his face red and sweat beading on the tip of his nose. Though nonplussed, we could see that he was genuinely excited, but we were not sure whether his excitement was induced by "patriotic zeal" or the pleasure of hearing grandiose sounds issued from his own lips. For my part, I suspected that verbal intoxication caused his excitement. Scanning the classroom, he seemed to bask in our admiration rather than to urge us to sacrifice our lives for the Party. He then translated the speech into Chinese and gave us another dose of eloquence:

> From now on, you are not pupils anymore, but soldiers—young, intellectual soldiers fighting at a special front. Neither is each English word you learn a mere word anymore. Each new word is a bullet shot at the enemy's chest, and each sentence a hand grenade.

Comrade Chang was from a "red" family. His name *hong* means red in Chinese, and *gen* means root, so literally, he was "Chang of Red Root." Students said that his father was a major in the People's Liberation Army, and his grandfather a general, and that both the father and the grandfather had "contributed a great deal to the Party, the Motherland, and the Chinese working people." When the "Great Proletarian Cultural Revolution" started, Mr. Chang had just graduated from the Beijing Foreign Languages Institute, a prestigious university in the capital where some thirty languages were taught to people "of red roots." Red youngsters were trained there to serve in the Foreign Ministry, mostly in Chinese embassies and consulates in foreign countries. We understood that Comrade Chang would work only for a token period in our ghetto middle school. At the time, the Foreign Ministry was too busy with the Cultural Revolution to hire new translators, but as soon as the "Movement" was over and everything back to normal, Comrade Chang, we knew, would leave us and begin his diplomatic career.

In the late 1960s the Revolution defined "intellectual" as "subversive." So my father, a university professor educated in a British missionary school in Tianjin, was regarded as a "black" element, an enemy of the people. In 1967, our family was driven out of our university faculty apartment, and I found myself in a ghetto middle school, an undeserving pupil of the red expert Comrade Chang.

In a shabby and ill-heated schoolroom I began my first English lesson, not "from the very beginning" by studying the alphabet, but with some powerful "hand grenades":

> Give up; no harm!
> Drop your guns!

Down with the Soviet Neo-Czarists!
Down with U.S. Imperialism!
Long live Chairman Mao!
We wish Chairman Mao a long, long life!
Victory belongs to our people!

6   These sentences turned out to be almost more difficult and more dangerous to handle than real grenades, for soon the words became mixed up in our heads. So much so that not a few "revolutionary pupils" reconstructed the slogans to the hearty satisfactions of themselves but to the horror of Comrade Chang:

Long live the Soviet Neo-Czarists!
Victory belongs to your guns!

Upon hearing this, Comrade Chang turned pale and shouted at us, "You idiots! Had you uttered anything like that in Chinese, young as you are, you could have been thrown into jail for years. Probably me too! Now you follow me closely: Long live Chairman Mao!"

7   "Long live Chairman Mao!" we shouted back.

8   "Long live Chairman Mao!"

9   "Long live Chairman Mao!"

10   "Down with the Soviet Neo-Czarists!"

11   "Down with the Soviet Neo-Czarists!"

12   Comrade Chang decided that those two sentences were enough for idiots to learn in one lesson, and he told us to forget the other sentences for the moment. Then he wrote the two sentences on the chalkboard and asked us to copy them in our English exercise books. Alas, how could anybody in our school know what that was!

13   I wrote the two sentences on my left palm and avoided putting my left hand in my pocket or mitten for the rest of the day. I also remembered what Comrade Chang said about being thrown into jail, for as the son of a "black, stinking bourgeois intellectual," I grasped the truth in his warning. The two English sentences were a long series of meaningless, unutterable sounds. Comrade Chang had the power to impose some Chinese meaning on my mind. So, before I forgot or confused the sounds, I invented a makeshift transliteration in Chinese for the phonetically difficult and politically dangerous parts of the sentences. I put the Chinese words *qui, mian,* and *mao* (cut, noodle, hair) under "Chairman Mao," and *niu za sui* (beef organ meat) under "Neo-Czarists." "Down with" were bad words applied to the enemies; "long live" were good words reserved for the great leader. These were easy to remember. So I went home with a sense of security, thinking the device helped me distinguish the Great Leader from the enemy.

14   The next morning, Comrade "Red Roots" asked us to try our weapons before the blackboard. Nobody volunteered. Then Comrade Chang began calling us by name. My friend "Calf" was the first to stand up. He did not

What does it mean to become literate? Are there significant differences in this process among cultures, nationalities? Compare your own experience of learning to read and write English or another language with the processes of language learning that Ning Yu describes in "Red and Black."

remember anything. He didn't try to learn the words, and he told me to "forget it" when I was trying to memorize the weird sounds. In fact, none of my classmates remembered the sentences.

My fellow pupils were all "red" theoretically. But they were not Comrade Chang's type of red. Their parents were coolies, candy-peddlers, or bricklayers. Poor and illiterate. Before the 1949 revolution, these people led miserable lives. Even the revolution didn't improve their lives much, and parents preferred their children to do chores at home rather than fool around with books, especially after the "Great Proletarian Cultural Revolution" started in 1966. Books were dangerous. Those who read books often ran into trouble for having ideas the Party didn't want them to have. "Look at the intellectuals," they said. "They suffer even more than us illiterates." They also knew that their children could not become "red experts" like Comrade Chang, because they themselves were working people who didn't contribute to the Party, the Motherland—or to the liberation of the working people themselves.

Thus my friends didn't waste time in remembering nonsense. Still Comrade Chang's questions had to be answered. Since I was the only one in class not from a red family, my opinion was always the last asked, if asked at all. I stood up when Comrade Chang called my name. I had

forgotten the English sounds too, for I took Calf's advice. But before I repeated the apology already repeated fifty times by my friends, I glanced
at my left palm and inspiration lit up my mind. "Long live *qie mian mao!*
Down with *niu za sui!*" My friends stared, and Comrade Chang glared at
me. He couldn't believe his ears. "Say that again." I did. This time my classmates burst into a roar of laughter. "Cut noodle hair! Beef organ meat!"
they shouted again and again.

17   "Shut up!" Comrade Chang yelled, trembling with anger and pointing at me with his right index finger. "What do you mean by 'cut noodle
hair'? That insults our great leader Chairman Mao." Hearing that, the class
suddenly became silent. The sons and daughters of the "Chinese working
people" knew how serious an accusation that could be. But Calf stood up
and said: "Comrade Teacher, it is truly a bad thing that Ning Yu should
associate Chairman Mao with such nonsense as 'cut noodle hair.' But he
didn't mean any harm. He was trying to throw a hand grenade at the
enemy. He also called the Soviets 'beef organ meat.' He said one bad thing
(not enough respect for Chairman Mao) but then said a good thing (condemning the Soviets). One take away one is zero. So he didn't really do
anything wrong, right?"

18   Again the room shook with laughter.

19   Now Comrade Chang flew into a rage and began to lecture us about
how class enemies often say good things to cover up evil intentions. Calf,
Chang said, was a red boy and should draw a line between himself and
me, the black boy. He also threatened to report my "evil words" to the revolutionary committee of the middle school. He said that in the "urgent
state of war" what I said could not be forgiven or overlooked. He told me
to examine my mind and conduct severe self-criticism before being punished. "The great proletarian dictatorship," he said, "is all-powerful. All
good will be rewarded and all evil punished when the right time comes."
He left the classroom in anger without giving us any new hand grenades.

20   I felt ruined. Destroyed. Undone. I could feel icy steel handcuffs
closing around my wrists. I could hear the revolutionary slogans that the
mobs would shout at me when I was dragged off by the iron hand of the
Proletarian Dictatorship. My legs almost failed me on my way home.

21   Calf knew better. "You have nothing to worry about, Third Ass."

22   I am the third child in my family, and it is a tradition of old Beijing
to call a boy by number. So usually my family called me Thirdy. But in my
ghetto, when the kids wanted to be really friendly, they added the word
"ass" to your number or name. This address upset me when I first moved
into the neighborhood. I was never comfortable with that affix during the
years I lived there, but at that moment I appreciated Calf's kindness in
using that affix. Words are empty shells. It's the feeling that people attach
to a word that counts.

23   "I'll be crushed like a rotten egg by the iron fist of the Great Proletarian Dictatorship," I said.

"No way. Red Rooty is not going to tell on you. Don't you know he 24
was more scared than you? He was responsible. How could you say such
things if he had not taught you? You get it? You relax. *Qie mian mao!* You
know, you really sounded like Rooty." Calf grinned.

Although Calf's wisdom helped me to "get it," relax I could not. 25
My legs were as stiff as sticks and my heart beat against my chest so hard
that I could hardly breathe. For many years I had tried to get rid of my
"blackness" by hard work and good manners. But I could not succeed.
No matter how hard I tried I could not change the fact that I was not
"red." The Party denied the existence of intermediate colors. If you were
not red, logically you could only be black. What Chang said proved what
I guessed. But, when cornered, even a rabbit may bite. Comrade Chang,
I silently imagined, if I have to be crushed, you can forget about your
diplomatic career. I created a drama in which Comrade Chang, the red
root, and I, the black root, were crushed into such fine powder that one
could hardly tell the red from the black. All one could see was a dark,
devilish purple.

The next morning, I went to school with a faltering heart, expecting 26
to be called out of the classroom and cuffed. Nothing happened. Comrade
Chang seemed to have forgotten my transgression and gave us three
handfuls of new "bullets." He slowed down too, placing more emphasis
on pronunciation. He cast the "bullets" into hand grenades only after he
was sure that we could shoot the "bullets" with certainty.

Nothing happened to me that day, or the next day, or the week after. 27
Calf was right. As weeks passed, my dislike of Chang dwindled and I
began to feel something akin to gratitude to him. Before learning his English tongue twisters, we only recited Chairman Mao's thirty-six poems.
We did that for so long that I memorized the annotations together with
the text. I also memorized how many copies were produced for the first,
the second, and the third printing. I was bored, and Teacher Chang's
tongue twisters brought me relief. Granted they were only old slogans in
new sounds. But the mere sounds and the new way of recording the
sounds challenged me. Still, as an old Chinese saying goes, good luck
never lasts long.

Forty hand grenades were as many as the Party thought proper for 28
us to hold. Before I mastered the fortieth tongue twister—"Revolutionary
committees are fine"—our "fine" revolutionary committee ordered Comrade Chang to stop English lessons and to make us dig holes for air raid
shelters. Comrade Chang approached this new task with just as much
"patriotic zeal" as he taught English. In truth he seemed content to let our
"bullets" and "hand grenades" rust in the bottom of the holes we dug. But
I was not willing to let my only fun slip away easily. When digging the
holes I repeated the forty slogans silently. I even said them at home in bed.
One night I uttered a sentence as I climbed onto my top bunk. Reading in
the bottom bunk, my father heard me and was surprised. He asked where

I had learned the words. Then for the first time I told him about Comrade Chang's English lessons.

29   Now it may seem strange for a middle school boy not to turn to his family during a "political crisis." But at that time, it was not strange at all. By then my mother, my sister, and my brother had already been sent to the countryside in two different remote provinces. Getting help from them was almost impossible, for they had enough pressing problems themselves. Help from my father was even more impractical: he was already "an enemy of the people," and therefore whatever he said or did for me could only complicate my problems rather than resolve them. So I kept him in the dark. Since we had only each other in the huge city of eight million people, we shared many things, but not political problems.

30   Our home in the working class neighborhood was a single seventeen-square-meter room. Kitchen, bathroom, sitting room, study, bedroom, all in one. There was no ceiling, so we could see the black beams and rafters when we lay in bed. The floor was a damp and sticky dirt, which defied attempts at sweeping and mopping. The walls were yellow and were as damp as the dirt floor. To partition the room was out of the question. Actually my parents had sold their king-sized bed and our single beds, and bought two bunk beds in their stead. My mother and sister each occupied a top bunk, my father slept in one bottom bunk, and my brother and I shared the other. Red Guards had confiscated and burned almost all of my father's Chinese books, but miraculously they left his English books intact. The English books were stuffed under the beds on the dirt floor. We lived in this manner for more than a year till the family members were scattered all over China, first my siblings to a province in the northwest, and then my mother to southern China. They were a thousand miles from us and fifteen hundred miles from each other. After they left, I moved to the top bunk over my father, and we piled the books on the other bed. Thanks to the hard covers, only the bottom two layers of the books had begun to mold.

31   That evening, after hearing me murmuring in English, my father gestured for me to sit down on his bunk. He asked me whether I knew any sentences other than the one he had heard. I jumped at the opportunity to go through the inventory of my English arsenal. After listening to my forty slogans my father said: "You have a very good English teacher. He has an excellent pronunciation, standard Oxford pronunciation. But the sentences are not likely to be found in any books written by native English speakers. Did he teach you how to read?"

32   "I can read all those sentences if you write them out."

33   "If *I* write them? But can't *you* write them by yourself?"

34   "No."

35   "Did he teach you grammar?"

36   "No."

37   "Did he teach you the alphabet?"

"No."   38

My father looked amused. Slowly he shook his head, and then asked: 39
"Can you recognize the words, the separate words, when they appear in
different contexts?"

"I think so, but I'm not sure."   40

He re-opened the book that he was reading and turned to the first   41
page and pointed with his index finger at the first word in the first sentence, signaling me to identify it.

I shook my head.   42

He moved the finger to the next word. I didn't know that either. Nor   43
did I know the third word, the shortest word in the line, the word made
up of a single letter. My father traced the whole sentence slowly, hoping
that I could identify some words. I recognized the bullet "in" and at once
threw a hand grenade at him: "Beloved Chairman Mao, you are the red
sun *in* our hearts." Encouraged, my father moved his finger back to the
second word in the sentence. This time I looked at the word more closely
but couldn't recognize it. "It's an 'is,'" he said. "You know 'are' but not
'is'! The third word in this sentence is an 'a'. It means 'one.'" It is the first
letter in the alphabet and you don't know that either! What a teacher! A
well-trained one too!" He then cleared his throat and read the whole sentence aloud: "It is a truth universally acknowledged, that a man in possession of a good fortune, must be in want of a wife."

The sounds he uttered reminded me of Chang's opening speech, but   44
they flowed out of my father's mouth smoothly. Without bothering about
the meaning of the sentence, I asked my father to repeat it several times
because I liked the rhythm. Pleased with my curiosity, my father began to
explain the grammatical structure of the sentence. His task turned out to
be much harder than he expected, for he had to explain terms such as "subject," "object," "nouns," "verbs" and "adjectives." To help me understand
the structure of the English sentence, he had to teach me Chinese grammar
first. He realized that the Great Proletarian Culture Revolution had made
his youngest son literally illiterate, in Chinese as well as English.

That night, our English lessons started. He taught me the letters A   45
through F. By the end of the week, I had learned my alphabet. Afterward
he taught the basics of grammar, sometimes using my hand grenades to
illustrate the rules. He also taught me the international phonetic symbols
and the way to use a dictionary. For reading materials, he excerpted simple
passages from whatever books were available. Some were short paragraphs while others just sentences. We started our lessons at a manageable
pace, but after a couple of months, for reasons he didn't tell me till the very
last, he speeded up the pace considerably. The new words that I had to
memorize increased from twenty words per day to fifty. To meet the challenge, I wrote the new words on small, thin slips of paper and hid them in
the little red book of Chairman Mao, so that I could memorize them during the political study hours at school. In hole-digging afternoons I recited

the sentences and sometimes even little paragraphs—aloud when I was sure that Chang was not around.

46   Before the sounds and shapes of English words became less elusive, before I could confidently study by myself, my father told me that I would have to continue on my own. He was going to join the "Mao Zedong Thought Study Group" at his university. In those years, "Mao Zedong Thought Study Group" was a broad term that could refer to many things. Used in reference to my father and people like him, it had only one meaning: a euphemism for imprisonment. He had been imprisoned once when my mother and siblings were still in Bejing. Now it had come again. I asked, "Are you detained or arrested?" "I don't know," he said. "It's just a Study Group." "Oh," I said, feeling the weight of the words. Legally, detention couldn't be any longer than fifteen days; arrest had to be followed by a conviction and a sentence, which also had a definite term. "Just a Study Group" could be a week or a lifetime. I was left on my own in a city of eight million people, my English lessons indefinitely postponed. What was worse, some people never returned alive from "Study Groups."

47   "When are you joining them?"

48   "Tomorrow."

49   I pretended to be "man" enough not to cry, but my father's eyes were wet when he made me promise to finish *Pride and Prejudice* by the time he came back.

50   After he left for the "Study Group," bedding roll on his shoulder, I took my first careful look at the book he had thrust into my hands. It was a small book with dark green cloth covers and gilt designs and letters on its spine. I lifted the front cover; the frontispiece had a flowery design and a woman figure on the upper right corner. Floating in the middle of the flowery design and as a mother, holding a baby, she held an armful of herbs, two apples or peaches, and a scroll. Her head tilted slightly toward her right, to an opened scroll intertwined with the flowers on the other side of the page. On the unrolled scroll, there were some words. I was thrilled to find that I could understand all the words in the top two lines with no difficulty except the last word: EVERYMAN, / I WILL GO WITH THEE. . . .

51   Two months after father entered the "Study Group," I stopped going to his university for my monthly allowance. The Party secretary of the bursar's office wore me out by telling me that my father and I didn't deserve to be fed by "working people." "Your father has never done any positive work," meaning the twenty years my father taught at the university undermined rather than contributed to socialist ideology. To avoid starvation, I picked up horse droppings in the streets and sold them to the farming communes in the suburb. Between the little cash savings my father left me and what I earned by selling dung, I managed an independent life. Meanwhile, I didn't forget my promise to my father. When I saw him again nineteen months later, I boasted of having thumbed his

dictionary to shreds and struggled through Austen's novel from cover to cover. I hadn't understood the story, but I had learned many words.

My father was not surprised to find that I took pleasure in drudgery. He knew that looking up English words in a dictionary and wrestling with an almost incomprehensible text could be an exciting challenge. It provided an intellectual relief for a teenager living at a time when the entire country read nothing but Chairman Mao's works. "Don't worry whether you are red or black," my father said. "Just be yourself. Just be an ordinary everyman. Keep up with your good work, and when you learn English well enough, you'll be sure of a guide 'in your most need.'" 52

Content

1. An essay of dividing its subject often draws rigid boundaries between its categories, so that they are mutually exclusive. Is that true in Ning Yu's essay? Are the "reds" in total opposition to the "blacks"? If there is any overlap or intermingling among these groups, where does it occur (see, for instance, ¶ 15)? Explain your answer.

2. Ning Yu is writing this essay for an American audience that he assumes is relatively unfamiliar with Red Chinese culture. What sorts of information does he need to supply each time he introduces an unfamiliar concept? Has he done this successfully? (An examination of ¶s 1–3 will help focus your answer.)

Strategies/Structures

3. Ning Yu can count on his American readers to make implicit comparisons between his childhood, schooling, and living conditions and their own. What sorts of comparisons do you make, and how do these enhance your understanding of "Red and Black"?

4. Ning Yu depends on Western readers, for political and cultural reasons, to be on the side of those persecuted by the People's Liberation Army, such as his father and, as a consequence, himself. Is this assumption accurate? What evidence from the text corroborates your answer? In what ways do your sympathies determine how you react to the characters and events in Ning Yu's account?

5. This essay gradually shifts from humor to somberness. In what ways does Ning Yu prepare his readers for this shift, and consequently, for the essay's conclusion?

Language

6. Much of the humor in "Red and Black" depends on the students' lack of understanding of the English slogans they are obliged to memorize, and their teacher's failure to teach them how to learn the language. Find some examples of this linguistic humor; why would it strike English-speaking readers as funny, but not the pupils who are trying to memorize the slogans?

7. Ning Yu's essay was written in English, not Chinese. Does his writing give any clues that his native language was not English? Explain your answer.

For Writing

8. Have you ever been given a "label"—based on your race, social class, gender, political or religious affiliation, place of residence (street or area, city or town, state)? If so, what was (or is) that label? How accurate are its connotations? Are they favorable, unfavorable, or a mixture? Does the label stereotype or limit the ways people are expected to react to it? Did (or do) you feel comfortable with that label? If not, what can you do to change it? Write a paper exploring these issues for an audience which includes at least some people whom that label doesn't fit.

9. Have you or anyone you know well ever experienced persecution or harassment—intellectual, political, economic, racial, religious, or for other reasons? If so, write a paper explaining the causes, effects, and resolution (if any) of the problem. If it's extremely complex, select one or two aspects to concentrate on in your paper. Can you count on your audience to be sympathetic to your point of view? If not, what will you need to do to win them to your side?

Additional Topics for Writing
Process Analysis   (For strategies for writing process analysis, see 157)

1. Write an essay in which you provide directions on how to perform a process—how to do or make something at which you are particularly skilled. In addition to the essential steps, you may wish to explain your own special technique or strategy that makes your method unique or better. Some possible subjects (which may be narrowed or adapted as you and your instructor wish) are these:

    a. How to get a good job, permanent or summer
    b. How to live meaningfully in a post 9/11 world (See the chapters "Terrorism" and "World Peace.")
    c. How to scuba dive, hang-glide, rappel, jog, lift weights, train for a marathon or triathlon
    d. How to make a good first impression (on a prospective employer, on a date, on your date's parents)
    e. How to do good for others, short term or long term
    f. How to be happy
    g. How to build a library of books, tapes, videocassettes, or CDs
    h. How to lose (or gain) weight
    i. How to shop at a garage sale or secondhand store
    j. How to repair your own car, bicycle, or other machine
    k. How to live cheaply (but enjoyably)
    l. How to study for a test
    m. How to administer first aid for choking, drowning, burns, or some other medical emergency
    n. How to get rich
    o. Anything else you know that others might want to learn

2. Write an informative essay in which you explain how one of the following occurs or works. Although you should pick a subject you know something about, you may need to supplement your information by consulting outside sources.

    a. How I made a major decision (to be—or not to be—a member of a particular profession, to practice a particular religion or lifestyle . . .)
    b. How a computer (or amplifier, piano, microwave oven, or other machine) works
    c. How a solar (or other) heating system works
    d. How a professional develops skill in his or her chosen field; i.e., how one becomes a skilled electrical engineer, geologist, chef, tennis coach, surgeon . . . ; pick a field in which you're interested
    e. How birds fly (or learn to fly), or some other process in the natural world
    f. How a system of the body (circulatory, digestive, respiratory, skeletal, neurological) works
    g. How the earth (or the solar system) was formed
    h. How the scientific method (or a particular variation of it) functions
    i. How a well-run business (pick one of your choice—manufacturing, restaurant, clothing or hardware store, television repair service . . .) functions

   j. How our federal government (or your particular local or state government) came into existence, or has changed over time

   k. How a system or process has gone wrong (may be satiric or humorous)

   l. How a particular drug or other medicine was developed

   m. How a great idea (on the nature of love, justice, truth, beauty . . .) found
acceptance

   n. How a particular culture (ethnic, regional, tribal, religious) or subculture
(preppies, yuppies, pacifists, punk rockers, motorcycle gangs . . .)
developed

3. Write a humorous paper explaining a process of the kind identified below.
You will need to provide a serious analysis of the method you propose, even
though the subject itself is intended to be amusing.

   a. How to make or do anything badly or inelegantly, without expertise or
ability

   b. How to be popular

   c. How to survive in college

   d. How to withstand an unhappy love affair

   e. How to be a model
babysitter/son/daughter/student/employee/lover/spouse/parent

   f. How to become a celebrity

   g. Any of the topics in Writing Suggestions 1 or 2 above

4. Write a seemingly objective account of a social phenomenon or some other aspect of human behavior of which you actually disapprove, either because the form
and context seem at variance (see Paul De Palma's critique of "computer literacy"
[168–78]), or because the phenomenon itself seems to you wrong, or to cause
problems, or otherwise inappropriate. Justify your opinion (and convince your
readers) through your choice of details and selection of a revealing incident or
several vignettes (brief glimpses of scenes or actions, such as Fadiman provides in
"Under Water" [128–32]). Social and cultural phenomena are particularly suitable
subjects for such an essay—nerd or geek or yuppie or twentysomething behavior,
ways of spending money and leisure time (and foolish, trivial, or wasteful things
to spend it on).

Cause and Effect

Writers concerned with cause and effect relationships ask, "*Why* did something happen?" or "*What* are its consequences?" or both. Both questions can be used to interpret the 1995 photograph of a Bosnian wedding celebration (above), held, judging from the rifle raised aloft by one of the celebrants, in a state of siege. Why did the United States develop as a democracy rather than as some other form of government? What have the effects of this form of government been on its population? Or you, as a writer, may choose to examine a chain reaction in which, like a Rube Goldberg cartoon device, Cause *A* produces Effect *B*, which in turn causes *C*, which produces Effect *D*: Peer pressure (Cause *A*) causes young men to drink to excess (Effect *B*), which causes them to drive unsafely (Cause *C*, a corollary of Effect *B*) and results in high accident rates in unmarried males under twenty-five (Effect *D*).

Although process analysis also deals with events or phenomena in sequence, it focuses on the *how* rather than the *why*. To focus on the process of drinking and driving would be to explain, as an accident report might, how Al C. O'Hall became intoxicated (he drank seventeen beers and a bourbon chaser in two hours at the Dun Inn) and how he then roared off at 120 miles an hour, lost control of his lightweight sports car on a curve, and plowed into an oncoming sedan.

Two conditions have to be met to prove a given cause:

B cannot occur without *A*.
Whenever *A* occurs, *B* must also occur.

Thus a biologist who observed, repeatedly, that photosynthesis *(B)* occurred in green plants whenever a light source *(A)* was present and that it only occurred under this condition could infer that light causes photosynthesis. This would be the immediate cause. The more *remote* or *ultimate cause* might be the source of the light if it were natural (the sun). Artificial light (electricity) would have a yet more remote cause, such as water or nuclear power.

But don't be misled by a coincidental time sequence. Just because *A* preceded *B* in time doesn't necessarily mean that *A* caused *B*. Although it may appear to rain every time you wash your car, the car wash doesn't cause the rain. To blame the car wash would be an example of the *post hoc, ergo propter hoc* fallacy (Latin for "after this, therefore because of this").

Indeed, in cause and effect papers ultimate causes may be of greater significance than immediate ones, especially when you're considering social, political, or psychological causes rather than exclusively physical phenomena. Looking for possible causes from multiple perspectives is a good way to develop ideas to write about. It's also a sure way to avoid oversimplification, attributing a single cause to an effect that results from several. Thus if you wanted to probe the causes of Al C. O'Hall's excessive drinking, looking at the phenomenon from the following perspectives would give you considerable breadth for discussion.

Perspective	*Reason (Attributed cause)*
Al, a twenty-one-year-old unmarried male:	"Because I like the taste."
Al's best friend:	"Because he thinks drinking is cool."
Al's mother:	"Because Al wants to defy me."
Al's father:	"Because Al wants to be my pal."
Physician:	"Because Al is addicted to alcohol. There's a strong probability that this is hereditary."
Sociologist:	"Because 79.2 percent of American males twenty-one and under drink at least once a week. It's a social trend encouraged by peer pressure."
Criminologist:	"Because Al derives antisocial pleasure from breaking the law."
Brewer or distiller:	"Because of my heavy advertising campaign."

All of these explanations may be partly right; none—not even the genetic explanation—is in itself sufficient. (Even if Al were genetically predisposed to alcoholism as the child of an alcoholic parent, he'd have to drink to become an alcoholic.) Taken together they, and perhaps still other explanations, can be considered the complex cause of Al's behavior. To write a paper on the subject, using Al as a case in point, you might decide to discuss all the causes. Or you might concentrate on the most important causes and weed out those that seem irrelevant or less significant. Or to handle a large, complex subject in a short paper you could limit your discussion to a particular cause or type of causes—say, the social or the psychological. You have the same options for selectivity in discussing multiple effects.

The essays that follow treat cause and effect in a variety of ways. Because causes and effects are invariably intertwined, writers usually acknowledge the causes even when they're emphasizing the effects, and vice versa.

Three of the five essays in this section deal with the causes and effects of education, formal and informal, on the students involved and with the consequences of that education—or lack of it—not only to the individual but to society. Jonathan Kozol's "The Human Cost of an Illiterate Society" (210–18) focuses on the enormous social costs—effects—of illiteracy on the 16 million Americans who cannot read or do math well enough to read or interpret prescriptions, insurance policies, medical warnings, bank regulations, telephone books, cookbooks, and a host of other printed materials that provide directions and information for everyday living. Illiteracy causes people to involuntarily relinquish their freedom of choice, their independence, their self-respect, their citizenship. The costs, in human, ethical, social, economic, and political terms, are enormous.

In "Framing My Father" (239–44), Leslie Moore offers a portrait of a complex man, "who has made a name for himself as a son-of-a-bitch." His uncompromising perfectionism as a teacher of his young daughter produces contradictory effects—anger, exhaustion, resistance—and in the process, a high level of learning and respect.

Excerpts from Zitkala-Sa's *The School Days of an Indian Girl* (218–26) illustrate a host of constraints that are placed on Native American children uprooted from their homes and sent far away to boarding schools run by whites. These are reflected in the photograph of young girls from Omaha at a boarding school in Carlisle, PA, in the 1880s (p. 221). Whether the efforts to acclimate these children to white middle-class culture (symbolized by cutting off their braids, making them wear Anglo clothing, and obliging them to speak English rather than their tribal languages) were made from benign or more sinister motives, the effects were the same: alienation from and marginalization in both cultures. In re-creating the child's point of view, intended to represent all children in such schools, the author does not offer solutions, though she implies them.

In "Blaming the Family for Economic Decline" (226–31) Stephanie Coontz argues that Americans consistently confuse effect with cause, wrongly blaming families' economic distress on "divorce and unwed motherhood." She offers considerable evidence to demonstrate that "in the majority of cases, it is poverty and social deprivation that cause unwed motherhood, not the other way around." There is no incentive for poor women to marry poor men. Marriage would not raise the poverty-level wages of undereducated men and women from low-income communities, and even if both parents were present, "two-thirds of the children who are poor today would *still* be poor." The scanty clothing and substandard housing in Walker Evans's striking portrait of a rural American family during the Depression (p. 228) puts a human face on poverty. Two-thirds of all families need more than one income to survive. The majority of single-parent heads of households are women, who are "paid far less than men." A woman's income plummets after divorce, whereas a man's rises. The solution, Coontz says, "does not lie in getting parents back together again but in raising real wages, equalizing the pay of men and women, and making child support . . . more fair."

"The Cancer-Cluster Myth" (231–39) by physician Atul Gawande examines a different sort of confusion between cause and effect. "A community that is afflicted with an unusual number of cancers quite naturally looks for a cause in the environment—in the ground, the water, the air." Because public health officials earnestly investigate outbreaks of other sorts of diseases—"Legionnaires' disease; mercury poisoning from contaminated fish; and HIV infection"—people also expect epidemiologists to come up with causes of local cancer "outbreaks." Citizens have a high stake in finding an environmental cause and thus look for meaning in the random variations that appear by chance in small samples. They misperceive patterns where none exist and become frustrated by the lack of conclusive evidence. The fault doesn't lie in the research but in the way cancer cells behave: "To produce a cancer cluster, a carcinogen has to hit a great many cells in a great many people. A brief, low-level exposure to a carcinogen is unlikely to do the job."

A paper of cause and effect analysis requires you, as a thoughtful and careful writer, to know your subject well enough to avoid oversimplification and to shore up your analysis with specific, convincing details. You won't be expected to explain all the causes or effects of a particular phenomenon; that might be impossible for most humans, even the experts. But you can do a sufficiently thorough job with your chosen segment of the subject to satisfy yourself and help your readers to see it your way. Maybe they'll even come to agree with your interpretation. Why? Because. . . .

STRATEGIES FOR WRITING— CAUSE AND EFFECT

1. What is the purpose of my cause and effect paper? Will I be focusing on the cause(s) of something, or its effect(s), short- or long-term? Will I be using cause and effect to explain a process? Analyze a situation? Present a prediction or an argument?

2. How much does my audience know about my subject? Will I have to explain some portions of the cause and effect relationship in more detail than others to compensate for their lack of knowledge? Or do they have sufficient background so I can focus primarily on new information or interpretations?
3. Is the cause and effect relationship I'm writing about valid? Or might there be other possible causes (or effects) that I'm overlooking? If I'm emphasizing causes, how far back do I want to go? If I'm focusing on effects, how many do I wish to discuss, and with how many examples?
4. Will I be using narration, description, definition, process analysis, argument, or other strategies in my explanation or analysis of cause(s) and effect(s)?
5. How technical or nontechnical will my language be? Will I need to qualify any of my claims or conclusions with "probably," or "in most cases," or other admissions that what I'm saying is not absolutely certain? What will my tone be—explanatory, persuasive, argumentative, humorous?

JONATHAN KOZOL

Kozol's first critique of American education, *Death at an Early Age: The Destruction of the Hearts and Minds of Negro Children in the Boston Public Schools* in 1967, won the National Book Award. Written during the civil rights and school desegregation movements in the 1960s, this book documents the repressive teaching methods in Boston's unintegrated public schools, designed, Kozol claimed, to reinforce a system that would keep the children separate but unequal. Kozol, himself a Harvard graduate (1958), Rhodes Scholar, and recipient of numerous prestigious fellowships (Gugenheim, Rockefeller, and Ford foundations), transcends his privileged background to address what he considers to be the failure of American education to reach minorities and the poor. Even his book on middle-class education, *The Night Is Dark and I Am Far from Home* (1975), expounds on his claim that because the schools reflect the inequities in society at large, the more affluent are educated at the expense of the poor. His recent books, *Savage Inequalities: Children in America's Schools* (1991), *Amazing Grace: The Lives of Children and the Conscience of a Nation* (1995), and *Ordinary Resurrections: Children in the Years of Hope* (2000) extend and reinforce these concerns.

Illiterate America (1985) analyzes the nature, causes, and effects of illiteracy, the ultimate and pervasive failure that, says Kozol, denies sixty million people "significant participation" in the government that "is neither of, nor for, nor by, the people." Kozol concludes with a call to action, a nationwide army of neighborhood volunteers who would teach people to read. Part of his strategy in arousing his own readers to action is to make them understand what it's like to be illiterate, on which this chapter (reprinted in full) focuses. Characteristically, Kozol interprets both the causes of illiteracy and the effects—discussed here—in human, moral terms. Kozol says, "I write as a witness. . . . This is what we have done. This is what we have permitted."

The Human Cost of an Illiterate Society

1   *PRECAUTIONS. READ BEFORE USING.*
Poison: Contains sodium hydroxide (caustic soda-lye).
Corrosive: Causes severe eye and skin damage, may cause blindness.
Harmful or fatal if swallowed.
If swallowed, give large quantities of milk or water.
Do not induce vomiting.
Important: Keep water out of can at all times to prevent contents from violently erupting . . .

WARNING ON A CAN OF DRĀNO

We are speaking here no longer of the dangers faced by passengers on   2
Eastern Airlines or the dollar costs incurred by U.S. corporations and taxpayers. We are speaking now of human suffering and of the ethical
dilemmas that are faced by a society that looks upon such suffering with
qualified concern but does not take those actions which its wealth and ingenuity would seemingly demand.

Questions of literacy, in Socrates' belief, must at length be judged as   3
matters of morality. Socrates could not have had in mind the moral com-
promise peculiar to a nation like our own. Some of our Founding Fathers
did, however, have this question in their minds. One of the wisest of those
Founding Fathers (one who may not have been most compassionate but
surely was more prescient than some of his peers) recognized the special
dangers that illiteracy would pose to basic equity in the political construction that he helped to shape.

"A people who mean to be their own governors," James Madison   4
wrote, "must arm themselves with the power knowledge gives. A popular
government without popular information or the means of acquiring it, is
but a prologue to a farce or a tragedy, or perhaps both."

Tragedy looms larger than farce in the United States today. Illiterate   5
citizens seldom vote. Those who do are forced to cast a vote of questionable worth. They cannot make informed decisions based on serious print
information. Sometimes they can be alerted to their interests by aggressive
voter education. More frequently, they vote for a face, a smile, or a style,
not for a mind or character or body of beliefs.

The number of illiterate adults exceeds by 16 million the entire vote   6
cast for the winner in the 1980 presidential contest. If even one third of all
illiterates could vote, and read enough and do sufficient math to vote in
their self-interest, Ronald Reagan would not likely have been chosen president. There is, of course, no way to know for sure. We do know this:
Democracy is a mendacious term when used by those who are prepared to
countenance the forced exclusion of one third of our electorate. So long as
60 million people are denied significant participation, the government is
neither of, nor for, nor by, the people. It is a government, at best, of those two
thirds whose wealth, skin color, or parental privilege allows them opportunity to profit from the provocation and instruction of the written word.

The undermining of democracy in the United States is one "expense"   7
that sensitive Americans can easily deplore because it represents a contradiction that endangers citizens of all political positions. The human price
is not so obvious at first.

Since I first immersed myself within this work I have often had the   8
following dream: I find that I am in a railroad station or a large department
store within a city that is utterly unknown to me and where I cannot
understand the printed words. None of the signs or symbols is familiar.
Everything looks strange: like mirror writing of some kind. Gradually I
understand that I am in the Soviet Union. All the letters on the walls

around me are Cyrillic. I look for my pocket dictionary but I find that it has been mislaid. Where have I left it? Then I recall that I forgot to bring it with me when I packed my bags in Boston. I struggle to remember the name of my hotel. I try to ask somebody for directions. One person stops and looks at me in a peculiar way. I lose the nerve to ask. At last I reach into my wallet for an ID card. The card is missing. Have I lost it? Then I remember that my card was confiscated for some reason, many years before. Around this point, I wake up in a panic.

9   This panic is not so different from the misery that millions of adult illiterates experience each day within the course of their routine existence in the U.S.A.

10   Illiterates cannot read the menu in a restaurant.

11   They cannot read the cost of items on the menu in the *window* of the restaurant before they enter.

12   Illiterates cannot read the letters that their children bring home from their teachers. They cannot study school department circulars that tell them of the courses that their children must be taking if they hope to pass the SAT exams. They cannot help with homework. They cannot write a letter to the teacher. They are afraid to visit in the classroom. They do not want to humiliate their child or themselves.

13   Illiterates cannot read instructions on a bottle of prescription medicine. They cannot find out when a medicine is past the year of safe consumption; nor can they read of allergenic risks, warnings to diabetics, or the potential sedative effect of certain kinds of nonprescription pills. They cannot observe preventive health care admonitions. They cannot read about "the seven warning signs of cancer" or the indications of blood-sugar fluctuations or the risks of eating certain foods that aggravate the likelihood of cardiac arrest.

14   Illiterates live, in more than literal ways, an uninsured existence. They cannot understand the written details on a health insurance form. They cannot read the waivers that they sign preceding surgical procedures. Several women I have known in Boston have entered a slum hospital with the intention of obtaining a tubal ligation and have emerged a few days later after having been subjected to a hysterectomy. Unaware of their rights, incognizant of jargon, intimidated by the unfamiliar air of fear and atmosphere of ether that so many of us find oppressive in the confines even of the most attractive and expensive medical facilities, they have signed their names to documents they could not read and which nobody, in the hectic situation that prevails so often in those overcrowded hospitals that serve the urban poor, had even bothered to explain.

15   Childbirth might seem to be the last inalienable right of any female citizen within a civilized society. Illiterate mothers, as we shall see, already have been cheated of the power to protect their progeny against the likelihood of demolition in deficient public schools and, as a result, against the verbal servitude within which they themselves exist. Surgical denial of

the right to bear that child in the first place represents an ultimate denial, an unspeakable metaphor, a final darkness that denies even the twilight gleamings of our own humanity. What greater violation of our biological, our biblical, our spiritual humanity could possibly exist than that which takes place nightly, perhaps hourly these days, within such overburdened and benighted institutions as the Boston City Hospital? Illiteracy has many costs; few are so irreversible as this.

Even the roof above one's head, the gas or other fuel for heating that 16 protects the residents of northern city slums against the threat of illness in the winter months become uncertain guarantees. Illiterates cannot read the lease that they must sign to live in an apartment which, too often, they cannot afford. The cannot manage check accounts and therefore seldom pay for anything by mail. Hours and entire days of difficult travel (and the cost of bus or other public transit) must be added to the real cost of whatever they consume. Loss of interest on the check accounts they do not have, and could not manage if they did, must be regarded as another of the excess costs paid by the citizen who is excluded from the common instruments of commerce in a numerate society.

"I couldn't understand the bills," a woman in Washington, D.C., re- 17 ports, "and then I couldn't write the checks to pay them. We signed things we didn't know what they were."

Illiterates cannot read the notices that they receive from welfare offices 18 or from the IRS. They must depend on word-of-mouth instruction from the welfare worker—or from other persons whom they have good reason to mistrust. They do not know what rights they have, what deadlines and re- quirements they face, what options they might choose to exercise. They are half-citizens. Their rights exist in print but not in fact.

Illiterates cannot look up numbers in a telephone directory. Even if 19 they can find the names of friends, few possess the sorting skills to make use of the yellow pages; categories are bewildering and trade names are beyond decoding capabilities for millions of nonreaders. Even the emergency num- bers listed on the first page of the phone book—"Ambulance," "Police," and "Fire"—are too frequently beyond the recognition of nonreaders.

Many illiterates cannot read the admonition on a pack of cigarettes. 20 Neither the Surgeon General's warning nor its reproduction on the package can alert them to the risks. Although most people learn by word of mouth that smoking is related to a number of grave physical disorders, they do not get the chance to read the detailed stories which can document this danger with the vividness that turns concern into determination to resist. They can see the handsome cowboy or the slim Virginia lady lighting up a filter cigarette; they cannot heed the words that tell them that this product is (not "may be") dangerous to their health. Sixty million men and women are condemned to be the unalerted, high-risk candidates for cancer.

Illiterates do not buy "no-name" products in the supermarkets. They 21 must depend on photographs or the familiar logos that are printed on the packages of brand-name groceries. The poorest people, therefore, are denied the benefits of the least costly products.

22   Illiterates depend almost entirely upon label recognition. Many labels, however, are not easy to distinguish. Dozens of different kinds of Campbell's soup appear identical to the nonreader. The purchaser who cannot read and does not dare to ask for help, out of the fear of being stigmatized (a fear which is unfortunately realistic), frequently comes home with something which she never wanted and her family never tasted.

23   Illiterates cannot read instructions on a pack of frozen food. Packages sometimes provide an illustration to explain the cooking preparations; but illustrations are of little help to someone who must "boil water, drop the food—*within* its plastic wrapper—in the boiling water, wait for it to simmer, instantly remove."

24   Even when labels are seemingly clear, they may be easily mistaken. A woman in Detroit brought home a gallon of Crisco for her children's dinner. She thought that she had bought the chicken that was pictured on the label. She had enough Crisco now to last a year—but no more money to go back and buy the food for dinner.

25   Recipes provided on the packages of certain staples sometimes tempt a semiliterate person to prepare a meal her children have not tasted. The longing to vary the uniform and often starchy content of low-budget meals provided to the family that relies on food stamps commonly leads to ruinous results. Scarce funds have been wasted and the food must be thrown out. The same applies to distribution of food-surplus produce in emergency conditions. Government inducements to poor people to "explore the ways" by which to make a tasty meal from tasteless noodles, surplus cheese, and powdered milk are useless to nonreaders. Intended as benevolent advice, such recommendations mock reality and foster deeper feelings of resentment and of inability to cope. (Those, on the other hand, who cautiously refrain from "innovative" recipes in preparation of their children's meals must suffer the opprobrium of "laziness," "lack of imagination . . .")

26   Illiterates cannot travel freely. When they attempt to do so, they encounter risks that few of us can dream of. They cannot read traffic signs and, while they often learn to recognize and to decipher symbols, they cannot manage street names which they haven't seen before. The same is true for bus and subway stops. While ingenuity can sometimes help a man or woman to discern directions from familiar landmarks, buildings, cemeteries, churches, and the like, most illiterates are virtually immobilized. They seldom wander past the streets and neighborhoods they know. Geographical paralysis becomes a bitter metaphor for their entire existence. They are immobilized in almost every sense we can imagine. They can't move up. They can't move out. They cannot see beyond. Illiterates may take an oral test for drivers' permits in most sections of America. It is a questionable concession. Where will they go? How will they get there?

How will they get home? Could it be that some of us might like it better if they stayed where they belong?

Travel is only one of many instances of circumscribed existence. 27 Choice, in almost all of its facets, is diminished in the life of an illiterate adult. Even the printed TV schedule, which provides most people with the luxury of preselection, does not belong within the arsenal of options in illiterate existence. One consequence is that the viewer watches only what appears at moments when he happens to have time to turn the switch. Another consequence, a lot more common, is that the TV set remains in operation night and day. Whatever the program offered at the hour when he walks into the room will be the nutriment that he accepts and swallows. Thus, to passivity, is added frequency—indeed, almost uninterrupted continuity. Freedom to select is no more possible here than in the choice of home or surgery or food.

"You don't choose," said one illiterate woman. "You take your wishes 28 from somebody else." Whether in perusal of a menu, selection of highways, purchase of groceries, or determination of affordable enjoyment, illiterate Americans must trust somebody else: a friend, a relative, a stranger on the street, a grocery clerk, a TV copywriter.

"All of our mail we get, it's hard for her to read. Sittin' down and 29 writing a letter, she can't do it. Like if we get a bill . . . we take it over to my sister-in-law . . . My sister-in-law reads it."

Billing agencies harass poor people for the payment of the bills for 30 purchases that might have taken place six months before. Utility companies offer an agreement for a staggered payment schedule on a bill past due. "You have to trust them," one man said. Precisely for this reason, you end up by trusting no one and suspecting everyone of possible deceit. A submerged sense of distrust becomes the corollary to a constant need to trust. "They are cheating me . . . I have been tricked . . . I do not know . . ."

Not knowing: This is a familiar theme. Not knowing the right word 31 for the right thing at the right time is one form of subjugation. Not knowing the world that lies concealed behind those words is a more terrifying feeling. The longitude and latitude of one's existence are beyond all easy apprehension. Even the hard, cold stars within the firmament above one's head begin to mock the possibilities for self-location. Where am I? Where did I come from? Where will I go?

"I've lost a lot of jobs," one man explains. "Today, even if you're a 32 janitor, there's still reading and writing . . . They leave a note saying, 'Go to room so-and-so . . .' You can't do it. You can't read it. You don't know."

"The hardest thing about it is that I've been places where I didn't 33 know where I was. You don't know where you are . . . You're lost."

"Like I said: I have two kids. What do I do if one of my kids starts 34 choking? I go running to the phone . . . I can't look up the hospital phone number. That's if we're at home. Out on the street, I can't read the sign. I

get to a pay phone. 'Okay, tell us where you are. We'll send an ambulance.'
I look at the street sign. Right there, I can't tell you what it says. I'd have to
spell it out, letter for letter. By that time, one of my kids would be dead . . .
These are the kinds of fears you go with, every single day . . ."

35   "Reading directions, I suffer with. I work with chemicals . . . That's
scary to begin with . . ."

36   "You sit down. They throw the menu in front of you. Where do you
go from there? Nine times out of ten you say, 'Go ahead. Pick out something for the both of us.' I've eaten some weird things, let me tell you!"

37   Menus. Chemicals. A child choking while his mother searches for a
word she does not know to find assistance that will come too late. Another mother speaks about the inability to help her kids to read: "I can't
read to them. Of course that's leaving them out of something they should
have. Oh, it matters. You *believe* it matters! I ordered all these books. The
kids belong to a book club. Donny wanted me to read a book to him. I told
Donny: 'I can't read.' He said: 'Mommy, you sit down. I'll read it to you.'
I tried it one day, reading from the pictures. Donny looked at me. He said,
'Mommy, that's not right.' He's only five. He knew I couldn't read . . ."

38   A landlord tells a woman that her lease allows him to evict her if her
baby cries and causes inconvenience to her neighbors. The consequence
of challenging his words conveys a danger which appears, unlikely as it
seems, even more alarming than the danger of eviction. Once she admits
that she can't read, in the desire to maneuver for the time in which to call
a friend, she will have defined herself in terms of an explicit impotence
that she cannot endure. Capitulation in this case is preferable to self-
humiliation. Resisting the definition of oneself in terms of what one cannot do, what others take for granted, represents a need so great that other
imperatives (even one so urgent as the need to keep one's home in winter's cold) evaporate and fall away in face of fear. Even the loss of home
and shelter, in this case, is not so terrifying as the loss of self.

39   "I come out of school. I was sixteen. They had their meetings. The
directors meet. They said that I was wasting their school paper. I was
wasting pencils . . ."

40   Another illiterate, looking back, believes she was not worthy of her
teacher's time. She believes that it was wrong of her to take up space
within her school. She believes that it was right to leave in order that
somebody more deserving could receive her place.

41   Children choke. Their mother chokes another way: on more than
chicken bones.

42   People eat what others order, know what others tell them, struggle
not to see themselves as they believe the world perceives them. A man in
California speaks about his own loss of identity, of self-location, definition:

43   "I stood at the bottom of the ramp. My car had broke down on the
freeway. There was a phone. I asked for the police. They was nice. They
said to tell them where I was. I looked up at the signs. There was one that

I had seen before. I read it to them: ONE WAY STREET. They thought it was a joke. I told them I couldn't read. There was other signs above the ramp. They told me to try. I looked around for somebody to help. All the cars was going by real fast. I couldn't make them understand that I was lost. The cop was nice. He told me: 'Try once more.' I did my best. I couldn't read. I only knew the sign above my head. The cop was trying to be nice. He knew that I was trapped. 'I can't send out a car to you if you can't tell me where you are.' I felt afraid. I nearly cried. I'm forty-eight years old. I only said: 'I'm on a one-way street . . .'"

Perhaps we might slow down a moment here and look at the reali- 44 ties described above. This is the nation that we live in. This is a society that most of us did not create but which our President and other leaders have been willing to sustain by virtue of malign neglect. Do we possess the character and courage to address a problem which so many nations, poorer than our own, have found it natural to correct?

The answers to these questions represent a reasonable test of our 45 belief in the democracy to which we have been asked in public school to swear allegiance.

Content

1. In earlier eras, explanations for illiteracy often implied considerable blame for the victims—they were seen as stupid, lazy, shiftless, imprudent, living only for the day but with no concern for the future. To what extent do these explanations confuse the effects of illiteracy with the causes? In what ways does Kozol's essay refute these stereotypes? In his opinion, who's to blame?

2. How does Kozol's chapter illustrate his assertion that 60 million illiterates in America are "denied significant participation" in the government "of those two thirds whose wealth, skin color, or parental privilege allows them the opportunity to profit from the provocation and instruction of the written word" (¶ 6)? What's provocative about literacy?

Strategies/Structures

3. Why does Kozol begin his chapter on the costs of illiteracy with the warning on a can of Drāno (a caustic chemical to unclog drains)? Why doesn't he say anything more about it—or about a great many of his other examples? To what extent can these (or any) examples be counted on to speak for themselves?

4. Kozol constructs his argument by using a myriad of examples of the effects of illiteracy. What determines the order of the examples? Which are the most memorable? Where in this chapter do they appear?

Language

5. Why does Kozol use so many direct quotations from the illiterate people whose experiences he cites as examples?

6. What clues in Kozol's language let his readers know that he's sympathetic toward his subjects and angry at the conditions that cause the class of people his readers represent?

For Writing

7. "Questions of literacy, in Socrates' belief, must at length be judged as matters of morality" (¶ 3). Write an essay in which you explain the connection between literacy and a moral society (and the converse, illiteracy and an immoral society), either for an audience you expect to agree with you or for readers who will disagree.

8. In the concluding vignette of the man unable to read the road signs to guide the police to his disabled car on the freeway (¶s 42–43), Kozol implicitly equates literacy with a sense of self-identity, self-location, self-definition. Write an essay exploring the question, How does being literate enable one to realize one's full human potential? When you're thinking about this, imagine what your life would be like if you couldn't read, write, or do math.

====

ZITKALA-SA

Zitkala-Sa (1878–1938) was the first Native American woman to write her autobiography by herself, without the help of an intermediary, such as an ethnographer, translator, editor, or oral historian. This unmediated authenticity gives her work unusual authority. She was a Yankton, born on the Pine Ridge Reservation in South Dakota, daughter of a full-blooded Sioux mother and a white father.

Zitkala-Sa wrote a number of autobiographical essays to call attention to the cultural dislocation and hardships caused when the whites in power sent Native American children to boarding schools hundreds of miles away from home and imposed western culture on them. In her own case, as she explains in "The Land of Red Apples," at the age of eight she left the reservation to attend a boarding school in Wabash, Indiana, run by Quaker missionaries. On her return, "neither a wild Indian nor a tame one," her distress and cultural displacement were acute, as "Four Strange Summers" makes clear. These were originally published in *Atlantic Monthly* (1900), as portions of *Impressions of an Indian Childhood* and *The School Days of an Indian Girl*.

Zitkala-Sa remained unhappily on the reservation for four years, then returned to the Quaker school, and at nineteen enrolled in the Quaker-run Earlham College in Indiana. Her marriage to Raymond Bonnin, a Sioux, enhanced her activism for Indian rights. She served as secretary of the Society of American Indians, and also edited *American Indian Magazine*. As a lobbyist and spokesperson for the National Council of American Indians, which she founded in 1926, she helped to secure passage of the Indian Citizenship Bill and other reforms. Yet she was an integrationist, not a separatist, and attempted to forge meaningful connections between cultures.

from The School Days of an Indian Girl

I   The Land of Red Apples

There were eight in our party of bronzed children who were going East   1
with the missionaries. Among us were three young braves, two tall
girls, and we three little ones, Judéwin, Thowin, and I.

We had been very impatient to start on our journey to the Red Apple   2
Country, which, we were told, lay a little beyond the great circular horizon of the Western prairie. Under a sky of rosy apples we dreamt of roam-
ing as freely and happily as we had chased the cloud shadows on the
Dakota plains. We had anticipated much pleasure from a ride on the iron
horse, but the throngs of staring palefaces disturbed and troubled us.

On the train, fair women, with tottering babies on each arm, stopped   3
their haste and scrutinized the children of absent mothers. Large men,
with heavy bundles in their hands, halted near by, and riveted their glassy
blue eyes upon us.

I sank deep into the corner of my seat, for I resented being watched.   4
Directly in front of me, children who were no larger than I hung themselves upon the backs of their seats, with their bold white faces toward
me. Sometimes they took their forefingers out of their mouths and pointed
at my moccasined feet. Their mothers, instead of reproving such rude
curiosity, looked closely at me, and attracted their children's further notice to my blanket. This embarrassed me, and kept me constantly on the
verge of tears.

I sat perfectly still, with my eyes downcast, daring only now and   5
then to shoot long glances around me. Chancing to turn to the window at
my side, I was quite breathless upon seeing one familiar object. It was the
telegraph pole which strode by at short paces. Very near my mother's
dwelling, along the edge of a road thickly bordered with wild sunflowers,
some poles like these had been planted by white men. Often I had
stopped, on my way down the road, to hold my ear against the pole, and,
hearing its low moaning, I used to wonder what the paleface had done to
hurt it. Now I sat watching for each pole that glided by to be the last one.

In this way I had forgotten my uncomfortable surroundings, when I   6
heard one of my comrades call out my name. I saw the missionary standing very near, tossing candies and gums into our midst. This amused us
all, and we tried to see who could catch the most of the sweet-meats. The
missionary's generous distribution of candies was impressed upon my
memory by a disastrous result which followed. I had caught more than
my share of candies and gums, and soon after our arrival at the school I
had a chance to disgrace myself, which, I am ashamed to say, I did.

7   Though we rode several days inside of the iron horse, I do not recall a single thing about our luncheons.

8   It was night when we reached the school grounds. The lights from the windows of the large buildings fell upon some of the icicled trees that stood beneath them. We were led toward an open door, where the brightness of the lights within flooded out over the heads of the excited palefaces who blocked the way. My body trembled more from fear than from the snow I trod upon.

9   Entering the house, I stood close against the wall. The strong glaring light in the large whitewashed room dazzled my eyes. The noisy hurrying of hard shoes upon a bare wooden floor increased the whirring in my ears. My only safety seemed to be in keeping next to the wall. As I was wondering in which direction to escape from all this confusion, two warm hands grasped me firmly, and in the same moment I was tossed high in midair. A rosy-checked paleface woman caught me in her arms. I was both frightened and insulted by such trifling. I stared into her eyes, wishing her to let me stand on my own feet, but she jumped me up and down with increasing enthusiasm. My mother had never made a plaything of her wee daughter. Remembering this I began to cry aloud.

10   They misunderstood the cause of my tears, and placed me at a white table loaded with food. There our party were united again. As I did not hush my crying, one of the older ones whispered to me, "Wait until you are alone in the night."

11   It was very little I could swallow besides my sobs, that evening.

12   "Oh, I want my mother and my brother Dawée! I want to go to my aunt!" I pleaded; but the ears of the palefaces could not hear me.

13   From the table we were taken along an upward incline of wooden boxes, which I learned afterward to call a stairway. At the top was a quiet hall, dimly lighted. Many narrow beds were in one straight line down the entire length of the wall. In them lay sleeping brown faces, which peeped just out of the coverings. I was tucked into bed with one of the tall girls, because she talked to me in my mother tongue and seemed to soothe me.

14   I had arrived in the wonderful land of rosy skies, but I was not happy, as I had thought I should be. My long travel and the bewildering sights had exhausted me. I fell asleep, heaving deep, tired sobs. My tears were left to dry themselves in streaks, because neither my aunt nor my mother was near to wipe them away.

II   The Cutting of My Long Hair

15   The first day in the land of the apples was a bitter-cold one; for the snow still covered the ground, and the trees were bare. A large bell rang for breakfast, its loud metallic voice crashing through the belfry overhead and into our sensitive ears. The annoying clatter of shoes on bare floors gave us no peace. The constant clash of harsh noises, with an undercurrent

How do you know these girls are Native Americans? What attributes of white middle-class culture are manifest in this photograph? How might the girls be expected to react to these attributes? How might their families be expected to regard the Anglicization of their daughters? How would the school personnel—then and now—interpret the girls' clothing, postures, and hair styles?

of many voices murmuring an unknown tongue, made a bedlam within which I was securely tied. And though my spirit tore itself in struggling for its lost freedom, all was useless.

A paleface woman, with white hair, came up after us. We were placed   16 in a line of girls who were marching into the dining room. These were Indian girls, in stiff shoes and closely clinging dresses. The small girls wore sleeved aprons and shingled hair. As I walked noiselessly in my soft moccasins, I felt like sinking to the floor, for my blanket had been stripped from my shoulders. I looked hard at the Indian girls, who seemed not to care that they were even more immodestly dressed than I, in their tightly fitting clothes. While we marched in, the boys entered at an opposite door. I watched for the three young braves who came in our party. I spied them in the rear ranks, looking as uncomfortable as I felt.

A small bell was tapped, and each of the pupils drew a chair from   17 under the table. Supposing this act meant they were to be seated, I pulled out mine and at once slipped into it from one side. But when I turned my head, I saw that I was the only one seated, and all the rest at our table remained standing. Just as I began to rise, looking shyly around to see how chairs were to be used, a second bell was sounded. All were seated at last, and I had to crawl back into my chair again. I heard a man's voice at one end of the hall, and I looked around to see him. But all the others hung their heads over their plates. As I glanced at the long chain of tables, I caught the eyes of a paleface woman upon me. Immediately I dropped my eyes, wondering why I was so keenly watched by the strange woman. The man ceased his mutterings, and then a third bell was tapped. Every one picked up his knife and fork and began eating. I began crying instead, for by this time I was afraid to venture anything more.

18   But this eating by formula was not the hardest trial in that first day. Late in the morning, my friend Judéwin gave me a terrible warning. Judéwin knew a few words of English; and she had overheard the paleface woman talk about cutting our long, heavy hair. Our mothers had taught us that only unskilled warriors who were captured had their hair shingled by the enemy. Among our people, short hair was worn by mourners, and shingled hair by cowards!

19   We discussed our fate some moments, and when Judéwin said, "We have to submit, because they are strong," I rebelled.

20   "No, I will not submit! I will struggle first!" I answered.

21   I watched my chance, and when no one noticed I disappeared. I crept up the stairs quietly as I could in my squeaking shoes,—my moccasins had been exchanged for shoes. Along the hall I passed, without knowing whither I was going. Turning aside to an open door, I found a large room with three white beds in it. The windows were covered with dark green curtains, which made the room very dim. Thankful that no one was there, I directed my steps toward the corner farthest from the door. On my hands and knees I crawled under the bed, and cuddled myself in the dark corner.

22   From my hiding place I peered out, shuddering with fear whenever I heard footsteps near by. Though in the hall loud voices were calling my name, and I knew that even Judéwin was searching for me, I did not open my mouth to answer. Then the steps were quickened and the voices became excited. The sounds came nearer and nearer. Woman and girls entered the room. I held my breath, and watched them open closet doors and peep behind large trunks. Some one threw up the curtains, and the room was filled with sudden light. What caused them to stoop and look under the bed I do not know. I remember being dragged out, though I resisted by kicking and scratching wildly. In spite of myself, I was carried downstairs and tied fast in a chair.

23   I cried aloud, shaking my head all the while until I felt the cold blades of the scissors against my neck, and heard them gnaw off one of my thick braids. Then I lost my spirit. Since the day I was taken from my mother I had suffered extreme indignities. People had stared at me. I had been tossed about in the air like a wooden puppet. And now my long hair was shingled like a coward's! In my anguish I moaned for my mother, but no one came to comfort me. Not a soul reasoned quietly with me, as my own mother used to do: for now I was only one of many little animals driven by a herder. . . .

VI   Four Strange Summers[1]

After my first three years of school, I roamed again in the Western coun- 24
try through four strange summers.

During this time I seemed to hang in the heart of chaos, beyond the 25
touch or voice of human aid. My brother, being almost ten years my senior,
did not quite understand my feelings. My mother had never gone inside
of a schoolhouse, and so she was not capable of comforting her daughter
who could read and write. Even nature seemed to have no place for me. I
was neither a wee girl nor a tall one; neither a wild Indian nor a tame one.
This deplorable situation was the effect of my brief course in the East, and
the unsatisfactory "teenth" in a girl's years.

It was under these trying conditions that, one bright afternoon, as I sat 26
restless and unhappy in my mother's cabin, I caught the sound of the spirited step of my brother's pony on the road which passed by our dwelling.
Soon I heard the wheels of a light buckboard, and Dawée's familiar "Ho!"
to his pony. He alighted upon the bare ground in front of our house. Tying
his pony to one of the projecting corner logs of the low-roofed cottage, he
stepped upon the wooden doorstep.

I met him there with a hurried greeting, and, as I passed by, he looked 27
a quiet "What?" into my eyes.

When he began talking with my mother, I slipped the rope from the 28
pony's bridle. Seizing the reins and bracing my feet against the dashboard,
I wheeled around in an instant. The pony was ever ready to try his speed.
Looking backward, I saw Dawée waving his hand to me. I turned with the
curve in the road and disappeared. I followed the winding road which
crawled upward between the bases of little hillocks. Deep water-worn
ditches ran parallel on either side. A strong wind blew against my cheeks
and fluttered my sleeves. The pony reached the top of the highest hill, and
began an even race on level lands. There was nothing moving within that
great circular horizon of the Dakota prairies save the tall grasses, over
which the wind blew and rolled off in long, shadowy waves.

Within this vast wigwam of blue and green I rode reckless and in- 29
significant. It satisfied my small consciousness to see the white foam fly
from the pony's mouth.

Suddenly, out of the earth a coyote came forth at a swinging trot that 30
was taking the cunning thief toward the hills and the village beyond. Upon
the moment's impulse, I gave him a long chase and a wholesome fright. As
I turned away to go back to the village, the wolf sank down upon his
haunches for a rest, for it was a hot summer day; and as I drove slowly
homeward, I saw his sharp nose still pointed at me, until I vanished below
the margin of the hilltops.

---

[1] Sections III, IV, and V are omitted.

31   In a little while I came in sight of my mother's house. Dawée stood in the yard, laughing at an old warrior who was pointing his forefinger, and again waving his whole hand, toward the hills. With his blanket drawn over one shoulder, he talked and motioned excitedly. Dawée turned the old man by the shoulder and pointed me out to him.

32   "Oh han!" (Oh yes) the warrior muttered, and went his way. He had climbed the top of his favorite barren hill to survey the surrounding prairies, when he spied my chase after the coyote. His keen eyes recognized the pony and driver. At once uneasy for my safety, he had come running to my mother's cabin to give her warning. I did not appreciate his kindly interest, for there was an unrest gnawing at my heart.

33   As soon as he went away, I asked Dawée about something else.

34   "No, my baby sister. I cannot take you with me to the party to-night," he replied. Though I was not far from fifteen, and I felt that before long I should enjoy all the privileges of my tall cousin, Dawée persisted in calling me his baby sister.

35   That moonlight night, I cried in my mother's presence when I heard the jolly young people pass by our cottage. There were no more young braves in blankets and eagle plumes, nor Indian maids with prettily painted cheeks. They had gone three years to school in the East, and had become civilized. The young men wore the white man's coat and trousers, with bright neckties. The girls wore tight muslin dresses, with ribbons at neck and waist. At these gatherings they talked English. I could speak English almost as well as my brother, but I was not properly dressed to be taken along. I had no hat, no ribbons, and no close-fitting gown. Since my return from school I had thrown away my shoes, and wore again the soft moccasins.

36   While Dawée was busily preparing to go I controlled my tears. But when I heard him bounding away on his pony, I buried my face in my arms and cried hot tears.

37   My mother was troubled by my unhappiness. Coming to my side, she offered me the only printed matter we had in our home. It was an Indian Bible, given her some years ago by a missionary. She tried to console me. "Here, my child, are the white man's papers. Read a little from them," she said most piously.

38   I took it from her hand, for her sake; but my enraged spirit felt more like burning the book, which afforded me no help, and was a perfect delusion to my mother. I did not read it, but laid it unopened on the floor, where I sat on my feet. The dim yellow light of the braided muslin burning in a small vessel of oil flickered and sizzled in the awful silent storm which followed my rejection of the Bible.

39   Now my wrath against the fates consumed my tears before they reached my eyes. I sat stony, with a bowed head. My mother threw a shawl over her head and shoulders, and stepped out into the night.

40   After an uncertain solitude, I was suddenly aroused by a loud cry piercing the night. It was my mother's voice wailing among the barren

hills which held the bones of buried warriors. She called aloud for her brothers' spirits to support her in her helpless misery. My fingers grew icy cold, as I realized that my unrestrained tears had betrayed my suffering to her, and she was grieving for me.

Before she returned, though I knew she was on her way, for she had   41 ceased her weeping, I extinguished the light, and leaned my head on the window sill.

Many schemes of running away from my surroundings hovered   42 about in my mind. A few more moons of such a turmoil drove me away to the Eastern school. I rode on the white man's iron steed, thinking it would bring me back to my mother in a few winters, when I should be grown tall, and there would be congenial friends awaiting me. . . .

Content

1. To an extent, leaving the security of home and its familiar culture to go to school, with its inevitably somewhat different culture, presents problems for any child. To what extent are Zitkala-Sa's memories of being uprooted and sent away to school similar to those of any child in a similar circumstance, and to what extent are they exacerbated by the alien culture to which she is expected to adapt?

2. What was the rationale of those in power for sending Native American children away to boarding school? Why did parents allow their children to be sent away (see "The Land of Red Apples")? In what ways did this contribute to the adulteration and breakup of Native American culture (see all sections)?

3. Historically, the Quakers have a reputation for being respectful of civil rights and very sympathetic to the preservation of minority cultures. Quaker households, for instance, were often places of shelter for slaves escaping along the Underground Railway. Was the Quaker school to which Zitkala-Sa went an exception? What factors influenced her perception of the school when she was in residence and later when she wrote about it?

Strategies/Structures

4. Zitkala-Sa is writing in English for an educated Anglo-American audience in 1900, many of whom might never have met a Native American, and who would have known very little about their schooling. What information does she need to supply to make the context of her narrative clear? Has she done this?

5. Zitkala-Sa's readers might be expected to share the viewpoint of the school personnel, in opposition to her own point of view, both as a character in her own story and the narrator of it. By what means does she try to win readers to her point of view? Is she successful?

Language

6. Why did Zitkala-Sa choose to write primarily in standard English, omitting the stereotypical features whites attribute, rightly or wrongly, to Native American speakers of English as a second language?

7. What are the effects of occasional passages in the language the Anglos attribute to Native Americans? See, for example, "palefaces" (¶ 2 and *passim*); "A few *more moons*. . . . I rode on the white man's *iron steed*, thinking it would bring me back to my mother in a *few winters*" (¶ 42).

8. Examine the language of the last paragraph of "The Cutting of My Long Hair" and analyze it in light of your answers to 1 and 2.

For Writing

9. Today many Native American children living on reservations can go to school there, sometimes from kindergarten through college. Write an essay for parents trying to decide what's best for their children in which you weigh the advantages of cultural integrity versus ghettoization that are inherent in this, or any system, of a closed-culture education—public or private (including parochial schooling). Feel free to draw on your own experiences in school. You may need to do some research on a particular school system to provide information for your argument.

10. As Zitkala-Sa does, tell the story of an experience of cultural displacement that you or someone you know well has experienced. Identify its causes and interpret its consequences, short- and long-term.

═══

STEPHANIE COONTZ

Coontz (born 1944) earned a B.A. at the University of California, Berkeley (1966), and an M.A. at the University of Washington (1970). A faculty member since 1975 at Evergreen State College in Olympia, Washington, her research in history and women's studies coalesce in work intended to correct misconceptions about American families. Her influential research includes *The Way We Never Were: American Families and the Nostalgia Trap* (1992) and *The Way We Really Are: Coming to Terms with America's Changing Families* (1997). Coontz is critical of the nostalgia that she sees as "very tempting to political and economic elitists who would like to avoid grappling with new demographic challenges. My favorite example," she told an interviewer, "is when people get nostalgic about the way elders were cared for in the past. Well, good Lord! Elders were the poorest, most abused sector of the population until the advent of Social Security."

The mythical American family, autonomous and independent, lives in legends from the early Puritans to the midwestern homesteaders to the rugged ranchers who "tamed" the Wild West. But people confuse the effect with the cause; the mythological characteristics of hard work and self-reliance are at odds with the facts—that the American family actually succeeded only with considerable outside help, particularly through federal policies. "Blaming the Family for Economic Decline" is an excerpt from Chapter 7, "Looking for Someone to Blame: Families and Economic Change," in *The Way We Really Are*. Here Coontz examines the popular and media confusion of the relationship between "poverty and single parenthood."

Blaming the Family for Economic Decline

The fallback position for those in denial about the socioeconomic transformation we are experiencing is to admit that many families are in economic stress but to blame their plight on divorce and unwed motherhood. Lawrence Mead of New York University argues that economic inequalities stemming from differences in wages and employment patterns "are now trivial in comparison to those stemming from family structure." David Blankenhorn claims that the "primary fault line" dividing privileged and nonprivileged Americans is no longer "race, religion, class, education, or gender" but family structure. Every major newspaper in the country has published editorials and opinion pieces along these lines. This "new consensus" produces a delightfully simple, inexpensive solution to the economic ills of America's families. From Republican Dan Quayle to the Democratic Party's Progressive Policy Institute, we hear the same words: "Marriage is the best anti-poverty program for children."

Now I am as horrified as anyone by irresponsible parents who yield to the temptations of our winner-take-all society and abandon their family obligations. But we are kidding ourselves if we think the solution to the economic difficulties of America's children lies in getting their parents back together. Single-parent families, it is true, are five to six times more likely to be poor than two-parent ones. But correlations are not the same as causes. The association between poverty and single parenthood has several different sources, suggesting that the battle to end child poverty needs to be fought on a number of different fronts.

One reason that single-parent families are more liable to be poor than two-parent families is because falling real wages have made it increasingly difficult for one earner to support a family. More than one-third of all *two-parent* families with children would be poor if both parents didn't work. In this case, the higher poverty rates of one-parent families are not caused by divorce or unwed motherhood per se but by the growing need for more than one income per household. Thus a good part of the gap between two-parent and one-parent families, which is much higher today than it was in the past, is the consequence rather than the cause of economic decline.

Another reason that one-parent families are likely to be poor is because the vast majority of single-parent heads of household are women, who continue to be paid far less than men. One study conducted during the highest period of divorce rates found that if women were paid the same as similarly qualified men, the number of poor families would be cut in half.

Many single-parent families fall into poverty, at least temporarily, because of unfair property divisions or inadequate enforcement of child support after a divorce. Although the figures were exaggerated in past

How many evidences of poverty can you find in this family portrait?
What might be its causes? What would photographer Walker Evans's
aims be in taking and publishing such a picture? Compare and contrast
this with a favorite photograph of your own family.

studies, the fact remains that women, especially women with children, usually lose income after a divorce. The most recent data show a 27 percent drop in women's standard of living in the first year after divorce and a 10 percent increase in that of men. In 1995, only 56 percent of custodial mothers were awarded child support, and only half of these received the full amount they were due.

6   In these examples, the solution to poverty in single-parent families does not lie in getting parents back together again but in raising real wages, equalizing the pay of men and women, and making child support and maintenance provisions more fair. In many cases, though, parents who don't earn enough to support two households *could* adequately support one. In such circumstances, it may be technically correct to say that marriage is the solution to child poverty. But even here, things are not always so simple.

7   Sometimes, for example, the causal arrow points in the opposite direction. Poor parents are twice as likely to divorce as more affluent ones, and job loss also increases divorce even among nonpoor families. Sociologist Scott South calculates that every time the unemployment rate rises by 1 percent, approximately 10,000 extra divorces occur. Jobless individuals are two to three times less likely to marry in the first place. And regardless of their individual values or personal characteristics, teens who live in

areas of high unemployment and inferior schools are five to seven times more likely to become unwed parents than more fortunately situated teens.

In the majority of cases, it is poverty and social deprivation that cause unwed motherhood, not the other way around. The fall in real wages and employment prospects for youth after 1970 *preceded* the rise in teen childbearing, which started after 1975 and accelerated in the 1980s. Indeed, reports researcher Mike Males, "the correlation between childhood poverty and later teenage childbearing is so strong that during the 1969–1993 period, the teen birth rate could be calculated with 90 percent accuracy from the previous decade's child poverty rate." According to a two-year study conducted by the Alan Guttmacher Institute, 38 percent of America's 15- to 19-year-old youths were poor in 1994. But of the one in forty teens who became an unwed parent, 85 percent were poor. 8

Of course causal relationships seldom flow entirely in one direction. Single parenthood can worsen poverty, educational failure, and low earnings capacity, creating a downward spiral. And I certainly wouldn't deny that values regarding marriage have changed, so that more men and women refuse to get married than in the past. But it's also true, as one poverty researcher has put it, that "almost no one volunteers for roles and duties they cannot fulfill." The fact is that fewer and fewer young men from low-income communities can *afford* to get married, or can be regarded by women as suitable marriage partners. 9

Today the real wages of a young male high school graduate are lower than those earned by a comparable worker back in 1963. Between 1972 and 1994 the percentage of men aged 25 to 34 with incomes *below* the poverty level for a family of four increased from 14 percent to 32 percent. When you realize that almost a third of all young men do not earn more than $15,141 a year, which is the figure defined as poverty level for a family of four in 1994, it's easier to understand why many young men are not rushing to get married, and why many young women don't bother to pursue them. By 1993, nearly half the African-American and Latino men aged 25 to 34 did not earn enough to support a family of four. 10

For African-American families in particular, the notion that family structure has replaced class and race as the main cause of poverty is absurd. The head of the U.S. Census Department Bureau of Marriage and Family Statistics estimates that at least one-half to three-fourths—perhaps more— of the black–white differential in childhood poverty would remain even if *all* children in African-American families had two parents present in the home. Nor do other family and cultural variations explain the high rates of African-American poverty: Youth poverty rates for African Americans have grown steadily over a period during which black teenage birth rates have dropped and high school graduation rates and test scores have risen. 11

The most recent and thorough review of the research on the links between poverty and family structure was issued by the Tufts University Center on Hunger, Poverty and Nutrition in 1995. After reviewing 12 seventy-three separate scholarly studies of the subject, the researchers concluded that "single-parent families are not a primary cause of the overall growth of poverty." Rather, poverty is increasing because of declines in employment, wages, and job training opportunities—"far-reaching changes in the economy . . . which hurt both poor and non-poor Americans." Most poverty, in other words, comes from our changing earnings structure, not our changing family structure.

13   Obviously, single parenthood and family instability intensify preexisting financial insecurity, throwing some people into economic distress and increasing the magnitude of poverty for those already impoverished. And equally obviously, those exceptional individuals who can construct a stable two-parent family in the absence of a stable community or a stable job will usually benefit from doing so. But marriage will not resolve this crisis of child well-being in our country. According to Donald Hernandez, chief of the U.S. Census Department Bureau of Marriage and Family Statistics, even if we could reunite every child in America with both biological parents—and any look at abuse statistics tells you that's certainly not in the best interest of every child—two-thirds of the children who are poor today would *still* be poor.

Content

1. "Most poverty," says Coontz, "comes from our changing earnings structure, not our changing family structure" (¶ 12), as people commonly believe. What kinds of evidence does Coontz provide to support her argument that the causes of family poverty are misunderstood and confused with the effects? Is her evidence convincing?

2. On what basis does Coontz dispute the claim that marriage is "'the best anti-poverty program for children'" (¶ 1)? She argues, "The association between poverty and single parenthood has several different sources, suggesting that the battle to end child poverty needs to be fought on a number of different fronts" (¶ 2). What are these fronts (see ¶ 6)?

3. What does Coontz suggest as appropriate remedies for the problems she identifies?

4. Which groups are responsible for the continued misunderstanding of the causes of poverty in families? Which groups are attempting to redress this misunderstanding—and what are they doing to make changes? In what ways has this essay affected your thinking about the relationship between cause and effect?

Strategies/Structures

5. At what point(s) does Coontz insert herself into her discussion? In what roles does she appear (expert authority, public citizen, private person of humanitarian views, other)? Explain how and why her presence either contributes to, or detracts from, the effectiveness of her argument.

6. Identify some of the places where Coontz uses figures and statistics, and show how these reinforce her point. Why don't these (or any) numbers speak for themselves? What sorts of analyses does the author need in order to give the numbers an eloquent voice?

Language

7. That "correlations are not the same as causes" (¶ 2) is an axiom of logic and of social science. What does this concept mean, and why is it so important? (For clues, see ¶s 3 and 8.)

For Writing

8. The causes of poverty in families may change over time and nationality, but it is a problem that continues to plague many societies. Consider the causes and solutions Jonathan Swift outlines in his "Modest Proposal" (491–99) and write an essay that discusses the similarities and differences between the causes of the poverty Swift identifies and the causes of the poverty with which Coontz is concerned. If you have firsthand knowledge of a particular family or community in which these problems are present, draw on this to illustrate your analysis.

9. As Coontz's essays illustrate, much of the confusion surrounding complex social problems results from a lack of the type of solid evidence she provides in her essay. Identify a commonly misunderstood social problem (such as hate crimes, the causes of illiteracy, or welfare reform) and, with classmates, research additional facets of that problem. Finally, present your findings to your classmates in either an oral or a written report that explains both the misconceptions surrounding the problem and the real causes you have identified through your research.

ATUL GAWANDE

Atul Gawande (born 1965) earned an M.A. in politics, philosophy, and economics from Oxford (1989), an M.D. from Harvard Medical School (1995), and an M.P.H. from the Harvard School of Public Health. He served as senior public health policy advisor during the Clinton administration, and is currently a surgical resident at Brigham & Women's Hospital in Boston, and a staff writer for *The New Yorker*. His collection of essays, *Complications: A Surgeon's Notes on an Imperfect Science* (2002), performs "exploratory surgery on medicine itself, laying bare a science not in its idealized form but as it actually is—complicated, perplexing, profoundly human." Thus in this "unflinching view from the scalpel's edge," Gawande takes readers into dramatic territory, the operating room, "where science is ambiguous, information is limited, the stakes are high, yet decisions must be made."

In "The Cancer-Cluster Myth," which originally appeared in *The New Yorker* (1999), Gawande considers the social implications of cancer-clusters—"communities in which there seems to be an unusual number of cancers"—whose residents suspect environmental factors in the water, soil, or air. However, identifying such environmental causes can be difficult because of the multitude of possible variables, including the length of the victim's exposure to the carcinogen. The costs are high, and the rate of success is nearly zero. Because people, as Gawande says, "have a deep-seated tendency to see meaning in the ordinary [random] variations that are bound to appear in small samples," the communities afflicted become frustrated and suspicious when correlations between, for example, cancer deaths and environmental conditions don't lead to the discovery of the causes.

The Cancer-Cluster Myth

1   Is it something in the water? During the past two decades, reports of cancer clusters—communities in which there seems to be an unusual number of cancers—have soared. The place-names and the suspects vary, but the basic story is nearly always the same. The Central Valley farming town of McFarland, California, came to national attention in the eighties after a woman whose child was found to have cancer learned of four other children with cancer in just a few blocks around her home. Soon doctors identified six more cases in the town, which had a population of 6,400. The childhood-cancer rate proved to be four times as high as expected. Suspicion fell on groundwater wells that had been contaminated by pesticides, and lawsuits were filed against six chemical companies.

2   In 1990, in Los Alamos, New Mexico, a local artist learned of seven cases of brain cancer among residents of a small section of the town's Western Area. How could seven cases of brain cancer in one neighborhood be merely a coincidence? "I think there is something seriously wrong with the Western Area," the artist, Tyler Mercier, told the *Times*. "The neighborhood may be contaminated." In fact, the Los Alamos National Laboratory, which was the birthplace of the atomic bomb, had once dumped millions of gallons of radioactive and toxic waste in the surrounding desert, without providing any solid documentation about precisely what was dumped or where. In San Ramon, California, a cluster of brain cancers was discovered at a high-school class reunion. On Long Island, federal, state, and local officials are currently spending $21 million to try to find out why towns like West Islip and Levittown have elevated rates of breast cancer.

3   I myself live in a cancer cluster. A resident in my town—Newton, Massachusetts—became suspicious of a decades-old dump next to an elementary school after her son developed cancer. She went from door to door and turned up forty-two cases of cancer within a few blocks of her home. The cluster is being investigated by the state health department.

4   No doubt, one reason for the veritable cluster of cancer clusters in recent years is the widespread attention that cases like those in McFarland

and Los Alamos received, and the ensuing increase in public awareness and concern. Another reason, though, is the way in which states have responded to that concern: they've made available to the public data on potential toxic sites, along with information from "cancer registries" about local cancer rates. The result has been to make it easier for people to find worrisome patterns, and, more and more, they've done so. In the late eighties, public-health departments were receiving between 1,300 and 1,600 reports of feared cancer clusters, or "cluster alarms," each year. Last year, in Massachusetts alone, the state health department responded to between 3,000 and 4,000 cluster alarms. Under public pressure, state and federal agencies throughout the country are engaging in "cancer mapping" to find clusters that nobody has yet reported.

A community that is afflicted with an unusual number of cancers   5 quite naturally looks for a cause in the environment—in the ground, the water, the air. And correlations are sometimes found: the cluster may arise after, say, contamination of the water supply by a possible carcinogen. The problem is that when scientists have tried to confirm such causes, they haven't been able to. Raymond Richard Neutra, California's chief environmental health investigator and an expert on cancer clusters, points out that among hundreds of exhaustive, published investigations of residential clusters in the United States, not one has convincingly identified an underlying environmental cause. Abroad, in only a handful of cases has a neighborhood cancer cluster been shown to arise from an environmental cause. And only one of these cases ended with the discovery of an unrecognized carcinogen. It was in a Turkish village called Karain, where twenty-five cases of mesothelioma, a rare form of lung cancer, cropped up among fewer than eight hundred villagers. (Scientists traced the cancer to a mineral called erionite, which is abundant in the soil there.) Given the exceedingly poor success rate of such investigations, epidemiologists tend to be skeptical about their worth.

When public-health investigators fail to turn up any explanation for the   6 appearance of a cancer cluster, communities can find it frustrating, even suspicious. After all, these investigators are highly efficient in tracking down the causes of other kinds of disease clusters. "Outbreak" stories usually start the same way: someone has an intuition that there are just too many people coming down with some illness and asks the health department to investigate. With outbreaks, though, such intuitions are vindicated in case after case. Consider the cluster of American Legionnaires who came down with an unusual lung disease in Philadelphia in 1976; the startling number of limb deformities among children born to Japanese women in the sixties; and the appearance of rare *Pneumocystis carinii* pneumonia in five young homosexual men in Los Angeles in 1981. All these clusters prompted what are called "hot-pursuit investigations" by public-health authorities, and all resulted in the definitive identification of a cause: namely, *Legionella* pneumonitis, or Legionnaires' disease; mercury poisoning from contaminated fish; and HIV infection. In fact, successful hot-pursuit investigations of disease clusters take place almost every day. A typical recent issue of the Centers for Disease Control's *Morbidity and Mortality Weekly Report* described a cluster of six patients who developed muscle pain after eating fried fish. Investigation by health authorities identified the condition as Haff disease, which is caused by a toxin sometimes present in buffalo fish. Four of the cases were traced to a single Louisiana wholesaler, whose suppliers fished the same tributaries of the Mississippi River.

7   What's more, for centuries scientists have succeeded in tracking down the causes of clusters of cancers that aren't residential. In 1775 the surgeon Percivall Pott discovered a cluster of scrotal-cancer cases among London chimney sweeps. It was common practice then for young boys to do their job naked, the better to slither down chimneys, and so high concentrations of carcinogenic coal dust would accumulate in the ridges of their scrota. Pott's chimney sweeps proved to be a classic example of an "occupational" cluster. Scientists have also been successful in investigating so-called medical clusters. In the late 1960s, for example, the pathologist Arthur Herbst was surprised to come across eight women between the ages of fifteen and twenty-two who had clear-cell adenocarcinoma, a type of cervical cancer that had never been seen in women so young. In 1971 he published a study linking the cases to an anti-miscarriage drug called diethylstilbestrol, or DES, which the mothers of these women had taken during pregnancy. Subsequent studies confirmed the link with DES, which was taken by some 5 million pregnant women between 1938 and 1971. The investigation of medical and occupational cancer clusters has led to the discovery of dozens of carcinogens, including asbestos, vinyl chloride, and certain artificial dyes.

8   So why don't hot-pursuit investigations of neighborhood cancer clusters yield such successes? For one thing, many clusters fall apart simply because they violate basic rules of cancer behavior. Cancer develops when a cell starts multiplying out of control, and the process by which this happens isn't straightforward. A carcinogen doesn't just flip some cancer switch to "on." Cells have a variety of genes that keep them functioning normally, and it takes an almost chance combination of successive mutations in these genes—multiple "hits," as cancer biologists put it—to make a cell cancerous rather than simply killing it. A carcinogen provides one hit. Other hits may come from a genetic defect, a further environmental exposure, a spontaneous mutation. Even when people have been subjected to a heavy dose of a carcinogen and many cells have been damaged, they will not all get cancer. (For example, DES causes clear-cell adenocarcinoma in only one out of a thousand women exposed to it in utero.) As a rule, it takes a long time before a cell receives enough hits to produce the cancer, and so, unlike infections or acute toxic reactions, the effect of a carcinogen

in a community won't be seen for years. Besides, in a mobile society like ours, cancer victims who seem to be clustered may not all have lived in an area long enough for their cancers to have a common cause.

To produce a cancer cluster, a carcinogen has to hit a great many 9 cells in a great many people. A brief, low-level exposure to a carcinogen is unlikely to do the job. Raymond Richard Neutra has calculated that for a carcinogen to produce a sevenfold increase in the occurrence of a cancer (a rate of increase not considered particularly high by epidemiologists) a population would have to be exposed to 70 percent of the maximum tolerated dose in the course of a full year, or the equivalent. "This kind of exposure is credible as part of chemotherapy or in some work settings," he wrote in a 1990 paper, "but it must be very rare for most neighborhood and school settings." For that reason, investigations of occupational cancer clusters have been vastly more successful than investigations of residential cancer clusters.

Matters are further complicated by the fact that cancer isn't one dis- 10 ease. What turns a breast cell into breast cancer isn't what turns a white blood cell into leukemia: the precise combination of hits varies. Yet some clusters lump together people with tumors that have entirely different biologies and are unlikely to have the same cause. The cluster in McFarland, for example, involved eleven children with nine kinds of cancer. Some of the brain-cancer cases in the Los Alamos cluster were really cancers of other organs that had metastasized to the brain.

If true neighborhood clusters—that is, local clusters arising from a com- 11 mon environmental cause—are so rare, why do we see so many? In a sense, we're programmed to: nearly all of them are the result of almost irresistible errors in perception. In a pioneering article published in 1971, the cognitive psychologists Daniel Kahneman and Amos Tversky identified a systematic error in human judgment, which they called the Belief in the Law of Small Numbers. People assume that the pattern of a large population will be replicated in all its subsets. But clusters will occur simply through chance. After seeing a long sequence of red on the roulette wheel, people find it hard to resist the idea that black is "due"—or else they start to wonder whether the wheel is rigged. We assume that a sequence of R-R-R-R-R-R is somehow less random than, say, R-R-B-R-B-B. But the two sequences are equally likely. (Casinos make a lot of money from the Belief in the Law of Small Numbers.) Truly random patterns often don't appear random to us. The statistician William Feller studied one classic example. During the Germans' intensive bombing of South London in the Second World War, a few areas were hit several times and others were not hit at all. The places that were not hit seemed to have been deliberately spared, and, Kahneman says, people became convinced that those places were where the Germans had their spies. When Feller analyzed the statistics of the bomb hits, however, he found that the distribution matched a random pattern.

12   Daniel Kahneman himself was involved in a similar case. "During the Yom Kippur War, in 1973, I was approached by people in the Israeli Air Force," he told me. "They had two squads that had left base, and when the squads came back one had lost four planes and the other had lost none. They wanted to investigate for all kinds of differences between the squadrons, like whether pilots in one squadron had seen their wives more than in the other. I told them to stop wasting their time." A difference of four lost planes could easily have occurred by chance. Yet Kahneman knew that if Air Force officials investigated they would inevitably find some measurable differences between the squadrons and feel compelled to act on them.

13   Human beings evidently have a deep-seated tendency to see meaning in the ordinary variations that are bound to appear in small samples. For example, most basketball players and fans believe that players have hot and cold streaks in shooting. In a paper entitled "The Hot Hand in Basketball," Tversky and two colleagues painstakingly analyzed the shooting of individual players in more than eighty games played by the Philadelphia 76ers, the New Jersey Nets, and the New York Knicks during the 1980–1981 season. It turned out that basketball players—even notorious "streak shooters"—have no more runs of hits or misses than would be expected by chance. Because of the human tendency to perceive clusters in random sequences, however, Tversky and his colleagues found that "no amount of exposure to such sequences will convince the player, the coach, or the fan that the sequences are in fact random. The more basketball one watches and plays, the more opportunities one has to observe what appears to be streak shooting."

14   In epidemiology, the tendency to isolate clusters from their context is known as the Texas sharpshooter fallacy. Like a Texas sharpshooter who shoots at the side of a barn and then draws a bull's-eye around the bullet holes, we tend to notice cases first—four cancer patients on one street— and then define the population base around them. With rare conditions, such as Haff disease or mercury poisoning, even a small clutch of cases really would represent a dramatic excess, no matter how much Texas sharpshooting we did. But most cancers are common enough that noticeable residential clusters are bound to occur. Raymond Richard Neutra points out that given a typical registry of eighty different cancers, you could expect 2,750 of California's 5,000 census tracts to have statistically significant but perfectly random elevations of cancer. So if you check to see whether your neighborhood has an elevated rate of a specific cancer, chances are better than even that it does—and it almost certainly won't mean a thing. Even when you've established a correlation between a specific cancer and a potential carcinogen, scientists have hardly any way to distinguish the "true" cancer cluster that's worth investigating from the crowd of cluster impostors.

15   One helpful tip-off is an extraordinarily high cancer rate. In Karain, Turkey, the incidence of mesothelioma was more than *seven thousand times*

as high as expected. In even the most serious cluster alarms that public-health departments have received, however, the cancer rate has been nowhere near that high. (The lawyer Jan Schlichtmann, of *Civil Action* fame, is now representing victims of a cancer cluster in Dover Township, New Jersey, where the childhood-cancer rate is 30 percent higher than expected.)

This isn't to say that carcinogens in the local environment can't raise   16
cancer rates; it's just that such increases disappear in all the background variation that occurs in small populations. In larger populations, it's a different story. The 1986 Chernobyl disaster exposed hundreds of thousands of people to radiation; scientists were able to establish that it caused a more than one-hundredfold increase in thyroid cancer among children years later. By contrast, investigating an isolated neighborhood cancer cluster is almost always a futile exercise. Investigators knock on doors, track down former residents, and check medical records. They sample air, soil, and water. Thousands, sometimes millions, of dollars are spent. And with all those tests, correlations inevitably turn up. Yet, years later, in case after case, nothing definite is confirmed.

"The reality is that they're an absolute, total, and complete waste of tax-   17
payer dollars," says Alan Bender, an epidemiologist with the Minnesota Department of Health, which investigated more than 1,000 cancer clusters in the state between 1984 and 1995. The problem of perception and politics, however, remains. If you're a public-health official, try explaining why a dozen children with cancer in one neighborhood doesn't warrant investigation. According to a national study, health departments have been able to reassure people by education in more than 70 percent of cluster alarms. Somewhere between 1 and 3 percent of alarms, however, result in expensive on-site investigations. And the cases that are investigated aren't even the best-grounded ones: they are the cases pushed by the media, enraged citizens, or politicians. "Look, you can't just kiss people off," Bender says. In fact, Minnesota has built such an effective public-response apparatus that it has not needed to conduct a formal cluster investigation in three years.

Public-health departments aren't lavishly funded, and scientists are   18
reluctant to see money spent on something that has proved to be as unproductive as neighborhood cluster alarms or cancer mapping. Still, public confidence is poorly served by officials who respond to inquiries with a scientific brushoff and a layer of bureaucracy. To be part of a cancer cluster is a frightening thing, and it magnifies our ordinary response when cancer strikes: we want to hold something or someone responsible, even allocate blame. Health officials who understand the fear and anger can have impressive success, as the ones in Minnesota have shown. But there are times when you cannot maintain public trust without acting on public concerns. Science alone won't put to rest questions like the one a McFarland mother posed to the *Los Angeles Times*: "How many more of our children must die before something is done?"

Content

1. Gawande notes, "A community that is afflicted with an unusual number of cancers quite naturally looks for a cause in the environment—in the ground, the water, the air. And correlations are sometimes found: the cluster may arise after, say, contamination of the water supply by a possible carcinogen. The problem is that when scientists have tried to confirm such causes, they haven't been able to" (¶ 5). Since the failure rate for identifying residential cancer clusters is so high, why do people continue to spend a great deal of time and money investigating them?

2. What should point investigators toward the "true" cancer clusters worth investigating and enable them to distinguish these "from the crowd of cluster impostors" (¶s 14–15)?

3. Why do the investigators of local cancer clusters so often confuse causes with effects? (Is that the same as confusing correlation with causation?) What does Gawande mean when he says, "Truly random patterns often don't appear random to us" (¶ 11)?

Strategies/Structures

4. Examine Gawande's evidence. From where does he draw the variety of examples he uses to illustrate his points? Has Gawande persuaded you that "investigating an isolated neighborhood cancer cluster is almost always a futile exercise" (¶ 16)? Would you agree with him if you lived "in a cancer cluster," as Gawande himself does (¶ 3)? Explain your answer.

5. As Gawande notes, "When public-health investigators fail to turn up any explanation for the appearance of a cancer cluster, communities can find it frustrating, even suspicious" (¶ 6). In a sense, Gawande's essay was written to alleviate such frustration and suspicion. How does his organizational strategy add to or detract from his ultimate success?

Language

6. What is the "Texas sharpshooter fallacy" (¶ 14)? Explain why it is or is not an effective analogy for the problem Gawande describes.

7. What is a myth? Why has Gawande entitled his piece "The Cancer-Cluster Myth"? Consider the kind of social myths Coontz investigates in "Blaming the Family for Economic Decline" (226–31). In what ways are they similar to the myths Gawande addresses in his work? In what ways are they different?

For Writing

8. Investigate the occurrence of some unusual phenomenon (cancer clusters in your area—this can be a neighborhood, a town, a county, a state) and the ways in which local or state officials (such as the police, social workers, school officials, public health departments) have handled such occurrences. What does your investigation reveal about its possible causes? Have these been addressed adequately by the investigators? Have they taken all of the major effects into account?

Is their emphasis in the investigation appropriate? If not, what have they missed that you've discovered?

9. How can nonscientists—for instance, the residents of the affected area—deal with local matters of potential life-and-death that depend both on their trust of scientific investigations and the accuracy of these? In respect to the subject of your investigation in #8, write a letter either to your representative in the state legislature or Congress, in which you analyze the appropriateness of the investigators' response in light of budget constraints, public concern, and other possibilities the investigation might have considered. Send a copy to the editor of your local newspaper.

10. Gawande claims that "public confidence is poorly served by officials who respond to inquiries with a scientific brushoff and a layer of bureaucracy" (¶ 18). Write an essay that considers the importance of maintaining public confidence when instances of a major social problem appear, and offer suggestions for doing so.

LESLIE S. MOORE

Moore (born 1954) grew up in California and majored in English at the University of California at Santa Cruz and at Berkeley, earning a B.A. in 1976 and an M.A.T. in 1982. She has served twice in the Peace Corps, first teaching English in Korea, 1977–1979. Six years later, she and her husband joined the Peace Corps together and were sent to Bamako, Mali, to teach composition and literature at the Ecole Normale Supérieure. The Moores then moved to Princeton, Massachusetts, where Leslie worked as a newspaper writer and photographer and later taught high school English. They now live in Brooksville, Maine, where she works for a social service agency.

Two writers influenced Moore's prizewinning "Framing My Father," Eudora Welty (see 22–26) and Scott Russell Sanders. She explains, "I used what Welty said in *One Writer's Beginnings* about the increasing importance of framing scene, situation, implication, and finally, 'a single, entire human being,' as a challenge to push me beyond merely describing scenes and situations to considering implications and to capturing more of the entire human being. Thus, Welty provided the shape for my essay. Sanders taught me another lesson in point of view with his two essays about his father: 'The Inheritance of Tools' (139–46) and 'Under the Influence: Paying the Price of My Father's Booze' (274–86). By first eulogizing his father as a mentor in carpentry and then lamenting his father's alcoholism, Sanders showed me two ways of looking at the same man and the divergent lessons he taught his son. In 'Framing My Father,' I used Sanders' two-pronged approach in reverse, first presenting my father and the lessons he taught me in a negative light, then shifting my perspective to the positive."

❄ *Framing My Father*

> *The frame through which I viewed the world changed too, with time. Greater than scene, I came to see, is situation. Greater than situation is implication. Greater than all of these is a single, entire human being, who will never be confined in any frame.*
> EUDORA WELTY, *One Writer's Beginnings*

First Frame: The Scene

1   My father, fierce as ever, sits in the center of our living room folded into the low-slung chair, his long frame scooped to its elliptical contours, his thin shoulders hunched around his ears, his white beard bristling against his chest. He's reading *The Bourne Ultimatum* by Robert Ludlum. "#1 New York Times Bestseller" announces the front cover; "VINTAGE LUDLUM" proclaims the back. He's wearing white leather athletic shoes, gray warm-up pants, a red-knit shirt with the collar turned up, and black-rimmed reading glasses—full-sized, not half glasses. At his right elbow a computerized chess set stands ready, the little plastic players guarding their squares: black king on white, white king on black, queens, bishops, knights, castles, and pawns ranged around them. To his left the wood stove ticks.

Second Frame: The Situation

2   On his visit to New England from California with his wife of only two months, my father commandeers the best chair in the house. An heirloom from my husband's side of the family, the chair is a citadel of security that no one vacates willingly. "Out!" my father orders the Scottie and she thumps down with a suffering sidelong glance. The Westie suffers his eviction with a great show of terrier ferocity that delights my father. My stepmother keeps out of the fray, opting for the second best chair in the house. Neither my husband nor I have a minute to dispute the chair with my father. My husband's not on vacation. When he's not reading or writing or teaching, he's harvesting firewood, loading stove lengths into the wheelbarrow in the woodlot then wheeling it to the woodshed in our garage. And I'm too busy entertaining—orchestrating meals and planning itineraries. I don't have the leisure to sit in the chair. So my father monopolizes the house favorite for ten days—from Friday, the eve of my April vacation, to Monday, the day I go back to teaching school. He gets up early each morning, brings one armload of wood in from the garage, stokes the stove next to the chair, and folds into it. Then he shifts his attention from bestsellers to chess problems.

Third Frame: The Implication

3   My father dominates our living room with his inertia. He forces us to move around him—around his feet, his books, his games—around a lifestyle that we don't share. Of course my husband and I both read. We have to. We

read for the courses we teach and take. We read our students' papers. We read each other's writing. We read with pencils in hand, underlining, taking notes, commenting in the margins. We read as a discipline. My father reads to escape. He has always read. He warned my mother early that marriage wasn't going to get in the way of his reading; the marriage ended in divorce. He reads widely and eclectically, balancing history, philosophy, and science on the one hand, science fiction, spy thrillers, and mysteries on the other. He used to read with a drink in one hand and a cigar in the other, but he has given up both—for health, not sociability. He avoids what he calls "classical literature," the sort I read. In a bookstore I point out Toni Morrison's *Beloved* but he ignores the suggestion and heads for the bestseller rack.

While my father sits folded into our favorite chair, my husband and 4
I fret over the school work we have to get done this week. My husband is writing papers, working on images of pride in seventeenth-century country house poems and analyzing Hawthorne's rhetorical stance in the introduction to *The Scarlet Letter*. He wants me to critique his writing. I have to wrench my thoughts from hostess problems—how much fresh pasta it takes to feed four, whether my stepmother has enough Swiss almond coffee beans to last the week, when I'll get to the store to buy my father his newspapers—to concentrate on houses of pride and phrases embedded within phrases. Plus I have my own work to do—*Romeo and Juliet* papers to grade and a high school murder mystery I've promised my students I'd write with them—but I don't have the psychic space to start either. Meanwhile my father gives up another game of chess to the computer, stokes the fire, and goes back to *The Bourne Ultimatum.*

"Why doesn't he put on a sweater?" asks my husband. "We've 5
burned more wood this week than we did in January."

We heat our house with wood that my husband cuts on our prop- 6
erty. It's a process that he works at year long and enjoys—felling oak, hickory, and maple with his chainsaw, limbing the trees, pulling and piling the brush to burn later, cutting the wood into stove lengths, stacking it to dry, splitting the dry wood with a sledge and steel wedges, then wheeling it into the woodshed. Once he leaves the full wheelbarrow nosed half-way into the garage. My father doesn't offer to help unload it.

We wait for my father to take an interest in us—to ask what we are 7
teaching, to inquire about books we have read, to wonder what we have written. Instead, near the end of his visit, he offers to buy us things. A microwave. We decline. A telephone answering machine. We shudder. We suggest rose bushes for our garden and he writes a check, then returns to his chair and his thriller.

Fourth Frame: The Human Being

My father has made a name for himself as a son-of-a-bitch. He has spent 8
a lifetime cultivating a fierceness that intimidates adults and terrorizes

children. That's one reason, I'm sure, he gave up pediatrics to go into public health. He honed this fierceness on his own four children. When my brothers and I were growing up, his favorite phrase was "Stop crying or I'll spank you again." His favorite epithet was "You dumb stupe!" We cringed at the sound of his explosive "God-damn-it-all-to-hells!" and ducked out of the reach of his backhands. Recently my father admitted to me that the way he treated us as children would be considered child abuse today.

9   The lessons my father taught me were stamped in fear and humiliation. Somehow I survived. Somehow the lessons stuck. Somehow I am grateful for the things I learned.

10   My father taught me how to body surf at Laguna Beach in Southern California. One moment I would be patting wet sand onto a castle, the next I would be tucked under his arm like a football and carried full speed into the surf kicking and screaming and swallowing salt water. Yet I learned how to body surf. I learned how to get out past the breakers, diving under walls of thundering surf. I learned what to look for in a wave—the green swell on the horizon, the slow build, the fingers of foam tickling the top. I learned how to time my take-off, poised under the wave's foaming lip, arms cocked for their furious windmilling, feet set to kick. I learned how to let the wave take me, my body rigid and horizontal, head jutting out of the wave, one arm straight-fisted before me, the other clasped to my side. Finally I learned how to finish, tucking and rolling out of the breaker as it ground its way onto the shore.

11   When I was an awkward thirteen-year-old seeking acceptance in a new school, my father taught me to throw a softball so that I could try out for Miss Sparks' all-star team. He began our first lesson with an insult. "You throw the ball just like a girl," he told me. "Here!" he ordered. "Hold it like this. Like *this*, I said. *Look* at me!" He taught me to hold the ball between my thumb and two fingers, to draw it back behind my ear, cocking my elbow, curling my arm like a snake ready to strike, then whipping it from my shoulder to my wrist. He also taught me to catch: to scoop up the grounders that skittered across the pavement, to glove the fast balls without flinching, to judge the high flies and get underneath them, to dive for the balls that curved out of reach. Finally he taught me to catch and throw in the same instant, to fire the ball back at him faster than thought, only a short skip between the crack in my mitt and its sendoff.

12   I don't know when I first showed my father my school papers, but by the time I was in high school we had established regular editing sessions. I slaved over my manuscripts in long-hand, leaving margins where my father wrote my literary pretensions clean off the page. He never commented on content—he'd rarely read the "classical literature" I was writing about—but he always had plenty to say about my style. None of it was complimentary. He muttered my sentences out loud, his pencil poised over the page, ready to attack my excesses—"You don't need *this*. Get rid

of *that*."—my obscurities—"What in the hell is *that* supposed to mean?"—
my stumblings—"You dumb stupe!"—my misspellings—"Look it up." He
jabbed holes through the paper where I used big words to conceal incomplete thoughts and demanded that I sort out my ideas on the spot. And so
we worked our way through my papers, paragraph by painful paragraph,
page after painful page. By the end of an editing session with my father,
my papers and my pretensions were returned to me, battered and bleeding, and I limped back to my room to start the rewrites.

My father's fierceness has cut both ways. It has cut all of his chil-   13
dren, leaving scars on each. Some of the scars have healed. It has also cut
him off, isolated him from human kindness, left him lonely and needy.
And so, like King Lear in his retirement, my father invites himself to his
grown children's houses. He commandeers the best chairs. He surrounds
himself with books and games. And then he folds in upon himself. He has
spent much of his fierceness and now he needs friends. Oscar Wilde says,
"Children begin by loving their parents; then they judge them; sometimes
they forgive them." As I trip over my father's feet in my living room, I
wonder if I've forgiven him.

I remember those editing sessions—my father's lessons in brevity,   14
clarity, grace, and precision. They were lessons in honesty, too. "Well then,
why in the hell don't you say what you mean?" I can still hear my father
demanding. And so I say it and I edit it and I rewrite it and I say it again.

I remember those softball practices—my father and I standing at op-   15
posite ends of stinging fast balls, the clap of leather against leather echoing
off houses, our own special pattern of plays back and forth, the pain that
numbed my throwing arm, yet still the "Just a few more, Dad, please?"
and the weight of acceptance that lone ball carried on its fleeting course
from hand to glove.

And I remember my brothers and me at Laguna Beach, called out of   16
the water at dusk and pleading to stay longer—"Just till the sun goes
down, please, Daddy?" Then we'd bob out there past the breakers, watching the sun sigh into the Pacific, firing its dark surface with one last
breath, until only a whisper of red remained, and we rode our last waves
in triumphantly.

Content

1. Was Dr. Smith, Moore's father, a good or bad teacher of his own children?
Does Moore view his lessons differently as an adult than she did at the time he
was teaching her?

2. Is it possible to sort out single causes and single effects from among the complex factors that influence the ways we learn anything and everything? Explain
your answer with reference to Moore's essay.

3. Moore says, "Recently my father admitted to me that the way he treated us as
children would be considered child abuse today" (¶ 8). Do you agree? Why do

you think Dr. Smith, a pediatrician and public health physician, treated his children so harshly? What was their reaction to him at the time?

Strategies/Structures

4. How does Moore's use, and labeling, of the four frames provide structure for her essay?

5. What does Moore think of her father? How do you know? Does she want you to share her opinion? Does her opinion actually change as the essay proceeds, or does she complicate it by showing more facets of a complicated parent-child relationship?

Language

6. Moore uses quotations from her father in all but the first of the essay's frames. What are these, how do they change as the essay proceeds, and what do they convey to you about the ambivalent relationship of Moore and her father?

7. If you (or anyone) had Dr. Smith for a writing tutor, would you have learned to write well? What is the effect of working one's way through a paper, under a mentor's unforgiving scrutiny, "paragraph by painful paragraph, page after painful page"?

For Writing

8. What makes parents good, or bad, teachers of their own children? Can they be both concurrently? Address this question, for an audience that doesn't know your parents (or other significant mentor) by identifying two or three of your major personal characteristics (such as honesty, curiosity, perseverance, loyalty, athletic ability, whatever) and show how a parent or mentor strongly influenced these while you were growing up. Show, as Moore does, through some characteristic incidents, what this person did (or did not do) to cause these effects. Do you consider the results good, bad, or a mixture? Explain why.

9. Try writing an essay by using a series of several frames, as Moore does, to establish and interpret a relationship, either between an older and younger person or between two age peers—grandparent-grandchild, teacher-student, a married couple, two friends or enemies of the same or opposite sex, or others. Whether or not you write about yourself, you should know both of your subjects very well. The frames may be the same as Moore's (scene, situation, implication, character) or others of your own choice.

10. Throughout America's history, harshness has alternated with gentleness as being for children's own good. Is the adage "No pain, no gain" a valid assertion, in teaching children or in learning anything else? What teaching/learning style suits you best? Why?

Additional Topics for Writing
Cause and Effect   (For strategies for writing cause and effect, see 208.)

Write an essay, adapted to an audience of your choice, explaining either the causes or the effects of one of the following:

1. Substance abuse by teenagers, young adults, or another group
2. America's 50 percent divorce rate
3. Genetic engineering
4. Teenage pregnancy
5. The popularity of a given television show, movie or rock star, film, book, or type of book (such as romance, Gothic, Western)
6. Current taste in clothing, food, cars, architecture, interior decoration
7. The Civil War, the Great Depression, World War II, the Vietnam War, the attack on the World Trade Center (see the chapter "Terrorism"), or other historical event
8. The popularity of a particular spectator or active sport
9. Your personality or temperament
10. Success in college or in business
11. Being "born again" or losing one's religious faith
12. Racial, sexual, or religious discrimination
13. An increasingly higher proportion of working women (or mothers of young children)
14. The computer revolution
15. The American Dream that "if you work hard you're bound to succeed"
16. America's disappearing farm land, and/or the decrease in the number of family farms (see Keifer, "The Death of a Farm" [475–77])
17. The actual or potential consequences of nuclear leaks, meltdowns, or global warming
18. Vanishing animal or plant species; or the depletion of natural resources
19. Decrease in the number of people in training for skilled labor—electricians, plumbers, carpenters, tool and die makers, and others
20. A sudden change in personal status (from being a high school student to being a college freshman, from living at home to living away from home; from being dependent to being self-supporting; from being single to being married; from being childless to being a parent; from being married to being divorced . . .)

Part **III**

Clarifying Ideas

Description

When you describe a person, place, thing, or phenomenon, you want your readers to see it as you do and to experience its sounds, tastes, smells, or textures. Since a writer can't include everything, the details you select, the information you impart, will determine your emphasis and should enable your readers to understand the subject as you do. You'll pick the details that matter most to your point of view—perhaps the dominant features, such as a volcano in the distance—but you may use small bits of material that together form a sparkling mosaic image of the subject—shards and swirls of lava at close range. No matter what the subject—whether readers are looking at lava, dwellings natural and manmade, fatness and obesity, alcoholism, life in China (as the essays in this chapter invite them to)—the author's rendering provides the lens through which the readers come to interpret it now and, if the writing is memorable and the description rings true, in the future.

You may or may not wish to provide an overt interpretation of the subject, as well. If you don't, you can describe something with seeming objectivity, impartially, sticking to the facts without evaluating them and letting your readers infer what they wish. (But bear in mind that by your very *selection and organization* of the facts you are implicitly evaluating them, deciding that some deserve emphasis, or mention, for whatever reasons, and others don't). Technical and scientific descriptions usually aim for objectivity, as would the author of a manual describing the components of a home computer, or an astronaut explaining the size, appearance, and composition of a newly discovered crater on the moon. So do some travel guides when describing places, for the authors cannot afford to let their personal preferences influence their presentations of Altoona and Oshkosh, which (bigosh!) must be described as impartially—or enthusiastically—as San Francisco and New Orleans.

However, most other descriptions of places, like descriptions of people, phenomena, processes, and other subjects, are strongly influenced by the observer's aims, experiences, and values. Thus in much nontechnical writing the descriptions you provide are bound to be subjective, intended both to guide and influence your readers to see the topic your way rather than theirs. As a writer you can't afford to leave critical spaces blank; you must provide direction to influence your readers' interpretations, as you would need to do when looking at the photograph of women making pottery (p. 247). If you "read" this picture to accompany Linda Hogan's "Dwellings" (259–65), you might interpret it differently than if you looked at it either in the abstract or in comparison to pictures of different activities in different places. Nevertheless, less is more. As all of the descriptive essays in this chapter reveal, writers supply what's necessary to sketch the picture, and they trust their readers' knowledge and judgment to expand the illustration according to the directions established in the text. Moreover, in descriptive writing the writer often interacts with what is being described instead of just viewing it from a detached perspective.

Even though Garrett Hongo assumes in "Pāhoehoe: Walking Over Lava" (253–59) that his readers haven't had this precise experience, he can take us with him on his expedition, confident that we can understand enough to be able to respond to this specific sojourn here on earth. He is not coming at us from outer space—a much more unfamiliar place that would require more explanation, even for people who have seen pictures or read astronauts' accounts. Hongo's description is, nevertheless, the story of an explorer eager for the adventure of going where he has never trod before, though he is wearing beach sandals rather than the hiking boots one might expect. Although Hongo could emphasize the danger— "lava had burned down a few homes and was pouring into the sea," as the photograph of the lava flow (p. 256) indicates—he chooses to concentrate on the properties of the lava itself, some of which are clearly visible in the photo. First he describes the lava's physical attributes through a series of familiar similes: the hardening lava "looked like the thick, fattened bodies of walruses and sea lions," "solidified like the weave of a basket," "little pans that seemed like a deck of black cards," "little toes of rock," "strings of silver sausages." Then he comes upon the remains of a house surrounded by corn and trucks that have been destroyed by the flowing lava. These he describes unemotionally, letting the images convey the sense: "I thought of Ice Age mammoths mired in pools of tar." He concludes with a description of walking "on the living rock,"—over the nearly molten surface where the lava was "cracking open a piece of its surface, stretching from the inside out, pouring through and dripping down, glowing from within." Hongo's piece is unusual, even for descriptions, in that it depends almost entirely on physical description embedded in his narrative of walking, a solitary man in a lonely yet pulsating terrain. Yet this is a molten jewel inset in a book otherwise alive with people and events—*Volcano*—the autobiographical account of Hongo's return to Hawaii, his native state.

Linda Hogan's "Dwellings" (259–65) reflects on a variety places to live from a range of perspectives—close up to long distance, immediate to remote in time, personal to anecdotal and legendary. This combination of points of view is common in description, just as it is in photography, where the interpreter employs a variety of angles and focuses to convey her personal vision. (In fact, the style of a distinctive photographer— Ansel Adams, Dorothea Lange, Cindy Sherman—is as individual and as immediately recognizable as a writer's characteristic literary style.) In her writing Hogan is always concerned with "the deepest questions, those of spirit, of shelter, of growth and movement toward peace and liberation, inner and outer," and it is these qualities she seeks in the environment, natural and manmade. As she explores the possibilities of ideal dwellings, Hogan looks first from long distance at "a broken wall of earth that contains old roots and pebbles woven together and exposed." Close up, however, this "rise of raw earth" becomes a bees' cliff dwelling, Anasazi-like, a sheltering hill of "tunneling rooms" that becomes a catacomb as the bees die. Inspired by this "intelligent architecture of memory," Hogan describes her own "dreams of peace," escaping to a wilderness sanctuary, a "nest inside stone or woods," "where a human hand has not been in everything." As she meditates on the goodness of fit between various shelters and their occupants—caves, fanciful bird houses, barn swallows' cluster nesting—Hogan discovers a great horned owl's nest adorned with a blue thread from one of Hogan's skirts and a "gnarl" of her daughter's hair. These specific details, primarily visual, lead her to contemplate the shelter that all living things find in the integrated universe, throbbing with life and possibility. Although Hogan's description throughout concentrates on precise physical details, the literal serves as a metaphor for the world beyond this world, and its effect is intensely spiritual: "The whole world was a nest . . . in the maze of the universe, holding us."

Poignant events can occur anywhere, in places as familiar as one's own backyard or in exotic spots halfway around the world. As intense as the message of Hogan's "Dwellings," but with complicated political undercurrents is Asiya Tschannerl's "One Remembers Most What One Loves" (287–92). Here she recalls incidents from her early childhood in Beijing to depict her life as a foreign schoolchild, "a little black [American] kid" who soon learned to speak "perfect Mandarin." She juxtaposes these with images of Tiananmen Square, initially a place of happy socialization, later tainted with the bloody massacre of the Chinese people by Chinese soldiers. Having become acculturated to life in China, she undergoes culture shock on return to her native country, with its noise, racism, and lack of respect for elders.

Thus through details, carefully chosen and arranged, description offers an interpretation, an understanding of its varied subjects. The subjects may be *places:* geographic (China), natural, or constructed by humans. The subjects may be *people:* characters in their own right or in relation to others (Eric Liu in "Notes of a Native Speaker," 410–20). An Asian American, Liu fights against being stereotyped Asian while he considers himself "white"—in lifestyle, values, clothing, jobs, ambition, language, groups he identifies with and respects. People are often described in relation to a particular place, role, occupation, or context. Like all the characters in this chapter, people are seen as experiencing change or understanding (or some other state of being) as a consequence of their reactions to or adventures in a particular setting or condition of life. The significance of descriptive details may be fairly obvious, whether stated or implied.

Liu's self-description begins with an overview of who he is now (whether "'an honorary white'" or "'a banana,'" a person who has "become white inside" in his assimilation of American culture) and then proceeds in historical order from his childhood through elementary school, high school, and college to the present.

Rarely do any literary techniques occur in isolation. Although the chapters in *The Essay Connection* are intended to highlight many of the major techniques of nonfiction writing, it is rare to find relatively pure types, such as the descriptive essays of Hongo and Hogan that you see here. Hogan's "Dwellings" may also be interpreted as an implied argument in favor of preserving a vulnerable, perhaps vanishing, ecosystem (see the introduction to the chapter "Appealing to Emotion and Ethics"). Essays that blend different techniques are far more common, as you may already have experienced if you've tried to write a narrative or, for example, an explanation, of cause and effect.

Each of the essays in the chapter titled "Cause and Effect" functions as an argument for the author's viewpoint. Likewise, Scott Russell Sanders's description of his father in "Under the Influence: Paying the Price of My Father's Booze" (274–86) presents an argument—and an *explanation*—and uses *comparison and contrast* to *illustrate cause-and-effect*. Sanders uses the single example of his father's alcoholism and its numerous, devastating effects on his family to serve as a description of alcoholism in general: the secret drinking, the reckless driving, the weaving walk, his mother's accusations and his father's rage, the children cowering in fear—at the fights, the sneakiness, the unseemly behavior. Sanders's reaction to his father's drinking, as both a child and as an adult, may also be generalized to describe the impact of parental drinking on the children of alcoholics: "I lie there [in bed] hating him, loving him, fearing him, knowing I have failed him. I tell myself he drinks to ease the ache . . . I must have caused by disappointing him somehow, a murderous ache I should be able to relieve by doing all my chores, earning A's in school. . . . He would not . . . drink himself to death, if only I were perfect." The accompanying photograph of a bartender in Cancun (p. 281) pouring tequila down the willing throat of an American college student engaging in a spring break ritual, implies an argument that corroborates Sanders's view of alcohol abuse, even if the participants in the ritual would disagree with this interpretation.

Sanders's account of alcoholism is personal and biographical, not medical. Scientific descriptions usually exclude the author-as-character and the author's personal reactions to the subject unless they are intended for general readers. Spencer Nadler's intensely human descriptions in "Fat" (265–74)—both of fat cells and his obese patient, Patti—are also intended for a nonscientific audience. Although his discussion of cells is technical ("the fat cell, or adipocyte, is buttressed by an external network of collagen fibers; myriad capillaries, even occasional nerve twigs, course in between"), he humanizes even the biological aspects of cells ("gregarious by nature, fat cells gather into millions of lobules . . . held together like a vital mosaic by miles of inflexible fibrous tracts"). Although nonscientists might not be able to draw a diagram of fat cells from Nadler's description, he provides a sense of what they look like, what they do, where they are located, and how they function—all significant attributes of descriptive writing. Indeed, he provides comparable information about Patti Fleming, even while using the most sympathetically presented case history as a case in point. His descriptive writing is saturated with admiration for the patient's character and determination, an appreciation of the bariatric surgery that enabled Patti to resume a healthy life, and a love of fat cells, both the problem and the solution: "Theirs is a glomerate beauty, an abundance or dearth of pure energy. . . . No other human cells can so rampantly rise or fall and, like millions of fiery suns burning bright or burning out, alter our universe." In contrast is the normative idea of a beautiful female body shape represented in the out-of-focus photograph of three women in brief bathing suits (p. 269). The blurring, in this case, aids the image, for viewers can supply the facial features that most closely conform to their ideal of women's beauty, and to the ideal underlying the aesthetic aim of the bariatric surgery Nadler describes. As these authors and photographers show us, there is a world of difference in descriptions, a compelling, complex world to explore.

STRATEGIES FOR WRITING— DESCRIPTION

1. What is my main purpose in writing this descriptive essay? To present and interpret factual information about the subject? To recreate its essence as I have experienced it, or the person, as I have known him or her? To form the basis for a narrative, or an argument—overt or implied? What mixture of objective information and subjective impressions will best fit my purpose?
2. If my audience is completely unfamiliar with the subject, how much and what kinds of basic information will I have to provide so they can understand what I'm talking about? (Can I assume that they've seen lakes, but not necessarily Lake Tahoe, the subject of my paper? Or that they know other grandmothers, but not mine, about whom I'm writing?) If my readers are familiar with the subject, in what ways can I describe it so they'll discover new aspects of it?
3. What particular characteristics of my subject do I wish to emphasize? Will I use in this description details revealed by the senses—sight, sound, taste, smell, touch? Any other sort of information, such as a person's characteristic behavior, gestures, ways of speaking or moving or dressing, values, companions, possessions, occupation, residence, style of spending money, beliefs, hopes, vulnerabilities? Nonsensory details will be particularly necessary in describing an abstraction, such as somebody's temperament or state of mind.
4. How will I organize my description? From the most dominant to the least dominant details? From the most to the least familiar aspects (or vice versa)? According to what an observer is likely to notice first, second . . . last? Or according to some other pattern?
5. Will I use much general language, or will my description be highly specific throughout? Do I want to evoke a clear, distinct image of the subject? Or a mood—nostalgic, thoughtful, happy, sad, or otherwise?

GARRETT HONGO

Hongo was born in 1951 in Volcano, Hawaii, a "chunk of the sublime," where he lived for six years until his Japanese parents moved to Los Angeles. He earned a B.A. in English from Pomona College (1973), studied at the University of Michigan and at the University of Irvine, earning an M.F.A. in 1980. After founding and directing the Asian Exclusion Act, a theater group in Seattle, Hongo taught at the University of Missouri and at UCLA before directing the creative writing program at the University of Oregon, where he is a professor of English. His major works are two books of poetry, *Yellow Light* (1982) and *The River of Heaven* (1988), and the nonfiction *Volcano: A Memoir of Hawai'i* (1995). "Pāhoehoe: Walking Over Lava" begins the chapter on "Volcanology," in which Hongo uses his senses to the utmost—sight, smell, and, especially, touch—to describe his first walk over fresh lava, destructive and beautiful, "alive under the surface of the flow."

What Hongo says of his poetry applies equally well to *Volcano*. He writes, he says, "to isolate and uphold cultural and moral value in a confusing time and environment, accommodating what I know of tradition and history to contemporary circumstances. . . . I write to be a voice that I can listen to, one that makes sense and raises my own consciousness. And I write for all the people who might want the same thing, no matter what race, class, or nationality. Finally, I write for my father in a very personal way. He was a great example to me of a man who refused to hate, or, being different himself, to be afraid of difference, who accepted the friendship of the strange and underprivileged people ostracized by the rest of society. I want my poems to be equal to his heart."

Pāhoehoe: Walking Over Lava

The first raw lava I saw close at hand was down alongside Highway 130 at the seacoast south of Kalapana in 1987. In April, I'd heard news reports that the flow had overrun the highway and that lava had burned down a few homes and was pouring into the sea. Curious to see it, I drove down from Volcano.

I went through the villages of Kea'au and Kapoho, by-passing Kaimū Black Sand Beach near Kalapana, stopping at the road barriers on the low hillocks of old lava flows. I was near an area along the seacoast called Kapa'ahu. The air was warm and humid, full of an ocean wind, but I could feel a singe and an acid in it, a weight in its vapor.

I stripped off my jacket and sweatshirt—the added layers of clothing I wore up in Volcano all the time—and parked the car along a line of other tourist rental cars pulled off by the shoulder of the road. They were parked beside the cutaway of a lava hill. I could see the layers and layers that had built up over time—a period which could have been centuries or merely a few years for all I knew then. I got out of my car and strolled down the center of the highway, still almost new, its asphalt the matte black of being freshly laid. I could see a spot of palm trees off in the distance, some smoke clouds below them, and a large white ribbon of steam trailing from a point that must have been the coast about two miles away. There was no glow of red, but I guessed the steam plume marked the point where lava was entering the sea.

4   I had to walk about a quarter mile downhill, cutting through the black expanse of a flow that was almost entirely new lavas, a wide sheeting over a swath in the land like a roof freshly drizzled with tar. It eddied in little fans and swirling shapes, mounding in doughy black hills beside the road. Close up, its sheen was silver and metallic, shining like the lead on a sharpened pencil, flaking like packed shards of ice, giving off a low heat and some sulphuric-smelling kind of gas. The highway surface was hot from the tropical sun, and there was something extra in the air—a sizzle of molecules stirring and restirring the atmosphere, heightening the senses, giving off a fume like ozone channeled down from the upper air.

5   Hummocks of new black rock rose up alongside the road, and I could see how it eddied in the flats, pouring like mud through gaps and shallows on the plain around me, fanning out and crusting, rippling into a hardened skin. This was called *pāhoehoe*, lava of the relatively fluid kind that congeals with a smooth and billowy surface. It cooled from its outside inward, at first forming a thin, sheetlike layer of crust on the large, flat flows. If it ran into an obstacle, the forward part of it blocked by a feature on the earth, or if it was slowed by a momentary slackening in the flow's volume or momentum, the crust might start to twist and curdle like a bedsheet lifted by one of its corners. *Pāhoehoe* would twist in ripples, gyring around a center of resistance, sending purling rays out from where it was being pulled and tugged, bending over itself, forming a littoral radiance that would be preserved. When it mounded, it made a wonderland of silvers and blacks, a topiary of fantasy shapes covering the land and everything on it. I saw *pāhoehoe* that looked like the thick, fattened bodies of walruses and sea lions. In other spots, the moving lava had buckled and rolled and solidified like the weave of a basket made from silvered fronds of palm. When it sluiced through a channel, it made frozen spillways and little pans that seemed like a deck of black cards fanned out and placed on a black slate table. Little toes of rock, shining like quicksilver and swelling from the inside out, dropped into the ditches alongside the road, cooling and hardening into strings of silver sausages that singed the asphalt boiling under them. A smell like a sauce of faint smog—I thought of the air around the L.A. airport at dawn—pervaded the atmosphere, and I rubbed at my eyes.

6   I'd been reading a textbook called *Geology of the State of Hawaii*, written by Harold T. Stearns. He wrote that its eruptive temperature—in a

fire-fountain or fissure eruption sending red gouts of it in a long curtain-of-fire sheeting upward—is over 2000 degrees Fahrenheit. The flow temperature, when it slides like a fluid red cream over the land, is no less hot. *Pāhoehoe* is emitted containing a lot of volcanic gases, which dissipate as the lava cools. If the lava cools and loses enough gas so that crystallization starts, *pāhoehoe* changes into *'a'ā*, the lava that is rough and clinkery. I had yet to encounter a live *'a'ā,* flow.

Pāhoehoe presents itself in a myriad of shapes and spreads from an   7
eruptive vent through a system of conduits that can range in size from a few inches to more than twenty-five feet in diameter. Nahuku, the Thurston Lava Tube, is that huge. There were layers of flowing *pāhoehoe* upslope of me then, made up of several smallish flow units spreading and forming glass skins a fraction of an inch thick, hardening over, then swelling open in squeeze ups (fractures in the hardened skin oozing fresh lava), or cooling down in blocks and slabs of tumuli and pressure domes where the land was flat and the lava had spread itself out in widening and thickening sheets. Up close, its surface could look like asphalt in one spot, then a shining elephant hide or sharkskin in another, crusting into shapes like entrails or a swirl of ropes and cords, tessellating in blistered and filamented surfaces, pumiceous, festooned, puffed up in small, intricate, and shelly chambers. When *pāhoehoe* pours over a cliff, it forms a lava cascade, a Niagara of molten red rock—a lava-fall. When it flows into the sea, it makes a lava delta that can be as big as a football field, a new piece of land that might suddenly crack away from its brittle tie and slide itself into the sea like a sounding whale. Or, if it maintains flowing in the shape of a tube all the way from vent to ocean waves, it can spew forth as a glowing fire hose of lava, *pāhoehoe* streaming in a sluice of lantern-orange sperm churning into rock and black sand in the liquid staggers of froth and spume from the sea.

After walking down the road awhile, I came upon a place where a   8
house had been. It looked like a junkyard or lot for auto wreckers, shells of scorched cars here and there in the black puddles of the flow, the blackened frame of a bench seat off by itself, round and rusted wheels half submerged in hardened lava. The flow had swung around a little hill and come down a gully—maybe there was a creek or small gulch here—and sliced through someone's property—someone who liked cars and trucks, someone who had to leave about half a dozen of them behind. There was the husk of a flatbed pickup immersed up to its wheel wells in lava. The steel on it looked like it had sat in rain for twenty years—all paint, upholstery, rubber belts and hoses and tires incinerated away. The hood was caved in and buckled. Its bed was buried under solidified lava. I thought of Ice Age mammoths mired in pools of tar. Ripped sheets of corrugated steel were strewn around too, sticking up out of the black puddings that held them at funny angles like stiffened sailboards, like metal sculpture left unbronzed. All was black and rust-colored. Pieces of flat metal like posters

Describe this photograph as fully as possible, and tell (or imagine) the story embedded in the lava encroaching on the stop sign at the intersection of Princess and Gardenia. What has occurred? How recently? Where were the residents of Princess and Gardenia at the time the photo was taken? What consequences can you imagine for this event?

or signs lay about, burned of their messages, black and rusting, pocked and curled from the heat. There was nothing like a house anymore—just a few steel pilings sticking up here and there, like the ribs of an old pier exposed at low tide. Indeed, the remnant world around the burning seemed like an eddied land of tidal flats after the ocean had pulled away, draining, full of things half-alive, exposed and shriven of their flesh.

9   I came to a black hump, like the carcass of a gigantic slug, lying across the road. This was where the flow finally cut off the rebuilt part of the highway. I'd heard that it had been rerouted each time that lava cut it off, keeping the way open for residents to come in and out. I'd heard there were people still living on the hillsides. They watched television while lava channeled through the slopes around them. Along the flatland that had been overrun with lava, other families who had evacuated were still coming back to pick up what was left of their things. I met a Hawaiian man who trekked miles across the flowfront just so he could get to what was left of his property—a crop of ripening mangoes hanging from trees still standing in a small pocket of green cut off from the road but left unscathed, an emerald island among the stark blacks and grays of the flow.

10   I stopped at a point where the flow had mounded up higher than the roof of a semi. It seemed the lava had crested here, burying the highway, inflating from inside until it grew higher than a man standing on another man's shoulders. I hopped up onto the edge of the flow, stepping on lava for the first time, worrying, gauging angles and footholds, measuring myself against its folds, crevices, and gaps.

It was still hot, giving off shimmers of heat, and I could feel the skin   11
on my face prickle, the heels of my feet getting warm. I wasn't wearing
shoes, just a thick pair of beach sandals. I wanted to *feel* that lava, would've
gone barefoot over it if I could've. It held me up, bearing my weight like a
mound of green Japanese floats held together with a seining net, crackling
under the spongy rubber of the sandals. It flaked and made a grinding
sound as I walked over it, building its heat up under my soft arches, keeping me on the move, taking me farther and farther away from the road. I
was spellbound out there, suddenly in a world strangified by this rare
phenomenon—a kind of silvery ocean on whose waters I could walk. I felt
wrapped inside of a brittle shroud of birthing. The heat did not matter,
nor did the faint charge of acidic air annoying my breathing. The sting in
my eyes seemed part of the awareness, the joy of feeling something was
new. I stalked from mound to mound, making little leaps across gaps and
gullies in the flow, playing like a child among fresh dunes of sand when
the tide was far, far out.

I came to a place where the skin of the flow was ripped. A red, dermal   12
gumminess glowed from within it. When I got close, I felt a radiant heat
as from an opened kiln. Lava was alive under the surface of the flow.
There was a thick red tatty of it still churned up inside the steel-colored
skin. What made things so hot out there, rock to rock, gray pillow to lead-
colored mound, was the inner paste still red and movable underneath like
a lagoon engorged with a tide of luminous plankton briefly masked and
then revealed by the sheet of hardened kelp that floated on its surface. I'd
walked on the living rock. I was separated from its temperatures only by
the thickness of what had cooled—perhaps inches, perhaps feet—a mere
skim of time for the cooling to take place, a dimension's distance between
the states of solid and of liquid. The radiance swam past my face and arms,
curling as the wind curled around me. I saw more streaks and scarrings of
red where the lava was inflating from underneath the hardened paddies of
rock, cracking open a piece of its surface, stretching from the inside out,
pouring through and dripping down, glowing from within.

There were soft sizzles of rose in the rock surrounding me. I'd walked   13
past the cooler point of the flow and stood alongside an expanding pond
of its red dough pushing upward through the gray coating of its surface.
Heat salved up the skin on my ankles and gripped my calves. My breath
shortened. A shimmer of sweat came to my brow, a cold spray of panic
broke through the skin on the back of my neck. I turned and moved back
the way I'd come, taking shorter steps, making fewer leaps, watching carefully the color under the surface of the silver rock I walked upon.

In minutes, I got back to the roadside. I'd only gone a few hundred   14
yards, but, within myself, I felt an upwelling like an orange glimmer of
pride. A globulous, cooling mass loomed beside me. I went and put my
hands on the lava again. It flaked and came off in my palms in gross scabs

the color of silver and black. Small fires touched off in the dry brush alongside the road. Around its bend, swizzles of burning grass sent up tiny flames and swirls of slate-gray smoke. The white plume of steam I'd seen ribboning out from the coastline was still a mile away across the shining gray sea of *pāhoehoe.*

Content

1. Hongo claims that his curiosity about raw lava is what impelled his journey. Has this curiosity been satisfied by the time he finishes examining the lava flow? What other types of feelings does Hongo express as he examines the lava from near and far? Has his description put you where he is? Has it made you want to go there to literally walk in his shoes?

2. Writers of description often draw upon their senses of sight, smell, taste, and touch. Which senses are the most useful to Hongo in describing the lava he encounters in "Volcanology"? What particular characteristics of lava has Hongo emphasized? Has his description enabled you to discriminate between the different types of lava that he encounters, *pāhoehoe* and *'a'ā*?

Strategies/Structures

3. People writing about places, particularly natural settings, often fade into the background as nature becomes prominent in their description. Is that true in "Pāhoehoe: Walking Over Lava"? What kind of person or character does Hongo appear to be in this essay? Under what circumstances is such self-effacement appropriate? Desirable? When is it better to get a clear picture of the author and his personality?

4. Is Hongo right in assuming that many of his readers have never seen lava? And that even those familiar with lava are likely to lump all kinds of lava together indiscriminately? What does he do in his writing to compensate for his readers' lack of knowledge? How can he (or any author) write about the unfamiliar without being condescending to the reader?

Language

5. Hongo uses a variety of similes to describe the lava. Identify several of them and discuss their effectiveness, either in enabling you to envision raw lava if you've never seen it or to reenvision raw lava if you are familiar with the sight. Were some similes more effective than others? Why?

6. In paragraph 5 Hongo uses a series of similes to describe the lava, ranging from "walruses and sea lions" to "a deck of black cards fanned out." Such an assemblage of images (what is sometimes referred to as a mixed metaphor) can at times be disorienting for a reader. Explain whether Hongo has avoided such disorientation.

7. In paragraphs 6 and 7 Hongo switches from first-person description of the lava to an overview of the properties of lava. What change in tone accompanies this switch? Contrast the tone in paragraphs 6 and 7 with the tone throughout the remainder of the essay.

8. Given the likelihood that Hongo's audience doesn't know much about lava, what justification has he for using such words and phrases as "purling rays" and "littoral radiance" (¶ 5) and "a word strangified" (¶ 11)?

For Writing

9. Hongo spends a great deal of time describing the texture of raw lava. Choose an object and, without naming it, describe its texture (and perhaps shape or other relevant properties) in as much detail as possible. Exchange descriptions with a classmate and see if you can deduce the object being described by each other.

10. Write a descriptive essay that incorporates sensory description and, as does Hongo's, a reference to an authoritative work on what is being described. At what point will you include your reference and how will you attempt to compensate for any change in tone? Your aim should be not only to explain the place or phenomenon to your readers, but to make them want to experience it for themselves.

LINDA HOGAN

Hogan's Chickasaw Indian heritage informs her work both as a creative writer and as a professor of American Indian studies, first at the University of Minnesota and currently at the University of Colorado. She was born in Denver in 1947, and earned a B.A. at the University of Colorado at Colorado Springs and an M.A. in English and creative writing at the University of Colorado, Boulder, in 1978. Her most recent book of poetry is *Book of Medicines* (1993). *Seeing Through the Sun* (1985) received an American Book Award for poetry. Her novels include *Mean Spirit* (1990), *Solar Storms* (1995), and *Power* (1998). Her most recent work is *The Woman Who Watches Over the World: A Native Memoir* (2001). "Dwellings" is the title essay of her collection *Dwellings: A Spiritual History of the Living World* (1995).

"As an Indian woman," the introduction to her book begins, "I question our responsibilities to the caretaking of the future and to the other species who share our journeys. These writings have grown out of these questions, out of wondering what makes us human, out of lifelong love for the living world and all its inhabitants. They have grown, too, out of my native understanding that there is a terrestrial intelligence that lies beyond our human knowing and grasping." She continues, "It has been my lifelong work to seek an understanding of the two views of the world, one as seen by native people and the other as seen by those who are new and young on this continent. It is clear that we have strayed from the treaties we once had with the land and with the animals. It is also clear, and heartening, that in our time there are many—Indian and non-Indian alike—who want to restore and honor these broken agreements."

Dwellings

1   Not far from where I live is a hill that was cut into by the moving water of a creek. Eroded this way, all that's left of it is a broken wall of earth that contains old roots and pebbles woven together and exposed. Seen from a distance, it is only a rise of raw earth. But up close it is something wonderful, a small cliff dwelling that looks almost as intricate and well made as those the Anasazi left behind when they vanished mysteriously centuries ago. This hill is a place that could be the starry skies of night turned inward into the thousand round holes where solitary bees have lived and died. It is a hill of tunneling rooms. At the mouths of some of the excavations, half-circles of clay beetle out like awnings shading a doorway. It is earth that was turned to clay in the mouths of the bees and spit out as they mined deeper into their dwelling places.

2   This place where the bees reside is at an angle safe from rain. It faces the southern sun. It is a warm and intelligent architecture of memory, learned by whatever memory lives in the blood. Many of the holes still contain the gold husks of dead bees, their faces dry and gone, their flat eyes gazing out from death's land toward the other uninhabited half of the hill that is across the creek from these catacombs.

3   The first time I found the residence of the bees, it was dusty summer. The sun was hot, and land was the dry color of rust. Now and then a car rumbled along the dirt road and dust rose up behind it before settling back down on older dust. In the silence, the bees made a soft droning hum. They were alive then, and working the hill, going out and returning with pollen, in and out through the holes, back and forth between daylight and the cooler, darker regions of inner earth. They were flying an invisible map through air, a map charted by landmarks, the slant of light, and a circling story they told one another about the direction of food held inside the center of yellow flowers.

4   Sitting in the hot sun, watching the small bees fly in and out around the hill, hearing the summer birds, the light breeze, I felt right in the world. I belonged there. I thought of my own dwelling places, those real and those imagined. Once I lived in a town called Manitou, which means "Great Spirit," and where hot mineral springwater gurgled beneath the streets and rose up into open wells. I felt safe there. With the underground movement of water and heat a constant reminder of other life, of what lives beneath us, it seemed to be the center of the world.

5   A few years after that, I wanted silence. My daydreams were full of places I longed to be, shelters and solitudes. I wanted a room apart from others, a hidden cabin to rest in. I wanted to be in a redwood forest with trees so tall the owls called out in the daytime. I daydreamed of living in a vapor cave a few hours away from here. Underground, warm, and moist,

I thought it would be the perfect world for staying out of cold winter, for escaping the noise of living.

And how often I've wanted to escape to a wilderness where a human 6 hand has not been in everything. But those were only dreams of peace, of comfort, of a nest inside stone or woods, a sanctuary where a dream or life wouldn't be invaded.

Years ago, in the next canyon west of here, there was a man who followed 7 one of those dreams and moved into a cave that could only be reached by climbing down a rope. For years he lived there in comfort, like a troglodite. The inner weather was stable, never too hot, too cold, too wet, or too dry. But then he felt lonely. His utopia needed a woman. He went to town until he found a wife. For a while after the marriage, his wife climbed down the rope along with him, but before long she didn't want the mice scurrying about in the cave, or the untidy bats that wanted to hang from stones of the ceiling. So they built a door. Because of the closed entryway, the temperature changed. They had to put in heat. Then the inner moisture of earth warped the door, so they had to have air-conditioning, and after that the earth wanted to go about life in its own way and it didn't give in to the people.

In other days and places, people paid more attention to the strong-headed 8 will of earth. Once homes were built of wood that had been felled from a single region in a forest. That way, it was thought, the house would hold together more harmoniously, and the family of walls would not fall or lend themselves to the unhappiness or arguments of the inhabitants.

An Italian immigrant to Chicago, Aldo Piacenzi, built birdhouses that 9 were dwellings of harmony and peace. They were the incredible spired shapes of cathedrals in Italy. They housed not only the birds, but also his memories, his own past. He painted them the watery blue of his Mediterranean, the wild rose of flowers in a summer field. Inside them was straw and the droppings of lives that layed eggs, fledglings who grew there. What places to inhabit, the bright and sunny birdhouses in dreary alleyways of the city.

One beautiful afternoon, cool and moist, with the kind of yellow light 10 that falls on earth in these arid regions, I waited for barn swallows to return from their daily work of food gathering. Inside the tunnel where they live, hundreds of swallows had mixed their saliva with mud and clay, much like the solitary bees, and formed nests that were perfect as a potter's bowl. At five in the evening, they returned all at once, a dark, flying shadow. Despite their enormous numbers and the crowding together of nests, they didn't pause for even a moment before entering the nests, nor did they crowd one another. Instantly they vanished into the nests. The tunnel went silent. It held no outward signs of life.

11   But I knew they were there, filled with the fire of living. And what a marriage of elements was in those nests. Not only mud's earth and water, the fire of sun and dry air, but even the elements contained one another. The bodies of prophets and crazy men were broken down in that soil.

12 I've noticed often how when a house is abandoned, it begins to sag. Without a tenant, it has no need to go on. If it were a person, we'd say it is depressed or lonely. The roof settles in, the paint cracks, the walls and floorboards warp and slope downward in their own natural ways, telling us that life must stay in everything as the world whirls and tilts and moves through boundless space.

13 One summer day, cleaning up after long-eared owls where I work at a rehabilitation facility for birds of prey, I was raking the gravel floor of a flight cage. Down on the ground, something looked like it was moving. I bent over to look into the pile of bones and pellets I'd just raked together. There, close to the ground, were two fetal mice. They were new to the planet, pink and hairless. They were so tenderly young. Their faces had swollen blue-veined eyes. They were nestled in a mound of feathers, soft as velvet, each one curled up smaller than an infant's ear, listening to the first sounds of earth. But the ants were biting them. They turned in agony, unable to pull away, not yet having the arms or legs to move, but feeling, twisting away from, the pain of the bites. I was horrified to see them bitten out of life that way. I dipped them in water, as if to take away the sting, and let the ants fall in the bucket. Then I held the tiny mice in the palm of my hand. Some of the ants were drowning in the water. I was trading one life for another, exchanging the lives of ants for those of mice, but I hated their suffering, and hated even more that they had not yet grown to a life, and already they inhabited the miserable world of pain. Death and life feed each other. I know that.

14   Inside these rooms where birds are healed, there are other lives besides those of mice. There are fine gray globes the wasps have woven together, the white cocoons of spiders in a corner, the downward tunneling anthills. All these dwellings are inside one small walled space, but I think most about the mice. Sometimes the downy nests fall out of the walls where their mothers have placed them out of the way of their enemies. When one of the nests falls, they are so well made and soft, woven mostly from the chest feathers of birds. Sometimes the leg of a small quail holds the nest together like a slender cornerstone with dry, bent claws. The mice have adapted to life in the presence of their enemies, adapted to living in the thin wall between beak and beak, claw and claw. They move their nests often, as if a new rafter or wall will protect them from

the inevitable fate of all our returns home to the deeper, wider nest of earth that houses us all.

One August at Zia Pueblo during the corn dance I noticed tourists pick- 15
ing up shards of all the old pottery that had been made and broken there. The residents of Zia know not to take the bowls and pots left behind by the older ones. They know that the fragments of those earlier lives need to be smoothed back to earth, but younger nations, travelers from conti-nents across the world who have come to inhabit this land, have little of their own to grow on. The pieces of earth that were formed into bowls, even on their way home to dust, provide the new people a lifeline to an unknown land, help them remember that they live in the old nest of earth.

It was in early February, during the mating season of the great horned 16
owls. It was dusk, and I hiked up the back of a mountain to where I'd heard the owls a year before. I wanted to hear them again, the voices so tender, so deep, like a memory of comfort. I was halfway up the trail when I found a soft, round nest. It had fallen from one of the bare-branched trees. It was a delicate nest, woven together of feathers, sage, and strands of wild grass. Holding it in my hand in the rosy twilight, I noticed that a blue thread was entwined with the other gatherings there. I pulled at the thread a little, and then I recognized it. It was a thread from one of my skirts. It was blue cotton. It was the unmistakable color and shape of a pattern I knew. I liked it, that a thread of my life was in an abandoned nest, one that had held eggs and new life. I took the nest home. At home, I held it to the light and looked more closely. There, to my surprise, nestled into the gray-green sage, was a gnarl of black hair. It was also unmistakable. It was my daughter's hair, cleaned from a brush and picked up out in the sun beneath the maple tree, or the pit cherry where birds eat from the overladen, fertile branches until only the seeds remain on the trees.

I didn't know what kind of nest it was, or who had lived there. It 17
didn't matter. I thought of the remnants of our lives carried up the hill that way and turned into shelter. That night, resting inside the walls of our home, the world outside weighed so heavily against the thin wood of the house. The sloped roof was the only thing between us and the universe. Everything outside of our wooden boundaries seemed so large. Filled with night's citizens, it all came alive. The world opened in the thickets of the dark. The wild grapes would soon ripen on the vines. The burrowing ones were emerging. Horned owls sat in treetops. Mice scurried here and there. Skunks, fox, the slow and holy porcupine, all were passing by this way. The young of the solitary bees were feeding on pollen in the dark. The whole world was a nest on its humble tilt, in the maze of the universe, holding us.

Content

1. Linda Hogan describes a variety of different types of dwellings. Choose two and explain what the relationship of these dwellings is to each other, and to the natural setting in which they appear. In what ways does Hogan's selection and organization of information, particularly sensory details, convey her implicit judgments of those dwellings?

2. Why does Hogan describe such a variety of dwellings—human and animal? What elements of nature connect them with one another and with the lives of their occupants? In what ways are the descriptions of animals' dwellings as vivid as those of humans?

3. In Hogan's description of the barn swallows' nests she notes that they contain "a marriage of elements. [. . .] Not only mud's earth and water, the fire of the sun and dry air" and that "even the elements contained one another. The bodies of prophets and crazy men were broken down in that soil" (¶ 11). What does Hogan mean by "the bodies of prophets and crazy men" and why does she claim that they are contained in the bird's nests?

4. What is the point of Hogan's detailed discussion of the "fetal mice" in the bird rehabilitation facility (¶s 13, 14)? What does this have to do with her topic of "Dwellings"?

Strategies/Structures

5. What determines the essay's overall order? To determine this, identify the topic of each paragraph in sequence. Which dwellings come first, in the middle, last? Which paragraphs don't discuss particular dwellings or types of dwellings— and where do they come?

6. When Hogan is describing a particular dwelling, what sort of details does she begin with? Conclude with? For instance, she might proceed from the most dominant or most familiar details to the least dominant or familiar—or vice versa. In what other ways might Hogan have organized her descriptions of dwellings? With what effects?

7. Towards the conclusion of her essay Hogan accidentally stumbles upon a thread from one of her own skirts and "a gnarl of black hair" from her daughter's brush contained in a bird's nest (¶ 16). Why doesn't it matter to her that she "didn't know what kind of nest it was, or who had lived there" (¶ 17)? What does she mean by ending her essay with "The whole world was a nest on its humble tilt, in the maze of the universe, holding us" (¶ 17)? In what ways throughout the essay has Hogan prepared her readers for this conclusion?

Language

8. Hogan uses many details as she describes both her own and others' dwellings. Is there a difference in the kind of details she uses to describe human dwellings and the kind of details she uses to describe non-human dwellings? If so, explain what the differences are. If not, identify the similarities.

9. In her discussion of the bees' tunnel Hogan notes that "Seen from a distance, it is only a rise of raw earth. But up close it is something wonderful, a small cliff

dwelling that looks almost as intricate and well made as those the Anasazi left behind when they vanished mysteriously centuries ago" (¶ 1). Who were the Anasazi and why does Hogan compare the bees' tunnels to their cliff dwellings? What does Hogan mean by the phrase "a warm and intelligent architecture of memory" (¶ 2)?

For Writing

10. Write an essay that describes your own dwelling (house, apartment, dorm room), or the house of another—human or animal. What details will you choose to include, and with what emphasis? What kinds of details will you leave out? Why? Do you want your readers to be attracted to your dwelling, or not? For what reasons?

Once you've written your essay, ask another student to read it and draw a sketch of the dwelling you've written about as she understands it. Does the sketch contain all the essential features? In the right proportions? Does it capture your attitude toward the dwelling? If not, what do you need to add to your essay to convey its meaning?

11. Draw up a detailed outline for a descriptive essay of, say, a person or place you know well, then revise that outline to reflect a different organizational pattern (see pp. 295–98 for a discussion of types of organizational patterns). In a brief essay, consider the differences between the two organizational outlines. What sorts of information do they highlight? For what types of audience might each be appropriate?

SPENCER NADLER

Nadler, a surgical pathologist born and raised in Montreal, has practiced in Palos Verdes, California, for over twenty-five years. "Choosing a career in medicine was easy," he writes in the introduction to *The Language of Cells* (2001). "I was enticed by a profession that was concerned for the welfare of others. And contact with patients promised more to me than the ethereal ministrations of the rabbinate." "What type of doctor did I want to be?" he asks. "This decision is critical, for it defines one's career, lifestyle, family life, modality of service to the sick, remuneration, even prestige. Some specialties harbor warrior qualities, and foremost among them is surgery. Back in the sixties when it was my time to choose, I opted for surgery; it seemed to me the other way to go to war." He served as a surgical resident at the Montreal General Hospital of McGill University and as a surgical pathologist at Albert Einstein College of Medicine (New York City). There he found his professional love in "the cellular world of biopsies," where magnified from forty to one hundred thousand times "were stark cellscapes filled with deep blue nuclei and scarlet cytoplasm." More recently, he "missed the bonding with patients that the intimacy of surgery engenders." To re-establish that intimacy, he was written essays which have appeared in *Harper's, The American Scholar* (where "Fat" was published in 2000), and several literary magazines. "Paradoxically," he writes, "the extraordinary people of whom I write have made me see the lives of cells in new and pertinent ways."

Morbid obesity—weighing 100 pounds more than normal body weight—afflicts four million Americans—"an illness without a cure." Nadler uses the case history of Patti Fleming, a sympathetic character, as an extended illustration to describe the pernicious effects, both physical and social, of such obesity, which is often complicated by heart disease, hypertension, diabetes, and other ailments. His orientation to her case is that of a surgical pathologist, and he describes her morbid obesity from both clinical and microscopic points of view. Nadler describes the bariatric surgery as a miniaturization of her stomach to drastically reduce its capacity to process, absorb, and propel foods, and a partial bypass of her small intestines to further reduce caloric absorption. Of the shrinking fat cells that ensue, Nadler states that "it is a courageous endeavor to pucker billions of . . . *your* . . . fat cells in the hope of renewal."

Fat

1   I spend much of my life looking at cells through a microscope. Of all the cells I see, few are as distinctive as the human fat cell. Inside, a large fat globule steamrolls the rest of the cell's contents flat against the outer membrane until the sphere bulges like a mozzarella. Freeze and section this cell through its nucleus and you see a signet ring snugly fit upon a plump finger. When the cell is prepared for the scanning electron microscope, so much fat is lost in the processing that what remains is a three-dimensional shell, the cytoplasm and cell membrane stretched into a rim.

2   In all its endeavors, the fat cell, or adipocyte, is buttressed by an external network of collagen fibers; myriad capillaries, even occasional nerve twigs, course in between. Gregarious by nature, fat cells gather into millions of lobules, separated from one another yet held together like a vital mosaic by miles of inflexible fibrous tracts.

3   We are steeped in fat cells. They pervade the great panniculus beneath our skin; they collect around our adrenals and kidneys, in our abdomen and chest and bone marrow, in the grooves of our heart and the subtle spaces of our neck and armpits and groin. Fat cells are everywhere but our central nervous system, lungs, eyelids, ears, penis, and the backs of our hands. They insulate, buffer, and energize us.

4   Yet when I look through my microscope, my eye often glosses over them. Seeking treachery, I am trained to look for more likely cellular culprits. Unlike cancer cells, fat cells are so often part of the mix in a tissue biopsy that a pathologist can easily take them for granted. Their aggregate

size, however, can affect our health; shape the way we think about ourselves and how others think of us; make our lives unbearable.

Patti Fleming is five feet eight inches tall. She once weighed 356 pounds.   5
She now weighs less than half that. Although her colossal subtraction yields no physical vestige of her former self, in her mind she remains a fat person.

Patti is reluctant to come to my hospital (any hospital) to talk with   6
me, so I take the afternoon off to visit her at work. I am not averse to searching out patients' stories on their own turf, where they are often more forthcoming than on mine. Patti and I have been introduced by one of my colleagues, a bariatric nurse who knows of my interest in breaking through a pathologist's ingrained clinical myopia. I wish to think of cells as more than something fixed beneath the lens of my microscope.

We sit in a sterile conference room in the Los Angeles law firm   7
where Patti, who is in her early forties, works as a legal secretary. She wears a short black pleated skirt and an ivory cashmere sweater; her face is pretty and her body trim. She says she can hardly believe she was ever so obese. Her maternal grandmother and her mother "carried weight in their stomachs," she tells me, but neither so extremely. "I was ten years old when I first noticed my weight," she says. "I couldn't get up on a horse as easily as the other girls." At camp, she ate the same portions of food as the others, and exercised every bit as much. Were "fat genes" beginning to express themselves?

"In high school, other kids first talked about me being fat, but I   8
wouldn't let it happen. I'd miss meals and was very active in sports. I knew that if I ate, I'd get fat." She laughs. "I felt like if I smelled a cake, I'd gain five pounds."

Her adipocytes' penchant for hoarding fat was a secret. Away at   9
work, her parents were unaware that she seldom ate breakfast or lunch. On the weekends, she was out of the house, skipping meals and trying to ignore her hunger. Her private starvation was a mind game, as impermanent as satiation.

The average-sized infant enters this world with approximately five billion   10
fat cells, one-sixth to one-seventh of the adult quota. During the first six months of life, these cells significantly sufflate with fat, but their numbers remain relatively constant. From that point until the end of puberty, the process flip-flops: the number of fat cells increases to adult proportion, but their size does not change. Then, throughout adulthood, we return to the pattern of infancy, plumping up mostly by adding to the fat in our adipocytes. Some of us are capable of distending them by a factor of three or four to a gargantuan three-hundred-micron diameter. If our thirty-five billion adult fat cells enlarge in this way and trigger the formation of

additional adipocytes, we can balloon to rotundity and come to resemble the cells themselves.

11   In human biopsies, normal fat is a glistening, uniform, cadmium yellow, its texture greasy and soft. In vivo, at body temperature, fat is liquid, oozing in and out of fat cells under neural and hormonal control. There is a perpetual ebb and flow of fat between its mobilized state in the blood (as free fatty acids) and its storage state in fat cells (most as triglycerides). The free fatty acids burn metabolically as a high-potency energy source; what is unused by the body gets restored as triglycerides in the fat cells. Such is the dynamism of fat, a flux complexly modified by how we eat and exercise, as well as by our genes.

12   When she was sixteen, Patti met Frank Fleming, her husband-to-be. He was unconcerned about her weight and encouraged her not to skip meals. "We enjoyed eating together," she says. "We ate the same amounts, but he stayed skinny and I got bigger and bigger."

13   They overate. Despite studies that suggest altered metabolism or disturbed satiety signals as predisposing factors, one must overeat to realize morbid obesity (which is defined as a weight of one hundred pounds or more above the norm). Whenever Frank gained a few pounds, he easily lost them by cutting out sweets for a week or two. Patti wasn't so fortunate. From the end of her teenage years until she was forty, she "pushed and shoved" her way through dozens of diets, spending thousands of dollars, losing and regaining hundreds of pounds. She tethered herself to diet food until she could no longer tolerate the tedium. The priceyness of those special packages angered her. Society did, too, for the stigma it placed on her body.

14   "I tried to exercise," she says, "but there are no commercial gyms that can hold people who are more than 250 pounds. You break their machines and they want you out of there." As her weight passed 300 pounds, she found exercise increasingly painful and finally impossible. Even walking down the street was a major effort. Her heart would pound; sweat would pour off her.

15   Her fat-cell aggregate was now so huge that she could barely keep her head above it. She seemed to be sinking inside herself, too mired to surface. Rather than garnering sympathy, she often repelled people; it was as if her globate habitus revealed all that was inside her, negating the need to look into her eyes or listen to a single word she spoke. It is hard for the morbidly obese to stand up for their rights when others consider their shape a character flaw rather than a disease or a disability. *Stop stuffing yourself,* people say, ignorant of the power of fat cells. *Do a little exercise once in a while. Don't be so damned lazy.*

16   Imagine fat as an organ tucked within our bodies, one that can rise to roll our features outward or shrink until it fades among the splay of protruding

If you see this as a photograph of beautiful young women, what does this picture imply about female beauty? Can you offer any alternative interpretations? Does the essence of this (or any) beauty reside in the figures, the viewer's eye (or imagination), in social norms, or some combination of these? Or somewhere else entirely?

bones. To make sense of this "organ" when it is a lipid-laden albatross, we must hark back to our distant hunter-gatherer ancestors. No fatness there. The constant trekking over long distances in search of scarce foods probably selected against obesity. It has been theorized that these ancestors acquired "thrifty genes" to store the fat of feasts in order to sustain them through famines. In our American surfeit, these ancestral adaptations have become liabilities. Fine-tuned by our individual genetic legacies, each of us settles into a metabolic equilibrium.

For those of us whose genes are all too thrifty, this settling point is a level of excess weight that we cannot reduce without sustained dietary effort. Today, the increasing consumption of cheap, readily available fatty foods is propelling the most metabolically susceptible of us into exorbitant obesity. Once our fat cells become extremely impacted, the recidivism rate of diets is almost 100 percent. For four million morbidly obese Americans, diets strict enough to succeed are by and large too uncomfortable to be feasible. These people have an illness without a cure, one that is often complicated by heart disease, hypertension, diabetes mellitus, sleep apnea, gallstones, degenerative arthritis of weight-bearing joints, and restrictive lung disease.

Sometimes we have the opposite problem. Markedly reduced or absent fat is usually a marker of serious illness or catastrophe. Cancer can cause weight loss; many physical and psychological ailments can erode the appetite; famine or subjugation can bring starvation. Seriously underweight people appear hollowed out, as if their flesh has sunk beneath their skeletons. We feel contempt for the obese but pity for those who have no fat, along with anger if their loss was engendered by tyranny.

19   Starving fat cells can shrink to a fraction of their former selves. With centrally placed nuclei and globule-free pink cytoplasm, they come to resemble tumor cells. Golden brown lipofuscin pigment granules—footprints of wear and tear—lightly disperse themselves throughout. As part of this involution, fat lobules can deflate into discrete, fat-free balls or, in the severest cachexia, into worm-like streaks as they distance themselves from one another. This fat loss is most apparent beneath the skin and in fat that hovers inside the abdomen.

20   When starvation remains unabated and the body's fat stores are eventually spent, proteins are burned to fuel the last, flickering glow of life force. But proteins are essential for maintaining cell function. When they are depleted to half their normal level, death ensues.

21   I ask Patti to recall a typical day lived inside her atypical body. She tells me that she always felt uncomfortable when she awoke. She slept on her side because she couldn't breathe on her back; her arms and hands often got caught underneath her body, cutting off her circulation and waking her. By morning, her upper limbs were numb and swollen, and her back and neck were sore. Her side of the mattress was cratered when she arose. She covered the sinkhole with a blanket so that Frank couldn't see it.

22   "I never ate breakfast," she says. "I got up, showered, and drove to work. The car seat creaked beneath me. I could hardly reach the steering wheel because my belly was in the way, and my feet went numb from body compression. Once I was rear-ended and my weight broke my seat in half."

23   Patti encountered little discrimination in her office, but lunches were difficult. She worried about fitting into a colleague's car en route to a restaurant. Once there, she prayed for a table and chairs because she couldn't wedge into a booth. Maître d's and waitresses ignored her. *Does anyone her size really want more food?* And sitting so close to others, she worried that the smell of her belly ooze would be detectable. Beneath her massive bulge of abdominal fat, ulcerated skin rashes wept until the itch was unbearable and the smell was rank. None of her medications brought relief. At home, she could raise the bulge of her abdomen and sit in the sway of a fan until the forced air dried her wounds, but at work there was no respite.

24   Patti also fretted about personal hygiene. "Morbidly obese people won't tell you this," she says, "but they can't wipe themselves properly after they use the bathroom. They can't reach their tush. At home I could clean my private parts with a hand shower. If I was sick, I had to rely on Frank to wipe me. He never said a word, but I was humiliated. At work,

I kept a bottle washer with me. I'd wipe myself with it the best I could, but how uncomfortable was that?"

By the afternoon, Patti was emotionally and physically exhausted. 25 Her legs swelled from supporting her body. Sciatica pierced her lower back like a fiery poker. She knew she would be too weary to cook dinner, so she usually bought fast food on the way home.

Some nights, parent meetings at the children's school could go on for 26 hours. "The chairs in the auditorium were little plastic things. I'd stand but eventually they'd say, 'Sit.'" So she would cautiously spread herself over the chair, her legs and thighs bearing much of her load while she braced her arms against the armrests.

"What about sex?" I ask, emboldened by her candor. 27

Patti gazes at me patiently. No question is too personal; she wants to 28 be as clear and open as she can in order to make people understand that morbid obesity is not a choice but an affliction. "I was pretty tired by then. Besides, it wasn't even enjoyable. I was confined to the missionary position and I couldn't stay there for long because I'd begin to choke."

Her lumbering lack of mobility in bed was just one more failure 29 among her many. Beaten daily into feelings of inferiority, Patti lost hope that she could ever change. "You're hardly alive when you're so huge," she says quietly. "I'd think about my kids, how embarrassed they were for me, how I couldn't really be there for them. I'd have given anything to lose weight permanently, but I just couldn't do it."

Surgeons fix bodily things. What is removable, if diseased or malfunc- 30 tioning, they can remove, and what is irremovable, they can sometimes imaginatively bypass. (Witness the skirting of coronary-artery blockages with leg-vein grafts.) The disappointing long-term results of medical, drug, and behavioral therapies for obesity in extremis have increased the number of referrals for a different kind of bypass: bariatric surgery, which circumnavigates portions of the stomach.

In 1997, Patti Fleming learned from her physicians that perhaps, after 31 all, she need not surrender all hope. Without bariatric surgery, she would not likely live to see her grandchildren; with it, she came to believe that she might prolong her future and even recapture her past, the years before her fat cells established an absolute dictatorship within her body.

The size and structure of the stomach pouch, the nature of the in- 32 testinal renovation, are intimately related and the subject of much surgical bandying. One such gastrointestinal resection—the Roux-en-Y gastric bypass—is currently the procedure of choice at UCLA; it is the one that Patti Fleming agreed to undergo. The bariatric team believed that she was a good candidate for the procedure, that she could commit herself to a draconian modification of her gastrointestinal tract and her life.

It is a courageous endeavor to submit one's obese body to the knife 33 in this way, to pucker billions of fat cells in the hope of renewal. None of

Patti's family or friends encouraged her to have the bypass. *Surely another diet is preferable to an operation.* She ignored them.

34   Patti awoke from the surgery frightened by what had been permanently perpetrated. Her 1,700-milliliter stomach had been miniaturized to 35 milliliters. The loss of 1,665 milliliters drastically reduced her stomach's capacity to process, absorb, and propel foods; her small intestines had been reconstructed to reduce the number of calories they could absorb. For the rest of her life, she would have to supplement her new diet with vitamin B_{12} injections. She would have to limit her food intake to frequent, small-portioned meals or suffer the consequences: the trim new stomach pouch, unable to handle at one sitting a food serving larger than a hard-boiled egg, or one that had been chewed fewer than thirty to forty times, would dump its unprocessed contents into the small bowel. The result would be abdominal pain, nausea, diarrhea, dizziness, heart palpitations, even loss of consciousness.

35   Patti's postoperative abdominal cramping was so severe that it made the deliveries of her children, without anesthetic, seem like child's play. Today, support groups are commonplace before and after bariatric surgery, but in 1997 they had not yet been organized, so Patti endured her flesh wounds as she had her obesity—largely on her own.

36   From minuscule drinks of water, she progressed to clear fluids and sugar-free Jell-O. By the third week, the cramping and wound pain had subsided and she could swallow liquid meals (Carnation Instant Breakfast, Slim-Fast). By the sixth week she was consuming high-protein, pureed foods along with a few soft foods (nonfat cottage cheese, water-packed canned tuna). By the eighth week she was eating fruits and vegetables. Pangs of withdrawal from fats and sweets seemed to rack every shriveling fat cell. She could not even drink a soda; the carbonated bubbles took up too much space.

37   Fat cells were releasing their stored triglycerides, and free fatty acids in the blood stream were burning like oil. Fat was melting into energy. Patti felt her clothes loosening. She still weighed more than 300 pounds, but Frank, who had opposed the surgery, noticed the shrinkage and cheered her on. For the first time in many years, she felt the urge to exercise. She swam in her apartment complex's outdoor pool at night, when the neighbors could not see her. As the pounds dropped, Patti's high blood pressure returned to normal and the arthritic pains in her feet, knees, back, and neck subsided. She was no longer primed for illness.

38   Six months after her surgery, Patti's jaw, elbows, shoulders, breasts, buttocks, knees, and even her lap emerged from her dwindling sphere. She could sit in a regular chair without bruising her hips; cross her legs; manipulate exercise equipment; climb in and out of a car with ease; fit into a restaurant booth.

39   "I lost so much weight in the early stages," she says, "that I didn't know what size I was. But it took my breath away when I first went to

Victoria's Secret to buy underwear and to Robinsons-May for my clothes. I never went back to Lane Bryant again."

The lighter she got, the greater her incentive to retrieve all that she   40
had missed. In her new 169-pound body—that is where she settled—Patti Fleming interacts casually with people and has rediscovered sports. She camps, water-skis, and kayaks, as she did in her youth. She often chooses tight-fitting dresses.

The Roux-en-Y is less a solution than a tool. It has allowed Patti to   41
deplete her fat cells and to sustain this reduction as long as she plays by the rules, most of which prevent her from taking as much pleasure from eating as she used to. "If I get stressed and forget to eat slowly," she says, "the food gets stuck. It's like an elephant walking on my sternum. Frank will quickly spot fast eating and hold my hand. It's one of our secret little communications. He knows how hard I've worked to get where I am."

On the stage of my microscope, fat cells, whether too large or too small,   42
aggregate in a lobular, geometric precision. Theirs is a glomerate beauty, an abundance or dearth of pure energy. In this microcosm I can see the power of their mutability. No other human cells can so rampantly rise or fall and, like millions of fiery suns burning bright or burning out, alter our universe.

Content

1. Nadler claims that "aggregate size [of fat cells] . . . can affect our health; shape the way we think about ourselves and how others think of us; make our lives unbearable" (¶ 4)? What information does he provide to convince readers of the truth of this statement? Explain your answer.

2. What is Nadler's purpose in writing this essay? What is his central argument? Is his argument implicit or explicit? How does his description—of fat cells and of Patti Fleming—contribute to or detract from the effectiveness of his argument?

3. Discuss the pros and cons of bariatric surgery as Nadler explains it (¶s 30–41). As a treatment for morbid obesity, would this operation be worth doing in spite of all the side effects?

4. Even though Patti Fleming has lost a great deal of weight, Nadler says that "in her mind she remains a fat person" (¶ 5). What does he mean? How is self-esteem related to a person's self-image?

Strategies/Structures

5. Nadler analyzes the case of Patti Fleming. In what ways is this a typical case history? In what ways does Nadler's presentation make it atypical? What does he do to make his subject such a sympathetic character in spite of a variety of unpleasant details about her case (and the difficulties morbidly obese people experience)?

6. Does a single case suffice to make the point about four million morbidly obese people?

7. What does Nadler mean when he says, "I wish to think of cells as more than something fixed beneath the lens of my microscope" (¶ 6)? How does he accomplish this?

Language

8. Nadler's essay alternates between scientific descriptions of fat cells and operations and compassionate description and analysis of Patti Fleming's life and her medical history. Identify and describe Nadler's tone in each type of writing, and explain how the tone reinforces the words. What effects does the tone have on you as a reader?

9. Why does Nadler italicize some of the language in paragraphs 15, 23, and 33?

For Writing

10. Obesity is a huge problem in our nation. One-third of the world population is identified as "obese," including 27 percent of ten-year-olds in the United States and 22 million children under age five worldwide ("U.N. Warns That Many Children, Rich and Poor, Are Obese," *New York Times*, May 17, 2002, A9). The World Health Organization identifies this as "an epidemic with a simple cure: Eat less fat, less sugar, less salt" (A9). Since most people know the medical consequences of obesity—diabetes, high blood pressure, strokes, heart attacks, among others—why do they persist in overeating? Write a workable proposal for obese (or potentially obese) people to follow to arrive at and maintain a healthy weight. If you personally have had problems with unwanted weight gain, draw on your own experience in explaining the problem and presenting the solution.

11. Write an essay that considers the impact of the mass media in shaping self-image in relation to appearance. For evidence, you might consider the appearance of popular film and television actors and the appearance of models in magazines such as *Vogue, Seventeen,* or *GQ*, which are directed toward a particular audience. If the media really exert such a powerful influence, why are so many Americans (four million, according to Nadler) morbidly obese?

SCOTT RUSSELL SANDERS

"Under the Influence," from *Secrets of the Universe* (1991), is full of examples that describe the effects of alcoholism—on the alcoholic father, on his wife, alternately distressed and defiant, and on his children, cowering with guilt and fear. Sanders uses especially the example of himself, the eldest son, who felt responsible for his father's drinking, guilty because he couldn't get him to stop, and obligated to atone for his father's sins through his own perfection and accomplishment. Although at the age of forty-four Sanders knows that his father was "consumed by disease rather than by disappointment," he writes to understand "the corrosive mixture of helplessness, responsibility, and shame that I learned to feel as the son of an alcoholic."

Through the highly specific example of his family's behavior, Sanders illustrates the general problem of alcoholism that afflicts some "ten or fifteen million people." He expects his readers to generalize and to learn from his understanding. (For more information about Sanders, see page 139).

Under the Influence: Paying the Price of My Father's Booze

My father drank. He drank as a gut-punched boxer gasps for breath, as a starving dog gobbles food—compulsively, secretly, in pain and trembling. I use the past tense not because he ever quit drinking but because he quit living. That is how the story ends for my father, age sixty-four, heart bursting, body cooling, slumped and forsaken on the linoleum of my brother's trailer. The story continues for my brother, my sister, my mother, and me, and will continue as long as memory holds.

In the perennial present of memory, I slip into the garage or barn to see my father tipping back the flat green bottles of wine, the brown cylinders of whiskey, the cans of beer disguised in paper bags. His Adam's apple bobs, the liquid gurgles, he wipes the sandy-haired back of a hand over his lips, and then, his bloodshot gaze bumping into me, he stashes the bottle or can inside his jacket, under the workbench, between two bales of hay, and we both pretend the moment has not occurred.

"What's up, buddy?" he says, thick-tongued and edgy.

"Sky's up," I answer, playing along.

"And don't forget prices," he grumbles. "Prices are always up. And taxes."

In memory, his white 1951 Pontiac with the stripes down the hood and the Indian head on the snout lurches to a stop in the driveway; or it is the 1956 Ford station wagon, or the 1963 Rambler shaped like a toad, or the sleek 1969 Bonneville that will do 120 miles per hour on straightaways; or it is the robin's-egg-blue pickup, new in 1980, battered in 1981, the year of his death. He climbs out, grinning dangerously, unsteady on his legs, and we children interrupt our game of catch, our building of snow forts, our picking of plums, to watch in silence as he weaves past us into the house, where he drops into his overstuffed chair and falls asleep. Shaking her head, our mother stubs out a cigarette he has left smoldering in the ashtray. All evening, until our bedtimes, we tiptoe past him, as past a snoring dragon. Then we curl fearfully in our sheets, listening. Eventually he wakes with a grunt, Mother slings accusations at him, he snarls back, she yells, he growls, their voices clashing. Before long, she retreats to their bedroom, sobbing—not from the blows of fists, for he never strikes her, but from the force of his words.

7   Left alone, our father prowls the house, thumping into furniture, rummaging in the kitchen, slamming doors, turning the pages of the newspaper with a savage crackle, muttering back at the late-night drivel from television. The roof might fly off, the walls might buckle from the pressure of his rage. Whatever my brother and sister and mother may be thinking on their own rumpled pillows, I lie there hating him, loving him, fearing him, knowing I have failed him. I tell myself he drinks to ease the ache that gnaws at his belly, an ache I must have caused by disappointing him somehow, a murderous ache I should be able to relieve by doing all my chores, earning A's in school, winning baseball games, fixing the broken washer and the burst pipes, bringing in the money to fill his empty wallet. He would not hide the green bottles in his toolbox, would not sneak off to the barn with a lump under his coat, would not fall asleep in the daylight, would not roar and fume, would not drink himself to death, if only I were perfect.

8   I am forty-four, and I know full well now that my father was an alcoholic, a man consumed by disease rather than by disappointment. What had seemed to me a private grief is in fact, of course, a public scourge. In the United States alone, some ten or fifteen million people share his ailment, and behind the doors they slam in fury or disgrace, countless other children tremble. I comfort myself with such knowledge, holding it against the throb of memory like an ice pack against a bruise. Other people have keener sources of grief: poverty, racism, rape, war. I do not wish to compete to determine who has suffered most. I am only trying to understand the corrosive mixture of helplessness, responsibility, and shame that I learned to feel as the son of an alcoholic. I realize now that I did not cause my father's illness, nor could I have cured it. Yet for all this grownup knowledge, I am still ten years old, my own son's age, and as that boy I struggle in guilt and confusion to save my father from pain.

9   Consider a few of our synonyms for *drunk:* tipsy, tight, pickled, soused, and plowed; stoned and stewed, lubricated and inebriated, juiced and sluiced; three sheets to the wind, in your cups, out of your mind, under the table; lit up, tanked up, wiped out; besotted, blotto, bombed, and buzzed; plastered, polluted, putrefied; loaded or looped, boozy, woozy, fuddled, or smashed; crocked and shit-faced, corked and pissed, snockered and sloshed.

10   It is a mostly humorous lexicon, as the lore that deals with drunks— in jokes and cartoons, in plays, films and television skits—is largely comic. Aunt Matilda nips elderberry wine from the sideboard and burps politely during supper. Uncle Fred slouches to the table glassy-eyed, wearing a lampshade for a hat and murmuring, "Candy is dandy, but liquor is quicker." Inspired by cocktails, Mrs. Somebody recounts the events of her day in a fuzzy dialect, while Mr. Somebody nibbles her ear and croons a bawdy song. On the sofa with Boyfriend, Daughter Somebody giggles,

licking gin from her lips, and loosens the bows in her hair. Junior knocks back some brews with his chums at the Leopard Lounge and stumbles home to the wrong house, wonders foggily why he cannot locate his pajamas, and crawls naked into bed with the ugliest girl in school. The family dog slurps from a neglected martini and wobbles to the nursery, where he vomits in Baby's shoe.

It is all great fun. But if in the audience you notice a few laughing 11
faces turn grim when the drunk lurches onstage, don't be surprised, for these are the children of alcoholics. Over the grinning mask of Dionysus, the leering face of Bacchus, these children cannot help seeing the bloated features of their own parents. Instead of laughing, they wince, they mourn. Instead of celebrating the drunk as one freed from constraints, they pity him as one enslaved. They refuse to believe *in vino veritas*, having seen their befuddled parents skid away from truth toward folly and oblivion. And so these children bite their lips until the lush staggers into the wings.

My father, when drunk, was neither funny nor honest; he was pa- 12
thetic, frightening, deceitful. There seemed to be a leak in him somewhere, and he poured in booze to keep from draining dry. Like a torture victim who refuses to squeal, he would never admit that he had touched a drop, not even in his last year, when he seemed to be dissolving in alcohol before our very eyes. I never knew him to lie about anything, ever, except about this one ruinous fact. Drowsy, clumsy, unable to fix a bicycle tire, balance a grocery sack, or walk across a room, he was stripped of his true self by drink. In a matter of minutes, the contents of a bottle could transform a brave man into a coward, a buddy into a bully, a gifted athlete and skilled carpenter and shrewd businessman into a bumbler. No dictionary of synonyms for *drunk* would soften the anguish of watching our prince turn into a frog.

Father's drinking became the family secret. While growing up, we 13
children never breathed a word of it beyond the four walls of our house. To this day, my brother and sister rarely mention it, and then only when I press them. I did not confess the ugly, bewildering fact to my wife until his wavering and slurred speech forced me to. Recently, on the seventh anniversary of my father's death, I asked my mother if she ever spoke of his drinking to friends. "No, no, never," she replied hastily. "I couldn't bear for anyone to know."

The secret bores under the skin, gets in the blood, into the bone, and 14
stays there. Long after you have supposedly been cured of malaria, the fever can flare up, the tremors can shake you. So it is with the fevers of shame. You swallow the bitter quinine of knowledge, and you learn to feel pity and compassion toward the drinker. Yet the shame lingers and, because of it, anger.

For a long stretch of my childhood we lived on a military reservation in 15
Ohio, an arsenal where bombs were stored underground in bunkers and

vintage airplanes burst into flames and unstable artillery shells boomed nightly at the dump. We had the feeling, as children, that we played within a minefield, where a heedless footfall could trigger an explosion. When Father was drinking, the house, too, became a minefield. The least bump could set off either parent.

16   The more he drank, the more obsessed Mother became with stopping him. She hunted for bottles, counted the cash in his wallet, sniffed at his breath. Without meaning to snoop, we children blundered left and right into damning evidence. On afternoons when he came home from work sober, we flung ourselves at him for hugs and felt against our ribs the telltale lump in his coat. In the barn we tumbled on the hay and heard beneath our sneakers the crunch of broken glass. We tugged open a drawer in his workbench, looking for screwdrivers or crescent wrenches, and spied a gleaming six-pack among the tools. Playing tag, we darted around the house just in time to see him sway on the rear stoop and heave a finished bottle into the woods. In his good-night kiss we smelled the cloying sweetness of Clorets, the mints he chewed to camouflage his dragon's breath.

17   I can summon up that kiss right now by recalling Theodore Roethke's lines about his own father:

> The whiskey on your breath
> Could make a small boy dizzy;
> But I hung on like death:
> Such waltzing was not easy.

Such waltzing was hard, terribly hard, for with a boy's scrawny arms I was trying to hold my tipsy father upright.

18   For years, the chief source of those incriminating bottles and cans was a grimy store a mile from us, a cinderblock place called Sly's, with two gas pumps outside and a mangy dog asleep in the window. Inside, on rusty metal shelves or in wheezing coolers, you could find pop and Popsicles, cigarettes, potato chips, canned soup, raunchy postcards, fishing gear, Twinkies, wine, and beer. When Father drove anywhere on errands, Mother would send us along as guards, warning us not to let him out of our sight. And so with one or more of us on board, Father would cruise up to Sly's, pump a dollar's worth of gas or plump the tires with air, and then, telling us to wait in the car, he would head for the doorway.

19   Dutiful and panicky, we cried, "Let us go with you!"

20   "No," he answered. "I'll be back in two shakes."

21   "Please!"

22   "No!" he roared. "Don't you budge or I'll jerk a knot in your tails!"

23   So we stayed put, kicking the seats, while he ducked inside. Often, when he had parked the car at a careless angle, we gazed in through the window and saw Mr. Sly fetching down from the shelf behind the cash register two green pints of Gallo wine. Father swigged one of them right

there at the counter, stuffed the other in his pocket, and then out he came, a bulge in his coat, a flustered look on his reddened face.

Because the mom and pop who ran the dump were neighbors of ours, 24 living just down the tar-blistered road, I hated them all the more for poisoning my father. I wanted to sneak in their store and smash the bottles and set fire to the place. I also hated the Gallo brothers, Ernest and Julio, whose jovial faces beamed from the labels of their wine, labels I would find, torn and curled, when I burned the trash. I noted the Gallo brothers' address in California and studied the road atlas to see how far that was from Ohio, because I meant to go out there and tell Ernest and Julio what they were doing to my father, and then, if they showed no mercy, I would kill them.

While growing up on the back roads and in the country schools and 25 cramped Methodist churches of Ohio and Tennessee, I never heard the word *alcoholic*, never happened across it in books or magazines. In the nearby towns, there were no addiction-treatment programs, no community mental-health centers, no Alcoholics Anonymous chapters, no therapists. Left alone with our grievous secret, we had no way of understanding Father's drinking except as an act of will, a deliberate folly or cruelty, a moral weakness, a sin. He drank because he chose to, pure and simple. Why our father, so playful and competent and kind when sober, would choose to ruin himself and punish his family we could not fathom.

Our neighborhood was high on the Bible, and the Bible was hard on 26 drunkards. "Woe to those who are heroes at drinking wine and valiant men in mixing strong drink," wrote Isaiah. "The priest and the prophet reel with strong drink, they are confused with wine, they err in vision, they stumble in giving judgment. For all tables are full of vomit, no place is without filthiness." We children had seen those fouled tables at the local truck stop where the notorious boozers hung out, our father occasionally among them. "Wine and new wine take away the understanding," declared the prophet Hosea. We had also seen evidence of that in our father, who could multiply seven-digit numbers in his head when sober but when drunk could not help us with fourth-grade math. Proverbs warned: "Do not look at wine when it is red, when it sparkles in the cup and goes down smoothly. At the last it bites like a serpent and stings like an adder. Your eyes will see strange things, and your mind utter perverse things." Woe, woe.

Dismayingly often, these biblical drunkards stirred up trouble for 27 their own kids. Noah made fresh wine after the flood, drank too much of it, fell asleep without any clothes on, and was glimpsed in the buff by his son Ham, whom Noah promptly cursed. In one passage—it was so shocking we had to read it under our blankets with flashlights—the patriarch Lot fell down drunk and slept with his daughters. The sins of the fathers set their children's teeth on edge.

Our ministers were fond of quoting St. Paul's pronouncement that 28 drunkards would not inherit the kingdom of God. These grave preachers assured us that the wine referred to in the Last Supper was in fact grape juice. Bible and sermons and hymns combined to give us the impression that Moses should have brought down from the mountain another stone tablet, bearing the Eleventh Commandment: Thou shalt not drink.

29   The scariest and most illuminating Bible story apropos of drunkards was the one about the lunatic and the swine. We knew it by heart: When Jesus climbed out of his boat one day, this lunatic came charging up from the graveyard, stark naked and filthy, frothing at the mouth, so violent that he broke the strongest chains. Nobody would go near him. Night and day for years, this madman had been wailing among the tombs and bruising himself with stones. Jesus took one look at him and said, "Come out of the man, you unclean spirits!" for he could see that the lunatic was possessed by demons. Meanwhile, some hogs were conveniently rooting nearby. "If we have to come out," begged the demons, "at least let us go into those swine." Jesus agreed, the unclean spirits entered the hogs, and the hogs raced straight off a cliff and plunged into a lake. Hearing the story in Sunday school, my friends thought mainly of the pigs. (How big a splash did they make? Who paid for the lost pork?) But I thought of the redeemed lunatic, who bathed himself and put on clothes and calmly sat at the feet of Jesus, restored—so the Bible said—to "his right mind."

30   When drunk, our father was clearly in his wrong mind. He became a stranger, as fearful to us as any graveyard lunatic, not quite frothing at the mouth but fierce enough, quick-tempered, explosive; or else he grew maudlin and weepy, which frightened us nearly as much. In my boyhood despair, I reasoned that maybe he wasn't to blame for turning into an ogre: Maybe, like the lunatic, he was possessed by demons.

31   If my father was indeed possessed, who would exorcise him? If he was a sinner, who would save him? If he was ill, who would cure him? If he suffered, who would ease his pain? Not ministers or doctors, for we could not bring ourselves to confide in them; not the neighbors, for we pretended they had never seen him drunk; not Mother, who fussed and pleaded but could not budge him; not my brother and sister, who were only kids. That left me. It did not matter that I, too, was only a child, and a bewildered one at that. I could not excuse myself.

32   On first reading a description of delirium tremens—in a book on alcoholism I smuggled from a university library—I thought immediately of the frothing lunatic and the frenzied swine. When I read stories or watched films about grisly metamorphoses—Dr. Jekyll and Mr. Hyde, the mild husband changing into a werewolf, the kindly neighbor inhabited by a brutal alien—I could not help but see my own father's mutation from sober to drunk. Even today, knowing better, I am attracted by the demonic theory of drink, for when I recall my father's transformation, the emergence of his ugly second self, I find it easy to believe in being possessed by unclean spirits. We never knew which version of Father would come home from

Describe and interpret this picture, with relevance to Sanders's essay "Under the Influence" and to your own experience. In what ways can this picture be read—and by whom—as an invitation to party? In what ways—and by whom—can this picture be read as a cautionary tale?

work, the true or the tainted, nor could we guess how far down the slope toward cruelty he would slide.

How far a man *could* slide we gauged by observing our backroad neighbors—the out-of-work miners who had dragged their families to our corner of Ohio from the desolate hollows of Appalachia, the tightfisted farmers, the surly mechanics, the balked and broken men. There was, for example, whiskey-soaked Mr. Jenkins, who beat his wife and kids so hard we could hear their screams from the road. There was Mr. Lavo the wino, who fell asleep smoking time and again, until one night his disgusted wife bundled up the children and went outside and left him in his easy chair to burn; he awoke on his own, staggered out coughing into the yard, and pounded her flat while the children looked on and the shack turned to ash. There was the truck driver, Mr. Sampson, who tripped over his son's tricycle one night while drunk and got mad, jumped into his semi, and drove away, shifting through the dozen gears, and never came back. We saw the bruised children of these fathers clump onto our school bus, we saw the abandoned children huddle in the pews at church, we saw the stunned and battered mothers begging for help at our doors.

Our own father never beat us, and I don't think he beat Mother, but he threatened often. The Old Testament Yahweh was not more terrible in His rage. Eyes blazing, voice booming, Father would pull out his belt and swear to give us a whipping, but he never followed through, never needed to, because we could imagine it so vividly. He shoved us, pawed us with the back of his hand, not to injure, just to clear a space. I can see him grabbing Mother by the hair as she cowers on a chair during a nightly quarrel. He twists her neck back until she gapes up at him, and then he lifts over her skull a glass quart bottle of milk, and milk spilling down his forearm, and he yells at her, "Say just one more word, one goddamn word, and I'll shut you up!" I fear she will prick him with her sharp tongue, but she is terrified into silence, and so am I, and the leaking bottle quivers in the air, and milk seeps through the red hair of my father's uplifted arm, and the entire scene is there to this moment, the head jerked back, the club raised.

35   When the drink made him weepy, Father would pack, kiss each of us children on the head, and announce from the front door that he was moving out. "Where to?" we demanded, fearful each time that he would leave for good, as Mr. Sampson had roared away for good in his diesel truck. "Someplace where I won't get hounded every minute," Father would answer, his jaw quivering. He stabbed a look at Mother, who might say, "Don't run into the ditch before you get there," or "Good riddance," and then he would slink away. Mother watched him go with arms crossed over her chest, her face closed like the lid on a box of snakes. We children bawled. Where could he go? To the truck stop, that den of iniquity? To one of those dark, ratty flophouses in town? Would he wind up sleeping under a railroad bridge or on a park bench or in a cardboard box, mummied in rags like the bums we had seen on our trips to Cleveland and Chicago? We bawled and bawled, wondering if he would ever come back.

36   He always did come back, a day or a week later, but each time there was a sliver less of him.

37   In Kafka's *Metamorphosis*, which opens famously with Gregor Samsa waking up from uneasy dreams to find himself transformed into an insect, Gregor's family keep reassuring themselves that things will be just fine again "when he comes back to us." Each time alcohol transformed our father we held out the same hope, that he would really and truly come back to us, our authentic father, the tender and playful and competent man, and then all things would be fine. We had grounds for such hope. After his tearful departures and chapfallen returns, he would sometimes go weeks, even months, without drinking. Those were glad times. Every day without the furtive glint of bottles, every meal without a fight, every bedtime without sobs encouraged us to believe that such bliss might go on forever.

38   Mother was fooled by such a hope all during the forty-odd years she knew Greeley Ray Sanders. Soon after she met him in a Chicago delicatessen on the eve of World War II and fell for his butter-melting Mississippi drawl and his wavy red hair, she learned that he drank heavily. But

then so did a lot of men. She would soon coax or scold him into breaking the nasty habit. She would point out to him how ugly and foolish it was, this bleary drinking, and then he would quit. He refused to quit during their engagement, however, still refused during the first years of marriage, refused until my older sister came along. The shock of fatherhood sobered him, and he remained sober through my birth at the end of the war and right on through until we moved in 1951 to the Ohio arsenal. The arsenal had more than its share of alcoholics, drug addicts, and other varieties of escape artists. There I turned six and started school and woke into a child's flickering awareness, just in time to see my father begin sneaking swigs in the garage.

He sobered up again for most of a year at the height of the Korean 39 War, to celebrate the birth of my brother. But aside from that dry spell, his only breaks from drinking before I graduated from high school were just long enough to raise and then dash our hopes. Then during the fall of my senior year—the time of the Cuban Missile Crisis, when it seemed that the nightly explosions at the munitions dump and the nightly rages in our household might spread to engulf the globe—Father collapsed. His liver, kidneys, and heart all conked out. The doctors saved him, but only by a hair. He stayed in the hospital for weeks, going through a withdrawal so terrible that Mother would not let us visit him. If he wanted to kill himself, the doctors solemnly warned him, all he had to do was hit the bottle again. One binge would finish him.

Father must have believed them, for he stayed dry the next fifteen 40 years. It was an answer to prayer, Mother said, it was a miracle. I believe it was a reflex of fear, which he sustained over the years through courage and pride. He knew a man could die from drink, for his brother Roscoe had. We children never laid eyes on doomed Uncle Roscoe, but in the stories Mother told us he became a fairy-tale figure, like a boy who took the wrong turn in the woods and was gobbled up by the wolf.

The fifteen-year dry spell came to an end with Father's retirement in 41 the spring of 1978. Like many men, he gave up his identity along with his job. One day he was a boss at the factory, with a brass plate on his door and a reputation to uphold; the next day he was a nobody at home. He and Mother were leaving Ontario, the last of the many places to which his job had carried them, and they were moving to a new house in Mississippi, his childhood stomping ground. As a boy in Mississippi, Father sold Coca-Cola during dances while the moonshiners peddled their brew in the parking lot; as a young blade, he fought in bars and in the ring, winning a state Golden Gloves championship; he gambled at poker, hunted pheasant, raced motorcycles and cars, played semiprofessional baseball, and, along with all his buddies—in the Black Cat Saloon, behind the cotton gin, in the woods—he drank hard. It was a perilous youth to dream of recovering.

After his final day of work, Mother drove on ahead with a car full of 42 begonias and violets, while Father stayed behind to oversee the packing.

When the van was loaded, the sweaty movers broke open a six-pack and offered him a beer.

43   "Let's drink to retirement!" they crowed. "Let's drink to freedom! to fishing! hunting! loafing! Let's drink to a guy who's going home!"

44   At least I imagine some such words, for that is all I can do, imagine, and I see Father's hand trembling in midair as he thinks about the fifteen sober years and about the doctors' warning, and he tells himself, *Goddamnit, I am a free man,* and *Why can't a free man drink one beer after a lifetime of hard work?* and I see his arm reaching, his fingers closing, the can tilting to his lips. I even supply a label for the beer, a swaggering brand that promises on television to deliver the essence of life. I watch the amber liquid pour down his throat, the alcohol steal into his blood, the key turn in his brain.

45   Soon after my parents moved back to Father's treacherous stomping ground, my wife and I visited them in Mississippi with our four-year-old daughter. Mother had been too distraught to warn me about the return of the demons. So when I climbed out of the car that bright July morning and saw my father napping in the hammock, I felt uneasy, and when he lurched upright and blinked his bloodshot eyes and greeted us in a syrupy voice, I was hurled back into childhood.

46   "What's the matter with Papaw?" our daughter asked.

47   "Nothing," I said. "Nothing!"

48   Like a child again, I pretended not to see him in his stupor, and behind my phony smile I grieved. On that visit and on the few that remained before his death, once again I found bottles in the workbench, bottles in the woods. Again his hands shook too much for him to run a saw, to make his precious miniature furniture, to drive straight down back roads. Again he wound up in the ditch, in the hospital, in jail, in the treatment center. Again he shouted and wept. Again he lied. "I never touched a drop," he swore. "Your mother's making it up."

49   I no longer fancied I could reason with the men whose names I found on the bottles—Jim Beam, Jack Daniel's—but I was able now to recall the cold statistics about alcoholism: ten million victims, fifteen million, twenty. And yet, in spite of my age, I reacted in the same blind way as I had in childhood, by vainly seeking to erase through my efforts whatever drove him to drink. I worked on their place twelve and sixteen hours a day, in the swelter of Mississippi summers, digging ditches, running electrical wires, planting trees, mowing grass, building sheds, as though what nagged at him was some list of chores, as though by taking his worries upon my shoulders I could redeem him. I was flung back into boyhood, acting as though my father would not drink himself to death if only I were perfect.

50   I failed of perfection; he succeeded in dying. To the end, he considered himself not sick but sinful. "Do you want to kill yourself?" I asked

him. "Why not?" he answered. "Why the hell not? What's there to save?" To the end, he would not speak about his feelings, would not or could not give a name to the beast that was devouring him.

In silence, he went rushing off to the cliff. Unlike the biblical swine, 51 however, he left behind a few of the demons to haunt his children. Life with him and the loss of him twisted us into shapes that will be familiar to other sons and daughters of alcoholics. My brother became a rebel, my sister retreated into shyness, I played the stalwart and dutiful son who would hold the family together. If my father was unstable, I would be a rock. If he squandered money on drink, I would pinch every penny. If he wept when drunk—and only when drunk—I would not let myself weep at all. If he roared at the Little League umpire for calling my pitches balls, I would throw nothing but strikes. Watching him flounder and rage, I came to dread the loss of control. I would go through life without making anyone mad. I vowed never to put in my mouth or veins any chemical that would banish my everyday self. I would never make a scene, never lash out at the ones I loved, never hurt a soul. Through hard work, relentless work, I would achieve something dazzling—in the classroom, on the basketball court, in the science lab, in the pages of books—and my achievement would distract the world's eyes from his humiliation. I would become a worthy sacrifice, and the smoke of my burning would please God.

It is far easier to recognize these twists in my character than to undo 52 them. Work has become an addiction for me, as drink was an addiction for my father. Knowing this, my daughter gave me a placard for the wall: WORKAHOLIC. The labor is endless and futile, for I can no more redeem myself through work than I could redeem my father. I still panic in the face of other people's anger, because his drunken temper was so terrible. I shrink from causing sadness or disappointment even to strangers, as though I were still concealing the family shame. I still notice every twitch of emotion in those faces around me, having learned as a child to read the weather in faces, and I blame myself for their least pang of unhappiness or anger. In certain moods I blame myself for everything. Guilt burns like acid in my veins.

I am moved to write these pages now because my own son, at the age of 53 ten, is taking on himself the griefs of the world, and in particular the griefs of his father. He tells me that when I am gripped by sadness, he feels responsible; he feels there must be something he can do to spring me from depression, to fix my life and that crushing sense of responsibility is exactly what I felt at the age of ten in the face of my father's drinking. My son wonders if I, too, am possessed. I write, therefore, to drag into the light what eats at me—the fear, the guilt, the shame—so that my own children may be spared.

54   I still shy away from nightclubs, from bars, from parties where the solvent is alcohol. My friends puzzle over this, but it is no more peculiar than for a man to shy away from the lions' den after seeing his father torn apart. I took my own first drink at the age of twenty-one, half a glass of burgundy. I knew the odds of my becoming an alcoholic were four times higher than for the children of nonalcoholic fathers. So I sipped warily.

55   I still do—once a week, perhaps, a glass of wine, a can of beer, nothing stronger, nothing more. I listen for the turning of a key in my brain.

Content

1. This essay abounds in examples of alcoholism. Which examples are the most memorable? Are these also the most painful? The most powerful? Explain why.

2. Sanders says that in spite of all his "grown-up knowledge" of alcoholism, "I am still ten years old, my own son's age" (¶ 8) as he writes this essay. What does he mean by this? What kind of a character is Sanders in this essay? What kind of a character is his father? Is there any resemblance between father and son?

Strategies/Structures

3. Is Sanders writing for alcoholic readers? Their families? People unfamiliar with the symptoms of alcoholism? Or is he writing mostly for himself, to try to come to terms with the effects of his father's alcoholism on him then and now?

4. Each section of this essay (¶s 1–8, 9–14, 15–24, 25–31, 32–36, 37–44, 45–52, 53–55) focuses on a different sort of example. What are they, and why are they arranged in this particular order?

5. Why does Sanders wait until late in the essay (¶ 39) to discuss his father's sobriety, and then devote only three paragraphs to a state that lasted fifteen years?

Language

6. What is the tone of this essay? How does Sanders, one of the victims of alcoholism as both a child and an adult, avoid being full of self-pity? Is he angry at his father? How can you tell?

For Writing

7. "Father's drinking became the family secret," says Sanders (¶ 13). Every family has significant secrets. Explain one of your family secrets, illustrating its effects on various family members, particularly on yourself. If you wish to keep the secret, don't show your essay to anyone; the point of writing this is to help yourself understand or come to terms with the matter.

8. Define an economic, political, ecological, social, or personal problem (unemployment, waste disposal, AIDS, hunger, housing, racism, or another subject of your choice) so your readers can understand it from an unusual perspective— your own or that of your sources. Illustrate its causes, effects, or implications with several significant examples.

ASIYA S. TSCHANNERL

Asiya Tschannerl was adopted soon after her birth in Philadelphia in 1977 by parents of Indian and Austrian nationalities (her Austrian last name, *Tschannerl*, rhymes with *chunnel*, as in the name of the tunnel under the English Channel). Having lived in China, India, and parts of Africa and Europe, she feels that her ethnicity extends well beyond her African-American roots. In 1998 she earned a B.Sc. in medical biochemistry from Royal Holloway, University of London, to which she has returned for graduate study in pursuit of a M.D. She is currently a certified emergency medical technician, and is an artist, composer, singer, cellist, and writer, as well.

Asiya believes that her best writing stems from subjects she knows well. As a consequence, she particularly enjoys writing short autobiographical pieces. As she composes these, she explains, she "retraces thoughts, smells, and touches from the past, since doing so usually brings a wealth of other memories along with the initial association." Indeed, through the "domino effect of remembrance," she claims even to remember her adoption at three months, the moment when her adoptive mother first held her. Her memories are evocative of the senses ("I remember leaning back against that wind and not being able to fall"), of pride, terror, disillusionment, and love. Through writing sketches such as "One Remembers Most What One Loves," Asiya hopes to "inspire readers with a willingness to embrace and love other cultures as their own."

❄ *One Remembers Most What One Loves*

I have often been commended for my memory. I can even remember being held when I was adopted at three months of age. Perhaps one only recalls events which profoundly change one's life.

I remember my youth very clearly. How the seasons would change! September would bring its chilly air and a nervous start of a new school year. November would be full of excitement, with its strong gusts of wind and swirling sandstorms. It was amazing to look at a grain of sand and know that it had come from over two thousand miles away, from the Gobi desert. I remember leaning back against that wind and not being able to fall. I can still see that stream of bicycles going to the city, every head clad with a thin scarf to protect against the sand.

How well I know that bitter coldness of the winter, bringing snowballs and ice-skating on the lake at the Summer Palace. February fireworks, noodles and mooncakes for the New Year, our home always filled with friendly visits. I remember the monsoon rains of April and how the rice fields behind our apartment would sway as if they had a life of their own. And how could I forget the long, hot summers of badminton, evening walks, and mosquito nets?

4   Perhaps my memory is fostered by the countless nights I spent memorizing Chinese characters, stroke after stroke. In any case, I cannot forget. I love my childhood. I love Beijing.

5   Bei sha tan nong ji xue yuan. This is the name of the Chinese compound we lived in, an agricultural mechanization institute on the outskirts of Beijing. During the day, my father worked there while I would accompany my mother into the city. My mother taught sociology at the Beijing Foreign Languages Institute and I attended its adjoining Chinese elementary school. At age nine, I was in a country I had not lived in since I was a toddler and my Chinese was very poor. Hence, I entered first grade having already had four years of American grade school.

6   I remember my apprehension when my teacher introduced me on the first day of school. A hush fell over the classroom as forty pairs of wide eyes beheld for the first time a person of African descent. After what seemed a long time, class went on as usual, and finding myself amidst a maze of unintelligible dialogue, I took out my coloring pencils and began to draw. The children around me smiled shyly at me, curious to see what I was drawing. Such was the beginning of enduring friendships.

7   As the months rolled by, the sea of gibberish slowly became a wealth of vocabulary. I never knew that a language could describe things so precisely—but this is not to be wondered at when one considers the 15,000 characters that comprise the Chinese language, of which one must know at least 3,000 to be literate.

8   There was a routine common to each day. Upon arriving at school in the morning, everyone assembled in the playground and did the morning exercises. This involved dance-like movements and several laps around the school, rain or shine. Once inside the building we would do a series of mental math computations as quickly as possible. Then everyone would assume the "correct posture" of arms folded behind the back—a posture I found exceedingly uncomfortable at first. This position had to be maintained throughout class except when raising a hand, which was done by putting the right elbow on the desk.

9   Chinese class would involve reading passages from our textbooks and learning new characters. Breaks between every class would be used to clean the classroom—sprinkling water on the concrete floor to dampen the famous Beijing dust before sweeping, washing the blackboards with wet cloths and neatening up the teacher's desk. One of these breaks was used for everyone to massage their heads while relaxing music wafted down from the announcement speaker attached to the ceiling. In the middle of the day, everybody went home to eat lunch and nap for a few hours, after which classes would continue till four in the afternoon.

After school I would always get a snack while I waited for my   10
mother to pick me up. In the fall there were glazed apple-like fruit which
were put on sticks, kebab style. In the winter there were dried, seasoned
fish slices, and dried plums. Summer always meant popsicles, peaches
and watermelon. I would eat my snack on the way home, watching the
city change into the corn and rice fields of our institute.

At first I found the idea of Saturday classes repelling but I soon for-   11
got that I ever had a two-day weekend. Sundays I looked forward to the
hour of Disney cartoons in Chinese. Every other weekend I visited a nearby
cow farm and helped feed the cows and calves. I remember talking at
length with a milkmaid who had never before heard of the African slave
trade, and her subsequent wishful disbelief.

I remember the proud feeling of putting on my red scarf for the first   12
time. By then, I had read a lot about Chairman Mao and talked to people
about the history of China. I felt a nationalist pride wearing this scarf, as
the Little Red Guards had forty years ago in helping to defeat the Japanese
militarists. The red scarf meant that one was committed to helping all
those in difficulty and I proceeded to do this with great zeal—picking up
watermelons for a man whose wheelbarrow wheels had split, helping old
people across busy roads, etc.

Third grade brought the advent of the English class. I was inwardly   13
amused by the children's accents but when I corrected them, I was astonished to find that my words differed very little from theirs. In fact, as a
grain of desert sand that has traveled many miles is indistinguishable
from surrounding indigenous earth, I felt no different from any other
Chinese child.

I can still see the faces of shopkeepers who had had their backs   14
turned when I had asked for an item and when they turned around, were
astounded to see a little black kid speaking perfect Mandarin. I think I
even delighted in shocking people, purposefully going on a raid of the
local shops. But I found that people were genuinely touched that I had
taken the time to study their difficult language. I was warmly embraced
as one of their children.

Fourth grade brought the Tiananmen massacre. Before the shoot-   15
ings, my mother and I had gone every day to visit her students and
friends at the square. My heart felt like it was bursting with love, so
strong was the feeling of community. There were so many people there
that every part of your body was in contact with someone else. Once I
looked triumphantly at my mother and exclaimed, "See? When you're
with the people, you can't fall!" I remember drawing an analogy between
the people and the November winds I could lean back against. Of course
it was also a political statement.

The night of the massacre, I could hear the firing of guns from our   16
home. My mother, who had been in the square at the time, managed to get

back safely. The silence the next day pervaded the whole city and the sadness was unbearable. I remember feeling betrayed. How could this happen to my people? For the first time in forty years, the army had gone against its people. The young said that this was what socialism had come to, but the elders, recognizing that this was a form of fascism, muttered softly that this would never have happened under Chairman Mao.

17   The vision of black marks on the roads made from burning vehicles is engraved in my mind. The pools of blood were quickly washed away, bullet holes patched and death tolls revised. Near our institute there was the distinct scent of decomposing bodies brought from the city. These may have been buried or set fire to—no one knew, no one asked or verified. No one dared to speak, but in everyone was a mixture of anger, anguish and horror.

18   My parents' following separation accentuated the sadness. I spent months trying to heal our broken family, almost believing that that achievement would heal the outside world as well. Fourth grade ended early and I longed to get away from the sadness. It was at this point that my mother decided to return to the U.S. I dreaded leaving but I anticipated the change of atmosphere. I was in for a surprise.

19   For more than a year, I experienced culture shock. Everything was familiar but new—the clothes, hairstyles, houses, toilets. People had so many things they never used or took for granted, and yet they considered themselves not to be well-off. I was incensed how little respect my peers had for their parents and elders. How anyone could hear what the teachers were saying when classes were so noisy was beyond me. Everyone seemed arrogant and ignorant of other cultures. Kids wouldn't believe I was American because they thought I "spoke weird." They asked me, "Why can't you talk normal?" I grew tired of explaining. Even African Americans thought I was from elsewhere. The pride I had felt when I represented Black America in China suffered a pang. I was disgusted by the racism against the Orient which I discovered to be rampant. I found myself pining for the comfortable existence I had come from.

20   Seven years later, I still like to surprise Chinese people with my knowledge of the language when I happen to meet them. I think it is important to show that cultural gaps can be crossed, and without much difficulty as long as there is an open mind. I go back to China when money is available—I visit Beijing and the cow farm, reliving old memories and making new ones. Perhaps one remembers most what one loves.

Content

1. Is it necessary to believe Tschannerl's claim in paragraph 1—"I can even remember being held when I was adopted at three months of age"—to trust her memories of life in China?

2. If you were to form your understanding of China only from Tschannerl's description, what would your impression of the country be?

3. What kind of a character is Tschannerl herself? What details, what incidents does she specifically present (as, for example, "I can still see the faces of shop-keepers who had their backs turned when I had asked for an item and when they turned around, were astounded to see a little black kid speaking perfect Mandarin," ¶ 14)? What else do you infer about her from reading between the lines?

4. Why did returning to the United States present such a culture shock (¶ 19) for Tschannerl?

Strategies/Structures

5. Throughout the essay (except for the last paragraph) Tschannerl appropriately sticks to her child's perspective. What would she have gained—or lost—if she had incorporated her more adult understanding of the country and the subject?

6. Based on your own experiences as identified in question 9 below, what can you conclude about the reliability of child witnesses? Do your conclusions affect the extent to which you trust other people's accounts of childhood incidents, not only Tschannerl's but those of Sanders (139–46 and 274–86) and Barry (500–04)? Might they be true to the spirit of the memories but weak on the specific details? Or vice versa?

Language

7. The prevailing tone of Tschannerl's recollection of China is one of love. How does she manage to convey this while at the same time acknowledging the harsh-ness of the political climate?

8. Tschannerl uses only a single Chinese expression, the name of the compound where her family lived (¶ 5), yet her immersion in China depends on fishing "a wealth of vocabulary" out of "a sea of gibberish" (¶ 7). This technique, of using a small fragment to indicate a much larger picture, delicate as a calligraphed scroll, conveys a wealth of meaning. Find other instances where she has used this tech-nique effectively.

For Writing

9. Many of the essays in *The Essay Connection,* such as this one (see also Sanders [139–46 and 274–86], Zitkala-Sa [218–26], Liu [410–20] and Barry [500–04]) rely on the memories of very young children for their details, incidents, even inter-pretations—though the meanings are often enhanced by the adult author's un-derstanding. Drawing primarily on your childhood memories, describe a place that is important to you, providing sufficient detail to convey its significance to readers who are unfamiliar with it. Can you rely entirely on your own memory, or do you need to consult other sources? If so, for what kinds of information?

10. All of us are continually in the process of shaping and being shaped by a par-ticular culture or cultures; identify some of the major features of this process and how this process works. For instance, if we live in a culture where high-tech

material comforts (such as TVs, stereos, computers, cell phones, and much much more) are commonplace in everyday life—at home, at school, and at work—we take them for granted. Yet their presence influences in obvious and more subtle ways how we do our work and spend our leisure time, even as we make individual choices about how much time to devote daily or weekly to any or all of these devices and for what purposes, as when we decide what to call up on the Internet, and then what to do with what we've found.

In your answer you could refer not only to Tschannerl's essay but to essays by any of the following: Zitkala-Sa (218–26), Liu (410–20), Santiago (420–24), Khan (330–35), or Barry (500–04). How is this process complicated when a person is multicultural and has lived in more than one country or culture?

Additional Topics for Writing
Description (For strategies for writing description, see 252.)

1. Places, for readers who haven't been there:

   a. Your dream house (or room)
   b. Your favorite spot on earth
   c. A ghost town, or a dying or decaying neighborhood
   d. A foreign city or country you have visited
   e. A shopping mall
   f. A factory, farm, store, or other place where you've worked
   g. The waiting room of a bus station, airport, hospital, or dentist's office
   h. A mountain, beach, lake, forest, desert, field, or other natural setting you know well
   i. Or, compare and contrast two places you know well—two churches, houses, restaurants, vacation spots, schools, or any of the places identified in parts a–h, above

2. People, for readers who don't know them:

   a. A close relative or friend
   b. A friend or relative with whom you were once very close but from whom you are presently separated, physically or psychologically
   c. An antagonist
   d. Someone with an occupation or skill you want to know more about— you may want to interview the person to learn what skills, training, and personal qualities the job or activity requires
   e. Someone who has participated, voluntarily or involuntarily, in a significant historical event
   f. A bizarre or eccentric person, a "character"
   g. A high achiever—in business, sports, the arts or sciences, politics, religion
   h. A person whose reputation, public or private, has changed dramatically, for better or worse

3. Situations or events, for readers who weren't there:

   a. A holiday, birthday, or community celebration
   b. A high school or college party
   c. A farmer's market, flea market, garage sale, swap meet, or auction
   d. An athletic event
   e. A performance of a play or concert
   f. A ceremony—a graduation, wedding, christening, bar or bat mitzvah, an initiation, the swearing-in of a public official
   g. A family or school reunion
   h. A confrontation—between team members and referees or the coach, strikers and scabs, protesters and police

4. Experiences or feelings, for readers with analogous experiences:

   a. Love—romantic, familial, patriotic, or religious (see Keifer, 475–77; Jefferson, 441–45)

b. Isolation or rejection (see Nadler, 265–74; Kozol, 210–18; Zitkala-Sa, 218–26)

c. Fear (see Barry, 500–04)

d. Aspiration (see Kleege, 12–22)

e. Success (see Liu, 410–20)

f. Anger (see Douglass, 133–38)

g. Peace, contentment, or happiness (see White, 122–28)

h. An encounter with birth or death (see Erdrich, 33–37)

i. Coping with a handicap or disability—yours or that of someone close to you (see Lamott, 56–60; Kleege, 12–22; Mairs, 364–75)

j. Knowledge and understanding—but after the fact (Fadiman, "Under Water," 128–32; Sanders, 274–86)

Division and
Classification

To divide something is to separate it into its component parts, as the above photograph of the periodic table displayed at University of California, Berkeley's Lawrence Hall of Science so graphically indicates. As a writer you can divide a large, complex subject into smaller segments, easier for you and your readers to deal with individually than to consider in a large, complicated whole. As the section on process analysis indicates (see 153–57), writers usually employ division to explain the individual stages of a process—how the earth was formed, how a professional jockey (or potter or surgeon) performs his or her job, how a heat pump works. Process analysis also underlies explanations of how to make or do something, how to train your dog, or make a cake, or cut gems.

You could also divide your subject in other ways—according to types of dogs, cakes, or gems. And there would be still different ways to divide a discussion of dogs—by their size (miniature, small, medium, large); by the length of their hair (short or long); or according to their suitability as working dogs, pets, or show dogs.

As you start to divide your subject, you almost naturally begin to *classify* it as well, to sort it into categories of groups or families. You'll probably determine the subcategories according to some logical principle or according to characteristics common to members of particular subgroups. Don't stretch to create esoteric groupings (dogs by hair color, for example) if your common sense suggests a more natural way. Some categories simply make more sense than others. A discussion of dogs by breeds could be logically arranged in alphabetical order—Afghan, borzoi, bulldog, collie, Weimaraner. But a discussion that grouped dogs by type first and then breed would be easier to understand and more economical to write. For instance, you could consider all the common features of spaniels first, before dividing them into breeds of spaniels—cocker, springer, water— and discussing the differences. In "Everything in Its Place" (314–22), Oliver Sacks explains the logic of the classification system of the periodic table. There were alternatives to the table chemists now know and use worldwide, as it proceeded in development so logical that vacant spaces could be left for elements yet to be discovered.

Again, how minutely you refine the subcategories of your classification system depends on the length of your writing, your focus, and your emphasis. You could use a *binary* (two-part) *classification*. This is a favorite technique of classifiers who wish to sort things into two categories, those with a particular characteristic and those without it (drinkers and nondrinkers, swimmers and nonswimmers). Thus, in an essay discussing the components of a large structure or organization—a farm, a corporation, a university—a binary classification might lead you to focus on management and labor, or the university's academic and nonacademic functions.

In "None of This Is Fair" (322–27), Richard Rodriguez adopts two binary classification systems: first dividing students into ethnic minorities and majorities to argue against affirmative action, and then in the last two paragraphs, dividing all children into two classes—the poor, irrespective of race, who "lack the confidence . . . to assume their right to a good education," and all other people, who feel entitled to a good education.

The two essays on wearing the *hijab,* Gelareh Asayesh's "Shrouded in Contradiction" (327–30) and Sumbul Khan's "'Mirror, Mirror on the Wall'" (330–35) examine the combination of restrictions and freedom, comfort and discomfort, that wearing the veil allows women in (and out of) Islamic societies. This is an issue freighted with intense religious, social, and political implications, and so full of controversy that the personal stories here can only begin to touch on it. All of these complications are reinforced by a photograph taken in Pakistan in 2002 (p. 329), in which veiled women, one carrying a child, pass in front of a phalanx of armed men in uniform.

Sometimes the divisions get more complicated because they are less clear-cut. In "Why Men Don't Last: Self-Destruction as a Way of Life" (299–304), Natalie Angier makes distinctions, based on biological and psychological research and statistical reports, between the self-destructive behavior of men and women—"women are about three times more likely than men to express suicidal thoughts or to attempt to kill themselves . . . but in the United States, four times more men than women die from the act each year." However, there are, she indicates, different ways to interpret these facts to show either that men are the greater risk takers ("given to showy displays of bravado, aggression and daring all for the sake of attracting a harem of mates") or that women are (because those who talk about suicide are more open to experience, including taking risks and seeking novelties). She makes other distinctions between men's and women's risk-taking behavior concerning homicide, alcohol and drug use, and gambling. For instance, while both men and women gamble, their "methods and preferences for throwing away big sums of money" are very different. Men try to "overcome the odds and beat the system" at table games "where they can feel powerful and omnipotent while everybody watches them," while women prefer "the solitary forms of gambling, the slot machines or video poker, where there isn't as much social scrutiny." Angier concludes by citing research that classifies boys by the extent to which they uphold traditional versus egalitarian views of masculinity; presumably the traditionalists would grow up to be more self-destructive than those who favored equal rights and responsibilities for women.

Deborah Tannen's works for general readers are characterized by numerous short divisions of the general topic, as both "Fast Forward: Technologically Enhanced Aggression" (304–14) and "Communication Styles" (391–97) indicate (both essays are graphically represented in the photograph of the tense angry man on p. 309). Each division makes her work easy to read and to understand. In particular, each division serves to classify the points in the arguments she makes, and each division is headed by a title that reinforces the point of that section. Although Tannen begins "Fast Forward" with positive examples of e-mail communication among coworkers and family members at short and long distance, the division titles reveal the way these divisions become an argument, that e-mail is really a form of "Technologically Enhanced Aggression" conducted through rapid and anonymous electronic communication. Thus the division titles claim, as they argue: "E-Mail Aggravates Aggression," "One-Way Communication Breeds Contempt," "Not So Fast!," "Stop That Law!" (What appears to legislators to be a "groundswell of popular protest is often the technologically enhanced protest of a few"—by fax, phone, letter, or e-mail), "Through the Magnifying Glass" (Technology makes it much easier for critics of public figures to "ferret out inconsistencies" and make them look "unreliable" or "dishonest"), "'Who Is This? Why Are You Calling Here?'" (New technology makes it easier to act on the anger towards intrusive phone calls), and "Training Our Children to Kill" (by allowing them to play war video games).

Obviously, you can create as many categories and subcategories as are useful in enabling you and your readers to understand and interpret the subject. If you wanted to concentrate on the academic aspects of your own university, you might categorize them according to academic divisions—arts and sciences, business, education, music, public health. A smaller classification would examine the academic disciplines within a division—biology, English, history, mathematics. Or smaller yet, depending on your purpose—English literature, American literature, creative writing, linguistics—*ad infinitum*, as the anonymous jingle observes:

> Big fleas have little fleas, and these
> Have littler fleas to bite 'em,
> And these have fleas, and these have fleas,
> And so on ad infinitum.

In all six of the essays in this chapter, the classification system provides the basis for the overall organization; but here as in most essays, the authors use many other techniques of writing in addition—narration, definition, description, analysis, illustration, and comparison and contrast.

In writing essays based on division, you might ask the following questions to help organize your materials: What are the parts of the total unit? How can these be subdivided to make the subject more understandable to my readers? In essays of classification, where you're sorting or grouping two or more things, you can ask: Into what categories can I sort these items? According to what principles—of logic, common characteristics, "fitness"? Do I want my classification to emphasize the similarities among groups or their differences? Once I've determined the groupings, am I organizing my discussion of each category in the same way, considering the same features in the same order? In many instances divisions and classifications are in the mind of the beholder. Is the glass half full or half empty? Your job as a writer is to help your readers recognize and accept the order of your universe.

STRATEGIES FOR WRITING— DIVISION AND CLASSIFICATION

1. Am I going to explain an existing system of classification, or am I going to invent a new one? Do I want to define a system by categorizing its components? Explain a process by dividing it into stages? Argue in favor of one category or another? Entertain through an amusing classification?
2. Do my readers know my subject but not my classification system? Know both subject and system? Or are they unacquainted with either? How will their knowledge (or lack of knowledge) of the subject or system influence how much I say about either? Will this influence the simplicity or complexity of my classification system?
3. According to what principle am I classifying or dividing my subject? Is it sensible? Significant? Does it emphasize the similarities or the differences among groups? Have I applied the principle consistently with respect to each category? How have I integrated my paper (to keep it from being just a long list), through providing interconnections among the parts and transitions between the divisions?
4. Have I organized my discussion of each category in the same way, considering the same features in the same order? Have I illustrated each category? Are the discussions of each category the same length? Should they be? Why or why not?
5. Have I used language similar in vocabulary level (equally technical, or equally informal) in each category? Have I defined any needed terms?

NATALIE ANGIER

Angier (born 1958), grew up in New York City, attended the University of Michigan and graduated from Barnard College in 1978. After working as a magazine staff writer at *Discover* and *Time* and as an editor at *Savvy*, she taught journalism at New York University before becoming a reporter for the *New York Times* in 1990. Her work as a *Times* science correspondent led to a Pulitzer Prize in 1991 and the publication of a collection of her columns, *The Beauty of the Beastly: New Views on the Nature of Life* (1995). Her topics include evolutionary biology ("Mating for Life?" "The Urge to Cuddle"), DNA, scorpions, hyenas, fish, and central issues of life, death (by suicide or AIDS) and creativity. *Woman: An Intimate Geography* (1999) offers a spirited and controversial celebration of "the female body—its anatomy, its chemistry, its evolution, and its laughter," including both traditional (the womb, the egg) and nontraditional elements ("movement, strength, aggression, and fury"). Angier, who lists her hobby as "weightlifting," recently became a mother; her work reflects the strengths of both.

Angier's writing is characteristically clear, precise, and witty. She explains the unfamiliar in terms of the familiar, giving research a memorably human perspective: "If stretched to its full length, a single molecule of human DNA would extend more than three feet, the height of the average nursery school child. But when squeezed and coiled and crammed into its rightful place in the bosom of the cell, the molecule of life measures about a hundred-thousandth of an inch across." With comparable precision and clarity in "Why Men Don't Last," first published in the *New York Times* (Feb. 17, 1999), Angier examines significant differences between the biology of men and women, translating statistical and psychological research (on risk taking, compulsive gambling, suicidal behavior, masculinity) into language and concepts general readers can readily understand—without oversimplifying the subject or demeaning the audience.

Why Men Don't Last:
Self-Destruction as a Way of Life

M y father had great habits. Long before ficus trees met weight ma- 1 chines, he was a dogged exerciser. He did push-ups and isometrics. He climbed rocks. He went for long, vigorous walks. He ate sparingly and avoided sweets and grease. He took such good care of his teeth that they looked fake.

My father had terrible habits. He was chronically angry. He threw 2 things around the house and broke them. He didn't drink often, but when he did, he turned more violent than usual. He didn't go to doctors, even when we begged him to. He let a big, ugly mole on his back grow bigger and bigger, and so he died of malignant melanoma, a curable cancer, at 51.

3   My father was a real man—so good and so bad. He was also Everyman.

4   Men by some measures take better care of themselves than women
do and are in better health. They are less likely to be fat, for example; they
exercise more, and suffer from fewer chronic diseases like diabetes, osteo-
porosis and arthritis.

5   By standard measures, men have less than half the rate of depression
seen in women. When men do feel depressed, they tend to seek distraction
in an activity, which, many psychologists say, can be a more effective technique for dispelling the mood than is a depressed woman's tendency to
turn inward and ruminate. In the United States and many other industrialized nations, women are about three times more likely than men to
express suicidal thoughts or to attempt to kill themselves.

6   And yet . . . men don't last. They die off in greater numbers than
women do at every stage of life, and thus their average life span is seven
years shorter. Women may attempt suicide relatively more often, but in the
United States, four times more men than women die from the act each year.

7   Men are also far more likely than women to die behind the wheel or
to kill others as a result of their driving. From 1977 to 1995, three and a half
times more male drivers than female drivers were involved in fatal car
crashes. Death by homicide also favors men; among those under 30, the
male-to-female ratio is 8 to 1.

8   Yes, men can be impressive in their tendency to self-destruct, ex-
plosively or gradually. They are at least twice as likely as women to be
alcoholics and three times more likely to be drug addicts. They have an
eightfold greater chance than women do of ending up in prison. Boys are
much more likely than girls to be thrown out of school for a conduct or
antisocial personality disorder, or to drop out on their own surly initiative. Men gamble themselves into a devastating economic and emotional
pit two to three times more often than women do.

9   "Between boys' suicide rates, dropout rates and homicide rates, and
men's self-destructive behaviors generally, we have a real crisis in America," said William S. Pollack, a psychologist at Harvard Medical School
and co-director of the Center for Men at McLean Hospital in Belmont,
Mass. "Until recently, the crisis has gone unheralded."

10   It is one thing to herald a presumed crisis, though, and to cite a
ream of gloomy statistics. It is quite another to understand the crisis, or
to figure out where it comes from or what to do about it. As those who
study the various forms of men's self-destructive behaviors realize, there
is not a single, glib, overarching explanation for the sex-specific patterns
they see.

11   A crude evolutionary hypothesis would have it that men are natural
risk-takers, given to showy displays of bravado, aggression and daring all
for the sake of attracting a harem of mates. By this premise, most of men's
self-destructive, violent tendencies are a manifestation of their need to take
big chances for the sake of passing their genes into the river of tomorrow.

Some of the data on men's bad habits fit the risk-taker model. For ex-   12
ample, those who study compulsive gambling have observed that men
and women tend to display very different methods and preferences for
throwing away big sums of money.

"Men get enamored of the action in gambling," said Linda Cham-   13
berlain, a psychologist at Regis University in Denver who specializes in
treating gambling disorders. "They describe an overwhelming rush of
feelings and excitement associated with the process of gambling. They
like the feeling of being a player, and taking on a struggle with the house
to show that they can overcome the odds and beat the system. They tend
to prefer the table games, where they can feel powerful and omnipotent
while everybody watches them."

Dr. Chamberlain noted that many male gamblers engage in other   14
risk-taking behaviors, like auto racing or hang gliding. By contrast, she
said, "Women tend to use gambling more as a sedative, to numb themselves and escape from daily responsibilities, or feelings of depression or
alienation. Women tend to prefer the solitary forms of gambling, the slot
machines or video poker, where there isn't as much social scrutiny."

Yet the risk-taking theory does not account for why men outnumber   15
women in the consumption of licit and illicit anodynes. Alcohol, heroin
and marijuana can be at least as numbing and sedating as repetitively
pulling the arm of a slot machine. And some studies have found that men
use drugs and alcohol for the same reasons that women often overeat: as
an attempt to self-medicate when they are feeling anxious or in despair.

"We can speculate all we want, but we really don't know why men   16
drink more than women," said Enoch Gordis, the head of the National Institute on Alcohol Abuse and Alcoholism. Nor does men's comparatively
higher rate of suicide appear linked to the risk-taking profile. To the contrary, Paul Duberstein, an assistant professor of psychiatry and oncology
at the University of Rochester School of Medicine, has found that people
who complete a suicidal act are often low in a personality trait referred
to as "openness to experience," tending to be rigid and inflexible in their
behaviors. By comparison, those who express suicidal thoughts tend to
score relatively high on the openness-to-experience scale.

Given that men commit suicide more often than women, and women   17
talk about it more, his research suggests that, in a sense, women are the
greater risk-takers and novelty seekers, while the men are likelier to feel
trapped and helpless in the face of changing circumstances.

Silvia Cara Canetto, an associate professor of psychology at Colo-   18
rado State University in Fort Collins, has extensively studied the role of
gender in suicidal behaviors. Dr. Canetto has found that cultural narratives may determine why women attempt suicide more often while men
kill themselves more often. She proposes that in Western countries, to talk
about suicide or to survive a suicidal act is often considered "feminine,"

hysterical, irrational and weak. To actually die by one's own hand may be viewed as "masculine," decisive, strong. Even the language conveys the polarized, weak-strong imagery: a "failed" suicide attempt as opposed to a "successful" one.

19   "There is indirect evidence that there is negative stigma toward men who survive suicide," Dr. Canetto said. "Men don't want to 'fail,' even though failing in this case means surviving." If the "suicidal script" that identifies completing the acts as "rational, courageous and masculine" can be "undermined and torn to pieces," she said, we might have a new approach to prevention.

20   Dr. Pollack of the Center for Men also blames many of men's self-destructive ways on the persistent image of the dispassionate, resilient, action-oriented male—the Marlboro Man who never even gasps for breath. For all the talk of the sensitive "new man," he argues, men have yet to catch up with women in expanding their range of acceptable emotions and behaviors. Men in our culture, Dr. Pollack says, are pretty much limited to a menu of three strong feelings: rage, triumph, lust. "Anything else and you risk being seen as a sissy," he said.

21   In a number of books, most recently "Real Boys: Rescuing Our Sons From the Myths of Boyhood," he proposes that boys "lose their voice, a whole half of their emotional selves," beginning at age 4 or 5. "Their vulnerable, sad feelings and sense of need are suppressed or shamed out of them," he said—by their peers, parents, the great wide televised fist in their face.

22   He added: "If you keep hammering it into a kid that he has to look tough and stop being a crybaby and a mama's boy, the boy will start creating a mask of bravado."

23   That boys and young men continue to feel confused over the proper harmonics of modern masculinity was revealed in a study that Dr. Pollack conducted of 200 eighth-grade boys. Through questionnaires, he determined their scores on two scales, one measuring their "egalitarianism"—the degree to which they think men and women are equal, that men should change a baby's diapers, that mothers should work and the like—and the other gauging their "traditionalism" as determined by their responses to conventional notions, like the premise that men must "stand on their own two feet" and must "always be willing to have sex if someone asks."

24   On average, the boys scored high on both scales. "They are split on what it means to be a man," said Dr. Pollack.

25   The cult of masculinity can beckon like a siren song in baritone. Dr. Franklin L. Nelson, a clinical psychologist at the Fairbanks Community Mental Health Center in Alaska, sees many men who get into trouble by adhering to sentimental notions of manhood. "A lot of men come up here hoping to get away from a wimpy world and live like pioneers by

old-fashioned masculine principles of individualism, strength and rugged-ness," he said. They learn that nothing is simple; even Alaska is part of a wider, interdependent world and they really do need friends, warmth and electricity.

"Right now, it's 35 degrees below zero outside," he said during a 26 January interview. "If you're not prepared, it doesn't take long at that temperature to freeze to death."

Content

1. Angier uses several categories of division in this piece: the "so good and so bad" habits of "Everyman" (¶ 3); the self-destructive habits and rates of men versus women (throughout); the division between the rugged individual versus the egali-tarian helpmeet roles today's men are expected to play (¶s 23–25). Why do such divisions enable readers to clearly recognize similarities as well as differences?

2. Angier's explanations for these divisions are equally divided. What evidence does she offer to support the "crude evolutionary hypothesis" that "men are nat-ural risk-takers, given to showy display of bravado, aggression and daring all for the sake of attracting a harem of mates" (¶ 11)? What evidence does she offer to contradict this hypothesis?

3. What do you make of the fact that women talk about committing suicide more than men do, but that men actually have a higher rate of suicide than women do (¶s 16–19)?

Strategies/Structures

4. Why does Angier begin this piece with a paragraph that lists her father's "great habits," followed by one listing his "terrible habits" (¶s 1–2)?

5. Why aren't the divisions and classifications Angier uses more clear-cut? Is this a phenomenon of the research she cites, of her writing, of the way things are in real life, or of some combination of the three?

6. Angier is writing as a reporter of other people's research. Although her writing begins with the personal example of her father, do we know where she stands on the subject—which hypothesis for men's risk-taking behavior she believes? Is her essay slanted in favor of one opinion or another, either in terms of her examples or her language?

7. Should a reporter be neutral? Isn't the selection of evidence in itself a form of tipping the scale in favor of one side or another?

8. What are the dangers and difficulties of categorizing behavior by gender?

For Writing

9. Have you ever done anything risky or dangerous to avoid looking like a wimp or to avoid falling into one or another stereotypical role for either men or women? Write a paper for an audience different from yourself; for instance, if you're a risk-taking man, write for a more prudent audience of women or men (if it makes a dif-ference to your argument, specify which gender).

10. Angier, like other science writers, had the difficult job of translating scientific research into language that newspaper readers can understand. From the following list of authors she cites on the role of gender in suicidal behaviors, choose one source and identify, with illustrations, the principles by which Angier works. Consider aspects such as document format, uses of evidence, presentation of data (via graphs, charts, statistics), technicality of language, definitions of scientific terms, citation of supporting research.

Canetto, Silvia Sara, and David Lester. "Gender, Culture, and Suicidal Behavior." Transcultural Psychiatry 35.2 (1998): 163–90.

Canetto, Silvia Sara, and Issac Sakinofsky. "The Gender Paradox in Suicide." *Suicide and Life-Threatening Behavior* 28.1 (Spring 1998): 1–23.

Chamberlain, Linda, Michael R. Ruetz, and William G. McCown. *Strange Attractors: Chaos, Complexity, and the Art of Family Therapy.* New York: Wiley, 1997.

Duberstein, Paul R., Yeates Conwell, and Christopher Cox. "Suicide in Widowed Persons." *American Journal of Geriatric Psychiatry* 6.4 (Fall 1998): 328–34.

Gordis, Enoch. "Alcohol Problems in Public Health Policy." *Journal of the American Medical Association.* (Dec. 1997) 1781–87.

Pollack, William S. *Real Boys: Rescuing Our Sons from the Myths of Boyhood.* New York: Random, 1998.

Pollack, William S., and Ronald F. Levant, eds. *New Psychotherapy for Men.* New York: Wiley, 1998.

DEBORAH TANNEN

Tannen, born in Brooklyn in 1945, was partially deafened by a childhood illness. Her consequent interest in nonverbal communication and other aspects of conversation led ultimately to a doctorate in linguistics (University of California, Berkeley, 1979) and professorship at Georgetown University. Tannen's numerous studies of gender-related speech patterns draw on the combined perspectives of anthropology, sociology, psychology, and women's studies, as well as linguistics. A poet and short story writer (*Greek Icons*) as well, Tannen brings a sensitive ear and keen analysis to *Gender and Conversational Interaction* (1993) among students from preschool through junior high, high school, and college. She also explores aspects of communication related to gender, power, and status in the best-selling *That's Not What I Meant!: How Conversational Style Makes or Breaks Your Relations with Others* (1986), *You Just Don't Understand: Women and Men in Conversation* (1990),*Talking from 9 to 5* (1994), *The Argument Culture: Moving from Debate to Dialogue* (1998), and *I Only Say This Because I Love You* (2001).

"Fast Forward: Technologically Enhanced Aggression" comes from *The Argument Culture: Moving from Debate to Dialogue*, a book devoted to analyzing the "pervasive warlike atmosphere that makes us approach public dialogue, and just about anything we need to accomplish, as if it were a fight." Our spirits, she says, are "corroded by living in an atmosphere of unrelenting contention—an argument culture" that "urges us to approach the world—and the people in it—in an adversarial frame of mind." Although argument can be useful, it often creates "more problems than it solves," as Tannen's analysis of various types of e-mail communication indicates. Each division of her analysis can be further categorized according to those who behave in the aggressive ways the section addresses and those who don't.

Fast Forward: Technologically Enhanced Aggression

I was the second person in my department to get a computer. The first 1
was my colleague Ralph. The year was 1980. Ralph got a Radio Shack TRS 80; I got a used Apple 2-Plus. He helped me get started and before long helped me get on e-mail, the precursor of the Internet. Though his office was next to mine, we rarely had extended conversations except about department business. Shy and soft-spoken, Ralph mumbled so, I could barely tell he was speaking. But when we both were using e-mail, we started communicating daily in this (then) leisurely medium. We could send each other messages without fear of imposing, since the receiver determines when to log on and read and respond. Soon I was getting long, self-revealing messages from Ralph. We moved effortlessly among discussions of department business, our work, and our lives. Through e-mail Ralph and I became friends.

Ralph recently forwarded to me a message he had received from his 2
niece, a college freshman. "How nice," I commented, "that you have such a close relationship with your niece. Do you think you'd be in touch with her if it weren't for e-mail?" "No," he replied. "I can't imagine we'd write each other letters regularly or call on the phone. No way." E-mail makes possible connections with relatives, acquaintances, or strangers that would not otherwise exist. And it enables more and different communication with people you are already close to. One woman discovered that e-mail brought her closer to her father. He would never talk much on the phone (as her mother would), but they have become close since they both got on line.

Everywhere e-mail is enhancing or even transforming relationships. 3
Parents keep in regular touch with children in college who would not be caught dead telephoning home every day. When I spent a year and a half in Greece in the late 1960s, I was out of touch with my family except for the mail—letters that took hours to compose and weeks to arrive. When my sister spent a year in Israel in the mid-1990s, we kept in touch nearly every day—and not only she and I. Prodded by her absence, within a month of

her departure our third sister and my sisters' daughters all started using e-mail. Though she was so far away, my sister was in some ways in closer touch with the family than she would have been had she stayed home.

4   And another surprise: My other sister, who generally is not eager to talk about her feelings, opened up on e-mail. One time I called her and we spoke on the phone; after we hung up, I checked my e-mail and found she had revealed information there that she hadn't mentioned when we spoke. I asked her about it (on e-mail), and she explained, "The telephone is so impersonal." At first this seemed absurd: How could the actual voice of a person right there be impersonal and the on-screen little letters detached from the writer be more personal? When I asked her about this, she explained: "The big advantage to e-mail is that you can do it at your time and pace; there is never the feeling that the phone is ringing and interrupting whatever it is you are doing." Writing e-mail is like writing in a journal; you're alone with your thoughts and your words, safe from the intrusive presence of another person.

E-Mail Aggravates Aggression

5 E-mail, and now the Internet and the World Wide Web, are creating networks of human connection unthinkable even a few years ago. But at the same time that technologically enhanced communication enables previously impossible loving contact, it also enhances hostile and distressing communication. Along with the voices of family members and friends, telephone lines bring into our homes the annoying voices of solicitors who want to sell something—generally at dinnertime. (My father-in-law startles a telephone solicitor by saying, "We're eating dinner, but I'll call you back. What's your home phone number?" To the nonplussed caller, he explains, "Well, you're calling me at home; I thought I'd call you at home, too.") Even more unnerving, in the middle of the night may come frightening obscene calls and stalkers. From time to time the public is horrified to learn that even the most respected citizens can succumb to the temptation of anonymity that the telephone seems to offer—like the New York State Supreme Court chief justice who was harassing a former lover by mail and phone and the president of American University in Washington, D.C., who was found to be the source of obscene telephone calls to a woman he didn't even know.

6   But telephone lines can be traced (as President Richard Berendzen learned) and voices can be recognized (as Judge Sol Wachtler discovered). The Internet ratchets up anonymity by homogenizing all messages into identical-appearing print and making it almost impossible to trace messages back to the computer that sent them. As the ease of using the Internet has resulted in more and more people logging on and sending messages to more and more others with whom they have a connection, it has also led to increased communication with strangers—and this has

resulted in "flaming": vituperative messages that verbally attack. Flaming results from the anonymity not only of the sender but also of the receiver. It is easier to feel and express hostility against someone far removed whom you do not know personally, like the rage that some drivers feel toward an anonymous car that cuts them off. If the anonymous driver to whom you've flipped the finger turns out to be someone you know, the rush of shame you experience is evidence that anonymity was essential for your expression—and experience—of rage.

One of the most effective ways to defuse antagonism between two groups is to provide a forum for individuals from those groups to get to know each other personally. This is the logic behind programs that bring together, for example, African-American and Jewish youths or Israeli and Palestinian women. It was the means by which a troubled Vietnam veteran finally achieved healing: through a friendship with a man who had been the enemy he was trying to kill—a retired Vietnamese officer whose diary the American had found during the war and managed to return to its owner nearly twenty-five years later. When you get to know members of an "enemy" group personally, it is hard to demonize them, to see them as less than human.

What is happening in our lives is just the opposite: More and more of our communication is not face to face, and not with people we know. The proliferation and increasing portability of technology isolate people in a bubble. When I was a child, my family got the first television on our block, and the neighborhood children gathered in our dining room to watch Howdy Doody. Before long, every family had its own TV—but each had just one, so, in order to watch it, families came together. Now it is common for families to have more than one television, so the adults can watch what they like in one room and the children can watch their choice in another—or maybe each child has a private TV to watch alone. The spread of radio has followed the same pattern. Early radios were like a piece of furniture around which a family had to gather in order to listen. Now radio listeners may have a radio in every room, one in the car, and yet another, equipped with headphones, for walking or jogging. Radio and television began as sources of information that drew people together physically, even if their attention was not on each other. Now these technologies are exerting a centrifugal force, pulling people apart—and, as a result, increasing the likelihood that their encounters will be agonistic.

One-Way Communication Breeds Contempt

The head of a small business had a reputation among his employees as being a Jekyll-and-Hyde personality. In person he was always mild-mannered and polite. But when his employees saw a memo from him in their mail, their backs stiffened. The boss was famous for composing angry, even vicious memos that he often had to temper and apologize for later. It seemed that the presence of a living, breathing person in front of him was a brake on his hostility. But seated before a faceless typewriter or computer screen, his anger built and overflowed. A woman who had worked as a dean at a small liberal arts college commented that all the major problems she encountered with faculty or other administrators resulted from written memos, not face-to-face communication.

10   Answering machines are also a form of one-way communication. A piano teacher named Craig was president of a piano teachers' association that sponsored a yearly competition. Craig had nothing to do with the competition—someone else had organized and overseen it. So he felt helpless and caught off guard when he came home to a message that laid out in detail the caller's grievances about how the competition had been handled, and ended, "That's no way to run an organization!" Slam! When he heard the message, Craig thought, "Here I am, being the president as a service to keep things together, and I'm being attacked for something I had no control over. It made me wonder," he commented, "why I was doing it at all." Craig refused a second term in large part because of attacks like this—even though they were infrequent, while he frequently received lavish praise. Being attacked is perhaps unavoidable for those in authority, but in this case the technology played a role as well. It is highly unlikely the caller would have worked herself up into quite this frenzy, or concluded the conversation by hanging up on Craig, if she had gotten Craig himself and not his answering machine, let alone if she had talked to him in person.

11   In the heat of anger, it is easy to pick up a phone and make a call. But when talking directly to someone, most people feel an impulse to tone down what they say. Even if they do not, the person they are attacking will respond after the first initial blast—by explaining, apologizing, or counterattacking. Whatever the response, it will redirect the attacker's speech, perhaps aggravating the anger but also perhaps deflating it. If you write an angry letter, you might decide later not to send it or to tone it down. But if you make a call and reach voice mail or an answering machine, it's the worst of both worlds: You spout off in the heat of anger, there is no way to take back what you said or correct misinterpretations, and there is no response to act as a brake. In my research on workplace communication, I found that a large percentage of serious conflicts had been sparked by one-way communication such as memos, voice mail, and e-mail.

12   An experienced reporter at a newspaper heard that one of his colleagues, a feature writer, was working on a story about a topic he knew well. He had done extensive research on a related topic in the course of his own reporting. So he thought he'd be helpful: He sent her a long e-mail message warning her of potential pitfalls and pointing out aspects she should bear in mind. Rather than thanks, he received a testy reply informing him that she was quite capable of watching out for these pitfalls without his expert guidance, and that she too was a seasoned reporter,

"Read" the picture as an illustration of either Angier's "Why Men Don't Last" or Tannen's "Fast Forward: Technologically Enhanced Aggression," or both. How can you tell he's angry? Would you interpret the picture the same way if the figure were a woman rather than a man? Or if the figure looked more like a college student than a career person?

even though she had been at the paper a shorter time than he. Reading her angry reply, he gulped and sent an apology.

An advantage of e-mail is its efficiency: The reporter was able to send his ideas without taking the time to walk to another floor and talk face to face with his colleague. But had he done so, he would probably have presented his ideas differently, and she would have seen the spirit in which the advice was given. If not, it is unlikely he would have gotten so far in his advice giving before picking up that he was not coming across the way he intended, that she was taking offense. He then could have backtracked and changed the tone of his communication rather than laying it on thicker and thicker, continuing and expanding in a vein that was making her angrier by the second. What's more, if people meet regularly face to face, friendships begin to build that lay the foundation for future communication. It's harder for e-mail and memos to do that.

Not So Fast!

The potential for misunderstandings and mishaps with electronic communication expands in proportion to the potential for positive exchanges. For example, two workers exchanged e-mail about a report that had to be submitted. One of them wrote that a portion could better be handled by a third person—but added an unflattering remark about her. The recipient received the message at a busy time, noticed that it called for Person 3 to do something—and quickly and efficiently forwarded it to her, disparaging remark and all. E-mail makes it too easy to forward messages, too easy to reply before your temper cools, too easy to broadcast messages to large numbers of people without thinking about how every sentence will strike every recipient. And there's plenty of opportunity for error: sending a message to the wrong person or having a message mysteriously appear on the screen of an unintended recipient.

15   Every improvement in technology makes possible new and scarier kinds of errors. In one company, a manager set up an e-mail user-group list, so his messages would go to everyone in the department at once and their replies would also get distributed to everyone on the list. But several people sent him replies that they thought were private, not realizing everyone in the office would see them. Like a private conversation overheard, these "overread" messages to the manager came across to colleagues as kissing up, since people tend to use a more deferential tone in addressing a boss than a peer. It was embarrassing, but not as bad as the job applicant who mistakenly sent a message including his uncensored judgment about the person who interviewed him to that person. . . .

Who's to Judge?

16 One of the great contributions of the Internet is that it enables ordinary people to put out information that previously would have been limited by such gatekeepers as newspaper editors and book publishers, or that would have required enormous amounts of time and money to publish and disseminate independently. In a few moments, anyone with the equipment and expertise can post information on the World Wide Web, and anyone else with the equipment and expertise can read it. This can be invaluable—for example, when individuals who have unusual medical conditions and their families exchange information and personal experience through specialized user groups. But there is a danger here as well. Editors, publishers, and other gatekeepers impose their judgment—for better or worse—on the accuracy of the material they publish. Those who download information from the Internet may be unable to judge the veracity and reliability of information.

17   A professor at a public university was assigned a student assistant who had excellent computer skills. The assistant offered to help her make reading materials available to her class by placing them on a class Web site. He began by putting on the site readings and secondary sources that the professor had assigned or recommended. But he did not stop there. He went on to scour the Internet for anything related to the course topic

and import it into the class Web site, too. When the professor discovered what he had done, she told him to remove these materials, since she did not have time to read everything he had imported to determine whether it was appropriate for the students to read. Some of it might have been irrelevant to the class and would distract them from the material she felt they should read. And some of it might be factually wrong. The idea that the professor thought she should read the material she was making available to her students in order to judge its accuracy and suitability was foreign to the student assistant—and offensive. He argued that she was trying to infringe on the students' First Amendment right to have access to any kind of information at all.

This is a danger inherent in the Internet: At the same time that the   18
ease of posting makes available enormous amounts of useful information, it also makes possible the dissemination of useless, false, or dangerous information—and makes it more difficult to distinguish between the two. To be sure, publishers and editors often make mistakes in publishing material they should not and rejecting material they should accept (as any author whose work has been rejected can tell you—and as evidenced by the many successful books that were rejected by dozens of editors before finally finding a home). Yet readers of reputable newspapers and magazines or books published by established presses know that what they are reading has been deemed reliable by professional editors. The Internet makes it more difficult for consumers to distinguish the veracity and reliability of information they come across.

The Internet can function as a giant and unstoppable rumor mill or   19
as a conduit for such dangerous information as how to build a bomb. It can also facilitate aggressive behavior, as author Elaine Showalter discovered when she published a book, *Hystories,* in which she included chronic fatigue syndrome among a list of phenomena, such as alien abduction and satanic ritual abuse, that she identified as hysterical epidemics. Sufferers from chronic fatigue syndrome who were angered by the label "hysterical" used the Internet to share information about the author's public appearances, so they could turn out in force to harass and even threaten her. Law enforcement authorities have been unable to identify members of the Animal Liberation Front, who use violence and terrorism in their efforts to halt what they see as cruelty to animals, because their communication with one another takes place for the most part on the Internet rather than at face-to-face meetings. . . .

Like Peas Out of a Pod

Flaming is only one aspect of electronic communication. E-mail makes pos-   20
sible extended interaction among people who are physically distant from each other. But it also makes possible anonymity and in some cases—as

with young people (mostly boys) who become computer "nerds"—begins
to substitute for human interaction. Following a tragic incident in which a
fifteen-year-old boy sexually assaulted and then murdered an eleven-year-
old boy who happened to ring his doorbell selling candy and wrapping
paper to raise money for his school, many people felt that the Internet
shared a portion of the blame, because the murderer had himself been sexually abused by a pedophile he had met through the Internet. An aspect of
this harrowing and bizarre event which received less comment was that as
the older boy had become obsessed with the Internet, he had gradually
withdrawn from social interaction with his peers.

21   Advances in technology are part of a larger complex of forces moving people away from face-to-face interaction and away from actual
experience—from hearing music performed, to hearing recordings of
performances, to hearing digital re-creations of performances that some
believe bear little resemblance to music as performed. From live dramatic
performances in theaters, to silent movies shown in theaters with the
accompaniment of live orchestras, to sound movies, to videos watched
in the isolation of one's home. From local stores privately owned and
owner-operated to chains owned by huge corporations based far away
and staffed by minimum-wage employees who know little about the
merchandise and have much less stake in whether customers leave the
store happy or offended.

22   All of these trends have complex implications—many positive, but
many troubling. Each new advance makes possible not only new levels of
connection but also new levels of hostility and enhanced means of expressing it. People who would not dream of cutting in front of others
waiting in a line think nothing of speeding along an empty traffic lane to
cut ahead of others waiting in a line of cars. It is easy to forget that inside
the car, or facing a computer screen, is a living, feeling person.

23   The rising level of public aggression in our society seems directly
related to the increasing isolation in our lives, which is helped along by
advances in technology. This isolation—and the technology that enhances it—is an ingredient in the argument culture. We seem to be better
at developing technological means of communication than at finding
ways to temper the hostility that sometimes accompanies them. We have
to work harder at finding those ways. That is the challenge we now face.

Content

1. What connections does Tannen make between "advances in technology," "the
increasing isolation in our lives," and "the rising level of public aggression in our
society" (¶ 23)? Which types of evidence that she uses to make her case do you find
the most convincing: personal anecdotes, contemporary news events, issues of
public policy, or analyses of the way Americans in general live and behave? Why?

2. What are some of the advantages of technology as outlined by Tannen? Some of its disadvantages? Do the gains outweigh the losses in Tannen's analysis? In yours?

3. Tannen opens her essay with a discussion of the advantages of e-mail in building and maintaining close relationships (¶s 1–4). In paragraph 13, she claims that "if people meet regularly face to face, friendships begin to build that lay the foundation for future communication. It's harder for e-mail and memos to do that." These positions are seemingly at odds with each other. Does she address or account for this apparent contradiction at any point in her essay?

4. What relationship does Tannen see between expressions of hostility such as "flaming" and "road rage" and the "anonymity not only of the sender but also of the receiver" (¶ 6)? Does your own experience corroborate her claim that "It is easier to feel and express hostility against someone far removed whom you do not know personally" (¶ 6) than it is to treat people with whom one has a personal connection in a hostile manner? Does Tannen offer any solutions to this problem? Can you or your fellow students resolve this issue, in discussion or in writing (see question 10).

Strategies/Structures

5. Each division of Tannen's analysis can be further divided according to people who behave in the aggressive ways the section addresses and people who don't. Is anonymity, coupled with the ease and speed of sending insults by e-mail, the most compelling reason for such hostile behavior? What evidence does she offer that personal acquaintance with "members of an 'enemy' group" will humanize them (¶ 7) and thus have the potential for transforming a hostile relationship into a friendly one? Under what circumstances could personal acquaintance make relations worse rather than better?

6. Tannen's writing in "Fast Forward" (304–14) and in "Communication Styles" (391–97) is characterized by numerous subdivisions of her topic, identified by witty slogans ("One-Way Communication Breeds Contempt") and breezy captions ("Not So Fast!"). What is the effect on the total piece of these subdivisions and of the language in which they're written?

Language

7. Do you use different language in e-mails than you do in conversation? In hardcopy letters? What consistencies do you find in the language and other conventions of all three forms of communication? What differences? (For evidence you could look at some messages you've written and perhaps tape a conversation for analysis.) Tabulate your results in lists or a chart.

8. Tannen claims that the use of language is influenced by the isolation that technology sometimes encourages. Keep a log of how many hours a day you spend by yourself using technology (playing video games, writing e-mails, listening to music or watching television alone), how many hours a day you spend with other people without the presence of technology, and how many hours a day you combine the two while still maintaining interaction (watching television with family or friends, listening to music with others, talking on the telephone).

For Writing

9. Use the data you and your classmates have collected in answering question 8 to write an essay that analyzes the use of technology by college students. You might, for example, set up a system of division and classification based on the categories suggested in question 8. Do you need to add other categories? You may wish to interview classmates to expand on their answers.

10. Tannen notes, "We seem to be better at developing technological means of communication than at finding ways to temper the hostility that sometimes accompanies them. We have to work harder at finding those ways. That is the challenge we now face" (¶ 23). If you use e-mail a lot (say, twenty or more messages a day), in collaboration with other e-mail users, draft a policy statement of appropriate e-mail etiquette for dealing with messages from people you don't know personally, such as those in your school or workplace to whom you are accountable. Would you recommend treating people you know personally any different from strangers? Incorporate some of the evidence you've gleaned in your answer to question 7.

OLIVER SACKS

Sacks was born in 1933 into a large family of "doctors, metallurgists, chemists, physicists, and teachers." Both parents were physicians and had their offices in the family home, "a huge, rambling Edwardian house" in London. This environment encouraged Sacks's scientific curiosity, including his passions "for numbers, metals, and for finding patterns in the world around him," so it is not surprising that Sacks, too, became a physician. After earning several degrees at Queen's College, Oxford (B.A., 1954; M.A., B.M., and B.Ch., all in 1958) he interned in medicine, surgery, and neurology in London before moving to New York for faculty appointments in neurology at the Albert Einstein College of Medicine and at New York University. Both his medical research and his writing for general readers focus on how people experience loss—of language, emotion, memory, perception, mobility—and learn to function with, or in spite of, these deficits. Among his best known works are *Migraine* (1970), *The Man Who Mistook His Wife for a Hat* (1985), and *A Leg to Stand On* (1984), an account of rehabilitating his leg after a mountain climbing accident.

Encouraged by his "chemical" uncle (for whom he named his childhood autobiography, *Uncle Tungsten*, published in 2001), as a child Sacks began to experiment with "the stinks and bangs that almost [always] define a first entry into chemistry." "There seemed to me," he explains in *Uncle Tungsten*, "an integrity, an essential goodness, about a life in science, a lifelong love affair," whose passion was inflamed by his first encounter with the periodic table that he explains here. "The beauty of science" was manifested in the periodic table, "so economical and simple" and precise a scheme of division and classification, "everything, the whole 92-ishness, reduced to two axes, and yet along each axis an ordered procession of different properties."

Everything in Its Place

It used to be said, when I was a boy, that there were 92 elements, each 1
with its own unique characteristics. These elements, which could combine with one another to form millions of compounds, were "the building blocks of the universe."

One knew, or suspected, that some of them were related. Tin and 2
lead, for example, were both soft metals, easily melted; copper, silver and gold—the "coinage" metals—could all be beaten into foils so thin that they transmitted green or blue light.

But I am not sure that it occurred to me that all the elements might be 3
related to one another until I went, at the age of 12, to the Science Museum in London (newly reopened after the end of the Second World War) and there saw an enormous cabinet labeled "The Periodic Table" hanging at the head of the stairs. Seeing the table, with its actual samples of the elements, was one of the formative experiences of my boyhood and showed me, with the force of revelation, the beauty of science. The periodic table seemed so economical and simple: everything, the whole 92-ishness, reduced to two axes, and yet along each axis an ordered procession of different properties.

Chemistry started to emerge from its alchemical roots in the 18th 4
century, partly with the discovery of new elements: between 1735 and 1826, no fewer than 40 were added to the 9 known to the ancients (copper, silver, gold, iron, mercury, lead, tin, sulphur and carbon) and the few discovered in the Middle Ages (arsenic, antimony and bismuth). The discovery of these new elements forced certain questions on every chemist: How many elements were there? Was there any limit to their number? Were they all related somehow? And if so, how could they be classified?

Kinships were recognized among some. Chlorine, bromine and io- 5
dine—all colored, volatile, hungrily reactive—seemed a natural family— the halogens. Calcium, strontium and barium, the alkaline earth metals were another family, for they were all light, soft, readily set alight and strongly reactive with water.

In 1817, a German chemist, Johann Döbereiner, observed that the 6
atomic weights of the alkaline earth metals formed a series, the atomic weight of strontium being just midway between those of calcium and barium. He later discovered other such triads, as well as triads in which the elements had similar properties but almost identical atomic weights.

Döbereiner's triads convinced many chemists that atomic weight 7
must represent a fundamental characteristic of all elements. But confusion about the basics remained—about the difference between atoms and molecules and about the combining power, or valency, of atoms. As a consequence, many accepted atomic weights were wrong. Dalton himself— the originator of the atomic hypothesis—assumed for instance, that the

formula of water was HO and not H_2O, giving him an atomic weight for oxygen that was only half the correct number.

8   In 1860, the first international gathering of chemists was convened in Karlsruhe, Germany, for the express purpose of clearing up this confusion. Here, Stanislao Cannizzaro proposed a reliable way of calculating atomic weights from vapor density, and his beautifully argued presentation carried the day, leading to a consensus: now, at last, with corrected atomic weights and a clear idea of valency, the way was open for a comprehensive classification of the elements.

9   It is a remarkable example of synchronicity that no fewer than six such classifications, all pointing toward the discovery of periodicity, were independently devised in the next decade. Of these, Dmitri Ivanovich Mendeleev's system was the most comprehensive, and also the most audacious, for it ventured to make detailed predictions of elements as yet unknown.

10   Mendeleev (whose name and wild bearded face were known to every schoolboy of my time) was a figure of heroic proportions. He was Russia's chief scientific adviser and closely involved with industry and agriculture, from coal and oil to cheese and beer. He was the author of the most delightful and vivid chemistry text ever published, "The Principles of Chemistry," and he had brooded since 1854 on how the chemical elements might be classified.

11   With the old, pre-Karlsruhe atomic weights, one could get, as Döbereiner did, a sense of local triads, or groups. But one could not easily see that there was a numerical relationship between the groups themselves. Only when Cannizzaro showed that the proper atomic weights for the alkaline earth metals, calcium, strontium and barium, were 40, 88 and 137 did it become clear how close these were to those of the alkali metals, potassium (39), rubidium (85) and cesium (133). It was this closeness, and the closeness of the atomic weights of the halogens—chlorine, bromine and iodine—that incited Mendeleev in 1868 to make a small, two-dimensional grid juxtaposing the three groups:

Cl	35.5	K	39	Ca	40
Br	80	Rb	85	Sr	88
I	127	Cs	133	Ba	137

12   And it was at this point, seeing that arranging the three groups of elements in order of atomic weight produced a repetitive pattern—a halogen followed by an alkali metal followed by an alkaline earth metal—that Mendeleev felt this must be a fragment of a larger pattern and leapt to the idea of a periodicity governing all the elements, a periodic law.

13   Mendeleev's first small table had to be filled in and then extended in all directions, as if filling up a crossword puzzle. Moving between conscious calculation and hunch, between intuition and analysis, Mendeleev arrived within a few weeks at a tabulation of 30-odd elements in order of

ascending atomic weight, a tabulation that suggested that there was a re-capitulation of properties with every eighth element.

On the night of Feb. 16, 1869, it is said, Mendeleev had a dream in 14 which he saw almost all of the 65 known elements arrayed in a grand table. The following morning, he committed this to paper.

This first table was to undergo considerable revision over the next few 15 years, but by 1871 it had taken its new familiar form of a chunky rectangle with intersecting groups and periods.

It was this table that I saw in the Science Museum and that was to be 16 found in every textbook, lecture room and museum for a century. One could read the table up and down, going from one group to another (each vertical group was a family of elements with similar reactivity and valency)—this was what Döbereiner and the pre-1860 chemists would have done. But one could also read it horizontally, getting a feel for each period as it moved through the eight groups. One could see the way in which the properties of the elements changed with each increment of atomic weight, until suddenly the period came to an end and one found oneself on the next period, where all the elements echoed the properties of those above. It was this, above all, that gave one a feel for the myste-rious periodicity of the table, the reality of the great law it enshrined.

I already had a little lab of my own, where I had spent many hours, and 17 I must have seen in books small versions of Mendeleev's table. But it was seeing the huge table in the museum, being enraptured, really assimilat-ing it for the first time, that moved me from a random or encyclopedic approach—collecting all the chemicals I could, doing all the experiments I could—to a more systematic one, exploring the trends of the elements for myself.

One simple, highly dramatic (and slightly dangerous) experiment 18 was putting small lumps of the alkali metals into water and seeing how they increased in reactivity as their atomic weight increased. One had to do this gingerly, with tongs, and to equip oneself and one's guests with goggles: lithium would move about the surface of the water sedately, reacting with it, emitting hydrogen, until it was all gone; a lump of sodium would move around the surface with an angry buzz, but would not catch fire if a small lump was used; potassium, in contrast, would catch fire the instant it hit the water, burning with a pale mauve flame and shooting globules of itself everywhere; rubidium was still more reactive, splutter-ing violently with a reddish violet flame, and cesium, I found, exploded when it hit the water, shattering its glass container. One never forgot the properties of the alkali metals after this.

The periodic table did not actually tell one the properties of the ele- 19 ments, but like a family tree, it assigned them places. The fun, for me, was to work backward from this, to see how an element's properties corre-sponded with its place. Tungsten, for example, was a favorite—no other metal had such a high melting point. This, I first thought, made it unique, but now I could compare it with its neighbors in the periodic table and see that the highest metallic melting points were all to be found in Group VI and Period 6. Tungsten, at VI:6, lay at the intersection of two mountain ranges, an Everest among other peaks, but not an anomaly.

20   I could plot the physical and chemical properties of all the elements against their atomic weights and obtain the most tantalizing graphs. If one plotted atomic volume against atomic weight, for example, one would get a many-peaked curve, with summits for the light Group I metals, valleys for the dense Group VIII metals. Every property, it seemed, varied periodically and was somehow linked with atomic weight. But why any of the elements should have the properties they had, and why such properties should recur in periodicity with atomic weight, were complete mysteries to me, as they had been to Mendeleev.

21   From 1869 to 1871, Mendeleev expanded the table, going so far as to reposition elements that did not fit, revising their accepted atomic weights to make them fit, an act that shocked some of his contemporaries. Further challenges were presented by two groups of elements, the transition elements (these included rare metals like vanadium and platinum, as well as common ones like iron and nickel) and the rare-earth elements. Neither of these seemed to fit in the neat octaves of the earlier periods. To accommodate them, Mendeleev and others experimented with new forms of the table—helical forms, pyramidal forms, etc.—that, in a sense, gave it extra dimensions.

22   In an act of supreme confidence, Mendeleev reserved several empty spaces in his table for elements "as yet unknown." He asserted that by extrapolating from the properties of the elements above and below (and also, to some extent, from those to either side), one might make a confident prediction as to what these unknown elements would be like. He did exactly this, predicting in great detail a new element that would follow aluminum in Group III: it would be a silvery metal, he thought, with a density of 6.0 and an atomic weight of 68. Four years later, in 1875, just such an element was found: gallium. He also predicted with equal precision the existence of scandium and germanium, and these too were soon discovered. It was this ability to predict elements in such detail that stunned his fellow chemists and convinced many of them that Mendeleev's system was not just an arbitrary ordering of the elements but a profound expression of reality.

23   But Mendeleev was astonished, as everyone was, by the discovery in the 1890's of an entire new family of elements, the inert gases. He was at first skeptical of their existence. (He initially thought that argon, the first found, was just a heavier form of nitrogen.) But with the discovery of helium, neon, krypton, xenon and finally radon, it was clear that they formed a perfect periodic group. They were identical in their inability to form compounds; they had a valency, it seemed, of zero. So to the eight groups of the table, Mendeleev now added a final Group 0.

With the inert gases in place, the number of elements in each period 24 stood out: 2 (hydrogen and helium) in the first period; 8 each in the second and third; 8 typical plus 10 transition elements, or 18 each, in the fourth and fifth periods; 8 plus 10 plus 14 rare-earth elements, or 32, in the sixth period. These were the magical numbers—2, 8, 8, 18, 18, 32. But what did they mean? And what, in broader terms, was the basis of chemical properties?

Mendeleev constantly returned to these questions. He yearned for 25 a new "chemical mechanics," comparable to the classical mechanics of Newton. And yet one wonders what he might have thought of the actual form of the revolution that took place after his death, a revolution wholly unimaginable in terms of classical mechanics.

The new insight into the internal constitution of atoms came in 1911, 26 four years after Mendeleev's death, when Ernest Rutherford (bombarding gold foil with alpha particles and finding that, very occasionally, one was deflected back) inferred that the atom must have a structure like a miniature solar system, with almost all of its mass concentrated in a minute, very dense, positively charged nucleus surrounded at great distances by relatively weightless electrons. But the very essence of atoms was their absolute stability. And such an atom as Rutherford's, if ruled by the laws of classical mechanics, would not be stable; its electrons would lose energy as they orbited, eventually diving into the nucleus.

Niels Bohr, working with Rutherford in 1912, was intensely aware of 27 this, and of the need for a radically new approach. This he found in quantum theory, which postulated that electromagnetic energy—light, radiation—was not continuous but emitted or absorbed in discrete packets, or "quanta." Bohr, by an astounding leap, connected these concepts with the Rutherford model and with the well-known but previously inexplicable nature of optical spectra—that these were not only characteristic for each element but consisted of a multitude of discrete lines or frequencies.

All of these considerations came together in the Bohr atom, where 28 electrons were conceived to occupy a series of orbits, or "shells," of differing energies about the nucleus. Unlike classical orbits, which decay, these quantum orbits had a stability that allowed them to maintain themselves, potentially, forever. (But if the atom was excited, some of its electrons might leap to higher energy orbits for a while and in returning to their ground state emit a quantum of energy of a certain frequency; it was this that caused the characteristic lines in their spectra.)

Bohr brought out his model of the atom in the spring of 1913. A few 29 months later, Henry Moseley found a most intimate relationship between the order of the elements and their X-ray spectra. These spectra could be correlated, Moseley thought, with the number of positive charges in the nucleus, and for this the term "atomic number" was used. With atomic numbers, there were no gaps or fractions or irregularities, as with atomic weights. It was atomic number, not atomic weight, that determined the order of the elements. And Moseley could now say with absolute confidence that there were only 92 elements between hydrogen and uranium, including half a dozen as yet undiscovered. (Three of these had been predicted, though vaguely, by Mendeleev.)

30   Bohr's model suggested that every element's chemical properties, its position in the periodic table, depended on the number of its electrons and how these were organized in successive shells. Valency and chemical reactivity, the definers of Mendeleev's groups, were correlated with the number of valence electrons in the outer shells: with the maximum of eight electrons, an atom was chemically inert; with more, or less, than the maximum, it would tend to be more reactive. Thus the halogens, only one electron short in their outermost shells, were avid to pick up an eighth electron, whereas the alkali metals, with only a single electron in their outer shells, were avid to get rid of it, to become stable in their own way.

31   To this basic eightness, extra shells were added in the later periods: 10-electron shells for the transition elements and 14-electron shells for the rare-earth elements.

32   Bohr and Moseley provided a spectacular confirmation of the periodic table, grounding it, as Mendeleev had hoped, in "the invisible world of chemical atoms." The periodicity of the elements, it was now clear, emerged from their electronic structure. And the mysterious numbers that governed the periodic table—2, 8, 8, 18, 18, 32—could now be understood as the number of electrons added in each period.

33   Such an electronic periodic table is basically identical with Mendeleev's table, posited nearly half a century earlier on purely chemical grounds. Moseley and Bohr worked from the inside, with the invisible world of chemical atoms, and Mendeleev and his contemporaries worked from the outside, with the visible and manifest properties of the elements—and yet they arrived at the same point. This is the beauty of the periodic table, indeed, that it looks both ways, uniting classical chemistry and quantum physics in a magical synthesis.

34   Given Bohr's orbits of different energy levels, one can, in principle, build up the whole periodic table by adding electrons one at a time, climbing the rungs of an atomic ladder from helium to uranium. And it is by such a building-up that we have been able to create new elements absent in nature, like the 20 elements (93–112) that now follow uranium in the periodic table, heavier atoms that do not depart from the regularities of the periodic law. In principle, one can work out the periodic table to element 200 and beyond and predict some of the properties of such elements. (These predictions are largely theoretical because the highly radioactive transuranic elements tend to get more and more unstable. One may only be able to produce an atom at a time, and this may be gone in a few millionths of a second.) But the idea of periodicity, it seems, has no discernible limits, and this, like all the confirmations of this century, would have delighted Mendeleev.

It is more than 50 years since I first saw the periodic table, and my 35
delight in it has never faded. It is still the icon of chemistry, as it has been
for 130 years; it continues to guide chemical research, to suggest new syn-
theses, to allow predictions of the properties of never-before-seen materials. It is a marvelous map to the whole geography of the elements.

My kitchen is papered with periodic tables of every size and sort— 36
oblongs, spirals, pyramids, weather vanes—and on the kitchen table, a
very favorite one, a round periodic table made of wood that I can spin
like a prayer wheel. I carry two tiny periodic tables in my wallet—a classical Mendeleevian one with antique lettering and a more modern one,
a beautiful colored spiral that shows the elements, their atomic numbers, like a great nebula, whirling out beyond uranium to who knows
what infinity.

Content

1. Sacks regards the periodic table as "the icon of chemistry . . . a marvelous
map to the whole geography of the elements" (¶ 35). Explain how his essay
illustrates this.
2. What system of classification did Mendeleev use for organizing the first periodic table? How was Mendeleev able to "predict elements in such detail that
. . . [he demonstrated that his] system was not just an arbitrary ordering of elements
but a profound expression of reality" (¶ 21)?
3. How can a system of division and classification of anything (not only chemical elements) be used to predict new components that haven't been discovered
yet? Explain how this system operated with reference to the work of Bohr and
Moseley on the elements (sees ¶ 29–32).

Strategies/Structures

4. Sacks begins and ends his essay on a personal note. How does this strategy
reflect his concept of his audience?
5. Sacks discusses the discovery of the periodic table and the systems of classification that have added to our knowledge of the table. How does his own organizational strategy enhance our understanding of this complex topic?

Language

6. Sacks uses many technical terms throughout his essay, which is intended for
general readers of the *New York Times*, where "Everything in its Place" was originally published. Identify some of these terms. In which instances does Sacks provide brief definitions or illustrations to aid readers unfamiliar with even the basics
of chemistry?
7. What else does Sacks do to make it possible for readers who are novices at
chemistry to understand the system of division and classification that underlies
the periodic table?

For Writing

8. Pick a system that provides order or that assembles diverse or unlike things into an orderly arrangement, and justify it. Test out your system on some of its potential users to see whether they can understand it, can suggest refinements and improvements, and would use it. Revise your paper accordingly.

9. Sacks's "kitchen is papered with periodic tables of every size and sort—oblongs, spirals, pyramids, weather vanes—and on the kitchen table, a very favorite one, a round periodic table made of wood that [he] can spin like a prayer wheel" (¶ 36). Following the suggestion of this illustration, pick a topic that is customarily organized or interpreted according to a particular classification system, and invent a new system for interpreting the same phenomenon. Discuss possibilities with your peers, for this requires new ways of looking at familiar things: the calendar; day and night; grammar systems; the sexes—including customs of dating, marriage, and childrearing; issues of work and play. Write a paper, either individually or with your group, justifying your new classification system and its advantages over the familiar system.

=======

RICHARD RODRIGUEZ

How Richard Rodriguez, born in San Francisco in 1944, the son of Mexican immigrants, should and can deal with his dual heritage is the subject of his autobiographical *Hunger of Memory: The Education of Richard Rodriguez* (1982). He spoke Spanish at home and didn't learn English until he began grammar school in Sacramento. Although for a time he refused to speak Spanish, he studied that language in high school as if it were a foreign language. Nevertheless, classified as Mexican-American, Rodriguez benefited from Affirmative Action programs, and on scholarships he earned a B.A. from Stanford (1967), and an M.A. from Columbia (1969). After that he studied Renaissance literature at the University of California, Berkeley— the site of the climactic event described in the following essay, later incorporated into *Hunger of Memory*. In 1992 he published *Days of Obligation: An Argument with my Mexican Father*, a collection of essays focusing on his complicated relations to the cultures of the Catholic Church, San Francisco's gay Castro District, and Mexico. *Brown* followed in 2002.

For two decades Rodriguez, now an educational consultant and freelance writer, has consistently—and controversially—argued against bilingual education, other programs that would separate minority students from the mainstream, and Affirmative Action. In this essay Rodriguez argues against the arbitrary—and divisive—classification of people into categories, by race, religion, or ethnic origin, for the purposes of Affirmative Action. But he concludes with a different classification of people on the basis of income, which lumps together "white, black, brown. Always poor. Silent." Hopeless. And untouched by Affirmative Action. He will be their spokesperson, too.

None of This Is Fair

M y plan to become a professor of English—my ambition during long   1
years in college at Stanford, then in graduate school at Columbia and
Berkeley—was complicated by feelings of embarrassment and guilt. So
many times I would see other Mexican-Americans and know we were
alike only in race. And yet, simply because our race was the same, I was,
during the last years of my schooling, the beneficiary of their situation. Affirmative Action programs had made it all possible. The disadvantages of
others permitted my promotion; the absence of many Mexican-Americans
from academic life allowed my designation as a "minority student."

For me opportunities had been extravagant. There were fellowships,   2
summer research grants, and teaching assistantships. After only two years
in graduate school, I was offered teaching jobs by several colleges. Invitations to Washington conferences arrived and I had the chance to travel
abroad as a "Mexican-American representative." The benefits were often,
however, too gaudy to please. In three published essays, in conversations
with teachers, in letters to politicians and at conferences, I worried the
issue of Affirmative Action. Often I proposed contradictory opinions.
Though consistent was the admission that—because of an early, excellent
education—I was no longer a principal victim of racism or any other social oppression. I said that but still I continued to indicate on applications
for financial aid that I was a Hispanic-American. It didn't really occur to
me to say anything else, or to leave the question unanswered.

Thus I complied with and encouraged the odd bureaucratic logic of   3
Affirmative Action. I let government officials treat the disadvantaged condition of many Mexican-Americans with my advancement. Each fall my
presence was noted by Health, Education, and Welfare department statis-
ticians. As I pursued advanced literary studies and learned the skill of
reading Spenser and Wordsworth and Empson, I would hear myself num-
bered among the culturally disadvantaged. Still, silent, I didn't object.

But the irony cut deep. And guilt would not be evaded by averting   4
my glance when I confronted a face like my own in a crowd. By late 1975,
nearing the completion of my graduate studies at Berkeley, I was so wary
of the benefits of Affirmative Action that I feared my inevitable success
as an applicant for a teaching position. The months of fall—traditionally
that time of academic job-searching—passed without my applying to a
single school. When one of my professors chanced to learn this in late
November, he was astonished, then furious. He yelled at me: Did I think
that because I was a minority student jobs would just come looking for
me? What was I thinking? Did I realize that he and several other faculty
members had already written letters on my behalf? Was I going to start
acting like some other minority students he had known? They struggled
for success and then, when it was almost within reach, grew strangely
afraid and let it pass. Was that it? Was I determined to fail?

5   I did not respond to his questions. I didn't want to admit to him, and thus to myself, the reason I delayed.

6   I merely agreed to write to several schools. (In my letter I wrote: "I cannot claim to represent disadvantaged Mexican-Americans. The very fact that I am in a position to apply for this job should make that clear.") After two or three days, there were telegrams and phone calls, invitations to interviews, then airplane trips. A blur of faces and the murmur of their soft questions. And, over someone's shoulder, the sight of campus buildings shadowing pictures I had seen years before when I leafed through Ivy League catalogues with great expectations. At the end of each visit, interviewers would smile and wonder if I had any questions. A few times I quietly wondered what advantage my race had given me over other applicants. But that was an impossible question for them to answer without embarrassing me. Quickly, several persons insisted that my ethnic identity had given me no more than a "foot inside the door"; at most, I had a "slight edge" over other applicants. "We just looked at your dossier with extra care and we like what we saw. There was never any question of having to alter our standards. You can be certain of that."

7   In the early part of January, offers arrived on stiffly elegant stationery. Most schools promised terms appropriate for any new assistant professor. A few made matters worse—and almost more tempting—by offering more: the use of university housing; an unusually large starting salary; a reduced teaching schedule. As the stack of letters mounted, my hesitation increased. I started calling department chairmen to ask for another week, then 10 more days—"more time to reach a decision"—to avoid the decision I would need to make.

8   At school, meantime, some students hadn't received a single job offer. One man, probably the best student in the department, did not even get a request for his dossier. He and I met outside a classroom one day and he asked about my opportunities. He seemed happy for me. Faculty members beamed. They said they had expected it. "After all, not many schools are going to pass up getting a Chicano with a Ph.D. in Renaissance literature," somebody said laughing. Friends wanted to know which of the offers I was going to accept. But I couldn't make up my mind. February came and I was running out of time and excuses. (One chairman guessed my delay was a bargaining ploy and increased his offer with each of my calls.) I had to promise a decision by the 10th; the 12th at the very latest.

9   On the 18th of February, late in the afternoon, I was in the office I shared with several other teaching assistants. Another graduate student was sitting across the room at his desk. When I got up to leave, he looked over to say in an uneventful voice that he had some big news. He had finally decided to accept a position at a faraway university. It was not a job he especially wanted, he admitted. But he had to take it because there hadn't been any other offers. He felt trapped, and depressed, since his job would separate him from his young daughter.

I tried to encourage him by remarking that he was lucky at least to   10
have found a job. So many others hadn't been able to get anything. But
before I finished speaking I realized that I had said the wrong thing. And
I anticipated his next question.

"What are your plans?" he wanted to know. "Is it true you've gotten   11
an offer from Yale?"

I said that it was. "Only, I still haven't made up my mind."   12

He stared at me as I put on my jacket. And smiling, then unsmiling,   13
he asked if I knew that he too had written to Yale. In his case, however, no
one had bothered to acknowledge his letter with even a postcard. What
did I think of that?

He gave me no time to answer.   14

"Damn!" he said sharply and his chair rasped the floor as he pushed   15
himself back. Suddenly, it was to *me* that he was complaining. "It's just not
right, Richard. None of this is fair. You've done some good work, but so
have I. I'll bet our records are just about equal. But when we look for jobs
this year, it's a different story. You get all of the breaks."

To evade his criticism, I wanted to side with him. I was about to   16
admit the injustice of Affirmative Action. But he went on, his voice hard
with accusation. "It's all very simple this year. You're a Chicano. And I am
a Jew. That's the only real difference between us."

His words stung me: there was nothing he was telling me that I didn't   17
know. I had admitted everything already. But to hear someone else say
these things, and in such an accusing tone, was suddenly hard to take. In
a deceptively calm voice, I responded that he had simplified the whole
issue. The phrases came like bubbles to the tip of my tongue: "new blood";
"the importance of cultural diversity"; "the goal of racial integration."
These were all the arguments I had proposed several years ago—and had
long since abandoned. Of course the offers were unjustifiable. I knew that.
All I was saying amounted to a frantic self-defense. I tried to find an end
to a sentence. My voice faltered to a stop.

"Yeah, sure," he said. "I've heard all that before. Nothing you say   18
really changes the fact that Affirmative Action is unfair. You see that, don't
you? There isn't any way for me to compete with you. Once there were
quotas to keep my parents out of certain schools; now there are quotas to
get you in and the effect on me is the same as it was for them."

I listened to every word he spoke. But my mind was really on some-   19
thing else. I knew at that moment that I would reject all of the offers. I
stood there silently surprised by what an easy conclusion it was. Having
prepared for so many years to teach, having trained myself to do nothing
else, I had hesitated out of practical fear. But now that it was made, the decision came with relief. I immediately knew I had made the right choice.

My colleague continued talking and I realized that he was simply   20
right. Affirmative Action programs *are* unfair to white students. But as I
listened to him assert his rights, I thought of the seriously disadvantaged.

How different they were from white, middle-class students who come armed with the testimony of their grades and aptitude scores and self-confidence to complain about the unequal treatment they now receive. I listen to them. I do not want to be careless about what they say. Their rights are important to protect. But inevitably when I hear them or their lawyers, I think about the most seriously disadvantaged, not simply Mexican-Americans, but of all those who do not ever imagine themselves going to college or becoming doctors: white, black, brown. Always poor. Silent. They are not plaintiffs before the court or against the misdirection of Affirmative Action. They lack the confidence (my confidence!) to assume their right to a good education. They lack the confidence and skills a good primary and secondary education provides and which are prerequisites for informed public life. They remain silent.

21   The debate drones on and surrounds them in stillness. They are distant, faraway figures like the boys I have seen peering down from freeway overpasses in some other part of town.

Content

1. What does Rodriguez mean by his fundamental premise, "None of this is fair" (¶ 15)?

2. What is Affirmative Action? What is reverse discrimination? What does Rodriguez's comparison of his job-seeking experience with those of his white male classmates illustrate about these terms?

3. Does Rodriguez intend that his readers generalize on the basis of the job-seeking experiences of himself and his two white male classmates, one Jewish?

4. What categories of people does Rodriguez claim are currently benefiting from Affirmative Action programs? What categories of people are the victims of reverse discrimination?

5. In Rodriguez's opinion, which people truly need Affirmative Action (¶ 20)? Why aren't they getting what they need? Why does he wait so long to get to this point?

Strategies/Structures

6. If Rodriguez believes that Affirmative Action doesn't benefit the "most seriously disadvantaged," the poor people of all races (¶ 20), why doesn't he illustrate the point with an example based on economics, rather than race? And devote more space to the economic issue?

7. Show how Rodriguez employs division and classification to conduct his argument.

For Writing

8. If you or someone you know has either benefited from Affirmative Action or experienced reverse discrimination, write an essay about that experience to illustrate a general point about it for readers unfamiliar with the issue.

9. Rodriguez has been attacked as an Uncle Juan (a Chicano Uncle Tom) for claiming that he and other middle-class minority students improperly benefit from Affirmative Action programs that do not aid "all those who never imagine themselves going to college or becoming doctors: white, black, brown. Always poor. Silent" (¶ 20). Discuss the issue with fellow students or other colleagues and write an essay on Rodriguez's position, summarizing either the consensus or the main lines of debate on this subject and indicating your position, as well. Do you, either individually or collectively, agree either with Rodriguez or with his critics?

GELAREH ASAYESH

"When a natural disaster hits, people talk for years about . . . the power of the earth tremor that remade the landscape of their lives. But the emotional disasters in our lives go largely unacknowledged, their repercussions unclaimed," says Asayesh, in *Saffron Sky,* of her parents' decision in 1977 to move the family from Tehran, Iran (where she was born in 1961), to Chapel Hill, North Carolina. In Iran they lived in material comfort but in political opposition to the repressive Shah. In Chapel Hill, as graduate students, they became outsiders, "wrenched from all that was loved and familiar" in Iran, "faced with an unspoken choice: to be alienated from the world around us or from our innermost selves." Although Asayesh was educated at the University of North Carolina-Chapel Hill, and went on to become a journalist, working for *The Boston Globe, The Miami Herald,* and *The Baltimore Sun,* the appeals and tensions of these contradictory cultures have never been fully resolved.

In *Saffron Sky: A Life Between Iran and America* (1999), Asayesh explores the contrasts between these two ways of life, her ambivalent attitude toward her homeland intensified by her marriage to an American and her own parenthood. Returning to Iran in October 1990, just before the Persian Gulf war, Asayesh is newly aware of the world of "rigidity and restriction"— rules against wearing lipstick, or too sheer stockings, or letting the hair show—enforced by the intrusive gender police. Yet, as "Shrouded in Contradiction," published in the *New York Times Magazine* (November 2001), reveals, "To wear *hijab* is to invite contradiction. Sometimes I hate it. Sometimes I value it"—as a covering of both restriction and freedom.

Shrouded in Contradiction

I grew up wearing the miniskirt to school, the veil to the mosque. In the Tehran of my childhood, women in bright sundresses shared the sidewalk with women swathed in black. The tension between the two ways of life was palpable. As a schoolgirl, I often cringed when my bare legs got leering or contemptuous glances. Yet, at times, I long for the days when I   1 could walk the streets of my country with the wind in my hair. When clothes were clothes. In today's Iran, whatever I wear sends a message. If it's a chador, it embarrasses my Westernized relatives. If it's a skimpy scarf, I risk being accused of stepping on the blood of the martyrs who died in the war with Iraq. Each time I return to Tehran, I wait until the last possible moment, when my plane lands on the tarmac, to don the scarf and long jacket that many Iranian women wear in lieu of a veil. To wear *hijab*—Islamic covering—is to invite contradiction. Sometimes I hate it. Sometimes I value it.

2   Most of the time, I don't even notice it. It's annoying, but so is wearing pantyhose to work. It ruins my hair, but so does the humidity in Florida, where I live. For many women, the veil is neither a symbol nor a statement. It's simply what they wear, as their mothers did before them. Something to dry your face with after your ablutions before prayer. A place for a toddler to hide when he's feeling shy. Even for a woman like me, who wears it with a hint of rebellion, *hijab* is just not that big a deal.

3   Except when it is.

4   "Sister, what kind of get-up is this?" a woman in black, one of a pair, asks me one summer day on the Caspian shore. I am standing in line to ride a gondola up a mountain, where I'll savor some ice cream along with vistas of sea and forest. Women in chadors stand wilting in the heat, faces gleaming with sweat. Women in makeup and clunky heels wear knee-length jackets with pants, their hair daringly exposed beneath sheer scarves.

5   None have been more daring than I. I've wound my scarf into a turban, leaving my neck bare to the breeze. The woman in black is a government employee paid to police public morals. "Fix your scarf at once!" she snaps.

6   "But I'm hot," I say.

7   "You're hot?" she exclaims. "Don't you think we all are?"

8   I start unwinding my makeshift turban. "The men aren't hot," I mutter.

9   Her companion looks at me in shocked reproach. "Sister, this isn't about men and women," she says, shaking her head. "This is about Islam."

10   I want to argue. I feel like a child. Defiant, but powerless. Burning with injustice, but also with a hint of shame. I do as I am told, feeling acutely conscious of the bare skin I am covering. In policing my sexuality, these women have made me more aware of it.

11   The veil masks erotic freedom, but its advocates believe *hijab* transcends the erotic—or expands it. In the West, we think of passion as a fever of the body, not the soul. In the East, Sufi poets used earthly passion as a metaphor; the beloved they celebrated was God. Where I come from, people are more likely to find delirious passion in the mosque than in the bedroom.

12   There are times when I feel a hint of this passion. A few years after my encounter on the Caspian, I go to the wake of a family friend. Sitting in a

In what ways is this photograph a graphic illustration of the elements of division and classification? Explain how it is a commentary on both "Shrouded in Contradiction" and "Mirror, Mirror on the Wall."

mosque in Mashhad, I grip a slippery black veil with one hand and a prayer book with the other. In the center of the hall, there's a stack of Koranic texts decorated with green-and-black calligraphy, a vase of white gladioluses and a large photograph of the dearly departed. Along the walls, women wait quietly.

From the men's side of the mosque, the mullah's voice rises in lament. His voice is deep and plaintive, oddly compelling. I bow my head, sequestered in my veil while at my side a community of women pray and weep with increasing abandon. I remember from girlhood this sense of being exquisitely alone in the company of others. Sometimes I have cried as well, free to weep without having to offer an explanation. Perhaps they are right, those mystics who believe that physical love is an obstacle to spiritual love; those architects of mosques who abstained from images of earthly life, decorating their work with geometric shapes that they believed freed the soul to slip from its worldly moorings. I do not aspire to such lofty sentiments. All I know is that such moments of passionate abandon, within the circle of invisibility created by the veil, offer an emotional catharsis every bit as potent as any sexual release.

Outside, the rain pours from a sullen sky. I make my farewells and walk toward the car, where my driver waits. My veil is wicking muddy water from the sidewalk. I gather up the wet and grimy folds with distaste,

13

14

longing to be home, where I can cast off this curtain of cloth that gives with one hand, takes away with the other.

[Suggestions for reading and writing about this essay are combined with those pertaining to Sumbul Khan's "Mirror, Mirror on the Wall" and appear on pages 334–35.]

SUMBUL KHAN

> Sumbul Khan, born in Karachi, Pakistan, in 1978, attended the Indus Valley School of Art and Architecture for three years before transferring to the University of Connecticut, where she is pursuing a B.F.A. "Mirror, Mirror on the Wall" was written in a freshman composition class during her first year at an American university. This was, Kahn says, "a tumultuous and yet very enriching time as it entailed adjusting to a completely different culture and finding my place in it as an international student." In writing the essay, she says, "I made a conscious effort to convey lucidly the logic behind the Muslim practice of wearing the veil and addressing the stereotypes that make it difficult sometimes to adhere to the practice, without alienating an audience that might have had varied perceptions of it."

❄ *Mirror, Mirror on the Wall, Who's the Fairest of Them All?*

1 "One of those international students, can't help looking at them, can you?"

2 The snigger repeats itself in her mind as her fingers fasten the dark strands of hair in silver barrettes. She looks at the girl on the other side of the mirror and watches her face change as the white folds of cloth crop her countenance closely around its contours. The resemblance is evident and yet it is not her she sees today but the girl they see.

3 Rambling through her mind, seeking to find words that describe her to them, she sets herself on a plane outside of herself. It is as if she does not reside in her own body anymore but somewhere beyond its physical dimensions, from where she stares down at the effigy she calls, I. Is it the I that keeps coming in the way of adopting their ways? What is the I? What is it made of?

4 The I, for the moment, is only the piece of cloth that covers her hair, the *hejaab*. The garb of bondage, the symbol of primitive conformity, the virgin white *hejaab* that enshrouds her body that breathes every breath in

self-abnegation. She wonders if that is what it really is? She peers into her eyes for an answer but the two pairs of eyes, both her own, stare trans-fixed at each other, neither knowing what to expect of which.

I was seventeen when it all began. Dunya had come home one day in tears: her husband had put a knife to her throat and threatened to kill her. They had been in the marriage for two years and not a day had gone by that he hadn't called her a whore and not meant it. *Was* Dunya a whore? Dunya was as untouched and pure as they come. Dunya was, however, a better doctor than him and, worse still, she belonged to a family that believed its daughters to be individual entities, not their husbands' doormats. The man was insecure. Having risen from adversity by dint of a little luck and a little help from kind relatives, his views were still as inflexible, as was typical of the men of his strata. Dunya, for him, was too self-sufficient for her culture and so Dunya was a whore. "It can't work, *Ammi*," she wept hysterically in their mother's arms.

That was the first failed marriage in the family and that too on the eve of the second daughter's wedding. Iman's wedding was fraught with uncertainty. It would have been postponed, for no one was up to cele-brating, but putting off a wedding was said to bring bad luck. Hence it was decided that the wedding would be held the very day that it had been scheduled. It was the day after Dunya's divorce papers were filed.

The irony of it all did not go unnoticed and much was said in the neighborhood about *Miyan Saheb's* misfortune. Of course the punch line was, "When girls get sent to college they lose sight of their real station in life. How then, can marriages last?" After a year and a half of turning a deaf ear to such shows of sympathy and keeping their chins up with all the integrity parents with girls can have in South Asia, they hadn't the faintest idea what more was about to come their way.

It wasn't long before Iman came home too. Her divorce was not stom-ached as well as Dunya's, after all there was a third's marriage prospects to consider: who would marry her knowing both her elder sisters had failed to keep their husbands happy. They wouldn't see that the decision to opt out had been the girls' in both cases because there was something wrong with the men, but that didn't matter. No matter what the men were like, the girls had failed. The third will probably not make it either. It took six months of Iman being tossed back and forth between her father's and husband's house, before it was decided that it was unfair to make Iman live through hell for the sake of the youngest. If Allah willed the youngest to be happy, she would find her happiness regardless of whether her sis-ters were divorced or not. So that was that.

It was sometime in the middle of this frenzy that I, the youngest, struggled with the travails of adolescent girlhood in a male-dominated culture. Disillusioned by my sisters' experiences, I was probably the most cynical nineteen-year-old of my lot. So while my friends were looking for flippant high school sweethearts, I found myself thinking of independence—financial, social, physical and emotional—a career began to take form in my mind. Perhaps it was the need for stability, external and internal, that made me start reading up on Islam, the religion I was born in. And then I woke up one day and donned the *hejaab*. I was not going to be sized up by men, I would take control of my body and defy the objectification I felt as a woman. I would decide who was worthy enough to share my person with. It was a step towards liberation, as the readings on feminism later suggested, from the masculine gaze.

10   America. The land of opportunity. The land where Feminism was born. The land I thought would embrace me with open arms because I had broken the shackles of male dependence by deciding to live on my own. I celebrated my twenty-second birthday here. Life takes a perverse delight, though, in proving us wrong just when we think we're on top of things.

11   Her finger tips trace the circles around her eyes. Age. Is this what they say they feel at the big thirty? She counts her years up to thirty—eight more to go—no, it must be another feeling, she was too far behind to know quite what thirty felt like. It has been a while since she has thought back to a past so carefully locked away in the deep recesses of her mind. Perhaps this is one of those moments, when one feels so overcome by vulnerability that the strength of the everyday façade refuses to stay up, and all one's insecurities float before one's face laughing demonically, with vengeance. She looks back at them, the tiny specters that loom so large before her.

12   "Afghanistan wages war on women" had been the subject of the e-mail her friend had forwarded her. It had jabbed like a dagger in her gut. Even now she could feel the bile rising to her throat as she imagined women, covered like herself, being sentenced to death for being out with a male friend.

13   It's not their fault. How can they help but think of me as a victim? I can't even blame them for seeing me as an accomplice in the savagery of the Muslim world for wearing my *hejaab* so confidently. How can I explain my position against a backdrop of such ignorant transgression? What is wrong with the Afghan government? This is not what Islam propounds. Islam was the religion to give women the right to vote, the right to conduct trade, the right to marry who they pleased when the West was still grappling with corseted, powdered and puffed to perfection, chaperoned, puppets of the male will. What a mockery we make of our religion now! How in the face of this does one propose to anyone the feminist implications of *hejaab*? The fact that it sets a woman free from having to conform to the male standards of feminine beauty. Even in the most traditional of

connotations, where it was a symbol of protection at a time against men who were at liberty to take any woman off the street, the *hejaab* was *for* the woman and now it is the very thing our men strangle us with! No, that isn't Islam, not to me, and not to a lot of Muslim men and women I know. There are those of us who still see the teachings in their true spirit. Yet, to a world that is fed only on the media, there appears to be no difference between those of us who understand their faith and those who warp it to suit their own interests.

Haven't there been transgressors in every religion, though? What of   14 the ethnic cleansing in Bosnia? Christ, who died for the sins of mankind, would not have proposed killing every non-Christian left, right and center, yet the world doesn't generalize Christians as bigoted terrorists. Why is that objectivity extended to Christians—the level-headedness that says not all are alike and what is being done is wrong, wrong even to the spirit of the religion, in the name of which it is being done—and not to Muslims?

Her eyes wander from her face to the rest of her form, to her practically   15 non-existent breasts. All through school if anyone had anything to say to her it was, "Honey, you need to let a man get to you." It was one of the gifts of repressed, single-sex, Convent schooling—girls deriding each other more openly than they would have were there boys around. Under the loose T-shirt however, they completely disappeared. Her thoughts drift to the pair of gray-green eyes that she had lately been seeking out in her drawing class. Eyes that barely ever rested on her longer than a second—how could they on a form so covered that it offered little incentive to look? Yet this is exactly what the point had been, to not allow a man to feast his eyes on her, but this one she was willing to give the prerogative to. The prerogative, however, only came with marriage and an American man was not about to forsake all the pleasures prettier girls may readily offer, just to have her.

It's something about the color of his eyes, I think, because in every other   16 sense he's just an ordinary looking male. All that is keeping me from those eyes is my *hejaab*.

Is it worth it? This whole deal that I make of it? Can not having pre-   17 marital sex guarantee that the man I ultimately choose to take would be right for me? He wasn't for Dunya or Iman. Yet would succumbing to this desire now guarantee that I would be able to secure a long-term relationship with this man-to-be?

No, if it failed, it would hurt all the more for then my husband's   18 touch would never suffice. Perhaps then the *hejaab* in a way protects one from getting hurt, too; if there is nothing to compare against, at least the physical aspect of a conjugal bond would most likely be pleasurable with whomever the husband might be.

19   And yet, there is the present, the sordidly hurtful present that yearns, that longs, and that doesn't quite taste that particular mouth.

20   Her mouth curves into a sad wishful smile as her lower lip curls under the sharp bite of her teeth. For now, reverie has seized reign of her conscious self as a whiff of the fresh, sweet air that would waft across her room at home when the window was opened on to the garden. Her senses give in to its heady, tantalizing allure, unable to keep her from smiling. Far, oh-so-far, is the misery, the torment of being misunderstood, being unread. The anticipation of a new day, of the possibility of seeing him, propels her away from the self-analytical mirror to gather her things for the Tuesday morning studio.

Content

1. For what purpose or purposes is the *hijab* (or *hejaab*) worn? Why does Asayesh write, "In today's Iran, whatever I wear sends a message" (¶ 1)? What is the "message"? To whom is a message being sent? Is the message the same to every viewer? Is this the same message that Khan sends when she wears the *hejaab* to class in America?

2. Both Asayesh and Khan have ambivalent feelings about wearing the *hijab,* the veil-like covering for women mandated in Islamic countries. What are these?

3. Both authors are bicultural: Asayesh is Iranian-American, and Khan, from Karachi, Pakistan, is studying in Connecticut. Are their conflicts related to the fact that they live in dual cultures? Or would these same conflicts exist if they lived in or held the values of a single culture?

Strategies/Structures

4. Asayesh introduces her subject with a reference to wearing both miniskirts and veils. How does this reference help to convey the forms of division and classification she will pursue in her discussion? How does her conclusion help to tie her essay together?

5. The essays by Asayesh and Khan contain several contradictions. Identify them and explain how they contribute to the project of division and classification each undertakes in her essay.

Language

6. Is Asayesh's definition of *hijab* adequate? Is Khan's? Do some research on *hijab* and explain why the definition each provides is either adequate or inadequate for the purposes of her essay.

7. In Asayesh's essay, who is "paid to police public morals" (¶ 5)? What does the policing of public morals entail? What is "the masculine gaze" to which Khan refers in paragraph 9? Is this also a form of control and "policing"? Compare and contrast, in discussion or in writing, the differences in the scrutiny of individual women's dress (and behavior) in the cultures depicted in these papers.

For Writing

8. Choose a particular article of clothing, describe it in detail (fabric, cost, quality, style), and trace the history of the changed messages it (as worn by a particular individual or group) has sent over time. You might consider the original purpose of the article (for example, a baseball cap, a fur coat, blue jeans, a military uniform) and then examine how and why the connotations of wearing this have changed— over time and when worn by different types of people. What message—cultural, economic, political, aesthetic, and/or other—is sent by each type of wearing?

9. What clothes do your fellow students wear? You can use the essays by Asayesh and Khan as points of reference. Analyze the clothing of a typical man and woman. In what respects are they similar? Different? Do any articles of clothing predominate? What "messages" do they send to particular audiences in particular contexts? What dictates this dress? Custom? Individual preference? Group behavior? Other factors?

10. Write an essay that proposes answers to Khan's questions in paragraph 13. How can those not familiar with the history of the *hejaab* "help but think of [Khan, Asayesh, or any women who wears a *hejaab*] as a victim"? How can these and other women who choose to wear a *hejaab* for the reasons these authors identify avoid being seen as "an accomplice in the savagery of the Muslim world for wearing [their] *hejaab* so confidently" (¶ 13)?

Additional Topics for Writing Division and Classification

(For strategies for writing division and classification, see 298)

1. Write an essay in which you use division to analyze one of the subjects below. Explain or illustrate each of the component parts, showing how each part functions or relates to the functioning or structure of the whole. Remember to adapt your analysis to your reader's assumed knowledge of the subject. Is it extensive? meager? or somewhere in between?

    a. The organization of the college or university you attend
    b. An organization of which you are a member—team, band or orchestra, fraternity or sorority, social or political action group
    c. A typical (or atypical) weekday or weekend in your life
    d. Your budget, or the federal budget
    e. Your family
    f. A farm, kibbutz, or factory
    g. Geologic periods
    h. A poem
    i. A provocative short story, novel, play, or television or film drama
    j. A hospital, city hall, bank, restaurant, supermarket, shopping mall
    k. The organizational structure of a particular corporation or government office

2. Write an essay, adapted to your reader's assumed knowledge of the subject, in which you classify members of one of the following subjects. Make the basis of your classification apparent, consistent, and logical. You may want to identify each group or subgroup by a name or relevant term, actual or invented.

    a. Types of cars (or sports cars), boats, or bicycles
    b. People's temperaments or personality types
    c. Vacations or holidays
    d. Styles of music, or types of a particular kind of music (classical, country and western, folk, rock)
    e. People's styles of spending money
    f. Types of restaurants, or subcategories (such as types of fast-food restaurants)
    g. Individual or family lifestyles
    h. Types of post–high school educational institutions, or types of courses a given school offers
    i. Clothing styles for your age group
    j. Tennis players, skiers, golfers, runners, or other sports stars; or television or movie stars
    k. Computers—types of hardware, software, or computer (or Internet) users
    l. Types of stores or shopping malls
    m. Some phenomenon, activity, types of people or literature or entertainment that you like or dislike a great deal
    n. Social or political groups

Definition

A definition can set limits or expand them. An objective definition may settle an argument; a subjective definition can provoke one. In either case, they answer the definer's fundamental question, What is X? The photograph above of the couple in the kitchen, for instance, might be interpreted as a visual definition of "love," "marriage," "domesticity," "sex roles," "materialism," "technology," "cleanliness," "wealth," or "the good life," among many possibilities. The easiest way to define something is to identify it as a member of a class and then specify the characteristics that make it distinctive from all the other members of that class. You could define yourself as a "student," but that wouldn't be sufficient to discriminate between you as a college undergraduate and pupils in kindergarten, elementary, junior high, or high school, graduate students, or, for that matter, a person independently studying aardvarks, gourmet cooking, or the nature of the universe.

As you make any kind of writing more specific, you lower the level of abstraction, usually a good idea in definition. So you could identify—and thereby define—yourself by specifying "college student," or more specifically yet, your class status, "college freshman." That might be sufficient for some contexts, such as filling out an application blank. Or you might need to indicate where you go to school "at Cuyahoga Community College" or "Michigan State University." (Initials won't always work—readers might think MSU means Memphis State, or Mississippi, or Montana.)

But if you're writing an entire essay devoted to defining exactly what kind of student you are, a phrase or sentence will be insufficient, even if expanded to include "a computer science major" or "a business major with an accounting specialty, and a varsity diver." Although the details of that definition would separate and thereby distinguish you from, certainly, most other members of your class, they wouldn't convey the essence of what you as a person are like in your student role.

You could consider that sentence your core definition, and expand each key word into a separate paragraph to create an essay-length definition that could include "college student," "accounting major," and "varsity diver." But that still might not cover it. You could approach the subject through considering *cause-and-effect*. Why did you decide to go to college? Because you love to learn? Because you need to get specialized training for your chosen career? To get away from home? What have been the short-term effects of your decision to attend college? What are the long-term effects likely to be—on yourself, on your chosen field, perhaps on the world?

Or you might define yourself as a college student by *comparing and contrasting* your current life with that of a friend still in high school, or with someone who hasn't gone to college, or with a person you admire who has already graduated. If you work part- or full-time while attending college, you could write an *analysis* of its effect on your studying; or an *argument*, using yourself as an *extended example*, stating why it's desirable (or undesirable) for college students to work. Or, among many other possibilities, you could write a *narrative* of a typical week or semester at college. Each of these modes of writing could be an essay of definition. Each could be only partial, unless you wrote a book, for every definition is, by definition, selective. But each would serve your intended purpose. Each essay in this section represents a different common type of definition, but most use other types as well.

Definition According to Purpose.   A definition according to purpose specifies the fundamental qualities an object, principle or policy, role, or literary or artistic work has—or should have—in order to fulfill its potential. Thus, such a definition might explicitly answer such questions as, What is the purpose of X? ("A parable is a simple story designed to teach a moral truth.") What is X for? ("Horror movies exist to scare the spectators.") Judy Brady's "I Want a Wife" (361–64) concentrates on two other aspects of definition according to purpose, What does X do? and What is the role of X? An ideal wife, says Brady, will serve as a wage-earner, secretary, housekeeper, "nurturant attendant" of the children, hostess, entertainer, and sexual companion, among other roles. Brady defines by both negative and positive examples: "I want a wife who will not bother me with rambling complaints about a wife's duties. But I want a wife who will listen to me when I feel the need to explain a rather difficult point I have come across in my course of studies." Because Brady is writing satirically, however, it is possible to interpret the positive examples as negative and vice versa, and still to agree with the emphatic conclusion of her definition, "My God, who *wouldn't* want a wife?"

Descriptive Definition.   A descriptive definition identifies the distinctive characteristics of an individual or group that set it apart from others. Thus a descriptive definition may begin by *naming* something, answering the question, What is X called? A possible answer might be Eudora Welty (unique among all other women); a walnut (as opposed to all other species of nuts); or *The Sound and the Fury* (and no other novel by William Faulkner). A descriptive definition may also *specify the relationship among the parts of a unit or group*, responding to the questions, What is the structure of X? How is X organized? How is X put together or constituted? In "Everything in Its Place" (314–22) Oliver Sacks explains the periodic table in these terms. Jasmine Innerarity, in "Code Blue" (376–80) claims that Code Blue is "well organized and well executed," as indeed the photograph of medical personnel administering CPR and other aid to a patient (p. 380) reveals.

Logical Definitions.   Logical definitions answer two related questions: Into what general category does X fall? and How does it differ from all other members of that category? ("A porpoise is a marine mammal but differs from whales, seals, dolphins, and the others in its. . . .") Logical definitions are often used in scientific and philosophical writing, and indeed form the basis for the functional definition Howard Gardner presents in "Who Owns Intelligence?" (349–61).

There are five key principles for writing logical definitions:

1. For economy's sake, use the most specific category to which the item to be defined belongs, rather than broader categories. Thus Gardner confines his discussion to human beings, not animals nor even all primates.
2. Any division of a class must include all members of that class. *Negative definitions* explain what is excluded from a given classification and what is not.
3. Subdivisions must be smaller than the class divided. Intelligence, says Gardner, can be divided into various functional categories: "linguistic and logical-mathematical, musical, spatial, bodily-kinesthetic, naturalist, interpersonal, and intrapersonal."
4. Categories should be mutually exclusive; they should not overlap.
5. The basis for subdividing categories must be consistent throughout each stage of subdivision. Thus, claiming that Daniel Goleman, in his

"otherwise admirable *Emotional Intelligence,*" confuses emotional intelligence with "certain preferred patterns of behavior," Gardner prefers the term "emotional sensitivity" because this includes both "interpersonal and intrapersonal intelligences" and therefore applies to "people who are sensitive to emotions in themselves and in others."

Essential or Existential Definition.   An essential definition might be considered a variation of a descriptive definition as it answers the question, "What is the essence, the fundamental nature of X?"—love, beauty, truth, justice, for instance. An existential definition presents the essence of its subject by answering the question, "What does it mean to be X?" or "What does it mean to live as an X" or "in a state of X?"—perhaps Chinese, supremely happy, married (or not), an AIDS victim. In "On Being a Cripple" (364–75) Nancy Mairs provides for an audience of people who can walk without aid a searing comprehensive definition of what it means to be "a cripple," the word she chooses to define herself—instead of "disabled," handicapped," or "differently abled." She examines head-on the symptoms from which those who can "pick up babies, play the piano" too often avert their eyes in embarrassment, ignorance, or fear. With humor and uncompromising integrity, this gutsy woman shows herself in action, grotesque ("I carry one arm bent in front of me, the fingers curled into a claw"), clumsy (falling over backward in a public toilet), fearful of others' pity: "If I had to have MS, by God I was going to do it well. This is a class act, ladies and gentlemen." In the process of explaining what it's like to live with MS, Mairs also shows what it's like to be a wife, a mother, a teacher, a writer. Her initial sense of "grief and fury and terror" has given way, over the years, to acceptance of the "change and loss" that are part of the human condition. Thus Mairs's thoroughly human definition of a particular disease expands to encompass a definition of what it means to be human.

Process Definitions.   These are concerned with how things or phenomena get to be the way they are. How is X produced? What causes X? How does it work? What does it do, or not do? With what effects? How does change affect X itself? Such questions are often the basis for scientific definitions, as Spencer Nadler's "Fat" (265–74) and Charles Darwin's "Understanding Natural Selection" (342–48) illustrate. Darwin's definition is composed of a series of illustrations of natural phenomena and processes (such as stags' horns, cocks' spurs, lions' manes, male peacocks' plumage) that lead to demonstrable effects, such as the propagation and survival of the species, as depicted in the photograph of the cape gannet pairs on p. 346. The two essays on "Code Blue" provide very different definitions of a dramatic medical process. In "Code Blue: The Process" (376–80), Jasmine Innerarity carefully explains, from her experience as a pediatric oncology nurse, the conditions for calling a "Code Blue," "the alert signal for a patient who has stopped breathing or whose heart has stopped." She identifies the medical personnel summoned in the process, the equipment needed, the processes involved ("sedating and intubating the patient"), the speed required, the decisions to be made (to take a patient to the operating room, or off a respirator), and the likely outcomes. Innerarity's language, precise and careful, identifies medical crises and explains the medical team's appropriate reactions—definition in the abstract. "Code Blue: The Story" (380–84), Dr. Abraham Verghese's fast-paced narrative, takes readers into the emergency room for a breathless re-enactment of the race to snatch life from death—definition in action.

Ultimately, when you're writing an extended definition, you'll need to make it as clear, real, and understandable as possible. You could define a dog as "a clawed, domesticated carnivorous mammal, *Canis familiaris.*" But would that abstract, technical definition get at your intended focus on working dogs (for instance, sheepherding border collies or seeing-eye German shepherds), or convey the essence of the family setter, Serendipity, who rescued you from drowning when you were five and has been your security blanket ever since? Your choices of specific details, illustrations, analogies, anecdotes, and the like will enable your readers to accept your definition, the ways you see the subject, the boundaries you set.

STRATEGIES FOR WRITING— DEFINITION

1. What is the purpose of the definition (or definitions) I'm writing about? Do I want to explain the subject's particular characteristics? Identify its nature? Persuade readers of my interpretation of its meaning? Entertain readers with a novel, bizarre, or highly personal meaning? How long will my essay be? (A short essay will require a restricted subject that you can cover in the limited space.)
2. For whom am I providing the definition? Why are they reading it? Do they know enough about the background of the subject to enable me to deal with it in a fairly technical way? Or must I stick to the basics—or at least begin there? If I wish to persuade or entertain my readers, can I count on them to have a pre-existing definition in mind against which I can match my own?
3. Will my entire essay be a definition, or will I incorporate definition(s) as part of a different type of essay? What proportion of my essay will be devoted to definition? Where will I include definitions? As I introduce new terms or concepts? Where else, if at all?
4. What techniques of definition will I use: naming; providing examples, brief or extended; comparing and contrasting; considering cause and effect; analysis; argument; narrative; analogy; or a mixture? Will I employ primarily positive or negative means (i.e., X is, or X is not)?
5. How much denotative (objective) definition will I use in my essay? How much connotative (subjective) definition? Will my tone be serious? Authoritative? Entertaining? Sarcastic? Or otherwise?

CHARLES DARWIN

Darwin (1809–1882) descended from a distinguished British scientific family; his father was a physician, and his grandfather was the renowned Erasmus Darwin, amateur naturalist. As a youth Darwin was most alert when studying natural phenomena, particularly beetles, even popping a rare specimen into his mouth to preserve it when his hands were full of other newly collected insects. So, despite his lackadaisical study of medicine at Edinburgh University (1825–1828) and equally indifferent preparation for the clergy at Cambridge (B.A., 1831), he shipped aboard the HMS *Beagle* on a scientific expedition around South America, 1831–1836. As the ship's naturalist, he recorded careful observations of plants, animals, and human behavior that were published in *The Voyage of the Beagle* (1839), and eventually led to his theories of natural selection (roughly translated as "the survival of the fittest") and evolution. The publication of the earthshaking *On the Origin of Species by Means of Natural Selection, or the Preservation of Favored Races in the Struggle for Life* (1859) was based on his painstaking observations of animals and plants, on land and sea and in the air.

"Understanding Natural Selection," a small portion of this work, contains the essence of Darwin's best-known and most revolutionary principles, that in natural selection those variations, "infinitesimally small inherited modifications," endure if they aid in survival. The claim that these modifications occur gradually, rather than being produced at a single stroke by a divine creator, is the basis for Darwin's theory of evolution, extended to humans in *The Descent of Man* (1871). Darwin's theories provoked the enormous controversy between theologians and scientists that continues to this day—as Gould's "Evolution as Fact and Theory" (401–10) makes clear.

Darwin's work continues to be read, as much for its clear and elegant literary style as for its content. Using the techniques of popular literature to explain sophisticated scientific concepts and to present mountains of detailed information, Darwin is a highly engaging writer. He uses the first person, metaphors, anecdotes, and numerous illustrations that overlap and reinforce one another—here as ways to define his subject. Because he is explaining a theory and concepts totally new to his audience, he has to ground them in the reality of numerous natural phenomena that can be seen and studied.

Understanding Natural Selection

1   It may be said that natural selection is daily and hourly scrutinizing, throughout the world, every variation, even the slightest; rejecting that which is bad, preserving and adding up all that is good; silently and insensibly working, whenever and wherever opportunity offers, at the improvement of each organic being in relation to its organic and inorganic conditions of life. We see nothing of these slow changes in progress, until

the hand of time has marked the long lapses of ages, and then so imperfect is our view into long past geological ages, that we only see that the forms of life are now different from what they formerly were.

Although natural selection can act only through and for the good of   2
each being, yet characters and structures, which we are apt to consider as of very trifling importance, may thus be acted on. When we see leaf-eating insects green, and bark-feeders mottled-grey; the alpine ptarmigan white in winter, the red-grouse the color of heather, and the black-grouse that of peaty earth, we must believe that these tints are of service to these birds and insects in preserving them from danger. Grouse, if not destroyed at some period of their lives, would increase in countless numbers; they are known to suffer largely from birds of prey; and hawks are guided by eyesight to their prey—so much so, that on parts of the Continent persons are warned not to keep white pigeons, as being the most liable to destruction. Hence I can see no reason to doubt that natural selection might be most effective in giving the proper color to each kind of grouse, and in keeping that color, when once acquired, true and constant. Nor ought we to think that the occasional destruction of an animal of any particular color would produce little effect: we should remember how essential it is in a flock of white sheep to destroy every lamb with the faintest trace of black. In plants the down on the fruit and the color of the flesh are considered by botanists as characters of the most trifling importance: yet we hear from an excellent horticulturist, Downing, that in the United States smooth-skinned fruits suffer far more from a beetle, a curculio, than those with down; that purple plums suffer far more from a certain disease than yellow plums; whereas another disease attacks yellow-fleshed peaches far more than those with other colored flesh. If, with all the aids of art, these slight differences make a great difference in cultivating the several varieties, assuredly, in a state of nature, where the trees would have to struggle with other trees and with a host of enemies, such differences would effectually settle which variety, whether a smooth or downy, a yellow or purple fleshed fruit, should succeed.

In looking at many small points of difference between species, which,   3
as far as our ignorance permits us to judge, seem to be quite unimportant, we must not forget that climate, food, and so on probably produce some slight and direct effect. It is, however, far more necessary to bear in mind that there are many unknown laws of correlation to growth, which, when one part of the organization is modified through variation, and the modifications are accumulated by natural selection for the good of the being, will cause other modifications, often of the most unexpected nature.

As we see that those variations which under domestication appear at   4
any particular period of life, tend to reappear in the offspring of the same period; for instance, in the seeds of the many varieties of our culinary and agricultural plants; in the caterpillar and cocoon stages of the varieties of the silkworm; in the eggs of poultry, and in the color of the down of their

chickens; in the horns of our sheep and cattle when nearly adult; so in a state of nature, natural selection will be enabled to act on and modify organic beings at any age, by the accumulation of profitable variations at that age, and by their inheritance at a corresponding age. If it profit a plant to have its seeds more and more widely disseminated by the wind, I can see no greater difficulty in this being effected through natural selection, than in the cotton-planter increasing and improving by selection the down in the pods on his cotton-trees. Natural selection may modify and adapt the larva of an insect to a score of contingencies, wholly different from those which concern the mature insect. These modifications will no doubt affect, through the laws of correlation, the structure of the adult; and probably in the case of those insects which live only for a few hours, and which never feed, a large part of their structure is merely the correlated result of successive changes in the structure of their larvae. So, conversely, modifications in the adult will probably often affect the structure of the larva; but in all cases natural selection will ensure that modifications consequent on other modifications at a different period of life, shall not be in the least degree injurious: for if they became so, they would cause the extinction of the species.

5   Natural selection will modify the structure of the young in relation to the parent, and of the parent in relation to the young. In social animals it will adapt the structure of each individual for the benefit of the community; if each in consequence profits by the selected change. What natural selection cannot do, is to modify the structure of one species, without giving it any advantage, for the good of another species; and though statements to this effect may be found in works of natural history, I cannot find one case which will bear investigation. A structure used only once in an animal's whole life, if of high importance to it, might be modified to any extent by natural selection; for instance, the great jaws possessed by certain insects, and used exclusively for opening the cocoon—or the hard tip to the beak of nestling birds, used for breaking the egg. It has been asserted, that of the best short-beaked tumbler pigeons more perish in the egg than are able to get out of it; so that fanciers assist in the act of hatching. Now, if nature had to make the beak of a full-grown pigeon very short for the bird's own advantage, the process of modification would be very slow, and there would be simultaneously the most rigorous selection of the young birds within the egg, which had the most powerful and hardest beaks, for all with weak beaks would inevitably perish: or, more delicate and more easily broken shells might be selected, the thickness of the shell being known to vary like every other structure.

Sexual Selection

6   Inasmuch as peculiarities often appear under domestication in one sex and become hereditarily attached to that sex, the same fact probably occurs

under nature, and if so, natural selection will be able to modify one sex in its functional relations to the other sex, or in relation to wholly different habits of life in the two sexes, as is sometimes the case with insects. And this leads me to say a few words on what I call sexual selection. This depends, not on a struggle for existence, but on a struggle between the males for possession of the females; the result is not death to the unsuccessful competitor, but few or no offspring. Sexual selection is, therefore, less rigorous than natural selection. Generally, the most vigorous males, those which are best fitted for their places in nature, will leave most progeny. But in many cases, victory will depend not on general vigor, but on having special weapons, confined to the male sex. A hornless stag or spurless cock would have a poor chance of leaving offspring. Sexual selection by always allowing the victor to breed might surely give indomitable courage, length to the spur, and strength to the wing to strike in the spurred leg, as well as the brutal cock-fighter, who knows well that he can improve his breed by careful selection of the best cocks. How low in the scale of nature this law of battle descends, I know not; male alligators have been described as fighting, bellowing, and whirling round, like Indians in a war dance, for the possession of the females; male salmons have been seen fighting all day long; male stag-beetles often bear wounds from the huge mandibles of other males. The war is, perhaps, severest between the males of polygamous animals, and these seem oftenest provided with special weapons. The males of carnivorous animals are already well armed; though to them and to others, special means of defence may be given through means of sexual selection, as the mane to the lion, the shoulder-pad to the boar, and the hooked jaw to the male salmon, for the shield may be as important for victory, as the sword or spear.

Amongst birds, the contest is often of a more peaceful character. All those who have attended to the subject, believe that there is the severest rivalry between the males of many species to attract by singing the females. The rock-thrush of Guiana, birds of Paradise, and some others, congregate; and successive males display their gorgeous plumage and perform strange antics before the females, which standing by as spectators, as last choose the most attractive partner. Those who have closely attended to birds in confinement well know that they often take individual preferences and dislikes: thus Sir R. Heron has described how one pied peacock was eminently attractive to all his hen birds. It may appear childish to attribute any effect to such apparently weak means: I cannot here enter on the details necessary to support this view; but if man can in a short time give elegant carriage and beauty to his bantams, according to his standard of beauty, I can see no good reason to doubt that female birds, by selecting, during thousands of generations, the most melodious or beautiful males, according to their standard of beauty, might produce a marked effect. I strongly suspect that some well-known laws with

What Darwinian observations or principles does this photograph illustrate?
Does each species, whose members bear a strong family resemblance, have
ways of detecting individuals that members of other species are unaware of?
How does this detection—and pairing—contribute to their survival?

respect to the plumage of male and female birds, in comparison with the
plumage of the young, can be explained on the view of plumage having
been chiefly modified by sexual selection, acting when the birds have
come to the breeding age or during the breeding season; the modifications
thus produced being inherited at corresponding ages or seasons, either by
the males alone, or by the males and females; but I have not space here to
enter on this subject.

8   Thus it is, as I believe, that when the males and females of any
animal have the same general habits of life, but differ in structure, color,
or ornament, such differences have been mainly caused by sexual selection; that is, individual males have had, in successive generations, some
slight advantage over other males, in their weapons, means of defence, or
charms; and have transmitted these advantages to their male offspring.
Yet, I would not wish to attribute all such sexual differences to this
agency: for we see peculiarities arising and becoming attached to the male
sex in our domestic animals (as the wattle in male carriers, horn-like pro-
tuberances in the cocks of certain fowls, and so on), which we cannot believe to be either useful to the males in battle, or attractive to the females.
We see analogous cases under nature, for instance, the tuft of hair on the

breast of the turkey-cock, which can hardly be either useful or ornamental to this bird; indeed, had the tuft appeared under domestication, it would have been called a monstrosity.

Illustration of the Action of Natural Selection

. . . Let us take the case of a wolf, which preys on various animals, securing some by craft, some by strength, and some by fleetness; and let us suppose that the fleetest prey, a deer for instance, had from any change in the country increased in numbers, or that other prey had decreased in numbers, during that season of the year when the wolf is hardest pressed for food. I can under such circumstances see no reason to doubt that the swiftest and slimmest wolves would have the best chance of surviving, and so be preserved or selected—provided always that they retain strength to master their prey at this or at some other period of the year, when they might be compelled to prey on other animals. I can see no more reason to doubt this, than that man can improve the fleetness of his greyhounds by careful and methodical selection, or by that unconscious selection which results from each man trying to keep the best dogs without any thought of modifying the breed.

Even without any change in the proportional numbers of the animals on which our wolf preyed, a cub might be born with an innate tendency to pursue certain kinds of prey. Nor can this be thought very improbable; for we often observe great differences in the natural tendencies of our domestic animals; one cat, for instance, taking to catch rats, another mice; one cat . . . bringing home winged game, another hares or rabbits, and another hunting on marshy ground and almost nightly catching woodcocks or snipes. The tendency to catch rats rather than mice is known to be inherited. Now, if any slight innate change of habit or of structure benefited an individual wolf, it would have the best chance of surviving and of leaving offspring. Some of its young would probably inherit the same habits or structure, and by the repetition of this process, a new variety might be formed which would either supplant or coexist with the parent-form of wolf. Or, again, the wolves inhabiting a mountainous district, and those frequenting the lowlands, would naturally be forced to hunt different prey; and from the continued preservation of the individuals best fitted for the two sites, two varieties might slowly be formed. These varieties would cross and blend where they met; but to this subject of intercrossing we shall soon have to return. I may add, that . . . there are two varieties of the wolf inhabiting the Catskill Mountains in the United States, one with a light greyhoundlike form, which pursues deer, and the other more bulky, with shorter legs, which more frequently attacks the shepherd's flocks.

Content

1. What does Darwin mean by "natural selection" (¶s 1–5)? How does "natural selection" differ from "sexual selection" (¶s 6–8)?

2. Although Darwin doesn't use the term "evolution," this piece clearly illustrates that concept. Define that term, using some of Darwin's illustrations. Does your definition anticipate creationists' objections? Should it? If you believe in creationism, how does this belief influence the way you define "evolution"?

3. Distinguish between theory, opinion, and fact in Darwin's presentation of the concepts of natural selection (¶s 1–5, 9–10).

Strategies/Structures

4. Darwin offers arguments on behalf of both natural selection and sexual selection. Which argument has the better supporting evidence? Which argument makes its case more compellingly? Why?

5. Darwin builds his case for the existence of natural selection by using numerous illustrations. Identify some. Explain how an argument can also, as in this case, be a definition.

6. What kind of authorial persona does Darwin present? In what ways is this "scientist figure" familiar today? How does this persona differ from the stereotype of the "mad scientist"?

Language

7. Is Darwin writing for an audience of other scientists? For a general readership? Or for both? What aspects of his language (choice of vocabulary, familiar or unfamiliar language and illustrations), tone, and sentence structure reinforce your answer?

8. Are there features of Darwin's language, and sentence and paragraph structure, that indicates that this excerpt was written in the nineteenth rather than the twentieth century? Illustrate your answer.

For Writing

9. Write a definition of something (a natural phenomenon, human or animal behavior you have observed carefully over time) for an audience of nonscientists. If you are writing about the behavior of college students in a particular type of situation—for example, some aspect(s) of test-taking, dating, dressing, eating—record your observations in as objective and "scientific" a manner as you can.

10. Every definition is an argument, overt or implied, for the definer's particular way of looking at the subject (for example, see Gould's "Evolution as Fact and Theory" [401–10]). For readers who might disagree with you, write a controversial definition of a subject about which you feel passionate—friendship, love, marriage, violence, war, an ideal—you name it (place to live, job to have, family life, public policy). If you are dealing in abstractions, as you are likely to do in an extended definition, you will need to shore up your generalizations with specific information and illustrations.

HOWARD GARDNER

Gardner (born 1943) studied cognitive and social psychology at Harvard (B.A., 1965, Ph.D., 1971) and with David Perkins became codirector of Project Zero at the Harvard Graduate School of Education, studying the ways children and adults learn. He is currently the Hobbs Professor in Cognition and Education at Harvard and an adjunct research professor of neurology at Boston University School of Medicine.

Gardner has written over twenty books and hundreds of articles, most of them focusing on creativity and intelligence. In his best known book, *Frames of Mind: The Theory of Multiple Intelligences* (1983), he postulates that there are seven distinct cognitive realms in the human brain and that each governs a particular kind of intelligence. Those intelligences most commonly considered—and tested—by the American educational establishment are *linguistic,* the ability to communicate through language, and *logical-mathematical,* the ability to come up with and use abstract concepts. To these Gardner adds five other intelligences: *spatial,* the ability to perceive and re-image the physical world; *bodily-kinesthetic,* the ability to use the body in skilled or creative ways; *musical,* the ability to distinguish, remember, and manipulate tone, melody, and rhythm; *interpersonal,* the ability to understand other people; and *intrapersonal,* the ability to understand one's self and have a conscious awareness of one's emotions. A decade later Gardner added an eighth intelligence, *naturalist,* the ability to have an intuitive understanding about plants and animals. Despite criticism from people who say Gardner's multiple intelligences are really talents (something we can get along without, as opposed to traditionally defined intelligence, which is indispensable) and that they can't be easily measured, to many educators he evokes "the reverence teenagers lavish on a rock star." "Who Owns Intelligence?" first published in the *Atlantic Monthly* in February 1999, addresses these issues in attempting, once again, to pin down intelligence and who owns it—a particularly significant issue as the twenty-first century grapples with expanding concepts of intellectual property, ranging from book manuscripts, musical compositions, and mechanical inventions to web sites, applications of gene therapy, and esoteric chemical and technical processes.

Who Owns Intelligence?

Almost a century ago Alfred Binet, a gifted psychologist, was asked by the French Ministry of Education to help determine who would experience difficulty in school. Given the influx of provincials to the capital, along with immigrants of uncertain stock, Parisian officials believed they needed to know who might not advance smoothly through the system. Proceeding in an empirical manner, Binet posed many questions to youngsters of different ages. He ascertained which questions when answered correctly predicted success in school, and which questions when answered incorrectly foretold school difficulties. The items that discriminated most clearly between the two groups became, in effect, the first test of intelligence.

2   Binet is a hero to many psychologists. He was a keen observer, a careful scholar, an inventive technologist. Perhaps even more important for his followers, he devised the instrument that is often considered psychology's greatest success story. Millions of people who have never heard Binet's name have had aspects of their fate influenced by instrumentation that the French psychologist inspired. And thousands of psychometricians—specialists in the measurement of psychological variables—earn their living courtesy of Binet's invention.

3   Although it has prevailed over the long run, the psychologists' version of intelligence is now facing its biggest threat. Many scholars and observers—and even some iconoclastic psychologists—feel that intelligence is too important to be left to the psychometricians. Experts are extending the breadth of the concept—proposing many intelligences, including emotional intelligence and moral intelligence. They are experimenting with new methods of ascertaining intelligence, including some that avoid tests altogether in favor of direct measures of brain activity. They are forcing citizens everywhere to confront a number of questions: What is intelligence? How ought it to be assessed? And how do our notions of intelligence fit with what we value about human beings? In short, experts are competing for the "ownership" of intelligence in the next century.

4   The outline of the psychometricians' success story is well known. Binet's colleagues in England and Germany contributed to the conceptualization and instrumentation of intelligence testing—which soon became known as IQ tests. (An IQ, or intelligence quotient, designates the ratio between mental age and chronological age. Clearly we'd prefer that a child in our care have an IQ of 120, being smarter than average for his or her years, than an IQ of 80, being older than average for his or her intelligence). Like other Parisian fashions of the period, the intelligence test migrated easily to the United States. First used to determine who was "feeble-minded," it was soon used to assess "normal" children, to identify the "gifted," and to determine who was fit to serve in the Army. By the 1920s the intelligence test had become a fixture in educational practice in the United States and much of Western Europe.

5   Early intelligence tests were not without their critics. Many enduring concerns were first raised by the influential journalist Walter Lippmann, in a series of published debates with Lewis Terman, of Stanford University, the father of IQ testing in America. Lippmann pointed out the superficiality of the questions, their possible cultural biases, and the risks of trying to

determine a person's intellectual potential with a brief oral or paper-and-pencil measure.

Perhaps surprisingly, the conceptualization of intelligence did not 6 advance much in the decades following Binet's and Terman's pioneering contributions. Intelligence tests came to be seen, rightly or wrongly, as primarily a tool for selecting people to fill academic or vocational niches. In one of the most famous—if irritating—remarks about intelligence testing, the influential Harvard psychologist E. G. Boring declared, "Intelligence is what the tests test." So long as these tests did what they were supposed to do (that is, give some indication of school success), it did not seem necessary or prudent to probe too deeply into their meaning or to explore alternative views of the human intellect.

Psychologists who study intelligence have argued chiefly about three 7 questions. The first: Is intelligence singular, or does it consist of various more or less independent intellectual faculties? The purists—ranging from the turn-of-the-century English psychologist Charles Spearman to his latter-day disciples Richard J. Herrnstein and Charles Murray (of *The Bell Curve* fame)—defend the notion of a single overarching "g," or general intelligence. The pluralists—ranging from L. L. Thurstone, of the University of Chicago, who posited seven vectors of the mind, to J. P. Guilford, of the University of Southern California, who discerned 150 factors of the intellect—construe intelligence as composed of some or even many dissociable components. In his much cited *The Mismeasure of Man* (1981) the paleontologist Stephen Jay Gould argued that the conflicting conclusions reached on this issue reflect alternative assumptions about statistical procedures rather than the way the mind is. Still, psychologists continue the debate, with a majority sympathetic to the general-intelligence perspective.

The public is more interested in the second question: Is intelligence 8 (or are intelligences) largely inherited? This is by and large a Western question. In the Confucian societies of East Asia individual differences in endowment are assumed to be modest, and differences in achievement are thought to be due largely to effort. In the West, however, many students of the subject sympathize with the view—defended within psychology by Lewis Terman, among others—that intelligence is inborn and one can do little to alter one's intellectual birthright.

Studies of identical twins reared apart provide surprisingly strong 9 support for the "heritability" of psychometric intelligence. That is, if one wants to predict someone's score on an intelligence test, the scores of the biological parents (even if the child has not had appreciable contact with them) are more likely to prove relevant than the scores of the adoptive parents. By the same token, the IQs of identical twins are more similar than the IQs of fraternal twins. And, contrary to common sense (and political correctness), the IQs of biologically related people grow closer in the later years of life. Still, because of the intricacies of behavioral genetics and the difficulties of conducting valid experiments with human child-rearing, a few defend the proposition that intelligence is largely environmental rather than heritable, and some believe that we cannot answer the question at all.

10   Most scholars agree that even if psychometric intelligence is largely inherited, it is not possible to pinpoint the sources of differences in average IQ between groups, such as the fifteen-point difference typically observed between African-American and white populations. That is because in our society the contemporary—let alone the historical—experiences of these two groups cannot be equated. One could ferret out the differences (if any) between black and white populations only in a society that was truly color-blind.

11   One other question has intrigued laypeople and psychologists: Are intelligence tests biased? Cultural assumptions are evident in early intelligence tests. Some class biases are obvious—who except the wealthy could readily answer a question about polo? Others are more subtle. Suppose the question is what one should do with money found on the street. Although ordinarily one might turn it over to the police, what if one had a hungry child? Or what if the police force were known to be hostile to members of one's ethnic group? Only the canonical response to such a question would be scored as correct.

12   Psychometricians have striven to remove the obviously biased items from such measures. But biases that are built into the test situation itself are far more difficult to deal with. For example, a person's background affects his or her reaction to being placed in an unfamiliar locale, being instructed by someone dressed in a certain way, and having a printed test booklet thrust into his or her hands. And as the psychologist Claude M. Steele has argued in these pages (see "Race and the Schooling of Black Americans," April, 1992), the biases prove even more acute when people know that their academic potential is being measured and that their racial or ethnic group is widely considered to be less intelligent than the dominant social group. . . .

13   Paradoxically, one of the clearest signs of the success of intelligence tests is that they are no longer widely administered. In the wake of legal cases about the propriety of making consequential decisions about education on the basis of IQ scores, many public school officials have become test-shy. By and large, the testing of IQ in the schools is restricted to cases involving a recognized problem (such as a learning disability) or a selection procedure (determining eligibility for a program that serves gifted children).

14   Despite this apparent setback, intelligence testing and the line of thinking that underlies it have actually triumphed. Many widely used scholastic measures, chief among them the SAT (renamed the Scholastic Assessment Test a few years ago), are thinly disguised intelligence tests that correlate highly with scores on standard psychometric instruments.

Virtually no one raised in the developed world today has gone untouched by Binet's seemingly simple invention of a century ago.

Multiple Intelligences

The concept of intelligence has in recent years undergone its most robust 15
challenge since the days of Walter Lippmann. Some who are informed by psychology but not bound by the assumptions of the psychometricians have invaded this formerly sacrosanct territory. They have put forth their own ideas of what intelligence is, how (and whether) it should be measured, and which values should be invoked in considerations of the human intellect. For the first time in many years the intelligence establishment is clearly on the defensive—and the new century seems likely to usher in quite different ways of thinking about intelligence.

One evident factor in the rethinking of intelligence is the perspec- 16
tive introduced by scholars who are not psychologists. Anthropologists have commented on the parochialism of the Western view of intelligence. Some cultures do not even have a concept called intelligence, and others define intelligence in terms of traits that we in the West might consider odd—obedience, good listening skills, or moral fiber, for example. Neuroscientists are skeptical that the highly differentiated and modular structure of the brain is consistent with a unitary form of intelligence. Computer scientists have devised programs deemed intelligent; these programs often go about problem-solving in ways quite different from those embraced by human beings or other animals.

Even within the field of psychology the natives have been getting 17
restless. Probably the most restless is the Yale psychologist Robert J. Sternberg. A prodigious scholar, Sternberg, who is forty-nine, has written dozens of books and hundreds of articles, the majority of them focusing in one or another way on intelligence. Sternberg began with the strategic goal of understanding the actual mental processes mobilized by standard test items, such as the solving of analogies. But he soon went beyond standard intelligence testing by insisting on two hitherto neglected forms of intelligence: the "practical" ability to adapt to varying contexts (as we all must in these days of divorcing and downsizing), and the capacity to automate familiar activities so that we can deal effectively with novelty and display "creative" intelligence.

Sternberg has gone to greater pains than many other critics of stan- 18
dard intelligence testing to measure these forms of intelligence with the paper-and-pencil laboratory methods favored by the profession. And he has found that a person's ability to adapt to diverse contexts or to deal with novel information can be differentiated from success at standard IQ-test problems. . . .

The psychologist and journalist Daniel Goleman has achieved world- 19
wide success with his book *Emotional Intelligence* (1995). Contending that

this new concept (sometimes nicknamed EQ) may matter as much as or more than IQ, Goleman draws attention to such pivotal human abilities as controlling one's emotional reactions and "reading" the signals of others. In the view of the noted psychiatrist Robert Coles, author of *The Moral Intelligence of Children* (1997), among many other books, we should prize character over intellect. He decries the amorality of our families, hence our children; he shows how we might cultivate human beings with a strong sense of right and wrong, who are willing to act on that sense even when it runs counter to self-interest. Other, frankly popular accounts deal with leadership intelligence (LQ), executive intelligence (EQ or ExQ), and even financial intelligence.

20   Like Coles's and Goleman's efforts, my work on "multiple intelligences" eschews the psychologists' credo of operationalization and test-making. I began by asking two questions: How did the human mind and brain evolve over millions of years? and How can we account for the diversity of skills and capacities that are or have been valued in different communities around the world?

21   Armed with these questions and a set of eight criteria, I have concluded that all human beings possess at least eight intelligences: linguistic and logical-mathematical (the two most prized in school and the ones central to success on standard intelligence tests), musical, spatial, bodily-kinesthetic, naturalist, interpersonal, and intrapersonal.

22   I make two complementary claims about intelligence. The first is universal. We all possess these eight intelligences—and possibly more. Indeed, rather than seeing us as "rational animals," I offer a new definition of what it means to be a human being, cognitively speaking: *Homo sapiens sapiens* is the animal that possesses these eight forms of mental representation.

23   My second claim concerns individual differences. Owing to the accidents of heredity, environment, and their interactions, no two of us exhibit the same intelligences in precisely the same proportions. Our "profiles of intelligence" differ from one another. This fact poses intriguing challenges and opportunities for our education system. We can ignore these differences and pretend that we are all the same; historically, that is what most education systems have done. Or we can fashion an education system that tries to exploit these differences, individualizing instruction and assessment as much as possible.

Intelligence and Morality

24 As the century of Binet and his successors draws to a close, we'd be wise to take stock of, and to anticipate, the course of thinking about intelligence. Although my crystal ball is no clearer than anyone else's (the species may lack "future intelligence"), it seems safe to predict that interest in intelligence will not go away.

To begin with, the psychometric community has scarcely laid down 25 its arms. New versions of the standard tests continue to be created, and occasionally new tests surface as well. Researchers in the psychometric tradition churn out fresh evidence of the predictive power of their instruments and the correlations between measured intelligence and one's life chances. And some in the psychometric tradition are searching for the biological basis of intelligence: the gene or complex of genes that may affect intelligence, and neural structures that are crucial for intelligence, or telltale brain-wave patterns that distinguish the bright from the less bright.

Beyond various psychometric twists, interest in intelligence is likely 26 to grow in other ways. It will be fed by the creation of machines that display intelligence and by the specific intelligence or intelligences. Moreover, observers as diverse as Richard Herrnstein and Robert B. Reich, President Clinton's first Secretary of Labor, have agreed that in coming years a large proportion of society's rewards will go to those people who are skilled symbol analysts—who can sit at a computer screen (or its technological successor), manipulate numbers and other kinds of symbols, and use the results of their operations to contrive plans, tactics, and strategies for enterprises ranging from business to science to war games. These people may well color how intelligence is conceived in decades to come—just as the need to provide good middle-level bureaucrats to run an empire served as a primary molder of intelligence tests in the early years of the century.

Surveying the landscape of intelligence, I discern three struggles be- 27 tween opposing forces. The extent to which, and the manner in which, these various struggles are resolved will influence the lives of millions of people. I believe that the three struggles are interrelated; that the first struggle provides the key to the other two; and that the ensemble of struggles can be resolved in an optimal way.

The first struggle concerns the breadth of our definition of intelli- 28 gence. One camp consists of the purists, who believe in a single form of intelligence—one that basically predicts success in school and in school-like activities. Arrayed against the purists are the progressive pluralists, who believe that many forms of intelligence exist. Some of these pluralists would like to broaden the definition of intelligence considerably, to include the abilities to create, to lead, and to stand out in terms of emotional sensitivity or moral excellence.

The second struggle concerns the assessment of intelligence. Again, 29 one readily encounters a traditional position. Once chiefly concerned with paper-and-pencil tests, the traditionally oriented practitioner is now likely to use computers to provide the same information more quickly and more accurately. But other positions abound. Purists disdain psychological tasks of any complexity, preferring to look instead at reaction time, brain waves, and other physiological measures of intellect. In contrast, simulators favor measures closely resembling the actual abilities that are prized.

And skeptics warn against the continued expansion of testing. They emphasize the damage often done to individual life chances and self-esteem by a regimen of psychological testing, and call for less technocratic, more humane methods—ranging from self assessment to the examination of portfolios of student work to selection in the service of social equity.

30   The final struggle concerns the relationship between intelligence and the qualities we value in human beings. Although no one would baldly equate intellect and human worth, nuanced positions have emerged on this issue. Some (in the *Bell Curve* mold) see intelligence as closely related to a person's ethics and values; they believe that brighter people are more likely to appreciate moral complexity and to behave judiciously. Some call for a sharp distinction between the realm of intellect on the one hand, and character, morality, or ethics on the other. Society's ambivalence on this issue can be discerned in the figures that become the culture's heroes. For every Albert Einstein or Bobby Fischer who is celebrated for his intellect, there is a Forrest Gump or a Chauncey Gardiner who is celebrated for human—and humane—traits that would never be captured on any kind of intelligence test. . . .

The Borders of Intelligence

31   Writing as a scholar rather than as a layperson, I see two problems with the notion of emotional intelligence. First, unlike language or space, the emotions are not contents to be processed; rather, cognition has evolved so that we can make sense of human beings (self and others) that possess and experience emotions. Emotions are part and parcel of all cognition, though they may well prove more salient at certain times or under certain circumstances: they accompany our interactions with others, our listening to great music, our feelings when we solve—or fail to solve—a difficult mathematical problem. If one calls some intelligences emotional, one suggests that other intelligences are not—and that implication flies in the face of experience and empirical data.

32   The second problem is the conflation of emotional intelligence and a certain preferred pattern of behavior. This is the trap that Daniel Goleman sometimes falls into in his otherwise admirable *Emotional Intelligence*. Goleman singles out as emotionally intelligent those people who use their understanding of emotions to make others feel better, to solve conflicts, or to cooperate in home or work situations. No one would dispute that such people are wanted. However, people who understand emotion may not necessarily use their skills for the benefit of society.

33   For this reason I prefer the term "emotional sensitivity"—a term (encompassing my interpersonal and intrapersonal intelligences) that could apply to people who are sensitive to emotions in themselves and in others. Presumably, clinicians and salespeople excel in sensitivity to

others, poets and mystics in sensitivity to themselves. And some autistic or psychopathological people seem completely insensitive to the emotional realm. I would insist, however, on a strict distinction between emotional sensitivity and being a "good" or "moral" person. A person may be sensitive to the emotions of others but use that sensitivity to manipulate or to deceive them, or to create hatred.

I call, then, for a delineation of intelligence that includes the full 34 range of contents to which human beings are sensitive, but at the same time designates as off limits such valued but separate human traits as creativity, morality, and emotional appropriateness. I believe that such a delineation makes scientific and epistemological sense. It reinvigorates the elastic band without stretching it to the breaking point. It helps to resolve the two remaining struggles: how to assess, and what kinds of human beings to admire.

Once we decide to restrict intelligence to human information- 35 processing and product-making capacities, we can make use of the established technology of assessment. That is, we can continue to use paper-and-pencil or computer-adapted testing techniques while looking at a broader range of capacities, such as musical sensitivity and empathy with others. And we can avoid ticklish and possibly unresolvable questions about the assessment of values and morality that may well be restricted to a particular culture and that may well change over time.

Still, even with a limited perspective on intelligence, important ques- 36 tions remain about which assessment path to follow—that of the purist, the simulator, or the skeptic. Here I have strong views. I question the wisdom of searching for a "pure" intelligence—be it general intelligence, musical intelligence, or interpersonal intelligence. I do not believe that such alchemical intellectual essences actually exist; they are a product of our penchant for creating terminology rather than determinable and measurable entities. Moreover, the correlations that have thus far been found between supposedly pure measures and the skills that we actually value in the world are too modest to be useful.

What does exist is the use of intelligences, individually and in con- 37 cert, to carry out tasks that are valued by a society. Accordingly, we should be assessing the extent to which human beings succeed in carrying out tasks of consequence that presumably involve certain intelligences. To be concrete, we should not test musical intelligence by looking at the ability to discriminate between two tones or timbres; rather, we should be teaching people to sing songs or play instruments or transform melodies and seeing how readily they master such feats. At the same time, we should abjure a search for pure emotional sensitivity—for example, a test that matches facial expressions to galvanic skin response. Rather, we should place (or observe) people in situations that call for them to be sensitive to the aspirations and motives of others. For example, we could see how they handle a situation in which they and colleagues have to break up a fight between two teenagers, or persuade a boss to change a policy of which they do not approve.

38   Here powerful new simulations can be invoked. We are now in a position to draw on technologies that can deliver realistic situations or problems and also record the success of subjects in dealing with them. A student can be presented with an unfamiliar tune on a computer and asked to learn that tune, transpose it, orchestrate it, and the like. Such exercises would reveal much about the student's intelligence in musical matters.

39   Turning to the social (or human, if you prefer) realm, subjects can be presented with simulated interactions and asked to judge the shifting motivations of each actor. Or they can be asked to work in an interactive hypermedia production with unfamiliar people who are trying to accomplish some sort of goal, and to respond to their various moves and countermoves. The program can alter responses in light of the moves of the subject. Like a high-stakes poker game, such a measure should reveal much about the interpersonal or emotional sensitivity of a subject.

40   A significant increase in the breadth—the elasticity—of our concept of intelligence, then, should open the possibility for innovative forms of assessment far more realistic than the classic short-answer examinations. Why settle for an IQ or an SAT test, in which the items are at best remote proxies for the ability to design experiments, write essays, critique musical performances, and so forth? Why not instead ask people actually (or virtually) to carry out such tasks? And yet by not opening up the Pandora's box of values and subjectivity, one can continue to make judicious use of the insights and technologies achieved by those who have devoted decades to perfecting mental measurement.

41   To be sure, one can create a psychometric instrument for any conceivable human virtue, including morality, creativity, and emotional intelligence in its several senses. Indeed, since the publication of Daniel Goleman's book dozens of efforts have been made to create tests for emotional intelligence. The resulting instruments are not, however, necessarily useful. Such instruments are far more likely to satisfy the test maker's desire for reliability (a subject gets roughly the same score on two separate administrations of the test) than the need for validity (the test measures the trait that it purports to measure).

42   Such instruments-on-demand prove dubious for two reasons. First, beyond some platitudes, few can agree on what it means to be moral, ethical, a good person: consider the differing values of Jesse Helms and Jesse Jackson, Margaret Thatcher and Margaret Mead. Second, scores on such tests are much more likely to reveal test-taking savvy (skills in language and logic) than fundamental character.

43   In speaking about character, I turn to a final concern: the relationship between intelligence and what I will call virtue—those qualities that we admire and wish to hold up as examples for our children. No doubt the desire to expand intelligence to encompass ethics and character represents

a direct response to the general feeling that our society is lacking in these dimensions; the expansionist view of intelligence reflects the hope that if we transmit the technology of intelligence to these virtues, we might in the end secure a more virtuous population.

I have already indicated my strong reservations about trying to make 44 the word "intelligence" all things to all people—the psychometric equivalent of the true, the beautiful, and the good. Yet the problem remains: how, in a post-Aristotelian, post-Confucian era in which psychometrics looms large, do we think about the virtuous human being?

My analysis suggests one promising approach. We should recognize 45 that intelligences, creativity, and morality—to mention just three desiderata—are separate. Each may require its own form of measurement or assessment, and some will prove far easier to assess objectively than others. Indeed, with respect to creativity and morality, we are more likely to rely on overall judgments by experts than on any putative test battery. At the same time, nothing prevents us from looking for people who combine several of these attributes—who have musical and interpersonal intelligence, who are psychometrically intelligent and creative in the arts, who combine emotional sensitivity and a high standard of moral conduct.

Let me introduce another analogy at this point. In college admis- 46 sions much attention is paid to scholastic performance, as measured by College Board examinations and grades. However, other features are also weighed, and sometimes a person with lower test scores is admitted if he or she proves exemplary in terms of citizenship or athletics or motivation. Admissions officers do not confound these virtues (indeed, they may use different scales and issue different grades), but they recognize the attractiveness of candidates who exemplify two or more desirable traits.

We have left the Eden of classical times, in which various intellectual 47 and ethical values necessarily commingled, and we are unlikely ever to re-create it. We should recognize that these virtues can be separate and will often prove to be remote from one another. When we attempt to aggregate them, through phrases like "emotional intelligence," "creative intelligence," and "moral intelligence," we should realize that we are expressing a wish rather than denoting a necessary or even a likely coupling.

We have an aid in converting this wish to reality: the existence of 48 powerful examples—people who succeed in exemplifying two or more cardinal human virtues. To name names is risky—particularly when one generation's heroes can become the subject of the next generation's pathographies. Even so, I can without apology mention Niels Bohr, George C. Marshall, Rachel Carson, Arthur Ashe, Louis Armstrong, Pablo Casals, Ella Fitzgerald.

In studying the lives of such people, we discover human possibili- 49 ties. Young human beings learn primarily from the examples of powerful adults around them—those who are admirable and also those who are simply glamorous. Sustained attention to admirable examples may well

increase the future incidence of people who actually do yoke capacities
that are scientifically and epistemologically separate.

50   In one of the most evocative phrases of the century the British novelist E. M. Forster counseled us, "Only connect." I believe that some expan-
sionists in the territory of intelligence, though well motivated, have
prematurely asserted connections that do not exist. But I also believe that
as human beings, we can help to forge connections that may be important
for our physical and psychic survival.

51   Just how the precise borders of intelligence are drawn is a question
we can leave to scholars. But the imperative to broaden our definition of
intelligence in a responsible way goes well beyond the academy. Who
"owns" intelligence promises to be an issue even more critical in the next
century than it has been in this era of the IQ test.

Content

1. What is intelligence? Compare and contrast some of the types Gardner refers
to, which may be divided into two groups, the sort that "predicts success in school
and in school-like activities" (¶s 4–10, 28) and all other kinds, including "the abilities to create, to lead, and to stand out in terms of emotional sensitivity or moral
excellence" (¶ 28).

2. How can intelligence of a particular sort best be measured?

3. Who owns intelligence? The people who possess it? The society or social subgroup that determines what sorts of intelligence are valuable, necessary, appreciated—and those that aren't? The testers? How does Gardner's essay address
this issue?

Strategies/Structures

4. Find examples in Gardner's essay of the following common techniques of definition, and comment on their effectiveness in conveying one or more meanings
of intelligence:

   a. Illustration
   b. Comparison and contrast
   c. Negation (saying what something is not)
   d. Analysis
   e. Explanation of a process (how something is measured or works)
   f. Identification of causes or effects
   g. Simile, metaphor, or analogy
   h. Reference to authority or the writer's own expertise
   i. Reference to the writer's or others' personal experience or observation

5. Gardner's essay is full of arguments: for his definition of intelligence, against
competing definitions; for various practical ways of measuring intelligence,
against particular sorts of testing. Identify some of the assertions and evidence he
uses to support his claims. Are they credible?

Language

6. Does Gardner believe it's possible to expand the definition of *intelligence* to include virtue (¶ 43), to make it encompass qualities he'd like it to have?

7. Can people change definitions of words to make them mean what they want them to mean? Or does every term have a border around it (¶ 50)? If so, who creates and enforces the boundaries?

For Writing

8. Write your own definition either of *intelligence* in general or of a specific type of intelligence such as one that Gardner discusses in his essay. You may need to define some of these yourself or consult other sources for the intelligences Gardner only touches on: a. psychometric intelligence (¶s 4–10); b. the "'practical'" ability to adapt to varying contexts (¶ 17); the "ability to deal with novel information" (¶ 18); emotional intelligence (¶s 19, 31–33); moral intelligence (¶s 19, 41–45); or creativity (¶s 41–45). Or define a form of intelligence on Gardner's personal list that includes: "linguistic, logical-mathematical, musical, spatial, bodily-kinesthetic, naturalist, interpersonal, and intrapersonal." (See Gardner's book *Frames of Mind* (1983) or any other of Gardner's numerous writings on the subject.) Use one or more techniques of definition identified in Strategies/Structures above, and, assuming that you yourself fulfill your own definition of *intelligent*, supplement your more general definition with a specific first-hand example.

9. Write a definition of an abstract concept for readers who may not have thought much about it—such as *love, truth, beauty, justice, greed, pride,* or *the good life*—but who have probably used it often in everyday life, something intangible that can be identified in terms of its effects, causes, manifestations, or other nonphysical properties. Use one or more techniques of definition identified in Strategies/Structures above and illustrate your definition with one or two specific examples with which you are familiar. Then use the examples as a basis for making generalizations that apply to other aspects of the concept.

JUDY BRADY

Brady was born in 1937 in San Francisco and earned a bachelor's degree in painting from the University of Iowa in 1962. Married in 1960 and now divorced, she raised two daughters as a "disenfranchised and fired housewife" while working full-time as a secretary and attending night school. Her activities in the women's movement led to political activism and a trip to Cuba in 1973 to study the influence of class relationships on social change.

Brady's definition of a wife, in the essay below, was first published in December 1971 in the inaugural issue of the feminist magazine *Ms.* That it has been widely reprinted ever since testifies to its appeal to a much wider audience than originally intended. This definition is comprehensive, though ironic, covering wifely behavior; temperament; domestic, social, and sexual tasks; and projected life span of eternal servitude; it justifies the title as well as the closing exclamation, "My God, who *wouldn't* want a wife?"

I Want a Wife

1   I belong to that classification of people known as wives. I am a Wife. And, not altogether incidentally, I am a mother.

2   Not too long ago a male friend of mine appeared on the scene fresh from a recent divorce. He had one child, who is, of course, with his ex-wife. He is obviously looking for another wife. As I thought about him while I was ironing one evening, it suddenly occurred to me that I, too, would like to have a wife. Why do I want a wife?

3   I would like to go back to school so that I can become economically independent, support myself, and, if need be, support those dependent upon me. I want a wife who will work and send me to school. And while I am going to school I want a wife to take care of my children. I want a wife to keep track of the children's doctor and dentist appointments. And to keep track of mine, too. I want a wife to make sure my children eat properly and are kept clean. I want a wife who will wash the children's clothes and keep them mended. I want a wife who is a good nurturant attendant to my children, who arranges for their schooling, makes sure that they have an adequate social life with their peers, takes them to the park, the zoo, etc. I want a wife who takes care of the children when they are sick, a wife who arranges to be around when the children need special care, because, of course, I cannot miss classes at school. My wife must arrange to lose time at work and not lose the job. It may mean a small cut in my wife's income from time to time, but I guess I can tolerate that. Needless to say, my wife will arrange and pay for the care of the children while my wife is working.

4   I want a wife who will take care of *my* physical needs. I want a wife who will keep my house clean. A wife who will pick up after me. I want a wife who will keep my clothes clean, ironed, mended, replaced when need be, and who will see to it that my personal things are kept in their proper place so that I can find what I need the minute I need it. I want a wife who cooks the meals, a wife who is a *good* cook. I want a wife who will plan the menus, do the necessary grocery shopping, prepare the meals, serve them pleasantly, and then do the cleaning up while I do my studying. I want a wife who will care for me when I am sick and sympathize with my pain and loss of time from school. I want a wife to go along when our family takes a vacation so that someone can continue to care for me and my children when I need a rest and change of scene.

I want a wife who will not bother me with rambling complaints   5
about a wife's duties. But I want a wife who will listen to me when I feel
the need to explain a rather difficult point I have come across in my course
of studies. And I want a wife who will type my papers for me when I have
written them.

I want a wife who will take care of the details of my social life. When   6
my wife and I are invited out by my friends, I want a wife who will take
care of the babysitting arrangements. When I meet people at school that I
like and want to entertain, I want a wife who will have the house clean,
will prepare a special meal, serve it to me and my friends, and not interrupt when I talk about the things that interest me and my friends. I want
a wife who will have arranged that the children are fed and ready for bed
before my guests arrive so that the children do not bother us. I want a wife
who takes care of the needs of my guests so that they feel comfortable,
who makes sure that they have an ashtray, that they are passed the hors
d'oeuvres, that they are offered a second helping of the food, that their
wine glasses are replenished when necessary, that their coffee is served to
them as they like it. And I want a wife who knows that sometimes I need
a night out by myself.

I want a wife who is sensitive to my sexual needs, a wife who makes   7
love passionately and eagerly when I feel like it, a wife who makes sure
that I am satisfied. And, of course, I want a wife who will not demand
sexual attention when I am not in the mood for it. I want a wife who assumes the complete responsibility for birth control, because I do not want
more children. I want a wife who will remain sexually faithful to me so
that I do not have to clutter up my intellectual life with jealousies. And I
want a wife who understands that *my* sexual needs may entail more than
strict adherence to monogamy. I must, after all, be able to relate to people
as fully as possible.

If, by chance, I find another person more suitable as a wife than the   8
wife I already have, I want the liberty to replace my present wife with another one. Naturally, I will expect a fresh, new life; my wife will take the
children and be solely responsible for them so that I am left free.

When I am through with school and have a job, I want my wife to   9
quit working and remain at home so that my wife can more fully and
completely take care of a wife's duties.

My God, who *wouldn't* want a wife?   10

Content

1. Brady defines *wife* in terms of the purpose(s), activities, and personality traits
of a person functioning in a wife's many roles. What are some of these?

2. What is the purpose of Brady's definition of *wife*? How could she expect her
intended audience of feminist women to react to this definition? How would more
traditional women be expected to respond to this definition? Would men be expected to react in ways similar to those of their female counterparts?

Strategies/Structures

3. In what order does Brady list the wife's expected services?

4. How do you know that Brady does not always mean what she says—for instance, that she does not really favor the sexual double standard identified in paragraphs 8 and 9?

Language

5. Brady always calls a *wife* by that label and never uses the pronouns *he* or *she*. Why not?

6. Why does Brady use the short, simple (almost simplistic) phrase "I want a wife," and why does she repeat it so often?

For Writing

7. Write your own ironic version of "I want a wife," or "I want a husband," aimed at your significant other, actual or imagined. Identify, as Brady does, the spouse's most important roles, activities, personality traits; this should imply or state the reciprocal way you would function as a spouse, for better or worse.

8. Write an essay in which you define the ideal relationship between husband and wife. How likely is this ideal to be realized? If you are married or engaged in a serious courtship, ask your partner to comment on a draft before you revise it.

===

NANCY MAIRS

Nancy Mairs (born 1943) defies conventional autobiography as she defies conventional life. In her major works, *Plaintext* (1986), *Remembering the Bone House* (1989), and *Ordinary Time* (1993), and *Waist-High in the World* (1997), all autobiographical, this candid writer presents herself as bitchy, whiny, self-indulgent—but with a redeeming spirituality and wry humor. Married at nineteen, Mairs finished college (Wheaton, 1964), and bore two children. Her reaction to marriage and motherhood ("I didn't know how to do it") resulted in a suicidal mixture of agoraphobia and anorexia. Hospitalized for six months, she has ever since coped with panic attacks and the worsening symptoms of multiple sclerosis. Yet she refuses to sentimentalize her physical state ("I hate it"), or to equate herself with MS: "I am not a disease. What I hate is not me but a disease."

In "On Being a Cripple," Nancy Mairs defines her subject through a series of illustrations to show what it means to live with multiple sclerosis, and to demonstrate what she can do (cook, write, be a wife, mother, teacher, and friend) and what she can't do (run, walk easily, vacuum). Some of these have a narrative structure that states a problem, shows the complications of the problem, and resolves it—all within a paragraph, such as the paragraph that opens the essay with a dramatic fall which Mairs transforms into a comic pratfall—"the old beetle-on-its-back routine." Together these illustrations comprise a partial autobiography that also incorporates thumbnail sketches of Mairs's husband and children. A major aspect of Mairs's essay is her attitude toward MS; she treats her subject as she treats herself, with honesty, anger, sardonic humor, and considerable vigor. Mairs's own life, her reactions to it, and her interpretations of it comprise her existential definition of multiple sclerosis.

On Being a Cripple

To escape is nothing. Not to escape is nothing.

LOUISE BOGAN

The other day I was thinking of writing an essay on being a cripple. I was thinking hard in one of the stalls of the women's room in my office building, as I was shoving my shirt into my jeans and tugging up my zipper. Preoccupied, I flushed, picked up my book bag, took my cane down from the hook, and unlatched the door. So many movements unbalanced me, and as I pulled the door open I fell over backward, landing fully clothed on the toilet seat with my legs splayed in front of me: the old beetle-on-its-back routine. Saturday afternoon, the building deserted, I was free to laugh aloud as I wriggled back to my feet, my voice bouncing off the yellowish tiles from all directions. Had anyone been there with me, I'd have been still and faint and hot with chagrin. I decided that it was high time to write the essay.

First, the matter of semantics. I am a cripple. I choose this word to name me. I choose from among several possibilities, the most common of which are "handicapped" and "disabled." I made the choice a number of years ago, without thinking, unaware of my motives for doing so. Even now, I'm not sure what those motives are, but I recognize that they are complex and not entirely flattering. People—crippled or not—wince at the word "cripple," as they do not at "handicapped" or "disabled." Perhaps I want them to wince. I want them to see me as a tough customer, one to whom the fates/gods/viruses have not been kind, but who can face the brutal truth of her existence squarely. As a cripple, I swagger.

But, to be fair to myself, a certain amount of honesty underlies my choice. "Cripple" seems to me a clean word, straightforward and precise. It has an honorable history, having made its first appearance in the Lindisfarne Gospel in the tenth century. As a lover of words, I like the accuracy with which it describes my condition: I have lost the full use of my limbs. "Disabled," by contrast, suggests any incapacity, physical or mental. And I certainly don't like "handicapped," which implies that I have deliberately been put at a disadvantage, by whom I can't imagine (my God is not a Handicapper General), in order to equalize chances in the great race of life. These words seem to me to be moving away from my condition, to be widening the gap between word and reality. Most remote is the recently coined euphemism "differently abled," which partakes of the same semantic hopefulness that transformed countries from "undeveloped" to "underdeveloped," then to "less developed," and finally to "developing" nations. People have continued to starve in those countries during the shift. Some realities do not obey the dictates of language.

4   Mine is one of them. Whatever you call me, I remain crippled. But I don't care what you call me, so long as it isn't "differently abled," which strikes me as pure verbal garbage designed, by its ability to describe anyone, to describe no one. I subscribe to George Orwell's thesis that "the slovenliness of our language makes it easier for us to have foolish thoughts." And I refuse to participate in the degeneration of the language to the extent that I deny that I have lost anything in the course of this calamitous disease; I refuse to pretend that the only differences between you and me are the various ordinary ones that distinguish any one person from another. But call me "disabled" or "handicapped" if you like. I have long since grown accustomed to them; and if they are vague, at least they hint at the truth. Moreover, I use them myself. Society is no readier to accept crippledness than to accept death, war, sex, sweat, or wrinkles. I would never refer to another person as a cripple. It is the word I use to name only myself.

5   I haven't always been crippled, a fact for which I am soundly grateful. To be whole of limb is, I know from experience, infinitely more pleasant and useful than to be crippled; and if that knowledge leaves me open to bitterness at my loss, the physical soundness I once enjoyed (though I did not enjoy it half enough) is well worth the occasional stab of regret. Though never any good at sports, I was a normally active child and young adult. I climbed trees, played hopscotch, jumped rope, skated, swam, rode my bicycle, sailed. I despised team sports, spending some of the wretchedest afternoons of my life, sweaty and humiliated, behind a field-hockey stick and under a basketball hoop. I tramped alone for miles along the bridle paths that webbed the woods behind the house I grew up in. I swayed through countless dim hours in the arms of one man or another under the scattered shot of light from mirrored balls, and gyrated through countless more as Tab Hunter and Johnny Mathis gave way to the Rolling Stones, Creedence Clearwater Revival, Cream. I walked down the aisle. I pushed baby carriages, changed tires in the rain, marched for peace.

6   When I was twenty-eight I started to trip and drop things. What at first seemed my natural clumsiness soon became too pronounced to shrug off. I consulted a neurologist, who told me that I had a brain tumor. A battery of tests, increasingly disagreeable, revealed no tumor. About a year and a half later I developed a blurred spot in one eye. I had, at last, the episodes "disseminated in space and time" requisite for a diagnosis: multiple sclerosis. I have never been sorry for the doctor's initial misdiagnosis,

however. For almost a week, until the negative results of tests were in, I thought that I was going to die right away. Every day for the past nearly ten years, then, has been a kind of gift. I accept all gifts.

Multiple sclerosis is a chronic degenerative disease of the central nervous system, in which the myelin that sheathes the nerves is somehow eaten away and scar tissue forms in its place, interrupting the nerves' signals. During its course, which is unpredictable and uncontrollable, one may lose vision, hearing, speech, the ability to walk, control of bladder and/or bowels, strength in any or all extremities, sensitivity to touch, vibration, and/or pain, potency, coordination of movements—the list of possibilities is lengthy and yes, horrifying. One may also lose one's sense of humor. That's the easiest to lose and the hardest to survive without.

In the past ten years, I have sustained some of these losses. Characteristic of MS are sudden attacks, called exacerbations, followed by remissions, and these I have not had. Instead, my disease has been slowly progressive. My left leg is now so weak that I walk with the aid of a brace and a cane; and for distances I use an Amigo, a variation on the electric wheelchair that looks rather like an electrified kiddie car. I no longer have much use of my left hand. Now my right side is weakening as well. I still have the blurred spot in my right eye. Overall, though, I've been lucky so far. My world has, of necessity, been circumscribed by my losses, but the terrain left me has been ample enough for me to continue many of the activities that absorb me: writing, teaching, raising children and cats and plants and snakes, reading, speaking publicly about MS and depression, even playing bridge with people patient and honorable enough to let me scatter cards every which way without sneaking a peek.

Lest I begin to sound like Pollyanna, however, let me say that I don't like having MS. I hate it. My life holds realities—harsh ones, some of them —that no right-minded human being ought to accept without grumbling. One of them is fatigue. I know of no one with MS who does not complain of bone-weariness; in a disease that presents an astonishing variety of symptoms, fatigue seems to be a common factor. I wake up in the morning feeling the way most people do at the end of a bad day, and I take it from there. As a result, I spend a lot of time *in extremis* and, impatient with limitation, I tend to ignore my fatigue until my body breaks down in some way and forces rest. Then I miss picnics, dinner parties, poetry readings, the brief visits of old friends from out of town. The offspring of a puritanical tradition of exceptional venerability, I cannot view these lapses without shame. My life often seems a series of small failures to do as I ought.

I lead, on the whole, an ordinary life, probably rather like the one I would have led had I not had MS. I am lucky that my predilections were already solitary, sedentary, and bookish—unlike the world-famous French cellist I have read about, or the young woman I talked with one long afternoon who wanted only to be a jockey. I had just begun graduate school when I found out something was wrong with me, and I have remained, interminably, a graduate student. Perhaps I would not have if I'd thought I had the stamina to return to a full-time job as a technical editor; but I've enjoyed my studies.

11   In addition to studying, I teach writing courses. I also teach medical students how to give neurological examinations. I pick up freelance editing jobs here and there. I have raised a foster son and sent him into the world, where he has made me two grandbabies, and I am still escorting my daughter and son through adolescence. I go to Mass every Saturday. I am a superb, if messy, cook. I am also an enthusiastic laundress, capable of sorting a hamper full of clothes into five subtly differentiated piles, but a terrible housekeeper. I can do italic writing and, in an emergency, bathe an oil-soaked cat. I play a fiendish game of Scrabble. When I have the time and money, I like to sit on my front steps with my husband, drinking Amaretto and smoking a cigar, as we imagine our counterparts in Leningrad and make sure that the sun gets down once more behind the sharp childish scrawl of the Tucson Mountains.

12   This lively plenty has its bleak complement, of course, in all the things I can no longer do. I will never run again, except in dreams, and one day I may have to write that I will never walk again. I like to go camping, but I can't follow George and the children along the trails that wander out of a campsite through the desert or into the mountains. In fact, even on the level I've learned never to check the weather or try to hold a coherent conversation: I need all my attention for my wayward feet. Of late, I have begun to catch myself wondering how people can propel themselves without canes. With only one usable hand, I have to select my clothing with care not so much for style as for ease of ingress and egress, and even so, dressing can be laborious. I can no longer do fine stitchery, pick up babies, play the piano, braid my hair. I am immobilized by acute attacks of depression, which may or may not be physiologically related to MS but are certainly its logical concomitant.

13   These two elements, the plenty and the privation, are never pure, nor are the delight and wretchedness that accompany them. Almost every pickle that I get into as a result of my weakness and clumsiness—and I get into plenty—is funny as well as maddening and sometimes painful. I recall one May afternoon when a friend and I were going out for a drink after finishing up at school. As we were climbing into opposite sides of my car, chatting, I tripped and fell, flat and hard, onto the asphalt parking lot, my abrupt departure interrupting him in mid-sentence. "Where'd you go?" he called as he came around the back of the car to find me hauling myself up by the door frame. "Are you all right?" Yes, I told him, I was fine, just a bit ratty, and we drove off to find a shady patio and some beer. When I got home an hour or so later, my daughter greeted me with "What have you done to yourself?" I looked down. One elbow of my white turtleneck with the green froggies, one knee of my white trousers, one white kneesock were bloodsoaked. We peeled off the clothes and inspected the damage,

which was nasty enough but not alarming. That part wasn't funny: The abrasions took a long time to heal, and one got a little infected. Even so, when I think of my friend talking earnestly, suddenly, to the hot thin air while I dropped from his view as though through a trap door, I find the image as silly as something from a Marx Brothers movie.

I may find it easier than other cripples to amuse myself because I 14 live propped by the acceptance and the assistance and, sometimes, the amusement of those around me. Grocery clerks tear my checks out of my checkbook for me, and sales clerks find chairs to put into dressing rooms when I want to try on clothes. The people I work with make sure I teach at times when I am least likely to be fatigued, in places I can get to, with the materials I need. My students, with one anonymous exception (in an end-of-the-semester evaluation), have been unperturbed by my disability. Some even like it. One was immensely cheered by the information that I paint my own fingernails; she decided, she told me, that if I could go to such trouble over fine details, she could keep on writing essays. I suppose I became some sort of bright-fingered muse. She wrote good essays, too.

The most important struts in the framework of my existence, of 15 course, are my husband and children. Dismayingly few marriages survive the MS test, and why should they? Most twenty-two- and nineteen-year-olds, like George and me, can vow in clear conscience, after a childhood of chickenpox and summer colds, to keep one another in sickness and in health so long as they both shall live. Not many are equipped for catastrophe: the dismay, the depression, the extra work, the boredom that a degenerative disease can insinuate into a relationship. And our society, with its emphasis on fun and its association of fun with physical performance, offers little encouragement for a whole spouse to stay with a crippled partner. Children experience similar stresses when faced with a crippled parent, and they are more helpless, since parents and children can't usually get divorced. They hate, of course, to be different from their peers, and the child whose mother is tacking down the aisle of a school auditorium packed with proud parents like a Cape Cod dinghy in a stiff breeze jolly well stands out in a crowd. Deprived of legal divorce, the child can at least deny the mother's disability, even her existence, forgetting to tell her about recitals and PTA meetings, refusing to accompany her to stores or church or the movies, never inviting friends to the house. Many do.

But I've been limping along for ten years now, and so far George and 16 the children are still at my left elbow, holding tight. Anne and Matthew vacuum floors and dust furniture and haul trash and rake up dog droppings and button my cuffs and bake lasagna and Toll House cookies with just enough grumbling so I know that they don't have brain fever. And far from hiding me, they're forever dragging me by racks of fancy clothes or through teeming school corridors, or welcoming gaggles of friends while I'm wandering through the house in Anne's filmy pink babydoll pajamas. George generally calls before he brings someone home, but he does just as many dumb thankless chores as the children. And they all yell at me, laugh at some of my jokes, write me funny letters when we're apart—in short, treat me as an ordinary human being for whom they have some use. I think they like me. Unless they're faking. . . .

17   Faking. There's the rub. Tugging at the fringes of my consciousness always is the terror that people are kind to me only because I'm a cripple. My mother almost shattered me once, with that instinct mothers have— blind, I think, in this case, but unerring nonetheless—for striking blows along the fault-lines of their children's hearts, by telling me, in an attack on my selfishness, "We all have to make allowances for you, of course, be- cause of the way you are." From the distance of a couple of years, I have to admit that I haven't any idea just what she meant, and I'm not sure that she knew either. She was awfully angry. But at the time, as the words thudded home, I felt my worst fear, suddenly realized. I could bear being called selfish: I am. But I couldn't bear the corroboration that those around me were doing in fact what I'd always suspected them of doing, profess- ing fondness while silently putting up with me because of the way I am. A cripple. I've been a little cracked ever since.

18   Along with this fear that people are secretly accepting shoddy goods comes a relentless pressure to please—to prove myself worth the burdens I impose, I guess, or to build a substantial account of goodwill against which I may write drafts in times of need. Part of the pressure arises from social expectations. In our society, anyone who deviates from the norm had better find some way to compensate. Like fat people, who are ex- pected to be jolly, cripples must bear their lot meekly and cheerfully. A grumpy cripple isn't playing by the rules. And much of the pressure is self-generated. Early on I vowed that, if I had to have MS, by God I was going to do it well. This is a class act, ladies and gentlemen. No tears, no recriminations, no faint-heartedness.

19   One way and another, then, I wind up feeling like Tiny Tim, peering over the edge of the table at the Christmas goose, waving my crutch, pip- ing down God's blessing on us all. Only sometimes I don't want to play Tiny Tim. I'd rather be Caliban, a most scurvy monster. Fortunately, at home no one much cares whether I'm a good cripple or a bad cripple as long as I make vichyssoise with fair regularity. One evening several years ago, Anne was reading at the dining-room table while I cooked dinner. As I opened a can of tomatoes, the can slipped in my left hand and juice spat- tered me and the counter with bloody spots. Fatigued and infuriated, I bellowed, "I'm so sick of being crippled!" Anne glanced at me over the top of her book. "There now," she said, "do you feel better?" "Yes," I said, "yes, I do." She went back to her reading. I felt better. That's about all the attention my scurviness ever gets.

20   Because I hate being crippled, I sometimes hate myself for being a cripple. Over the years I have come to expect—even accept—attacks of violent self-loathing. Luckily, in general our society no longer connects

deformity and disease directly with evil (though a charismatic once told me that I have MS because a devil is in me) and so I'm allowed to move largely at will, even among small children. But I'm not sure that this revision of attitude has been particularly helpful. Physical imperfection, even freed of moral disapprobation, still defies and violates the ideal, especially for women, whose confinement in their bodies as objects of desire is far from over. Each age, of course, has its ideal, and I doubt that ours is any better or worse than any other. Today's ideal woman, who lives on the glossy pages of dozens of magazines, seems to be between the ages of eighteen and twenty-five; her hair has body, her teeth flash white, her breath smells minty, her underarms are dry, she has a career but is still a fabulous cook, especially of meals that take less than twenty minutes to prepare; she does not ordinarily appear to have a husband or children; she is trim and deeply tanned; she jogs, swims, plays tennis, rides a bicycle, sails, but does not bowl; she travels widely, even to out-of-the-way places like Finland and Samoa, always in the company of the ideal man, who possesses a nearly identical set of characteristics. There are a few exceptions. Though usually white and often blonde, she may be black, Hispanic, Asian, or Native American, so long as she is unusually sleek. She may be old, provided she is selling a laxative or is Lauren Bacall. If she is selling a detergent, she may be married and have a flock of strikingly messy children. But she is never a cripple.

Like many women I know, I have always had an uneasy relationship 21 with my body. I was not a popular child, largely, I think now, because I was peculiar: intelligent, intense, moody, shy, given to unexpected actions and inexplicable notions and emotions. But as I entered adolescence, I believed myself unpopular because I was homely: my breasts too flat, my mouth too wide, my hips too narrow, my clothing never quite right in fit or style. I was not, in fact, particularly ugly, old photographs inform me, though I was well off the ideal; but I carried this sense of self-alienation with me into adulthood, where it regenerated in response to the depredations of MS. Even with my brace I walk with a limp so pronounced that, seeing myself on the videotape of a television program on the disabled, I couldn't believe that anything but an inchworm could make progress humping along like that. My shoulders droop and my pelvis thrusts forward as I try to balance myself upright, throwing my frame into a bony S. As a result of contractures, one shoulder is higher than the other and I carry one arm bent in front of me, the fingers curled into a claw. My left arm and leg have wasted into pipe-stems, and I try always to keep them covered. When I think about how my body must look to others, especially to men, to whom I have been trained to display myself, I feel ludicrous, even loathsome.

At my age, however, I don't spend much time thinking about my 22 appearance. The burning egocentricity of adolescence, which assures one that all the world is looking all the time, has passed, thank God, and I'm generally too caught up in what I'm doing to step back, as I used to, and watch myself as though upon a stage. I'm also too old to believe in the accuracy of self-image. I know that I'm not a hideous crone, that in fact, when I'm rested, well dressed, and well made up, I look fine. The self-loathing I feel is neither physically nor intellectually substantial. What I hate is not me but a disease.

23   I am not a disease.

24   And a disease is not—at least not singlehandedly—going to determine who I am, though at first it seemed to be going to. Adjusting to a chronic incurable illness, I have moved through a process similar to that outlined by Elizabeth Kübler-Ross in *On Death and Dying*. The major difference—and it is far more significant than most people recognize—is that I can't be sure of the outcome, as the terminally ill cancer patient can. Research studies indicate that, with proper medical care, I may achieve a "normal" life span. And in our society, with its vision of death as the ultimate evil, worse even than decrepitude, the response to such news is, "Oh well, at least you're not going to *die.*" Are there worse things than dying? I think that there may be.

25   I think of two women I know, both with MS, both enough older than I to have served me as models. One took to her bed several years ago and has been there ever since. Although she can sit in a high-backed wheelchair, because she is incontinent she refuses to go out at all, even though incontinent pants, which are readily available at any pharmacy, could protect her from embarrassment. Instead, she stays at home and insists that her husband, a small quiet man, a retired civil servant, stay there with her except for a quick weekly foray to the supermarket. The other woman, whose illness was diagnosed when she was eighteen, a nursing student engaged to a young doctor, finished her training, married her doctor, accompanied him to Germany when he was in the service, bore three sons and a daughter, now grown and gone. When she can, she travels with her husband; she plays bridge, embroiders, swims regularly; she works, like me, as a symptomatic-patient instructor of medical students in neurology. Guess which woman I hope to be.

26   At the beginning, I thought about having MS almost incessantly. And because of the unpredictable course of the disease, my thoughts were always terrified. Each night I'd get into bed wondering whether I'd get out again the next morning, whether I'd be able to see, to speak, to hold a pen between my fingers. Knowing that the day might come when I'd be physically incapable of killing myself, I thought perhaps I ought to do so right away, while I still had the strength. Gradually I came to understand that the Nancy who might one day lie inert under a bedsheet, arms and legs paralyzed, unable to feed or bathe herself, unable to reach out for a gun, a bottle of pills, was not the Nancy I was at present, and that I could not presume to make decisions for that future Nancy, who might well not want in the least to die. Now the only provision I've made for the future Nancy is that when the time comes—and it is likely to come in the form

of pneumonia, friend to the weak and the old—I am not to be treated with machines and medications. If she is unable to communicate by then, I hope she will be satisfied with these terms.

Thinking all the time about having MS grew tiresome and intrusive, 27 especially in the large and tragic mode in which I was accustomed to considering my plight. Months and even years went by without catastrophe (at least without one related to MS), and really I was awfully busy, what with George and children and snakes and students and poems, and I hadn't the time, let alone the inclination, to devote myself to being a disease. Too, the richer my life became, the funnier it seemed, as though there were some connection between largesse and laughter, and so my tragic stance began to waver until, even with the aid of a brace and cane, I couldn't hold it for very long at a time.

After several years I was satisfied with my adjustment. I had suffered 28 my grief and fury and terror, I thought, but now I was at ease with my lot. Then one summer day I set out with George and the children across the desert for a vacation in California. Part way to Yuma I became aware that my right leg felt funny. "I think I've had an exacerbation," I told George. "What shall we do?" he asked. "I think we'd better get the hell to California," I said, "because I don't know whether I'll ever make it again." So we went on to San Diego and then to Orange, and up the Pacific Coast Highway to Santa Cruz, across to Yosemite, down to Sequoia and Joshua Tree, and so back over the desert to home. It was a fine two-week trip, filled with friends and fair weather, and I wouldn't have missed it for the world, though I did in fact make it back to California two years later. Nor would there have been any point in missing it, since in MS, once the symptoms have appeared, the neurological damage has been done, and there's no way to predict or prevent that damage.

The incident spoiled my self-satisfaction, however. It renewed my 29 grief and fury and terror, and I learned that one never finishes adjusting to MS. I don't know now why I thought one would. One does not, after all, finish adjusting to life, and MS is simply a fact of my life—not my favorite fact, of course—but as ordinary as my nose and my tropical fish and my yellow Mazda station wagon. It may at any time get worse, but no amount of worry or anticipation can prepare me for a new loss. My life is a lesson in losses. I learn one at a time.

And I had best be patient in the learning, since I'll have to do it like 30 it or not. As any rock fan knows, you can't always get what you want. Particularly when you have MS. You can't, for example, get cured. In recent years researchers and the organizations that fund research have started to pay MS some attention even though it isn't fatal; perhaps they have begun to see that life is something other than a quantitative phenomenon, that one may be very much alive for a very long time in a life that isn't worth living. The researchers have made some progress toward understanding the mechanism of the disease: It may well be an autoimmune reaction triggered by a slow-acting virus. But they are nowhere near its prevention, control, or cure. And most of us want to be cured. Some, unable to accept incurability, grasp at one treatment after another, no matter how bizarre: megavitamin therapy, gluten-free diet, injections of cobra venom, hypothermal suits, lymphocytopharesis, hyperbaric chambers. Many treatments are probably harmless enough, but none are curative.

31   The absence of a cure often makes MS patients bitter toward their doctors. Doctors are, after all, the priests of modern society, the new shamans, whose business is to heal, and many an MS patient roves from one to another, searching for the "good" doctor who will make him well. Doctors too think of themselves as healers, and for this reason many have trouble dealing with MS patients, whose disease in its intransigence defeats their aims and mocks their skills. Too few doctors, it is true, treat their patients as whole human beings, but the reverse is also true. I have always tried to be gentle with my doctors, who often have more at stake in terms of ego than I do. I may be frustrated, maddened, depressed by the incurability of my disease, but I am not diminished by it, and they are. When I push myself up from my seat in the waiting room and stumble toward them, I incarnate the limitation of their powers. The least I can do is refuse to press on their tenderest spots.

32   This gentleness is part of the reason that I'm not sorry to be a cripple. I didn't have it before. Perhaps I'd have developed it anyway—how could I know such a thing?—and I wish I had more of it, but I'm glad of what I have. It has opened and enriched my life enormously, this sense that my frailty and need must be mirrored in others, that in searching for and shaping a stable core in a life wrenched by change and loss, change and loss, I must recognize the same process, under individual conditions, in the lives around me. I do not deprecate such knowledge, however I've come by it.

33   All the same, if a cure were found, would I take it? In a minute. I may be a cripple, but I'm only occasionally a loony and never a saint. Anyway, in my brand of theology God doesn't give bonus points for a limp. I'd take a cure; I just don't need one. A friend who also has MS startled me once by asking, "Do you ever say to yourself, 'Why me, Lord?'" "No, Michael, I don't," I told him, "because whenever I try, the only response I can think of is 'Why not?'" If I could make a cosmic deal, who would I put in my place? What in my life would I give up in exchange for sound limbs and a thrilling rush of energy? No one. Nothing. I might as well do the job myself. Now that I'm getting the hang of it.

Content

1. Mairs uses a number of illustrations to compose her definition of "being a cripple," many of them involving physical failure or physical difficulty. Identify some of these. Given the fact that they represent recurring problems that will only

get worse and will never be solved, how do you account for the ultimately positive, affirmative tone of the essay?

2. Mairs is very candid about her body, with which she has "always had an uneasy relationship" (¶ 21). What features of American culture and values cause people to be dissatisfied with their bodies? Is this as true of men as of women, of adults as well as teenagers? How has Mairs come to terms with her appearance, which is, in fact, continuing to deteriorate (¶ 22)? What could others, "crippled" or not, learn from her example?

Strategies/Structures

3. This essay involves considerable comparison and contrast, overt and implied, between being crippled and not crippled. Why is it important for Mairs to establish the fact that she "was a normally active child and young adult" (¶ 5)? How can we tell that she is writing for an audience "whole of limb," who will as they read be comparing their state with hers?

4. This essay is full of examples of Mairs in a variety of roles—wife, mother, friend, teacher, writer. What examples of activities does Mairs use to characterize herself in these roles as an adult with MS? Why are these varied examples important to her definition of "being crippled"?

Language

5. Why does Mairs choose for herself the label of "cripple" (¶s 2–4) rather than the alternative labels—"disabled," "handicapped," "differently abled"—that she rejects? Why does she put that word, sure to offend some readers, in the title?

6. Mairs wants our sympathetic understanding but not our pity. What language does she use to obtain this? What is her essay's prevailing tone? Is Mairs a person you'd like to know? Why or why not? Which of your reasons are related to her handicap?

For Writing

7. A disability of any kind makes the victim different from people without it. Mairs's essay shows the positive as well as negative effects of being different, and she also shows how these differences can be transcended, in spirit and in action. Have you ever felt different enough from your peers to be uncomfortable? If so, for mainstream readers, write a definition of "being different," and illustrate its effects, for better and/or worse. Make some connections between your case and larger groups. (See Lamott, "Polaroids" [56–60] or Liu and Santiago on being American [410–24], for instance.)

8. Mairs says, "Every day for the past ten years," since her symptoms were diagnosed as MS rather than a malignant brain tumor, "has been a kind of gift" (¶ 6). If you (or someone you know well) have had an experience that has made you grateful for every day thereafter, explain the nature of that experience and show why its effects have been so profound.

Code Blue: Two Definitions

JASMINE INNERARITY

Innerarity, born (1968) and raised in Jamaica, studied at the University of Toronto and earned from the University of Connecticut a B.S. in nursing (1989) and an M.S. in nursing/public health (1999). A pediatric oncology nurse, she has served as president of the Connecticut chapter of the Society of Pediatric Nurses and has written movingly of her compassionate care of young patients—those who would survive, and those who would not.

The writing of "Code Blue: The Process" presented problems for Innerarity. She wanted to present an accurate and precise definition of what happens during this emergency procedure that would be clear to an audience of undergraduates, who needed further definitions of terms such as "intubation," "crash cart," and "ambu bag." During the course of several revisions, to ensure that her writing was both accurate and ethical, she checked her work with nursing colleagues (was she revealing medical secrets? no!). She also provided additional definitions of key terms and more illustrations because of her realization that what she as a professional nurse could take for granted was not always common knowledge. To avoid giving the impression of medical infallibilty, her last revision was to include an example of the fact that despite a medical team's best efforts Code Blue procedures do not always succeed.

❄ Code Blue: The Process

1   An unforgettable moment in caring for the sick in the hospital or any institutional setting is the Code Blue Process. Code Blue is the alert signal for a patient who has stopped breathing or whose heart has stopped. This signal is universal throughout hospitals in the U.S. The alert is given via the physicians' private beepers and the overhead intercom within hospitals. This process is always associated with what seems like chaos to the outsider but to the health team, it is well organized and well executed.

2   Code Blue is usually initiated by the nurse. There are many reasons for this. First, the nurse spends more time with the patient than any other member of the health team. In addition, the nurse is continuously assessing the patient's condition. The nurse usually detects small changes in vital signs or physical conditions at crucial times when other members of the health team are absent.

3   Within the hospital, a patient who has stopped breathing or who is in cardiac arrest is quickly discovered because the circular arrangement of the floor allows all patients to be seen from the nursing station. In addition, those patients who are unstable are placed on cardiac monitors with audio

alarms which alert the medical team to changes in their health status if medical personnel is not present in the room.

A cart which is equipped with all the necessary equipment to initiate 4 the Code Blue response is also placed in a central region on each hospital floor. This cart called the "Code cart," usually contains intravenous fluids, emergency medications, and equipment used for intubating the patient. In the event of a Code Blue, this cart is immediately brought into the patient's room.

Example of Code Blue Process

Timmy was a two-year-old boy. He was in the Intensive Care Unit for a 5 neurological condition which affects his breathing patterns. He has been doing well. I have been caring for him for the past week and have watched his progress with great joy. He was still being monitored before being released from the Intensive Care Unit to the regular Hospital Unit.

One morning, I walked in to see Timmy five minutes after his mother 6 had left the room. I had heard them playing together minutes before she left. As I entered the room, I noticed that Timmy was lying still and his lips were turning blue. "Timmy! Timmy!" I shouted, while shaking him. He did not respond. "I have a Code Blue," I called out.

My shout of "Code Blue!" was the warning to the rest of the health 7 team to get someone else into the room while the secretary announces the alert to the Code Blue team. In a Code Blue situation, a member from several different medical teams appears. The teams are designed to ensure that in an emergency situation, such as this one, each physician or health care member essential to getting this patient back to health is present. Although the medical personnel who arrive vary by hospitals, there is usually a surgeon, a cardiologist, a respiratory therapist, an anesthesiologist, an intensivist, and the patient's primary or attending physician for the day. The primary physician leads the Code team by getting a quick history of what precipitated the patient's cessation of breathing and tries to determine how to reverse this crisis. His role is to give the orders in the code.

The surgeon arrives to insert central lines—a plastic tubing going 8 from the outside of the body to the inside that is used to infuse medication, fluids, and blood products quickly into the body and heart. A cardiologist has the role of prescribing medications to ensure that the most central organ in the body (the heart) is functioning.

The anesthesiologist has the role of sedating and intubating the patient who has stopped breathing. Intubation involves placing a plastic 9 tubing through the patient's mouth and into his or her lungs. This process requires considerable skill, because one has to take care to insert the tube into the trachea, and not into the esophagus which leads to the stomach. Once the tube is placed into the lungs, an X-ray is taken of the chest to confirm that this tube is in fact where it belongs, in the lungs. The end of the tubing which projects from the mouth is connected to a respirator, a computerized machine that breathes for the patient. The respiratory therapist is in charge of monitoring the respirator.

10   Accessory personnel, such as members of the fire department or EMT team from the hospital, may arrive to assist in a Code Blue situation. In fact, it is not unusual after the initial assessment of the situation to ask some health personnel who are not needed to leave the room. The aim is to prevent clutter and maximize efficiency in responding to the Code.

11   A series of quick actions is executed within a minute of the Code Blue call. A team of health professionals rushes into the room. As I try to instill air into Timmy's lungs, using a mechanical device called an "ambu bag," another nurse feels for pulses, and the physician prepares to intubate Timmy. An ambu bag is a pressure bag made of rubber (it looks like an inflated balloon) that has two ends. One end has a long plastic tubing which connects to an oxygen tank or oxygen outlet in the wall, and the other end has a mouthpiece which fits over the patient's face and mouth. When the middle part of the balloon is squeezed, oxygen is expelled into the patient's mouth and ultimately into the lungs.

12   The physician in charge of Timmy gives the orders:

> "500 ml of I.V. fluids wide open stat!"
> "What's his pressure?"
> "Does he have a pulse?"
> "Yes."
> "Okay, let's have a blood gas."

Each member of the team rushes to fulfill their role.

13   The series of quick necessary motions, as well as the numerous health professionals in the patient's room, give the impression of disorder. On the contrary, the process is very orderly: Blood is being drawn, phone calls are being made to get lab results quickly, and the physician is speaking loudly so that everyone can hear what to do and when. There is no time for mishaps. It is an assembly line and everyone must be alert. Each team member must mesh into this new team, the team of people trying to save the patient's life.

14   Timmy starts to cry after three minutes of resuscitation. His lips are no longer blue. "Good job, team," says the physician.

15   The team rushes out and back to their original stations. The nurses stay behind to do what they do best, care for Timmy and comfort his family. Timmy's mother has been brought down to the lounge during the code. Timmy will be in an oxygen tent for the night. "What's that?" she asks, pointing to the tent. The oxygen tent is made of plastic and is in the shape of a tent (hence the name). It delivers a continuous supply of oxygen to Timmy, which will help with his breathing overnight. I sit to explain to her what just happened to Timmy and to answer any questions she may have. Timmy's mother takes my hand, "Thanks for saving him."

The process of Code Blue in this instance is short, lasting for fifteen   16
minutes only. Timmy responded well to the medical interventions. In other
cases, however, the outcome can be grave. Mark was a twelve-year-old boy
with a brain tumor. His family had agonized about the decision to make
him a "Do not resuscitate" (DNR) patient. This status implies that if he
should stop breathing, then the Code Blue process would not be initiated.
DNR is attributed to patients who are gravely ill and for whom medical
interventions have proven ineffective. The decision to make a patient a
DNR however, is ultimately that of the family. Mark's parents wanted
everything to be done for him despite the recommendation of DNR status
by the physicians. Thus, Mark was not a DNR.

When Mark stopped breathing one evening, a Code Blue was called.   17
Again the group of medical personnel arrived to save Mark's life. In this
case and unlike Timmy, Mark responded poorly to the use of the ambu
bag. His heart stopped. He was intubated by the anesthesiologist and
was placed on a respirator. The private physician shouted: "We need
to take him to the operating room (OR), he's bleeding." The physicians
debated whether Mark's heart was strong enough for the OR. Despite
several medications, Mark's heart would not return to the normal sinus
rhythm.

The health team rushed to get blood into his body. The surgeons de-   18
bated whether they could stop the bleeding, which they found was in his
brain. After forty-five minutes of medications and mechanical ventilation,
Mark still did not respond. The primary physician and the family talked
about the grave outcome for Mark. After a half hour had passed since the
Code Blue, the parents decided to let Mark go. He was taken off the respirator and died immediately.

The timing for the Code Blue process is as varied as the patients in-   19
volved in the process. The two examples above showed the difference in
response to medical interventions, which determine how long the process
is continued. In many instances, the team will continue the process for up
to an hour if the patient responds to medication. The patient will then be
transferred to an Intensive Care Unit where he will be monitored closely
until he is stable.

There are many emotions involved in a Code Blue process, depend-   20
ing on whether the outcome is good or poor. Initially, the team members
experience a rush of adrenalin. This occurs because a Code Blue does not
happen daily, so the nervousness, yet urgency of the situation takes one
by surprise. There is also the continuous struggle with the ethical issues
involved in Code Blue situations. For example, in each Code Blue situation, the determination must be made whether or not that patient is a
DNR status. Usually the primary nurse and physician are aware of this
status. At times, however, the determination must be made immediately.
Nurses as well as family members struggle with the decision to make
someone a DNR or a full code status.

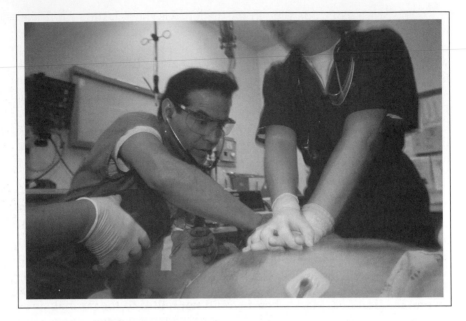

What's going on here? How many people are present? What are the mode, tone, and energy level of the activities depicted here? What is the relation of teamwork to this matter of life and death?

21   One of the biggest rewards in caring for the sick is the miracle of seeing a person who has stopped breathing and who looks lifeless return to life. After ten years of being involved in the nursing process, my natural instinct is to care for those who are sick. I genuinely believe that caring for the sick makes them better. Of course, the Code Blue process shows that this is not always true. However, in my experience, the positive outcomes disproportionately overshadow the very small number of morbid outcomes.

[Suggestions for reading and writing about this essay are combined with those pertaining to Abraham Verghese's "Code Blue: The Story" and appear on pages 383–84.]

ABRAHAM VERGHESE

Verghese was born in Addis Ababa, Ethiopia (1955), where his expatriate Indian parents were teachers, but he returned to India to study medicine (M.D., Madras University, 1979). In 1980 he began a three-year residency in internal medicine at East Tennessee State University, then switched to infectious diseases because, he says, "it offered the promise of a cure. In the early 1980s infectious disease was the one discipline where a cure was common." But in August, 1985, the local hospital in rural Johnson City treated its first AIDS patient, and soon the crisis that had once seemed an urban problem spread to the small town, as well. *My Own Country: A Doctor's Story* (1994) describes how Verghese, as a specialist in infectious diseases, gradually became drawn into the treatment of the "shocking number" of male and female patients who took over not only his professional life but also his compassionate imagination.

Of this experience, Verghese, now chief of infectious diseases at Texas Technological Regional Academic Health Center in El Paso, says, "Today I am a doctor who is unable to cure." He explains, "You're suddenly dealing with people your own age whose plight makes you reflect on your ideas about sex, about social issues and, of course, about your own mortality. Almost every emotion is magnified and brought into sharp relief with AIDS." He began writing nonfiction, now published in the *New Yorker* and many other places, aided by a year's Michener Fellowship to the Writers' Workshop at the University of Iowa (1990–1991), as a way to deal with "some of my frustrations at work. I can't reverse death, I can't get into a patient's mind and think his thoughts. But with writing, the boundaries are virtually limitless," as Verghese's most recent book, *The Tennis Partner: A Doctor's Story of Friendship and Loss* (1998) also illustrates. "Code Blue: The Story" opens *My Own Country,* putting into dramatic action—with characters, dialogue, and frenetic activity—the definition that Innerarity has explained in a more formal manner.

Code Blue: The Story

I n the early evening of August 11, 1985, he was rolled into the emergency room (ER) of the Johnson City Medical Center—the "Miracle Center," as we referred to it when we were interns. Puffing like an overheated steam engine, he was squeezing in forty-five breaths a minute. Or so Claire Bellamy, the nurse, told me later. It had shocked her to see a thirty-two-year-old man in such severe respiratory distress.   1

He sat bolt upright on the stretcher, his arms propped behind him like struts that braced his heaving chest. His blond hair was wet and stuck to his forehead; his skin, Claire recalled, was gunmetal gray, his lips and nail beds blue.   2

She had slapped an oxygen mask on him and hollered for someone to pull the duty physician away from the wound he was suturing. A genuine emergency was at hand, something she realized, even as it overtook her, she was not fully comprehending. She knew what it was not: it was *not* severe asthma, status asthmaticus; it was *not* a heart attack. She could not stop to take it all in. Everything was happening too quickly.   3

With every breath he sucked in, his nostrils flared. The strap muscles of his neck stood out like cables. He pursed his lips when he exhaled, as if he was loath to let the oxygen go, hanging on to it as long as he could.   4

5   Electrodes placed on his chest and hooked to a monitor showed his heart fluttering at a desperate 160 beats per minute.

6   On his chest x-ray, the lungs that should have been dark as the night were instead whited out by a veritable snowstorm.

7   My friend Ray, a pulmonary physician was immediately summoned. While Ray listened to his chest, the phlebotomist drew blood for serum electrolytes and red and white blood cell counts. The respiratory therapist punctured the radial artery at the wrist to measure blood oxygen levels. Claire started an intravenous line. And the young man slumped on the stretcher. He stopped breathing.

8   Claire punched the "Code Blue" button on the cubicle wall and an operator's voice sounded through the six-story hospital building: "Code Blue, emergency room!"

9   The code team—an intern, a senior resident, two intensive care unit nurses, a respiratory therapist, a pharmacist—thundered down the hallway.

10   Patients in their rooms watching TV sat up in their beds; visitors froze in place in the corridors.

11   More doctors arrived; some came in street clothes, having heard the call as they headed for the parking lot. Others came in scrub suits. Ray was "running" the code; he called for boluses of bicarbonate and epinephrine, for a second intravenous line to be secured, and for Claire to increase the vigor but slow down the rate of her chest compressions.

12   The code team took their positions. The beefy intern with Nautilus shoulders took off his jacket and climbed onto a step stool. He moved in just as Claire stepped back, picking up the rhythm of chest compressions without missing a beat, calling the cadence out loud. With locked elbows, one palm over the back of the other, he squished the heart between breastbone and spine, trying to squirt enough blood out of it to supply the brain.

13   The ER physician unbuttoned the young man's pants and cut away the underwear, now soiled with urine. His fingers reached for the groin, feeling for the femoral artery to assess the adequacy of the chest compressions.

14   A "crash cart" stocked with ampules of every variety, its defibrillator paddles charged and ready, stood at the foot of the bed as the pharmacist recorded each medication given and the exact time it was administered.

15   The clock above the stretcher had been automatically zeroed when the Code Blue was called. A code nurse called out the elapsed time at thirty-second intervals. The resident and another nurse from the code team probed with a needle for a vein to establish the second "line."

16   Ray "bagged" the patient with a tight-fitting mask and hand-held squeeze bag as the respiratory therapist readied an endotracheal tube and laryngoscope.

17   At a signal from Ray, the players froze in midair while he bent the young man's head back over the edge of the stretcher. Ray slid the laryngoscope in between tongue and palate and heaved up with his left hand,

pulling the base of the tongue up and forward until the leaf-shaped epiglottis appeared.

Behind it, the light at the tip of the laryngoscope showed glimpses of 18
the voice box and the vocal cords. With his right hand, Ray fed the endotracheal tube alongside the laryngoscope, down the back of the throat, past the epiglottis, and past the vocal cords—this part done almost blindly and with a prayer—and into the trachea. Then he connected the squeeze bag to the end of the endotracheal tube and watched the chest rise as he pumped air into the lungs. He nodded, giving the signal for the action to resume.

Now Ray listened with his stethoscope over both sides of the chest as 19
the respiratory therapist bagged the limp young man. He listened for the muffled *whoosh* of air, listened to see if it was equally loud over both lungs.

He heard sounds only over the right lung. The tube had gone down 20
the right main bronchus, a straighter shot than the left.

He pulled the tube back an inch, listened again, and heard air enter- 21
ing both sides. The tube was sitting above the carina, above the point where the trachea bifurcates. He called for another chest x-ray; a radiopaque marker at the end of the tube would confirm its exact position.

With a syringe he inflated the balloon cuff at the end of the endo- 22
tracheal tube that would keep it snugly in the trachea. Claire wound tape around the tube and plastered it down across the young man's cheeks and behind his neck.

The blue in the young man's skin began to wash out and a faint pink 23
appeared in his cheeks. The ECG machine, which had spewed paper into a curly mound on the floor, now showed the original rapid heart rhythm restored.

At this point the young man was alive again, but just barely. The 24
Code Blue had been a success.

Content

1. What is *Code Blue* according to Innerarity's definition?

2. Is it possible to infer a definition of *Code Blue* from Verghese's illustration of *Code Blue* in action? What additional information do you need?

3. After she had written several versions of "Code Blue" that contained only positive examples, Innerarity added a negative example—of Code Blue not working—at her teacher's insistence. Does the negative example undercut the positive?

4. Why, in medical and science writing, are there usually many more positive examples (successful processes and procedures) than negative ones? Do the essays by Innerarity and Verghese bear this out?

Strategies/Structures

5. Why would nonmedical people want to know the details of a procedure that can be performed only by a medical team?

6. Innerarity offers a textbook definition of the process, personnel, and equipment used to carry out a Code Blue. In contrast, Verghese shows Code Blue in action. Explain how his narrative also functions as a definition.

7. Which version of "Code Blue" are you more likely to remember? Why?

Language

8. Innerarity had difficulty translating medical terminology into everyday language and wrote several drafts to simplify and clarify the language. Has she succeeded? Has she used any terms that still need definition?

For Writing

9. Define a specialized technical or scientific term or process so a nonspecialist can understand it. See De Palma (168–78), the Magliozzis (178–84), Innerarity and Verghese (376–84), Gardner (349–61), Brand (397–401).

10. Write a narrative (that is, tell a true story), as Innerarity and Verghese do, that through its characters and action implies a definition of a significant term—such as *love* (or *hate*), *beauty* (or *ugliness*), *fidelity* (or *betrayal*), *honesty* (or *dishonesty*)—or of a process (how to form or destroy a friendship, how to travel); or of some other concept that you expect to learn to understand in the process of writing about it.

Additional Topics for Writing

Definition   (For strategies for writing definition, see 341)

1. Write an extended definition of one or more of the following trends, concepts, abstractions, phenomena, or institutions. Be sure to identify your audience, limit your subject, and illustrate your essay with specific examples.

   a. Peace (see the "World Peace" chapter; Kleege, 12–22)
   b. Terrorism, national or international (see the "Terrorism" chapter)
   c. Intelligence (see Gardner, 349–61)
   d. Physical fitness (see Lamott, 56–60; Mairs 364–75)
   e. Personality
   f. Character
   g. Optimism
   h Depression (economic or psychological) (see Angier, 299–304)
   i. The nature of friendship
   j. Marriage (either, the ideal marriage, or the ideal versus the reality—see Brady, 361–64)
   k. Parenthood (see Erdrich, 33–37; White, 122–28; Sanders, 139–46 and 274–86; Spinner, 424–32)
   l. Education—formal or informal (see Kozol, 210–18; Zitkala-Sa, 218–26; Barry, 500–04)
   m. A good job or profession; work
   n. A sport, game, hobby, or recreational activity
   o. A Northerner, Southerner, Midwesterner, Texan, Californian, or person from some other state or region
   p. A scientific or technical phenomenon of your choice (an eclipse, the "big bang" theory of creation, genetic engineering, DNA, the MX missile)

2. Explain a particular value system or belief system, such as:

   a. Democracy, communism, socialism, or some other political theory or form of government
   b. Protestantism (or a particular sect), Catholicism, Judaism (or a particular branch—Orthodox, Conservative, Reform), Buddhism (or a particular sort), Islam, or some other religion
   c. A theoretical system and some of its major ramifications (feminism, post-colonialism, Freudianism)

3. Prepare a dictionary of ten jargon or slang words used in your academic major, in your hobby, or in some other activity you enjoy, such as playing a particular sport or game, listening to a specific type of music, or working on a computer system.

Comparison and
Contrast

Writers compare people, places, things, or qualities to identify their similarities, and contrast them to identify the differences. What you say about one subject usually helps to illuminate or explain the other, as a commentary on the five college graduates pictured above might do. Although all are happy—presumably because they are celebrating graduation—their diverse appearances imply different individualities, heritages, lives. Such explanations have the added advantage of answering questions that hinge on the similarities and differences under consideration. Your commentary can also provide the basis for judging the relative merits and demerits of the subject at hand.

For instance, comparison and contrast can help you determine whether to choose a liberal arts or technical education, and what your future will be like with whichever you select. It can help you explain the resemblances between the works of Faulkner and Hemingway, and the differences—and to justify your preference for one author over the other. Comparison and contrast can help you decide whom to vote for, what movie to see (or avoid), where to spend your next vacation, what car to buy, which person to marry. A thoroughgoing, detailed comparison and contrast of the reasons for the quality of life with and without handguns, conservation of natural resources, or nuclear power can provide a convincing argument for your choice.

But not everything will work. The subjects you select should have some obvious qualities in common to make the comparison and contrast fruitful. If you try to compare very dissimilar things, as the Mad Hatter does in *Alice in Wonderland* ("Why is a raven like a writing desk?"), you'll have to stretch for an answer ("Because they both begin with an *r* sound.") that may be either silly or irrelevant. But other comparisons by their very nature can command appropriate contrasts. Deborah Tannen's "Communication Styles" (391–97) is based on an extended exploration of differences in the way men and women students behave in the classroom. For instance, Tannen has found that men speak in class more often than women do. They're more at ease in the "public" classroom setting and enjoy the "debate-like form that discussion may take," while women students are "more comfortable speaking in private to a small group of people they know well" in nonconfrontational dialogue.

Stewart Brand's "Written on the Wind" (397–401) and Jenny Spinner's "In Search of a Past" (424–32) abound in comparisons and contrasts, explicit and implied. Brand deals with life before and during the digital age; different stages of digital sophistication; digital continuity and discontinuity ("The great creator becomes the great eraser."); timeliness and obsolescence; a unified versus a fragmented network of computer systems; past, present, and future ("How can we invest in a future we know is structurally incapable of keeping faith with its past?"); and many more. Likewise, Spinner's essay explores the bonds and similarities between her twin sister and herself and her adoptive parents; fantasy versions of her birth parents in contrast with the unknown (to her) reality of their lives; negative comparisons between the twins and schoolmates certain of their ancestry; choosing to know and not know—all embedded in a narrative that proceeds chronologically through the essay, from before her birth, through her school and college years, to the present.

In writing an essay of comparison and contrast you'll need to justify your choice of subject, unless the grounds for comparison are obvious. Thus in "Evolution as Fact and Theory" (401–10), the late Stephen Jay Gould explains a contrast that is not necessarily apparent to general readers—that evolution as a theory and evolution as a fact are "different things, not rungs in a hierarchy of increasing certainty." Facts are the data which theories try to explain, as evolutionists have always made clear "from the very beginning, if only because we have always acknowledged how far we are from completely understanding the mechanisms (theory) by which evolution (fact) occurred." He then uses these definitions as the basis for refuting the contrasting view of "scientific creationism," a "self-contradictory, nonsense" set of beliefs. What theory could explain the existence of the 130-million-year-old fossil dinosaur pictured on p. 406, covered from head to tail with downy fluff and primitive feathers? Might alternative theories compete for an evolutionary explanation?

You'll also have to limit your comparison. It would take a book or more to compare and contrast all the relevant aspects of the People's Republic of China and Taiwan. In an essay—short or long, or even treatise-length—on the subject you could focus instead on their relative educational systems, on their relations with the United Sates, or on the everyday life of the average worker in each country. Both Eric Liu, in "Notes of a Native Speaker" (410–20), and Esmeralda Santiago, in "Race . . . Other" (420–24), compare their race, heritage, and lifestyle to other native-born Americans with whiter skins. At times both identify strongly with the values of their lily-white comparison group and yearn to assimilate—and succeed in doing so. Yet at other times they assert their ethnic and cultural heritage. Both processes are implied in the photograph of the young couple on p. 412. The couple appear to be of different ethnicities—but which ones? As Liu says, "What was it, in my blind journey [toward assimilation], that I felt I should leave behind? And what *did* I leave behind? This, the jettisoning of one mode of life to send another aloft, is not only the immigrant's tale; it is the son's tale, too." It is useful to compare the ways in which Liu and Santiago write about common issues and to contrast their differences as well, some based on the writers' gender, others on the differences in their parents' social class and occupations. In a short paper, you're better off to compare the relevant aspects of two entities. The more items you add, the more complicated the comparison becomes, as you try to deal with the political system in the People's Republic of China, and Taiwan, and Russia, and Poland, and Romania, and. . . .

There are three common ways to organize an essay of comparison and contrast. Let's say you're in the market for a car and are writing an essay to help you make decisions on type (minivan, pickup, sportscar, sedan), make and model, age (new or used), cost, special features (four wheel drive, built-in CD player), and financing (buy or lease). If you've just begun to think about the subject, you could deal with each issue topic by topic, most usefully in the order listed here: type, make and model, etc. Or you could deal with each subject as a whole before moving on to the next. If you've already decided on the particular type and price of car, say, a small used vehicle costing between $6,000 and $8,000, then you might find it more useful to devote one section, say, to the Honda Civic, another to the GEO Prizm, and a third to the Toyota Celica, considering all features of each car in the same order: size, handling, reliability, fuel economy, safety, sportiness, and final cost. Why the same order for each car? Because you'll confuse yourself and your readers if you follow a different organizational pattern for each car; everyone needs to know where to look in each discussion to find comparable information. Another way to organize the information would be to group all the similarities about the cars in one section and all the differences in another, arranged in order from the most important (to you) to the least. Eventually, you'll summarize your conclusion: "While I like the first car better because it's sportier and more fun to drive, and the second is great on hills and curves, I guess I'm stuck with the third because I know I can get a good deal from my great uncle, who kept it in his garage all winter and never drove it over fifty."

The pattern of comparison and contrast that emerges may depend on how long the paper is; the longer the discussion, the less easy it is for readers to remember what they need to. Try out a sample section on members of your class or writing group and see whether they can understand the points of comparison you're trying to make; if they can't, then try another method of arrangement.

Whatever pattern of comparison and contrast you use, a topic outline can help you to organize such papers, and to make sure you've covered equivalent points for each item in the comparison. However you organize the paper, you don't have to give such equal emphasis to the similarities and to the differences; some may simply be more important than others. But you do have to make your chosen points of comparison relevant. Comparison and contrast is particularly useful as a technique in explanations. You can compare something that readers don't know much about (foreign sportscars) with something that's familiar (family sedans).

As we've seen, essays of comparison and contrast may include other types of writing, particularly description, narration, and analysis. Classification and division often determine the points to be covered in such essays: my actual life versus my ideal life, country living versus city living, life on the East (or West) coast versus life in the Midwest, middle-class life versus upper-class life. . . . And essays of comparison and contrast themselves become, at times, illustrations or arguments, direct or indirect, overt or more subtle. Long live the differences and the zest they provide.

STRATEGIES FOR WRITING—
COMPARISON AND CONTRAST

1. Will my essay focus on the similarities between two or more things (comparison) or the differences (contrast), or will I be discussing both similarities and differences? Why do I want to make the comparison or contrast? To find, explore, or deny overt or less apparent resemblances among the items? To decide which one of a pair or group is better or preferable? Or to use the comparison or contrast to argue for my preference?
2. Are my readers familiar with one or more of the objects of my comparison? If they are familiar with them all, then can I concentrate on the unique features of my analysis? (If they are familiar with only one item, start with the known before discussing the unknown. If they are unacquainted with everything, for

purposes of explanation you might wish to begin with a comparison that focuses on the common elements among the items under discussion.)

3. How global or minute will my comparison be (i.e., do I want to make only a few points of comparison or contrast, or many)? Will my essay make more sense to my readers if I present each subject as a complete unit before discussing the next? Or will the comparison or contrast be more meaningful if I proceed point by point?

4. Have I ruled out trivial and irrelevant comparisons? Does each point have a counterpart that I have treated in an equivalent manner, through comparable analysis or illustration, length, and language?

5. Suppose I like or favor one item of the comparison or contrast over the others? Am I obliged to treat every item equally in language and tone, or can my tone vary to reinforce my interpretation?

DEBORAH TANNEN

For biographical information, see page 304.

Much of Tannen's research, like her writing, is based on comparative analyses of the contrasting behavior of men and women in a variety of situations. "Communication Styles" was originally published as "Teachers' Classroom Strategies Should Recognize that Men and Women Use Language Differently" in the *Chronicle of Higher Education* (June 19, 1991). Here Tannen explores differences in the ways that men and women students interact, and how the size, informality, and composition of the group influences who speaks up and who remains silent.

Communication Styles

When I researched and wrote my book, *You Just Don't Understand: Women and Men in Conversation,* the furthest thing from my mind was reevaluating my teaching strategies. But that has been one of the direct benefits of having written the book. 1

The primary focus of my linguistic research always has been the language of everyday conversation. One facet of this is conversational style: how different regional, ethnic, and class backgrounds, as well as age and gender, result in different ways of using language to communicate. *You Just Don't Understand* is about the conversational styles of women and men. As I gained more insight into typically male and female ways of using language, I began to suspect some of the causes of the troubling facts that women who go to single-sex schools do better in later life, and that when young women sit next to young men in classrooms, the males talk more. This is not to say that all men talk in class, nor that no women do. It is simply that a greater percentage of discussion time is taken by men's voices. 2

The research of sociologists and anthropologists such as Janet Lever, Marjorie Harness Goodwin, and Donna Eder has shown that girls and boys learn to use language differently in their sex-separate peer groups. Typically, a girl has a best friend with whom she sits and talks, frequently telling secrets. It's the telling of secrets, the fact and the way that they talk to each other, that makes them best friends. For boys, activities are central: Their best friends are the ones they do things with. Boys also tend to play in larger groups that are hierarchical. High-status boys give orders and push low-status boys around. So boys are expected to use language to seize center stage: by exhibiting their skills, displaying their knowledge, and challenging and resisting challenges. 3

These patterns have stunning implications for classroom interaction. Most faculty members assume that participating in class discussion is a 4 necessary part of successful performance. Yet speaking in a classroom is more congenial to boys' language experience than to girls', since it entails putting oneself forward in front of a large group of people, many of whom are strangers and at least one of whom is sure to judge speakers' knowledge and intelligence by their verbal display.

5   Another aspect of many classrooms that makes them more hospitable to most men than to most women is the use of debate-like formats as a learning tool. Our educational system, as Walter Ong argues persuasively in his book *Fighting for Life* (Cornell University Press, 1981), is fundamentally male in that the pursuit of knowledge is believed to be achieved by ritual opposition: public display followed by argument and challenge. Father Ong demonstrates that ritual opposition—what he calls "adversativeness" or "agonism"—is fundamental to the way most males approach almost any activity. (Consider, for example, the little boy who shows he likes a little girl by pulling her braids and shoving her.) But ritual opposition is antithetical to the way most females learn and like to interact. It is not that females don't fight, but that they don't fight for fun. They don't *ritualize* opposition.

6   Anthropologists working in widely disparate parts of the world have found contrasting verbal rituals for women and men. Women in completely unrelated cultures (for example, Greece and Bali) engage in ritual laments: spontaneously produced rhyming couplets that express their pain, for example, over the loss of loved ones. Men do not take part in laments. They have their own, very different verbal ritual: a contest, a war of words in which they vie with each other to devise clever insults.

7   When discussing these phenomena with a colleague, I commented that I see these two styles in American conversation: Many women bond by talking about troubles, and many men bond by exchanging playful insults and put-downs, and other sorts of verbal sparring. He exclaimed: "I never thought of this, but that's the way I teach: I have students read an article, and then I invite them to tear it apart. After we've torn it to shreds, we talk about how to build a better model."

8   This contrasts sharply with the way I teach: I open the discussion of readings by asking, "What did you find useful in this? What can we use in our own theory building and our own methods?" I note what I see as weaknesses in the author's approach, but I also point out that the writer's discipline and purposes might be different from ours. Finally, I offer personal anecdotes illustrating the phenomena under discussion and praise students' anecdotes as well as their critical acumen.

9   These different teaching styles must make our classrooms wildly different places and hospitable to different students. Male students are more likely to be comfortable attacking the readings and might find the inclusion of personal anecdotes irrelevant and "soft." Women are more likely to resist

discussion they perceive as hostile, and, indeed, it is women in my classes who are most likely to offer personal anecdotes.

A colleague who read my book commented that he had always taken for   10
granted that the best way to deal with students' comments is to challenge them; this, he felt it was self-evident, sharpens their minds and helps them develop debating skills. But he had noticed that women were relatively silent in his classes, so he decided to try beginning discussion with relatively open-ended questions and letting comments go unchallenged. He found, to his amazement and satisfaction, that more women began to speak up.

Though some women in his class clearly liked this better, perhaps   11
some of the men liked it less. One young man in my class wrote in a questionnaire about a history professor who gave students questions to think about and called on people to answer them: "He would then play devil's advocate . . . *i.e.*, he debated us. . . . That class *really* sharpened me intellectually. . . . We as students do need to know how to defend ourselves." This young man valued the experience of being attacked and challenged publicly. Many, if not most, women would shrink from such "challenge," experiencing it as public humiliation.

A professor at Hamilton College told me of a young man who was   12
upset because he felt his class presentation had been a failure. The professor was puzzled because he had observed that class members had listened attentively and agreed with the student's observations. It turned out that it was this very agreement that the student interpreted as failure: Since no one had engaged his ideas by arguing with him, he felt they had found them unworthy of attention.

So one reason men speak in class more than women is that many of   13
them find the "public" classroom setting more conducive to speaking, whereas most women are more comfortable speaking in private to a small group of people they know well. A second reason is that men are more likely to be comfortable with the debate-like form that discussion may take. Yet another reason is the different attitudes toward speaking in class that typify women and men.

Students who speak frequently in class, many of whom are men, as-   14
sume that it is their job to think of contributions and try to get the floor to express them. But many women monitor their participation not only to get the floor but to avoid getting it. Women students in my class tell me that if they have spoken up once or twice, they hold back for the rest of the class because they don't want to dominate. If they have spoken a lot one week, they will remain silent the next. These different ethics of participation are, of course, unstated, so those who speak freely assume that those who remain silent have nothing to say, and those who are reining themselves in assume that the big talkers are selfish and hoggish.

15   When I looked around my classes, I could see these differing ethics and habits at work. For example, my graduate class in analyzing conversation had 20 students, 11 women and 9 men. Of the men, four were foreign students: two Japanese, one Chinese, and one Syrian. With the exception of the three Asian men, all the men spoke in class at least occasionally. The biggest talker in the class was a woman, but there were also five women who never spoke at all, only one of whom was Japanese. I decided to try something different.

16   I broke the class into small groups to discuss the issues raised in the readings and to analyze their own conversational transcripts. I devised three ways of dividing the students into groups: one by the degree program they were in, one by gender, and one by conversational style, as closely as I could guess it. This meant that when the class was grouped according to conversational style, I put Asian students together, fast talkers together, and quiet students together. The class split into groups six times during the semester, so they met in each grouping twice. I told students to regard the groups as examples of interactional data and to note the different ways they participated in different groups. Toward the end of the term, I gave them a questionnaire asking about their class and group participation.

17   I could see plainly from my observation of the groups at work that women who never opened their mouths in class were talking away in the small groups. In fact, the Japanese woman commented that she found it particularly hard to contribute to the all-woman group she was in because "I was overwhelmed by how talkative the female students were in the female-only group." This is particularly revealing because it highlights that the same person who can be "oppressed" into silence in one context can become the talkative "oppressor" in another. No one's conversational style is absolute; everyone's style changes in response to the context and others' styles.

18   Some of the students (seven) said that they preferred the same-gender groups; others preferred the same-style groups. In answer to the question "Would you have liked to speak in class more than you did?" six of the seven who said Yes were women; the one man was Japanese. Most startlingly, this response did not come only from quiet women; it came from women who had indicated they had spoken in class never, rarely, sometimes, and often. Of the 11 students who said the amount they had spoken was fine, 7 were men. Of the four women who checked "fine," two added qualifications indicating it wasn't completely fine: One wrote in "maybe more," and one wrote, "I have an urge to participate but often feel I should have something more interesting/relevant/wonderful/intelligent to say!!"

19   I counted my experiment a success. Everyone in the class found the small groups interesting, and no one indicated he or she would have preferred that the class not break into groups. Perhaps most instructive, however, was the fact that the experience of breaking into groups, and of talking about participation in class, raised everyone's awareness about

classroom participation. After we had talked about it, some of the quietest women in the class made a few voluntary contributions, though sometimes I had to insure their participation by interrupting the students who were exuberantly speaking out.

Americans are often proud that they discount the significance of cultural differences: "We are all individuals," many people boast. Ignoring such issues as gender and ethnicity becomes a source of pride: "I treat everyone the same." But treating people the same is not equal treatment if they are not the same.   20

The classroom is a different environment for those who feel comfortable putting themselves forward in a group than it is for those who find the prospect of doing so chastening, or even terrifying. When a professor asks, "Are there any questions?," students who can formulate statements the fastest have the greatest opportunity to respond. Those who need significant time to do so have not really been given a chance at all, since by the time they are ready to speak, someone else has the floor.   21

In a class where some students speak out without raising hands, those who feel they must raise their hands and wait to be recognized do not have equal opportunity to speak. Telling them to feel free to jump in will not make them feel free; one's sense of timing, of one's rights and obligations in a classroom, are automatic, learned over years of interaction. They may be changed over time, with motivation and effort, but they cannot be changed on the spot. And everyone assumes his or her own way is best. When I asked my students how the class could be changed to make it easier for them to speak more, the most talkative woman said she would prefer it if no one had to raise hands, and a foreign student said he wished people would raise their hands and wait to be recognized.   22

My experience in this class has convinced me that small-group interaction should be part of any class that is not a small seminar. I also am convinced that having the students become observers of their own interaction is a crucial part of their education. Talking about ways of talking in class makes students aware that their ways of talking affect other students, that the motivations they impute to others may not truly reflect others' motives, and that the behaviors they assume to be self-evidently right are not universal norms.   23

The goal of complete equal opportunity in class may not be attainable, but realizing that one monolithic classroom-participation structure is not equal opportunity is itself a powerful motivation to find more-diverse methods to serve diverse students—and every classroom is diverse.   24

Content

1. In your experience, are boys (more often than girls) "expected to use language to seize center stage: by exhibiting their skill, displaying their knowledge, and

challenging and resisting challenges" (¶ 3)? How does this translate into class-room performance (¶s 4, 7)? In your experience, is Walter Ong's claim true that "ritual opposition . . . is fundamental to the way most males approach almost any activity" (¶ 5)?

2. "Treating people the same is not equal treatment if they are not the same" (¶ 20). Explain how this idea applies in a classroom.

3. Does Tannen equate student talkativeness in class with an inquiring mind? With intelligent preparation? If so, is she justified in equating the two? Or does she base her equation exclusively on gender?

4. Does Tannen argue that the differences between men's and women's commu-nication styles are biologically or culturally determined? Explain your answer.

Strategies/Structures

5. Tannen's article follows the format of physical science and social research: state-ment of the problem, review of the literature, identification of research methodology, explanation of the research procedure, interpretation of the research findings, and generalizations to other situations or recommendations for either further research or practical applications or both. Show where each stage occurs in this article.

Language

6. "No one's conversational style is absolute; everyone's style changes in response to the context and others' styles" (¶ 17). Explain, with reference to your own expe-rience and other students' behavior in your classes—and out.

For Writing

7. If you go to a co-ed school, do some primary investigation to replicate Tannen's observation that "when young women sit next to [presumably she means *share the same classroom*, not necessarily *sit in immediate proximity to*] young men in class-rooms, the males talk more" (¶ 2). Is this true in any or all of your classes? Typically, do men speak more than women in classes taught by men? Do women speak more or less than men in classes taught by women? Do the ages and life experiences of men and women influence the extent of their class participation? Generalize from your findings and interpret them with regard to Tannen's findings. Do you think the men and women students at your school are typical of students at all American col-leges or only at colleges of the type that yours represents (private or public com-munity college, four-year undergraduate school, research university)?

8. Do you agree with Tannen's conclusion that "small-group interaction should be part of any class that is not a small seminar" (¶ 23)? If so, why? If not, why not? What demands does this format place on the students? What does this format imply about the way we learn?

9. Write an essay about any of the Content questions. Base your essay on your own experience, and reinforce it with three interviews—one with a student of a dif-ferent gender from yours, another with a student of a different racial background, another with a student from a different socio-economic class. (To control for teach-ing style and content, all the students should be enrolled in the same course at the

same time.) To what extent are your conclusions influenced by your informants' class and ethnicity, in comparison with their gender?

10. Examine a class in which you wanted to talk more (or at all), but did not do so. Why were you more silent than you wanted to be? What in the class format—teacher's instructional style, other students' behavior, your own preparation or maturity—would have had to change in order for you to have been willing to talk more? Would you have gained more from the class if you'd been a more talkative (and hence, more active) participant?

STEWART BRAND

Brand—writer, consultant, gadfly, and futurist—founded *The Whole Earth Catalog* in the late 1960s, an award-winning compendium of book reviews, recommendations for tools, alternative energy sources, natural fibers, and personal testimonials such as, "Here are the tools" (a key word of Brand's) to make your life go better. And to make the world go better. That they're the same tools is our theory of civilization." Despite the book's counterculture orientation, Brand (born 1938) himself grew up in Rockford, Illinois, was educated at Phillips Exeter Academy and Stanford (B.S., 1960), and served in the Army, training to be a paratrooper, before a stint as a psychedelic member of Ken Kesey's Merry Pranksters. Today he lives on a houseboat in Sausalito, California; his office is in a crumbling fishing boat moored in a parking lot, flanked by two cargo containers that house his vast library.

In recent years Brand, who remains independent-minded though no longer psychedelic, has edited the *Coevolution Quarterly,* a think-tank journal that publishes a mix of left, right, and mainstream opinions; founded the WELL, a teleconference system that has become "a seminal institution of cyberspace"; and also founded Global Business Network, an organization that helps businesses and industries anticipate the future with creative innovations. One of his early predictions, for instance, was that the first e-mail system in the country would be provided not by AT&T, which had been proceeding slowly, step-by-step to figure out the optimal system, but by the Internet, which was quickly up and running and then tinkered with through a process of trial-and-error. "Written on the Wind," first published in the Library of Congress's magazine *Civilization,* "the cultural search engine," in November, 1998, addresses problems caused by rapid technological changes that make digital information "irretrievable almost as soon as it is stored."

Written on the Wind

The promise has been made: "Digital information is forever. It doesn't deteriorate and requires little in the way of material media." So said one of the chieftains of the emerging digital age, computer-chip maker Andy Grove, the head of the Intel Corporation. Another chieftain, Librarian of

Congress James H. Billington, has set about digitizing the world's largest library so that its contents can become accessible by anyone, from anywhere, forever.

2　　　But a shadow has fallen. "It is only slightly facetious," wrote RAND researcher Jeff Rothenberg in *Scientific American*, "to say that digital information lasts forever—or five years, whichever comes first."

3　　　Digitized media do have some attributes of immortality. They possess great clarity, great universality, great reliability and great economy— digital storage is already so compact and cheap it is essentially free. Many people have found themselves surprised and embarrassed by the reemergence of perfectly preserved e-mail or online newsgroup comments they wrote nonchalantly years ago and forgot about.

4　　　Yet those same people discover that they cannot revisit their own word-processor files or computerized financial records from ten years before. It turns out that what was so carefully stored was written with a now-obsolete application, in a now-obsolete operating system, on a long-vanished make of computer, using a now-antique storage medium (where do you find a drive for a 5 ¼-inch floppy disk?)

5　　　Fixing digital discontinuity sounds like exactly the kind of problem that fast-moving computer technology should be able to solve. But fast-moving computer technology is the problem: By constantly accelerating its own capabilities (making faster, cheaper, sharper tools that make ever faster, cheaper, sharper tools), the technology is just as constantly self-obsolescing. The great creator becomes the great eraser.

6　　　Behind every hot new working computer is a trail of bodies of extinct computers, extinct storage media, extinct applications, extinct files. Science fiction writer Bruce Sterling refers to our time as "the Golden Age of dead media, most of them with the working lifespan of a pack of Twinkies." On the Internet, Sterling is amassing a roll call of their once-honored personal computer names: Altair, Amiga, Amstrad, Apples I, II and III, Apple Lisa, Apricot, Atari, AT&T, Commodore, CompuPro, Cromemco, Epson, Franklin, Grid, IBM PCjr, IBM XT, Kaypro, Morrow, NEC PC-8081, North-Star, Osborne, Sinclair, Tandy, Wang, Xerox Star, Yamaha CX5M. Buried with them are whole clans of programming languages, operating systems, storage formats, and countless rotting applications in an infinite variety of mutually incompatible versions. Everything written on them was written on the wind, leaving not a trace.

7　　　Computer scientist Danny Hillis notes that we have good raw data from previous ages written on clay, on stone, on parchment and paper, but from the 1950s to the present, recorded information increasingly disappears into a digital gap. Historians will consider this a dark age. Science historians can read Galileo's technical correspondence from the 1590s but not Marvin Minsky's from the 1960s.

8　　　It's not just that file formats quickly become obsolete; the physical media themselves are short-lived. Magnetic media, such as disks and tape, lose their integrity in 5 to 10 years. Optically etched media, such as CD-ROMS, if used only once, last only 5 to 15 years before they degrade. And digital files do not degrade gracefully like analog audio tapes. When they fail, they fail utterly.

Beyond the evanescence of data formats and digital storage media lies   9
a deeper problem. Computer systems of large scale are at the core of driving corporations, public institutions, and indeed whole sectors of the economy. Over time, these gargantuan systems become dauntingly complex and unknowable, as new features are added, old bugs are worked around with layers of "patches," generations of programmers add new programming tools and styles, and portions of the system are repurposed to take on novel functions. With both respect and loathing, computer professionals call these monsters "legacy systems." Teasing a new function out of a legacy system is not done by command, but by conducting cautious alchemic experiments that, with luck, converge toward the desired outcome.

And the larger fear looms: We are in the process of building one vast   10
global computer, which could easily become The Legacy System from Hell that holds civilization hostage—the system doesn't really work; it can't be fixed; no one understands it; no one is in charge of it; it can't be lived without; and it gets worse every year.

Today's bleeding-edge technology is tomorrow's broken legacy system.   11
Commercial software is almost always written in enormous haste, at ever-accelerating market velocity; it can foresee an "upgrade path" to next year's version, but decades are outside its scope. And societies live by decades, civilizations by centuries.

Digital archivists thus join an ancient lineage of copyists and trans-   12
lators. The process, now as always, can introduce copying errors and spurious "improvements," and can lose the equivalent of volumes of Aristotle. But the practice also builds the bridge between human language eras—from Greek to Latin, to English, to whatever's next.

Archivist Howard Besser points out that digital artifacts are increas-   13
ingly complex to revive. First there is the viewing problem—a book displays itself, but the contents of a CD-ROM are invisible until opened on something. Then there's the scrambling problem—the innumerable ways that files are compressed and, increasingly, encrypted. There are interrelationship problems—hypertext or Web-site links that were active in the original, now dead ends. And translation problems occur in the way different media behave—just as a photograph of a painting is not the same experience as the painting, looking through a screen is not the same as experiencing an immersion medium, watching a game is not the same as playing it.

Gradually a set of best practices is emerging for ensuring digital   14
continuity: Use the most common file formats, avoid compression where possible, keep a log of changes to a file, employ standard metadata, make multiple copies and so forth.

15   Another approach is through core standards, like the DNA code in genes or written Chinese in Asia, readable through epochs while everything changes around and through them. The platform-independent programming language called Java boasts the motto "Write Once, Run Anywhere." One of Java's creators, Bill Joy, asserts that the language "is so well specified that if you write a simple version of Java in Java, it becomes a Rosetta Stone. Aliens, or a sufficiently smart human, could eventually figure it out because it's an implementation of itself." We'll see.

16   Exercise is always the best preserver. Major religious works are impressively persistent because each age copies, analyzes and uses them. The books live and are kept contemporary by frequent use.

17   Since digital artifacts are quickly outnumbering all possible human users, Jaron Lanier recommends employing artificial intelligences to keep the artifacts exercised through centuries of forced contemporaneity. Still, even robot users might break continuity. Most reliable of all would be a two-path strategy: To keep a digital artifact perpetually accessible, record the current version of it on a physically permanent medium, such as silicon disks microetched by Norsam Technologies in New Mexico, then go ahead and let users, robot or human, migrate the artifact through generations of versions and platforms, pausing from time to time to record the new manifestation on a Norsam disk. One path is slow, periodic and conservative; the other, fast, constant and adaptive. When the chain of use is eventually broken, it leaves a permanent record of the chain until then, so the artifact can be revived to begin the chain anew.

18   How can we invest in a future we know is structurally incapable of keeping faith with its past? The digital industries must shift from being the main source of society's ever-shortening attention span to becoming a reliable guarantor of long-term perspective. We'll know that shift has happened when programmers begin to anticipate the Year 10,000 Problem, and assign five digits instead of four to year dates. "01998" they'll write, at first frivolously, then seriously.

Content

1. "Behind every hot new working computer is a trail of bodies of extinct computers, extinct storage media, extinct applications, extinct files. . . . Everything written on them was written on the wind, leaving not a trace" (¶ 6). What does this trail of obsolescence from the past imply for the future?

2. Brand summarizes, "We are in the process of building one vast global computer, which could easily become The Legacy System from Hell that holds civilization hostage—the system doesn't really work; it can't be fixed; no one understands it; no one is in charge of it; it can't be lived without; and it gets worse every year" (¶ 10). Does the evidence Brand cites in the essay's opening (¶s 1–2), or the solutions he proposes at the end provide a reassuring solution to the problem? In your answer, draw on your own knowledge and experience to assess his evidence. What does Brand himself think ought to be done?

Strategies/Structures

3. Explain the paradox that Brand points out, "It is only slightly facetious . . . to say that digital information lasts forever—or five years, whichever comes first" (¶ 2).

4. Brand devotes twice as much space to stating the problem (¶s 1–13) as to identifying possible solutions (¶s 14–18). Does the proportioning of the space convey the message that the problems are of greater magnitude than the solutions?

5. In what ways (if any) does Brand establish his authority to write about this subject?

Language

6. Brand uses quite breezy language in discussing a problem of great seriousness. Find examples of his breezy language, and decide whether the language undercuts or reinforces his point.

7. Brand invents memorable paradoxical epigrams, "The great creator becomes the great eraser" (¶ 5). What's gained with an epigrammatic statement? What's lost?

For Writing

8. Elaborate on both halves of a paradox in the essay—or anywhere else—such as Brand's observations that "digitized media do have some attributes of immortality" while concurrently possessing the potential for great (self-) destruction.

9. Pick a current invention or discovery, such as cloning, genetic alteration, innovations in computer technology, and discuss its worst case/best case scenario.

STEPHEN JAY GOULD

Gould (born 1941) graduated from Antioch in 1963, earned a Ph.D. from Columbia in 1967, and since then was a geology professor at Harvard, where he taught paleontology, biology, and history of science until his death in 2002. He provides exceptionally clear definitions, explanations, and arguments in his writings for students, colleagues, and general readers of his columns in *Natural History*. These have been collected in several volumes, including *Ever Since Darwin* (1977); *Hen's Teeth and Horse's Toes* (1983); *Bully for Brontosaurus* (1991); *Eight Little Piggies* (1993); *Leonardo's Mountain of Clams and the Diet of Worms* (1998); and *The Lying Stones of Marrakech* (2001). Gould's scientific orientation favors the underdog, as is evident in *The Mismeasure of Man* (1981). There he reinterprets two centuries of IQ testing and other quantitative ways of determining intelligence to show how flawed measurement procedures and wrong interpretations of information invariably favored educated white Anglo-Saxon males and contributed to the oppression of everyone else. Gould has received numerous honors, including the American Book Award in Science and a MacArthur Fellowship (a "genius grant").

Gould's analysis of the qualities of great scientific essayists (T. H. Huxley, J. B. S. Haldane, P. B. Medawar) applies equally well to his own writings:

> All write about the simplest things and draw from them a universe of implications. . . . All maintain an unflinching commitment to rationality amid the soft attractions of an uncritical mysticism. . . . All demonstrate a deep commitment to the demystification of science by cutting through jargon; they show by example rather than exhortation that the most complex concepts can be rendered intelligible to everyone.

These qualities are apparent in "Evolution as Fact and Theory," originally published in *Discover* (1981), a journal of popular science. Gould uses the crucial definitions and distinctions between fact and theory as the basis for contrasting the evolutionists' scientific position with the creationists' pseudoscientific position, which he argues against in most of the rest of the essay. He contends—by means of another contrast—that " 'scientific creationism' is a self-contradictory, nonsense phrase precisely because it cannot be falsified."

Evolution as Fact and Theory

1   Kirtley Mather, who died last year at age 89, was a pillar of both science and the Christian religion in America and one of my dearest friends. The difference of half a century in our ages evaporated before our common interests. The most curious thing we shared was a battle we each fought at the same age. For Kirtley had gone to Tennessee with Clarence Darrow to testify for evolution at the Scopes trial of 1925. When I think that we are enmeshed again in the same struggle for one of the best documented, most compelling and exciting concepts in all of science, I don't know whether to laugh or cry.

2   According to idealized principles of scientific discourse, the arousal of dormant issues should reflect fresh data that give renewed life to abandoned notions. Those outside the current debate may therefore be excused for suspecting that creationists have come up with something new, or that evolutionists have generated some serious internal trouble. But nothing has changed; the creationists have not a single new fact or argument. Darrow and Bryan were at least more entertaining than we lesser antagonists today. The rise of creationism is politics, pure and simple; it represents one issue (and by no means the major concern) of the resurgent evangelical right. Arguments that seemed kooky just a decade ago have re-entered the mainstream.

Creationism Is Not Science

3   The basic attack of the creationists falls apart on two general counts before we even reach the supposed factual details of their complaints against

evolution. First, they play upon a vernacular misunderstanding of the word "theory" to convey the false impression that we evolutionists are covering up the rotten core of our edifice. Second, they misuse a popular philosophy of science to argue that they are behaving scientifically in attacking evolution. Yet the same philosophy demonstrates that their own belief is not science, and that "scientific creationism" is therefore meaningless and self-contradictory, a superb example of what Orwell called "newspeak."

In the American vernacular, "theory" often means "imperfect fact"— part of a hierarchy of confidence running downhill from fact to theory to hypothesis to guess. Thus the power of the creationist argument: evolution is "only" a theory, and intense debate now rages about many aspects of the theory. If evolution is less than a fact, and scientists can't even make up their minds about the theory, then what confidence can we have in it? Indeed, President Reagan echoed this argument before an evangelical group in Dallas when he said (in what I devoutly hope was campaign rhetoric): "Well, it is a theory. It is a scientific theory only, and it has in recent years been challenged in the world of science—that is, not believed in the scientific community to be as infallible as it once was."

Well, evolution *is* a theory. It is also a fact. And facts and theories are different things, not rungs in a hierarchy of increasing certainty. Facts are the world's data. Theories are structures of ideas that explain and interpret facts. Facts do not go away when scientists debate rival theories to explain them. Einstein's theory of gravitation replaced Newton's, but apples did not suspend themselves in mid-air pending the outcome. And human beings evolved from apelike ancestors whether they did so by Darwin's proposed mechanism or by some other, yet to be discovered.

Moreover, "fact" does not mean "absolute certainty." The final proofs of logic and mathematics flow deductively from stated premises and achieve certainty only because they are *not* about the empirical world. Evolutionists make no claim for perpetual truth, though creationists often do (and then attack us for a style of argument that they themselves favor). In science, "fact" can only mean "confirmed to such a degree that it would be perverse to withhold provisional assent." I suppose that apples might start to rise tomorrow, but the possibility does not merit equal time in physics classrooms.

Evolutionists have been clear about this distinction between fact and theory from the very beginning, if only because we have always acknowledged how far we are from completely understanding the mechanisms (theory) by which evolution (fact) occurred. Darwin continually emphasized the difference between his two great and separate accomplishments: establishing the fact of evolution, and proposing a theory—natural selection—to explain the mechanism of evolution. He wrote in *The Descent of Man*: "I had two distinct objects in view; firstly, to show that species had not been separately created, and secondly, that natural selection had been the chief agent of change . . . Hence if I have erred in . . . having exaggerated its [natural selection's] power . . . I have at least, as I hope, done good service in aiding to overthrow the dogma of separate creations."

8   Thus Darwin acknowledged the provisional nature of natural selection while affirming the fact of evolution. The fruitful theoretical debate that Darwin initiated has never ceased. From the 1940s through the 1960s, Darwin's own theory of natural selection did achieve a temporary hegemony that it never enjoyed in his lifetime. But renewed debate characterizes our decade, and, while no biologist questions the importance of natural selection, many now doubt its ubiquity. In particular, many evolutionists argue that substantial amounts of genetic change may not be subject to natural selection and may spread through populations at random. Others are challenging Darwin's linking of natural selection with gradual, imperceptible change through all intermediary degrees; they are arguing that most evolutionary events may occur far more rapidly than Darwin envisioned.

9   Scientists regard debates on fundamental issues of theory as a sign of intellectual health and a source of excitement. Science is—and how else can I say it?—most fun when it plays with interesting ideas, examines their implications, and recognizes that old information may be explained in surprisingly new ways. Evolutionary theory is now enjoying this uncommon vigor. Yet amidst all this turmoil no biologist has been led to doubt the fact that evolution occurred; we are debating *how* it happened. We are all trying to explain the same thing: the tree of evolutionary descent linking all organisms by ties of genealogy. Creationists pervert and caricature this debate by conveniently neglecting the common conviction that underlies it, and by falsely suggesting that we now doubt the very phenomenon we are struggling to understand.

10   Using another invalid argument, creationists claim that "the dogma of separate creations," as Darwin characterized it a century ago, is a scientific theory meriting equal time with evolution in high school biology curricula. But a prevailing viewpoint among philosophers of science belies this creationist argument. Philosopher Karl Popper has argued for decades that the primary criterion of science is the falsifiability of its theories. We can never prove absolutely, but we can falsify. A set of ideas that cannot, in principle, be falsified is not science.

11   The entire creationist argument involves little more than a rhetorical attempt to falsify evolution by presenting supposed contradictions among its supporters. Their brand of creationism, they claim, is "scientific" because it follows the Popperian model in trying to demolish evolution. Yet Popper's argument must apply in both directions. One does not become a scientist by the simple act of trying to falsify another scientific system; one has to present an alternative system that also meets Popper's criterion—it too must be falsifiable in principle.

12   "Scientific creationism" is a self-contradictory, nonsense phrase precisely because it cannot be falsified. I can envision observations and

experiments that would disprove any evolutionary theory I know, but I cannot imagine what potential data could lead creationists to abandon their beliefs. Unbeatable systems are dogma, not science. Lest I seem harsh or rhetorical, I quote creationism's leading intellectual, Duane Gish, Ph.D., from his recent (1978) book *Evolution? The Fossils Say No!* "By creation we mean the bringing into being by a supernatural Creator of the basic kinds of plants and animals by the process of sudden, or fiat, creation. We do not know how the Creator created, what processes He used, *for He used processes which are not now operating anywhere in the natural universe* [Gish's italics]. This is why we refer to creation as special creation. We cannot discover by scientific investigations anything about the creative processes used by the Creator." Pray tell, Dr. Gish, in the light of your last sentence, what then is "scientific" creationism?

The Fact of Evolution

Our confidence that evolution occurred centers upon three general argu-   13
ments. First, we have abundant, direct, observational evidence of evolution in action, from both the field and the laboratory. It ranges from countless experiments on change in nearly everything about fruit flies subjected to artificial selection in the laboratory to the famous British moths that turned black when industrial soot darkened the trees upon which they rest. (The moths gain protection from sharp-sighted bird predators by blending into the background.) Creationists do not deny these observations; how could they? Creationists have tightened their act. They now argue that God only created "basic kinds," and allowed for limited evolutionary meandering within them. Thus toy poodles and Great Danes come from the dog kind and moths can change color, but nature cannot convert a dog to a cat or a monkey to a man.

The second and third arguments for evolution—the case for major   14
changes—do not involve direct observation of evolution in action. They rest upon inference, but are no less secure for that reason. Major evolutionary change requires too much time for direct observation on the scale of recorded human history. All historical sciences rest upon inference, and evolution is no different from geology, cosmology, or human history in this respect. In principle, we cannot observe processes that operated in the past. We must infer them from results that still survive: living and fossil organisms for evolution, documents and artifacts for human history, strata and topography for geology.

The second argument—that the imperfection of nature reveals evo-   15
lution—strikes many people as ironic, for they feel that evolution should be most elegantly displayed in the nearly perfect adaptation expressed by some organisms—the chamber of a gull's wing, or butterflies that cannot be seen in ground litter because they mimic leaves so precisely. But perfection could be imposed by a wise creator or evolved by natural selection.

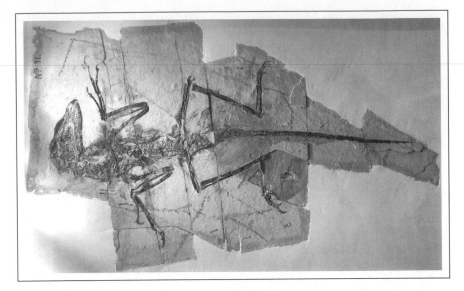

What is the significance of the downy fluff and feathers on this 130 million-year-old dinosaur skeleton? What explanation(s) would Darwin's theory reinforce? What explanation(s) would Gould's analysis address?

Perfection covers the tracks of past history. And past history—the evidence of descent—is our mark of evolution.

16   Evolution lies exposed in the *imperfections* that record a history of descent. Why should a rat run, a bat fly, a porpoise swim, and I type this essay with structures built of the same bones unless we all inherited them from a common ancestor? An engineer, starting from scratch, could design better limbs in each case. Why should all the large native mammals of Australia be marsupials, unless they descended from a common ancestor isolated on this island continent? Marsupials are not "better," or ideally suited for Australia; many have been wiped out by placental mammals imported by man from other continents. This principle of imperfection extends to all historical sciences. When we recognize the etymology of September, October, November, and December (seventh, eighth, ninth, and tenth, from the Latin), we know that two additional items (January and February) must have been added to an original calendar of ten months.

17   The third argument is more direct: transitions are often found in the fossil record. Preserved transitions are not common—and should not be, according to our understanding of evolution (see next section)—but they are not entirely wanting, as creationists often claim. The lower jaw of reptiles contains several bones, that of mammals only one. The non-mammalian jawbones are reduced, step by step, in mammalian ancestors until they become tiny nubbins located at the back of the jaw. The "hammer" and

"anvil" bones of the mammalian ear are descendants of these nubbins. How could such a transition be accomplished? the creationists ask. Surely a bone is either entirely in the jaw or in the ear. Yet paleontologists have discovered two transitional lineages or therapsids (the so-called mammal-like reptiles) with a double jaw joint—one composed of the old quadrate and articular bones (soon to become the hammer and anvil), the other of the squamosal and dentary bones (as in modern mammals). For that matter, what better transitional form could we desire than the oldest human, *Australopithecus afarensis*, with its apelike palate, its human upright stance, and a cranial capacity larger than any ape's of the same body size but a full 1,000 cubic centimeters below ours? If God made each of the half dozen human species discovered in ancient rocks, why did he create in an unbroken temporal sequence of progressively more modern features—increasing cranial capacity, reduced face and teeth, larger body size? Did he create to mimic evolution and test our faith thereby?

An Example of Creationist Argument

Faced with these facts of evolution and the philosophical bankruptcy of   18
their own position, creationists rely upon distortion and innuendo to buttress their rhetorical claim. If I should sound sharp or bitter, indeed I am—for I have become a major target of these practices.

   I count myself among the evolutionists who argue for a jerky, or epi-   19
sodic, rather than a smoothly gradual, pace of change. In 1972 my colleague Niles Eldredge and I developed the theory of punctuated equilibrium. We argued that two outstanding facts of the fossil record—geologically "sudden" origin of new species and failure to change thereafter (stasis)—reflect the predictions of evolutionary theory, not the imperfections of the fossil record. In most theories, small isolated populations are the source of new species, and the process of speciation takes thousands or tens of thousands of years. This amount of time, so long when measured against our lives, is a geological microsecond. It represents much less than 1 percent of the average life span for a fossil invertebrate species—more than 10 million years. Large, widespread, and well-established species, on the other hand, are not expected to change very much. We believe that the inertia of large populations explains the stasis of most fossil species over millions of years.

   We proposed the theory of punctuated equilibrium largely to provide   20
a different explanation for pervasive trends in the fossil record. Trends, we argued, cannot be attributed to gradual transformation within lineages, but must arise from the differential success of certain kinds of species. A trend, we argued, is more like climbing a flight of stairs (punctuations and stasis) than rolling up an inclined plane.

   Since we proposed punctuated equilibria to explain trends, it is in-   21
furiating to be quoted again and again by creationists—whether through

design or stupidity, I do not know—as admitting that the fossil record includes no transitional forms. Transitional forms are generally lacking at
the species level, but are abundant between larger groups. The evolution
from reptiles to mammals, as mentioned earlier, is well documented. Yet a
pamphlet entitled "Harvard Scientists Agree Evolution Is a Hoax" states:
"The facts of punctuated equilibrium which Gould and Eldredge . . . are
forcing Darwinists to swallow fit the picture that Bryan insisted on, and
which God has revealed to us in the Bible."

22　　　Continuing the distortion, several creationists have equated the
theory of punctuated equilibrium with a caricature of the beliefs of
Richard Goldschmidt, a great early geneticist. Goldschmidt argued, in a
famous book published in 1940, that new groups can arise all at once
through major mutations. He referred to these suddenly transformed
creatures as "hopeful monsters." (I am attracted to some aspects of the
non-caricatured version, but Goldschmidt's theory still has nothing to do
with punctuated equilibrium.) Creationist Luther Sunderland talks of the
"punctuated equilibrium hopeful monster theory" and tells his hopeful
readers that "it amounts to tacit admission that anti-evolutionists are correct in asserting there is no fossil evidence supporting the theory that all
life is connected to a common ancestor." Duane Gish writes, "According
to Goldschmidt, and now apparently according to Gould, a reptile laid
an egg from which the first bird, feathers and all, was produced." Any
evolutionist who believed such nonsense would rightly be laughed off the
intellectual stage; yet the only theory that could ever envision such a scenario for the evolution of birds is creationism—God acts in the egg.

Conclusion

23　I am both angry at and amused by the creationists; but mostly I am deeply
sad. Sad for many reasons. Sad because so many people who respond to
creationist appeals are troubled for the right reason, but venting their
anger at the wrong target. It is true that scientists have often been dogmatic
and elitist. It is true that we have often allowed the white-coated, advertising image to represent us—"Scientists say that Brand X cures bunions
ten times faster than . . ." We have not fought it adequately because we
derive benefits from appearing as a new priesthood. It is also true that
faceless bureaucratic state power intrudes more and more into our lives
and removes choices that should belong to individuals and communities.
I can understand that requiring that evolution be taught in schools might
be seen as one more insult on all these grounds. But the culprit is not, and
cannot be, evolution or any other fact of the natural world. Identify and
fight your legitimate enemies by all means, but we are not among them.

24　　　I am sad because the practical result of this brouhaha will not be expanded coverage to include creationism (that would also make me sad), but
the reduction or excision of evolution from high school curricula. Evolution

is one of the half dozen "great ideas" developed by science. It speaks to the profound issues of genealogy that fascinate all of us—the "roots" phenomenon writ large. Where did we come from? Where did life arise? How did it develop? How are organisms related? It forces us to think, ponder, and wonder. Shall we deprive millions of this knowledge and once again teach biology as a set of dull and unconnected facts, without the thread that weaves diverse material into a supple unity?

But most of all I am saddened by a trend I am just beginning to dis- 25
cern among my colleagues. I sense that some now wish to mute the healthy debate about theory that has brought new life to evolutionary biology. It provides grist for creationist mills, they say, even if only by distortion. Perhaps we should lie low and rally round the flag of strict Darwinism, at least for the moment—a kind of old-time religion on our part.

But we should borrow another metaphor and recognize that we too 26
have to tread a straight and narrow path, surrounded by roads to perdition. For if we ever begin to suppress our search to understand nature, to quench our own intellectual excitement in a misguided effort to present a united front where it does not and should not exist, then we are truly lost.

Content

1. Identify Gould's two different definitions of "theory," one scientific, the other vernacular (common, everyday) (¶s 3–4, and elsewhere). Define what he means by a "fact" (¶s 5–7). Using these definitions, explain what he means by "Well, evolution *is* a theory. It is also a fact." What differentiation does Gould make between evolution as a fact and evolution as a theory (¶s 5–7 and throughout)?

2. What does Gould mean by insisting that any set of scientific ideas must be able to be falsified? Why does he identify creationism as an "unbeatable system" that cannot be falsified?

3. "Scientists regard debates on fundamental issues of theory as a sign of intellectual health and a source of excitement," says Gould (¶ 9). Why is this so? Why is evolutionary theory so much fun, in Gould's view? Why would creationist theories stifle debate and take the "fun" out of doing science (¶s 9–12)?

Strategies/Structures

4. How does Gould use definitions in constructing his argument against creationism?

5. Using Gould's definitions, derive Gould's rules for scientific debate. Does he follow his own rules in this essay?

Language

6. Gould says, "The rise of creationism is politics, pure and simple" (¶ 2). What does he mean by this? How does politics influence the language we use?

7. How does the language we use influence our beliefs about a particular subject? In reference to this essay, you could talk about *science* and *creationism*, but there are many other possibilities for discussion.

8. Gould says, "I am both angry at and amused by the creationists; but mostly I am deeply sad" (¶ 23). Does the language Gould uses in addressing the ideas of his opponents (both creationists and fellow strict Darwinist geologists who dispute his theories and would suppress them for different reasons [¶s 23–26]) reflect any or all of these attitudes? Does he treat his opponents with courtesy? With respect?

For Writing

9. Science, like any other body of knowledge, is ever-changing. Facts can be reassessed, reinterpreted; intellectual constructs can be reconfigured—suppose someone redrew the constellations to represent great works of art instead of mythological stories. New contexts can be provided to enable new ways to understand familiar information. Select a definition of a term central to medicine, psychology, sociology, or an empirically oriented science, that has undergone major changes (*race, homosexual, family,* are among the possible terms). Trace the history of this definition to highlight the changes in the word's meaning, and explore some of the implications of the old and new definitions.

10. Judging from Gould's practice in this essay, construct a set of rules for appropriate treatment of one's opponents in an argument. (You could use your answers to Language question 8 as a point of departure.) Under what, if any, circumstances are irony, sarcasm, invective, humor suitable in referring to ideas or people with whom you disagree?

Becoming an American:
Two Contrasts for Comparison

ERIC LIU

> Liu (born 1968) grew up in Wappingers Falls, New York, near Poughkeepsie where his father, a Taiwanese immigrant, worked as an account executive at IBM until his death. His mother, also Taiwanese, is a computer programmer. After graduating from Yale in 1990, Liu worked as a legislative assistant to Senator David Boren and started a magazine of writings from people age twenty-four to thirty-two, positive views of society and politics designed to contradict the negative stereotypes of Generation X as self-centered hedonists (compiled in 1994 in *Next: Young American Writers on the New Generation*). Consequently, he became a speechwriter, first for Secretary of State Warren Christopher (1993), and then for President Bill Clinton, before entering Harvard Law School at age twenty-five.
>
> In his autobiography *The Accidental Asian: Notes of a Native Speaker* (1998), published when he was twenty-nine, Liu (pronounced LOO)

explores what it means to grow up as an Asian in America. Should he, like other children of immigrants, embrace, resist, or redefine assimilation? In "Notes of a Native Speaker" (a chapter from *The Accidental Asian*), Liu defines himself as an "accidental Asian," someone who has stumbled upon a sense of race and tries to describe it in order to define and live with it. This isn't always easy. "If Asians were shy and retiring," he says, "I'd try to be exuberant and jocular. If they were narrow-minded specialists, I'd be a well-rounded generalist." He realizes, "The irony is that in working so hard to defy stereotype, I became a slave to it. . . . I could have spared myself a great deal of heartache had I understood . . . that the choice of race is not simply 'embrace or efface.'"

Notes of a Native Speaker

1.

Here are some of the ways you could say I am "white":

> I listen to National Public Radio.
> I wear khaki Dockers.
> I own brown suede bucks.
> I eat gourmet greens.
> I have few close friends "of color."
> I married a white woman.
> I am a child of the suburbs.
> I furnish my condo à la Crate & Barrel.
> I vacation in charming bed-and-breakfasts.
> I have never once been the victim of blatant discrimination.
> I am a member of several exclusive institutions.
> I have been in the inner sanctums of political power.
> I have been there as something other than an attendant.
> I have the ambition to return.
> I am a producer of the culture.
> I expect my voice to be heard.
> I speak flawless, unaccented English.
> I subscribe to *Foreign Affairs*.
> I do not mind when editorialists write in the first person plural.
> I do not mind how white television casts are.
> I am not too ethnic.
> I am wary of minority militants.
> I consider myself neither in exile nor in opposition.
> I am considered "a credit to my race."

I never asked to be white. I am not literally white. That is, I do not have white skin or white ancestors. I have yellow skin and yellow ancestors, hundreds of generations of them. But like so many other Asian Americans

What mixture of ethnicities and cultures do this young man and woman represent? Where do you think this photograph was taken? What are they doing? What does this imply about their relationship? What evidence can you offer for your interpretations?

of the second generation, I find myself now the bearer of a strange new status: white, by acclamation. Thus it is that I have been described as an "honorary white," by other whites, and as a "banana," by other Asians. Both the honorific and the epithet take as a given this idea: to the extent that I have moved away from the periphery and toward the center of American life, I have become white inside. *Some are born white, others achieve whiteness, still others have whiteness thrust upon them.* This, supposedly, is what it means to assimilate.

2   There was a time when assimilation did quite strictly mean whitening. In fact, well into the first half of this century, mimicry of the stylized standards of the WASP gentry was the proper, dominant, perhaps even sole method of ensuring that your origins would not be held against you. You "made it" in society not only by putting on airs of anglitude, but also by assiduously bleaching out the marks of a darker, dirtier past. And this bargain, stifling as it was, was open to European immigrants almost exclusively; to blacks, only on the passing occasion; to Asians, hardly at all.

3   Times have changed, and I suppose you could call it progress that a Chinaman, too, may now aspire to whiteness. But precisely because the times have changed, that aspiration—and the *imputation* of the aspiration—now seems astonishingly outmoded. The meaning of "American" has undergone a revolution in the twenty-nine years I have been alive, a

revolution of color, class, and culture. Yet the vocabulary of "assimilation" has remained fixed all this time: fixed in whiteness, which is still our metonym for power; and fixed in shame, which is what the colored are expected to feel for embracing the power.

I have assimilated. I am of the mainstream. In many ways I fit the   4
psychological profile of the so-called banana: imitative, impressionable, rootless, eager to please. As I will admit in this essay, I have at times gone to great lengths to downplay my difference, the better to penetrate the "establishment" of the moment. Yet I'm not sure that what I did was so cut-and-dried as "becoming white." I plead guilty to the charges above: achieving, learning the ways of the upper middle class, distancing myself from radicals of any hue. But having confessed, I still do not know my crime.

To be an accused banana is to stand at the ill-fated intersection of   5
class and race. And because class is the only thing Americans have more trouble talking about than race, a minority's climb up the social ladder is often willfully misnamed and wrongly portrayed. There is usually, in the portrayal, a strong whiff of betrayal: the assimilist is a traitor to his kind, to his class, to his own family. He cannot gain the world without losing his soul. To be sure, something *is* lost in any migration, whether from place to place or from class to class. But something is gained as well. And the result is always more complicated than the monochrome language of "whiteness" and "authenticity" would suggest.

My own assimilation began long before I was born. It began with my   6
parents, who came here with an appetite for Western ways already whetted by films and books and music and, in my mother's case, by a father who'd been to the West. My parents, who traded Chinese formality for the more laissez-faire stance of this country. Who made their way by hard work and quiet adaptation. Who fashioned a comfortable life in a quiet development in a second-tier suburb. Who, unlike your "typical" Chinese parents, were not pushy, status-obsessed, rigid, disciplined, or prepared. Who were haphazard about passing down ancestral traditions and "lessons" to their children. Who did pass down, however, the sense that their children were entitled to mix and match, as they saw fit, whatever aspects of whatever cultures they encountered.

I was raised, in short, to assimilate, to claim this place as mine. I   7
don't mean that my parents told me to act like an American. That's partly the point: they didn't tell me to do anything except to be a good boy. They trusted I would find my way, and I did, following their example and navigating by the lights of the culture that encircled me like a dome. As a function of my parents' own half-conscious, half-finished acculturation, I grew up feeling that my life was Book II of an ongoing saga. Or that I was running the second leg of a relay race. *Slap!* I was out of the womb and sprinting, baton in hand. Gradually more sure of my stride, my breathing, the feel of the track beneath me. Eyes forward, never backward.

8   Today, nearly seven years after my father's death and two years after my marriage into a large white family, it is as if I have come round a bend and realized that I am no longer sure where I am running or why. My sprint slows to a trot. I scan the unfamiliar vista that is opening up. I am somewhere else now, somewhere far from the China that yielded my mother and father; far, as well, from the modest horizons I knew as a boy. I look at my limbs and realize I am no longer that boy; my gait and grasp exceed his by an order of magnitude. Now I want desperately to see my face, to see what time has marked and what it has erased. But I can find no mirror except the people who surround me. And they are mainly pale, powerful.

9   How did I end up here, standing in what seems the very seat of whiteness, gazing from the promontory of social privilege? How did I cover so much ground so quickly? What was it, in my blind journey, that I felt I should leave behind? And what *did* I leave behind? This, the jettisoning of one mode of life to send another aloft, is not only the immigrant's tale; it is the son's tale, too. By coming to America, my parents made themselves into citizens of a new country. By traveling the trajectory of an assimilist, so did I.

2.

10   As a child, I lived in a state of "amoebic bliss," to borrow the felicitous phrase of the author of *Nisei Daughter*, Monica Sone. The world was a gossamer web of wonder that began with life at home, extended to my friendships, and made the imaginary realm of daydream seem as immediate as the real. If something or someone was in my personal web of meaning, then color or station was irrelevant. I made no distinctions in fourth grade between my best friend, a black boy named Kimathi, and my next-best friend, a white boy named Charlie—other than the fact that one was number one, the other number two. I did not feel, or feel for, a seam that separated the textures of my Chinese life from those of my American life. I was not "bicultural" but omnicultural, and omnivorous, too. To my mind, I differed from others in only two ways that counted: I was a faster runner than most, and a better student. Thus did work blend happily with play, school with home, Western culture with Eastern: it was all the same to a self-confident boy who believed he'd always be at the center of his own universe.

11   As I approached adolescence, though, things shifted. Suddenly, I could no longer subsume the public world under my private concept of self. Suddenly, the public world was more complicated than just a parade of smiling teachers and a few affirming friends. Now I had to contend with the unstated, inchoate, but inescapable standards of *cool*. The essence of cool was the ability to conform. The essence of conformity was the ability to anticipate what was cool. And I wasn't so good at that. For the first time, I had found something that did not come effortlessly to me. No one had

warned me about this transition from happy amoeboid to social animal; no one had prepared me for the great labors of fitting in.

And so in three adjoining arenas—my looks, my loves, my manners— 12 I suffered a bruising adolescent education. I don't mean to overdramatize: there was, in these teenage banalities, usually something humorous and nothing particularly tragic. But in each of these realms, I came to feel I was not normal. And obtusely, I ascribed the difficulties of that age not to my age but to my color. I came to suspect that there was an order to things, an order that I, as someone Chinese, could perceive but not quite crack. I responded not by exploding in rebellion but by dedicating myself, quietly and sometimes angrily, to learning the order as best I could. I was never ashamed of being Chinese; I was, in fact, rather proud to be linked to a great civilization. But I was mad that my difference should matter now. And if it had to matter, I did not want it to defeat me.

Consider, if you will, my hair. For the first eleven years of my life, I 13 sported what was essentially the same hairstyle: a tapered bowl cut, the handiwork of my mother. For those eleven joyful years, this low-maintenance do was entirely satisfactory. But in my twelfth year, as sixth grade got under way, I became aware—gradually at first, then urgently—that bangs were no longer the look for boys. This was the year when certain early bloomers first made the height-weight-physique distribution in our class seem startlingly wide—and when I first realized that I was lingering near the bottom. It was essential that I compensate for my childlike mien by cultivating at least a patina of teenage style.

This is where my hair betrayed me. For some readers the words 14 "Chinese hair" should suffice as explanation. For the rest, particularly those who have spent all your lives with the ability to comb back, style, and part your hair *at will*, what follows should make you count your blessings. As you may recall, 1980 was a vintage year for hair that was parted straight down the middle, then feathered on each side, feathered so immaculately that the ends would meet in the back like the closed wings of angels. I dreamed of such hair. I imagined tossing my head back casually, to ease into place the one or two strands that had drifted from their positions. I dreamed of wearing the fluffy, tailored locks of the blessed.

Instead, I was cursed. My hair was straight, rigid, and wiry. Not only 15 did it fail to feather back; it would not even bend. Worse still, it grew the wrong way. That is, it all emanated from a single swirl near the rear edge of my scalp. Parting my hair in any direction except back to front, the way certain balding men stage their final retreat, was a physical impossibility. It should go without saying that this was a disaster. For the next three years, I experimented with a variety of hairstyles that ranged from the ridiculous to the sublimely bad. There was the stringy pothead look. The mushroom do. Helmet head. Bangs folded back like curtains. I enlisted a blow-dryer, a Conair set on high heat, to force my hair into stiff postures of submission. The results, though sometimes innovative, fell always far short of cool.

16   I feigned nonchalance, and no one ever said anything about it. But make no mistake: this was one of the most consuming crises of my inner life as a young teen. Though neither of my parents had ever had such troubles, I blamed this predicament squarely on my Chinese genes. And I could not abide my fate. At a time when homogeneity was the highest virtue, I felt I stood out like a pigtailed Manchu.

17   My salvation didn't come until the end of junior high, when one of my buddies, in an epiphany as we walked past the Palace of Hair Design, dared me to get my head shaved. Without hesitation, I did it—to the tearful laughter of my friends and, soon afterward, the tearful horror of my mother. Of course, I had moments of doubt the next few days as I rubbed my peach-fuzzed skull. But what I liked was this: I had managed, without losing face, to rid myself of my greatest social burden. What's more, in the eyes of some classmates, I was now a bold (if bald) iconoclast. I've worn a crew cut ever since.

18   Well-styled hair was only one part of a much larger preoccupation during the ensuing years: wooing girls. In this realm I experienced a most frustrating kind of success. I was the boy that girls always found "sweet" and "funny" and "smart" and "nice." Which, to my highly sensitive ear, sounded like "leprous." Time and again, I would charm a girl into deep friendship. Time and again, as the possibility of romance came within reach, I would smash into what I took to be a glass ceiling.

19   The girls were white, you see; such were the demographics of my school. I was Chinese. And I was convinced that this was the sole obstacle to my advancement. It made sense, did it not? I was, after all, sweet and funny and smart and nice. Hair notwithstanding, I was not unattractive, at least compared with some of the beasts who had started "going out" with girls. There was simply no other explanation. Yet I could never say this out loud: it would have been the whining of a loser. My response, then, was to secretly scorn the girls I coveted. It was *they* who were subpar, whose small-mindedness and veiled prejudice made them unworthy.

20   My response, too, was to take refuge in my talents. I made myself into a Renaissance boy, playing in the orchestra but also joining the wrestling team, winning science prizes but also editing the school paper. I thought I was defying the stereotype of the Asian American male as a one-dimensional nerd. But in the eyes of some, I suppose, I was simply another "Asian overachiever."

21   In hindsight, it's hard to know exactly how great a romantic penalty I paid for being Chinese. There may have been girls who would have had nothing to do with me on account of my race, but I never knew them. There were probably girls who, race aside, simply didn't like me. And then there were girls who liked me well enough but who also shied from the prospect of being part of an interracial couple. With so many boys out there, they probably reasoned, why take the path of greater resistance? Why risk so many status points? Why not be "just friends" with this Chinese boy?

Maybe this stigma was more imagined than real. But being an ABC   22
("American-born Chinese," as our parents called us) certainly affected me
another way. It made me feel like something of a greenhorn, a social immigrant. I wanted so greatly to be liked. And my earnestness, though en-
dearing, was not the sort of demeanor that won girls' hearts. Though I was
observant enough to notice how people talked when flirting, astute enough
to mimic the forms, I was oblivious to the subterranean levels of courtship,
blind to the more subtle rituals of "getting chicks" by spurning them. I held
the view that if you were manifestly a good person, eventually someone of
the opposite sex would do the rational thing and be smitten with you. I
was clueless. Many years would pass before I'd wise up.

3.

I recently dug up a photograph of myself from freshman year of college that   23
made me smile. I have on the wrong shoes, the wrong socks, the wrong
checkered shirt tucked the wrong way into the wrong slacks. I look like
what I was: a boy sprung from a middlebrow burg who affected a second-
hand preppiness. I look nervous. Compare that image to one from my
senior-class dinner: now I am attired in a gray tweed jacket with a green
plaid bow tie and a sensible button-down shirt, all purchased at the Yale
Co-op. I look confident, and more than a bit contrived.

What happened in between those two photographs is that I expe-   24
rienced, then overcame, what the poet Meena Alexander has called "the
shock of arrival." When I was deposited at the wrought-iron gates of my
residential college as a freshman, I felt more like an outsider than I'd
thought possible. It wasn't just that I was a small Chinese boy standing at
a grand WASP temple; nor simply that I was a hayseed neophyte puzzled
by the refinements of college style. It was *both:* color and class were all
twisted together in a double helix of felt inadequacy.

For a while I coped with the shock by retreating to a group of my   25
own kind—not fellow Asians, but fellow marginal public-school grads
who resented the rah-rah Yalies to whom everything came so effortlessly.
Aligning myself this way was bearable —I was hiding, but at least I could
place myself in a long tradition of underdog exiles at Yale. Aligning myself by race, on the other hand, would have seemed too inhibiting.

I know this doesn't make much sense. I know also that college, in the   26
multicultural era, is supposed to be where the deracinated minority youth
discovers the "person of color" inside. To a point, I did. I studied Chinese,
took an Asian American history course, a seminar on race politics. But
ultimately, college was where the unconscious habits of my adolescent
assimilation hardened into self-conscious strategy.

I still remember the moment, in the first week of school, when I came   27
upon a table in Yale Station set up by the Asian American Student Association. The upperclassman staffing the table was pleasant enough. He

certainly did not strike me as a fanatic. Yet, for some reason, I flashed immediately to a scene I'd witnessed days earlier, on the corner outside. Several Lubavitcher Jews, dressed in black, their faces bracketed by dangling side curls, were looking for fellow travelers at this busy crossroads. Their method was crude but memorable. As any vaguely Jewish-looking male walked past, the zealots would quickly approach, extend a pamphlet, and ask, "Excuse me, sir, are you Jewish?" Since most were not, and since those who were weren't about to stop, the result was a frantic, nervous, almost comical buzz all about the corner: Excuse me, are you Jewish? Are you Jewish? Excuse me. Are you Jewish?

28   I looked now at the clean-cut Korean boy at the AASA table (I think I can distinguish among Asian ethnicities as readily as those Hasidim thought they could tell Gentile from Jew), and though he had merely offered an introductory hello and was now smiling mutely at me, in the back of my mind I heard only this: *Excuse me, are you Asian? Are you Asian? Excuse me. Are you Asian?* I took one of the flyers on the table, even put my name on a mailing list, so as not to appear impolite. But I had already resolved not to be active in any Asians-only group. I thought then: I would never *choose* to be so pigeonholed.

29   This allergic sensitivity to "pigeonholing" is one of the unhappy hallmarks of the banana mentality. What does the banana fear? That is, what did *I* fear? The possibility of being mistaken for someone more Chinese. The possibility of being known only, or even primarily, for being Asian. The possibility of being written off by whites as a self-segregating ethnic clumper. These were the threats—unseen and, frankly, unsubstantiated— that I felt I should keep at bay.

30   I didn't avoid making Asian friends in college or working with Asian classmates; I simply never went out of my way to do so. This distinction seemed important—it marked, to my mind, the difference between self-hate and self-respect. That the two should have been so proximate in the first place never struck me as odd, or telling. Nor did it ever occur to me that the reasons I gave myself for dissociating from Asians as a group— that I didn't want to be part of a clique, that I didn't want to get absorbed and lose my individuality—were the very developments that marked my own assimilation. I simply hewed to my ideology of race neutrality and self-reliance. I didn't need that crutch, I told myself nervously, that crutch of racial affinity. What's more, I was vaguely insulted by the presumption that I might.

31   But again: Who was making the presumption? Who more than I was taking the mere existence of Korean volleyball leagues or Taiwanese social sets or pan-Asian student clubs to mean that *all* people of Asian descent, myself included, needed such quasi-kinship groups? And who more than I interpreted this need as infirmity, as a failure to fit in? I resented the faintly sneering way that some whites regarded Asians as an undifferentiated mass. But whose sneer, really, did I resent more than my own?

I was keenly aware of the unflattering mythologies that attach to   32
Asian Americans: that we are indelibly foreign, exotic, math and science
geeks, numbers people rather than people people, followers and not leaders, physically frail but devious and sneaky, unknowable and potentially
treacherous. These stereotypes of Asian otherness and inferiority were like
immense blocks of ice sitting before me, challenging me to chip away at
them. And I did, tirelessly. All the while, though, I was oblivious to rumors
of my *own* otherness and inferiority, rumors that rose off those blocks like
a fog, wafting into my consciousness and chilling my sense of self.

As I had done in high school, I combated the stereotypes in part by   33
trying to disprove them. If Asians were reputed to be math and science
geeks, I would be a student of history and politics. If Asians were supposed to be feeble subalterns, I'd lift weights and go to Marine officer
candidate school. If Asians were alien, I'd be ardently patriotic. If Asians
were shy and retiring, I'd try to be exuberant and jocular. If they were
narrow-minded specialists, I'd be a well-rounded generalist. If they were
perpetual outsiders, I'd join every establishment outfit I could and show
that I, too, could run with the swift.

I overstate, of course. It wasn't that I chose to do all these things with   34
no other purpose than to cut against a supposed convention. I was neither
so Pavlovian nor so calculating that I would simply remake myself into
the opposite of what people expected. I actually *liked* history, and wasn't
especially good at math. As the grandson of a military officer, I *wanted* to
see what officer candidates school would be like, and I enjoyed it, at least
once I'd finished. I am *by nature* enthusiastic and allegiant, a joiner, and a
bit of a jingo.

At the same time, I was often aware, sometimes even hopeful, that   35
others might think me "exceptional" for my race. I derived satisfaction
from being the "atypical" Asian, the only Chinese face at OCS or in this
club or that.

The irony is that in working so duteously to defy stereotype, I be-   36
came a slave to it. For to act self-consciously against Asian "tendencies" is
not to break loose from the cage of myth and legend; it is to turn the very
key that locks you inside. What spontaneity is there when the value of
every act is measured, at least in part, by its power to refute a presumption
about why you act? The *typical Asian* I imagined, and the *atypical Asian* I
imagined myself to be, were identical in this sense: neither was as much a
creature of free will as a human being ought to be.

Let me say it plainly, then: I am not proud to have had this mentality.   37
I believe I have outgrown it. And I expose it now not to justify it but to
detoxify it, to prevent its further spread.

Yet it would be misleading, I think, to suggest that my education cen-   38
tered solely on the discomfort caused by race. The fact is, when I first got
to college I felt deficient compared with people of *every* color. Part of why
I believed it so necessary to achieve was that I lacked the connections, the

wealth, the experience, the sophistication that so many of my classmates seemed to have. I didn't get the jokes or the intellectual references. I didn't have the canny attitude. So in addition to all my coursework, I began to puzzle over this, the culture of the influential class.

39   Over time, I suppose, I learned the culture. My interests and vocabulary became ever more worldly. I made my way onto what Calvin Trillin once described as the "magic escalator" of a Yale education. Extracurriculars opened the door to an alumni internship, which brought me to Capitol Hill, which led to a job and a life in Washington after commencement. Gradually, very gradually, I found that I was not so much of an outsider anymore. I found that by almost any standard, but particularly by the standards of my younger self, I was actually beginning to "make it."

40   It has taken me until now, however, to appraise the thoughts and acts of that younger self. I can see now that the straitening path I took was not the only or even the best path. For while it may be possible to transcend race, *it is not always necessary to try.* And while racial identity is sometimes a shackle, it is not *only* a shackle. I could have spared myself a great deal of heartache had I understood this earlier, that the choice of race is not simply "embrace or efface."

41   I wonder sometimes how I would have turned out had I been, from the start, more comfortable in my own skin. What did I miss by distancing myself from race? What friendships did I forgo, what self-knowledge did I defer? Had certain accidents of privilege been accidents of privation or exclusion, I might well have developed a different view of the world. But I do not know just how my view would have differed.

42   What I know is that through all those years of shadow-dancing with my identity, something happened, something that had only partially to do with color. By the time I left Yale I was no longer the scared boy of that freshman photo. I had become more sure of myself and of my place—sure enough, indeed, to perceive the folly of my fears. And in the years since, I have assumed as sense of expectation, of access and *belonging,* that my younger self could scarcely have imagined. All this happened incrementally. There was no clear tipping point, no obvious moment of mutation. The shock of arrival, it would seem, is simply that I arrived.

[Suggestions for reading and writing about this essay are combined with those pertaining to Esmeralda Santiago's "Race . . . Other" and appear on pages 423–24.]

ESMERALDA SANTIAGO

Santiago (born 1948) in San Juan, Puerto Rico, earned an A.B. from Harvard (1976) and a M.F.A. from Sarah Lawrence. Santiago's works, which often examine cross-cultural conflicts, include *When I Was Puerto Rican* (memoir,

1993), *American Dream* (novel, 1996), and *Almost a Woman* (memoir, 1998). Santiago details such conflicts when she notes, "I was told I was no longer Puerto Rican because my Spanish was rusty, my gaze too direct, my personality too assertive. . . . Yet in the United States, my darkness, my accented speech, my frequent lapses into confused silence between English and Spanish identified me as foreign, non-American. In writing [*When I Was Puerto Rican*] I wanted to get back to that feeling of Puertoricanness I had before I came here." She has also written screenplays (*Beverly Hills Supper Club*, 1980, and *Button, Button,* 1982) and short stories.

In "Race . . . Other" (which originally appeared in *Almost a Woman*) Santiago compares her old life in Puerto Rico with her new life in New York, highlighting the contrasts between the two. As she becomes "Americanized" her ideas and desires change, as do her relationships with her family members: "I wanted a different life from the one I had. I wanted my own bed in my own room. I wanted to be able to take a bath without having to shoo the whole family out of the kitchen."

Race . . . Other

"I don't know what's with you," Mami muttered as we walked back to   1
Ellery Street. "You've changed."

I hugged the plastic bag with my yellow dress. "I'm getting older,   2
Mami." I chuckled, to make light of it, so she wouldn't accuse me of talking back.

"Older, yes," she continued, unappeased. "And stubborn, and dis-   3
respectful." She looked at me from the corner of her eye. "Don't think just because you're going to that school for *blanquitos* I'm going to put up with any *pocavergüenzas* from you." She turned the corner, and I dawdled after, trapped between thoughts.

When Mami and I went to the welfare or unemployment office, a   4
box in the forms asked us to identify our race: White, Black, Other. Technically, Mami was white. Her skin was creamy beige, lacked the warm brown tones her children with Papi had inherited. My memory of my paternal grandparents was that they were white, but Papi and some of his sisters and brothers were dark brown, evoking a not-too-distant African ancestor. Franky, Mami's son with Francisco, was lighter-skinned than the seven older brothers and sisters. He had his father's pale complexion, dark eyes and hair.

When I had to indicate my race, I always marked "Other," because   5
neither black nor white was appropriate. Pretending to be white when I was clearly not was wrong. If I could "pass," which I couldn't, there was always the question Puerto Ricans asked when someone became too arrogant about the value of their white skin: "*Y tu abuela, ¿donde está?*" Asking "Where is your grandmother?" implied that in Puerto Rico no one really knew the total racial picture and claims of racial purity were suspect.

6   I was not oblivious to race in Puerto Rico. I'd noticed that white skin was coveted by those who didn't have it and that those who did looked down on those who didn't. Light-skinned babies in a family were doted on more than dark ones. "Good" hair was straight, not kinky, and much more desirable than the tightly coiled strands of "bad" hair, which at its tightest was called *pasitas,* raisins. Blue or green eyes proclaimed whiteness, even when surrounded by dark skin.

7   I was neither black nor white; I was *trigueña,* wheat-colored. I had "good" hair, and my features were neither African nor European but a combination of both. In Puerto Rican schools I had not stood out because of the color of my skin or my features. I never had either the darkest or the lightest skin in a room. But when we lived in the city, I was teased for being a *jíbara* from the country. When in the country, my city experience made me suspicious to others.

8   At junior high schools 49 and 33 in Brooklyn, I was a recently arrived Puerto Rican in a school where most students were Puerto Rican, Italian, or black. I stood apart with the other recent arrivals because of my struggle to speak English. The few Americans in our schools, who were all white-skinned, lived and moved in their own neighborhoods and groups, closed to the rest of us.

9   When Mami accused me of wanting to go to a school for *blanquitos,* she guessed that most of the people at Performing Arts would be white and, therefore, richer than we were. In Puerto Rico, as in the United States, whiteness meant economic advantage, and when Mami talked about *los blanquitos,* she referred to people of superior social status more than to skin color.

10   The implication that I was reaching higher than I ought to by going to Performing Arts stung, but I wasn't about to defend myself to Mami. Any response to her assessment of me and what I wanted to do with my life would have confirmed her conclusions that I'd changed since we came to the United States. I had become too independent, she claimed, too bent on my own way, too demanding. All the attention around my application to Performing Arts High School had gone to my head. I had become ambitious and hard to please, always wanting more than I had or was entitled to.

11   She was right. I had changed. Some nights I lay in bed next to my sister wondering if she was changing too, if the Delsa in Brooklyn was different from the Delsa in Puerto Rico. Other than her growing ease with English, Delsa was the same high-strung, responsible, hardworking girl she'd always been. *She* wasn't applying to a high school in Manhattan. She was going to Eli Whitney to study nursing, a real profession that would bring her a good salary and steady employment. If I thought about it, none of my sisters or brothers seemed to feel the dissatisfaction with their lives that I felt.

12   I wanted a different life from the one I had. I wanted my own bed in my own room. I wanted to be able to take a bath without having to shoo the whole family out of the kitchen. I wanted books without a date due. I

wanted pretty clothes that I chose for myself. I wanted to wear makeup and do my hair and teeter on high heels. I wanted my own radio so that I could listen to La Lupe on the Spanish station or Cousin Brucie's Top 40 countdown on the American one. I wanted to be able to buy a Pepsi or a Baby Ruth any time I craved one. In Puerto Rico I hadn't wanted any of those things. In Puerto Rico, I didn't know they were within my reach. But in Brooklyn every day was filled with want, even though Mami made sure we had everything we needed. Yes, I had changed. And it wasn't for the better. Every time Mami said I had changed, it was because I'd done something wrong. I defied her, or was disrespectful, or didn't like the same things as before. When she said I had changed, she meant I was becoming Americanized, that I thought I deserved more and was better than everyone else, better than her. She looked at me resentfully, as if I had betrayed her, as if I could help who I was becoming, as if I knew.

Content

1. Why is it so important for Liu and Santiago to label and analyze their racial identity? Why is each concerned with defying the stereotypes attributed to "Asian," "white," "black"? In what ways does Santiago define herself as "Other"— or different from those with whom she comes into contact? In what ways is Liu's "otherness" different from Santiago's? Similar to hers?

2. Why is "white" the norm with which these authors (or people of any race other than white) compare their own racial status? Given the variability of white (or any) culture, what aspects of white culture does Liu claim he has assimilated? Is assimilation more a matter of class than race for Liu (see ¶s 6–7) For Santiago (see ¶s 8–12)? What traits commonly associated with race are, in these author's estimations, actually linked to social status?

3. Look up *race* in a reliable online or paper dictionary. Copy the definitions you find (remember to cite your source correctly). Think about these definitions as you answer the following questions. What markers are used to determine race? What is "racial purity" (Santiago, ¶ 5)? Liu refers to people having a "choice of race" when he says "the choice of race is not simply 'embrace or efface'" (¶ 40). Do his meanings correspond to those dictionary definitions? To Santiago's definition? In what ways do both authors complicate the idea of race?

4. Since both authors are Americans, why don't they concentrate on nationality rather than race in their self-descriptions? What does Santiago mean by the term "becoming Americanized" (¶ 12)? In what ways is Liu "American"?

Strategies/Structures

5. What kinds of comparisons and contrasts do Liu and Santiago make, either implicitly or explicitly, between Puerto Rican and Chinese cultures and the culture of the continental United States?

6. Are these authors writing primarily for themselves? For an audience of white Americans? For an audience of their racial and cultural peers? For what social and economic class? What clues in their essays reveal their intended audience?

Language

7. What does Liu mean by "assimilation" (see ¶ 1)? Is the assimilationist "a traitor to his kind, to his class, to his own family" (¶ 5)? Does Santiago share this view?

8. Liu refers to himself as an "Asian American" (¶ 1), "an 'honorary white'" (¶ 1), "a 'banana'" (¶ 1), an "Asian" (¶ 2), a "Chinaman" (¶ 3), an "assimilist" (¶ 5). Substitute Puerto Rican for Asian, as you compare Liu and Santiago. Do all of these labels fit equally well? Or are some better than others? For what purposes? Which of these are labels that only others of the same race or ethnicity can use in talking about themselves?

9. Santiago uses several terms that may not be familiar to an English-speaking audience. Which of these does she define and which does she leave it up to her audience to define? Why does she define some and not others?

For Writing

10. "How did I cover so much ground so quickly [in my quest for assimilation]?" asks Liu. "What was it, in my blind journey, that I felt I should leave behind? And what *did* I leave behind? This, the jettisoning of one mode of life to send another aloft, is not only the immigrant's tale; it is the son's tale, too" (¶ 9). Santiago's account is similar in some ways. Identify a culture (of family, gender, race, class, occupation, nationality) that helped to shape you and that to an extent you have resisted. What did you take from it and what about it did you resist? If you have made deliberate choices, on what basis did you do so? If the shaping was unavoidable, explain why this was so. If stereotyping played any role in either your acceptance or resistance, identify the stereotype and the nature of its influence.

11. Liu's list of the ways in which he is "white" (¶ 1) covers food, clothing, shelter, entertainment, affiliations, jobs, ambition, language, groups he identifies with and rejects, measures of self-esteem, and attitudes toward himself and his status. Why is he making this comparison? Make a list of the ways in which you are "white" that address these same topic areas, and other significant ones (note, for instance, that Liu omits a spiritual dimension) if you wish. In what ways are you non-white (identify these on another list). Write a paper of self-description in which you compare your list with Liu's, and show how each list defines its author. If you wish, write the paper with a classmate or friend of a different race from your own and, using the same considerations, examine the ways in which you two are similar and different in significant ways.

JENNY SPINNER

> An essayist and poet, Spinner (born 1970) attended the University of Illinois and Oxford University (England), earned a B.A. at Millikin University (1992), an M.F.A. in nonfiction writing at Pennsylvania State University (1995), and an M.A. at the University of Connecticut (1999), where she is currently completing a Ph.D. in English. Her columns, often about her

sister and her family in Illinois, have appeared in the *Washington Post*, the *Hartford Courant*, and on National Public Radio.

Spinner grew up in Decatur, Illinois, a sprawling factory town on the Central Illinois prairie. In much of her writing, Spinner returns to this setting and to the large extended family of her childhood days. The most frequently appearing "character" in her personal essays—besides herself—is her twin sister Jackie. "I use the word *character* on purpose," Spinner explains. "In many of my essays, Jackie is a true wit. Of course she's charming and funny in reality, but she's extraordinarily charming and funny in my essays. She's there to make the reader laugh, to make me look good, and in a technical sense, to act as a transition between two paragraphs.

"It is when I write seriously about her, when I try to describe our unique relationship as twins, adopted twins for that matter, that I most struggle. I was twenty-eight when I began writing "In Search of Our Past." I had been writing since I was 18. It took me ten years to find the courage to write the story of our beginning. Our relationship is so powerful, and so powerfully embedded in who I am, that I was almost afraid to touch it, as if touching it would either cheapen it or prove entirely inadequate.

"I had to remind myself, as I remind my students, that 'I am not the page.' In other words, my writing is a construction of myself, of my sister, of our relationship. I am not writing a life; I am writing *about* a life (and in writing about a life, creating a new life, in print). To that end, I cannot possibly write about our life in a single essay, or even in a book of essays. The initial drafts of "In Search of Our Past" include too much detail, too many stories, too many angles on our relationship. . . . I'd lost track of my readers—who didn't need them—and of my focus for this essay: to write about our adoption.

"When revising "In Search of Our Past," as is the case each time I write about my sister, I had to forgive myself: for not being able to write perfectly about what means most to me. In the process, I also felt relieved. After all, my readers have access only to that which I give them. I, the writer and chief engineer, remain in control of construction. My writing about my sister, and about myself, represents many choices. I choose to include some details, leave behind others. I choose to make my sister savvy and myself a bit awkward. These choices are grounded in reality, in what is true, but they remain creations I create."

❄ *In Search of Our Past*

W hen we were young, my twin sister Jackie and I shared everything. Although our childhood years were not the last we shared, they were the least divided. We had the same Baby Alives dolls that burbled slime which Grandpa Spinner once heroically ate; same Buster Browns, brown, narrow, fitted with arch supports for flat feet; same cotton dresses that barely touched the knees; same Trixie Belden books bought for us to share. And share we did: the dresser, its drawers; bathroom towels; gum sometimes; earrings, make-up, the car during high school; perfectionism, ambition and eating disorders after that. But what really mattered is that we shared the door to our bedroom, the way in, the way out, the lock that could be opened with a toothpick: one door, one way, one lock. There is little dignity in running to a room mid-tantrum, sobbing, slamming a door so hard that the second-floor windows rattle, only to turn around and find someone sitting in the middle of her bed watching you unfold.

2   It seems fitting that we shared so much of our lives together in our strawberry pink room with its strawberry walls, strawberry carpet, strawberry gingham bedspreads and curtains. What came before the pink was colorless, blank, *tabula rasa* in its purest sense, and we shared that blankness, too. Unlike our brother Tim, twenty months younger and biological child of our parents, we had no roots before birth. The first few weeks following that birth hinged on tiny, gathered bits of information. Adopted at twenty-three days old, we came into the world free of any heritage other than the one we chose for ourselves.

3   It was something we always knew: adoption. One of my earliest memories is of the two of us begging my parents to "tell the story." "Don't you ever get tired of hearing it?" my mother asked, amused. "No." No, even though there was not much to it, or to the answers we sought: A poor young woman and her husband could not afford two infants. They loved them, yes, enough to give them up—because that is what you do, when you love something more than yourself. And so, after repeated tellings, the myth of our birth evolved, out of one "lady," whom we carefully never called mother and one man who soon disappeared from the stories we told ourselves.

4   For my parents, the story actually began two years before my sister and I were born. In June 1968, three years after they were married, my mother lay in bed trying not to bleed. She was three months pregnant with their first child. Trying hard to save the baby, to go twenty-four hours without spotting, she stayed in bed for several days. On the black-and-white Zenith at the edge of the bed, she watched as Sirhan B. Sirhan shot Bobby Kennedy two thousand miles away in a Los Angeles hotel. Kennedy did not survive; neither did my parents' baby. For a long time, my sister and I celebrated quietly the death of this child. Beneath a blanket tent on one of our beds, we whispered our understanding: Had the baby lived, we would not have—at least not in the lives we knew.

5   In 1969, after four years of trying to conceive, my parents contacted Lutheran Child and Family Services—a private adoption agency affiliated with the Lutheran Church Missouri Synod. At that time, my mother's oldest sister already had three children; my father's oldest brother, two. My parents so desperately wanted to contribute a baby to the family that when their adoption counselor asked if they were willing to adopt multiple birth babies, they agreed. So rare was this possibility that the question was more formality than reality.

That reality soon reordered itself, however, when my mother re- 6
ceived a telephone call from their counselor on July 28, 1970. Would she
and my father be interested in adopting twin girls born on the fifteenth?
This phone call is the closest thing my sister and I have to a conception.
It is the moment in which the idea of us was first presented to our parents, and it is the moment we call birth. Details about the days before are
scattered and incomplete. According to information given to my parents
by the adoption agency, I had been living in a foster home in the Chicago
area since July 24. Not released until July 31, my sister (four pounds at
birth compared to my plumper five) was still in the hospital when my
mother received the counselor's phone call.

Thinking about these early days creates questions for which there are 7
few answers. We do know on July 15, 1970, at 2:08 and 2:10 P.M. we were
delivered by cesarean in the former Chicago Masonic Medical Center (now
Illinois Masonic Medical Center). Cesarean is important because it indicates a trace of permanence, a visible scar. On our birthday each year, we
imagined her, "the lady," running her fingers across that scar, feeling the
hard skin, wondering. Because of the scar, she can't forget. The hospital is
important, too, because it means a place exists, means in some building we
were there, all three of us. One year, during a visit to Chicago relatives, our
parents drove us by the Medical Center. Intimidated by the hospital's reality, we didn't ask to go inside. Behind closed eyes, I imagined pale green
walls and gray filing cabinets hiding manila folders. In those folders were
names—and a past. A few years later I ventured inside, just to see, but I
wasn't allowed on the maternity ward. A nurse told me visitors might in-
fect new mothers and babies. I paced the main lobby for an hour trying to
find something that "she" saw, too. When my parents, waiting in the car,
came in to find me, my mother tried to cheer me by buying me a pink baby
shirt that she would have bought herself had I been hers at that hospital.
Back in the car, I hid my face from her good intentions and swallowed sobs.

When I was twelve, I went searching for names and didn't find 8
them. I did discover several pages of biographical data which the adoption agency had given to my parents and which my parents chose not to
share with us—perhaps because we never asked, careful not to hurt their
feelings by reminding them that we were not biologically theirs. In the
bottom drawer of a filing cabinet, behind tax records, insurance papers
and department store bills, I found a folder marked in my dad's neat
block-letter hand: "GIRLS ADOPTION." I sat on his office floor for several minutes, unable to open the folder, the weight of my past leaning
hard against my chest. When I finally peered inside, a twenty-seven-year-
old man and a twenty-three-year-old woman stepped out to greet me,
brushing the dust from their clothes—or trying to pull it back around
them. She was tiny with dark brown hair and blue-green eyes. He was
tall, had blond hair and blue eyes. These physical details were important.
Ever since we were old enough to realize what we were doing, my sister

and I had been searching crowds for the woman who gave birth to us. At the World's Fair in Tennessee we thought we saw her, but she disappeared before we could be sure.

9   When we were younger, a number of people told us we looked like our adoptive mother, and we did. We shared her straight brown hair, cut boyishly short like hers, parted in the middle, her brown eyes and fair skin. Our father and brother, with their dark blond hair and green eyes, were their own perfect match. When required to fill out heredity worksheets during what became the dreaded genetics unit in grade- and high-school science classes, we came close, pretending our parents' and grandparents' blood was really ours, at least by association. But the widows' peaks never matched; neither did the blood. In the end, those nights we spent in our pink room filling out our biological family trees were unhappy ones, and we wondered why it never occurred to our teachers that not everyone lived by science.

10   I memorized other details in the file, adding them to the pictures in my head and measuring myself. A talented cartoonist and fiction writer, the woman graduated from college and planned to attend graduate school. The man was a college graduate, manager of a bank, dabbled in photography and art. They both swam and played tennis. The tomboy in me who loved taking pictures and writing beamed—until I read the next lines. Although they were college sweethearts and intended to marry, the man changed his mind after learning about the woman's pregnancy. "He didn't reject her but tried to help," the black ink scrawled onto my heart. "Mother felt best thing to do was give up for adoption." I realized then that my biological parents were not married, that what changed the man's mind was my sister and me. Moreover, the vision of them sharing a life together was a myth, even though my mother always referred to him as the lady's husband. Probably she gave birth, they parted and went on with their lives, trying not to remind themselves of what they had done. Probably. Nothing is sure. It was a lot to swallow at twelve, especially for someone surrounded in school and at home by a conservative religious doctrine that demanded men and women have sex only after marriage, that chastised people who ran from pregnancies. Until I was old enough to establish my own rules, make mistakes, understand, then forgive, I lived with the burden of sin. At the very least, I knew we were a mistake.

11   Near the bottom of the papers I found a physical description of Jackie and me at birth: petite feminine build, fair complexions, brown hair with blond highlights, dark blue eyes. When I shared my findings with my sister, we wondered if that description was all the woman knew. How soon did they take us away? Did she ask to hold us? Did she cry? We wondered, of course, if she now wondered, too. But most of our questions were not grounded in a dramatic fairy tale of two happy people ready to apologize and explain once discovered by their progeny. We simply wanted to color in a black hole that swallowed the beginning of our lives. "Dear Lady," I

wrote to her when I was thirteen, "Some day my sister and I will open our adoption records and find out your name. We won't try to contact you. We just want a name. We're not looking for a mother because we have one. We're looking for some answers to questions we've had for a long time, questions that might remain unanswered forever." Every year I wrote to her a version of that letter, always addressed "Dear Lady." I never put the letter in an envelope, and every year it asked fewer questions and told more about me and my sister. I wasn't bragging as much as insisting: that we turned out okay, that she would be proud.

Although the darkness surrounding our birth bothered us, my sister   12
and I never opened our adoption records, even after we turned twenty-one and were old enough to do so. The desire for name finally lost its pull. Mostly we didn't want to hurt our parents. The hole, after all, had nothing to do with them, and we had no intention of creating a new one—in their hearts. A few years ago, I ran into a childhood friend in a bar in my home-town. She had recently been hired by Lutheran Child and Family Services, and, she told me excitedly, she'd read our file. She knew our original names. Leaning close, smiling, she asked, "Do you want to know anything else?" I set my glass on the table and told her I needed a minute to think. I walked to the back of the bar, found a pay phone and called my sister. At first I thought she couldn't hear me over the juke box. Neither of us said anything for a long time. Finally I understood her silence as "no," told our friend "no" and left. Our past stayed behind in the bar, washed down by glass after glass of ordinary beer.

From the time we began attending elementary school and our class-   13
mates learned of our adoption—how, I don't remember—we knew we were different. One morning in third grade, I stood in front of a long mir-ror in the girls' bathroom alongside Karen, both of us examining our faces.

"Do you ever wonder if you look like her?" she asked.   14

"Who?" I replied, avoiding her eyes, and my own.   15

"Your mother."   16

"I do look like my mother."   17

"Really? Have you seen a picture?"   18

"No."   19

"Then how do you know?"   20

"Because I see her every day." I knew what she was asking but I was   21
determined not to let her make me feel different than she, the tall, skinny girl with long brown flapping braids who was a miniature version of her mother.

"I mean your real mother, not Mrs. Spinner," she said, turning away   22
from the mirror.

"She is my real mother."   23

"It's not the same," she said, walking away and tossing her braids.   24

Although I hated Karen then, I knew she was right. But my sister and   25
I were good at pretending.

26   Our brother Tim was not always as skilled. In angry moods, he reminded us that we did not belong as much as he did. We, too, were good at throwing an occasional "You love him better because he's yours" tantrum. Usually, however, we kept such comparisons inside. In trips to the grocery store or K Mart, Tim pushed ahead of us, pointing out boxes of cold cereal and stuffed bears he wanted. Jackie and I hung back, reluctant to ask for too much, afraid the expense would force my parents to give us back. We were eleven before we understood adoption well enough to know they couldn't return us. "Don't ask for anything," I whispered to my sister beneath a row of blonde Barbies. "Timmy can afford to, but not us."

27   One afternoon, we kneeled in front of the couch in our basement, tallying how much we had cost our parents since they brought us home. "Did you pay anything to get us?" my sister asked, nervously eyeing the lengthening expense column. "A little," my father said, buried in his own stack of bills and unaware of why she asked. In actuality, they paid $1,000 to the adoption agency and about $300 in lawyer's fees. The thought of any money at all, however, even "a little," was a shock to my sister and me who viewed the transaction as one of love—poor parents handing over their babies to richer ones. Money turned love into business. It made us bought.

28   "All things considered," I asked my father when I was older, "do you think your investment has paid off?"

29   "Of course," he laughed. It wasn't always that easy. Yet it was. The adoption story we lived was nothing like the dramas that entertained television audiences in the late 1980s, especially following the Baby M and Baby Jessica cases. For people who know nothing about it, adoption is fascinating, embarrassing or sad; for people who do, it just is. No woman ever demanded us back. We never considered going back. Our parents loved us completely, loved us as much as our brother. We also had a wonderful relationship with both sets of grandparents with whom we spent a great deal of time and considered best friends as we grew older. Only once did I feel the awkwardness of being an adopted child in my family. I had just returned home from the first three weeks of my freshman year at college—they were actually my only three weeks as I withdrew, homesick and disenchanted, a failure. I'd always made good grades and given my family reasons to be proud. Now, in the dark of my grandmother's living room, I tried to explain what went wrong. Reaching out from her chair to touch my hand, she told me, "We don't know certain things about you girls that could explain a lot. There could be ugly things in your past." Her explanation startled me. Later I realized she was right, not about why I left college, but in some sense still right. My sister and I didn't know anything beyond what we created for ourselves.

30 What we *had* created was each other. Eventually I learned there would be gaps even in what we constructed, times when I would be left alone to

make sense of the absence that thrust us into this world. Until that time, the only world I knew contained my sister and what we held together—and I could not imagine any experience outside that bond. What lay outside was nothing we could name, touch, hold onto. Nothing would belong only to me, or to her, until we moved away from one another and began to create our own lives.

Those lives remain a curious mix of fervent attachment and the desire to be individuals. We are both writers, she a journalist, I, an essayist. We both run, physically and emotionally, until exhausted. She injures herself, and hundreds of miles away, I feel her pain. I cry, and she calls to ask what's wrong. We fight tortured fights. We make up like lovers, whispering over and over, "Don't leave me," "I won't," until we are convinced that we will be okay, that no one, that nothing, can destroy us. Together, separately we live, stepping carefully from our shared past, from that dry well falling deep into the dark. 31

Content

1. As young girls, Spinner and her sister, twins adopted as infants, spent considerable time speculating on their heritage. What couldn't they take for granted, or even know, that children living with their birth parents know and accept? Why, when Spinner finally has the chance to learn her birth parents' names and other information about them (¶ 12), does she reject the opportunity?

2. Why did Spinner write this essay? What is its thesis? Is it implied or stated explicitly?

3. This essay could be interpreted from the perspective of contrasts: insiders/outsiders; people with an identifiable past/people without; people with twin siblings/people without; adoptive siblings/birth siblings living in the same family. Explain how these divisions govern what Spinner tells us about these relationships, and what she implies.

Strategies/Structures

4. Show through an analysis of "In Search of Our Past" the implicit and explicit comparisons between the lives of children living with their birth parents and of adoptive children.

5. What does Spinner choose to tell us about her adoptive parents? What sorts of information does she omit? Why?

Language

6. What's the meaning of Spinner's concluding paradox, "Together, separately we [Jenny and her twin sister] live, stepping carefully from our shared past, from that dry well falling deep into the dark" (¶ 31)? Is the essay's ending optimistic, pessimistic, realistic?

For Writing

7. What problems exist for school children who are asked to write family histories when they don't know those histories? Or when the family stories are difficult to understand or full of problems? How can teachers adjust their assignments to be sensitive to issues of individual and family heritages? Construct such an assignment, and explain why you've written it in the way you have. Elicit responses to it from your fellow students before showing it to your instructor.

8. Write an essay that explores the relations between outsiders and a particular insider group such as a family; a group united by race, religion, ethnicity, class, or immigrant status; a gang; a club, a residence-hall group, a sorority or fraternity; or people of particular geographic area whether urban, suburban, or rural, in a particular state or country. See essays by Wallace (69–74), Tan (6–12), Wiesel (38–43), Rodriguez (322–27), among others. Consider your audience to be outsiders to the group you are discussing.

Additional Topics for Writing Comparison and Contrast

(For strategies for writing comparison and contrast, see 389–90.)

1. Write an essay, full of examples, that compares and contrasts any of the following pairs:

   a. Two people with a number of relevant characteristics in common (two of your teachers, roommates, friends, relatives playing the same role—i.e., two of your sisters or brothers, two of your grandparents, a father or mother and a stepparent)

   b. Two cities or regions of the country you know well, or two neighborhoods you have lived in

   c. Two comparable historical figures with similar positions, such as two presidents, two senators, two generals, two explorers, or others

   d. Two religions or two sects or churches within the same religion

   e. Two utopian communities (real or imaginary)

   f. Two explanations or interpretations of the same scientific, economic, religious, psychological, or political phenomenon (for instance, creationism versus Darwinism; Freudian versus Skinnerian theory of behavior)

   g. The cuisine of two different countries or two or more parts of a country (Greek versus French cooking; Szechuan, Cantonese, and Peking Chinese food)

2. Write a balanced essay involving a comparison and contrast of one of the subjects below that justifies your preference for one over the other. Write for a reader who is likely to debate your choice.

   a. American-made versus foreign-made cars (specify the country and the manufacturer)

   b. The styles of two performers—musicians, actors or actresses, dancers, athletes participating in the same sport, comedians

   c. The work of two writers, painters, theater or film directors; or two (or three) works by the same writer or painter

   d. Two political parties, campaigns, or machines, past or present

   e. Two colleges or universities (or programs or sports teams within them) that you know well

   f. Two styles of friendship, courtship, marriage, or family (both may be contemporary, or you may compare and contrast past and present styles)

   g. Two academic majors, professions, or careers

   h. Life in the mainstream or on the margin (specify of which group, community, or society)

3. Write an essay, for an audience of fellow students, comparing the reality with the ideal of one of the following:

   a. Dating or courtship styles

   b. Your current job and the most satisfying job you could have

    c. Your current accomplishment in a particular area (sports, a performing art, a skill, or a level of knowledge) with what you hope to attain

    d. Friendship

    e. Parenthood

    f. Your present dwelling and your dream house

    g. The way you currently spend your leisure time and the way you'd like to spend it

    h. The present state of affairs versus the future prospects of some issue of social significance, such as world population, ecology, the control of nuclear arms, the activities and treatment of hijackers and other international terrorists, an appropriate climate for world peace

Part IV

Arguing Directly and Indirectly

Appealing to Reason: Deductive and Inductive Arguments

12

When you write persuasively you're trying to move your readers to either belief or action or both, as the Declaration of Independence (441–45; Jefferson's working draft is depicted in the photo on p. 435) reveals. You can do this through appealing to their reasons, their emotions, or their sense of ethics, as you know if you've ever tried to prove a point on an exam or change an attitude in a letter to the editor. The next section discusses appeals to emotion and ethics; here we'll concentrate on argumentation.

An argument, as we're using the term here, does not mean a knock-down confrontation over an issue: "Philadelphia is the most wonderful place in the world to live!" "No, it's not. Social snobbery has ruined the City of Brotherly Love." Nor is an argument hard-sell brainwashing that admits of no alternatives: "America—love it or leave it!" When you write an argument, however, as a reasonable writer you'll present a reasonable proposition that states what you believe ("In the twenty-first century, the United States will continue to remain the best country in the world for freedom, democracy, and the opportunity to succeed."). You'll need to offer logic, evidence, and perhaps emotional appeals, to try to convince your readers of the merits of what you say. Sometimes, but not always, you'll also argue that they should adopt a particular course of action. ("Consequently, the United States should establish an 'open door' immigration policy to enable the less fortunate to enjoy these benefits, too." Or "Consequently, the United States should severely restrict immigration, to prevent overcrowding and enable every citizen to enjoy these hard-won benefits.")

Unless you're writing an indirect argument that makes its point through satire, irony, an imagined character whose actions or life story illustrate a point (see Jonathan Swift, "A Modest Proposal," [491–99]), or some other oblique means, you'll probably want to identify the issue at hand and justify its significance early in the essay: "Mandatory drug-testing is essential for public officials with access to classified information." If it's a touchy subject, you may wish at this point to demonstrate good will toward readers likely to disagree with you by showing the basis for your common concern: "Most people would agree that it's important to protect children and adolescents from harmful influences." You could follow this by acknowledging the merits of their valid points: "And it's also true that drug abuse is currently a national crisis, and deserves immediate remedy." You'll need to follow this with an explanation of why, nevertheless, your position is better than theirs: "But mandatory drug testing for everyone would be a violation of their civil liberties, incredibly costly, and subject to abuse through misuse of the data."

There are a number of suitable ways to organize the body of your argument. If your audience is inclined to agree with much of what you say, you might want to put your strongest point first and provide the most evidence for that, before proceeding to the lesser points, arranged in order of descending importance:

1. Mandatory drug testing for everyone is unconstitutional.
   (three paragraphs)
2. Mandatory drug testing would be extremely costly, an expense grossly disproportionate to the results.
   (two paragraphs)
3. The results of mandatory drug testing would be easy to abuse—to falsify, to misreport, to misinterpret.
   (one paragraph)
4. Consequently, mandatory drug testing for everyone would cause more problems than it would solve.
   (conclusion—one paragraph)

For an antagonistic audience you could do the reverse, beginning with the points easiest to accept or agree with and concluding with the most difficult. Or you could work from the most familiar to the least familiar parts.

No matter what organizational pattern you choose, you'll need to provide supporting evidence—through specific examples, facts and figures, the opinions of experts, case histories, narratives, analogies, considerations of cause and effect. Any or all of these techniques can be employed in either *inductive* or *deductive* reasoning. Chances are that most of your arguments will proceed by induction. You might use an individual example intended as representative of the whole, as Scott Russell Sanders does in anatomizing his father's alcoholism to illustrate the alcoholic's characteristic behavior (274–86).

Or you might use a larger number of examples and apply inductive reasoning to prove a general proposition. Research scientists and detectives work this way, as do some social commentators and political theorists. Robert Reich identifies the characteristics of "The Global Elite" (461–71) and uses them both to counteract the myths that the United States is a benevolent, egalitarian society and to argue against the separatism—moral and economic secession—that upper-income Americans currently practice to dissociate themselves from responsibilities toward the rest of society.

An essay of deductive reasoning proceeds from a general proposition to a specific conclusion. The model for a deductive argument is the syllogism, a three-part sequence that begins with a major premise, is followed by a minor premise, and leads to a conclusion. Aristotle's classic example of this basic logical pattern is

Major premise: All men are mortal.
Minor premise: Socrates is a man.
Conclusion: Therefore, Socrates is mortal.

Sometimes an essay will identify all parts of the syllogism; sometimes one or more parts will be implied. In "The Declaration of Independence" (441–45), Thomas Jefferson and his coauthors explore the consequences of the explicitly stated propositions that "all men are created equal" and that, as a consequence, their "unalienable Rights" cannot be denied. Likewise, in "Uncle Sam and Aunt Samantha" (471–75) Anna Quindlen's argument offers a classic example of deductive reasoning, reinforced by the photograph (p. 473) of Cathy De La Garza, one of only seven women F-15 Air Force pilots in 1999.

> Major premise: All U.S. citizens between the ages of eighteen and twenty-five should be subject to the draft
> Minor premise: Women between the ages of eighteen and twenty-five are citizens of the United States.
> Conclusion: Therefore, women between the ages of eighteen and twenty-five should be subject to the draft.

To do otherwise is insulting to women, deeming them "lesser citizens." In "Letter from Birmingham Jail" (445–61), Martin Luther King, Jr., shown in a 1960 photograph on p. 447 on his way to an Atlanta court as a consequence of his civil rights activities, argues for the proposition that "one has a moral responsibility to disobey unjust laws" and uses a vast range of resources to demonstrate his point. He uses biblical and historical examples to explain the situation in Birmingham; illustrations from his own life and from the lives of his own children and other victims of racial segregation; and more generalized incidents of brutal treatment of "unarmed, nonviolent Negroes."

Amy Jo Keifer in "The Death of a Farm" (475–77) implies a number of fundamental principles that could be parts of syllogisms. Which of the following incorporate still other principles?

1. A family heritage has a right to be preserved.
2. Hard work should be rewarded.
3. Land is a sacred trust, to be held and treated with respect.
4. Those who love the land have a right to live on it—and to make a living from it.
5. A heritage of family possession should take precedence over a land developer's right to make money.
6. A farm, if run with appropriate intelligence and effort, should enable farmers to be self-sustaining.
7. Something is fundamentally wrong with a society that lets down small farmers in hard times
8. Something is fundamentally wrong with a society that favors big developers over small farmers.

No matter what your argumentative strategy, you will want to avoid *logical fallacies,* errors of reasoning that can lead you to the wrong conclusion. The most common logical fallacies to be aware of are the following:

- *Arguing from analogy:* Comparing only similarities between things, concepts, or situations while overlooking significant differences that might weaken the argument. "Having a standing army is just like having a loaded gun in the house. If it's around, people will want to use it."

- *Argumentation ad hominem* (from Latin, "argument to the man"): Attacking a person's ideas or opinions by discrediting him or her as a person. "Napoleon was too short to be a distinguished general." "She was seen at the Kit Kat Lounge three nights last week; she can't possibly be a good mother."
- *Argument from doubtful or unidentified authority:* Treating an unqualified, unreliable, or unidentified source as an expert on the subject at hand. "They say you can't get pregnant the first time." "'History is bunk!' said Henry Ford."
- *Begging the question:* Regarding as true from the start what you set out to prove; asserting that what is true is true. "Rapists and murderers awaiting trial shouldn't be let out on bail" assumes that the suspects have already been proven guilty, which is the point of the impending trial.
- *Arguing in a circle:* Demonstrating a premise by a conclusion and a conclusion by a premise. "People should give 10 percent of their income to charity because that is the right thing to do. Giving 10 percent of one's income to charity is the right thing to do because it is expected."
- *Either/or reasoning:* Restricting the complex aspects of a difficult problem or issue to only one of two possible solutions. "You're not getting any younger. Marry me or you'll end up single forever."
- *Hasty generalization:* Erroneously applying information or knowledge of one or a limited number of representative instances to an entire, much larger category. "Poor people on welfare cheat. Why, just yesterday I saw an SUV parked in front of the tenement at 9th and Main."
- *Non sequitur* (from the Latin, "it does not follow"): Asserting as a conclusion something that doesn't follow from the first premise or premises. "The Senator must be in cahoots with that shyster developer, Landphill. After all, they were college fraternity brothers."
- *Oversimplification:* Providing simplistic answers to complex problems. "Ban handguns and stop murderous assaults in public schools."
- *Post hoc ergo propter hoc* (from Latin, "after this, therefore because of this"): Confusing a cause with an effect and vice versa. "Bicyclists are terribly unsafe riders. They're always getting into accidents with cars." Or confusing causality with proximity: just because two events occur in sequence doesn't necessarily mean that the first caused the second. Does war cause famine, or is famine sometimes the cause of war?

After you've written a logical argument, have someone who disagrees with you read it critically to look for loopholes. Your critic's guidelines could be the same questions you might ask yourself while writing the paper, as indicated in the process strategies below. If you can satisfy yourself and a critic, you can take on the world. Or is that a logical fallacy?

STRATEGIES FOR WRITING— APPEALING TO REASON: DEDUCTIVE AND INDUCTIVE ARGUMENTS

1. Do I want to convince my audience of the truth of a particular matter? Do I want essentially to raise their consciousness of an issue? Do I want to promote a belief or refute a theory? Or do I want to move my readers to action? If action, what kind? To change their minds, attitudes, or behavior? To right a wrong, or alter a situation?
2. At the outset, do I expect my audience to agree with my ideas? To be neutral about the issues at hand? Or to be opposed to my views? Can I build into my essay responses to my readers' anticipated reactions, such as rebuttals to their possible objections? Do I know enough about my subject to be able to do this?
3. What is my strongest (and presumably most controversial) point, and where should I put it? At the beginning, if my audience agrees with my views? At the end, after a gradual build-up, for an antagonistic audience? How much development (and consequent emphasis) should each point have? Will a deductive or inductive format best express my thesis?
4. What will be my best sources of evidence? My own experience? The experiences of people I know? Common sense or common knowledge? Opinion from experts in a relevant field? Scientific evidence? Historic records? Economic, anthropological, or statistical data?
5. What tone will best reinforce my evidence? Will my audience also find this tone appealing? Convincing? Would an appropriate tone be sincere? Straightforward? Objective? Reassuring? Confident? Placating? What language can I use to most appropriately convey this tone?

THOMAS JEFFERSON

Politician, philosopher, architect, inventor, and writer, Jefferson (1743–1826) was born near Charlottesville, Virginia, and was educated at the College of William and Mary. He served as a delegate to the Continental Congress in 1775, as governor of the Commonwealth of Virginia, and as third president of the United States. With help from Benjamin Franklin and John Adams, he wrote *The Declaration of Independence* in mid-June 1776, and after further revision by the Continental Congress in Philadelphia, it was signed on July 4. Frequently called "an expression of the American mind," Jefferson's Declaration is based on his acceptance of democracy as the ideal form of government, a belief also evidenced in his refusal to sign the Constitution until the Bill of Rights was added. Jefferson died at Monticello, his home in Charlottesville, on July 4, 1826, the fiftieth anniversary of the signing of the Declaration.

The Declaration is based on a deductive argument, with the fundamental premises stated in the first sentence of the second paragraph, "We hold these truths to be self-evident. . . ." The rest of the argument follows logically—patriots among the Colonists who read this might say inevitably—from the premises of this emphatic, plainspoken document. What evidence is there in the Declaration that the British might react to it as a hot-headed manifesto, perhaps even a declaration of war? Can a cluster of colonies simply secede by fiat?

The Declaration of Independence

When in the course of human events, it becomes necessary for one people to dissolve the political bands which have connected them with another, and to assume among the Powers of the earth, the separate and equal station to which the Laws of Nature and of Nature's God entitle them, a decent respect to the opinions of mankind requires that they should declare the causes which impel them to the separation.

We hold these truths to be self-evident, that all men are created equal, that they are endowed by their Creator with certain unalienable Rights, that among these are Life, Liberty and the pursuit of Happiness. That to secure these rights, Governments are instituted among Men deriving their just powers from the consent of the governed. That whenever any Form of Government becomes destructive of these ends, it is the Right of People to alter or to abolish it, and to institute new Government, laying its foundation on such principles and organizing its powers in such form, as to them shall seem most likely to effect their Safety and Happiness. Prudence, indeed, will dictate that Governments long established should not be changed for light and transient causes; and accordingly all experience hath shown, that mankind are more disposed to suffer, while evils are sufferable, than to right themselves by abolishing the forms to which they are accustomed. But when a long train of abuses and usurpations pursuing invariably the same Object evinces a design to reduce them under absolute Despotism, it is their right, it is their duty, to throw off such government, and to provide new Guards for their future security. Such has been the patient sufferance of these Colonies; and such is now the necessity which constrains them to alter their former Systems of Government. The history of the present King of Great Britain is a history of repeated injuries and usurpations, all having in direct object the establishment of an absolute Tyranny over these States. To prove this, let Facts be submitted to a candid world.

3   He has refused his Assent to Laws, the most wholesome and necessary for the public good.

4   He had forbidden his Governors to pass Laws of immediate and pressing importance, unless suspended in their operation till his Assent should be obtained; and when so suspended, he has utterly neglected to attend them.

5   He has refused to pass other Laws for the accommodation of large districts of people, unless those people would relinquish the right of Representation in the Legislature, a right inestimable to them and formidable to tyrants only.

6   He has called together legislative bodies at places unusual, uncomfortable, and distant from the depository of their Public Records, for the sole purpose of fatiguing them into compliance with his measures.

7   He has dissolved Representative Houses repeatedly, for opposing with manly firmness his invasions on the rights of the people.

8   He has refused for a long time, after such dissolutions, to cause others to be elected; whereby the Legislative Powers, incapable of Annihilation, have returned to the People at large for their exercise; the State remaining in the mean time exposed to all the dangers of invasion from without, and convulsions within.

9   He has endeavoured to prevent the population of these States; for that purpose obstructing the Laws of Naturalization of Foreigners; refusing to pass others to encourage their migration hither, and raising the conditions of new Appropriations of Lands.

10   He has obstructed the Administration of Justice, by refusing his Assent to Laws for establishing Judiciary Powers.

11   He has made Judges dependent on his Will alone, for the tenure of their offices, and the amount and payment of their salaries.

12   He has erected a multitude of New Offices, and sent hither swarms of Officers to harass our People, and eat out their substance.

13   He has kept among us, in time of peace, Standing Armies without the Consent of our Legislature.

14   He has affected to render the Military independent of and superior to the Civil Power.

He has combined with others to subject us to jurisdictions foreign to 15
our constitution, and unacknowledged by our laws; giving his Assent to
their acts of pretended Legislation:

For quartering large bodies of armed troops among us: 16

For protecting them, by a mock Trial, from Punishment for any 17
Murders which they should commit on the Inhabitants of these States:

For cutting off our Trade with all parts of the world: 18

For imposing Taxes on us without our Consent: 19

For depriving us in many cases, of the benefits of Trial by Jury: 20

For transporting us beyond Seas to be tried for pretended offenses: 21

For abolishing the free System of English Laws in a Neighbouring 22
Province, establishing therein an Arbitrary government, and enlarging its
boundaries so as to render it at once an example and fit instrument for
introducing the same absolute rule into these Colonies:

For taking away our Charters, abolishing our most valuable Laws, 23
and altering fundamentally the Forms of our Governments:

For suspending our own Legislatures, and declaring themselves in- 24
vested with Power to legislate for us in all cases whatsoever.

He has abdicated Government here, by declaring us out of his Pro- 25
tection and waging War against us.

He has plundered our seas, ravaged our Coasts, burnt our towns and 26
destroyed the Lives of our people.

He is at this time transporting large Armies of foreign Mercenaries 27
to compleat works of death, desolation and tyranny, already begun with
circumstances of Cruelty & perfidy scarcely paralleled in the most bar-
barous ages, and totally unworthy the Head of a civilized nation.

He has constrained our fellow Citizens taken Captive on the high 28
Seas to bear Arms against their Country, to become the executioners of
their friends and Brethren, or to fall themselves by their Hands.

He has excited domestic insurrections amongst us, and has endeav- 29
oured to bring on the inhabitants of our frontiers, the merciless Indian
Savages, whose known rule of warfare, is an undistinguished destruction
of all ages, sexes and conditions.

In every stage of these Oppressions We Have Petitioned for Redress 30
in the most humble terms: Our repeated petitions have been answered
only be repeated injury. A Prince, whose character is thus marked by every
act which may define a Tyrant, is unfit to be the ruler of a free People.

Not have We been wanting in attention to our British brethren. We 31
have warned them from time to time of attempts by their legislature to
extend an unwarrantable jurisdiction over us. We have reminded them of
the circumstances of our emigration and settlement here. We have ap-
pealed to their native justice and magnanimity and we have conjured
them by the ties of our common kindred to disavow these usurpations,
which would inevitably interrupt our connections and correspondence.

They too have been deaf to the voice of justice and of consanguinity. We must, therefore acquiesce in the necessity, which denounces our Separation, and hold them, as we hold the rest of mankind, Enemies in War, in Peace Friends.

32   We, therefore, the Representatives of the United States of America, in General Congress, Assembled, appealing to the Supreme Judge of the world for the rectitude of our intentions, do, in the Name, and by Authority of the good People of these Colonies, solemnly publish and declare, That these United Colonies are, and of Right ought to be Free and Independent States; that they are Absolved from all Allegiance to the British Crown and that all political connection between them and the State of Great Britain, is and ought to be totally dissolved; and that as Free and Independent States, they have full power to levy War, conclude Peace, contract Alliances, establish Commerce, and to do all other Acts and Things which Independent States may of right do. And for the support of this Declaration, with a firm reliance on the protection of Divine Providence, we mutually pledge to each other our lives, our Fortunes and our sacred Honor.

Content

1. What are "the Laws of Nature and of Nature's God" to which Jefferson refers in paragraph 1? Why doesn't he specify what they are? Is a brief allusion to them in the first paragraph sufficient support for the fundamental premise of the second paragraph?

2. What is Jefferson's fundamental premise (¶ 2)? Does he ever prove it? Does he need to?

3. In paragraphs 3–31 the Declaration states a series of the American colonists' grievances against the British King, George III. What are some of these grievances? Can they be grouped into categories related to the "unalienable rights" Jefferson has specified at the outset, the rights to "Life, Liberty and the pursuit of Happiness"?

4. From the nature of the grievances Jefferson identifies, what ideal of government does he have in mind? Can such a government exist among colonial peoples, or only in an independent nation?

5. Is the conclusion (¶ 32) the inevitable consequence of the reasoning that precedes it? Are there any feasible alternatives?

Strategies/Structures

6. Why has Jefferson listed the grievances in the order in which they appear?

7. Is *The Declaration of Independence* written primarily for an audience of the British King and his advisors? Who else would be likely to be vitally involved?

8. Could the American colonists have expected the British simply to agree with what they said? Or is *The Declaration of Independence* in effect a declaration of war?

Language

9. What is the tone of this document? How would Jefferson have expected this tone to have affected King George III and associates? How might the same tone have affected the American patriots of 1776?

10. Look up in a good college dictionary the meanings of any problematic words, such as station (¶ 1), unalienable (¶ 2), despotism (¶ 2), usurpations (¶ 2), abdicated (¶ 25), perfidy (¶ 27), redress (¶ 30), magnanimity (¶ 31), rectitude (¶ 32).

For Writing

11. Write an essay in which you discuss the extent to which the federal government of the United States exhibits the ideals of government that Jefferson promoted in *The Declaration of Independence*.

12. Write your own "declaration of independence," in which you justify setting yourself (or yourself as a member of a particular social, occupational, economic, ethnic, or cultural group) free from an oppressor or oppressive group.

13. Is colonialism ever justified? In an essay on this issue, supplement your knowledge of history with *The Declaration of Independence*, Zitkala-Sa's excerpts from *The School Days of an Indian Girl* (218–26), and King's "Letter from Birmingham Jail" (445–61). Bear in mind that each was written from the viewpoint of considerable sympathy with oppressed people.

MARTIN LUTHER KING, JR.

"Letter from Birmingham Jail," a literary and humanitarian masterpiece, reveals why Martin Luther King, Jr. was the most influential leader of the American civil rights movement in the 1950s and 1960s, and, why, with Mahatma Gandhi, he was one of this century's most influential advocates for human rights. King was born in Atlanta in 1929, the son of a well-known Baptist clergyman, educated at Morehouse College, and ordained in his father's denomination.

A forceful and charismatic leader, Dr. King became at twenty-six a national spokesperson for the civil rights movement when in 1955 he led a successful boycott of the segregated bus system of Montgomery, Alabama. Dr. King became president of the Southern Christian Leadership Conference and led the sit-ins and demonstrations—including the 1964 march on Washington, D.C., which climaxed with his famous "I Have a Dream" speech—that helped to ensure passage of the 1964 Civil Rights Act and the Voting Rights Act of 1965. He received the Nobel Peace Prize in 1964, its youngest winner. Toward the end of his life, cut short by assassination in 1968, Dr. King was increasingly concerned with improving the rights and the lives of the nation's poor, irrespective of race, and with ending the war in Vietnam. His birthday became a national holiday in 1986.

In 1963 King wrote the letter reprinted below while imprisoned for "parading without a permit." Though ostensibly replying to eight clergymen—Protestant, Catholic, and Jewish—who feared violence in the Birmingham desegregation demonstrations, King actually intended his letter for the worldwide audience his civil rights activities commanded. Warning that America had more to fear from passive moderates ("the appalling silence of good people") than from extremists, King defended his policy of "nonviolent direct action" and explained why he was compelled to disobey "unjust laws"—supporting his argument with references to Protestant, Catholic, and Jewish examples ("Was not Jesus an extremist for love. . . ."), as well as to the painful examples of segregation in his own life.

Letter from Birmingham Jail[1]

April 16, 1963

My Dear Fellow Clergymen:

1   While confined here in the Birmingham city jail, I came across your recent statement calling my present activities "unwise and untimely." Seldom do I pause to answer criticism of my work and ideas. If I sought to answer all the criticisms that cross my desk, my secretaries would have little time for anything other than such correspondence in the course of the day, and I would have no time for constructive work. But since I feel that you are men of genuine good will and that your criticisms are sincerely set forth, I want to try to answer your statement in what I hope will be patient and reasonable terms.

2   I think I should indicate why I am here in Birmingham, since you have been influenced by the view which argues against "outsiders coming in." I have the honor of serving as president of the Southern Christian Leadership Conference, an organization operating in every southern state, with headquarters in Atlanta, Georgia. We have some eighty-five affiliated organizations across the South, and one of them is the Alabama Christian

---

[1] AUTHOR'S NOTE: This response to a published statement by eight fellow clergymen from Alabama (Bishop C. C. J. Carpenter, Bishop Joseph A. Durick, Rabbi Hilton L. Grafman, Bishop Paul Hardin, Bishop Holan B. Harmon, the Reverend George M. Murray, the Reverend Edward V. Ramage and the Reverend Earl Stallings) was composed under somewhat constricting circumstances. Begun on the margins of the newspaper in which the statement appeared while I was in jail, the letter was continued on scraps of writing paper supplied by a friendly Negro trusty, and concluded on a pad my attorneys were eventually permitted to leave me. Although the text remains in substance unaltered, I have indulged in the author's prerogative of polishing it for publication.

This photograph shows Martin Luther King, Jr. being escorted by two officers on October 25, 1960 in Atlanta, Georgia. What arguments are embedded in this picture? Compare and contrast the body language of each of the three figures.

Movement for Human Rights. Frequently we share staff, educational and financial resources with our affiliates. Several months ago the affiliate here in Birmingham asked us to be on call to engage in a nonviolent direct-action program if such were deemed necessary. We readily consented, and when the hour came we lived up to our promise. So I, along with several members of my staff, am here because I was invited here. I am here because I have organizational ties here.

But more basically, I am in Birmingham because injustice is here. 3 Just as the prophets of the eighth century B.C. left their villages and carried their "thus saith the Lord" far beyond the boundaries of their home towns, and, just as the Apostle Paul left his village of Tarsus and carried the gospel of Jesus Christ to the far corners of the Greco-Roman world, so am I compelled to carry the gospel of freedom beyond my own home town. Like Paul, I must constantly respond to the Macedonian call for aid.

Moreover, I am cognizant of the interrelatedness of all communities 4 and states. I cannot sit idly by in Atlanta and not be concerned about what happens in Birmingham. Injustice anywhere is a threat to justice everywhere. We are caught in an inescapable network of mutuality, tied in a single garment of destiny. Whatever affects one directly, affects all indirectly. Never again can we afford to live with the narrow, provincial "outside agitator" idea. Anyone who lives inside the United States can never be considered an outsider anywhere within its bounds.

5   You deplore the demonstrations taking place in Birmingham. But your statement, I am sorry to say, fails to express a similar concern for the conditions that brought about the demonstrations. I am sure that none of you would want to rest content with the superficial kind of social analysis that deals merely with effects and does not grapple with underlying causes. It is unfortunate that demonstrations are taking place in Birmingham, but it is even more unfortunate that the city's white power structure left the Negro community with no alternative.

6   In any nonviolent campaign there are four basic steps: collection of the facts to determine whether injustices exist; negotiation; self-purification; and direct action. We have gone through all these steps in Birmingham. There can be no gainsaying the fact that racial injustice engulfs this community. Birmingham is probably the most thoroughly segregated city in the United States. An ugly record of brutality is widely known. Negroes have experienced grossly unjust treatment in the courts. There have been more unsolved bombings of Negro homes and churches in Birmingham than in any other city in the nation. These are the hard brutal facts of the case. On the basis of these conditions, Negro leaders sought to negotiate with the city fathers. But the latter consistently refused to engage in good-faith negotiation.

7   Then, last September, came the opportunity to talk with leaders of Birmingham's economic community. In the course of the negotiations, certain promises were made by the merchants—for example, to remove the stores' humiliating racial signs. On the basis of these promises, the Reverend Fred Shuttlesworth and the leaders of the Alabama Christian Movement for Human Rights agreed to a moratorium on all demonstrations. As the weeks and months went by, we realized that we were the victims of a broken promise. A few signs, briefly removed, returned; the others remained.

8   As in so many past experiences, our hopes had been blasted, and the shadow of deep disappointment settled upon us. We had no alternative except to prepare for direct action, whereby we would present our very bodies as a means of laying our case before the conscience of the local and the national community. Mindful of the difficulties involved, we decided to undertake a process of self-purification. We began a series of workshops on nonviolence, and we repeatedly asked ourselves: "Are you able to accept blows without retaliating?" "Are you able to endure the ordeal of jail?" We decided to schedule our direct-action program for the Easter season, realizing that except for Christmas, this is the main shopping period of the year. Knowing that a strong economic-withdrawal program would be the by-product of direct action, we felt that this would be the best time to bring pressure to bear on the merchants for the needed change.

9   Then it occurred to us that Birmingham's mayoralty election was coming up in March, and we speedily decided to postpone action until after election day. When we discovered that the Commissioner of Public Safety, Eugene "Bull" Connor, had piled up enough votes to be in the run-off, we

decided again to postpone action until the day after the run-off so that the demonstrations could not be used to cloud the issues. Like many others, we waited to see Mr. Connor defeated, and to this end we endured postponement after postponement. Having aided in this community need, we felt that our direct-action program could be delayed no longer.

You may well ask: "Why direct action? Why sit-ins, marches and so forth? Isn't negotiation a better path?" You are quite right in calling for negotiation. Indeed this is the very purpose of direct action. Nonviolent direct action seeks to create such a crisis and foster such a tension that a community which has constantly refused to negotiate is forced to confront the issue. It seeks so to dramatize the issue that it can no longer be ignored. My citing the creation of tension as part of the work of the nonviolent-resister may sound rather shocking. But I must confess that I am not afraid of the word "tension." I have earnestly opposed violent tension, but there is a type of nonviolent tension which is necessary for growth. Just as Socrates felt that it was necessary to create a tension in the mind so that individuals could rise from the bondage of myths and half-truths to the unfettered realm of creative analysis and objective appraisal, so must we see the need for nonviolent gadflies to create the kind of tension in society that will help men rise from the dark depths of prejudice and racism to the majestic heights of understanding and brotherhood.

The purpose of our direct-action program is to create a situation so crisis-packed that it will inevitably open the door to negotiation. I therefore concur with you in your call for negotiation. Too long has our beloved Southland been bogged down in a tragic effort to live in monologue rather than dialogue.

One of the basic points in your statement is that the action that I and my associates have taken in Birmingham is untimely. Some have asked: "Why didn't you give the new city administration time to act?" The only answer that I can give to this query is that the new Birmingham administration must be prodded about as much as the outgoing one, before it will act. We are sadly mistaken if we feel that the election of Albert Boutwell as mayor will bring the millennium to Birmingham. While Mr. Boutwell is a much more gentle person than Mr. Connor, they are both segregationists, dedicated to maintenance of the status quo. I have hope that Mr. Boutwell will be reasonable enough to see the futility of massive resistance to desegregation. But he will not see this without pressure from devotees of civil rights. My friends, I must say to you that we have not made a single gain in civil rights without determined legal and nonviolent pressure. Lamentably, it is an historical fact that privileged groups seldom give up their privileges voluntarily. Individuals may see the moral light and voluntarily give up their unjust posture; but, as Reinhold Niebuhr has reminded us, groups tend to be more immoral than individuals.

We know through painful experience that freedom is never voluntarily given by the oppressor; it must be demanded by the oppressed. Frankly,

I have yet to engage in a direct-action campaign that was "well-timed" in the view of those who have not suffered unduly from the disease of segregation. For years now I have heard the word "Wait!" It rings in the ear of every Negro with piercing familiarity. This "Wait" has almost always meant "Never." We must come to see, with one of our distinguished jurists, that "justice too long delayed is justice denied."

14   We have waited for more than 340 years for our constitutional and Godgiven rights. The nations of Asia and Africa are moving with jetlike speed toward gaining political independence, but we still creep at horse-and-buggy pace toward gaining a cup of coffee at a lunch counter. Perhaps it is easy for those who have never felt the stinging darts of segregation to say, "Wait." But when you have seen vicious mobs lynch your mothers and fathers at will and drown your sisters and brothers at whim; when you have seen hate-filled policemen curse, kick and even kill your black brothers and sisters; when you see the vast majority of your twenty million Negro brothers smothering in an airtight cage of poverty in the midst of an affluent society; when you suddenly find your tongue twisted and your speech stammering as you seek to explain to your six-year-old daughter why she can't go to the public amusement park that has just been advertised on television, and see tears welling up in her eyes when she is told that Funtown is closed to colored children, and see ominous clouds of inferiority beginning to form in her little mental sky, and see her beginning to distort her personality by developing an unconscious bitterness toward white people; when you have to concoct an answer for a five-year-old son who is asking: "Daddy, why do white people treat colored people so mean?"; when you take a cross-country drive and find it necessary to sleep night after night in the uncomfortable corners of your automobile because no motel will accept you; when you are humiliated day in and day out by nagging signs reading "white" and "colored"; when your first name becomes "nigger," your middle name becomes "boy" (however old you are) and your last name becomes "John," and your wife and mother are never given the respected title "Mrs."; when you are harried by day and haunted by night by the fact that you are a Negro, living constantly at tiptoe stance, never quite knowing what to expect next, and are plagued with inner fears and outer resentments; when you are forever fighting a degenerating sense of "nobodiness"—then you will understand why we find it difficult to wait. There comes a time when the cup of endurance runs over, and men are no longer willing to be plunged into the abyss of despair. I hope, sirs, you can understand our legitimate and unavoidable impatience.

15   You express a great deal of anxiety over our willingness to break laws. This is certainly a legitimate concern. Since we so diligently urge people to obey the Supreme Court's decision of 1954 outlawing segregation in the public schools, at first glance it may seem rather paradoxical for us consciously to break laws. One may well ask: "How can you advocate breaking some laws and obeying others?" The answer lies in the fact that there

are two types of laws: just and unjust. I would be the first to advocate obeying just laws. One has not only a legal but a moral responsibility to obey
just laws. Conversely, one has a moral responsibility to disobey unjust
laws. I would agree with St. Augustine that "an unjust law is no law at all."

Now, what is the difference between the two? How does one deter- 16
mine whether a law is just or unjust? A just law is a man-made code that
squares with the moral law or the law of God. An unjust law is a code that
is out of harmony with the moral law. To put it in the terms of St. Thomas
Aquinas: An unjust law is a human law that is not rooted in eternal law and
natural law. Any law that uplifts human personality is just. Any law that
degrades human personality is unjust. All segregation statutes are unjust
because segregation distorts the soul and damages the personality. It gives
the segregator a false sense of superiority and the segregated a false sense
of inferiority. Segregation, to use the terminology of the Jewish philosopher
Martin Buber, substitutes an "I-it" relationship for an "I-thou" relationship
and ends up relegating persons to the status of things. Hence segregation
is not only politically, economically and sociologically unsound, it is
morally wrong and sinful. Paul Tillich has said that sin is separation. Is not
segregation an existential expression of man's tragic separation, his awful
estrangement, his terrible sinfulness? Thus it is that I can urge men to obey
the 1954 decision of the Supreme Court, for it is morally right; and I can
urge them to disobey segregation ordinances, for they are morally wrong.

Let us consider a more concrete example of just and unjust laws. An 17
unjust law is a code that a numerical or power majority group compels a
minority group to obey but does not make binding on itself. This is *difference* made legal. By the same token, a just law is a code that a majority
compels a minority to follow and that it is willing to follow itself. This is
sameness made legal.

Let me give another explanation. A law is unjust if it is inflicted on a 18
minority that, as a result of being denied the right to vote, had no part in
enacting or devising the law. Who can say that the legislature of Alabama
which set up that state's segregation laws was democratically elected?
Throughout Alabama all sorts of devious methods are used to prevent
Negroes from becoming registered voters, and there are some counties in
which even though Negroes constitute a majority of the population, not a
single Negro is registered. Can any law enacted under such circumstances
be considered democratically structured?

Sometimes a law is just on its face and unjust in its application. For 19
instance, I have been arrested on a charge of parading without a permit.
Now, there is nothing wrong in having an ordinance which requires a permit for a parade. But such an ordinance becomes unjust when it is used to
maintain segregation and to deny citizens the First-Amendment privilege
of peaceful assembly and protest.

I hope you are able to see the distinction I am trying to point out. In 20
no sense do I advocate evading or defying the law, as would the rabid

segregationist. That would lead to anarchy. One who breaks an unjust law must do so openly, lovingly, and with a willingness to accept the penalty. I submit that an individual who breaks a law that conscience tells him is unjust, and who willingly accepts the penalty of imprisonment in order to arouse the conscience of the community over its injustice, is in reality expressing the highest respect for the law.

21   Of course, there is nothing new about this kind of civil disobedience. It was evidenced sublimely in the refusal of Shadrach, Meshach and Abednego to obey the laws of Nebuchadnezzar, on the ground that a higher moral law was at stake. It was practiced superbly by the early Christians, who were willing to face hungry lions and the excruciating pain of chopping blocks rather than submit to certain unjust laws of the Roman Empire. To a degree, academic freedom is a reality today because Socrates practiced civil disobedience. In our own nation, the Boston Tea Party represented a massive act of civil disobedience.

22   We should never forget that everything Adolf Hitler did in Germany was "legal" and everything the Hungarian freedom fighters did in Hungary was "illegal." It was "illegal" to aid and comfort a Jew in Hitler's Germany. Even so, I am sure that, had I lived in Germany at the time, I would have aided and comforted my Jewish brothers. If today I lived in a Communist country where certain principles dear to the Christian faith are suppressed, I would openly advocate disobeying that country's anti-religious laws.

23   I must make two honest confessions to you, my Christian and Jewish brothers. First, I must confess that over the past few years I have been gravely disappointed with the white moderate. I have almost reached the regrettable conclusion that the Negro's great stumbling block in his stride toward freedom is not the White Citizen's Counciler or the Ku Klux Klanner, but the white moderate, who is more devoted to "order" than to justice; who prefers a negative peace which is the absence of tension to a positive peace which is the presence of justice; who constantly says: "I agree with you in the goal you seek, but I cannot agree with your methods of direct action"; who paternalistically believes he can set the timetable for another man's freedom; who lives by a mythical concept of time and who constantly advises the Negro to wait for a "more convenient season." Shallow understanding from people of good will is more frustrating than absolute misunderstanding from people of ill will. Lukewarm acceptance is much more bewildering than outright rejection.

24   I had hoped that the white moderate would understand that law and order exist for the purpose of establishing justice and that when they fail in this purpose they become the dangerously structured dams that block the flow of social progress. I had hoped that the white moderate would understand that the present tension in the South is a necessary phase of the transition from an obnoxious negative peace, in which the Negro passively accepted his unjust plight, to a substantive and positive peace, in which all

men will respect the dignity and worth of human personality. Actually, we who engage in non-violent direct action are not the creators of tension. We merely bring to the surface the hidden tension that is already alive. We bring it out in the open, where it can be seen and dealt with. Like a boil that can never be cured so long as it is covered up but must be opened with all its ugliness to the natural medicines of air and light, injustice must be exposed, with all the tension its exposure creates, to the light of human conscience and the air of national opinion before it can be cured.

In your statement you assert that our actions, even though peaceful, 25 must be condemned because they precipitate violence. But is this a logical assertion? Isn't this like condemning a robbed man because his possession of money precipitated the evil act of robbery? Isn't this like condemning Socrates because his unswerving commitment to truth and his philosophical inquiries precipitated the act by the misguided populace in which they made him drink hemlock? Isn't this like condemning Jesus because his unique God-consciousness and never-ceasing devotion to God's will precipitated the evil act of crucifixion? We must come to see that, as the federal courts have consistently affirmed, it is wrong to urge an individual to cease his efforts to gain his basic constitutional rights because the quest may precipitate violence. Society must protect the robbed and punish the robber.

I had also hoped that the white moderate would reject the myth con- 26 cerning time in relation to the struggle for freedom. I have just received a letter from a white brother in Texas. He writes: "All Christians know that the colored people will receive equal rights eventually, but it is possible that you are in too great a religious hurry. It has taken Christianity almost two thousand years to accomplish what it has. The teachings of Christ take time to come to earth." Such an attitude stems from a tragic misconception of time, from the strangely irrational notion that there is something in the very flow of time that will inevitably cure all ills. Actually, time itself is neutral; it can be used either destructively or constructively. More and more I feel that the people of ill will have used time much more effectively than have the people of good will. We will have to repent in this generation not merely for the hateful words and actions of the bad people but for the appalling silence of the good people. Human progress never rolls in on wheels of inevitability; it comes through the tireless efforts of men willing to be coworkers with God, and without this hard work, time itself becomes an ally of the forces of social stagnation. We must use time creatively, in the knowledge that the time is always ripe to do right. Now is the time to make real the promise of democracy and transform our pending national elegy into a creative psalm of brotherhood. Now is the time to lift our national policy from the quicksand of racial injustice to the solid rock of human dignity.

You speak of our activity in Birmingham as extreme. At first I was 27 rather disappointed that fellow clergymen would see my nonviolent efforts as those of an extremist. I began thinking about the fact that I stand in the middle of two opposing forces in the Negro community. One is a force of complacency, made up in part of Negroes who, as a result of long years of oppression, are so drained of self-respect and a sense of "somebodiness" that they have adjusted to segregation; and in part of a few middle-class Negroes who, because of a degree of academic and economic security and because in some ways they profit by segregation, have become insensitive to the problems of the masses. The other force is one of bitterness and hatred, and it comes perilously close to advocating violence. It is expressed in the various black nationalist groups that are springing up across the nation, the largest and best-known being Elijah Muhammad's Muslim movement. Nourished by the Negro's frustration over the continued exis-tence of racial discrimination, this movement is made up of people who have lost faith in America, who have absolutely repudiated Christianity, and who have concluded that the white man is an incorrigible "devil."

28   I have tried to stand between these two forces, saying that we need emulate neither the "do-nothingism" of the complacent nor the hatred and despair of the black nationalist. For there is the more excellent way of love and nonviolent protest. I am grateful to God that, through the influence of the Negro church, the way of nonviolence became an integral part of our struggle.

29   If this philosophy had not emerged, by now many streets of the South would, I am convinced, be flowing with blood. And I am further convinced that if our white brothers dismiss as "rabble-rousers" and "out-side agitators" those of us who employ nonviolent direct action, and if they refuse to support our non-violent efforts, millions of Negroes will, out of frustration and despair, seek solace and security in black-nationalist ideologies—a development that would inevitably lead to a frightening racial nightmare.

30   Oppressed people cannot remain oppressed forever. The yearning for freedom eventually manifests itself, and that is what has happened to the American Negro. Something within has reminded him of his birthright of freedom, and something without has reminded him that it can be gained. Consciously or unconsciously, he has been caught up by the *Zeit-geist*, and with his black brothers of Africa and his brown and yellow brothers of Asia, South America and the Caribbean, the United States Negro is moving with a sense of great urgency toward the promised land of racial justice. If one recognizes this vital urge that has engulfed the Negro community, one should readily understand why public demon-strations are taking place. The Negro has many pent-up resentments and latent frustrations, and he must release them. So let him march; let him make prayer pilgrimages to the city hall; let him go on freedom rides—and try to understand why he must do so. If his repressed emotions are not re-leased in nonviolent ways, they will seek expression through violence; this is not a threat but a fact of history. So I have not said to my people: "Get rid of your discontent." Rather, I have tried to say that this normal and

healthy discontent can be channeled into the creative outlet of nonviolent direct action. And now this approach is being termed extremist.

But though I was initially disappointed at being categorized as an extremist, as I continued to think about the matter I gradually gained a measure of satisfaction from the label. Was not Jesus an extremist for love: "Love your enemies, bless them that curse you, do good to them that hate you, and pray for them which despitefully use you, and persecute you." Was not Amos an extremist for justice: "Let justice roll down like waters and righteousness like an ever-flowing stream." Was not Paul an extremist for the Christian gospel: "I bear in my body the marks of the Lord Jesus." Was not Martin Luther an extremist: "Here I stand; I cannot do otherwise, so help me God." And John Bunyan: "I will stay in jail to the end of my days before I make a butchery of my conscience." And Abraham Lincoln: "This nation cannot survive half slave and half free." And Thomas Jefferson: "We hold these truths to be self-evident, that all men are created equal. . . ." So the question is not whether we will be extremists, but what kind of extremists we will be. Will we be extremists for hate or for love? Will we be extremists for the preservation of injustice or for the extension of justice? In that dramatic scene on Calvary's hill three men were crucified. We must never forget that all three were crucified for the same crime—the crime of extremism. Two were extremists for immorality, and thus fell below their environment. The other, Jesus Christ, was an extremist for love, truth and goodness, and thereby rose above his environment. Perhaps the South, the nation and the world are in dire need of creative extremists.

I had hoped that the white moderate would see this need. Perhaps I was too optimistic; perhaps I expected too much. I suppose I should have realized that few members of the oppressor race can understand the deep groans and passionate yearnings of the oppressed race, and still fewer have the vision to see that injustice must be rooted out by strong, persistent and determined action. I am thankful, however, that some of our white brothers in the South have grasped the meaning of this social revolution and committed themselves to it. They are still all too few in quantity, but they are big in quality. Some—such as Ralph McGill, Lillian Smith, Harry Golden, James McBride Dabbs, Ann Braden and Sarah Patton Boyle—have written about our struggle in eloquent and prophetic terms. Others have marched with us down nameless streets of the South. They have languished in filthy, roach-infested jails, suffering the abuse and brutality of policemen who view them as "dirty nigger-lovers." Unlike so many of their moderate brothers and sisters, they have recognized the urgency of the moment and sensed the need for powerful "action" antidotes to combat the disease of segregation.

Let me take note of my other major disappointment. I have been so greatly disappointed with the white church and its leadership. Of course, there are some notable exceptions. I am not unmindful of the fact that each of you has taken some significant stands on this issue. I commend

31

32

33

you, Reverend Stallings, for your Christian stand on this past Sunday, in welcoming Negroes to your worship service on a nonsegregated basis. I commend the Catholic leaders of this state for integrating Spring Hill College several years ago.

34   But despite these notable exceptions, I must honestly reiterate that I have been disappointed with the church. I do not say this as one of those negative critics who can always find something wrong with the church. I say this as a minister of the gospel, who loves the church; who was nurtured in its bosom; who has been sustained by its spiritual blessings and who will remain true to it as long as the cord of life shall lengthen.

35   When I was suddenly catapulted into the leadership of the bus protest in Montgomery, Alabama, a few years ago, I felt we would be supported by the white church. I felt that the white ministers, priests and rabbis of the South would be among our strongest allies. Instead, some have been outright opponents, refusing to understand the freedom movement and misrepresenting its leaders; all too many others have been more cautious than courageous and have remained silent behind the anesthetizing security of stained-glass windows.

36   In spite of my shattered dreams, I came to Birmingham with the hope that the white religious leadership of this community would see the justice of our cause and, with deep moral concern, would serve as the channel through which our just grievances could reach the power structure. I had hoped that each of you would understand. But again I have been disappointed.

37   I have heard numerous southern religious leaders admonish their worshipers to comply with a desegregation decision because it is the law, but I have longed to hear white ministers declare: "Follow this decree because integration is morally right and because the Negro is your brother." In the midst of blatant injustices inflicted upon the Negro, I have watched white churchmen stand on the sideline and mouth pious irrelevancies and sanctimonious trivialities. In the midst of a mighty struggle to rid our nation of racial and economic injustice, I have heard many ministers say: "Those are social issues, with which the gospel has no real concern." And I have watched many churches commit themselves to completely otherworldly religion which makes a strange, un-Biblical distinction between body and soul, between the sacred and the secular.

38   I have traveled the length and breadth of Alabama, Mississippi and all the other southern states. On sweltering summer days and crisp autumn mornings I have looked at the South's beautiful churches with their lofty spires pointing heavenward. I have beheld the impressive outlines of her massive religious-education buildings. Over and over I have found myself asking: "What kind of people worship here? Who is their God? Where were their voices when the lips of Governor Barnett dripped with words of interposition and nullification? Where were they when Governor Wallace gave a clarion call for defiance and hatred? Where were their

voices of support when bruised and weary Negro men and women decided to rise from the dark dungeons of complacency to the bright hills of creative protest?"

Yes, these questions are still in my mind. In deep disappointment I 39 have wept over the laxity of the church. But be assured that my tears have been tears of love. There can be no deep disappointment where there is not deep love. Yes, I love the church. How could I do otherwise? I am in the rather unique position of being the son, the grandson and the great-grandson of preachers. Yes, I see the church as the body of Christ. But, oh! How we have blemished and scarred that body through social neglect and through fear of being nonconformists.

There was a time when the church was very powerful—in the time 40 when the early Christians rejoiced at being deemed worthy to suffer for what they believed. In those days the church was not merely a thermometer that recorded the ideas and principles of popular opinion; it was a thermostat that transformed the mores of society. Whenever the early Christians entered a town, the people in power became disturbed and immediately sought to convict the Christians for being "disturbers of the peace" and "outside agitators." But the Christians pressed on, in the conviction that they were "a colony of heaven," called to obey God rather than man. Small in number, they were big in commitment. They were too God-intoxicated to be "astronomically intimidated." By their effort and example they brought an end to such ancient evils as infanticide and gladiatorial contests.

Things are different now. So often the contemporary church is a 41 weak, ineffectual voice with an uncertain sound. So often it is an arch-defender of the status quo. Far from being disturbed by the presence of the church, the power structure of the average community is consoled by the church's silent—and often even vocal—sanction of things as they are.

But the judgment of God is upon the church as never before. If 42 today's church does not recapture the sacrificial spirit of the early church, it will lose its authenticity, forfeit the loyalty of millions, and be dismissed as an irrelevant social club with no meaning for the twentieth century. Every day I meet young people whose disappointment with the church has turned into outright disgust.

Perhaps I have once again been too optimistic. Is organized religion 43 too inextricably bound to the status quo to save our nation and the world? Perhaps I must turn my faith to the inner spiritual church, the church within the church, as the true *ekklesia* and the hope of the world. But again I am thankful to God that some noble souls from the ranks of organized religion have broken loose from the paralyzing chains of conformity and joined us as active partners in the struggle for freedom. They have left their secure congregations and walked the streets of Albany, Georgia, with us. They have gone down the highways of the South on tortuous rides for freedom. Yes, they have gone to jail with us. Some have been dismissed from their churches, have lost the support of their bishops and fellow ministers. But they have acted in the faith that right defeated is stronger than evil triumphant. Their witness has been the spiritual salt that has preserved the true meaning of the gospel in these troubled times. They have carved a tunnel of hope through the dark mountain of disappointment.

44   I hope the church as a whole will meet the challenge of this decisive hour. But even if the church does not come to the aid of justice, I have no despair about the future. I have no fear about the outcome of our struggle in Birmingham, even if our motives are at present misunderstood. We will reach the goal of freedom in Birmingham and all over the nation, because the goal of America is freedom. Abused and scorned though we may be, our destiny is tied up with America's destiny. Before the pilgrims landed at Plymouth, we were here. Before the pen of Jefferson etched the majestic words of the Declaration of Independence across the pages of history, we were here. For more than two centuries our forebears labored in this country without wages; they made cotton king; they built the homes of their masters while suffering gross injustice and shameful humiliation— and yet out of a bottomless vitality they continued to thrive and develop. If the inexpressible cruelties of slavery could not stop us, the opposition we now face will surely fail. We will win our freedom because the sacred heritage of our nation and the eternal will of God are embodied in our echoing demands.

45   Before closing I feel impelled to mention one other point in your statement that has troubled me profoundly. You warmly commended the Birmingham police force for keeping "order" and "preventing violence." I doubt that you would have so warmly commended the police force if you had seen its dogs sinking their teeth into unarmed, nonviolent Negroes. I doubt that you would so quickly commend the policemen if you were to observe their ugly and inhumane treatment of Negroes here in the city jail; if you were to watch them push and curse old Negro women and young Negro girls; if you were to see them slap and kick old Negro men and young boys; if you were to observe them as they did on two occasions, refuse to give us food because we wanted to sing our grace together. I cannot join you in your praise of the Birmingham police department.

46   It is true that the police have exercised a degree of discipline in handling the demonstrators. In this sense they have conducted themselves rather "nonviolently" in public. But for what purpose? To preserve the evil system of segregation. Over the past few years I have consistently preached that nonviolence demands that the means we use must be as pure as the ends we seek. I have tried to make clear that it is wrong to use immoral means to attain moral ends. But now I must affirm that it is just as wrong, or perhaps even more so, to use moral means to preserve immoral ends. Perhaps Mr. Connor and his policemen have been rather nonviolent in public, as was Chief Pritchett in Albany, Georgia, but they have

used the moral means of nonviolence to maintain the immoral end of racial injustice. As T. S. Eliot has said: "The last temptation is the greatest treason: To do the right deed for the wrong reason."

I wish you had commended the Negro sit-inners and demonstrators 47 of Birmingham for their sublime courage, their willingness to suffer and their amazing discipline in the midst of great provocation. One day the South will recognize its real heroes. They will be the James Merediths, with the noble sense of purpose that enables them to face jeering and hostile mobs, and with the agonizing loneliness that characterizes the life of the pioneer. They will be old, oppressed, battered Negro women, symbolized in a seventy-two-year-old woman in Montgomery, Alabama, who rose up with a sense of dignity and with her people decided not to ride segregated buses, and who responded with ungrammatical profundity to one who inquired about her weariness: "My feet is tired, but my soul is at rest." They will be the young high school and college students, the young ministers of the gospel and a host of their elders, courageously and nonviolently sitting in at lunch counters and willingly going to jail for conscience' sake. One day the South will know that when these disinherited children of God sat down at lunch counters, they were in reality standing up for what is best in the American dream and for the most sacred values in our Judaeo-Christian heritage, thereby bringing our nation back to those great wells of democracy which were dug deep by the founding fathers in their formulation of the Constitution and the Declaration of Independence.

Never before have I written so long a letter. I'm afraid it is much too 48 long to take your precious time. I can assure you that it would have been much shorter if I had been writing from a comfortable desk, but what else can one do when he is alone in a narrow jail cell, other than write long letters, think long thoughts and pray long prayers?

If I have said anything in this letter that overstates the truth and in- 49 dicates an unreasonable impatience, I beg you to forgive me. If I have said anything that understates the truth and indicates my having a patience that allows me to settle for anything less than brotherhood, I beg God to forgive me.

I hope this letter finds you strong in faith. I also hope that circum- 50 stances will soon make it possible for me to meet each of you, not as an integrationist or a civil-rights leader but as a fellow clergyman and a Christian brother. Let us all hope that the dark clouds of racial prejudice will soon pass away and the deep fog of misunderstanding will be lifted from our fear-drenched communities, and in some not too distant tomorrow the radiant stars of love and brotherhood will shine over our great nation with all their scintillating beauty.

Yours for the cause of Peace and Brotherhood,
Martin Luther King, Jr.

Content

1. In paragraph 4 King makes several assertions on which he bases the rest of his argument. What are they? Does he ever prove them, or does he assume that readers will take them for granted?

2. In paragraph 5 King asserts that Birmingham's "white power structure left the Negro community with no alternative" but to commit civil disobedience. Does he ever prove this? Does he need to? Is it a debatable statement?

3. What, according to King, are the "four basic steps" in "any nonviolent campaign" (¶ 6)? What is the goal of "nonviolent direct action" (¶ 10)? What is the constructive, "nonviolent tension" (¶ 10) King favors?

4. Why has King been disappointed by white moderates (¶s 23–32)? By the white church (¶s 33–44)? What does he want white moderates to do? What does he claim that the church should do?

5. How does King deal with the argument that civil rights activists are too impatient, that they should go slow because "It has taken Christianity almost two thousand years to accomplish what it has" (¶ 26)? How does he refute the argument that he is an extremist (¶ 27)?

Strategies/Structures

6. How does King establish, in the salutation and first paragraph, his reasons for writing? The setting in which he writes? His intended audience? In what ways does he demonstrate a sensitive, reasonable tone?

7. King's letter ostensibly replies to that of the eight clergymen. Find passages in which he addresses them, and analyze the voice he uses. In what relation to the clergymen does King see himself? He also has a secondary audience; who are its members? Locate passages that seem especially directed to this second audience. In what relation to this audience does King see himself?

8. Why does King cite the theologians Aquinas (a Catholic), Buber (a Jew), and Tillich (a Protestant) in paragraph 16? What similarities link the three?

9. After defending his actions against the criticisms of the clergymen, King takes the offensive in paragraphs 23–44. How does he signal this change?

10. Which parts of King's letter appeal chiefly to reason? To emotion? How are the two types of appeals interrelated?

11. King uses large numbers of rhetorical questions throughout this essay (see ¶s 18, 25, 31, 38, 39). Why? With what effects?

Language

12. How does King define a "just law" (¶s 16, 17)? An "unjust law" (¶s 16, 17)? Why are these definitions crucial to the argument that follows?

13. Consult your dictionary, if necessary, for the meanings of the following words or others you do not understand: cognizant (¶ 4), gainsaying (¶ 6), moratorium (¶ 7), gadflies (¶ 10), harried (¶ 14), degenerating (¶ 14), abyss (¶ 14), incorrigible (¶ 27), *Zeitgeist* (¶ 30), scintillating (¶ 50).

For Writing

14. Under what circumstances, if any, is breaking the law justifiable? If you use Dr. King's definition of just and unjust law (¶s 15–20), or make any distinction, say, between moral law and civil law, be sure to explain what you mean. You may, if you wish, use examples with which you are personally familiar. Or you may elaborate on some of the examples King uses (¶ 22) or on examples from King's own civil-rights activities, such as the boycotts in the early 1950s of the legally segregated Montgomery bus system (¶ 35).

15. If you are a member of a church, or attend a church regularly, address members of the congregation on what, if any, commitment you think your church should make to better the lives of other groups who do not attend that church. Does this commitment extend to civil disobedience?

16. Would you ever be willing to go to jail for a cause? What cause? Under what circumstances? If you knew that a prison record might bar you from some privileges in some states (such as practicing law or medicine), would you still be willing to take such a risk?

ROBERT REICH

Reich (born 1946), earned a B.A. at Dartmouth College (1968) and a J.D. degree from Yale Law School (1973), was a Rhodes scholar at Oxford, taught at Harvard's John F. Kennedy School of Government, and is currently a professor of social and economic policy at Brandeis University. Active in politics since his student days, Reich has served as summer intern for Senator Robert Kennedy; coordinator of Eugene McCarthy's 1968 presidential campaign; and as economic advisor to presidential candidates Walter Mondale and Michael Dukakis. He was U.S. Secretary of Labor during Clinton's first term as president, 1993–96; *Locked in the Cabinet* (1997) discusses his experiences.

Many of Reich's books on economics have been intended for a general audience, including *Tales of a New America: The Anxious Liberal's Guide to the Future* (1988); and *The Work of Nations: Preparing Ourselves for 21st-Century Capitalism* (1991). *The Next American Frontier* (1983) provided a rationale for the Democratic party's economic policy, explaining that "government intervention sets the boundaries, decides what's going to be marketed, sets the rules of the game through procurement policies, tax credits, depreciation allowances, loans and loan guarantees." *Tales of a New America*, also popular with Democrats, defines four economic myths: "Mob at the Gate" labels foreigners as adversaries to American citizens; "The Triumphant Individual" reinforces the myth of the American Dream; "The Benevolent Community" claims that Americans act out of social responsibility to one another; and "The Rot at the Top" accuses the elite class of corruption and abuse of their power. "The Global Elite," first published in the *New York*

Times Magazine (1991) provides factual information to counteract the myths of a benevolent, egalitarian society and implicitly argues for a more equitable—and democratic—distribution of our country's wealth.

The Global Elite

1   The idea of "community" has always held a special attraction for Americans. In a 1984 speech, President Ronald Reagan celebrated America's "bedrock"—"its communities where neighbors help one another, where families bring up kids together, where American values are born." Governor Mario M. Cuomo of New York, with a very different political leaning, has been almost as lyrical. "Community . . . is the reality on which our national life has been founded," he said in 1987.

2   There is only one problem with this picture. Most Americans no longer live in traditional communities. They live in suburban subdivisions bordered by highways and sprinkled with shopping malls, or in tony condominiums and residential clusters, or in ramshackle apartment buildings and housing projects. Most of them commute to work and socialize on some basis other than geographic proximity. And most people pick up and move to a different neighborhood every five years or so.

3   But Americans generally have one thing in common with their neighbors: They have similar incomes. And that simple fact lies at the heart of the new community. This means that their educational backgrounds are likely to be similar, that they pay roughly the same in taxes, and that they indulge in the same consumer impulses. "Tell me someone's ZIP code," the founder of a direct-mail company once bragged, "and I can predict what they eat, drink, drive—even think."

4   Americans who own their homes usually share one political cause with their neighbors: a near obsessive concern with maintaining or upgrading property values. And this common interest is responsible for much of what has brought neighbors together in recent years. Complete strangers, although they may live on the same street or in the same condominium complex, suddenly feel intense solidarity when it is rumored that low-income housing will be constructed in their midst or that a poorer school district will be consolidated with their own.

5   The renewed emphasis on "community" in American life has justified and legitimized these economic enclaves. If generosity and solidarity end at the border of similarly valued properties, then the most fortunate can be virtuous citizens at little cost. Since most people in one neighborhood or town are equally well off, there is no cause for a guilty conscience. If inhabitants of another area are poorer, let them look to one another. Why should *we* pay for *their* schools?

So the argument goes, without acknowledging that the critical 6
assumption has already been made: "We" and "they" belong to fundamentally different communities. Through such reasoning, it has become
possible to maintain a self-image of generosity toward, and solidarity
with, one's "community" without bearing any responsibility to "them"—
the other "community."

America's high earners—the fortunate top fifth—thus feel increas- 7
ingly justified in paying only what is necessary to insure that everyone
in their community is sufficiently well educated and has access to the
public services they need to succeed.

Last year, the top fifth of working Americans took home more money 8
than the other four-fifths put together—the highest portion in postwar
history. These high earners will relinquish somewhat more of their income to the Federal Government this year than in 1990 as a result of last
fall's tax changes, although considerably less than in the late 1970s, when
the tax code was more progressive. But the continuing debate over
whether the wealthy are paying their fair share of taxes obscures a larger
issue, with more profound implications for America: The fortunate fifth
is quietly seceding from the rest of the nation.

This is occurring gradually, without much awareness by members of 9
the top group—or, for that matter, by anyone else. And the Government is
speeding this process as Washington shifts responsibility for many public
services to state and local governments.

The secession is taking several forms. In many cities and towns, the 10
wealthy have in effect withdrawn their dollars from the support of public
spaces and institutions shared by all and dedicated the savings to their
own private services. As public parks and playgrounds deteriorate, there
is a proliferation of private health clubs, golf clubs, tennis clubs, skating
clubs, and every other type of recreational association in which costs are
shared among members. Condominiums and the omnipresent residential
communities dun their members to undertake work that financially
strapped local governments can no longer afford to do well—maintaining
roads, mending sidewalks, pruning trees, repairing street lights, cleaning
swimming pools, paying for lifeguards, and, notably, hiring security
guards to protect life and property. (The number of private security guards
in the United States now exceeds the number of public police officers.)

Of course, wealthier Americans have been withdrawing into their 11
own neighborhoods and clubs for generations. But the new secession is
more dramatic because the highest earners now inhabit a different economy
from other Americans. The new elite is linked by jet, modem, fax, satellite,
and fiber-optic cable to the great commercial and recreational centers of the
world, but it is not particularly connected to the rest of the nation.

That is because the work this group does is becoming less tied to the 12
activities of other Americans. Most of their jobs consist of analyzing and

manipulating symbols—words, numbers, or visual images. Among the most prominent of these "symbolic analysts" are management consultants, lawyers, software and design engineers, research scientists, corporate executives, financial advisors, strategic planners, advertising executives, television and movie producers, and other workers whose job titles include terms like "strategy," "planning," "consultant," "policy," "resources," or "engineer."

13   These workers typically spend long hours in meetings or on the telephone and even longer hours in planes or hotels—advising, making presentations, giving briefings, and making deals. Periodically, they issue reports, plans, designs, drafts, briefs, blueprints, analyses, memorandums, layouts, renderings, scripts, or projections. In contrast with people whose jobs tend to be tedious and repetitive, symbolic analysts find their work varied and intellectually challenging. In fact, the work is often enjoyable.

14   These symbolic analysts are in ever greater demand in a world market that places an increasing value on identifying and solving problems. Requests for their software designs, financial advice, or engineering blueprints come from all parts of the globe. This largely explains why most (but by no means all) symbolic analysts have become wealthier, even as the ever-growing worldwide supply of unskilled labor continues to depress the wages of other Americans.

15   Successful Americans have not completely disengaged themselves from the lives of their less fortunate compatriots. Some devote substantial resources and energies to helping the rest of society, not through their tax payments, but through voluntary efforts. "Generosity is a reflection of what one does with his or her resources—and not what he or she advocates the government do with everyone's money," Ronald Reagan said in 1984.

16   The argument is fair enough. Government is not the only device for redistributing wealth. In his speech accepting the Presidential nomination at the Republican National Convention in 1988, George Bush said that the real magnanimity of America was to be found in a "brilliant diversity" of private charities, "spread like stars, like a thousand points of light in a broad and peaceful sky."

17   No nation congratulates itself more enthusiastically on its charitable acts than America; none engages in a greater number of charity balls, bake sales, benefit auctions, and border-to-border hand holdings for good causes. Much of this is sincerely motivated and admirable.

18   But close examination reveals that many of these acts of benevolence do not help the needy. Particularly suspect is the private givings of those in the top income-tax bracket. Studies have revealed that their largess does not flow mainly to social services for the poor—to better schools, health clinics, or recreational centers. Instead, most voluntary contributions of wealthy Americans go to the places and institutions that entertain, inspire, cure, or educate wealthy Americans—art museums,

opera houses, theaters, orchestras, ballet companies, private hospitals, and elite universities.

And even these charitable contributions are relatively skimpy. Last 19 year, American households with incomes of less than $10,000 gave an average of 5.5 percent of their earnings to charity or to a religious organization; those making more than $100,000 a year gave only 2.9 percent. After the 1986 tax-code overhaul reduced the benefits of charitable giving, the very rich became even stingier. According to Internal Revenue Service data, taxpayers earning $500,000 or more slashed their average donations to $16,062 in 1988 from $47,432 in 1980.

Corporate philanthropy is following the same general pattern. In 20 recent years, the largest American corporations have been sounding the alarm about the nation's fast deteriorating primary and secondary schools. Few are more eloquent and impassioned about the need for better schools than American executives. "How well we educate all of our children will determine our competitiveness globally, and our economic health domestically, and our communities' character and vitality," said a report of The Business Roundtable, a New York–based association of top executives.

Accordingly, there are numerous "partnerships" between corpora- 21 tions and public schools: scholarships for poor children qualified to attend college, and programs in which businesses adopt individual schools by making conspicuous donations of computers, books, and, on occasion, even money. That such activities are loudly touted by public relations staffs should not detract from the good they do.

Despite the hoopla, business donations to education and charitable 22 causes actually tapered off markedly in the 1980s, even as the economy boomed. In the 1970s, corporate giving to education jumped an average of 15 percent a year. In 1990, however, giving was only 5 percent over that in 1989; and in 1989 it was 3 percent over 1988. Moreover, most of this money goes to colleges and universities—in particular, to the alma maters of symbolic analysts, who expect their children and grandchildren to follow in their footsteps. Only 1.5 percent of corporate giving in the late 1980s was to public primary and secondary schools.

Notably, these contributions have been smaller than the amounts 23 corporations are receiving from states and communities in the form of subsidies or tax breaks. Companies are quietly procuring such deals by threatening to move their operations—and jobs—to places around the world with a more congenial tax climate. The paradoxical result has been even less corporate revenue to spend on schools and other community services than before. The executives of General Motors, for example, who have been among the loudest to proclaim the need for better schools, have also been among the most relentless in pursuing local tax abatements and in challenging their tax assessments. G.M.'s successful efforts to reduce its taxes in North Tarrytown, N.Y., where the company has had a factory since 1914, cut local revenues by $1 million in 1990, part of a larger short-fall that forced the town to lay off scores of teachers.

24   The secession of the fortunate fifth has been apparent in how and where they have chosen to work and live. In effect, most of America's large urban centers have splintered into two separate cities. One is composed of those whose symbolic and analytic services are linked to the world economy. The other consists of local service workers—custodians, security guards, taxi drivers, clerical aides, parking attendants, salespeople, restaurant employees—whose jobs are dependent on the symbolic analysts. Few blue-collar manufacturing workers remain in American cities. Between 1953 and 1984, for example, New York City lost 600,000 factory jobs; in the same interval, it added about 700,000 jobs for symbolic analysts and service workers.

25   The separation of symbolic analysts from local service workers within cities has been reinforced in several ways. Most large cities now possess two school systems—a private one for the children of the top-earning group and a public one for the children of service workers, the remaining blue-collar workers, and the unemployed. Symbolic analysts spend considerable time and energy insuring that their children gain entrance to good private schools, and then small fortunes keeping them there—dollars that under a more progressive tax code might finance better public education.

26   People with high incomes live, shop, and work within areas of cities that, if not beautiful, are at least esthetically tolerable and reasonably safe; precincts not meeting these minimum standards of charm and security have been left to the less fortunate.

27   Here again, symbolic analysts have pooled their resources to the exclusive benefit of themselves. Public funds have been spent in earnest on downtown "revitalization" projects, entailing the construction of clusters of post-modern office buildings (complete with fiber-optic cables, private branch exchanges, satellite dishes, and other communications equipment linking them to the rest of the world), multilevel parking garages, hotels with glass enclosed atriums, upscale shopping plazas and galleries, theaters, convention centers, and luxury condominiums.

28   Ideally, these complexes are entirely self-contained, with air-conditioned walkways linking residences, businesses, and recreational space. The lucky resident is able to shop, work, and attend the theater without risking direct contact with the outside world—that is, the other city.

29   When not living in urban enclaves, symbolic analysts are increasingly congregating in suburbs and exurbs where corporate headquarters have been relocated, research parks have been created, and where bucolic universities have spawned entrepreneurial ventures. Among the most desirable of such locations are Princeton, N.J.; northern Westchester and Putnam Counties in New York; Palo Alto, Calif.; Austin, Tex.; Bethesda, Md.; and Raleigh-Durham, N.C.

Engineers and strategists of American auto companies, for example, 30
do not live in Flint or Saginaw, Mich., where the blue-collar workers reside;
they cluster in their own towns of Troy, Warren, and Auburn Hills. Likewise, the vast majority of financial specialists, lawyers, and executives
working for the insurance companies of Hartford would never consider
living there; after all, Hartford is the nation's fourth-poorest city. Instead,
they flock to Windsor, Middlebury, West Hartford, and other towns that
are among the wealthiest in the country.

This trend, too, has been growing for decades. But technology has 31
accelerated it. Today's symbolic analysts linked directly to the rest of the
globe can choose to live and work in the most pastoral of settings.

The secession has been encouraged by the Federal Government. For 32
the last decade, Washington has in effect shifted responsibility for many
public services to local governments. At their peak, Federal grants made up
25 percent of state and local spending in the late 1970s. Today, the Federal
share has dwindled to 17 percent. Direct aid to local governments, in the
form of programs introduced in the Johnson and Nixon Administrations,
has been the hardest hit by budget cuts. In the 1980s, Federal dollars for
clean water, job training and transfers, low-income housing, sewage treatment, and garbage disposal shrank by some $50 billion a year, and Wash-
ington's share of spending on local transit declined by 50 percent. (The Bush
Administration has proposed that states and localities take on even more
of the costs of building and maintaining roads, and wants to cut Federal aid
for mass transit.) In 1990, New York City received only 9.6 percent of all its
revenue from the Federal Government, compared with 16 percent in 1981.

States have quickly transferred many of these new expenses to fis- 33
cally strapped cities and towns, with a result that by the start of the 1990s,
localities were bearing more than half the costs of water and sewage,
roads, parks, welfare, and public schools. In New York State, the local
communities' share has risen to about 75 percent of these costs.

Cities and towns with affluent inhabitants can bear these burdens 34
relatively easily. Poorer ones, faced with the twin problem of lower incomes and greater demand for social services, have had far more difficulty.
And as the gap between the richest and poorest communities has widened,
the shift in responsibility for public services to cities and towns has func-
tioned as another means of relieving wealthier Americans of the cost of
aiding less fortunate citizens.

The result has been a growing inequality in basic social and com- 35
munity services. While the city tax rate in Philadelphia, for example, is
about triple that of communities around it, the suburbs enjoy far better
schools, hospitals, recreation, and police protection. Eighty-five percent of
the richest families in the greater Philadelphia area live outside the city
limits, and 80 percent of the region's poorest live inside. The quality of a
city's infrastructure—roads, bridges, sewage, water treatment—is likewise related to the average income of its inhabitants.

36   The growing inequality in government services has been most apparent in the public schools. The Federal Government's share of the costs of primary and secondary education has dwindled to about 6 percent. The bulk of the cost is divided about equally between the states and local school districts. States with a higher concentration of wealthy residents can afford to spend more on their schools than other states. In 1989, the average public-school teacher in Arkansas, for example, received $21,700; in Connecticut, $37,300.

37   Even among adjoining suburban towns in the same state the differences can be quite large. Consider three Boston-area communities located within minutes of one another. All are predominantly white, and most residents within each town earn about the same as their neighbors. But the disparity of incomes between towns is substantial.

38   Belmont, northwest of Boston, is inhabited mainly by symbolic analysts and their families. In 1988, the average teacher in its public schools earned $36,100. Only 3 percent of Belmont's eighteen-year-olds dropped out of high school, and more than 80 percent of graduating seniors chose to go on to a four-year college.

39   Just east of Belmont is Somerville, most of whose residents are low-wage service workers. In 1988, the average Somerville teacher earned $29,400. A third of the town's eighteen-year-olds did not finish high school, and fewer than a third planned to attend college.

40   Chelsea, across the Mystic River from Somerville, is the poorest of the three towns. Most of its inhabitants are unskilled, and many are unemployed or only employed part time. The average teacher in Chelsea, facing tougher educational challenges than his or her counterparts in Belmont, earned $26,200 in 1988, almost a third less than the average teacher in the more affluent town just a few miles away. More than half of Chelsea's eighteen-year-olds did not graduate from high school, and only 10 percent planned to attend college.

41   Similar disparities can be found all over the nation. Students at Highland Park High School in a wealthy suburb of Dallas, for example, enjoy a campus with a planetarium, indoor swimming pool, closed-circuit television studio and state-of-the-art science laboratory. Highland Park spends about $6,000 a year to educate each student. This is almost twice that spent per pupil by the towns of Wilmer and Hutchins in southern Dallas County. According to Texas education officials, the richest school district in the state spends $19,300 a year per pupil; its poorest, $2,100 a year.

42   The courts have become involved in trying to repair such imbalances, but the issues are not open to easy judicial remedy.

43   The four-fifths of Americans left in the wake of the secession of the fortunate fifth include many poor blacks, but racial exclusion is neither the primary motive for the separation not a necessary consequence. Lower-income whites are similarly excluded, and high-income black symbolic analysts are often welcomed. The segregation is economic rather

than racial, although economically motivated separation often results in *de facto* racial segregation. Where courts have found a pattern of racially motivated segregation, it usually has involved lower-income white communities bordering on lower-income black neighborhoods.

In states where courts have ordered equalized state spending in   44
school districts, the vast differences in a town's property values—and thus local tax revenues—continue to result in substantial inequities. Where courts or state governments have tried to impose limits on what affluent communities can pay their teachers, not a few parents in upscale towns have simply removed their children from the public schools and applied the money they might otherwise have willingly paid in higher taxes to private school tuitions instead. And, of course, even if statewide expenditures were better equalized, poorer states would continue to be at a substantial disadvantage.

In all these ways, the gap between America's symbolic analysts and   45
everyone else is widening into a chasm. Their secession from the rest of the population raises fundamental questions about the future of American society. In the new global economy—in which money, technologies, and corporations cross borders effortlessly—a citizen's standard of living depends more and more on skills and insights, and on the infrastructure needed to link these abilities to the rest of the world. But the most skilled and insightful Americans, who are already positioned to thrive in the world market, are now able to slip the bonds of national allegiance, and by so doing disengage themselves from their less-favored fellows. The stark political challenge in the decades ahead will be to reaffirm that, even though America is no longer a separate and distinct economy, it is still a society whose members have abiding obligations to one another.

Content

1. Does Reich prove convincingly that "the fortunate fifth [those Americans with the highest income] is quietly seceding from the rest of the nation" (¶ 8)? To what extent does your receptivity to his argument depend on whether or not you consider yourself or your family a member of the "fortunate fifth"?

2. Who are "symbolic analysts" (¶s 12–14, 25–31)? Does Reich demonstrate that these persons comprise a significant portion of the "fortunate fifth"? Why does he identify their job titles (¶ 12), activities (¶ 13), lifestyles (¶s 25–28), and places of work and residence (¶s 28–30) in long lists? In what ways does he expect his readers to interpret these lists?

3. Reich illustrates many of the points of his argument with reference to the public schools in rich and poor districts (¶s 36–44, for example). Why does he focus on schools?

4. If Reich has convinced you of his premise (see question 1 above), has he also convinced you of his conclusion that "the most skilled and insightful Americans . . . are now able to slip the bonds of national allegiance, and by so doing disengage themselves from their less-favored fellows. The stark political challenge . . .

will be to reaffirm that . . . [America] is still a society whose members have abiding obligations to one another" (¶ 45)? If he has convinced you, what does he want
you to do as a consequence? If he hasn't convinced you, why hasn't he?

Strategies/Structures

5. The specific statistical information and other figures in Reich's 1991 article
change annually, if not more often. Is their alteration within the next decade
likely to affect either Reich's argument or your receptivity to it? Since numbers
are always in flux, why use them in an argument?

6. Reich says that corporations threaten to move to a "more congenial tax climate" unless they get substantial tax breaks from the communities in which
they're located. But what they return to the communities in philanthropic contributions is much less than they receive: "G.M.'s successful efforts to reduce its
taxes in North Tarrytown, N.Y., where the company has had a factory since 1914,
cut local revenues by $1 million in 1990, part of a larger shortfall that forced the
town to lay off scores of teachers" (¶ 23). What is the point of including this and
comparable information? What response from readers is Reich looking for?

7. Reich's sentences are fairly long, but his paragraphs are short, usually from
one to three sentences. (The longest paragraph, ¶ 32, has eight sentences.) This is
because the article was originally published in a newspaper, the *New York Times
Magazine*; newspapers provide paragraph breaks not to indicate where the material logically breaks or changes course but to rest readers' eyes as they roam the
page. What is the effect, if any, of such a large number of short paragraphs in a
serious article?

8. Which side does Reich favor? At what point in the argument does he expect
his readers to realize this?

Language

9. Does Reich's division of workers into "symbolic and analytic services" and
"local service workers" cover most people in cities? Where do "blue-collar manufacturing workers" live (see ¶ 24)? Are such labels necessary or helpful in constructing the argument Reich makes?

For Writing

10. Argue, as Reich does but using your own examples (and some of his factual information, among other sources) that, as Reich concludes, "even though America is
no longer a separate and distinct economy, it is still a society whose members have
abiding obligations to one another" (¶ 45). One way to address the subject is to consider the implications of a particular public policy issue (such as school vouchers,
school busing, property taxation, equalization of school funding across rich and
poor districts, gated residential communities with private security guards). See, for
example, Martin Luther King, Jr.'s, "Letter from Birmingham Jail" (445–61), and the
essays by Kozol, Coontz, and Nocton identified in the next question.

11. Is it socially desirable for the upper fifth in income to "secede," however
quietly, "from the rest of the nation," as Reich asserts in paragraph 8? Shouldn't

everyone have the right to live where they want to? Should people be required to live in the same geographical area where they work? If you wish, supplement your argument with reference to the essays by Jonathan Kozol, "The Human Cost of an Illiterate Society," 210–18; Stephanie Coontz, "Blaming the Family for Economic Decline," 226–31; and Matt Nocton, "Harvest of Gold, Harvest of Shame," 515–21.

ANNA QUINDLEN

Quindlen, born in Philadelphia in 1953, became a reporter for the *New York Times* within three years of graduating from Barnard (B.A., 1974). Her columns "About New York," "Life in the 30s," and "Public & Private"— which won a Pulitzer Prize in 1992—made her "the unintended voice of the baby boom generation." These have been collected in her books *Living Out Loud* (1988) and *Thinking Out Loud* (1993). From a perspective at once in-cisive and thoroughly alert to the perplexities of being human—a daughter, a happily-married mother of three, a Roman Catholic, a liberal feminist— she focuses on, as *Newsweek* said, "the rocky emotional terrain of marriage, parenthood, secret desires and self-doubts." Leaving the *Times* in 1994 to write fiction and children's stories, she published best-selling novels about complications of family life: *Object Lessons* (1991), on the "dislocations of growing up"; *One True Thing* (1995), on right-to-die issues; and *Black and Blue* (1998), on domestic violence. Her most recent book is *A Short Guide to a Happy Life* (2000).

In 1999 she resumed her journalistic career as a columnist at *Newsweek*, where "Uncle Sam and Aunt Samantha" appeared on November 5, 2001. Here she argues—as the mother of teenage children—against the sexist U.S. policy of mandatory draft for men only. If men and women truly have equal rights, they should bear equal responsibility to serve their country. A double standard "makes a mockery not only of the standards of this household but of the standards of this nation."

Uncle Sam and Aunt Samantha

O ne out of every five new recruits in the United States military is female.   1

The Marines gave the Combat Action Ribbon for service in the Per-   2
sian Gulf to 23 women.

Two female soldiers were killed in the bombing of the USS Cole.   3

The Selective Service registers for the draft all male citizens between   4
the ages of 18 and 25.

What's wrong with this picture?   5

6   As Americans read and realize that the lives of most women in this country are as different from those of Afghan women as a Cunard cruise is from maximum-security lockdown, there has nonetheless been little attention paid to one persistent gender inequity in U.S. public policy. An astonishing anachronism, really: while women are represented today in virtually all fields, including the armed forces, only men are required to register for the military draft that would be used in the event of a national-security crisis.

7   Since the nation is as close to such a crisis as it has been in more than 60 years, it's a good moment to consider how the draft wound up in this particular time warp. It's not the time warp of the Taliban, certainly, stuck in the worst part of the 13th century, forbidding women to attend school or hold jobs or even reveal their arms, forcing them into sex and marriage. Our own time warp is several decades old. The last time the draft was considered seriously was 20 years ago, when registration with the Selective Service was restored by Jimmy Carter after the Soviet invasion of, yep, Afghanistan. The president, as well as the Army chief of staff, asked at the time for the registration of women as well as men.

8   Amid a welter of arguments—women interfere with esprit de corps, women don't have the physical strength, women prisoners could be sexually assaulted, women soldiers would distract male soldiers from their mission—Congress shot down the notion of gender-blind registration. So did the Supreme Court, ruling that since women were forbidden to serve in combat positions and the purpose of the draft was to create a combat-ready force, it made sense not to register them.

9   But that was then, and this is now. Women have indeed served in combat positions, in the Balkans and the Middle East. More than 40,000 managed to serve in the Persian Gulf without destroying unit cohesion or failing because of upper-body strength. Some are even now taking out targets in Afghanistan from fighter jets, and apparently without any male soldier's falling prey to some predicted excess of chivalry or lust.

10   Talk about cognitive dissonance. All these military personnel, male and female alike, have come of age at a time when a significant level of parity was taken for granted. Yet they are supposed to accept that only males will be required to defend their country in a time of national emergency. This is insulting to men. And it is insulting to women. Caroline Forell, an expert on women's legal rights and a professor at the University of Oregon School of Law, puts it bluntly: "Failing to require this of women makes us lesser citizens."

11   Neither the left nor the right has been particularly inclined to consider this issue judiciously. Many feminists came from the antiwar movement and have let their distaste for the military in general and the draft in particular mute their response. In 1980 NOW released a resolution that buried support for the registration of women beneath opposition to the draft, despite the fact that the draft had been redesigned to eliminate the

*Look at this photograph of F-15 Air Force pilot Cathy De La Garza,
taken on March 10, 1999. At the time, Ms. De La Garza was one of only
seven such women pilots. What appeals—to reason, to emotion—does this
photograph convey?*

vexing inequities of Vietnam, when the sons of the working class served
and the sons of the Ivy League did not. Conservatives, meanwhile, used an
equal-opportunity draft as the linchpin of opposition to the Equal Rights
Amendment, along with the terrifying specter of unisex bathrooms. (I
have seen the urinal, and it is benign.) The legislative director of the right-
wing group Concerned Women for America once defended the existing
regulations by saying that most women "don't want to be included in the
draft." All those young men who went to Canada during Vietnam and
those who today register with fear and trembling in the face of the Trade
Center devastation might be amazed to discover that lack of desire is an
affirmative defense.

Parents face a series of unique new challenges in this more egalitarian   12
world, not the least of which would be sending a daughter off to war. But
parents all over this country are doing that right now, with daughters who
enlisted; some have even expressed surprise that young women, in this day
and age, are not required to register alongside their brothers and friends.
While all involved in this debate over the years have invoked the assumed
opposition of the people, even 10 years ago more than half of all Americans
polled believed women should be made eligible for the draft. Besides, this
is not about comfort but about fairness. My son has to register with the
Selective Service this year, and if his sister does not when she turns 18, it

makes a mockery not only of the standards of this household but of the standards of this nation.

13   It is possible in Afghanistan for women to be treated like little more than fecund pack animals precisely because gender fear and ignorance and hatred have been codified and permitted to hold sway. In this country, largely because of the concerted efforts of those allied with the women's movement over a century of struggle, much of that bigotry has been beaten back, even buried. Yet in improbable places the creaky old ways surface, the ways suggesting that we women were made of finer stuff. The finer stuff was usually porcelain, decorative and on the shelf, suitable for meals and show. Happily, the finer stuff has been transmuted into the right stuff. But with rights come responsibilities, as teachers like to tell their students. This is a responsibility that should fall equally upon all, male and female alike. If the empirical evidence is considered rationally, if the decision is divested of outmoded stereotypes, that's the only possible conclusion to be reached.

Content

1. Why is it that until now "only men [have been] required to register for the military draft that would be used in the event of a national-security crisis" (¶ 6)? What evidence does Quindlen use to make her point that not requiring women to register for the draft is wrong?

2. Why does Quindlen believe that not requiring women to defend their country "in a time of national emergency" is insulting to both men and women (¶ 10)?

3. Why did Quindlen write this essay, originally published in *Newsweek*? To what extent might she believe her readers would agree with her viewpoint at the outset? After reading her essay? Would an audience of college students be expected to respond in the same way?

Strategies/Structures

4. Quindlen begins her essay with a series of factual statements that lead to a question: "What's wrong with this picture?" (¶ 5). What are the advantages of this type of introductory strategy in writing an argumentative essay? Are there disadvantages as well?

5. Quindlen sums up her argument by stating, "If the empirical evidence is considered rationally, if the decision is divested of outmoded stereotypes, that's the only possible conclusion to be reached" (¶ 13). Do most arguments admit of only a single conclusion? Does this one? Explain.

6. What is the point of Quindlen's comparisons between women in America and in Afghanistan (¶s 6, 7, 13)?

Language

7. Quindlen uses straightforward statements, anger, sarcasm, and irony in making her argument. Show where these occur and how they work together to reinforce her point.

8. Quindlen ends the essay with two metaphors (¶ 13): "It is possible in Afghanistan for women to be treated like little more than fecund pack animals. . . ." in contrast to American women "made of finer stuff [than men]. The finer stuff was usually porcelain, decorative and on the shelf. . . ." Then she transmutes "the finer stuff" of the latter metaphor into "the right stuff." Explain the significance and appropriateness of these metaphors, and show how they convey complicated ideas in an economical way.

For Writing

9. Quindlen claims that "even 10 years ago more than half of all Americans polled believed women should be made eligible for the draft" (¶ 12). The results Quindlen cites are derived from a poll of approximately 1,500 respondents in which 52 percent believed women should register for the draft. Conduct your own poll, both on and off campus, to find out whether the figure Quindlen states is still accurate in light of current events.

10. With a peer of the opposite gender, write an essay that discusses your own willingness—whether man or woman—to serve in the military during a period of national emergency.

AMY JO KEIFER

Keifer was born in 1972, and grew up on her family's farm in Bangor, Pennsylvania. She wrote "The Death of a Farm" in 1991 at American University, Washington, D.C., in a freshman composition course, "Writing About Contemporary Issues." Her instructor required all his students to submit a piece of writing to either the *Washington Post* or the *New York Times*, and promised an A for the semester to anyone whose work got published. However, he originally gave Keifer an F on the paper; at three pages it was too short, he said, for an op-ed (opposite the editorial page) piece.

Keifer trusted her own judgment, a good lesson for the readers of *The Essay Connection*. Although the *Times* receives hundreds of op-ed submissions each month, mostly by experienced writers and professionals in various fields, Keifer submitted her paper to the *Times* exactly as she had written it. It was published as an op-ed article on June 30, 1991, and the following semester the instructor changed her grade to an A. In 1993 Keifer graduated from American University with a B.A. in International Relations, and a strong interest in multicultural education and in the agricultural aspects of international trade.

"The Death of a Farm" was read by many people in the United States Department of Agriculture, and landed Keifer a summer internship on the *Express-Times* (Easton, Pennsylvania). Keifer's essay indeed proves that her personal experience has given her an expert's understanding of her subject. "It was easy to write," she says, "because it's a subject I know a lot about, although it was hard to get the tone right because I am so emotionally involved with the subject. We are near the Delaware Water Gap, and the land is beautiful at all seasons, especially in the fall. The farm's status today is as it was eight years ago. My younger brother will keep the family farm going, but he will have to work at a full-time job elsewhere in order to do so."

❄ *The Death of a Farm*

1   I am a farmer's daughter. I am also a 4-H member, breeder and showman of sheep and showman of cattle. My family's farm is dying and I have watched it, and my family, suffer.

2   Our eastern Pennsylvania farm is a mere 60 acres. The green rolling hills and forested land are worth a minimum of $300,000 to developers, but no longer provide my family with the means to survive. It's a condition called asset rich and cash poor, and it's a hard way of life.

3   My grandfather bought our farm when he and my grandmother were first married. He raised dairy cattle and harvested the land full time for more than 20 years. When he died, my father took over and changed the farm to beef cattle, horses and pigs, and kept the crops. But it wasn't enough to provide for a young family, so he took on a full-time job, too.

4   I can remember, when I was young, sitting on the fence with my sister and picking out a name for each calf. My sister's favorite cow was named Flower, and so we named her calves Buttercup, Daisy, Rose and Violet. Flower was the leader of a herd of more than 20. The only cattle left on our farm now are my younger sister's and brother's 4-H projects.

5   I can remember a huge tractor-trailer backed into the loading chute of our barn on days when more than 200 pigs had to be taken to market. That was before the prices went down and my father let the barn go empty rather than take on more debt.

6   I can remember my father riding on the tractor, larger than life, baling hay or planting corn. When prices started dropping, we began to rent some land to other farmers, so they could harvest from it. But prices have dropped so low this year there are no takers. The land will go unused; the tractor and the equipment have long since been sold off.

7   I don't remember the horses. I've seen a few pictures in which my father, slim and dark, is holding his newborn daughter on horseback amid a small herd. And I've heard stories of his delivering hay to farms all over the state, but I can't ever remember his loading up a truck to do it.

8   Piece by piece, our farm has deteriorated. We started breeding sheep and now have about 25 head, but they yield little revenue. My mother, who works as a registered nurse, once said something that will remain with me forever: "Your father works full-time to support the farm. I work full-time to support the family."

9   I've seen movies like "The River" and "Places in the Heart." They tell the real struggle. But people can leave a movie theater, and there's a happy

ending for them. There aren't many happy endings in a real farmer's life. I was reared hearing that hard work paid off, while seeing that it didn't. My younger brother would like to take over the farm some day, but I'm not sure it will hold on much longer. Its final breath is near.

Content

1. Keifer's family history is embedded in the story of the family farm. Explain how they are interrelated.
2. What's the point of Keifer's mother's observation, "Your father works full-time to support the farm. I work full-time to support the family" (¶ 8)?
3. Why is Keifer telling this story? To whom is she telling it? Is she trying to influence any individual action? Public policy? Is this a cautionary tale, a warning? Why would an urban newspaper, the *New York Times*, print this story?

Strategies/Structures

4. Why is it important for Keifer to state her credentials at the very outset of the essay?
5. Is it appropriate for Keifer to tip her hand in the second sentence: "My family's farm is dying and I have watched it, and my family, suffer" (¶ 1)? Or would the essay be more effective if she waited until the end, to make this the inevitable conclusion to the series of steps of the progressive deterioration of the farm which in fact she presents as the essay proceeds?
6. Keifer provides a series of snapshots of the farm and farm life. Identify some and show how they reinforce her case.

Language

7. What is the effect of beginning paragraphs 4, 5, and 6 with "I can remember"? And then of varying this pattern with "I don't remember the horses"?
8. In what ways does Keifer's simple, unadorned language convince us that she's "been there"? How does that language put her readers there as well?

For Writing

9. Keifer says, "I was reared hearing that hard work paid off, while seeing that it didn't" (¶ 9). Tell a story whose thesis contradicts conventional wisdom, as Keifer's does. Since your readers will probably be prepared, initially, to accept the conventional view, you'll have to use signals throughout (incidents, natural symbols, connotative language) that point in the opposite direction.
10. Write an essay to protest "the death of . . ." a subject close to your heart, though not necessarily close to your reader's heart or conscience. (This might be an endangered species; a vanishing way of life; a lost art or profession; a major change in the way people do things—for instance, have e-mail and the telephone meant the death of personal letters? Or of even face-to-face conversations? Avoid sentimentality.

Additional Topics for Writing
Appealing to Reason:
Deductive and Inductive Arguments

(For strategies for appealing to reason, see 440.)

1. Write a logical, clearly reasoned, well-supported argument appropriate in organization, language, and tone to the subject and appealing to your designated audience. Be sure you have in mind a particular reader or group of readers whom you know (or suspect) are likely to be receptive or hostile to your position, or uncommitted people whose opinion you're trying to influence.

   a. A college education is (or is not) worth the effort and expense.
   b. Smoking, drinking, or using "recreational" drugs is (is not) worth the risks.
   c. Economic prosperity is (is not) more important to our country than conservation and preservation of our country's resources.
   d. The Social Security system should (should not) be preserved at all costs.
   e. Everyone should (should not) be entitled to comprehensive medical care (supply one: from the cradle to the grave; in early childhood; while a student; in old age).
   f. Drunk drivers should (should not) be jailed, even for a first offense.
   g. Auto safety belts should (should not) be mandatory.
   h. Companies manufacturing products that may affect consumers' health or safety (such as food, drugs, liquor, automobiles, pesticides) should (should not) have consumer representatives on their boards of directors.
   i. The civil rights, women's liberation, gay liberation, or some comparable movement has (has not) accomplished major and long- lasting benefits for the group it represents.
   j. Intercollegiate athletic teams that are big business should (should not) hire their players; intercollegiate athletes should (should not) have professional status.
   k. Strong labor unions should (should not) be preserved at all costs.
   l. The costs of America's manned space program are worth (far exceed) the benefits.
   m. The federal government should (should not) take over the nation's health care system.
   n. The postal service should (should not) be privatized.

2. Write a letter to your campus, city, or area newspaper in which you take a stand on an issue, defending or attacking it. You could write on one of the topics in Additional Topics 1 above, or differ with a recent column or editorial. Send in your letter (keep a copy for yourself) and see if it is published. If so, what kind of response did it attract?

3. Write to your state or federal legislator urging the passage or defeat of a particular piece of legislation currently being considered. (You will probably find at least one side of the issue being reported in the newspapers or a newsmagazine.) An extra: If you receive a reply, analyze it to see whether it addresses the specific points you raise. In what fashion? Does it sound like an individual response or a form letter?

Appealing to Emotion and Ethics

The essence of an emotional appeal is passion. You write from passion, and you expect your readers to respond with equal fervor. "I have a dream." "The only thing we have to fear is fear itself." "We have nothing to offer but blood, toil, tears, and sweat." "The West wasn't won with a loaded gun!" "We shall overcome." The importance of freedom of artistic expression, as argued by the protesters and their banner in the photograph above, is compelled as much—if not more—by emotion as by logical argument. You'll be making your case in specific, concrete, memorable ways that you expect to have an unusually powerful impact on your readers. So your writing will probably be more colorful than it might be in less emotional circumstances, with a high proportion of vivid examples, narratives, anecdotes, character sketches, analogies ("Will Bosnia or Rwanda or X be another Vietnam?"), and figures of speech, including metaphors ("a knee-jerk liberal"), and similes ("The Southern Senator had a face like an old Virginia ham and a personality to match.").

You can't incite your readers, either to agree with you or to take action on behalf of the cause you favor, by simply bleeding all over the page. The process of writing and rewriting and revising again (see the chapter "Writing: Re-Vision and Revision") will act to cool your red-hot emotion and will enable you to modulate in subsequent drafts what you might have written the first time just to get out of your system. "Hell, no! We won't go!" As the essays in this section and elsewhere reveal, writers who appeal most effectively to their readers' emotions themselves exercise considerable control over the organization and examples they use to make their points.

They also keep particularly tight rein over their own emotions, as revealed in the tone and connotations of their language, crucial in an emotional appeal. Tone, the prevailing mood of the essay, like a tone of voice conveys your attitude toward your subject and toward the evidence you present in support of your point. It is clear from the tone of all the essays in this chapter—indeed, all the essays in the entire *Essay Connection*—that the authors care deeply about their subjects. Amy Jo Keifer's tone in "The Death of a Farm" (475–77) might almost be objective, but the technique she uses throughout, comparing the invariably better past, almost a golden era, with the deteriorating conditions for farmers in the present, evokes considerable emotion in the reader: "Your father works full time to support the farm," says Keifer's mother. "I work full time to support the family." Matt Nocton's "Harvest of Gold, Harvest of Shame" (515–21) is a useful companion piece to Keifer's (see also Ntozake Shange's "What Is It We Really Harvestin' Here?" [184–91]). Like Keifer, Nocton reports in a relatively objective tone on his personal experience with an aspect of farming—in this case, the harvesting of tobacco by a business that employs migrant and contract laborers, racial and ethnic minorities overseen by white bosses. Keeping himself out of the essay, he does not say in the essay that as a teenager, after two days on the job he was promoted to "bentkeeper" over the heads of minority employees with far more experience. Nevertheless, Nocton's concern for the workers and anger over their exploitation is apparent in the way he recounts the harvesting process, detail by detail, dirty, dusty, hot, and humiliating: each worker "must tie [a burlap sack] around his waist as a source of protection against the dirt and rocks that he will be dragging himself through for the next eight hours." The essays by Keifer and Nocton illustrate that these days, in nonfiction, anyway, unless it's satire, readers generally prefer understatement to overkill. To establish a climate that encourages readers to sympathize emotionally, you as a writer can present telling facts and allow the readers to interpret them, rather than continually nudging the audience with verbal reminders to see the subject your way.

If you are appealing to your readers' emotions through irony, the tone of your words, their music, is likely to be at variance with their overt message—and to intentionally undermine it. Thus the narrator of Swift's "A Modest Proposal" (491–99) can, with an impassive face, advocate that year-old children of the poor Irish peasants be sold for "a most delicious, nourishing, and wholesome food, whether stewed, roasted, baked, or broiled"; and, in an additional inhumane observation, "I make no doubt that it will equally serve in a fricassee or a ragout."

The connotations, overtones of the language, are equally significant in emotional appeals, as they subtly (or not so subtly) reinforce the overt, literal meanings of the words. Lincoln, shown (in the photograph on p. 485) arriving at Gettysburg in 1863 to deliver the speech that would rank among the most memorable in American history, deliberately uses biblical language ("Fourscore" instead of "eighty"), biblical phrasing, biblical cadences to reinforce the solemnity of the occasion—dedication of the graveyard at Gettysburg. This language also underscores the seriousness of the Civil War, then in progress, and its profound consequences.

For additional analysis see Gilbert Highet's elegant, eloquent "The Gettysburg Address" (486–91), an exemplary model of literary criticism. Here Highet gracefully combines history, biography, and an understanding of the Bible and various literary conventions while keeping the focus on this most human of subjects, Lincoln himself. In contrast to the majesty of Lincoln's language, Swift's narrator depersonalizes human beings, always calling the children *it*, with an impersonal connotation, and never employing the humanizing terms of *he*, *she*, or *baby*. The *it* emphasizes the animalistic connotations of the narrator's references to a newborn as "a child just dropped from its dam," further dehumanizing both mother and child.

Language, tone, and message often combine to present an *ethical appeal*—a way of impressing your readers that you as the author (and perhaps as a character in your own essay) are a knowledgeable person of good moral character, good will, and good sense. Consequently, you are a person of integrity, and to be believed as a credible, reasonable advocate of the position you take in your essay. In "None of This Is Fair" (322–27), Richard Rodriguez explains that as a Mexican-American he benefited considerably from Affirmative Action programs to gain financial aid in college and to get highly competitive job offers afterward. Having thus established his fitness to discuss the subject, Rodriguez agrees with the critics of Affirmative Action, that "none of this is fair." His actions reinforce his words. Not only does he decide to reject all the job offers obtained by his "unfair" means; he turns his attention, at the conclusion, to the "seriously disadvantaged," irrespective of color, the poor on whom he wishes us all to focus our best efforts.

In "Losing: An American Tradition" (504–15), Charles M. Young identifies himself early in the essay: "I may not be the worst college football player of all time. . . . I may be only the worst college football player of 1972." Thus he establishes his firsthand understanding of the subject, and his orientation to it—profound sympathy for the underdogs, thereby including most of his readers. "Losing" thus becomes an ethical analysis of the phenomenon of losing in sports (and by extrapolation, in the rest of life), the corruption of the language employed in calling people "losers," and other negative consequences of losing. Losers (nearly everyone who plays any sport) suffer from the stigmatizing effects of shame, as depicted in the photograph (p. 508) of two college football players, hunched over on the bench, faces hidden in their hands, suffering the effects of a loss. Winners lose as well, because "The kids who win are being taught that they are good only to the extent that they continue to beat other people." The sense of community is destroyed: "'We're all losers in the race to win.'" Young is not opposed to playing sports per se, but to the emphasis on winning.

Because they usually make their point indirectly, fables, parables, and other stories with subtle moral points are often used to appeal to readers' emotions and ethical sense. The photographs of winsome (never repulsive, never ugly!) waifs often grace fund-raising advertisements for famine relief, amplified by biographies of their pitiful lives; only our contributions can save them. One of the dangers in using such poster-child appeals is the possibility that you'll include too many emotional signals or ultraheavy emotional language and thereby write a paper that repels your readers by either excessive sentimentality or overkill. Lynda Barry's "The Sanctuary of School" (500–04) uses at the beginning techniques similar to the famine relief ads to present a dramatic and moving picture of herself (and her brother) as young children: "In an overcrowded and unhappy home, it's incredibly easy for any child to slip away. The high levels of frustration, depression, and anger in my house made my brother and me invisible. We were children with the sound turned off." The beginning of the essay reflects the emotional level of Barry's panic as a young child after her parents "had been fighting all night." Realizing she was "lost," she headed for "the sanctuary of school," with its host of reassuring teachers, janitor, and secretary. As the school day unfolded, so did the predictable opportunity "to sit at my desk, with my crayons and pencils and books and classmates all around me, and for the next six hours I was going to enjoy a thoroughly secure, warm, and stable world." The tone shifts gradually to reflect the calmness of the "world that I absolutely relied on," and the essay ends with an emphatic, unsentimental plea for our country to pledge allegiance to its schoolchildren. How readily we accept these arguments depends, in part, on the values, beliefs, and other experiences we bring to our reading of the work at hand. The more emotionally engaged we are at the outset, the easier it will be for such writers to enlist us in their cause.

Although ethical appeals usually tap our most profound moral values, they can be made in humorous ways, as in Judy Brady's "I Want a Wife" (361–64), which argues, implicitly, that given all the work they do—housekeeping, cleaning, cooking, childrearing, hostessing, nurturing—everyone, wives included, wants a "wife."

Appeals to emotion and ethics are often intertwined. Such appeals are everywhere, for example, in the connotations of descriptions and definitions. Furthermore, if your readers like and trust you, they're more likely to believe what you say and to be moved to agree with your point of view. The evidence in a scientific report, however strong in itself, is buttressed by the credibility of the researcher. The sense of realism, the truth of a narrative, is enhanced by the credibility of the narrator. We believe Lincoln and Barry and Nocton; and we trust the spirit of satirist Swift, even if we believe he is are exaggerating, if not downright inventing, the substance of his narrative. Hearts compel agreement where minds hesitate. Don't hesitate to make ethical use of this understanding.

STRATEGIES FOR WRITING— APPEALING TO EMOTION AND ETHICS

1. Do I want to appeal primarily to my readers' emotions (and which emotions) or to their ethical sense of how people ought to behave? (Remember that in either case the appeals are intertwined with reason—see the chapter "Appealing to Reason: Deductive and Inductive Arguments.")
2. To what kinds of readers am I making these appeals? What ethical or other personal qualities should I as an author exhibit? How can I lead my readers to believe that I am a person of sound character and good judgment?
3. What evidence can I choose to reinforce my appeals and my authorial image? Examples from my own life? The experiences of others? References to literature or scientific research? What order of arrangement would be most convincing? From the least emotionally moving or involving to the most? Or vice versa?
4. How can I interpret my evidence to move my readers to accept it? Should I explain very elaborately, or should I let the examples speak for themselves? If you decide on the latter, try out your essay on someone unfamiliar with the examples to see if they are in fact self-evident.
5. Do I want my audience to react with sympathy? Pity? Anger? Fear? Horror? To accomplish this, should I use much emotional language? Should my appeal be overt, direct? Or would indirection, understatement, be more effective? Would irony, saying the opposite of what I really mean (as Swift does), be more appropriate than a direct approach? Could I make my point more effectively with a fable, parable, comic tale, or invented persona than with a straightforward analysis and overt commentary?

ABRAHAM LINCOLN

Lincoln (1809–1865) was a self-made, self-taught son of Kentucky pioneers. He served four terms in the Illinois state legislature before being elected to Congress in 1847. As sixteenth president of the United States (1861–1865), Lincoln's supreme efforts were devoted to trying to secure the passage of the Thirteenth Amendment to outlaw slavery and to preserve the still young United States of America from the forces expressed through and beyond the bloody Civil War that threatened to destroy its young men, its economy, and the very government itself.

For a discussion of the biographical, political, historical, and literary aspects of this speech, see Gilbert Highet's "The Gettysburg Address" immediately following the questions for this essay. You may wish to defer addressing these questions until after you've read Highet's perceptive analysis.

The Gettysburg Address

1   Four score and seven years ago our fathers brought forth on this continent, a new nation, conceived in liberty, and dedicated to the proposition that all men are created equal.

2   Now we are engaged in a great civil war, testing whether that nation, or any nation so conceived and so dedicated, can long endure. We are met on a great battlefield of that war. We have come to dedicate a portion of that field, as a final resting place for those who here gave their lives that the nation might live. It is altogether fitting and proper that we should do this.

3   But, in a larger sense, we cannot dedicate—we cannot consecrate—we cannot hallow—this ground. The brave men, living and dead, who struggled here, have consecrated it, far above our poor power to add or detract. The world will little note, nor long remember what we say here, but it can never forget what they did here. It is for us the living, rather, to be dedicated here to the unfinished work which they who fought here have thus far so nobly advanced. It is rather for us to be here dedicated to the great task remaining before us—that from these honored dead we take increased devotion—that we here highly resolve that these dead shall not have died in vain—that this nation, under God, shall have a new birth of freedom—and that the government of the people, by the people, for the people, shall not perish from the earth.

Content

1. What principles of the founding of the United States does Lincoln emphasize in the first sentence? Why are these so important to the occasion of his address? To the theme of this address?

2. What does Lincoln imply and assert is the relation of life and death? Birth and rebirth?

This classic photograph of President Abraham Lincoln arriving at Gettysburg, a significant event in American history, requires the viewer to know and understand both the event at hand and its historical context. Drawing on your understanding of the events that goes well beyond this photograph, interpret its emotional as well as its historical impact.

Strategies/Structures

3. Why would Lincoln, knowing that his audience expected longer orations, deliberately have decided to make his speech so short?

4. Lincoln's speech commemorated a solemn occasion: the dedication of a major battlefield of the ongoing Civil War. Wouldn't such a short speech have undermined the significance of the event?

Language

5. Identify the language and metaphors of birth that Lincoln uses throughout this address. For what purpose? With what effect?

6. Why did Lincoln use biblical language and phrasing conspicuously at the beginning and end of the address, such as "four score and seven years ago" instead of the more common "eighty-seven"?

7. Lincoln uses many *antitheses*—oppositions, contrasts. Identify some and show how they reinforce the meaning.

8. Another important rhetorical device is the *tricolon*, "the division of an idea into three harmonious parts, usually of increasing power,"—for example, "government of the people, by the people, for the people. . . ." Find others and show why they are so memorable.

For Writing

9. Write a short, dignified speech for a solemn occasion, real or imaginary. Let the majesty of your language and the conspicuous rhetorical patterns of your sentences and paragraphs (through such devices as antithesis and parallelism) reinforce your point.

10. Rewrite the "Gettysburg Address" as it might have been spoken by a more recent president or other politician, using language, paragraphing, and sentence structures characteristic of the speaker and the times. One such speech, a parody, is William Safire's "Carter's Gettysburg Address," which begins: "Exactly two hundred and one years, five months and one day ago, our forefathers—and our foremothers, too, as my wife, the First Lady, reminds me—our highly competent Founding Persons brought forth on this land mass a new nation, or entity, dreamed up in liberty and dedicated to the comprehensive program of insuring that all of us are created with the same basic human rights."

GILBERT HIGHET

> Highet (1906–1978) took "all literature for his province." As Anthon Professor of Latin Language and Literature at Columbia University, where he taught from 1938 to 1972 (with time out for military service during World War II), he wrote and edited critical works on poetry, satire, literary history, criticism, classicism, and "the joy of teaching and learning." He wrote "the English language with affectionate ease," from a personal, enthusiastic, anecdotal perspective that charmed general readers and antagonized literary scholars who objected to his popular treatment of canonical works—as the erudite often do when laypeople are invited into their exclusive circle. Born in Glasgow, Scotland, Highet emigrated to the United States in 1937, after an education at Glasgow and Oxford. Among his most popular works are *The Art of Teaching* (1950) and *The Anatomy of Satire* (1962).
>
> With the same understated eloquence and ease that Lincoln used in "The Gettysburg Address," Highet places the speech and the speaker in their biographical, historical, literary, and political contexts. Highet's knowledge of his subject is equaled by his love of Lincoln and profound respect for his work, indeed a work of art as well as oratory.

The Gettysburg Address

1   Fourscore and seven years ago . . .

2   These five words stand at the entrance to the best-known monument of American prose, one of the finest utterances in the entire language and surely one of the greatest speeches in all history. Greatness is like granite: it is molded in fire, and it lasts for many centuries.

Fourscore and seven years ago. . . . It is strange to think that President Lincoln was looking back to the 4th of July 1776, and that he and his speech are now further removed from us than he himself was from George Washington and the Declaration of Independence. Fourscore and seven years before the Gettysburg Address, a small group of patriots signed the Declaration. Fourscore and seven years after the Gettysburg Address, it was the year 1950,[1] and that date is already receding rapidly into our troubled, adventurous, and valiant past.

Inadequately prepared and at first scarcely realized in its full importance, the dedication of the graveyard at Gettysburg was one of the supreme moments of American history. The battle itself had been a turning point of the war. On the 4th of July 1863, General Meade repelled Lee's invasion of Pennsylvania. Although he did not follow up his victory, he had broken one of the most formidable aggressive enterprises of the Confederate armies. Losses were heavy on both sides. Thousands of dead were left on the field, and thousands of wounded died in the hot days following the battle. At first, their burial was more or less haphazard; but thoughtful men gradually came to feel that an adequate burying place and memorial were required. These were established by an interstate commission that autumn, and the finest speaker in the North was invited to dedicate them. This was the scholar and statesman Edward Everett of Harvard. He made a good speech—which is still extant: not at all academic, it is full of close strategic analysis and deep historical understanding.

Lincoln was not invited to speak, at first. Although people knew him as an effective debater, they were not sure whether he was capable of making a serious speech on such a solemn occasion. But one of the impressive things about Lincoln's career is that he constantly strove to *grow*. He was anxious to appear on that occasion and to say something worthy of it. (Also, it has been suggested, he was anxious to remove the impression that he did not know how to behave properly—an impression which had been strengthened by a shocking story about his clowning on the battlefield of Antietam the previous year.) Therefore when he was invited he took considerable care with his speech. He drafted rather more than half of it in the White House before leaving, finished it in the hotel at Gettysburg the night before the ceremony (not in the train, as sometimes reported), and wrote out a fair copy the next morning.

There are many accounts of the day itself, 19 November 1863. There are many descriptions of Lincoln, all showing the same curious blend of grandeur and awkwardness, or lack of dignity, or—it would be best to call it humility. In the procession he rode horseback: a tall lean man in a high plug hat, straddling a short horse, with his feet too near the ground. He arrived before the chief speaker, and had to wait patiently for half an hour

---

[1] In November 1950 the Chinese had just entered the war in Korea.

or more. His own speech came right at the end of a long and exhausting ceremony, lasted less than three minutes, and made little impression on the audience. In part this was because they were tired, in part because (as eye-witnesses said) he ended almost before they knew he had begun, and in part because he did not speak the Address, but read it, very slowly, in a thin high voice, with a marked Kentucky accent, pronouncing "to" as "toe" and dropping his final R's.

7   Some people of course were alert enough to be impressed. Everett congratulated him at once. But most of the newspapers paid little attention to the speech, and some sneered at it. The *Patriot and Union* of Harrisburg wrote, "We pass over the silly remarks of the President; for the credit of the nation we are willing . . . that they shall be no more repeated or thought of"; and the London *Times* said, "The ceremony was rendered ludicrous by some of the sallies of that poor President Lincoln," calling his remarks "dull and commonplace." The first commendation of the Address came in a single sentence of the Chicago *Tribune,* and the first discriminating and detailed praise of it appeared in the Springfield *Republican,* the Providence *Journal,* and the Philadelphia *Bulletin.* However, three weeks after the ceremony and then again the following spring, the editor of *Harper's Weekly* published a sincere and thorough eulogy of the Address, and soon it was attaining recognition as a masterpiece.

8   At the time, Lincoln could not care much about the reception of his words. He was exhausted and ill. In the train back to Washington, he lay down with a wet towel on his head. He had caught smallpox. At that moment he was incubating it, and he was stricken down soon after he re-entered the White House. Fortunately it was a mild attack, and it evoked one of his best jokes: he told his visitors, "At last I have something I can give to everybody."

9   He had more than that to give to everybody. He was a unique person, far greater than most people realize until they read his life with care. The wisdom of his policy, the sources of his statesmanship—these were things too complex to be discussed in a brief essay. But we can say something about the Gettysburg Address as a work of art.

10   A work of art. Yes: for Lincoln was a literary artist, trained both by others and by himself. The textbooks he used as a boy were full of difficult exercises and skillful devices in formal rhetoric, stressing the qualities he practiced in his own speaking: antithesis, parallelism, and verbal harmony. Then he read and reread many admirable models of thought and expression: the King James Bible, the essays of Bacon, the best plays of Shakespeare. His favorites were *Hamlet, Lear, Macbeth, Richard III,* and *Henry VIII,* which he had read dozens of times. He loved reading aloud, too, and spent hours reading poetry to his friends. (He told his partner Herndon that he preferred getting the sense of any document by reading it aloud.) Therefore his serious speeches are important parts of the long and noble classical tradition of oratory which begins in Greece, runs

through Rome to the modern world, and is still capable (if we do not neglect it) of producing masterpieces.

The first proof of this is that the Gettysburg Address is full of quo-   11
tations—or rather of adaptations—which give it strength. It is partly religious, partly (in the highest sense) political: therefore it is interwoven
with memories of the Bible and memories of American history. The first
and last words are Biblical cadences. Normally Lincoln did not say "fourscore" when he meant eighty; but on this solemn occasion he recalled the
important dates in the Bible—such as the age of Abram when his first son
was born to him, and he was "fourscore and six years old."[2] Similarly he
did not say there was a chance that democracy might die out: he recalled
the somber phrasing of the Book of Job—where Bildad speaks of the destruction of one who shall vanish without a trace, and says that "his
branch shall be cut off: his remembrance shall perish from the earth."[3]
Then again, the famous description of our State as "government of the
people, by the people, for the people" was adumbrated by Daniel Webster
in 1830 (he spoke of "the people's government, made for the people, made
by the people, and answerable to the people") and then elaborated in 1854
by the abolitionist Theodore Parker (as "government of all the people, by
all the people, for all the people"). There is good reason to think that Lincoln took the important phrase "under God" (which he interpolated at the
last moment) from Weems, the biographer of Washington; and we know
that it had been used at least once by Washington himself.

Analyzing the address further, we find that it is based on a highly imagi-   12
native theme, or group of themes. The subject is—how can we put it, so
as not to disfigure it?—the subject is the kinship of life and death, that
mysterious linkage which we see sometimes as the physical succession of
birth and death in our world, sometimes as the contrast, which is perhaps
a unity, between death and immortality. The first sentence is concerned
with birth:

Our *fathers brought forth* a *new* nation, *conceived* in liberty.

The final phrase but one expresses the hope that

this nation, under God, shall have a *new birth* of freedom.

And the last phrase of all speaks of continuing life as the triumph over
death. Again and again throughout the speech, this mystical contrast and
kinship reappear: "those who *gave their lives* that that nation might *live*,"
"the brave men *living* and *dead*," and so in the central assertion that the
dead have already consecrated their own burial place, while "it is for us,
the *living*, rather to be dedicated . . . to the great task remaining." The

---

[2] Genesis 16:16; and Exodus 7:7.
[3] Job 18:16–17; Jeremiah 10:11; Micah 7:2

Gettysburg Address is a prose poem; it belongs to the same world as the great elegies, and the adagios of Beethoven.

13   Its structure, however, is that of a skillfully contrived speech. The oratorical pattern is perfectly clear. Lincoln describes the occasion, dedicates the ground, and then draws a larger conclusion by calling on his hearers to dedicate themselves to the preservation of the Union. But within that, we can trace his constant use of at least two important rhetorical devices.

14   The first of these two is *antithesis:* opposition, contrast. The speech is full of it. Listen:

> The world will little *note*
> 　　　　　nor long *remember*　　　what *we say* here
> 　but　　　it can never *forget*　　　what *they did* here.

And so in nearly every sentence: "brave men, *living* and *dead*"; "to *add* or *detract.*" There is the antithesis of the Founding Fathers and the men of Lincoln's own time:

> Our *fathers brought forth* a new nation . . .
> now *we* are testing whether that nation . . . can *long endure.*

And there is the more terrible antithesis of those who have already died and those who still live to do their duty. Now, antithesis is the figure of contrast and conflict. Lincoln was speaking in the midst of a great civil war.

15   The other important pattern is different. It is technically called *tricolon* —the division of an idea into three harmonious parts, usually of increasing power. The most famous phrase of the Address is a tricolon:

> government of the people
> 　　　　　by the people
> 　and　　　for the people.

The most solemn sentence is a tricolon:

> we cannot dedicate
> we cannot consecrate
> we cannot hallow this ground.

And above all, the last sentence (which has sometimes been criticized as too complex) is essentially two parallel phrases, with a tricolon growing out of the second and then producing another tricolon: a trunk, three branches, and a cluster of flowers. Lincoln says that it is for his hearers to be dedicated to the great task remaining before them. Then he goes on,

> that from these honored dead

—apparently he means "in such a way that from these honored dead"—

> we take increased devotion to that cause.

Next, he restates this more briefly:

> that we here highly resolve . . .

And now the actual resolution follows, in three parts of growing intensity:

> that these dead shall not have died in vain
> that this nation, under God, shall have a new birth
> of freedom

and that (one more tricolon)

> government of the people
>   by the people
> and   for the people
> shall not perish from the earth.

Now the tricolon is the figure which, through division, emphasizes basic harmony and unity. Lincoln used antithesis because he was speaking to people at war. He used the tricolon because he was hoping, planning, praying for peace.

No one thinks that when he was drafting the Gettysburg Address, Lincoln 16 deliberately looked up these quotations and consciously chose these particular patterns of thought. No, he chose the theme. From its development and from the emotional tone of the entire occasion, all the rest followed, or grew—by that marvelous process of choice and rejection which is essential to artistic creation. It does not spoil such a work of art to analyze it as closely as we have done; it is altogether fitting and proper that we should do this: for it helps us to penetrate more deeply into the rich meaning of the Gettysburg Address, and it allows us the very rare privilege of watching the workings of a great man's mind.

Sources

W. E. Barton. *Lincoln at Gettysburg*. Bobbs-Merrill. 1930.

R. P. Basler. "Abraham Lincoln's Rhetoric." *American Literature:* 11:1939–40, 167–82.

L. E. Robinson. *Abraham Lincoln as a Man of Letters*. Chicago, 1918.

See questions following Lincoln's "The Gettysburg Address" (484–85).

JONATHAN SWIFT

Swift, author of *Gulliver's Travels* (1726) and other satiric essays, poems, and tracts, was well acquainted with irony. Born in Dublin in 1667, the son of impoverished English Anglicans, he obtained a degree from Trinity College, Dublin, in 1685 only by "special grace." When James II arrived in Ireland in 1688, he initiated pro-Catholic, anti-Protestant policies that remained in force until the ascendancy of William III. Swift, along with many Anglo-Irish, was forced to flee to England, was eventually ordained as an Anglican priest, and rose prominently in London literary and political circles until 1713. Although he had hoped for a church appointment in England, his desertion of the Whig Party for the Tories was ironically rewarded with an appointment as dean of St. Patrick's (Anglican) Cathedral in Dublin, which he regarded as virtual exile. Nevertheless, despite his religious differences with the Irish people, Swift became a beloved leader in the Irish resistance to English oppression, motivated less by partisan emotions than by his own "savage indignation" against injustice. He died in 1745.

Swift wrote "A Modest Proposal" in the summer of 1729, after three years of drought and crop failure had forced over 35,000 peasants to leave their homes and wander the countryside looking for work, food, and shelter for their starving families, ignored by the insensitive absentee landowners. The "Proposal" carries the English landowners' treatment of the Irish to its logical—but repugnant—extreme: if they are going to devour any hope the Irish have of living decently, why don't they literally eat the Irish children? The persona Swift creates is logical, consistent, seemingly rational—and utterly inhumane, an advocate of infanticide and cannibalism. Yet nowhere in the "Proposal" does the satirist condemn the speaker; he relies on the readers' sense of morality for that. This tactic can be dangerous, for a reader who misses the irony may take the "Proposal" at face value. But Swift's intended readers, English (landlords included) as well as Irish who could act to alleviate the people's suffering, understood very well what he meant. The victims themselves, largely illiterate, would probably have been unaware of this forceful plea on their behalf.

A Modest Proposal

1   It is a melancholy object to those who walk through this great town or travel in the country, when they see the streets, the roads, and cabin doors, crowded with beggars of the female sex, followed by three, four, or six children, all in rags and importuning every passenger for an alms. These mothers, instead of being able to work for their honest livelihood, are forced to employ all their time in strolling to beg sustenance for their helpless infants: who as they grow up either turn thieves for want of work, or leave their dear native country to fight for the pretender in Spain, or sell themselves to the Barbadoes.

2   I think it is agreed by all parties that this prodigious number of children in the arms, or on the backs, or at the heels of their mothers, and frequently of their fathers, is in the present deplorable state of the kingdom a very great additional grievance; and, therefore, whoever could find out a fair, cheap, and easy method of making these children sound, useful members of the commonwealth, would deserve so well of the public as to have his statue set up for a preserver of the nation.

But my intention is very far from being confined to provide only for the children of professed beggars; it is of a much greater extent, and shall take in the whole number of infants at a certain age who are born of parents in effect as little able to support them as those who demand our charity in the streets.

As to my own part, having turned my thoughts for many years upon this important subject, and maturely weighed the several schemes of our projectors, I have always found them grossly mistaken in their computation. It is true, a child just dropped from its dam may be supported by her milk for a solar year, with little other nourishment; at most not above the value of two shillings, which the mother may certainly get, or the value in scraps, by her lawful occupation of begging; and it is exactly at one year old that I propose to provide for them in such a manner as instead of being a charge upon their parents or the parish, or wanting food and raiment for the rest of their lives, they shall on the contrary contribute to the feeding, and partly to the clothing, of many thousands.

There is likewise another great advantage in my scheme, that it will prevent those voluntary abortions, and that horrid practice of women murdering their bastard children, alas! too frequent among us! sacrificing the poor innocent babes I doubt more to avoid the expense than the shame, which would move tears and pity in the most savage and inhuman breast.

The number of souls in this kingdom being usually reckoned one million and half, of these I calculate there may be about two hundred thousand couple whose wives are breeders; from which number I subtract thirty thousand couple who are able to maintain their own children (although I apprehend there cannot be so many, under the present distress of the kingdom); but this being granted, there will remain an hundred and seventy thousand breeders. I again subtract fifty thousand for those women who miscarry, or whose children die by accident or disease within the year. There only remain an hundred and twenty thousand children of poor parents annually born. The question therefore is, how this number shall be reared and provided for? which, as I have already said, under the present situation of affairs, is utterly impossible by all the methods hitherto proposed. For we can neither employ them in handicraft or agriculture; we neither build houses (I mean in the country) nor cultivate land; they can very seldom pick up a livelihood by stealing, till they arrive at six years old, except where they are of towardly parts; although I confess they learn the rudiments much earlier; during which time they can, however, be properly looked upon only as probationers; as I have been informed by a principal gentleman in the country of Cavan, who protested to me that he never knew above one or two instances under the age of six, even in a part of the kingdom so renowned for the quickest proficiency in that art.

I am assured by our merchants, that a boy or a girl before twelve years old is no saleable commodity; and even when they come to this age they will not yield above three pounds, or three pounds and a half a crown at most on the Exchange; which cannot turn to account either to the parents or kingdom, the charge of nutriment and rags having been at least four times that value.

8   I shall now therefore humbly propose my own thoughts, which I hope will not be liable to the least objection.

9   I have been assured by a very knowing American of my acquaintance in London, that a young healthy child well nursed is at a year old the most delicious, nourishing, and wholesome food, whether stewed, roasted, baked, or broiled; and I make no doubt that it will equally serve in a fricassee or a ragout.

10   I do therefore humbly offer it to public consideration that of the hundred and twenty thousand children already computed, twenty thousand may be reserved for breed, whereof only one fourth part to be males; which is more than we allow to sheep, black cattle, or swine; and my reason is, that these children are seldom the fruits of marriage, a circumstance not much regarded by our savages; therefore, one male will be sufficient to serve four females. That the remaining hundred thousand may, at a year old, be offered in sale to the persons of quality and fortune through the kingdom; always advising the mother to let them suck plentifully in the last month, so as to render them plump and fat for a good table. A child will make two dishes at an entertainment for friends; and when the family dines alone, the fore or hind quarter will make a reasonable dish, and seasoned with a little pepper or salt will be very good boiled on the fourth day, especially in winter.

11   I have reckoned upon a medium that a child just born will weigh twelve pounds, and in a solar year, if tolerably nursed, will increase to twenty-eight pounds.

12   I grant this food will be somewhat dear, and therefore very proper for landlords, who, as they have already devoured most of the parents, seem to have the best title to the children.

13   Infant's flesh will be in season throughout the year, but more plentiful in March, and a little before and after: for we are told by a grave author, an eminent French physician, that fish being a prolific diet, there are more children born in Roman Catholic countries about nine months after Lent than at any other season; therefore, reckoning a year after Lent, the markets will be more glutted than usual, because the number of popish infants is at least three to one in this kingdom: and therefore it will have one other collateral advantage, by lessening the number of papists among us.

14   I have already computed the charge of nursing a beggar's child (in which list I reckon all cottagers, laborers, and four-fifths of the farmers) to be about two shillings per annum, rags included; and I believe no gentleman would repine to give ten shillings for the carcass of a good fat child, which, as I have said, will make four dishes of excellent nutritive meat, when he has only some particular friend or his own family to dine with him. Thus the squire will learn to be a good landlord, and grow popular

among the tenants; the mother will have eight shillings net profit, and be fit for work till she produces another child.

Those who are more thrifty (as I must confess the times require) may flay the carcass; the skin of which artificially dressed will make admirable gloves for ladies, and summer boots for fine gentlemen. 15

As to our city of Dublin, shambles may be appointed for this purpose in the most convenient parts of it, and butchers we may be assured will not be wanting: although I rather recommend buying the children alive, and dressing them hot from the knife as we do roasting pigs. 16

A very worthy person, a true lover of his country, and whose virtues I highly esteem, was lately pleased in discoursing on this matter to offer a refinement upon my scheme. He said that many gentlemen of this kingdom, having of late destroyed their deer, he conceived that the want of venison might be well supplied by the bodies of young lads and maidens, not exceeding fourteen years of age nor under twelve; so great a number of both sexes in every country being now ready to starve for want of work and service; and these to be disposed of by their parents, if alive, or otherwise by their nearest relations. But with due deference to so excellent a friend and so deserving a patriot, I cannot be altogether in his sentiments; for as to the males, my American acquaintance assured me from frequent experience that their flesh was generally tough and lean, like that of our schoolboys by continual exercise, and their taste disagreeable; and to fatten them would not answer the charge. Then as to the females, it would, I think, with humble submission be a loss to the public, because they soon would become breeders themselves: and besides, it is not improbable that some scrupulous people might be apt to censure such a practice (although indeed very unjustly), as a little bordering upon cruelty; which, I confess, has always been with me the strongest objection against any project, how well soever intended. 17

But in order to justify my friend, he confessed that this expedient was put into his head by the famous Psalmanazar, a native of the island Formosa, who came from thence to London about twenty years ago: and in conversation told my friend, that in his country when any young person happened to be put to death, the executioner sold the carcass to persons of quality as a prime dainty; and that in his time the body of a plump girl of fifteen, who was crucified for an attempt to poison the emperor, was sold to his imperial majesty's prime minister of state, and other great mandarins of the court, in joints from the gibbet, at four hundred crowns. Neither indeed can I deny, that if the same use were made of several plump young girls in this town, who without one single groat to their fortunes cannot stir abroad without a chair, and appear at the playhouse and assemblies in foreign fineries which they never will pay for, the kingdom would not be the worse. 18

Some persons of a desponding spirit are in great concern about that vast number of poor people, who are aged, diseased, or maimed, and I have 19 been desired to employ my thoughts what course may be taken to ease the nation of so grievous an encumbrance. But I am not in the least pain upon that matter, because it is very well known that they are every day dying and rotting by cold and famine, and filth and vermin, as fast as can be reasonably expected. And as to the young laborers, they are now in as hopeful a condition: they cannot get work, and consequently pine away for want of nourishment, to a degree that if at any time they are accidentally hired to common labor, they have not strength to perform it; and thus the country and themselves are happily delivered from the evils to come.

20   I have too long digressed, and therefore shall return to my subject. I think the advantages by the proposal which I have made are obvious and many, as well as of the highest importance.

21   For first, as I have already observed, it would greatly lessen the number of papists, with whom we are yearly overrun, being the principal breeders of the nation as well as our most dangerous enemies; and who stay at home on purpose to deliver the kingdom to the Pretender, hoping to take their advantage by the absence of so many good Protestants, who have chosen rather to leave their country than stay at home and pay tithes against their conscience to an Episcopal curate.

22   Secondly, The poor tenants will have something valuable of their own, which by law may be made liable to distress and help to pay their landlord's rent, their corn and cattle being already seized, and money a thing unknown.

23   Thirdly, Whereas the maintenance of a hundred thousand children from two years old and upward, cannot be computed at less than ten shillings a piece per annum, the nation's stock will be thereby increased fifty thousand pounds per annum, beside the profit of a new dish introduced to the tables of all gentlemen of fortune in the kingdom who have any refinement in taste. And the money will circulate among ourselves, the goods being entirely of our own growth and manufacture.

24   Fourthly, The constant breeders beside the gain of eight shillings sterling per annum by the sale of their children, will be rid of the charge of maintaining them after the first year.

25   Fifthly, This food would likewise bring great custom to taverns, where the vintners will certainly be so prudent as to procure the best receipts for dressing it to perfection, and consequently have their houses frequented by all the fine gentlemen, who justly value themselves upon their knowledge in good eating; and a skillful cook who understands how to oblige his guests, will contrive to make it as expensive as they please.

26   Sixthly, This would be a great inducement to marriage, which all wise nations have either encouraged by rewards or enforced by laws and penalties. It would increase the care and tenderness of mothers toward their children, when they were sure of a settlement for life to the poor babes, provided in some sort by the public, to their annual profit instead of expense. We should see an honest emulation among the married women,

which of them would bring the fattest child to the market. Men would become as fond of their wives during the time of their pregnancy as they are now of their mares in foal, their cows in calf, their sows when they are ready to farrow; nor offer to beat or kick them (as is too frequent a practice) for fear of a miscarriage.

Many other advantages might be enumerated. For instance, the addition of some thousand carcasses in our exportation of barreled beef, the propagation of swine's flesh, and improvement in the art of making good bacon, so much wanted among us by the great destruction of pigs, too frequent at our table; which are no way comparable in taste or magnificence to a well-grown, fat, yearling child, which roasted whole will make a considerable figure at a lord mayor's feast or any other public entertainment. But this and many others I omit, being studious of brevity.

Supposing that one thousand families in this city would be constant customers for infants' flesh, besides others who might have it at merry-meetings, particularly at weddings and christenings, I compute that Dublin would take off annually about twenty thousand carcasses; and the rest of the kingdom (where probably they will be sold somewhat cheaper) the remaining eighty thousand.

I can think of no one objection that will possibly be raised against this proposal, unless it should be urged that the number of people will be thereby much lessened in the kingdom. This I freely own, and it was indeed one principal design in offering it to the world. I desire the reader will observe, that I calculate my remedy for this one individual kingdom of Ireland and for no other that ever was, is, or I think ever can be upon earth. Therefore let no man talk to me of other expedients; of taxing our absentees at five shillings a pound: of using neither clothes nor household furniture except what is of our own growth and manufacture: of utterly rejecting the materials and instruments that promote foreign luxury: of curing the expensiveness of pride, vanity, idleness, and gaming in our women: of introducing a vein of parsimony, prudence, and temperance: of learning to love our country, in the want of which we differ even from Laplanders and the inhabitants of Topinamboo: of quitting our animosities and factions, nor acting any longer like the Jews, who were murdering one another at the very moment their city was taken: of being a little cautious not to sell our country and conscience for nothing: of teaching landlords to have at least one degree of mercy toward their tenants; lastly, of putting a spirit of honesty, industry, and skill into our shopkeepers; who, if a resolution could now be taken to buy only our native goods, would immediately unite to cheat and exact upon us in the price, the measure, and the goodness, nor could ever yet be brought to make one fair proposal of just dealing, though often and earnestly invited to it.

Therefore I repeat, let no man talk to me of these and the like expedients, till he has at least some glimpse of hope that there will be ever some hearty and sincere attempts to put them in practice.

31   But as to myself, having been wearied out for many years with offering vain, idle, visionary thoughts, and at length utterly despairing of success, I fortunately fell upon this proposal; which, as it is wholly new, so it has something solid and real, of no expense and little trouble, full in our own power, and whereby we can incur no danger in disobliging England. For this kind of commodity will not bear exportation, the flesh being of too tender a consistence to admit a long continuance in salt, although perhaps I could name a country which would be glad to eat up our whole nation without it.

32   After all, I am not so violently bent upon my own opinion as to reject any offer proposed by wise men, which shall be found equally innocent, cheap, easy, and effectual. But before something of that kind shall be advanced in contradiction to my scheme, and offering a better, I desire the author or authors will be pleased maturely to consider two points. First, as things now stand, how they will be able to find food and raiment for a hundred thousand useless mouths and backs. And secondly, there being a round million of creatures in human figure throughout this kingdom, whose subsistence put into a common stock would leave them in debt two millions of pounds sterling, adding those who are beggars by profession to the bulk of farmers, cottagers, and laborers, with the wives and children who are beggars in effect; I desire those politicians who dislike my overture, and may perhaps be so bold as to attempt an answer, that they will first ask the parents of these mortals, whether they would not at this day think it a great happiness to have been sold for food at a year old in the manner I prescribe, and thereby have avoided such a perpetual scene of misfortunes as they have since gone through by the oppression of landlords, the impossibility of paying rent without money or trade, the want of common sustenance, with neither house nor clothes to cover them from the inclemencies of the weather, and the most inevitable prospect of entailing the like or greater miseries upon their breed for ever.

33   I profess, in the sincerity of my heart, that I have not the least personal interest in endeavoring to promote this necessary work, having no other motive than the public good of my country, by advancing our trade, providing for infants, relieving the poor, and giving some pleasure to the rich. I have no children by which I can propose to get a single penny; the youngest being nine years old, and my wife past child-bearing.

Content

1. What is the overt thesis of Swift's essay? What is its implied (and real) thesis? In what ways do these theses differ?

2. What are the primary aims and values of the narrator of the essay? Identify the economic advantages of his proposal that he offers in paragraphs 9–16. How

do the narrator's alleged aims and values differ from the aims and values of Swift as the essay's author?

3. What do the advantages that the narrator offers for his proposal (¶s 21–26) reveal about the social and economic conditions of Ireland when Swift was writing?

4. Why is it a "very knowing *American*" who has assured the narrator of the suitability of year-old infants for food (¶ 9)?

5. Swift as the author of the essay expects his readers to respond to the narrator's cold economic arguments on a humane, moral level. What might such an appropriate response be?

Strategies/Structures

6. What persona (a created character) does the speaker of Swift's essay have? How are readers to know that this character is not Swift himself?

7. Why does the narrator use so many mathematical computations throughout? How do they reinforce his economic argument? How do they enhance the image of his cold-bloodedness?

8. Why did Swift choose to present his argument indirectly rather than overtly? What advantages does this indirect, consistently ironic technique provide? What disadvantages does it have (for instance, do you think Swift's readers are likely to believe he really advocated eating babies)?

Language

9. What is the prevailing tone of the essay? How does it undermine what the narrator says? How does the tone reinforce Swift's implied meaning?

10. Why does Swift say "a child just dropped from its dam" (¶ 4) instead of "just born from his mother"? What other language reinforces the animalistic associations (see, for instance, "breeders" in ¶ 17)?

11. In paragraph 21 Swift refers to Roman Catholics by the common term "papists." What clues does the context provide as to whether this usage is complimentary or derogatory? How does this emphasize the sense of a split between the English Anglican landowners and the Irish Catholic tenants that prevails throughout the essay?

For Writing

12. Write a modest proposal of your own. Pick some problem that you think needs to be solved, and propose, for a critical audience, a radical solution—perhaps a dramatic way to bring about world peace, preserve endangered species, dispose of chemical or nuclear waste, or use genetic engineering.

13. Write an essay in which a created character, a narrative persona, speaks ironically (as Swift's narrator does) about your subject. The character's values should be at variance with the values you and your audience share. For instance, if you want to propose stiff penalties for drunk driving, your narrator could be a firm advocate of drinking, and of driving without restraint, and could be shown driving unsafely while under the influence of alcohol, indifferent to the dangers.

LYNDA BARRY

Lynda Barry (born 1956), daughter of a Filipino mother and an American father, grew up in an interracial neighborhood in Seattle. She told an interviewer, "There was always a lot of commotion in the house, mostly in the kitchen. We didn't have a set dinner or lunch or breakfast time; when we wanted to eat there was always food on the stove. . . . At the time it was a little frustrating for me, because I looked to all the world like a regular little white American kid, but at home we were eating real different food and there was sometimes octopus in the refrigerator and stuff that was scary looking to my friends. . . . We ate with our hands, and when you say that, people think that you're also squatting on the floor . . . but it wasn't like that. There's a whole etiquette to the way that you eat with your hands, just like you hold a fork. And it was lively and unusual, an atmosphere where I . . . could pretty much do whatever I wanted to do."

As "The Sanctuary of School" indicates, "drawing came to mean everything" to the little girl who grew up to be a cartoonist. Nevertheless, when she began Evergreen State College she "wanted to be a fine artist," she says. "Cartoons to me were really base." Then she realized that her drawings could make her friends laugh, and shortly after she graduated, in 1978, she created "Ernie Pook's Comeek," a wry, witty, and feminist strip now syndicated in over sixty newspapers in the United States, Canada, Russia, and Hungary. Barry's eighth comic collection is *It's So Magic* (1994); her second novel is *Cruddy* (1998). *One Hundred Demons*, her autobiography in graphic novel format, was published in 2003. She is also a commentator for National Public Radio's *Morning Edition*. Her first novel, *The Good Times Are Killing Me,* was published in 1988. Like many satirists, Barry cares deeply about her subjects, as illustrated in her compassionate plea for social justice for children that permeates "The Sanctuary of School," first published in the *New York Times* Education Section, January 5, 1992.

The Sanctuary of School

1   I was 7 years old the first time I snuck out of the house in the dark. It was winter and my parents had been fighting all night. They were short on money and long on relatives who kept "temporarily" moving into our house because they had nowhere else to go.

2   My brother and I were used to giving up our bedroom. We slept on the couch, something we actually liked because it put us that much closer to the light of our lives, our television.

3   At night when everyone was asleep, we lay on our pillows watching it with the sound off. We watched Steve Allen's mouth moving. We watched Johnny Carson's mouth moving. We watched movies filled with gangsters

shooting machine guns into packed rooms, dying solders hurling a last grenade and beautiful women crying at windows. Then the sign-off finally came and we tried to sleep.

The morning I snuck out, I woke up filled with a panic about needing to get to school. The sun wasn't quite up yet but my anxiety was so fierce that I just got dressed, walked quietly across the kitchen and let myself out the back door. [4]

It was quiet outside. Stars were still out. Nothing moved and no one was in the street. It was as if someone had turned the sound off on the world. [5]

I walked the alley, breaking thin ice over the puddles with my shoes. I didn't know why I was walking to school in the dark. I didn't think about it. All I knew was a feeling of panic, like the panic that strikes kids when they realize they are lost. [6]

That feeling eased the moment I turned the corner and saw the dark outline of my school at the top of the hill. My school was made up of about 15 nondescript portable classrooms set down on a fenced concrete lot in a rundown Seattle neighborhood, but it had the most beautiful view of the Cascade Mountains. You could see them from anywhere on the playfield and you could see them from the windows of my classroom—Room 2. [7]

I walked over to the monkey bars and hooked my arms around the cold metal. I stood for a long time just looking across Rainier Valley. The sky was beginning to whiten and I could hear a few birds. [8]

In a perfect world my absence at home would not have gone unnoticed. I would have had two parents in a panic to locate me, instead of two parents in a panic to locate an answer to the hard question of survival during a deep financial and emotional crisis. [9]

But in an overcrowded and unhappy home, it's incredibly easy for any child to slip away. The high levels of frustration, depression and anger in my house made my brother and me invisible. We were children with the sound turned off. And for us, as for the steadily increasing number of neglected children in this country, the only place where we could count on being noticed was at school. [10]

"Hey there, young lady. Did you forget to go home last night?" It was Mr. Gunderson, our janitor, whom we all loved. He was nice and he was funny and he was old with white hair, thick glasses and an unbelievable number of keys. I could hear them jingling as he walked across the playfield. I felt incredibly happy to see him. [11]

He let me push his wheeled garbage can between the different portables as he unlocked each room. He let me turn on the lights and raise the window shades and I saw my school slowly come to life. I saw Mrs. Holman, our school secretary, walk into the office without her orange lipstick on yet. She waved. [12]

13   I saw the fifth-grade teacher, Mr. Cunningham, walking under the breezeway eating a hard roll. He waved.

14   And I saw my teacher, Mrs. Claire LeSane, walking toward us in a red coat and calling my name in a very happy and surprised way, and suddenly my throat got tight and my eyes stung and I ran toward her crying. It was something that surprised us both.

15   It's only thinking about it now, 28 years later, that I realize I was crying from relief. I was with my teacher, and in a while I was going to sit at my desk, with my crayons and pencils and books and classmates all around me, and for the next six hours I was going to enjoy a thoroughly secure, warm and stable world. It was a world I absolutely relied on. Without it, I don't know where I would have gone that morning.

16   Mrs. LeSane asked me what was wrong and when I said "Nothing," she seemingly left it at that. But she asked me if I would carry her purse for her, an honor above all honors, and she asked if I wanted to come into Room 2 early and paint.

17 She believed in the natural healing power of painting and drawing for troubled children. In the back of her room there was always a drawing table and an easel with plenty of supplies, and sometimes during the day she would come up to you for what seemed like no good reason and quietly ask if you wanted to go to the back table and "make some pictures for Mrs. LeSane." We all had a chance at it—to sit apart from the class for a while to paint, draw and silently work out impossible problems on 11 × 17 sheets of newsprint.

18   Drawing came to mean everything to me. At the back table in Room 2, I learned to build myself a life preserver that I could carry into my home.

19   We all know that a good education system saves lives, but the people of this country are still told that cutting the budget for public schools is necessary, that poor salaries for teachers are all we can manage and that art, music and all creative activities must be the first to go when times are lean.

20 Before- and after-school programs are cut and we are told that public schools are not made for baby-sitting children. If parents are neglectful temporarily or permanently, for whatever reason, it's certainly sad, but their unlucky children must fend for themselves. Or slip through the cracks. Or wander in a dark night alone.

21   We are told in a thousand ways that not only are public schools not important, but that the children who attend them, the children who need them most, are not important either. We leave them to learn from the blind eye of a television, or to the mercy of "a thousand points of light" that can be as far away as stars.

22   I was lucky. I had Mrs. LeSane. I had Mr. Gunderson. I had an abundance of art supplies. And I had a particular brand of neglect in my home

that allowed me to slip away and get to them. But what about the rest of the kids who weren't as lucky? What happened to them?

By the time the bell rang that morning I had finished my drawing and 23 Mrs. LeSane pinned it up on the special bulletin board she reserved for drawings from the back table. It was the same picture I always drew—a sun in the corner of a blue sky over a nice house with flowers all around it.

Mrs. LeSane asked us to please stand, face the flag, place our right 24 hands over our hearts and say the Pledge of Allegiance. Children across the country do it faithfully. I wonder now when the country will face its children and say a pledge right back.

Content

1. What is the point of calling school a "sanctuary" (in the title)? How does Barry reinforce this image throughout the essay? Identify some of the life-saving features of Barry's second grade. Is Barry's view likely to convince even those readers whose elementary school experiences were quite different from hers, for instance, readers who regarded school as a form of prison or punishment?

2. Barry tells a personal story to make a general point about the values and economic priorities of the entire country. What is her point? Is it appropriate to make such a sweeping generalization on the basis of a single incident from one person's experience?

Strategies/Structures

3. How does Barry manage to tell an extremely painful and moving tale without lapsing into either sentimentality (emotion disproportionate to the subject) or self-pity?

4. Barry compresses her family history into a single sentence: "[My parents] were short on money and long on relatives who kept 'temporarily' moving into our house because they had nowhere else to go" (¶ 1). What is the effect of reading the rest of the essay through the lens of this statement? What additional dimensions does the essay's opening sentence add: "I was 7 years old the first time I snuck out of the house in the dark" (¶ 1)?

5. By analogy with the sentence quoted in question 4 above, are readers to believe that Barry compresses her childhood into this story of a single morning in second grade? Why or why not?

6. Barry explains, "[Mrs. LeSane] asked me if I would carry her purse for her, an honor above all honors, and she asked if I wanted to come into Room 2 early and paint" (¶ 16). She expects her readers to interpret this and the entire piece from two perspectives: that of the seven-year-old child who experienced "the sanctuary of school," and their own viewpoint as adults. Is this expectation justified? What does Barry do to reinforce this dual perspective? (See Language question 7 below.)

Language

7. If Barry's conversational language occasionally sounds childlike, "I snuck out of the house" (¶ 1), "[Mr. Gunderson] was nice and he was funny and he was old

with white hair . . ." (¶ 11), what features of her vocabulary, sentence structure, and point of view remind us that "The Sanctuary of School" is written by an adult and for adult readers?

8. "The Sanctuary of School" is full of natural symbols. Among these are watching TV with the sound off (¶ 3)—echoed in "We were children with the sound turned off" (¶ 10); "walking to school in the dark" (¶ 6) and watching the sun rise over the "beautiful view of the Cascade Mountains" (¶ 7); seeing her teacher (is it a happy accident or Barry's invention that she was named "Claire LeSane"?) "calling my name in a very happy and surprised way" (¶ 14); saying the Pledge of Allegiance (¶ 24). Explain the literal and symbolic meanings of these and others in the essay.

For Writing

9. Tell a story of your own experience—as a child, teenager, or adult—that throughout implies a social or political message. Although your message may be familiar to your audience, as Barry's is, the story itself should render the experience in a new and meaningful way. Select details to reinforce your point, but don't preach.

10. Write an essay that employs several natural symbols (see Language question 8, above) or an elaboration of a single natural symbol to make a point about which you can generalize (see Ruffin, "Mama's Smoke" [107–15]).

CHARLES M. YOUNG

Young (born 1951), grew up in Waukesha, Wisconsin, and graduated from Macalester College with a B.A. in 1973. For two years, as "the only guy on third string" on the Macalester Scots, a football team with "barely enough players for one string," Young says although he may not have been "the worst college football player of all time," he "may be only the worst player on the Macalester College Scots" in 1972. But, he says, "I do think I made a huge contribution to the atmosphere of despair and futility" that led to the team's NCAA record losing streak of "fifty straight losses."

Cutting his own losses, he headed for Columbia University, where he earned an M.S. in 1975 and soon got a job as an editor at *Rolling Stone* magazine. At the time he commented, "I try to write from a rock and roll sensibility, which at its best finds humor in the absurdity of life. A friend once accused me of liking punk rock because I never outgrew being fourteen. This is true, and there is nothing more absurd than being an adolescent in America. I aspire to play typewriter as well as Charlie Watts plays the drums." He succeeded. "Losing," first published in *Men's Journal* 2000, was selected for inclusion in *Best American Sports Writing 2000.* Young says he's "grateful to win an award for losing." In this essay Young analyzes the concepts embedded in the language of "losing"—"to call someone a loser is probably the worst insult in the United States today," the shame associated with losing, and the hypocritical paradox of athletic contests that produce losers in abundance, yet stigmatize the losers, those who call them "losers," and the winners as well. "We're all losers in the race to win."

Losing: An American Tradition

Somebody's got to lose. Don't we all know the feeling? —B.C.

J ust north of the north end zone of Blackshear Stadium at Prairie View 1
A&M University in Texas is an unmarked grave.

"We buried last season," said Greg Johnson, the Prairie View Pan- 2
thers' coach, during a break in football practice. "In March, just before the
start of spring practice, we had them write down everything they didn't
like about the past—being 0–9 last season, the record losing streak. We
used the example of Superman, this guy that nobody could stop unless
you got him near some green kryptonite. We asked them, 'Well, what's
your green kryptonite? What is it that keeps you from doing what you
need to do in the classroom and on the football field? Is it a female? Is it
your friends? Is it a drug? Is it alcohol? Lack of dedication? Not enough
time in the weight room? You got a nagging injury that you didn't rehab?'
Whatever they wanted to bury, they wrote it down on a piece of paper.
And the last thing we did, we looked at the HBO tape. The segment that
Bryant Gumbel did on us for *Real Sports,* where they laughed at us and
ridiculed us as the worst team in the country—'How does it feel to be
0–75 since 1989?' or whatever it was at that point. I said, 'That's the last
we'll ever see of that tape,' and I put it in a big plastic trash bag with the
paper. We took it to a hole I had dug near the gate, and we threw it in. All
the players and all the coaches walked by. Some of them kicked dirt on it,
some of them spit on it. Some of them probably thought I was crazy. I
said, 'This is the last time we're going to talk about last year. This is the
last time we're going to talk about the losing streak. The past is dead, and
anything that's dead ought to be buried. It's history. It's gone.'"

That took place in September 1998, when Prairie View's NCAA- 3
record losing streak stood at 0–77. Now skip ahead to the postgame interviews of the January 9, 1999, AFC playoff game, in which the Denver
Broncos beat the Miami Dolphins 38–3. Shannon Sharpe, the Broncos' tight
end, called Miami's Dan Marino a "loser." Universally, this was viewed as
a mortal insult, far beyond the bounds of acceptable trash talk.

"I cringed when I read that," said Mike Shanahan, the Broncos' 4
coach. "I was really disappointed. Dan Marino's no loser."

So Sharpe, much humbled (and probably at Shanahan's insistence), 5
groveled after the next Denver practice: "In no way, shape, or form is Dan
Marino a loser. Dan, if I offended you or your family, your wife, your kids,
your mother or father, your brothers or sisters, I apologize. I stand before
you and sincerely apologize. I would never disrespect you as a person."

Which is odd. Football, along with every other major sport, is con- 6
structed to create losers. On any given game day, half the teams win, and
half the teams lose. By the end of the playoffs, exactly one team can be
called a winner, while thirty other teams are, literally, losers. So given that

96.7 percent of the players in the NFL can't help but be losers, why should calling somebody a loser be considered such an egregious violation of propriety that the guy who won must debase himself in public for pointing out that the guy who lost, lost?

7   Consider *Patton,* winner of the 1971 Academy Award for Best Picture and a favorite of coaches, team owners, and politicians ever since. It opens with George C. Scott standing in front of a screen-size American flag in the role of General George S. Patton, giving a pep talk to his troops. Using sports imagery to describe war (mirroring the sportswriters who use war imagery to describe sports), Patton delivers a succinct sociology lesson: "Americans love a winner, and will not tolerate a loser. Americans play to win all the time. I wouldn't give a hoot in hell for a man who lost and laughed. That's why Americans have never lost, and will never lose a war—because the very thought of losing is hateful to Americans."

8   Which is a view of most Americans that's shared by most Americans. Certain women of my acquaintance refer to men who score low on the Multiphasic Boyfriend Potentiality Scale as losers. *Cosmopolitan* has run articles on how to identify and dump losers before they have a chance to inseminate the unwary.

9   In *Jerry Maguire,* Tom Cruise suffers his worst humiliation when he spots his former girlfriend dating a rival agent at a *Monday Night Football* game. She makes an L with her fingers and mouths, "Loser."

10   In *American Beauty,* Kevin Spacey announces during his midlife crisis: "Both my wife and daughter think I'm this gigantic loser."

11   In *Gods and Monsters,* Lolita Davidovich, playing a bartender, dismisses the possibility of sex with her sometime lover, played by Brendan Fraser: "From now on, you're just another loser on the other side of the bar."

12   In *200 Cigarettes,* set in the ostensibly alternative subculture of Manhattan's Lower East Side, Martha Plimpton works herself into a state of despair considering the idea that no one will come to her New Year's Eve party. Then, considering an even worse possibility, she weeps: "All the losers will be here!"

13   At the real-life sentencing last February of Austin Offen for bashing a man over the head with a metal bar outside a Long Island night club, Assistant District Attorney Stephen O'Brien said that Offen was "vicious and brutal. He's a coward and a loser." Offen, displaying no shame over having crippled a man for life, screamed back: "I am not a loser!"

14   In his book *Turbo Capitalism: Winners and Losers in the Global Economy,* Edward Luttwak equates losing with poverty and observes that Americans believe that "failure is the result not of misfortune or injustice, but of divine disfavor."

15   I could list a hundred more examples, but you get the point.

16   Shannon Sharpe, in using the word *loser,* implied that Dan Marino was: unworthy of sex or love or friendship or progeny, socially clueless,

stupid, parasitical, pathetic, poverty-stricken, cowardly, violent, felonious, bereft of all forms of status, beneath all consideration, hated by himself, hated by all good Americans, hated by God. And Dan Marino is one of the best quarterbacks ever to play football. . . .

The literal truth is, I may not be the worst college football player of all [17] time. I've claimed that occasionally in the course of conversation, but I may be only the worst college football player of 1972. I was definitely the worst player on the Macalester College of Scots of St. Paul, Minnesota, and we lost all of our games that season by an aggregate score of 312–46. The team went on to win one game in each of the following two seasons (after I graduated), then set the NCAA record with fifty straight losses. So, strictly speaking, the losing streak wasn't my fault. I do think I made a huge contribution to the atmosphere of despair and futility that led to the losing streak. I think that as Prairie View was to the '90s, Macalester was to the '70s. But in the final analysis, I think that over two decades at both schools, some athlete may have failed more than I did.

I may therefore merely be one of the worst, a weaker distinction that [18] makes me even more pathetic than whoever it is who can make the case for sole possession of the superlative—if someone wants to make that case. . . .

A couple weeks after I left PVU, the Panthers won a football game, 14–12, [19] against Langston University, ending the losing streak at eighty. The campus erupted in a victory celebration that was typical of the orgiastic outpourings that people all over the world feel entitled to after an important win. I was happy for them. I felt bad for Langston, having to carry the stigma of losing to the losers of all time.

There being virtually no literature of losing, I became obsessed with [20] reading books about winning, some by coaches and some by self-help gurus. All of them advised me to forget about losing. If you want to join the winners, they said, don't dwell on your past humiliations. Then I thought of George Santayana's dictum: "Those who forget the past are condemned to repeat it." So If I remembered losing, I'd be a loser. And if I forgot losing, I'd be a loser. Finally, I remembered a dictum of my own: "Anybody who quotes George Santayana about repeating the past will soon be repeating even worse clichés."

That Christmas, my local Barnes & Noble installed a new section [21] called "Lessons from the Winners." Publishers put out staggering numbers of books with "win" in the title (as they do with *Zen and Any Stupid Thing*), and they make money because there's a bottomless market of losers who want to be winners. Almost all of these books are incoherent lists of aphorisms and advice on how to behave like a CEO ("Memorize the keypad on your cell phone so you dial and drive without taking your

How do you know that this photograph depicts losers? Could it represent anything else? Although it depicts two Florida State players in 1997, do the date, location, even the sport itself, actually matter in this portrait of losing?

eyes off the road"). Most of these books are written by men who have made vast fortunes polluting the groundwater and screwing people who work for a living, and these men want to air out their opinions, chiefly that they aren't admired enough for polluting the groundwater and screwing people who work for a living. I thought of the ultimate winner, Howard Hughes, who was once the richest man in the world, who had several presidents catering to his every whim, who stored his feces in jars. I got more and more depressed.

22   Maybe I was just hypnotized by my own history of failure, character defects, and left-wing politics. Maybe what I needed was a pep talk. Maybe what I needed was Ray Pelletier, a motivational speaker who has made a lot of money raising morale for large corporations and athletic teams. Pelletier, a member of the National Speakers Association Hall of Fame, wrote a book, *Permission to Win*, that Coach Johnson had recommended to me. Basically an exhortation to feel like a winner no matter how disastrous your circumstances happen to be, the book deals with losing as a problem of individual psychology. I asked Pelletier if he thought that the emphasis American culture places on competition was creating vast numbers of people who, on the basis of having lost, quite logically think of themselves as losers.

23   "I don't think you have to think of yourself as a loser," he said. "I think competition causes you to reach down inside and challenges you to be at your very best. The key is not to beat yourself. If you're better than I am and you're more prepared to play that day, you deserve to win. I

have no problem with that. Every time I give a presentation, I want it to be better than the last one. I want to be sure I'm winning in everything that I do."

Yeah, but wasn't there a difference between excellence and winning?   24

"No, that's why I say that if I get beat by a team that's more talented,   25 I don't have a problem with that."

When one guy won, was he not inflicting defeat on the other guy?   26

"No. I'll give you an example. The first time I worked with a female   27 team before a big game, I was getting them all riled up and playing on their emotions, telling them how they deserved this win and how they worked really hard. A rah-rah, goose-pimple kind of speech. Just before we went on the court, the point guard said, 'Can I ask a question? Haven't the girls in the other locker room worked really hard, too? Don't they deserve to win, too?'"

Pelletier then veered off into a discussion of how the game teaches   28 you about life, of how his talks are really for fifteen years down the line when your wife leaves you, or the IRS calls for an audit, or you can't pay your mortgage. I asked him how he replied to the point guard in the locker room.

"I said, 'Absolutely the other team deserves to win, too. What we   29 have to do is find out if we can play together tonight as a team.' See, that's the biggest challenge facing corporate America today. We talk about teamwork but we don't understand the concept of team. Most of us have never been coached in anything. We've been taught, but not coached. There's a big difference. Great coaches challenge you to play at your best. The key is, you're in the game, trying to better yourself."

But Bill Parcells, the former coach of the Jets, is famous for saying   30 that you are what the standings say you are . . .

"Winning is playing at your best. Do you know the number one rea-   31 son why an athlete plays his sport? Recognition. Once you understand that, everything else becomes easy. Lou Holtz says that win means 'What's Important Now.'"

That's just standard practice in books about winning, I told him.   32 They redefine the word to include all human behavior with a good connotation. In *The Psychology of Winning,* Dr. Denis Waitley writes that winning is "unconditional love." Winning could hardly be a more conditional form of love. You are loved if you win, and scorned if you lose.

"I don't believe that."   33

If athletes play for recognition, don't they want to be recognized as   34 winners? And if you've lost, won't you be recognized as a loser?

"I don't think they're labeled that way."   35

By the press? By the fans?   36

"To me, unconditional love is an aspect of winning. The problem   37 is that you and I have not been trained to think positively. In one of my corporate seminars, I ask people to write down all the advantages there are to being negative. I want them to think about it seriously. It's an exercise that can take fifteen or twenty minutes, and then they have the 'Aha!' There is no advantage to negative thinking. None. And yet the biggest problem we face in America is low self-esteem."

38   Low self-esteem has its uses, though. Whenever you see a couple of male animals on a PBS nature special duking it out for the privilege of having sex with some female of the species, one of the males is going to dominate and the other male is either going to die or get low self-esteem and crawl off making obsequious gestures to the winner. The evolutionary value is obvious: Fight to the death and your genes die with you; admit you're a loser and you may recover to fight again or find another strategy for passing on your genes through some less selective female. Species in which one alpha male gets to have sex with most of the females—elephant seals are a good example—need a lot of low self-esteem among the beta males for social stability.

39   With 1 percent of the population possessing more wealth than the bottom 95 percent, the American economy operates a lot like a bunch of elephant seals on a rock in the ocean. And it simply must mass-produce low self-esteem in order to maintain social stability amidst such colossal unfairness.

40   According to the World Health Organization, mood disorders are the number-one cause worldwide of people's normal activities being impaired. In the United States alone, the WHO estimates, depression costs $53 billion a year in worker absenteeism and lost productivity. While that's a hell of a market for Ray Pelletier and the National Speakers Association, which has more than three thousand people giving pep talks to demoralized companies and sports teams, doled-out enthusiasm is a palliative, not a curative. In fact, demoralization is a familiar management tool; the trick is creating just enough. Too much and you have work paralysis, mass depression, and suicide. Too little and you have a revolution. Ever hear a boss brag that he doesn't *have* ulcers, he *gives* them? He's making sure his employees are demoralized enough to stay in their place.

41   Consider the book *Shame and Pride,* by Dr. Donald L. Nathanson, a psychiatrist and the executive director of the Silvan S. Tomkins Institute in Philadelphia. Starting in the mid-1940s, Dr. Tomkins watched babies for thousands of hours and made a convincing case that humans are born preprogrammed with nine "affects"—potential states of emotion that can be triggered by a stimulus or memory. These affects are: interest-excitement, enjoyment-joy, surprise-startle, fear-terror, distress-anguish, anger-rage, dissmell (*dissmell* is similar to *distaste,* but related to the sense of smell), disgust, and shame-humiliation. These affects "amplify" an outside stimulus or memory to give you an increase in brain activity that eventually becomes full-blown emotion.

Until recent years, shame was the "ignored emotion" in psychol- 42
ogy. But a few people, Nathanson most prominently, built on Tomkins
and discovered the key to . . . well, not quite everything, but an awful lot.
According to Tomkins and Nathanson, shame erupts whenever "desire
outruns fulfillment." An impediment arises to the two positive affects
(interest-excitement and enjoyment-joy), and suddenly your eyes drop,
your head and body slump, your face turns red, and your brain is confused to the point of paralysis. . . .

I called up Nathanson and asked if he had any thoughts about [ath- 43
letes and shame]. . . .

Sports events are often described as a morality play, I said, but there's 44
nothing moral about it. Sports decide who will participate in power and
who will be humiliated.

"That's understandable when you recognize that our sense of place 45
in society is maintained by shame. Keeping people in their place is maintaining them at certain levels of shaming interaction at which they can be
controlled. This issue of winning and losing, it throws us. It defines our
identity, doesn't it?"

Calling someone a loser is probably the worst insult in the United 46
States today.

"If you're calling someone that, the person must live in a perpetual 47
state of shame. The only way he can live with himself is to have massive
denial, disavowal of his real identity. He has to make his way in the
world somehow, and he can't walk around constantly thinking of himself as a loser. Yet if someone in our eyes is a loser and he refuses to admit
it, this is narcissism. He has an identity that can't be sustained by con-
sensual validation."

Is there some value in competition, in creating all these losers? 48

"When you're young and you're learning and it's just a bunch of 49
guys playing a game, that's not shame. That's just figuring out that Billy
is faster than Johnny. When parents and schools and bureaucracies start
getting involved and demanding wins, then it gets pathological."

Playing for the Chicago Bears, the Philadelphia Eagles, and the Dallas 50
Cowboys from 1961 to 1972, Mike Ditka was All-Pro five times as a tight
end, won an NFL championship with the Bears in 1963, won Super Bowl
VI with the Cowboys, and was elected to the Hall of Fame. As the coach
of the Bears from 1982 to 1992, he won Super Bowl XX with an 18–1 team
generally acknowledged as one of the greatest ever and was named Coach
of the Year twice. As the coach of the New Orleans Saints for the past three
seasons, he had a 15–33 record and is now most vividly remembered for
flipping off the fans and grabbing his crotch during and after an especially inept defeat. (He was fined $20,000.) I asked him if he thinks that
football fans are inherently interested in the game, or in the hallucination
of power they get when their team wins?

51   "They relate to the winning. Well, you can't say they aren't interested in the game. They watch the game. But the excitement comes from winning."

52   When football players snap at journalists in the locker room after a loss . . .

53   "That's only human nature. They probably snap at their wives when they get home, too. Are you saying, Does losing bother people? Sure it does. It's no different from a guy at IBM who loses a sale to a competitor. You just don't like to lose. Most people want to be associated with winning. When you work your butt off and don't get the results you want, you might be a little short-tempered as a coach. That's only life. But that's no different than any other segment of life. Football parallels society, period."

54   I've noticed that the worst thing you can call somebody in the United States is a loser.

55   "No. The word *quitter* is the worst thing you can call somebody. Lemme ask you something: If two teams play all year, and they reach the Super Bowl, the one that loses is a loser? Come on.

56   "I don't like the term. . . . It's not fair. I think as long as you compete and you do your best, if the other team is better, I don't think you really lose. I think you lose when you quit trying."

57   The problem with declaring a quitter to be a lower form of dirt than a loser is that you're still stigmatizing almost everybody. Studies indicate that up to 90 percent of children drop out of organized competitive sports by the age of fifteen. Extrapolating from my own experience, I would guess that they don't enjoy feeling like losers so that the jocks can feel like winners. Since they associate intense physical activity with feeling rotten, they grow up having problems with obesity and depression, both of which have become epidemic in the United States.

58   As Mike Ditka would say, it's not fair. But I think there's a way out. And I think that Alfie Kohn has seen it. Kohn, an educational philosopher, has helped inspire the opposition to standardized tests, an especially pernicious form of competition. His first book, *No Contest: The Case Against Competition,* cites study after study demonstrating that competition hinders work, play, learning, and creativity in people of all ages. (In fact, there is almost no evidence to the contrary in the social sciences.) The book is wonderfully validating for anyone who ever had doubts about the ostensible fun of gym class and spelling bees. I told Kohn that in my experience, people get unhinged when you question the value of making other people fail.

59   "Absolutely. It calls into question America's state religion, which is practiced not only on the playing field but in the classroom and the workplace, and even in the family. The considerable body of evidence demonstrating that this is self-defeating makes very little impression on people who are psychologically invested in a desperate way in the idea of winning.

The real alternative to being number one is not being number two, but being able to dispense with these pathological ratings altogether. If people accepted the research on the destructiveness of competition, you wouldn't see all these books teaching how to compete more effectively. I hear from a lot of teachers and parents whose kids fall apart after losing in spelling bees and awards assemblies, and they feel dreadful about it. The adults start to think, *Hmm, maybe competition isn't such a good thing, at least for those kids*. It took me years to see that the same harms were being visited upon the winners. The kids who win are being taught that they are good only to the extent that they continue to beat other people. They're being taught that other people are obstacles to their own success, which destroys a sense of community as effectively as when we teach losers that lesson. And finally, the winners are being taught that the point of what they are doing is to win, which leads to diminished achievement and interest in what they are doing. What's true for kids is also true for adults. It's not a problem peculiar to those who lose. We're all losers in the race to win."

I'm very blessed that way. I didn't have the perspective to spell it   60 out like Alfie Kohn, but I've known I was a total loser since my first college football practice. I've admitted it here publicly, and I am free. You, you're probably holding on to some putrefying little shred of self-esteem, denying that you're a loser in a country inhabited by Bill Gates and 260 million losers. You're still hoping to beat your friend at racquetball and make him feel as bad as you do when you lose, still looking to flatten some rival with just the right factoid in an argument, still craving the sports car in the commercial that accurately announces, "There's no such thing as a gracious winner." Give up, I say. Join me. Losers of the world, unite! You have nothing to lose but your shame.

Content

1. Young asserts, "Calling someone a loser is probably the worst insult in the United States today" (¶ 46) and "Football, along with every other major sport, is constructed to create losers" (¶ 6). Explain why you either agree or disagree with Young's assertions. Comment on Young's question: "So given that 96.7 percent of the players in the NFL can't help but be losers, why should calling somebody a loser be considered such an egregious violation of propriety that the guy who won must debase himself in public for pointing out that the guy who lost, lost?" (¶ 6).

2. How, as Young points out, can "books about winning" get away with redefining "the word to include all human behavior with a good connotation," such as "winning is 'unconditional love.' Winning could hardly be a more conditional form of love. You are loved if you win, and scorned if you lose" (¶ 32)? Which definition of winning is more accurate—Young's or those books'? Cite the best evidence you can to prove your point.

3. Young asserts, "Sports events are often described as a morality play . . . but there's nothing moral about it. Sports decide who will participate in power and who will be humiliated" (¶ 44). Do you agree or disagree? On what evidence? How

can a country such as the United States, which promises "freedom and justice to all," perpetuate a sports culture devoted to the exercise of power and humiliation as Young describes?

Strategies/Structure

4. In paragraph 15, which follows several examples of losing, Young writes, "I could list a hundred more examples, but you get the point." What is "the point"? Is his use of evidence to make this point adequate?

5. In his final paragraph Young proudly declares himself a "total loser," thereby departing from our traditional conception of equating shame with losing (¶ 60). He then makes a direct appeal to his audience with "Give up, I say. Join me. Losers of the world, unite! You have nothing to lose but your shame." Discuss the effectiveness of such a concluding strategy in an essay that appeals to emotions and ethics.

Language

6. Young's definition of the word *loser* (¶ 16) includes "unworthy of sex or love or friendship or progeny, socially clueless, stupid, parasitical, pathetic, poverty-stricken, cowardly. . . ." Compare his definition to a dictionary definition. Do they contain common elements? What are the significant differences? Are there qualities that should either be added to or deleted from Young's definition? What are these?

7. In many respects this entire essay is about language, slippery definitions of losing and winning, low self-esteem, shame, and quitting. Given that "Losing" was originally published in *Men's Journal,* does this mean that Young thinks men in general hold definitions of these terms in some commonly accepted sense? How does Young redefine these terms? Does he expect women as well as men to agree with him?

8. Young's tone varies throughout the essay, from comic to dead serious and in between. What is the tone of his opening examples of the Prairie View Panthers' burial of their losing streak (¶ 2) and the discussion of "losers" that begins and ends with Dan Marino (¶s 3–16)? Why does he describe his own lack of athletic success in a comic tone ("I may not be the worst college football player of all time . . . but I may be only the worst college player of 1972" (¶17)? At what points is he the most serious? In what ways does his variable tone reinforce his argument?

For Writing

9. Alfie Kohn, an educational philosopher, argues that "kids who win are being taught that they are good only to the extent that they continue to beat other people. They're being taught that other people are obstacles to their own success, which destroys a sense of community as effectively as when we teach losers that lesson" and that "we're all losers in the race to win" (¶ 59). Write an essay that uses a wide variety of examples, ranging from the personal to examples from the media to those provided by experts, in arguing for or against Kohn's position.

10. With a partner, write an essay in which you discuss two or three key experiences you have each had with winning and losing in light of Young's argument.

(You will need to identify the significant features of these experiences. One person's experiences may corroborate the other's, or they may differ significantly.) In what ways has Young reinforced what you already believed to be true in relation to these experiences with winning and losing? In what ways has Young helped you to see these experiences in a new light? What advice for others can you draw from your analysis?

MATT NOCTON

Nocton (born 1975) has spent most of his life in the vicinity of his hometown, Simsbury, Connecticut, except for a year's sojourn in California—a cross-country trek that stimulated some of his best writing. An English major at the University of Connecticut, he explained "Why I Write" in the short paper, whose essence is quoted here:

> I write to dispel lies. I write because I seek the truth. Writing for me is a source of discovery. I write because I feel a sense of freedom and adventure in writing. To me writing is a place that I can return to again and again where the scenery of my life is always new and exciting. I write because I am always in the process of changing, and writing is a way to take a snapshot of who I am today. I want to rediscover myself and remind myself of who I was. I like to discover where I am going and where I am coming from. I write because I find it relaxing and it takes my mind off the dreadful events in the world today. I write to prove that I exist.
>
> I write because I can express myself in ways I find impossible with spoken words. I write to prove a fact or sway an opinion. Through writing, I find that I can put things in perspective and see things differently, more clearly. I write to express my ideas or feelings. I write to emulate the styles of writers I admire. I write to delve into places that I have never been, and to explore new places within myself. I also write for others. I write to apologize and I write to forgive. I write to greet people and I write to amuse. I write to sustain my mind with the exercise and nourishment that it needs to stay healthy.
>
> Being a quiet person, one thing I most enjoy about writing is the ability to avoid interruptions that occur in conversation. Arguing with words on paper can be an excellent method for waging war while eluding enemy fire, at least temporarily.

Nocton himself worked harvesting tobacco in Connecticut; the tobacco fields are adjacent to the state's largest airport, Bradley International Airport. "Harvest of Gold, Harvest of Shame" is the seventh revision Nocton submitted, every draft reinforcing the gulf between the bosses and the workers in the tobacco fields and sheds, every draft increasing his own awareness of the workers' exploited and powerless condition.

❄ *Harvest of Gold, Harvest of Shame*

1   Simsbury is a small affluent town located in the heart of the Connecticut River Valley. It is not a particularly exciting place and its high school students refer to it as "Simsboring." But in fact there is something unique about this quiet town. Simsbury is home to Culbro Tobacco Company's Farm No. 2. The Culbro Tobacco Company prides itself on growing the finest shade tobacco in the world. Its leaves are used to wrap expensive cigars.

2   Culbro employs three kinds of people: migrant workers, most of whom are from Jamaica and live on the farm headquarters, inner-city people, most of whom are Hispanic and are bussed from Hartford to Simsbury at 6:15 in the morning; and finally, a few local white residents. The latter are typically the men who oversee all of the other employees. Each supervisor is referred to as the "boss man" by the less fortunate workers. When a boss man speaks to one of his subordinates, the usual response comes either in the form of Spanglish, which most of the Hispanics speak, or Patoi, which is what the Jamaicans speak.

3   Working in tobacco fields is demanding and repetitious and the pay is minimum wage. In a typical day, a field worker is bussed to the field where he will be working with his group of roughly fifty to two hundred workers. When he gets off the bus he will find a pick-up truck parked nearby full of burlap and twine. He must tie this burlap around his waist as a source of protection against the dirt and rocks that he will be dragging himself through for the next eight hours. He will then find another pick-up truck containing wooden stakes with numbers on them. There he will find the stake with his number and stick it into the ground before the row of tobacco plants where he is about to work. A recorder or "bent-keeper" (so called because the distance between two tobacco posts is called a bent) stands under the blazing sun and monitors all the workers. He does this by looking at the numbers of each stake in each row. He flips through the pages on his clipboard until he finds the corresponding employee number. Then he checks the number of poles in the row and adds the number of "bents" in the row to a particular worker's sum total. He does this for fifty to two hundred laborers. At times when the rows are very short it is difficult to add all of the numbers fast enough to keep up with the pace of the pickers. The pickers who complete the most bents earn the most money. The bentkeeper is the only one authorized to carry the clipboard and add the bent numbers. Every so often the unshaven field boss man with the coarse black mustache and cowboy hat calls the bentkeeper. "Hey, who was working in this row? Twelve six-four-five is still staked in here. Who was working next to twelve six-four-five?" The bentkeeper nervously hands over his clipboard and the boss man takes off his sunglasses and draws on his cigarette while he examines it.

"What the hell is this!?! This is an eight bent row! You've been add- 4
ing nine! It changed from nine to eight way the hell back there! Look at
the goddamn post! Goddamn are you blind or can't you read!?! Go fix it!"
He shoves the clipboard into the bentkeeper's stomach and jumps in his
truck. The truck kicks up dirt and a cloud of dust as it speeds down the
rocky dirt road. It comes to an abrupt halt about one hundred yards
down. As the bentkeeper tries to figure out where the bents changed from
nine to eight and from which numbers he must deduct points, he hears
the boss man in the distance. "Hey eleven two-nine-two! Were you working next to twelve six-four-five?! You're bruising the leaves! Look at this?
See this? This is from your row! We can't use these! You're going too fast.
Stop bruising the goddamn leaves or I'm going to dock ten bents from
your total!"

The humiliated bentkeeper tries not to listen as he attempts to cor- 5
rect his blunder while keeping pace with the pickers at the same time. A
tough looking Hispanic kid breaks his concentration. "Hey bentkeeper!
How many I got?" He holds up his stake so the bentkeeper can see the
number.

The bentkeeper flips through the pages, "Uhhmm . . . sixty-eight." 6
"What!? I got more than that!" 7
"No, you've got sixty-eight." 8
"Ahh man this is bullshit. How'd you get that job anyway?" The 9
complaining worker walks over to the water truck to get a drink.

In the middle of two towering tobacco plants under the white net- 10
ting eleven two-nine-two mumbles slowly in a deep raspy voice with
smoke in his breath "Duh boss mon is crazy mon." He finishes his row and
approaches the bentkeeper. "Hey mon, eleven two-nine-two, how many I
got now?"

The bentkeeper replies "Yeah I know your number Stanley, you have 11
one-hundred and fifteen."

Stanley's smile reveals a gold front tooth with a black clover on it, 12
"Ohkay mon, yuh shades uh looking fat mon. All shades uh fat in my
book mon."

After field "asparagus 1032," is finished, the nets are dropped and 13
the boss man selects two unlucky souls to spray the field. They reluctantly
don cumbersome yellow suits that resemble something NASA designed
for the planned mission to Mars. The only obvious difference is that the
sprayers wear back packs of insecticides rather than oxygen.

Beneath the foggy mask of his suit, David's pockmarked hairy face 14
contorts into a nasty expression as he argues with his partner. Everyone
hated David. He talked in the belligerent tongue of a junkyard dog. He
was likened to a Neanderthal, though an allusion to something more ancient would probably suit him better. In the middle of the argument David
blurts out, "I was in prison you know. . . . you know why I was there? . . .
I killed a cop. . . . strangled him. . . . I'm on parole now." The significance

of his comment seemed to bear no relation to the argument and his partner ignored it. He wasn't afraid of David.

15   All of the leaves from "asparagus 1032" are transported to the shed on a trailer pulled by a big blue Ford tractor. The shed operations are run by a short stocky Hispanic man who wears a blue Hawaiian tee shirt with buttons and flowers. Working in the shed is better than working in the field. Many women work in the shed. There, by means of a giant sewing machine, they monotonously sew tobacco leaves to a stick called a "lath." Every time a worker finishes fifty laths she gets credit for one bundle. That is recorded by the bundlekeeper who patrols the shed monitoring daily progress. When a sewer calls out "bundle!" the bundlekeeper acknowledges "bundle!" and he hurries over to the end of the shed and hoists the heavy bundle from the bundle stockpile onto his shoulder. He then carries it to the idle sewer and he drops the bundle of fifty laths on top of her sewing machine. He then withdraws his hole puncher and he punches a hole in her card. Every time he punches a sewer's card he punches the master card which he wears around his neck. The master card shows how many bundles the shed completes on a daily basis. The bundlekeeper is the only one authorized to carry the hole puncher and the master card. Every so often a "boss man" will summon the bundlekeeper over and yank the master card from the bundlekeeper's neck to examine it. Then the boss man marches up and down the shed to exercise his authority. Then he stops in a thick cloud of dust to bark his favorite motivational speech "you not gonna get paid if you don't speed up!" The sewers ignore him and try to keep up with their mindless sewing machines. Those who complete the most bundles make the most money.

16   Every time a lath is completed it is racked. Then a man who has precariously positioned himself on the bottom level of rafters in the shed reaches down to the rack and picks it up. He then passes it to his partner above him on the next level who passes it up to the man above him and so on until the lath reaches the highest level that is available for another row of lath. Each lath is suspended between two rafters in the barn. They are carefully packed about a foot and a half apart across the width of the shed on every level of rafters and along the length of the barn. It normally takes about three days or a million and a half tobacco leaves to fill a shed.

17   On the dry dusty floor of the shed, the sweaty bundlekeeper looks up and admires the beautiful ceiling as it is painted with enormous green leaves with a splotch of a red shirt on one level and a yellow shirt above it and black arms with extended hands reaching to one another. For a moment he is gazing at the ceiling of the Sistine Chapel in Rome. He can imagine he is actually witnessing Michelangelo paint his masterpiece. For a moment the two men with extended hands remind the bundlekeeper of God in the heavens reaching to Adam. His imagination is suddenly snapped by a falling lath misplaced by an imperfect human being hanging

from the rafters. The bundlekeeper ducks and after a loud 'thump!' he thanks God for his green hard hat.

As the clock rolls onto ten o'clock the boss man calls out "Coffee! Last lath!" The sewers finish sewing their last fifty leaves and the squeaky machines fall silent. The silence is invaded by the chatter of relieved sewers who have temporarily escaped the heat and dust in the shed to drink their coffee outside under the shade of a nearby tree or the side of the barn. The men in the rafters descend to retrieve their coolers to snack on bread and beer for a leisurely ten minutes. [18]

Work resumes promptly at ten after ten with the boss man's "back to work!" The dissipating dust is replenished by a fresh cloud churned from the feet of a tired troop heading back to the barn. Next to the crack in the shed where a ray of sunlight illuminates floating dust particles, an old machine resumes its monotonous humming and clicking as a carefree Jamaican man whistles while feeding it leaves. [19]

The boss man steps outside his dark shed for a breath of fresh air and a chance to blow his nose and spit the gritty sand from his mouth. Then he sees the next load of green leaves preceding a light brown dust cloud in field "Ketchen 918" with the new hybrid seed. Those leaves cannot be mixed. He grows red in the face because the next shed has not yet been prepared for those leaves. He stomps over to his dust colored pickup truck to call base. After talking to the base coordinator he realizes that he will have to divide his crew into two sections with one half in one shed and another in the other shed. Now the bundlekeeper will have to run back and forth between the two sheds because of the field boss man's mistake. The stressed-out shed boss man invents another motivational speech "Hey, dees is not a carnival! dees is not the beach!" By lunch time the boss man has resumed his composure. He sneaks a peek at his watch and yells "last lath! break time! last lath!" [20]

The shed workers rush to the water truck outside to wash their hands before lunch. They sit in the weeds against the shady side of the shed and eat their lunches. The bundlekeeper and the shed boss eat in the pickup truck and listen to the Spanish radio. Out in the field the boss man calls "lunch time! Finish your rows!" The dirty and smelly pickers crawl out from underneath the nets and remove the tape from their fingers and try to wash the sticky tape, tobacco juices, and dirt from their finger tips. Then they head to the bus to find their coolers of beer and candy bars. They eat and drink for half an hour. Stanley puffs his harsh "Craven A" cigarette between mouthfuls of ham and cheese and tries not to think about tobacco. [21]

The bentkeeper and the field boss eat in the dusty pickup and the field boss lights his Marlboro and explains: "You know, when I yell at you it's nothing personal. I have to yell at you because it's my job. Man I know how it is, I was in your shoes once." The bentkeeper nods in agreement. [22]

His mind is on his lunch. It appears inedible. After growing tired of drinks and sandwiches that became warm and soggy in the hot sun for the past month, he has devised an unreliable system to solve that problem. Instead of just packing his lunch in ice, he actually freezes his entire lunch overnight. Unfortunately, when he opened his cooler on this hot day he discovered his peanut butter and jelly to be hard as a brick. Likewise his Boku juice boxes were still frozen solid.

23   As he sits there listening to his boss's rambling, he places his sandwich on the dash and he peels away the walls of his juice box and gnaws on it as if it were some kind of primitive popsicle. No matter how he prepares his lunch he can never seem to achieve a proper balance between hot and cold. When the sun is high and it's time to eat, he discovers either a frozen block of bread and jam or a soggy something suffering heat stroke.

24   At half past the hour Stanley strikes his stake into the dirt with a swift robotic motion. He sucks deeply on his cigarette and marches down to the end of the row. Large veins puff out of his forearm like the veins on the bottom green leaf that he snaps from the lower stalk of a thriving tobacco plant. Three more hours to go.

25   At the shed yet another blue tractor arrives with its precious load of fresh leaves. The shed boss man orders two rafter men down to disperse the containers of tobacco among the sewers. The bundlekeeper manages to help with the heavy containers between bundle runs. He is thoroughly exhausted and his eyes are bloodshot from the irritating smoke and dust in the shed. Although three hours remain every shed laborer is anticipating the boss man's "last lath! Get on the bus!"

26   At three-thirty in the hot afternoon three buses and two Chevy pickup trucks carry exhausted tobacco workers back to farm headquarters where the workers can rest before returning to work early tomorrow in the cool morning hours.

Content

1. Nocton identifies a variety of tasks the tobacco farm workers perform. What similarities are there among the jobs? What differences? Are readers to assume that all jobs are "demanding and repetitious and the pay is minimum wage" (¶ 3)? What's the difference between the tobacco harvesting process and the harvesting activities that Shange describes (184–91)?

2. Which workers are Hispanics and Jamaicans? Are any white Americans? Who performs which tasks?

3. Nocton evidently doesn't expect his readers to know much about the work of harvesting tobacco. What does he expect them to learn from reading his essay? What does he expect them to do?

4. Is Nocton himself a worker in the scene he describes? If so, can you ascertain what his job is? What are your clues? In what ways, if any, does the effectiveness of his argument depend on the authority of his personal experience?

Strategies/Structures

5. Where does Nocton use dialogue? With what effects?
6. What is the point of comparing the ceiling of the shed with Michelangelo's painting on the Sistine Chapel ceiling (¶ 17)?

Language

7. Nocton's language is slow and repetitive. How does the style fit the subject?
8. Why does Nocton call the shed boss's speeches "motivational" (¶s 15, 20)? Are there other ironies present in this account?

For Writing

9. Have you ever thought about how any crop that provides common raw materials—wheat, sugar, potatoes, rice, coffee, cotton—is grown and harvested? Have you or your relatives ever worked in such harvests? Find out about the production of one of these crops and compare it with the tobacco harvest that Nocton describes. On the basis of your investigation, formulate some principles of how agricultural workers should be treated and what their compensation and protection should be.
10. Have you or any family members ever had a minimum-wage job, or do you currently hold such a job? What elements, if any, does it have in common with the jobs Nocton describes? Are there any significant differences? Write a satiric paper about a day on the job, intended to serve as a critique and to imply a plan for better working conditions or employee benefits.

Additional Topics for Writing
Appealing to Emotion and Ethics

(For strategies for appealing to emotion and ethics, see 483.)

Write an essay that attempts to persuade one of the following audiences through a combination of appeals to reason, emotion, and ethics.

1. To someone you'd like for a friend, fiancé(e), or spouse: Love me.
2. To an athlete, or to an athletic coach: Play according to the rules, even when the referee (umpire, or other judge) isn't looking.
3. To a prospective employer: I'm the best person for the job. Hire me.
4. To a police officer: I shouldn't receive this traffic ticket. Or, to a judge or jury: I am innocent of the crime of which I'm accused.
5. To the voters: Vote for me (or for a candidate of my choice).
6. To admissions officers of a particular college, university, or of a program within that institution (such as medical or law school, graduate program, or a division with a special undergraduate degree): Let me in.
7. To the prospective buyer of something you want to sell or service you can perform: Buy this.
8. To an audience prejudiced against a particular group or simply to a majority audience: X is beautiful. (X may be black, yellow, Hispanic, female, a member of a particular national or religious group . . .)
9. To an antagonist on any issue: As Joan Didion says, *"Listen to me, see it my way, change your mind."*
10. To people engaging in behavior that threatens their lives or their health: Stop doing X (or stop doing X to excess)—smoking, drinking, overeating, undereating, or using drugs. Or: Start doing X—exercising regularly, using bike helmets or seatbelts, planning for the future by getting—an education, a stable job, an investment plan, a retirement plan . . .
11. Pick a work of fiction or nonfiction whose content intrigues you and whose style you admire and write a brief parody (probably involving considerable exaggeration) of it to show your understanding of the content and your appreciation of the style.
12. Write a satire to argue implicity for a point, as Swift does in "A Modest Proposal" (491–99). Use whatever techniques seem appropriate, such as creating a character who does the talking for you; setting a scene (such as of pathos or misery) that helps make your point; using a tone involving understatement, irony, or exaggeration. Be sure to supply enough clues to enable your readers to understand what you really mean.

Controversy in Context:
Implications of World Terrorism and World Peace

AN ARGUMENT CASEBOOK

Terrorism

For most Americans, indeed for much of the world, the attacks on the World Trade Center and the Pentagon on September 11, 2001, like the attack on Pearl Harbor on December 7, 1941, make it a day that like few others, will long live in infamy as we realize, in poet Seamus Heaney's words, "Anything can happen, the tallest things/Be overturned. . . ." This is illustrated in the photograph (p. 523) of the remains of the World Trade Center, disintegrating amidst the ash and debris of that fateful attack. As with every other earth-shaking event, we looked at our world one way before the cataclysm and another way—or many other ways—afterward. Did the world change? Or did we? And in what ways—significant, casual, even trivial? Given where we have been, where we are going (and where exactly that will be) depends to an extent on the viewer's stance. Will our sojourn involve nation with (or against) nation; culture with (or against) culture; technology, economy, or ideology with (or against) its counterpart? How will terrorist attacks, and the infinite possibilities of future terrorism, specific or vague, affect the ways we live our lives, our plans for the future, and how we look at our neighbors, our friends—and our enemies? What can we, as individuals and as a nation, do to balance the free and open nature of our hospitable society against needs for protection and security? How can we avoid dividing the world into "us" against "them"? How can we temper suspicion and paranoia, and nevertheless be on guard—but against what?

The chapter "Terrorism" explores these questions, with specific issues embedded in the details not only of the terrorist attacks of September 11, but in earlier manifestations of violence and terrorism throughout the world. The eight pieces that comprise this chapter—a poem, six essays, and an excerpt from a book—are representative of the more reasoned, balanced, analytic views of events of this incendiary nature, among hundreds of thousands of outpourings. Yet, with the possible exception of Heaney's poem, all of these writings could be interpreted as incendiary, provocative of argument and conflict by readers who disagree, or who interpret flashpoint words such as *terrorism, war,* even *peace,* from different perspectives.

This first inclination of many, along with a surge of sympathy for the victims, is to try to understand what happened. "Where were you when . . . ?" "What did you do?" "Do you know anybody who . . . ?" We talk about it, we listen to the incessant media reports, we write to try to make sense of things that don't make sense, which Heaney's brief reflection on "Horace and Thunder" attempts to do. The world, says Heaney, is suddenly "overturned," "Capstones shift, nothing resettles right." And in a time of terror, when "telluric ash and fire-spores darken day," it is tempting, as many writers and media commentators do, to divide the world into "us"—the innocent, beleaguered victims of a horrific attack—and "them" the vile denizens of an evil empire who hate us all and will stop at nothing to destroy our free society (as, for example, Don DeLillo does in "In the Ruins of the Future," *Harper's,* 2002). This is not a good way to conduct any argument, although this kind of thinking is often the basis for initiating and conducting a war, emanating from the halls of Congress, the Oval Office, branches of the military, with reverberations throughout the press and television, domestic and international.

Because the "us" versus "them" view is so popular, it cannot be overlooked. Nevertheless, as the immediate impact of the events is somewhat mitigated by time, we realize that this is not the only perspective and war is not the only alternative. Even if we can't change the past, or prevent the World Trade Center's destruction, we can interpret the present in ways that we hope will prepare us for the future. In "History Overcomes Stories" (529–32), an eyewitness commentary on her experience of living ten blocks from "what used to be the World Trade Center towers" (an experience shared by the men fleeing the collapse of the first tower in the photograph on p. 530), Laurie Fendrich, a painter and fine arts professor, writes a counternarrative to combat media overkill, to interpret stories that "are polluted and demeaned by having been reduced to fodder for television, movie, and slick magazine entertainment." She looks, as people do in times of trauma, for guidance "to see if we can now act the way we ought to have been acting all along," and finds focus and stability in a reaffirmation of the core values of Western culture, which trendy postmodern theory has undervalued: "individual liberty, coupled with obligations to virtue, democracy coupled with responsibility, the requirement of courage, an acknowledgement—always tempered by reason—of duty, and an assertion of basic, not jingoistic, patriotism."

Those who examine the causes of international terrorism, as does Bernard Lewis in "What Went Wrong?" (532–38), are aware that there is no single interpretation and that all explanations are controversial. Even for those who concede the truth of Lewis's first premise, that by the twentieth century "Compared with Christendom, its rival for more than a millennium, the world of Islam had become poor, weak, and ignorant," the reasons for this decline are in dispute. Because "it is usually easier and always more satisfying to blame others for one's misfortunes," the Middle East could blame the thirteenth-century Mongol invasions "for the destruction of both Muslim power and Islamic civilization"; the Arabs, Turks, and Persians could blame each other for "the loss of their ancient glories" and blame the British and French for nineteenth-century depredations. Current scapegoats include America, and "the Jews." Self-blame includes attacks on Islam in general, or on fanatics, or "the relegation of women to an inferior position in Muslim society," thereby depriving "the Islamic world of the talents and energies of half its people." Because "Who did this to us?" leads only to "neurotic fantasies and conspiracy theories," concludes Lewis, the question "What did we do wrong?" leads naturally to the search for a solution. This is difficult because the condition of freedom in the Middle East is fragile and full of complications.

Lewis's answer, that the peoples of the Middle East should establish a free society where people have the freedom "to question and inquire and speak; freedom of the economy from corrupt and pervasive mismanagement; freedom of women from male oppression; freedom of citizens from tyranny," provides the perspective that underlies the interpretation of the subject by many pro-Westerners. Nevertheless, critics such as Palestinian scholar Edward Said (not included here) strongly object to such solutions, which they interpret as the efforts of Westerners attempting to dominate an Eastern culture.

Terror in the Mind of God (538–50), Mark Juergensmeyer's analysis of the "exaggerated violence" of terrorist attacks such as the 1993 World Trade Center bombing, eerily prescient of its 2001 successor, explains them as "constructed events: they are mind-numbing, mesmerizing theater. At center stage are the acts themselves—stunning, abnormal, and outrageous murders carried out in a way that graphically displays the awful power of violence—set within grand scenarios of conflict and proclamation." Horrifically violent acts that "surpass the wounds inflicted during warfare" because of their demonstrative "secondary impact . . . elicit feelings of revulsion and anger in those who witness them." Indeed, claims Juergensmeyer, "terrorism is always part of a political strategy," performed not only to "fulfill political ends" but to "have a direct impact on public policy."

Wendell Berry's "Thoughts in the Presence of Fear" (550–55) itemizes twenty-seven reflections on the aftermath of "the horrors of September 11." Each paragraph could be the basis for a policy statement, an argument, an essay, a book, so concentrated is Berry's discussion of topics ranging from the end of "technological and economic optimism" (I), to the view that "The 'developed' nations had given to the 'free market' the status of a god, and were sacrificing to it their farmers, farmlands, and communities" (IV). He questions the view that "The aim and result of war necessarily is not peace but victory, and any victory won by violence necessarily justifies the violence that won it and leads to further violence. If we are serious about innovation," he says, "must we not conclude that we need something new to replace our perpetual 'war to end war'?" (XX). Although Berry's tone is moderate, his rural, agrarian (Berry is a farmer as well as a poet and essayist), pacifistic, Christian views are bound to anger some whose values conflict with these perspectives, however appreciative they might be of peaceful views such as the sunset on Mt. McKinley depicted in the photograph on p. 553.

Are there no solutions to matters of terrorism on which all right-minded, principled people can agree? Many of the possible solutions, ranging from all-out war to racial profiling to severe restraints on the freedoms of speech, the press, assembly, worship, and travel—among others—are problematic, as Berry has indicated. How are we, as individuals and a nation, to balance individual needs against the requirements of national security in a world that is never static, but always in motion? In "The Information Wars" (555–58), Mary Graham identifies a number of ways in which the federal government has, swiftly and silently, restricted public access to information, such as removing from its Web site "maps of the nation's 2.2 million miles of pipe lines" that would enable people to "identify places where ruptures in pipes that carry oil, natural gas, or hazardous chemicals could endanger lives, property, or drinking water," on the grounds that these and many other types of reports—"thousands of pages of information about health and safety risks to Americans"—might "somehow aid terrorists." She concludes that in the nominal interest of "national security," "temporary emergency actions have evolved into fundamental changes in the public's right to know, and the restrictions have been driven as much by familiar politics and bureaucratic instincts as by national security"—a threat not only to civil liberties, but to the health and welfare of all of America's residents.

In "The Futility of 'Homeland Defense'" (558–63), David Carr addresses the issue of national security from an economic perspective. He contends that ours is "a big society designed to be open"—to commerce (two billion tons in 1999), mail (the U.S. Postal Service processes 680 million pieces of mail per day), immigrants and foreign visitors (some 350 million in 2000 alone)—and thus it is impossible to close. Homeland security may operate in limited venues, such as airports and the testing of postal workers for biological agents. But because "America will continue to be a place of tremendous economic dynamism and openness," our culture cannot be re-engineered to make it less porous: "The very small percentage of unwanted people and substances that arrive with all the people and things we do want is part of the cost of being America, Inc."

Susan Sontag's op-ed commentary in the *New York Times*, published on September 10, 2002, a year after the terrorist attacks, addresses the issue of "WAR? Real Battles and Empty Metaphors" (563–66). Sontag, quite moderate here in comparison to her earlier incendiary statements, explores the implications of the meaning of war, as a figurative concept and as a literal activity. When the government declares war on something, whether "cancer or poverty or drugs . . . it means that the government is asking that new forces be mobilized to address the problem" and that "the government cannot do a whole lot to solve it." She continues, "When the government declares war on terrorism—terrorism being a multinational, largely clandestine network of enemies—it means that the government is giving itself permission to do what it wants. When it wants to intervene somewhere, it will. It will brook no limits on its power." Although she does not "for a moment question the obligation of the American government to protect the lives of its citizens," she does question the "pseudo-declaration of pseudo-war," "the dangerous, lobotomizing notion of endless war," and its consequences so "destructive of constitutional rights and of international agreements that serve the public interest of all."

There are no suggestions for reading or writing following the pieces in this chapter; the topic is too fluid to permit closure at this time. More general suggestions for writing about terrorism and/or peace appear at the end of the "World Peace" chapter (567–606). Each raises issues capable of multiple interpretations and debate. Wendell Berry's "Thoughts in the Presence of Fear" permits infinite discussion of a wide range of issues; he raises subjects that the other essayists here deal with at greater length, and supplies key words and concepts necessary to pursue a train of thought in a subject that continues to change even as we write about it.

SEAMUS HEANEY

Seamus Heaney, Ireland's best-known contemporary poet, was born in 1939 on a farm in County Derry, Northern Ireland. He considers the fact that his heritage includes "both the Ireland of the cattle-herding Gaelic past and the Ulster of the Industrial Revolution" to be significant in his work. For the past thirty years he has lived alternately in Dublin and the United States. Since 1981 he has taught for one semester a year at Harvard, as Boylston Professor of Rhetoric and Oratory (1984–1997), and as Ralph Waldo Emerson Poet in Residence. Like his predecessor and countryman, W. B. Yeats, Heaney's poetry deals in passionate yet clear language with love and loss, peace and war as interpreted through Irish history and lore. And, like Yeats, Heaney received the Nobel Prize in Literature (1985) for his poetry, the year he published *Station Island*. Other recent books include *The Haw Lantern* (1987), *Seeing Things* (1991), *The Spirit Level* (1996), and a translation of Beowulf (1999). Heaney's work has won a rare combination of critical esteem—as signaled by numerous awards and prestigious academic appointments (including five years as professor of poetry at Oxford)—and great popular acclaim, as attested by the large sales of his books and the hundreds of fans ("Heanyboppers" included) who attend his readings.

Horace and the Thunder

After Horace, Odes, 1, 34.

1   Anything can happen. You know how Jupiter
       Will mostly wait for clouds to gather head
       Before he hurls the lightning? Well, just now,
       He galloped his thunder-cart and his horses

2   Across a clear blue sky. It shook the earth
       And the clogged underearth, the River Styx,
       The winding streams, the Atlantic shore itself.
       Anything can happen, the tallest things

3   Be overturned, those in high places daunted,
       Those overlooked regarded. Stropped-beak Fortune
       Swoops, making the air gasp, tearing off the crest of one,
       Setting it down bleeding on the next.

4   Ground gives. The heaven's weight
       Lifts up off Atlas like a kettle lid,
       Capstones shift, nothing resettles right.
       Smoke-furl and boiling ashes darken day.

LAURIE FENDRICH

Laurie Fendrich, a professor of fine arts at Hofstra University, was born in Paterson, New Jersey, in 1948. She earned a B.A. in political science at Mount Holyoke College in 1970 and an M.F.A. in painting at the School of the Art Institute of Chicago in 1978. She is also an abstract painter who lives and works in New York, where she was on September 11, 2001, an eyewitness to the events in "History Overcomes Stories." This was commissioned by *The Chronicle of Higher Education,* to which she has been a contributor since 1999. *Why Painting Still Matters* was published in 2000 by Phi Delta Kappa.

She explains, "I began painting while I was in college, in the late 1960s. Since then, painting has steadily declined in cultural importance. Artists have turned to newer art forms, such as photography, sound and video installations, and computer art. The prevailing outlook of artists has also changed—from modern to postmodern. Modern art had been about the free exploration of forms within ever-widening ideas about beauty. Postmodern art turned its back on beauty almost entirely, focusing instead on popular culture, identity politics, social issues, technology and science. It reflects diverse, often previously ignored voices in society, each of which lays claim to a partial or fragmentary truth about a world continuously in flux. My writing focuses on painting's predicament in the postmodern environment.

"The essay 'History Overcomes Stories' was not about painting, however, and I wrote it under unusual circumstances. Like many people, I was numb during the days immediately following the September 11th attacks. Because I was asked to deliver a completed essay in just a few days, I didn't have much time to mull over different ideas. I had been asked to write something about the images of the imploding World Trade Center towers. Although I had seen the images over and over again, I didn't have any opinion about them other than that they were horrible. After several hours of struggling to write a personal narrative about what I had seen and felt during the attack and its immediate aftermath, I was getting nowhere. The essay seemed puny in the face of what had happened because it did no more than reiterate that we all felt a sense of shock, grief and fear. Suddenly it hit me that my whole approach was wrong. Artists and writers like to make images and stories, but these are limited, especially when used to excess, in helping us to be good citizens. We need something else in order to participate in politics and history."

History Overcomes Stories

I live about 10 blocks north of what used to be the World Trade Center towers, in an area of New York City called Tribeca. Three mornings ago was September 11, 2001.

My neighborhood is populated with artists like myself and my husband. Artists first started living in lofts in this former manufacturing district

*In what ways does this photograph of people running after the collapse
of the first tower of the World Trade Center on September 11, 2001,
augment and reinforce Fendrich's observations?*

sometime in the late 1960s. Later, they started families, and the neighbor-
hood filled up with children and stores and flowers in the windows.
When my own daughter was ready for kindergarten, we walked her to
P.S. 234, then a brand-new school built a few blocks north of the World
Trade Center. To us, it was practically Mr. Rogers's neighborhood.

3   Ours was a good life. My husband and I have never even had to own
a car. Within the past few years, rich newcomers began developing large
luxury lofts in buildings all over the neighborhood. Recently, they've been
adding spectacular penthouses. We artists grumbled, but most of us con-
ceded that cities must change even along these lines in order to stay vibrant.

4   An account of my life in lower Manhattan, what I've been through in
this calamity, and the sights I've seen don't really count for much. There are
thousands of other stories, many very terrible and dramatic, that are unfortunately more representative of the horror that New York, and the country, has suffered. And there is the question of when necessary, informative
storytelling disintegrates into a kind of entertainment. No amount of my
artist's experience in thinking about images adds relevance. In short, my
story contributes nothing to history.

5   Experiences and stories were once, however, the heart of history. That
was how Thucydides told history. Now stories are polluted and demeaned
by having been reduced to fodder for television, movie, and slick magazine

entertainment. At this point, hardly anybody's story can guide us in how to act. All we known, dimly, is that we have passed the end of an era, and face a probably very grim new one. The past 25 years, which so many saw as an eternal history-less present, turn out to have been a fleeting grace, a blip of peace in an inexorable continuum of war. The only redemption for the sin of having thought this eternally present tense could be true is to see if we can now act the way we ought to have been acting all along.

Until Tuesday, I was part of a ridiculously lucky generation. For me, 6 war was what I knew about from movies, reading, and the distant (before my birth) loss to my mother of her brother in World War II. Now, like all Americans, I know something directly about war. I know it as a civilian, having been attacked here, in my own country, my own city, my own neighborhood. All my strivings as an artist and a teacher seem to have been deprived of meaning. I've experienced a very small slice of Theodor Adorno's conclusion that "to write poetry after Auschwitz is barbaric." I, like many others, must try to figure out all over again what truly matters. After Tuesday, I can no longer speak as a woman, or an artist, or a New Yorker. Speaking in those ways—"speaking personally"—will no longer do. I have to learn how to speak as a citizen.

We have been seduced by television and computers into believing it 7 is images and stories, not ideas, that count. We have bought the party line that ours is the age of the computer and simulacra, not nature and physical reality; we've traded slow, sure ideas for "instant communication." We have deluded ourselves that the older, more complicated concepts of good, evil, beauty, and, above all, nature, are old-fashioned. Thinking we could, as Horace put it, drive nature out with a pitchfork, we moved into such quagmires as genetic manipulation. Not that microbiology in the service of medicine is automatically wrong. But Horace was right about the power of things that are the givens in life. In this case, Nature in its simple, oldest form—some people hating others—has come running back in.

In the din of postmodernism, we dismissed all voices celebrating 8 Western culture as reactionary and logocentric. Many of those voices revealed a profound bigotry, hatred, and fear of other cultures and ways of life. But the self-castigation that has been going on since the Vietnam War has gotten to the point where we have been throwing out almost everything that is Western except its material goods. What now ought to be clear as a bell is that it is precisely in our freedom to criticize ourselves that we locate the values of Western culture. Self-criticism is our freedom, but it, too, must be modified by restraint.

The universal values of freedom and democracy, originating with the 9 ancient Greeks, modified by Christianity and Judaism, and maturing with the ideas of humanism and liberalism, are now nourished by the streaming energy and beauty coming from non-Western cultures. That complex structure is the 21st-century foundation for any viable, modern civilization. At its bottom layer still sits our need for the Western values of individual

liberty, coupled with obligations to virtue, democracy coupled with responsibility, the requirement of courage, an acknowledgment—always tempered
by reason—of duty, and an assertion of basic, not jingoistic, patriotism.

10   Art and images need to be postponed. (I certainly can't think of
painting right now.) We need, I think, to achieve intellectual control of our
feelings, and direct our actions according to what is right and just, instead
of to what pleases us as "personal expression" or intrigues us as convo-
luted theory. Our unfamiliarity with how to use history correctly, and our
forgetfulness when it comes to our own values, have resulted in this unspeakable historical moment being at risk of degenerating into hundreds
of personal "survival" or "coping" stories, the sort that turn into television
movies on the Lifetime network. Worse, the images of our current disaster
will be aestheticized into "unforgettable" or "iconic" images. As I write,
television news is already adding music to montages of horror.

11   A perhaps impenetrable boundary exists—or should exist—between
the thousands of real lives that were brutally destroyed on Tuesday, and
art. And that slovenly province of art known as entertainment should not
dare to touch what has happened. Mine is not a postmodernist response,
of course, and it is, admittedly, written under the stress of being an immediate neighbor to calamity. But I do not see myself ever shrinking from
the renewed convictions put forth in this essay—one for which, I wish
with all my heart, there had never been an occasion to write.

BERNARD LEWIS

> Bernard Lewis (born in London, 1916) was educated at the University of
> London School of Oriental and African Studies, specializing in the history
> of Islam. He began his lifelong teaching career at his alma mater in 1938,
> where—with five years' absence during World War II to serve as a special-
> ist in Middle Eastern matters for the British Foreign Office—he taught until
> 1974. Thereafter, he taught at Princeton until retirement in 1986, where he
> remains an emeritus professor of Near Eastern studies. His numerous
> books on the Middle East span fifty-two years, from *The Arabs in History*
> (1950) to *The Political Language of Islam* (1988) to *What Went Wrong?* (2002),
> dealing with issues addressed in the chapter included here. Indeed, this
> chapter touches briefly on the range of topics Lewis examines in his other
> works: Islam's thousand-year domination of the West in culture, science,
> and military prowess and the retreat of Islam from the West after the failed
> Turkish siege of Vienna in 1683, "dominated and bettered by the West"
> according to "every possible measure. Because the Islamic world has an
> acute sense of history and America does not, this reversal has fed centuries
> of acrimony." America is the current object of Islamic rage because it is seen
> as "imperialistic," supportive of oppressive Middle Eastern governments
> for its own ends and fostering "a culture of temptation and seduction."

What Went Wrong?

In the course of the twentieth century it became abundantly clear that 1
things had gone badly wrong in the Middle East—and, indeed, in all the
lands of Islam. Compared with Christendom, its rival for more than a millennium, the world of Islam had become poor, weak, and ignorant. The
primacy and therefore the dominance of the West was clear for all to see,
invading every aspect of the Muslim's public and even—more painfully—
his private life.

Muslim modernizers—by reform or revolution—concentrated their 2
efforts in three main areas: military, economic, and political. The results
achieved were, to say the least, disappointing. The quest for victory by up-
dated armies brought a series of humiliating defeats. The quest for prosperity through development brought in some countries impoverished and
corrupt economies in recurring need of external aid, in others an unhealthy
dependence on a single resource—oil. And even this was discovered, ex-
tracted, and put to use by Western ingenuity and industry, and is doomed,
sooner or later, to be exhausted, or, more probably, superseded, as the international community grows weary of a fuel that pollutes the land, the
sea, and the air wherever it is used or transported, and that puts the world
economy at the mercy of a clique of capricious autocrats. Worst of all are
the political results: the long quest for freedom has left a string of shabby
tyrannies, ranging from traditional autocracies to dictatorships that are
modern only in their apparatus of repression and indoctrination.

Many remedies were tried—weapons and factories, schools and par- 3
liaments—but none achieved the desired result. Here and there they
brought some alleviation and, to limited elements of the population, some
benefit. But they failed to remedy or even to halt the increasing imbalance
between Islam and the Western world.

There was worse to come. It was bad enough for Muslims to feel poor 4
and weak after centuries of being rich and strong, to lose the position of
leadership that they had come to regard as their right, and to be reduced
to the role of followers of the West. But the twentieth century, particularly
the second half, brought further humiliation—the awareness that they
were no longer even the first among followers but were falling back in a
lengthening line of eager and more successful Westernizers, notably in
East Asia. The rise of Japan had been an encouragement but also a reproach.
The later rise of other Asian economic powers brought only reproach. The
proud heirs of ancient civilizations had gotten used to hiring Western firms
to carry out tasks of which their own contractors and technicians were apparently incapable. Now Middle Eastern rulers and businessmen found
themselves inviting contractors and technicians from Korea—only recently
emerged from Japanese colonial rule—to perform these tasks. Following
is bad enough; limping in the rear is far worse. By all the standards that

matter in the modern world—economic development and job creation, literacy, educational and scientific achievement, political freedom and respect for human rights—what was once a mighty civilization has indeed fallen low.

5   "Who did this to us?" is of course a common human response when things are going badly, and many in the Middle East, past and present, have asked this question. They have found several different answers. It is usually easier and always more satisfying to blame others for one's misfortunes. For a long time the Mongols were the favorite villains. The Mongol invasions of the thirteen century were blamed for the destruction of both Muslim power and Islamic civilization, and for what was seen as the ensuing weakness and stagnation. But after a while historians, Muslims and others, pointed to two flaws in this argument. The first was that some of the greatest cultural achievements of Islam, notably in Iran, came after, not before, the Mongol invasions. The second, more difficult to accept but nevertheless undeniable, was that the Mongols overthrew an empire that was already fatally weakened; indeed, it is hard to see how the once mighty empire of the caliphs would otherwise have succumbed to a horde of nomadic horsemen riding across the steppes from East Asia.

6   The rise of nationalism—itself an import from Europe—produced new perceptions. Arabs could lay the blame for their troubles on the Turks, who had ruled them for many centuries. Turks could lay the blame for the stagnation of their civilization on the dead weight of the Arab past, in which the creative energies of the Turkish people were caught and immobilized. Persians could lay the blame for the loss of their ancient glories on Arabs, Turks, and Mongols impartially.

7   In the nineteenth and twentieth centuries British and French paramountcy [sic] in much of the Arab world produced a new and more plausible scapegoat—Western imperialism. In the Middle East there have been good reasons for such blame. Western political domination, economic penetration, and—longest, deepest, and most insidious of all—cultural influence changed the face of the region and transformed the lives of its people, turning them in new directions, arousing new hopes and fears, creating new dangers and new expectations without precedent in their cultural past.

8   But the Anglo-French interlude was comparatively brief, and ended half a century ago; Islam's change for the worse began long before and continued unabated afterward. Inevitably, the role of the British and the French as villains was taken over by the United States, along with other aspects of Western leadership. The attempt to transfer the guilt to America has won considerable support but, for similar reasons, remains unconvincing. Anglo-French rule and American influence, like the Mongol invasions, were a consequence, not a cause, of the inner weakness of Middle Eastern states and societies. Some observers, both inside and outside the region, have pointed to differences in the post-colonial development of

former British possessions—for example, between Aden, in the Middle East, and Singapore or Hong Kong; or between the various lands that once made up the British Empire in India.

Another European contribution to this debate is anti-Semitism, and 9 blaming "the Jews" for all that goes wrong. Jews in traditional Islamic societies experienced the normal constraints and occasional hazards of minority status. Until the rise and spread of Western tolerance in the seventeenth and eighteenth centuries, they were better off under Muslim than under Christian rule in most significant respects. With rare exceptions, where hostile stereotypes of the Jew existed in the Islamic tradition, Islamic societies tended to be contemptuous and dismissive rather than suspicious and obsessive. This made the events of 1948—the failure to prevent the establishment of the state of Israel—all the more of a shock. As some writers observed at the time, it was humiliating enough to be defeated by the great imperial powers of the West; to suffer the same fate at the hands of a contemptible gang of Jews was intolerable. Anti-Semitism and its image of the Jew as a scheming, evil monster provided a soothing antidote.

The earliest specifically anti-Semitic statements in the Middle East 10 occurred among Christian minorities, and can usually be traced back to European originals. They had limited impact, during the Dreyfus trial in France, for example, when a Jewish officer was unjustly accused and condemned by a hostile court, Muslim comments usually favored the persecuted Jew against his Christian persecutors. But the poison continued to spread, and starting in 1933, Nazi Germany and its various agencies made a concerted and on the whole remarkably successful effort to promote European-style anti-Semitism in the Arab world. The struggle for Palestine greatly facilitated the acceptance of the anti-Semitic interpretation of history, and led some to attribute all evil in the Middle East—and, indeed, in the world—to secret Jewish plots. This interpretation has pervaded much of the public discourse in the region, including that seen in education, the media, and even entertainment.

An argument sometimes adduced is that the cause of the changed 11 relationship between East and West is not a Middle Eastern decline but a Western upsurge—the discoveries and the scientific, technological, industrial, and political revolutions that transformed the West and vastly increased its wealth and power. But this is merely to restate the question: Why did the discoverers of America sail from Spain rather than from a Muslim Atlantic port, out of which such voyages were indeed attempted in earlier times? Why did the great scientific breakthrough occur in Europe and not, as one might reasonably have expected, in the richer, more advanced, and in most respects more enlightened realm of Islam?

A more sophisticated form of the blame game finds its targets inside, 12 rather than outside, Islamic society. One such target is religion—for some, specifically Islam. But to blame Islam as such is usually hazardous and not often attempted. Nor is it very plausible. For most of the Middle Ages it was neither the older cultures of the Orient nor the newer cultures of the West that were the major centers of civilization and progress but the world of Islam. There old sciences were recovered and developed and new sciences were created; there new industries were born and manufactures and commerce were expanded to a level without precedent. There, too, governments and societies achieved a freedom of thought and expression that led persecuted Jews and even dissident Christians to flee Christendom for refuge in Islam. In comparison with modern ideals, and even with modern practice in the more advanced democracies, the medieval Islamic world offered only limited freedom, but that was vastly more than was offered by any of its predecessors, its contemporaries, or most of its successors.

13   The point has often been made: If Islam is an obstacle to freedom, to science, to economic development, how is it that Muslim society in the past was a pioneer in all three—and this when Muslims were much closer in time to the sources and inspiration of their faith than they are now? Some have posed the question in a different form—not "What has Islam done to the Muslims?" but "What have the Muslims done to Islam?"—and have answered by laying the blame on specific teachers and doctrines and groups.

14   For those known nowadays as Islamists or fundamentalists, the failures and shortcomings of modern Islamic lands afflict those lands because they adopted alien notions and practices. They fell away from authentic Islam and thus lost their former greatness. Those known as modernists or reformers take the opposite view, seeing the cause of this loss not in the abandonment but in the retention of old ways, and especially in the inflexibility and ubiquity of the Islamic clergy, who, they say, are responsible for the persistence of beliefs and practices that might have been creative and progressive a thousand years ago but are neither today. The modernists' usual tactic is not to denounce religion as such, still less Islam in particular, but to level their criticism against fanaticism. It is to fanaticism—and more particularly to fanatical religious authorities—that they attribute the stifling of the once great Islamic scientific movement and, more generally, of the freedom of thought and expression.

15   A more common approach to this theme has been to discuss a specific problem: the place of religion and of its professional exponents in the political order. In this view a principal cause of Western progress is the separation of Church and State and the creation of a civil society governed by secular laws. Another approach has been to view the main culprit as the relegation of women to an inferior position in Muslim society, which deprives the Islamic world of the talents and energies of half its people and entrusts the other half's crucial early years of upbringing to illiterate and downtrodden mothers. The products of such an education, it has been said, are likely to grow up either arrogant or submissive, and unfit for a free, open society. However one evaluates the views of secularists

and feminists, their success or failure will be a major factor in shaping the Middle Eastern future.

Some solutions that once commanded passionate support have been discarded. The two dominant movements in the twentieth century were socialism and nationalism. Both have been discredited—the first by its failure, the second by its success and consequent exposure as ineffective. Freedom, interpreted to mean national independence, was seen as the great talisman that would bring all other benefits. The overwhelming majority of Muslims now live in independent states, but this has brought no solutions to their problems. National socialism, the bastard offspring of both ideologies, persists in a few states that have preserved the Nazi-Fascist style of dictatorial government and indoctrination through a vast security apparatus and a single all-powerful party. These regimes have failed every test except survival, and have brought none of the promised benefits. If anything, their infrastructures are even more antiquated than those of other Muslim states, their armed forces designed primarily for terror and repression. [16]

At present two answers to the question of what went wrong command widespread support in the Middle East, each with its own diagnosis and corresponding prescription. One attributes all evil to the abandonment of the divine heritage of Islam and advocates return to a real or imagined past. That is the way of the Iranian revolution and of the so-called fundamentalist movements and regimes in various Muslim countries. The other condemns the past and advocates secular democracy, best embodied in the Turkish Republic, proclaimed in 1923 by Kemal Atatürk. [17]

For the oppressive but ineffectual governments that rule much of the Middle East, finding targets to blame serves a useful, indeed an essential, purpose—to explain the poverty that they have failed to alleviate and to justify the tyranny that they have introduced. They seek to deflect the mounting anger of their unhappy subjects toward other, outside targets. [18]

But growing numbers of Middle Easterners are adopting a more self-critical approach. The question "Who did this to us?" has led only to neurotic fantasies and conspiracy theories. And the question "What did we do wrong?" has led naturally to a second question: "How do we put it right?" In that question, and in the various answers that are being found, lie the best hopes for the future. [19]

During the past few weeks the worldwide exposure given to the views and actions of Osama bin Laden and his hosts the Taliban has provided a new and vivid insight into the eclipse of what was once the greatest, most advanced, and most open civilization in human history. [20]

To a Western observer, schooled in the theory and practice of Western freedom, it is precisely the lack of freedom—freedom of the mind from constraint and indoctrination, to question and inquire and speak; freedom of the economy from corrupt and pervasive mismanagement; freedom of women from male oppression; freedom of citizens from tyranny—that underlies so many of the troubles of the Muslim world. But the road to [21] democracy, as the Western experience amply demonstrates, is long and hard, full of pitfalls and obstacles.

22   If the peoples of the Middle East continue on their present path, the suicide bomber may become a metaphor for the whole region, and there will be no escape from a downward spiral of hate and spite, rage and self-pity, poverty and oppression, culminating sooner or later in yet another alien domination—perhaps from a new Europe reverting to old ways, perhaps from a resurgent Russia, perhaps from some expanding super-power in the East. But if they can abandon grievance and victimhood, settle their differences, and join their talents, energies, and resources in a common creative endeavor, they can once again make the Middle East, in modern times as it was in antiquity and in the Middle Ages, a major cen-ter of civilization. For the time being, the choice is theirs.

MARK JUERGENSMEYER

Mark Juergensmeyer (born in 1940 in southern Illinois) earned a Master's in divinity from Union Theological Seminary (1965) and a Ph.D. in political science from Berkeley (1974). He is currently Director of Global and Inter-national Studies and professor of sociology and religious studies at the University of California, Santa Barbara. An expert on religious violence, conflict resolution, and South Asian religion and politics, he has pub-lished more than two hundred articles and a dozen books. He has received research fellowships from the Guggenheim Foundation, the U.S. Institute of Peace, and the American Council of Learned Societies. *The New Cold War? Religious Nationalism Confronts the Secular State* (1993) covers the rise of religious activism and its confrontation with secular modernity. His widely read *Terror in the Mind of God: The Global Rise of Religious Violence* (2000), from which these excerpts are taken, is based on interviews with violent religious activists around the world—including people convicted of the 1993 World Trade Center bombing, leaders of Hamas, and abortion clinic bombers in the United States.

from Terror in the Mind of God

1   . . . Instances of exaggerated violence are constructed events: they are mind-numbing, mesmerizing theater. At center stage are the acts themselves—stunning, abnormal, and outrageous murders carried out in a way that graphically displays the awful power of violence—set within grand sce-narios of conflict and proclamation. Killing or maiming of any sort is vio-lent, of course, but these acts surpass the wounds inflicted during warfare

or death delivered through capital punishment, in large part because they have a secondary impact. By their demonstrative nature, they elicit feelings of revulsion and anger in those who witness them.

Performance Violence

How do we make sense of such theatrical forms of violence? One way of answering this is to view dramatic violence as part of a strategic plan. This viewpoint assumes that terrorism is always part of a political strategy—and, in fact, some social scientists have defined terrorism in just this way: "the use of covert violence by a group for political ends." In some cases this definition is indeed appropriate, for an act of violence can fulfill political ends and have a direct impact on public policy.

The Israeli elections in 1996 provided a case in point. Shortly after the assassination of Yitzhak Rabin, his successor, Shimon Peres, held a 20 percent lead in the polls over his rival, Benjamin Netanyahu, but this lead vanished following a series of Hamas suicide attacks on Jerusalem buses. Netanyahu narrowly edged out Peres in the May elections. Many observers concluded that Netanyahu—no friend of Islamic radicals—had the terrorists of Hamas to thank for his victory.

When the Hamas operative who planned the 1996 attacks was later caught and imprisoned, he was asked whether he had intended to affect the outcome of the elections. "No," he responded, explaining that the internal affairs of Israelis did not matter much to him. This operative was a fairly low-level figure, however, and one might conjecture that his superiors had a more specific goal in mind. But when I put the same question to the political leader of Hamas, Dr. Abdul Aziz Rantisi, his answer was almost precisely the same: these attacks were not aimed at Israeli internal politics, since Hamas did not differentiate between Peres and Netanyahu. In the Hamas view, the two Israeli leaders were equally opposed to Islam. "Maybe God wanted it," the Hamas operative said of Netanyahu's election victory. Even if the Hamas leaders were being disingenuous, the fact remains that most of their suicide bombings have served no direct political purpose.

Other examples of religious terrorism have also shown little strategic value. The release of nerve gas in the Tokyo subways and the bombing of the World Trade Center did not provide any immediate political benefits to those who caused them. Although Mahmud Abouhalima, convicted for his part in the World Trade Center bombing, told me that assaults on public buildings did have a long-range strategic value in that they helped to "identify the government as enemy," in general the "political ends" for which these acts were committed seemed distant indeed.

A political scientist, Martha Crenshaw, has shown that the notion of "strategic" thinking can be construed in a broad sense to cover not just immediate political achievements but also the internal logic that propels a group into perpetrating terrorist acts. As Abouhalima said, many of those who committed them felt they were justified by the broad, long-range benefits to be gained. My investigations indicate that Crenshaw is right—acts of terrorism are usually the products of an internal logic and not of random or crazy thinking—but I hesitate to use the term *strategy* for all rationales for terrorist actions. *Strategy* implies a degree of calculation and an expectation of accomplishing a clear objective that does not jibe with such dramatic displays of power as the World Trade Center bombing. These creations of terror are done not to achieve a strategic goal but to make a symbolic statement.

7   By calling acts of religious terrorism "symbolic," I mean that they are intended to illustrate or refer to something beyond their immediate target: a grander conquest, for instance, or a struggle more awesome than meets the eye. As Abouhalima said, the bombing of a public building may dramatically indicate to the populace that the government or the economic forces behind the building were seen as enemies, to show the world that they were targeted as satanic foes. The point of the attack, then, was to produce a graphic and easily understandable object lesson. Such explosive scenarios are not *tactics* directed toward an immediate, earthly, or strategic goal, but *dramatic events* intended to impress for their symbolic significance. As such, they can be analyzed as one would any other symbol, ritual, or sacred drama.

8   I can imagine a line with "strategic" on the one side and "symbolic" on the other, with various acts of terrorism located in between. The hostage taking in the Japanese embassy by the Tupac Amaru in Peru in 1997—clearly an attempt to leverage power in order to win the release of members of the movement held prisoner by the Peruvian government—might be placed closer to the political, strategic side. The Aum Shinrikyo nerve gas attack in 1995 might be closer to the symbolic, religious side. Each was the product of logical thought, and each had an internal rationale. In cases such as the Tokyo nerve gas attack that were more symbolic than strategic, however, the logic was focused not on an immediate political acquisition, but at a larger, less tangible goal.

9   The very adjectives used to describe acts of religious terrorism—symbolic, dramatic, theatrical—suggest that we look at them not as tactics but as *performance violence.* In speaking of terrorism as "performance," I am not suggesting that such acts are undertaken lightly or capriciously. Rather, like religious ritual or street theater, they are dramas designed to have an impact on the several audiences that they affect. Those who witness the violence—even at a distance, via the news media—are therefore a part of what occurs. Moreover, like other forms of public ritual, the symbolic significance of such events is multifaceted; they mean different things to different observers. . . .

10   In addition to referring to drama, the term *performance* also implies the notion of "performative"—as in the concept of "performative acts." This

is an idea developed by language philosophers regarding certain kinds of speech that are able to perform social functions: their very utterance has a transformative impact. Like vows recited during marriage rites, certain words not only represent reality but also shape it: they contain a certain power of their own. The same is true of some nonverbal symbolic actions, such as the gunshot that begins a race, the raising of a white flag to show defeat, or acts of terrorism.

Terrorist acts, then, can be both *performance events,* in that they make   11 a symbolic statement, and *performative acts,* insofar as they try to change things. When Yigal Amir aimed his pistol at Israel's prime minister, Yitzhak Rabin, and when Sikh activists targeted Punjab's chief minister with a car bomb in front of the state's office buildings, the activists were aware that they were creating enormous spectacles. They probably also hoped that their actions would make a difference—if not in a direct, strategic sense, then in an indirect way as a dramatic show so powerful as to change people's perceptions of the world.

But the fact that the assassins of Prime Minister Rabin and Chief Min-   12 ister Beant Singh hoped that their acts would make such a statement does not mean that they in fact did. As I noted, public symbols mean different things to different people, and a symbolic performance may not have the intended effect. The way the act is perceived—by both the perpetrators and those who are affected by it—makes all the difference. In fact, the same is true of performance speech. One of the leading language philosophers, J. L. Austin, has qualified the notion that some speech acts are performative by observing that the power of the act is related to the perception of it. Children, for example, playing at marriage are not wedded by merely reciting the vows and going through the motions, nor is a ship christened by just anyone who gives it a name.[1]

The French sociologist Pierre Bourdieu, carrying further the idea that   13 statements are given credibility by their social context, has insisted that the power of performative speech—vows and christenings—is rooted in social reality and is given currency by the laws and social customs that stand behind it.[2] Similarly, an act of terrorism usually implies an underlying power and legitimizing ideology. But whether the power and legitimacy implicit in acts of terrorism are like play-acted marriage vows or are the real thing depends in part on how the acts are perceived. It depends, in part, on whether their significance is believed.

This brings us back to the realm of faith. Public ritual has traditionally   14 been the province of religion, and this is one of the reasons that performance

---

[1] See J. L. Austin, *How to Do Things with Words* (Oxford: Clarendon Press, 1962), 4.
[2] Pierre Bourdieu, *Language and Symbolic Power* (Cambridge, MA: Harvard University Press, 1991) (translated from the 1982 French original by Gino Raymond and Matthew Adamson, edited by John B. Thompson), 117.

violence comes so naturally to activists from a religious background. In a collection of essays on the connection between religion and terrorism published some years ago, one of the editors, David C. Rapoport, observed— accurately, I think—that the two topics fit together not only because there is a violent streak in the history of religion, but also because terrorist acts have a symbolic side and in that sense mimic religious rites. The victims of terrorism are targeted not because they are threatening to the perpetrators, he said, but because they are "symbols, tools, animals or corrupt beings" that tie into "a special picture of the world, a specific consciousness" that the activist possesses.[3]

15   The street theater of performance violence forces those who witness it directly or indirectly into that "consciousness"—that alternative view of the world. This gives the perpetrators of terrorism a kind of celebrity status and their actions an illusion of importance. The novelist Don DeLillo goes so far as to say that "only the lethal believer, the person who kills and dies for faith," is taken seriously in modern society.[4] When we who observe these acts take them seriously—are disgusted and repelled by them, and begin to distrust the peacefulness of the world around us— the purposes of this theater are achieved.

Setting the Stage

16   In looking at religious terrorism as theater, the appropriate place to begin is the stage—the location where the acts are committed, or rather, performed. When followers of an expatriate Muslim sheik living in New Jersey chose to make a statement about their unhappiness with American and Jewish support for Middle East leaders whom they perceived to be enemies of Islam, they found the most dramatic stage in sight: the World Trade Center. It turned out to be an apt location for a variety of symbolic reasons.

17   Designed to be the tallest buildings in New York City, and at one time the highest in the world, the 110-story twin towers of the World Trade Center house the headquarters of international businesses and financial corporations. Among its many offices are quarters for the federal Secret Service and the governor of the state of New York. More than fifty thousand employees daily enter the huge edifice, which also includes a hotel, shops, and several restaurants. From the windows of the penthouse restaurant, Windows on the World, the executives who come to lunch can scarcely identify Jersey City and the other industrial areas stretched out across the Hudson River in a distant haze.

---

[3] David C. Rapoport, "Introduction," in David C. Rapoport and Yonah Alexander, eds., *The Morality of Terrorism: Religious and Secular Justifications* (New York: Pergamon Press, 1982), xiii.

[4] Don DeLillo, *Mao II* (New York: Penguin, 1991), 157.

From across the river in Jersey City, the twin towers of the build-   18
ing are so tall that when no other part of the skyline in New York City is
visible, the tower tops are seen ethereally suspended above the eastern
horizon. When Muhammad A. Salameh came to the Ryder Truck Rental
lot on Jersey City's busy Kennedy Boulevard on Wednesday, February 24,
1993, to rent a ten-foot Ford Econoline van, therefore, he could catch
glimpses of the World Trade Center in the distance.

Two days later, at noon, shortly after the van was driven to level B2   19
of the parking basement of the World Trade Center, an enormous blast
shuddered through the basement levels, collapsing several floors, killing
several workers instantly, and ripping a 180-foot hole in the wall of the
underground Port Authority Trans-Hudson train station. On the 110th
floor, in the Windows on the World restaurant, young executives who
were attending a career-launching lunch felt a thump and heard what
seemed to be a mild earthquake or a clap of thunder. When the electricity
went off and they were told to evacuate the building, they headed downstairs jauntily singing "One Hundred Bottles of Beer on the Wall." Their
joviality turned to nervous apprehension when they were greeted with
clouds of soot and smoke as they groped their way down 110 flights of
stairs into a scene of confusion and suffering on the ground floor.

Throughout the world the news media projected images of American   20
power and civic order undermined. Based on the belief by government
officials that the World Trade Center was targeted primarily as a public
symbol, security was rushed to federal monuments and memorials in
Washington, DC, later that afternoon. Although six people were killed in
the blast, it was the assault on the building itself that received the most
prominent reportage. Within an hour of the World Trade Center bombing,
a coffeehouse in Cairo was attacked—allegedly by the same group implicated in the World Trade Center incident. This bombing killed more
people but garnered very little attention outside of Cairo. Regardless of the
number killed, a coffeehouse is not the World Trade Center. The towers are
in their own way as American as the Statue of Liberty or the Washington
Monument, and by assaulting them activists put their mark on a visibly
American symbol.

The same can be said about the bombing of the Alfred P. Murrah Fed-   21
eral Building in Oklahoma City on April 19, 1995, by Timothy McVeigh and
Terry Nichols. In this case the number killed was much greater than at the
World Trade Center, and an enormous outpouring of public sympathy for
the victims overshadowed any concern about damage done to the building. Yet there were several similarities between the two events: McVeigh
and Nichols used a mixture of ammonium nitrate fertilizer and diesel fuel
not unlike that used in the World Trade Center blast, and they mimicked
the World Trade Center bombers by employing a Ryder rental truck. Like
Mahmud Abouhalima and his colleagues, these self-designated soldiers
were fighting a quasi-religious war against the American government, and

they chose a building that symbolized what they regarded as an oppressive government force. . . .

22   If one had to choose a single building that symbolized the presence of centralized federal governmental power in this region of mid-America, the Murrah building in Oklahoma City would be it. When the dust settled after the devastating roar of the enormous explosion on Wednesday morning, April 19, 1995, the entire front of the building had been sheared off, killing 168 and injuring more than five hundred. Among the dead and injured were scores of children in the building's day care center, but only four ATF officials were injured, and none were killed. Clearly, the target of the attack was not so much the government agents, or even an agency such as the ATF, as it was the building itself and its everyday staff of government workers.

23   What was targeted was a symbol of normal government operations. In this scenario of terrorism, the lives of the workers were, like the building, a part of the scenery: they and the edifice constituted the stage on which the dramatic act was to be performed. If the building were attacked at night without the workers present, the explosion would not have been a serious blow to government operations, nor would the pain of the event be felt as acutely by society at large. If the building's employees had been machine-gunned as they left their offices, with the building itself left unscathed, the symbolism of an attack on normal government operations would have been incomplete. Such targets as the World Trade Center and the Oklahoma City federal building have provided striking images of a stable, seemingly invulnerable economic and political power. Yet all buildings are ultimately vulnerable, a fact that performers of terror such as Abouhalima and McVeigh have been eager to demonstrate. . . .

24   Because air traffic itself is indicative of a society's economic vitality, often airplanes rather than airports have provided terrorism's stage. The most dramatic example is Ramzi Yousef's Bojinka plot, aimed at eleven U.S. trans-Pacific passenger airplanes and alleged to have been funded by Saudi millionaire Osama bin Laden, which would have created a catastrophic event on one fateful day in 1995. The term *Bojinka* was one that Yousef himself had chosen and was the label for the file in the hard disk of his white Toshiba laptop computer that listed the details of the plot— where flights would depart, what routes they would take, and where the participants in the plot should deplane in order to escape the explosions caused by the bombs that they were to leave behind. In the trail that convicted him of conspiring to commit these acts of terrorism, Yousef, acting as his own lawyer, offered as his main defense the notion that anyone with computer expertise could have planted such information on his hard disk. Yet he was not able to refute the testimony of witnesses who heard him talk about the plot and the Philippines airline stewardess who saw him sitting in the very seat under which a bomb exploded on a later leg of the flight, after Yousef had departed. In December 1994, Yousef is said to have

boarded the plane and, once it was aloft, entered one of the bathrooms and mixed a highly inflammable cocktail involving a liquid form of nitroglycerin. He sealed it in a container and attached a blasting cap and a timer. Returning to his seat, he strapped the device underneath the cushion and departed the plane at its next stop, leaving the bomb beneath the seat to explode in midair as the plane journeyed on to its next destination. . . .

According to a chronology of terrorist acts maintained by Bruce Hoffman at the RAND Corporation and St. Andrews University, twenty-two airliners were bombed worldwide from 1969 to 1996, and many others were hijacked. A nation can feel dishonored by the bombing of one of its airlines even when the plane, such as the downed Pan Am 103, is far from home. In that case the bomb—plastic explosives hidden in a portable radio–tape player, allegedly placed by Libyan intelligence agencies operating out of Malta—blew up the aircraft as it flew above Scotland in 1988, the shredded pieces of the plane landing near the small town of Lockerbie. . . .   25

The symbolism of other locations has been more general: the locations represented the power and stability of the society itself. As we have seen, buildings such as the World Trade Center and the Oklahoma City federal building, along with transportation systems, are examples of such general symbols. . . . Computer networks and Internet channels are also symbols of a society's centrality—its central communication system. As the Melissa virus in 1999 demonstrated, acts of sabotage can cripple large corporations and government agencies. In response to NATO's bombing in Serbia and Kosovo in May 1999, hackers electronically entered the computer systems of several United States government agencies, leaving antiwar messages in their wake.   26

By revealing the vulnerability of a nation's most stable and powerful entities, movements that undertake these acts of sabotage have touched virtually everyone in the nation's society. Any person in the United States could have been riding the elevator in the World Trade Center, visiting the Oklahoma City federal building, traveling on Pan Am 103, or using a computer when a virus invaded it, and everyone in the United States will look differently at the stability of public buildings, transportation networks, and communication systems as a result of these violent incidents.   27

Why is the location of terrorist events—of performance violence—so important? . . . Such central places—even if they exist only in cyberspace—are symbols of power, and acts of terrorism claim them in a symbolic way. That is, they express for a moment the power of terrorist groups to control central locations—by damaging, terrorizing, and assaulting them—even when in fact most of the time they do not control them at all. Even before the smoke had cleared at the World Trade Center, life inside was returning to normal. Although the Murrah Federal Building was destroyed, the governmental functions that had been conducted there continued unabated. Yet during that brief dramatic moment when a terrorist act levels a building or damages some entity that a society regards as central to its existence, the   28 perpetrators of the act assert that they—and not the secular government—have ultimate control over that entity and its centrality.

29   The very act, however, is sometimes more than symbolic: by demonstrating the vulnerability of governmental power, to some degree it weakens that power. Because power is largely a matter of perception, symbolic statements can lead to real results. On the whole, however, the small degree to which a government's authority is discredited by a terrorist act does not warrant the massive destructiveness of the act itself. More significant is the impression—in most cases it is simply an illusion—that the movements perpetrating the acts have enormous power and that the ideologies behind them have cosmic importance. In the war between religious and secular authority, the loss of a secular government's ability to control and secure public spaces, even for a terrible moment, is ground gained for religion's side. . . .

America as Enemy

30 More than any other government, America has been assigned the role of primary or secondary foe. The wrath has been directed largely toward political leaders and governmental symbols, but the wider circle has included American businessmen, American culture, and the American "system"—a generic term that has included all responsible persons and every entity that has kept the country functioning as a political, economic, and social unit. According to the RAND Chronicle of International Terrorism, since 1968 the United States each year has headed the list of countries whose citizens and property were most frequently attacked. The U.S. State Department's counterterrorism unit reported that during the 1990s, 40 percent of all acts of terrorism worldwide have been against American citizens and facilities.[5]

31   Mahmud Abouhalima has said that he regards America as a worldwide enemy. The reason, he says, is not only because the United States supports the secular Egyptian government that he and his colleagues find directly oppressive, but also because of its history of terrorist acts. The bombing of Hiroshima, for instance, Abouhalima compared with the bombing of the Oklahoma City federal building.[6] Abouhalima's spiritual leader, Sheik Omar Abdul Rahman, during a lengthy courtroom speech at the end of the trial convicting him of conspiring to bomb the World Trade Center, predicted that a "revengeful" God would "scratch" America from the face of the earth.[7]

---

[5] Robin Wright, "Prophetic 'Terror 2000' Mapped Evolving Threat," *Los Angeles Times*, August 9, 1998, A16.
[6] Interview with Abouhalima, September 30, 1997.
[7] John J. Goldman, "Defendants Given 25 years to Life in New York Terror Plot," *Los Angeles Times*, January 18, 1996, A1.

Osama bin Laden, implicated in the bombing of the American em-   32
bassies in Kenya and Tanzania in 1998, explained in an interview a year
before the bombing that America deserved to be targeted because it was
"the biggest terrorist in the world."[8] It may be only coincidence that after
the embassy bombings U.S. National Security Advisor Samuel Berger
called Osama "the most dangerous nonstate terrorist in the world."[9] The
reason bin Laden gave for targeting America was its list of "crimes,"
which included "occupying the lands of Islam in the holist of places, the
Arabian Peninsula, plundering its riches, dictating to its rulers, humiliating its people, terrorizing its neighbors and turning its bases in the peninsula into a spearhead through which to fight the neighboring Muslim
peoples."[10] In response to what bin Laden regarded as a declaration of war
on Muslims by America, he issued a fatwa calling on "every Muslim" as
"an individual duty" to join him in a righteous war "to kill the Americans
and their allies." Their obligation was not only "to kill the Americans" but
also to "plunder their money wherever and whenever they find it." He
sealed his fatwa with the reassurance that "this is in accordance with the
words of Almighty God" and that "every Muslim who believes in God and
wishes to be rewarded" should "comply with God's order."[11]

Why is America the enemy? This question is hard for observers of   33
international politics to answer, and harder still for ordinary Americans to
fathom. Many have watched with horror as their compatriots and symbols of their country have been destroyed by people whom they do not
know, from cultures they can scarcely identify on a global atlas, and for
reasons that do not seem readily apparent. From the frames of reference
of those who regard America as enemy, however, several motives appear.

One reason we have already mentioned: America is often a second-   34
ary enemy. In its role as trading partner and political ally, America has a
vested interest in shoring up the stability of regimes around the world.
This has often put the United States in the unhappy position of being a de-
fender and promoter of secular governments regarded by their religious
opponents as primary foes. Long before the bombing of the World Trade
Center, Sheik Omar Abdul Rahman expressed his disdain for the United
States because of its role in propping up the Mubarak regime in Egypt.
"America is behind all these un-Islamic governments," the Sheik explained, arguing that the purpose of American political and economic
support was "to keep them strong" and to try to "defeat the Islamic movements."[12] In the case of Iran prior to the Islamic revolution, Ayatollah

---

[8] Osama bin Laden, interviewed on an ABC News report rebroadcast on August 9, 1998.
[9] Samel Berger, quoted in *"Jihad* Is an Individual Duty," *Los Angeles Times,* August 13, 1998, B9.
[10] *"Jihad* Is an Individual Duty," B9.
[11] *"Jihad* Is an Individual Duty," B9.
[12] Sheik Omar Abdul Rahman, quoted in Kim Murphy, "Have the Islamic Militants
Turned to a New Battlefront in the US?" *Los Angeles Times,* March 3, 1993, A20.

Khomeini saw the shah and the American government linked as evil twins: American was tarred by its association with the shah, and the shah, in turn, was corrupted by being a "companion of satanic forces"—that is, of America.[13] When Khomeini prayed to his "noble God for protection from the evil of every wicked traitor" and asked Him to "destroy the enemies," the primary traitor he had in mind was the shah and the chief enemy America.[14]

35   A second reason America is regarded as enemy is that both directly and indirectly it has supported modern culture. In a world where villagers in remote corners of the world increasingly have access to MTV, Hollywood movies, and the Internet, the images and values that have been projected globally have been American. It was this cultural threat that brought an orthodox rabbi, Manachem Fruman, who lived in a Jewish settlement on the West Bank of Israel near Hebron, to regular meetings with Hamas-related mullahs in nearby villages. What they had in common, Rabbi Fruman told me, was their common dislike of the "American-style" traits of individualism, the abuse of alcohol, and sexy movies that were widespread in modern cities such as Tel Aviv. Rabbi Fruman told me that "when the mullahs asked, who brought all this corruption here, they answered, 'the Jews.' But," Fruman continued, "rabbis like me don't like this corruption either." Hence the rabbi and the mullahs agreed about the degradation of modern urban values, and they concurred over which country was ultimately responsible. When the mullahs asserted that the United States was the "capital of the devil," Rabbi Fruman told me, he could agree.[15] In a similar vein, Mahmud Abouhalima told me he was bitter that Islam did not have influence over the global media the way that secular America did. America, he believed, was using its power of information to promote the immoral values of secular society.[16]

36   The third reason for the disdain of America is economic. Although most corporations that trade internationally are multinational, with personnel and legal ties to more than one country, many are based in the United States or have American associations. Even those that were identifiably European or Japanese are thought to be American-like and implicitly American in attitude and style. When Ayatollah Khomeini identified the "satanic" forces that were out to destroy Islam, he included not only Jews but also the even "more satanic" Westerners—especially corporate leaders with "no religious belief" who saw Islam as "the major

---

[13] Ayatollah Khomeini, *Collection of Speeches, Position Statements* (Arlington, VA: Joint Publications Research Service, 1979), 24.
[14] Khomeini, *Collection*, 30.
[15] Interview with Rabbi Manachem Fruman, Tuqua settlement, West Bank, Israel, August 14, 1995.
[16] Interview with Abouhalima, September 30, 1997.

obstacle in the path of their materialistic ambitions and the chief threat to their political power."[17] The ayatollah went on to claim that "all the problems of Iran" were due to the treachery of "foreign colonialists."[18] On another occasion, the ayatollah blended political, personal, and spiritual issues in generalizing about the cosmic foe—Western colonialism—and about "the black and dreadful future" that "the agents of colonialism, may God Almighty abandon them all," have in mind for Islam and the Muslim people."[19]

What the ayatollah was thinking of when he prophesied a "black and dreadful future" for Islam was the global domination of American economy and culture. This fear of globalization is the fourth reason America is often targeted as an enemy. The apprehensions of Ayatollah Khomeini were shared by many not only in the Muslim world but elsewhere, including the United States. There right-wing militias were convinced that the "new world order" proclaimed by President George Bush was more than a mood of global cooperation: it was a conspiratorial plot to control the world. Accepting this paranoid vision of American leaders' global designs, the Aum Shinrikyo master Shoko Asahara linked the U.S. army with the Japanese government, Freemasons, and Jews in the image of a global conspiratorial band. 37

Like all stereotypes, each of these characterizations holds a certain amount of truth. America's culture and economy have dominated societies around the world in ways that have caused concern to protectors of local societies. The vast financial and media networks of American-backed corporations and information systems have affected the whole of the globe. There has indeed been a great conflict between secular and religious life throughout the world, and America does ordinarily support the secular side of the fight. Financial aid provided to leaders such as Israel's Benjamin Netanyahu and Egypt's Hosni Mubarak has shored up the political power of politicians opposed to religious nationalism. Moreover, after the fall of the Soviet Union, the United States has been virtually the only coherent military power in the world. Hence it has been an easy target for blame when people have felt that their lives were going askew or were being controlled by forces they could not readily see. Yet to dislike America is one thing; to regard it as a cosmic enemy is quite another. 38

When the United States has been branded as an enemy in a cosmic war, it has been endowed with superhuman—or perhaps subhuman— qualities, ones that have had little to do with the people who actually live 39

---

17 Imam [Ayatollah] Khomeini, *Islam and Revolution: Writings and Declarations,* Hamid Algar, trans., annot. (London: Routledge and Kegan Paul, 1985) (orig. published by Mizan Press, Berkeley, in 1981), 27–28.

18 Khomeini, *Collection,* 3.

19 Khomeini, *Collection,* 25.

in America. It is the image of the country that has been despised—a reified notion of Americanism, not its people. Individual Americans have often been warmly accepted by those who hate the collective image that they hold as cosmic enemy. This was brought home to me in Gaza when I talked with Dr. Abdul Aziz Rantisi about the Hamas movement's attitude toward America and its pro-Israeli stance. As Dr. Rantisi offered me coffee in the comfortable living room of his home, he acknowledged that the United States was a secondary enemy because of its complicity in Israel's existence and its oppression of Palestinian Arabs. From his point of view, it deserved to be treated as an enemy. What about individual Americans, I cautiously asked him, raising the example of American professors. Would such people be targeted?

40   "You?" Rantisi responded, somewhat surprised. "You don't count. You're our guest."[20]

====

WENDELL BERRY

Called by the *New York Times* the "prophet of rural America," Berry was born in 1934 on a farm in Henry County, Kentucky where he has lived for most of his life, except for a year at Stanford (1958–1959) on a creative writing fellowship and a short stint teaching at New York University. He earned a B.A. (1956) and M.A. in English (1957) from the University of Kentucky, where he taught from 1964–1977. He then returned to his 125-acre farm to devote full time to laboring—literally and figuratively—in the fields as a farmer, conservationist, philosopher, and visionary, and to writing novels (*Remembering*, 1988; *A World Lost*, 1996), poetry (*The Country of Marriage*, 1973; *The Kentucky River: Two Poems*, 1975), and essays (*The Unsettling of America: Culture and Agriculture*, 1977). His commitment to the land and community he loves, as expressed in his writings and social philosophy, is intended to inspire others to act for the common good. His many awards include Guggenheim and Rockefeller fellowships and the Thomas Merton Award, given to people who "advance the transformation of the world." Berry's philosophy of education is to "make the standard the health of the community" rather than "the career of the student." Once you do this, he says, "you can't rule out any kind of knowledge. You need to know everything you possibly can know. . . . All the departmental walls fall down, because you can no longer feel that it's safe not to know something. And then you begin to see that . . . these specializations aren't separate at all, but are connected."

"Thoughts in the Presence of Fear," which appeared in the fall of 2001 on the OrionOnline.org Web site as "Thoughts on America," was

---

[20] Interview with Rantisi, March 2, 1989.

published in the *South Atlantic Quarterly,* Spring 2002. This comprehensive response to "the horrors of September 11" represents a distillation of Berry's philosophical principles. Here he reflects on the implications of the end of "the unquestioning technological and economic optimism that ended on that day." He explores the largely undesirable consequences of the belief that "we should go on and on from one technological innovation to the next, which would cause the economy to 'grow' and make every-thing better and better. This of course implied at every point a hatred of the past, of all things inherited and free" (V). He patiently explains why these values are wrong, and makes the case for a peaceable, self-sufficient economy, based on "thrift and care, on saving and conserving, not on excess and waste" (XXVII).

Thoughts in the Presence of Fear

I. The time will soon come when we will not be able to remember the horrors of September 11 without remembering also the unquestioning technologi-cal and economic optimism that ended on that day.

II. This optimism rested on the proposition that we were living in a "new world order" and a "new economy" that would "grow" on and on, bring-ing a prosperity of which every new increment would be "unprecedented."

III. The dominant politicians, corporate officers, and investors who believed this proposition did not acknowledge that the prosperity was limited to a tiny percent of the world's people, and to an ever smaller number of people even in the United States; that it was founded upon the oppressive labor of poor people all over the world; and that its ecological costs increasingly threatened all life, including the lives of the supposedly prosperous.

IV. The "developed" nations had given to the "free market" the status of a god, and were sacrificing to it their farmers, farmlands, and communi-ties, their forests, wetlands, and prairies, their ecosystems and watersheds. They had accepted universal pollution and global warming as normal costs of doing business.

V. There was, as a consequence, a growing worldwide effort on behalf of economic decentralization, economic justice, and ecological responsi-bility. We must recognize that the events of September 11 make this effort more necessary than ever. We citizens of the industrial countries must continue the labor of self-criticism and self-correction. We must recognize our mistakes.

VI. The paramount doctrine of the economic and technological eu-phoria of recent decades has been that everything depends on innovation. It was understood as desirable, and even necessary, that we should go on and on from one technological innovation to the next, which would cause the economy to "grow" and make everything better and better. This of course implied at every point a hatred of the past, of all things inherited and free. All things superceded in our progress of innovations, whatever their value might have been, were discounted as of no value at all.

7   VII. We did not anticipate anything like what has now happened. We did not foresee that all our sequence of innovations might be at once overridden by a greater one: the invention of a new kind of war that would turn our previous innovations against us, discovering and exploiting the debits and the dangers that we had ignored. We never considered the possibility that we might be trapped in the webwork of communication and transport that was supposed to make us free.

8   VIII. Nor did we foresee that the weaponry and the war science that we marketed and taught to the world would become available, not just to recognized national governments, which possess so uncannily the power to legitimate large-scale violence, but also to "rogue nations," dissident or fanatical groups and individuals—whose violence, though never worse than that of nations, is judged by the nations to be illegitimate.

9   IX. We had accepted uncritically the belief that technology is only good; that it cannot serve evil as well as good; that it cannot serve our enemies as well as ourselves; that it cannot be used to destroy what is good, including our homelands and our lives.

10   X. We had accepted too the corollary belief that an economy (either as a money economy or as a life-support system) that is global in extent, technologically complex, and centralized is invulnerable to terrorism, sabotage, or war, and that is protectable by "national defense."

11   XI. We now have a clear, inescapable choice that we must make. We can continue to promote a global economic system of unlimited "free trade" among corporations, held together by long and highly vulnerable lines of communication and supply, but now recognizing that such a system will have to be protected by a hugely expensive police force that will be worldwide, whether maintained by one nation or several or all, and that such a police force will be effective precisely to the extent that it oversways the freedom and privacy of the citizens of every nation.

12   XII. Or we can promote a decentralized world economy which would have the aim of assuring to every nation and region a local self-sufficiency in life-supporting goods. This would not eliminate international trade, but it would tend toward a trade in surpluses after local needs had been met.

13   XIII. One of the gravest dangers to us now, second only to further terrorist attacks against our people, is that we will attempt to go on as before with the corporate program of global "free trade," whatever the cost in freedom and civil rights, without self-questioning or self-criticism or public debate.

14   XIV. This is why the substitution of rhetoric for thought, always a temptation in a national crisis, must be resisted by officials and citizens alike. It is hard for ordinary citizens to know what is actually happening

Compare and contrast this photograph of a magnificent natural phenomenon (sunset on Mt. McKinley) with the former and transient magnificence of the man-made World Trade Center. In what ways do Berry's views amplify, reinforce, or contradict your own?

in Washington in a time of such great trouble; for all we know, serious and difficult thought may be taking place there. But the talk that we are hearing from politicians, bureaucrats, and commentators has so far tended to reduce the complex problems now facing us to issues of unity, security, normality, and retaliation.

XV. National self-righteousness, like personal self-righteousness, is a 15 mistake. It is misleading. It is a sign of weakness. Any war that we may make now against terrorism will come as a new installment in a history of war in which we have fully participated. We are not innocent of making war against civilian populations. The modern doctrine of such warfare was set forth and enacted by General William Tecumseh Sherman, who held that a civilian population could be declared guilty and rightly subjected to military punishment. We have never repudiated that doctrine.

XVI. It is a mistake also—as events since September 11 have shown— 16 to suppose that a government can promote and participate in a global economy and at the same time act exclusively in its own interest by abrogating its international treaties and standing apart from international cooperation on moral issues.

XVII. And surely, in our country, under our Constitution, it is a fundamental error to suppose that any crisis or emergency can justify any 17 form of political oppression. Since September 11, far too many public voices have presumed to "speak for us" in saying that Americans will gladly accept a reduction of freedom in exchange for greater "security." Some would, maybe. But some others would accept a reduction in security (and in global trade) far more willingly than they would accept any abridgement of our Constitutional rights.

18   XVIII. In a time such as this, when we have been seriously and most cruelly hurt by those who hate us, and when we must consider ourselves to be gravely threatened by those same people, it is hard to speak of the ways of peace and to remember that Christ enjoined us to love our enemies, but this is no less necessary for being difficult.

19   XIX. Even now we dare not forget that since the attack of Pearl Harbor—to which the present attack has been often and not usefully compared—we humans have suffered an almost uninterrupted sequence of wars, none of which has brought peace or made us more peaceable.

20   XX. The aim and result of war necessarily is not peace but victory, and any victory won by violence necessarily justifies the violence that won it and leads to further violence. If we are serious about innovation, must we not conclude that we need something new to replace our perpetual "war to end war"?

21   XXI. What leads to peace is not violence but peaceableness, which is not passivity, but an alert, informed, practiced, and active state of being. We should recognize that while we have extravagantly subsidized the means of war, we have almost totally neglected the ways of peaceableness. We have, for example, several national military academies, but not one peace academy. We have ignored the teachings and the examples of Christ, Gandhi, Martin Luther King, and other peaceable leaders. And here we have an inescapable duty to notice also that war is profitable, whereas the means of peaceableness, being cheap or free, make no money.

22   XXII. The key to peaceableness is continuous practice. It is wrong to suppose that we can exploit and impoverish the poorer countries, while arming them and instructing them in the newest means of war, and then reasonably expect them to be peaceable.

23   XXIII. We must not again allow public emotion or the public media to caricature our enemies. If our enemies are now to be some nations of Islam, then we should undertake to know those enemies. Our schools should begin to teach the histories, cultures, arts, and language of the Islamic nations. And our leaders should have the humility and the wisdom to ask the reasons some of those people have for hating us.

24   XXIV. Starting with the economies of food and farming, we should promote at home, and encourage abroad, the ideal of local self-sufficiency. We should recognize that this is the surest, the safest, and the cheapest way for the world to live. We should not countenance the loss or destruction of any local capacity to produce necessary goods.

XXV. We should reconsider and renew and extend our efforts to pro- 25
tect the natural foundations of the human economy: soil, water, and air.
We should protect every intact ecosystem and watershed that we have
left, and begin restoration of those that have been damaged.

XXVI. The complexity of our present trouble suggests as never before 26
that we need to change our present concept of education. Education is not
properly an industry, and its proper use is not to serve industries, either by
job-training or by industry-subsidized research. [Its] proper use is to enable citizens to live lives that are economically, politically, socially, and
culturally responsible. This cannot be done by gathering or "accessing"
what we now call "information"—which is to say facts without context
and therefore without priority. A proper education enables young people
to put their lives in order, which means knowing what things are more
important than other things; it means putting first things first.

XXVII. The first thing we must begin to teach our children (and learn 27
ourselves) is that we cannot spend and consume endlessly. We have got
to learn to save and conserve. We do need a "new economy," but one that
is founded on thrift and care, on saving and conserving, not on excess and
waste. An economy based on waste is inherently and hopelessly violent,
and war is its inevitable by-product. We need a peaceable economy.

<hr>

MARY GRAHAM

Mary Graham is a lawyer (J.D., Georgetown University Law Center, 1970)
and Visiting Fellow in Governance Studies at the Brookings Institution,
specializing in environmental policy, public access to information, regula-
tory policy, and U.S. politics more generally. Born in 1945, she earned a
B.A. at Harvard/Radcliffe in 1966. She worked for the federal government as a budget examiner in the U.S. Office of Management and Budget
and as a program analyst in the U.S. Department of Transportation before
becoming a research fellow at the John F. Kennedy School of Government
at Harvard, where she is currently co-director of the Transparency Policy
Project. Through the Brookings Institute she has published *The Morning
After Earth Day: New Pragmatism in Environmental Politics* (1999) and
Democracy by Disclosure: The Rise of Technopopulism (2002).

"The Information Wars," first published in the *Atlantic Monthly*
(September 2002) cites telling instances of the restrictions, swift and seemingly permanent, that the federal government under the Bush administration has imposed on public access to information since September 11,
2001—vastly extending and expanding practices begun earlier. For instance,
"the Justice Department initiated work on a new policy to support agency
actions to keep secret *any* government information, as long as agency

heads had a 'sound legal basis' for withholding it." Thus the previous policy, of honoring the public's right to know "unless the government could show 'foreseeable harm'" was reversed in a single stroke. Graham's understated conclusion, "the idea that openness can be more effective than secrecy in reducing risks," should, she claims, get far more attention than it currently receives.

The Information Wars

1　Within twenty-four hours of the terrorist attacks on the World Trade Center the federal Department of Transportation had removed maps of the nation's 2.2 million miles of pipe lines from its Web site. The government had created the maps only recently, to identify places where ruptures in pipes that carry oil, natural gas, or hazardous chemicals could endanger lives, property, or drinking water. In the 1990s an average of four accidents a week caused property damage of more than $5,000, injury, or death.

2　The removal of the maps was hardly an isolated incident. Since September federal and state officials have stricken from Web sites and public reports thousands of pages of information about health and safety risks to Americans—information, officials say, that might somehow aid terrorists. The Environmental Protection Agency withdrew from its Web site information about accidents, risks, and emergency plans at factories that handle dangerous chemicals. Energy regulators removed reports on power plants, transmission lines, and the transportation of radioactive materials. The Federal Aviation Administration stopped posting enforcement information about security breaches at airports and incidents that threatened airline safety. The U.S. Geological Survey removed reports on water resources and asked libraries to destroy all copies of a CD-ROM that described the characteristics of reservoirs.

3　Some state governments went further. Florida not only restricted access to security plans for hospitals and state facilities but also gave the president of the state senate authority to close formerly public meetings. In a directive that was itself intended to be secret, New York State's directors of public security and state operations ordered agency heads to curb public access to all "sensitive information." What, exactly, was "sensitive"? "Information related to systems, structures, individuals and services essential to the security, government or economy of the State, including telecommunications . . . electrical power, gas and oil storage and transportation, banking and finance, transportation, water supply, emergency services . . . and the continuity of government operations." Just about everything, that is.

4　These were extraordinary measures for extraordinary times. Administration officials moved quickly and appropriately to remove from the Web maps of nuclear-power plants and defense installations, for example. The Web, they argued, transformed previously scattered information into mosaics of opportunity for extremists. But a year after the terrorist attacks temporary emergency actions have evolved into fundamental changes in the public's right to know, and the restrictions have been driven as much by familiar politics and bureaucratic instincts as by national security. The problem comes because a new and uncertain threat has provided cover for legitimate and opportunistic measures alike.

Even before September 11 the Bush Administration had taken un-   5
precedented steps to expand official secrecy. Early last year Vice President Dick Cheney refused to provide to Congress the names of energy-industry executives who had advised the energy-policy task force he headed. That action provoked the first lawsuit ever by the General Accounting Office against the executive branch. Also before September 11 the Justice Department initiated work on a new policy to support agency actions to keep secret *any* government information, as long as agency heads had a "sound legal basis" for withholding it. This reversed a presumption in favor of disclosure unless the government could show "foreseeable harm."

By October, President Bush was calling for new policies to shield in-   6
formation voluntarily provided by private companies about weaknesses in "critical infrastructure"—a malleable term that the Administration said should include telecommunications, energy, financial services, transportation, and health care. In March, Andrew Card, the White House chief of staff, ordered all agencies to adopt guidelines to prevent inappropriate disclosure of "sensitive but unclassified" information—without actually defining the term.

Typically, these new rules have been put into effect by memorandum,   7
without public explanation. Missing has been any forum for weighing the risks of shutting off public access. Recent congressional debate about restricting access to critical infrastructure information under the Freedom of Information Act provided one limited step in the right direction, producing constructive ideas about how to narrow the definition of what is critical while still satisfying the concerns of national-security agencies.

Zealous secrecy in response to a foreign threat is not new, of course.   8
In a Harvard commencement address this past June, Senator Daniel Patrick Moynihan reminded students that the Cold War had produced a culture of secrecy that outlived the conflict and at times actually impaired security. That culture had largely disappeared by the end of the 1990s, as a better-informed public and the growth of the Internet drove advances toward openness. The Clinton Administration declassified millions of pages of historical records, and Congress approved the Electronic Freedom of Information Act, which encouraged agencies to put information online even before it was requested.

The wholesale censorship of information on Web sites and in gov-   9
ernment reports carries insidious costs. Current government proposals to

bar foreign nationals from working on scientific projects and to restrict publication of government-funded research could actually decrease national security. Relying on partial truths and official conclusions can create needless scares, increase risks, and ultimately change the political process.

10   Compromises that deem some members of the public more worthy than others violate basic fairness. The Environmental Protection Agency, for example, long known for its openness, now requires researchers to register before it gives them direct access to its enormous Envirofacts database. It also requires them to obtain sponsorship from a senior official and have their requests approved in advance. "The danger is that right to know is replaced by need to know," says Gary D. Bass, the director of OMB Watch and the organizer of a new coalition of environmental, health, labor, journalist, and library groups tracking secrecy changes.

11   An administration that prides itself on conducting business like a well-run corporation naturally thinks that sensitive information can and should remain proprietary. But national security is everyone's concern, and the idea that openness can be more effective than secrecy in reducing risks has received too little attention.

DAVID CARR

> David Carr (born 1956) received a B.A. from the University of Minnesota in journalism and economics. Currently a reporter who covers media for the *New York Times,* he is a former contributor to the *Atlantic Monthly* and *New York* magazine. Carr also worked for Inside.com, a media news site, and was editor of the *Washington City Paper,* a weekly in Washington, D.C. After the events of September 11, Michael Kelly, then editor of the *Atlantic,* asked Carr and others to take a step back and look at the stories that would reflect the American response to those unprecedented events. "The Futility of 'Homeland Defense'" writes Carr, "was conceived as an argument, based in both numbers and reality, that suggested buttoning-up America against further attacks might be more complicated than the political rhetoric of the time indicated."

The Futility of "Homeland Defense"

1   Get over thinking that America can be made safe. Defending a country as big and commercially robust as the United States raises profound, and profoundly insurmountable, issues of scale. There has been much talk of "Israelifying" the United States, but America has about forty-seven times

as many people as Israel, and roughly 441 times the amount of territory to be defended. New Jersey alone is 753 square miles bigger than Israel, and home to nearly 2.5 million more people. Beyond problems of size, it's all too reasonable to assume that America won't be safe. Righting various asymmetries merely designs—as opposed to prevents—the next attack. When one target is shored up, nimble transnational cells that can turn on a dime simply find new bull's-eyes. Up against those practical realities, homeland security is the national version of the gas mask in the desk drawer—something that lets people feel safer without actually making them so.

If America is riddled with holes and targets, it's because a big society   2
designed to be open is hard to change—impossible, probably. In 2000 more than 350 million non-U.S. citizens entered the country. In 1999 Americans made 5.2 billion phone calls to locations outside the United States. Federal Express handles nearly five million packages every business day, UPS accounts for 13.6 million, and until it became a portal for terror, the Postal Service processed 680 million pieces of mail a day. More than two billion tons of cargo ran in and out of U.S. ports in 1999, and about 7.5 million North Americans got on and off cruise ships last year.

Group targets are plentiful. There are eighty-six college and pro-   3
fessional stadiums that seat more than 60,000 people, and ten motor speedways with capacities greater than 100,000; the Indianapolis Motor Speedway seats more than 250,000. Few other countries offer the opportunity to take aim at a quarter million people at once. Also plentiful are tall buildings—until just yesterday the dominant symbol of civic pride. Fifty of the hundred tallest buildings in the world are on U.S. soil. Minneapolis, a mid-size city that doesn't leap to mind as a target, has three of them. And one of its suburbs has the largest shopping mall in the country, the Mall of America, with at least 600,000 visitors a week.

As for trained personnel to defend our borders and targets, the Im-   4
migration and Naturalization Service, which oversees the inspection of half a billion people a year, has only 2,000 agents to investigate violations of immigration law. The Postal Service has only 1,900 inspectors to investigate the misuse of mail. According to one estimate, it would take 14,000 air marshals to cover every domestic flight—more than the total number of special agents in the FBI. The former drug czar General Barry McCaffrey has pointed out that at least four different agencies oversee 303 official points of entry into the United States. After staffing increases over the past three years there are 334 U.S. Border Patrol agents guarding the 4,000 miles of Canadian border. The nation has 95,000 miles of shoreline to protect. "No one is in charge," McCaffrey says.

In all the discussion of building a homeland-security apparatus, very   5
little attention has been paid to the fundamental question of whether 100 percent more effort will make people even one percent safer. The current version of America can no more button up its borders than mid-empire Britain could. Not just cultural imperatives are at stake. America makes its

living by exporting technology and pop culture while importing hard goods and unskilled labor. The very small percentage of unwanted people and substances that arrive with all the people and things we do want is part of the cost of being America, Inc.

6   This is not the first time a President has declared a war within U.S. borders. In 1969 President Richard Nixon promised a "new urgency and concerted national policy" to combat the scourge of drugs—an initiative that has lurched along for more than three decades, growing to the point where the government spent $18.8 billion in 2000 trying to solve America's drug problem.

7   The drug war is progressing only marginally better than the one in Vietnam did. Adolescent use of most drugs has tailed off in the past year or two, but the hard-core population of 10 to 15 million American users can always find narcotics—and at a price that continues to drop. From 1981 to 1998 the price of both cocaine and heroin dropped substantially, while the purity of both drugs rose. From 1978 to 1998 the number of people dying from overdoses doubled, according to the Office of National Drug Control Policy. The Drug Enforcement Agency estimates that 331 tons of cocaine were consumed in the United States in 2000.

8   Counterterrorism is the ultimate zero-tolerance affair. Yet the same federal assets deployed in the war on drugs—the Coast Guard, U.S. Customs, the INS, the Border Patrol, the CIA, the FBI, and the DEA—are the first and last lines of defense in this new war. The fight against terror involves a triad that drug warriors can recite in their sleep: global source management, border interdiction, and domestic harm reduction.

9   In both wars human ingenuity is a relentless foe. Create a new blockade and some opportunist will survey the landscape for an alternative path. "What the war on drugs tells us," says Eric E. Sterling, of The Criminal Justice Policy Foundation, "is that people motivated by the most elementary of capitalist motives are constantly testing and finding ways to get in. Terrorists are as motivated as the most avaricious drug importer, if not more—and they are not going to be deterred by whatever barriers are put up."

10   Less than ten miles southwest of where the World Trade Center towers stood, the part of the Port of New York and New Jersey that occupies sections of Newark and Elizabeth is back to work. On the day I went there in October, straddle carriers—leggy, improbable contraptions that lift and cradle containers—buzzed around in the shadow of the *Monet,* a large cargo ship. The *Monet* is a floating lesson in friction-free commerce. It is operated by CMA CGM, a French company, but owned by the U.S. subsidiary of a German firm; it is registered in Monrovia, and it sails under the Liberian flag. Like everything else in view, it's massive, capable of holding 2,480 twenty-foot-long container units—the kind familiar from flatbed

trucks and freight trains. It left Pusan, Korea, on September 19, stopping in three Chinese cities before sailing across the Pacific and through the Panama Canal and coming to rest in New Jersey on October 22.

The Port of New York and New Jersey is no less international. It's 11 the busiest port on the East Coast. In 2000 the port moved approximately 70 million tons of general and bulk cargo, the equivalent of three million containers, from hundreds of cities around the globe, and half a million freshly built cars. The large containers it processes are stuffed, sealed, and tagged in far-flung locations, and their contents move, mostly unchecked, into the hands of consumers. A conga line of trains and trucks snakes out of the port, bound for a metropolitan market of some 18 million people.

Smuggling goods in containers probably started the day after ship- 12 ping goods in them did. In a sting last January, U.S. Customs and the DEA seized 126 pounds of heroin concealed in twelve bales of cotton towels on a container ship at the port. That same month two men were charged with importing 3.25 million steroid pills that were seized during a customs examination of a container shipped from Moldavia. And in May of 1999 the DEA and Customs seized 100 kilograms of cocaine hidden under 40,000 pounds of bananas in two refrigerated containers. Sometimes the cargo isn't cargo at all. In October, Italian authorities found a suspected terrorist—an Egyptian-born Canadian dressed in a business suit—ensconced in a shipping container. His travel amenities included a makeshift toilet, a bed, a laptop computer, two cell phones, a Canadian passport, security passes for airports in three countries, a certificate identifying him as an airline mechanic, and airport maps. The container was headed for Toronto from Port Said, Egypt.

Before September 11 only about two percent of all the containers that 13 move through ports were actually inspected. At Port Newark Elizabeth there is a single giant on-site x-ray machine to see inside the containers; since September 11 two portable machines have been brought in to supplement it. The Customs Service enforcement team has been temporarily increased by 30 percent, but even that means that a mere 100 inspectors are responsible for more than 5,000 containers every day. The service has been on Alert Level One, which theoretically means that more containers are being inspected. But not even that vigilance—let alone the overtime—can continue indefinitely.

By reputation and appearance, the port is extremely well run, and it 14 had tightened up security even before September 11. In the mid-1990s port officials began requiring every incoming truck driver to obtain an ID badge. One fall morning a man who appeared to be a Sikh, in a brilliant-orange turban and a lengthy beard, drew double takes from the other truckers—as he would anyplace else—when he stopped by the administration building to get his credential. When I was there, foreign crews were restricted from leaving their ships. The Coast Guard required ninety-six hours' notice before a ship arrived, and boarded every vessel before it was allowed into port. Two tugs accompanied each ship on its way in; if the ship were to head toward, say, a bridge support or some other target, the tugs would muscle the ship away.

15   But commerce, by definition, requires access. The port offers obvious targets because it is a place of business, not a fortified military installation. Tanks of edible oils sit behind a single cyclone fence; tankers of orange-juice concentrate from Brazil stand unguarded in parking lots. Two squad cars, one belonging to the port and the other on loan from the Department of Corrections, were parked at one of the port's major intersections, but anyone can drive around much of the facility without having to pass a single checkpoint. A train moves in or out of the port four times a day, crossing under the New Jersey Turnpike and through a tangle of bridges and elevated freeways that carries 630,000 cars every day. Just across the turnpike, Newark Airport handles roughly 1,000 flights a day.

16   Testifying one month after the September attacks, Rear Admiral Richard Larrabee, the port commerce director, told a Senate Commerce, Science, and Transportation subcommittee, "As a port director, I cannot give you or my superiors a fair assessment today of the adequacy of current security procedures in place, because I am not provided with information on the risk analysis conducted to institute these measures."

17   If a container holding heroin slips into the United States, the street price may go down, gangs may be enriched, and drug use may rise. If that same container held chemical or biological agents, or a nuclear weapon, the social costs would be incalculable. Doing nothing to deter such events would be foolish, but doing everything possible would be more foolish still. "There are two things to be considered with regard to any scheme," Jean Jacques Rousseau once observed. "In the first place, 'Is it good in itself?' In the second, 'Can it be easily put into practice?'" In the case of homeland security the answers are yes, and absolutely not.

18   Some measures, both quotidian and provident, will be taken. Practical approaches to making air travel safe again will emerge incrementally. Newly integrated databases will prevent a recurrence of the dark comedy of errors that allowed many of the hijackers into the country in the first place. Postal workers, it is to be hoped, will be tested for the presence of biological agents with the same alacrity that senators are. But the culture itself will not be re-engineered. America will continue to be a place of tremendous economic dynamism and openness.

19   At the port the country's muscular determination to remain in business is manifest on every loading dock. But if one looks hard enough, the cost of openness is there to see. In a quiet spot amid the industrial bustle— behind Metro Metals, on the north side of the port facility—is a nasty clump of twisted metal. Some of the girders from the World Trade Center,

another brawny symbol of U.S. economic strength that also happens to be owned by the Port Authority, have come to rest here. The stink of that day—the burnt smell of implacable mayhem—hangs near, reminding us that great symbols make irresistible targets.

SUSAN SONTAG

Sontag (born in New York, 1933), earned a B.A. in 1951 (at the age of 18) from the University of Chicago, and master's degrees from Harvard in English (1954) and philosophy (1955). She quickly attained the status—rare in the United States—of a public intellectual as a consequence of her provocative cultural commentary—left-wing, feminist, often strident, and relentlessly intellectual—for which she received a MacArthur "genius" grant. From multiple perspectives—political, philosophical, aesthetic, literary, and moral—she addresses a wide range of topics: including camp ("Notes on Camp"), pornographic literature and fascist aesthetics (*Styles of Radical Will*, 1969), photography (*On Photography*, 1976), cancer (*Illness and Metaphor*, 1978) and AIDS (*AIDS and Its Metaphors*, 1988). Her novels include *The Death Kit* (1963), *The Volcano Lover* (1992), and *In America* (1999), winner of the National Book Award.

Her own experience of cancer contributed to her understanding of the relation between metaphor and reality. Cancer, for instance, is likened to invasions described in science fiction narratives, the AIDS epidemic is understood in light of the history and fear surrounding the term *plague*— "metaphorically . . . the highest standard of collective calamity, evil, scourge. . . ." Thus her extensive analyses of metaphor are preparation for "WAR? Real Battles and Empty Metaphors," originally published as an op-ed article in the *New York Times* on September 10, 2002 as a commentary on the language accompanying the politics as the United States "declares a war on terrorism . . . a multinational, largely clandestine network" of ill-defined, shadowy enemies. This essay expresses a much more moderate interpretation of events than did Sontag's comments of a year earlier, in the *New Yorker* (Sept. 21, 2001), where she said: "The voices licensed to follow the event [public figures and TV commentators] seem to have joined together in a campaign to infantalize the public. Where is the acknowledgment that this was not a 'cowardly' attack on 'civilization' or 'liberty' or 'humanity' or 'the free world' but an attack on the world's self-proclaimed superpower, undertaken as a consequence of specific American alliances and actions? How many citizens are aware of the ongoing American bombing of Iraq? And if the word 'cowardly' is to be used, it might be more aptly applied to those who kill from beyond the range of retaliation, high in the sky, than to those willing to die themselves in order to kill others. In the matter of courage . . . the perpetrators of Tuesday's slaughter . . . were not cowards." "WAR? Real Battles and Empty Metaphors" does not specify why Sontag moderated her tone, if not her views, but the contrast between the two pieces is emphatic.

WAR? Real Battles and Empty Metaphors

1   Since last Sept. 11, the Bush administration has told the American people that America is at war. But this war is of a peculiar nature. It seems to be, given the nature of the enemy, a war with no foreseeable end. What kind of war is that?

2   There are precedents. Wars on such enemies as cancer, poverty and drugs are understood to be endless wars. There will always be cancer, poverty and drugs. And there will always be despicable terrorists, mass murderers like those who perpetrated the attack a year ago tomorrow— as well as freedom fighters (like the French Resistance and the African National Congress) who were once called terrorists by those they opposed but were relabeled by history.

3   When a president of the United States declares war on cancer or poverty or drugs, we know that "war" is a metaphor. Does anyone think that this war—the war that America has declared on terrorism—is a metaphor? But it is, and one with powerful consequences. War has been disclosed, not actually declared, since the threat is deemed to be self-evident.

4   Real wars are not metaphors. And real wars have a beginning and an end. Even the horrendous, intractable conflict between Israel and Palestine will end one day. But this antiterror war can never end. That is one sign that it is not a war but, rather, a mandate for expanding the use of American power.

5   When the government declares war on cancer or poverty or drugs it means the government is asking that new forces be mobilized to address the problem. It also means that the government cannot do a whole lot to solve it. When the government declares war on terrorism—terrorism being a multinational, largely clandestine network of enemies—it means that the government is giving itself permission to do what it wants. When it wants to intervene somewhere, it will. It will brook no limits on its power.

6   The American suspicion of foreign "entanglements" is very old. But this administration has taken the radical position that *all* international treaties are potentially inimical to the interests of the United States—since by signing a treaty on anything (whether environmental issues or the conduct of war and the treatment of prisoners) the United States is binding itself to obey conventions that might one day be invoked to limit America's freedom of action to do whatever the government thinks is in the

country's interests. Indeed, that's what a treaty is: it limits the right of its signatories to complete freedom of action on the subject of the treaty. Up to now, it has not been the avowed position of any respectable nation-state that this is a reason for eschewing treaties.

Describing America's new foreign policy as actions undertaken in wartime is a powerful disincentive to having a mainstream debate about what is actually happening. This reluctance to ask questions was already apparent in the immediate aftermath of the attacks last Sept. 11. Those who objected to the jihad language used by the American government (good versus evil, civilization versus barbarism) were accused of condoning the attacks, or at least the legitimacy of the grievances behind the attacks. 7

Under the slogan United We Stand, the call to reflectiveness was equated with dissent, dissent with lack of patriotism. The indignation suited those who have taken charge of the Bush administration's foreign policy. The aversion to debate among the principal figures in the two parties continues to be apparent in the run-up to the commemorative ceremonies on the anniversary of the attacks—ceremonies that are viewed as part of the continuing affirmation of American solidarity against the enemy. The comparison between Sept. 11, 2001, and Dec. 7, 1941, has never been far from mind. 8

Once again, America was the object of a lethal surprise attack that cost many—in this case, civilian—lives, more than the number of soldiers and sailors who died at Pearl Harbor. However, I doubt that great commemorative ceremonies were felt to be needed to keep up morale and unite the country on Dec. 7, 1942. That was a real war, and one year later it was very much still going on. 9

This is a phantom war and therefore in need of an anniversary. Such an anniversary serves a number of purposes. It is a day of mourning. It is an affirmation of national solidarity. But of one thing we can be sure. It is not a day of national reflection. Reflection, it has been said, might impair our "moral clarity." It is necessary to be simple, clear, united. Hence, there will be borrowed words, like the Gettysburg Address, from that bygone era when great rhetoric was possible. 10

Abraham Lincoln's speeches were not just inspirational prose. They were bold statements of new national goals in a time of real, terrible war. The Second Inaugural Address dared to herald the reconciliation that must follow Northern victory in the Civil War. The primacy of the commitment to end slavery was the point of Lincoln's exaltation of freedom in the Gettysburg Address. But when the great Lincoln speeches are ritually cited, or recycled for commemoration, they have become completely emptied of meaning. They are now gestures of nobility, of greatness of spirit. The reasons for their greatness are irrelevant. 11

Such an anachronistic borrowing of eloquence is in the grand tradition of American anti-intellectualism: the suspicion of thought, of words. Hiding behind the humbug that the attack of last Sept. 11 was too horrible, 12 too devastating, too painful, too tragic for words, that words could not possibly express our grief and indignation, our leaders have a perfect excuse to drape themselves in others' words, now voided of content. To say something might be controversial. It might actually drift into some kind of statement and therefore invite rebuttal. Not saying anything is best.

13   I do not question that we have a vicious, abhorrent enemy that opposes most of what I cherish—including democracy, pluralism, secularism, the equality of the sexes, beardless men, dancing (all kinds), skimpy clothing and, well, fun. And not for a moment do I question the obligation of the American government to protect the lives of its citizens. What I do question is the pseudo-declaration of pseudo-war. These necessary actions should not be called a "war." There are no endless wars; but there are declarations of the extension of power by a state that believes it cannot be challenged.

14   America has every right to hunt down the perpetrators of these crimes and their accomplices. But this determination is not necessarily a war. Limited, focused military engagements do not translate into "wartime" at home. There are better ways to check America's enemies, less destructive of constitutional rights and of international agreements that serve the public interest of all, than continuing to invoke the dangerous, lobotomizing notion of endless war.

World Peace:
Nobel Peace Prize
Awards and Speeches

In this final chapter it is fitting to balance terrorism against tranquility, war against peace. To focus only on the negative would be to ignore the best that is represented by the recipients of the Nobel Prize, whose acceptance speeches comprise this chapter. Goodness, selflessness, adherence to high moral principles, as the lives and works of the Nobel Prize winners reveal, can emerge even in times of trauma—often in responses to the challenges of trauma itself. Their talks, like their works, are beacons of faith, hope, and good will. If, as Franklin Roosevelt said, "the only thing we have to fear is fear itself," we need to reinforce a value system that will enable us to lead lives governed by principles and values that bring out the best rather than the worst of our common humanity. This is the message, implied and stated overtly, by every one of these Nobel Prize winners.

These Nobel winners form an international spectrum of the brave, the bold, the morally beautiful. Some of these Nobelists are people of high visibility and power—United Nations Secretary General Kofi Annan (Egypt; photograph p. 567); and national leaders Jimmy Carter (U.S.A.), Yitzak Rabin (Israel), and Frederik Willem de Klerk (South Africa). Others are religious and political leaders who have suffered extensive privations for living their beliefs: the 14th Dalai Lama (Tibet), sentenced by the Chinese to lifetime exile as the embodiment of the Tibetan Buddhists; Nelson Mandela (South Africa; see photograph with de Klerk on p. 588), anti-apartheid head of the African National Congress who was under harsh imprisonment for over a quarter century; and Aung San Suu Kyi (Myanmar; photograph p. 593), Burmese pro-democracy leader confined by the military junta to house arrest for nearly ten years. Still others are people of humble origins whose advocacy of human rights and reconciliation catapulted them into international prominence—housewife turned peace activist Betty Williams (Northern Ireland); and Guatemalan champion of Mayan rights and culture, Rigoberta Menchú. Activist humanitarian organizations are represented by Doctors Without Borders (Médecins Sans Frontières), whose members risk their own lives to travel to embattled parts of the world, providing medical aid to victims of genocide, massacre, rape, and other war crimes. "Ours is an ethic of refusal," explains James Orbinski. "It will not allow any moral political failure or injustice to be sanitized or cleansed of its meaning."

All of these Nobel recipients, and others (like Martin Luther King, Jr.), are "witnesses to the truth of injustice," as Orbinski says, willing to lay their lives on the line—and to lose them, as Rabin and Dr. King have done—for a moral cause. Like their lives, their words in these inspiring speeches can guide us to some answers. How we as individuals, family members, friends, and citizens can do our best not only to lead the good life but to make that life better for humankind is one of the aims of a liberal education and of this book.

Following the readings in this chapter you will find suggestions for discussion and writing. As with the readings on terrorism, the individual speeches presented here may be read in connection with or opposition to one another or the essays in the "Terrorism" chapter, and in relation to other works throughout the book, such as "The Declaration of Independence" (441–45), "The Gettysburg Address" (484–86), and Martin Luther King, Jr.'s "Letter From Birmingham Jail" (445–61).

JIMMY CARTER

Jimmy Carter, the thirty-ninth President of the United States, was born (1924) and raised in Plains, Georgia, where peanut farming, politics, and devotion to the Baptist faith were the pillars of his upbringing and have remained paramount throughout his life. He graduated in 1946 from the U.S. Naval Academy, married Rosalynn Smith, who became his partner in all activities, and served seven years as a naval officer. The Carters then returned to Plains, where they ran the family peanut farm and entered politics. In 1970 Carter was elected Governor of Georgia; his administration emphasized ecology, efficiency in government, and civil rights—an orientation that led to his nomination as the Democratic candidate for President and his election in 1976. He served a single term during a period of high inflation and unemployment; although jobs increased by eight million during his presidency, efforts to reduce inflation resulted in a brief recession (coupled with the Iranian holding of the American embassy staff as hostages for fourteen months) that contributed to Ronald Reagan's landslide victory in 1980.

In the years since then, Carter has "stretched the gravitas and star power of the Oval Office to promote democratic values across the world," says the *New York Times* (Oct. 12, 2002, A8); Carter himself agrees that he has been "a better former president than president." In 1982 he founded the Carter Center, a research group at Emory University (noted in the Nobel citation); and in 1984 the Carters became leaders of Habitat for Humanity, an organization that since that time has sponsored house renovation and home ownership for more than 110,000 dwellings worldwide. Carter has been instrumental in conflict resolution throughout the world, including brokering the Camp David accords between Israel and Egypt in 1978 (see Rabin and Arafat 579–86); seeking to settle the civil war between the Ethiopian central government and Eritrean rebels (1989); attempting to resolve the controversy over the North Korean suspected nuclear weapons program (1994); negotiating a four-month cease-fire in the civil war in Bosnia (1994); and becoming the first sitting or former president to visit Cuba since Fidel Castro took power (2002). Over the years, he has monitored elections in Liberia, Panama, Mexico, Peru, Paraguay, Nicaragua, Venezuela, East Timor, and Jamaica. Although he has written several books, including *Keeping Faith: Memoirs of a President* (1982), *Living Faith* (1996), and *An Hour Before Daylight: Memories of a Rural Boyhood* (2001), Carter has never exploited his worldwide recognition for personal gain.

The Nobel Peace Prize for 2002

. . . The world has changed greatly since I left the White House. Now there   1
is only one superpower, with unprecedented military and economic strength. The coming budget for American armaments will be greater than those of the next fifteen nations combined, and there are troops from

the United States in many countries throughout the world. Our gross national economy exceeds that of the three countries that follow us, and our nation's voice most often prevails as decisions are made concerning trade, humanitarian assistance, and the allocation of global wealth. This dominant status is unlikely to change in our lifetimes.

2   Great American power and responsibility are not unprecedented, and have been used with restraint and great benefit in the past. We have not assumed that super strength guarantees super wisdom, and we have consistently reached out to the international community to ensure that our own power and influence are tempered by the best common judgment.

3   Within our country, ultimate decisions are made through democratic means, which tend to moderate radical or ill-advised proposals. Constrained and inspired by historic constitutional principles, our nation has endeavored for more than two hundred years to follow the now almost universal ideals of freedom, human rights, and justice for all. . . .

4   Ladies and gentlemen: Twelve years ago, President Mikhail Gorbachev received your recognition for his preeminent role in ending the Cold War that had lasted fifty years.

5   But instead of entering a millennium of peace, the world is now, in many ways, a more dangerous place. The greater ease of travel and communication has not been matched by equal understanding and mutual respect. There is a plethora of civil wars, unrestrained by rules of the Geneva Convention, within which an overwhelming portion of the casualties are unarmed civilians who have no ability to defend themselves. And recent appalling acts of terrorism have reminded us that no nations, even superpowers, are invulnerable.

6   It is clear that global challenges must be met with an emphasis on peace, in harmony with others, with strong alliances and international consensus. Imperfect as it may be, there is no doubt that this can best be done through the United Nations, which Ralph Bunche described here in this same forum as exhibiting a "fortunate flexibility"—not merely to preserve peace but also to make change, even radical change, without violence.

7   He went on to say: "To suggest that war can prevent war is a base play on words and a despicable form of warmongering. The objective of any who sincerely believe in peace clearly must be to exhaust every honorable recourse in the effort to save the peace. The world has had ample evidence that war begets only conditions that beget further war."

8   We must remember that today there are at least eight nuclear powers on earth, and three of them are threatening to their neighbors in areas of great international tension. For powerful countries to adopt a principle of preventive war may well set an example that can have catastrophic consequences.

9   If we accept the premise that the United Nations is the best avenue for the maintenance of peace, then the carefully considered decisions of the United Nations Security Council must be enforced. All too often, the

alternative has proven to be uncontrollable violence and expanding spheres
of hostility. . . .

I am not here as a public official, but as a citizen of a troubled world 10
who finds hope in a growing consensus that the generally accepted goals
of society are peace, freedom, human rights, environmental quality, the
alleviation of suffering, and the rule of law.

During the past decades, the international community, usually under 11
the auspices of the United Nations, has struggled to negotiate global
standards that can help us achieve these essential goals. They include: the
abolition of land mines and chemical weapons; an end to the testing, proliferation, and further deployment of nuclear warheads; constraints on
global warming; prohibition of the death penalty, at least for children; and
an international criminal court to deter and to punish war crimes and
genocide. Those agreements already adopted must be fully implemented,
and others should be pursued aggressively.

We must also strive to correct the injustice of economic sanctions 12
that seek to penalize abusive leaders but all too often inflict punishment
on those who arc already suffering from the abuse. . . .

Despite theological differences, all great religions share common 13
commitments that define our ideal secular relationships. I am convinced
that Christians, Muslims, Buddhists, Hindus, Jews, and others can embrace each other in a common effort to alleviate human suffering and to
espouse peace.

But the present era is a challenging and disturbing time for those 14
whose lives are shaped by religious faith based on kindness toward each
other. We have been reminded that cruel and inhuman acts can be derived from distorted theological beliefs, as suicide bombers take the lives
of innocent human beings, draped falsely in the cloak of God's will. With
horrible brutality, neighbors have massacred neighbors in Europe, Asia,
and Africa.

In order for us human beings to commit ourselves personally to the 15
inhumanity of war, we find it necessary first to dehumanize our opponents, which is in itself a violation of the beliefs of all religions. Once we
characterize our adversaries as beyond the scope of God's mercy and
grace, their lives lose all value. We deny personal responsibility when we
plant landmines and, days or years later, a stranger to us—often a child—
is crippled or killed. From a great distance, we launch bombs or missiles
with almost total impunity, and never want to know the number or identity of the victims.

. . . The most serious and universal problem [today] is the growing 16
chasm between the richest and poorest people on earth. Citizens of the ten
wealthiest countries are now seventy-five times richer than those who live
in the ten poorest ones, and the separation is increasing every year, not
only between nations but also within them. The results of this disparity
are root causes of most of the world's unresolved problems, including

starvation, illiteracy, environmental degradation, violent conflict, and unnecessary illnesses that range from Guinea worm to HIV/AIDS.

17   Most work of The Carter Center is in remote villages in the poorest nations of Africa, and there I have witnessed the capacity of destitute people to persevere under heartbreaking conditions. I have come to admire their judgment and wisdom, their courage and faith, and their awesome accomplishments when given a chance to use their innate abilities.

18   But tragically, in the industrialized world there is a terrible absence of understanding or concern about those who are enduring lives of despair and hopelessness. We have not yet made the commitment to share with others an appreciable part of our excessive wealth. This is a potentially rewarding burden that we should all be willing to assume.

19   Ladies and gentlemen:

20   War may sometimes be a necessary evil. But no matter how necessary, it is always an evil, never a good. We will not learn how to live together in peace by killing each other's children.

21   The bond of our common humanity is stronger than the divisiveness of our fears and prejudices. God gives us the capacity for choice. We can choose to alleviate suffering. We can choose to work together for peace. We can make these changes—and we must.

22   Thank you.

KOFI ANNAN

Since 1997 Kofi Annan of Ghana has been the Secretary-General of the United Nations, where he has spent his entire career. Born in 1938 in Kumasi, Ghana, Kofi Annan completed an undergraduate degree in economics at Macalester College in St. Paul, Minnesota in 1961 and studied economics in Geneva from 1961 to 1962 before beginning work at the UN as a budget officer with the World Health Organization in Geneva. As a Sloan Fellow (1971–1972) he earned a M.S. in Management from M.I.T. He later served with the UN Economic Commission for Africa in Addis Ababa; the UN Emergency Force in Ismailia; and the Office of the UN High Commissioner for Refugees in Geneva. At the UN in New York he held a variety of posts, among them Assistant Secretary-General for Human Resources Management, Controller, Assistant Secretary-General for Peacekeeping, and Under Secretary-General during a period of unprecedented growth in UN peacekeeping operations around the world. He was chosen as the seventh Secretary-General of the UN in January of 1997. The 2001 Nobel Peace Prize was awarded to both the United Nations and to Kofi Annan for "their work for a better organized and more peaceful world. For one hundred years," says the citation, "the Norwegian Nobel Committee has sought to strengthen organized cooperation between states. The end of the cold war has at last made it possible for the U.N. to perform more fully the part it was originally intended to play. Today the organization is at the forefront of efforts to achieve peace and security in the world," and of international efforts to meet the world's economic, social, and environmental challenges. These include significant action on human rights and providing humanitarian aid to countries experiencing famine, drought, and medical epidemics such as HIV/AIDS. Since 1998 Annan's particular emphasis has been on "The Causes of Conflict and the Promotion of Durable Peace and Sustainable Development in Africa," "the most disadvantaged of the world's regions." During his tenure as Under Secretary-General, Annan supervised the expansion of UN peacekeeping operations around the world (including Kuwait, Iraq, Bosnia and Herzegovina) to, in 1995, 70,000 military and civilian personnel from 77 countries.

The United Nations in the 21st Century

We have entered the third millennium through a gate of fire. If today, after the horror of 11 September, we see better, and we see further— we will realize that humanity is indivisible. New threats make no distinction between races, nations or regions. A new insecurity has entered every mind, regardless of wealth or status. A deeper awareness of the bonds that bind us all—in pain as in prosperity—has gripped young and old.

In the early beginnings of the 21st century—a century already violently disabused of any hopes that progress towards global peace and prosperity is inevitable—this new reality can no longer be ignored. It must be confronted.

The 20th century was perhaps the deadliest in human history, devastated by innumerable conflicts, untold suffering, and unimaginable crimes. Time after time, a group or a nation inflicted extreme violence on another, often driven by irrational hatred and suspicion, or unbounded arrogance and thirst for power and resources. In response to these cataclysms, the leaders of the world came together at mid-century to unite the nations as never before.

A forum was created—the United Nations—where all nations could join forces to affirm the dignity and worth of every person, and to secure peace and development for all peoples. Here States could unite to strengthen the rule of law, recognize and address the needs of the poor, restrain man's brutality and greed, conserve the resources and beauty of nature, sustain the equal rights of men *and* women, and provide for the safety of future generations.

We thus inherit from the 20th century the political, as well as the scientific and technological power, which—if only we have the will to use them—give us the chance to vanquish poverty, ignorance and disease.

6   In the 21st Century I believe the mission of the United Nations will be defined by a new, more profound, awareness of the sanctity and dignity of every human life, regardless of race or religion. This will require us to look beyond the framework of States, and beneath the surface of nations or communities. We must focus, as never before, on improving the conditions of the individual men and women who give the state or nation its richness and character. We must begin with the young Afghan girl [born in poverty], recognizing that saving that one life is to save humanity itself.

7   Over the past five years, I have often recalled that the United Nations' Charter begins with the words: "We the peoples." What is not always recognized is that "we the peoples" are made up of individuals whose claims to the most fundamental rights have too often been sacrificed in the supposed interests of the state or the nation.

8   A genocide begins with the killing of one man—not for what he has done, but because of who he is. A campaign of "ethnic cleansing" begins with one neighbour turning on another. Poverty begins when even one child is denied his or her fundamental right to education. What begins with the failure to uphold the dignity of one life, all too often ends with a calamity for entire nations.

9   In this new century, we must start from the understanding that peace belongs not only to states or peoples, but to each and every member of those communities. The sovereignty of States must no longer be used as a shield for gross violations of human rights. Peace must be made real and tangible in the daily existence of every individual in need. Peace must be sought, above all, because it is the condition for every member of the human family to live a life of dignity and security.

10   The rights of the individual are of no less importance to immigrants and minorities in Europe and the Americas than to women in Afghanistan or children in Africa. They are as fundamental to the poor as to the rich; they are as necessary to the security of the developed world as to that of the developing world.

11   From this vision of the role of the United Nations in the next century flow three key priorities for the future: eradicating poverty, preventing conflict, and promoting democracy. Only in a world that is rid of poverty can all men and women make the most of their abilities. Only where individual rights are respected can differences be channelled politically and resolved peacefully. Only in a democratic environment, based on respect for diversity and dialogue, can individual self-expression and self-government be secured, and freedom of association be upheld. . . .

12   The idea that there is one people in possession of the truth, one answer to the world's ills, or one solution to humanity's needs, has done untold harm throughout history—especially in the last century. Today, however, even amidst continuing ethnic conflict around the world, there is a growing understanding that human diversity is both the reality that makes dialogue necessary, and the very basis for that dialogue.

We understand, as never before, that each of us is fully worthy of the 13
respect and dignity essential to our common humanity. We recognize that
we are the products of many cultures, traditions and memories; that mutual respect allows us to study and learn from other cultures; and that we
gain strength by combining the foreign with the familiar.

In every great faith and tradition one can find the values of tolerance 14
and mutual understanding. The Qur'an, for example, tells us that "We
created you from a single pair of male and female and made you into
nations and tribes, that you may know each other." Confucius urged his
followers: "when the good way prevails in the state, speak boldly and act
boldly. When the state has lost the way, act boldly and speak softly." In the
Jewish tradition, the injunction to "love thy neighbour as thyself," is considered to be the very essence of the Torah.

This thought is reflected in the Christian Gospel, which also teaches us 15
to love our enemies and pray for those who wish to persecute us. Hindus
are taught that "truth is one, the sages give it various names." And in the
Buddhist tradition, individuals are urged to act with compassion in every
facet of life.

Each of us has the right to take pride in our particular faith or heri- 16
tage. But the notion that what is ours is necessarily in conflict with what
is theirs is both false and dangerous. It has resulted in endless enmity and
conflict, leading men to commit the greatest of crimes in the name of a
higher power.

It need not be so. People of different religions and cultures live side by 17
side in almost every part of the world, and most of us have overlapping
identities which unite us with very different groups. We *can* love what we
are, without hating what—and who—we are *not*. We can thrive in our own
tradition, even as we learn from others, and come to respect their teachings.

This will not be possible, however, without freedom of religion, of 18
expression, of assembly, and basic equality under the law. Indeed, the lesson of the past century has been that where the dignity of the individual
has been trampled or threatened—where citizens have not enjoyed the
basic right to choose their government, or the right to change it regularly—conflict has too often followed, with innocent civilians paying the
price, in lives cut short and communities destroyed.

The obstacles to democracy have little to do with culture or religion, 19
and much more to do with the desire of those in power to maintain their
position at any cost. This is neither a new phenomenon nor one confined to
any particular part of the world. People of all cultures value their freedom
of choice, and feel the need to have a say in decisions affecting their lives.

The United Nations, whose membership comprises almost all the 20
States in the world, is founded on the principle of the equal worth of every
human being. It is the nearest thing we have to a representative institution
that can address the interests of all states, and all peoples. Through this
universal, indispensable instrument of human progress, States can serve

the interests of their citizens by recognizing common interests and pursuing them in unity. No doubt, that is why the Nobel Committee says that it "wishes, in its centenary year, to proclaim that the only negotiable route to global peace and cooperation goes by way of the United Nations."

21   I believe the Committee also recognized that this era of global challenges leaves no choice but cooperation at the global level. When States undermine the rule of law and violate the rights of their individual citizens, they become a menace not only to their own people, but also to their neighbours, and indeed the world. What we need today is better governance—legitimate, democratic governance that allows each individual to flourish, and each State to thrive.

JAMES ORBINSKI, M.D., AND MÉDECINS SANS FRONTIÈRES (DOCTORS WITHOUT BORDERS)

"Médecins Sans Frontières" ("Doctors Without Borders") received the Nobel Peace Prize in 1999 for "pioneering humanitarian work on several continents." The Nobel citation explains, "Since its foundation in the early 1970s, Médecins Sans Frontières has adhered to the fundamental principle that all disaster victims, whether the disaster is natural or human in origin, have a right to professional assistance, delivered as quickly and efficiently as possible. National boundaries and political circumstances or sympathies must have no influence on who is to receive humanitarian help." MSF has remained independent. It moves into hostile and dangerous situations rapidly, and in the process of treating victims of crisis, pinpoints the causes of such catastrophes and helps to influence public opinion to oppose violations and abuses of power and to effect reconciliation among warring parties. "At the same time, each fearless and self-sacrificing" helper—doctor, nurse, aide—"shows each victim a human face, stands for respect for that person's dignity, and is a source of hope for peace and reconciliation."

James Orbinski, M.D., president of Médecins Sans Frontières from 1998 to 2000, accepted the award on behalf of the organization. Born in the United Kingdom in 1960, Orbinski moved to Montreal in 1968, earned a bachelor's degree from Trent College in 1984 and an M.D. from McMaster Medical School in 1990. After spending his final year of medical school in Rwanda doing pediatric AIDS research, he formed MSF Canada in 1990 and worked with MSF during the Somalian civil war (1992), in Afghanistan during the civil war (1993), in Rwanda during the genocide (1994), in Zaire during the early stages of the civil war (1996), and in Zaire on the National Immunization program. After a year at the University of Toronto (1997–1998) to earn an M.A. in international relations, as MSF president Orbinski spent time in—among other places—Sudan, Kosovo, Albania, Russia, Cambodia, and South Africa.

Humanitarianism

The honor you give us today could so easily go to so many organiza- 1
tions, or worthy individuals, who struggle in their own society. But
clearly, you have made a choice to recognize MSF. We began formally in
1971 as a group of French doctors and journalists who decided to make
themselves available to assist. This meant sometimes a rejection of the
practices of states that directly assault the dignity of people. Silence has
long been confused with neutrality, and has been presented as a necessary
condition for humanitarian action. From its beginning, MSF was created in
opposition to this assumption. We are not sure that words can always save
lives, but we know that silence can certainly kill. Over our 28 years we
have been—and are today—firmly and irrevocably committed to this ethic
of refusal. This is the proud genesis of our identity, and today we struggle
as an imperfect movement, but strong in thousands of volunteers and national staff, and with millions of donors who support both financially and
morally, the project that is MSF. This honor is shared with all who in one
way or another, have struggled and do struggle every day to make live
the fragile reality that is MSF.

Humanitarianism occurs where the political has failed or is in crisis. 2
We act not to assume political responsibility, but firstly to relieve the inhuman suffering of failure. The act must be free of political influence, and the
political must recognize its responsibility to ensure that the humanitarian
can exist. Humanitarian action requires a framework in which to act.

In conflict, this framework is international humanitarian law. It es- 3
tablishes rights for victims and humanitarian organisations and fixes the
responsibility of states to ensure respect of these rights and to sanction their
violation as war crimes. Today this framework is clearly dysfunctional. Access to victims of conflict is often refused. Humanitarian assistance is even
used as a tool of war by belligerents. And more seriously, we are seeing the
militarisation of humanitarian action by the international community.

In this dysfunction, we will speak-out to push the political to assume 4
its inescapable responsibility. Humanitarianism is not a tool to end war or
to create peace. It is a citizen's response to political failure. It is an immediate, short term act that cannot erase the long term necessity of political
responsibility.

And ours is an ethic of refusal. It will not allow any moral political 5
failure or injustice to be sanitized or cleansed of its meaning. The 1992
crimes against humanity in Bosnia-Herzegovina. The 1994 genocide in
Rwanda. The 1997 massacres in Zaire. The 1999 actual attacks on civilians
in Chechnya. These cannot be masked by terms like "Complex Humanitarian Emergency," or "Internal Security Crisis." Or by any other such euphemism—as though they are some random, politically undetermined event.
Language is determinant. It frames the problem and defines response, rights

and therefore responsibilities. It defines whether a medical or humanitarian response is adequate. And it defines whether a political response is inadequate. No one calls a rape a complex gynecologic emergency. A rape is a rape, just as a genocide is a genocide. And both are a crime. For MSF, this is the humanitarian act: to seek to relieve suffering, to seek to restore autonomy, to witness to the truth of injustice, and to insist on political responsibility.

6   The work that MSF chooses does not occur in a vacuum, but in a social order that both includes and excludes, that both affirms and denies, and that both protects and attacks. Our daily work is a struggle, and it is intensely medical, and it is intensely personal. MSF is not a formal institution, and with any luck at all, it never will be. It is a civil society organization, and today civil society has a new global role, a new informal legitimacy that is rooted in its action and in its support from public opinion. It is also rooted in the maturity of its intent, in for example the human rights, the environmental and the humanitarian movements, and of course, the movement for equitable trade. Conflict and violence are not the only subjects of concern. We, as members of civil society, will maintain our role and our power if we remain lucid in our intent and independence.

7   As civil society we exist relative to the state, to its institutions and its power. We also exist relative to other non-state actors such as the private sector. Ours is not to displace the responsibility of the state. Ours is not to allow a humanitarian alibi to mask the state responsibility to ensure justice and security. And ours is not to be co-managers of misery with the state. If civil society identifies a problem, it is not theirs to provide a solution, but it is theirs to expect that states will translate this into concrete and just solutions. Only the state has the legitimacy and power to do this. Today, a growing injustice confronts us. More than 90% of all death and suffering from infectious diseases occurs in the developing world. Some of the reasons that people die from diseases like AIDS, TB, Sleeping Sickness and other tropical diseases is that life saving essential medicines are either too expensive, are not available because they are not seen as financially viable, or because there is virtually no new research and development for priority tropical diseases. This market failure is our next challenge. The challenge however, is not ours alone. It is also for governments, International Government Institutions, the Pharmaceutical Industry and other NGOs to confront this injustice. What we as a civil society movement demand is change, not charity.

8   We affirm the independence of the humanitarian from the political, but this is not to polarize the "good" NGO against "bad" governments, or the "virtue" of civil society against the "vice" of political power. Such a polemic is false and dangerous. As with slavery and welfare rights, history has shown that humanitarian preoccupations born in civil society have gained influence until they reach the political agenda. But these convergences should not mask the distinctions that exist between the political and the humanitarian. Humanitarian action takes place in the short term, for

limited groups and for limited objectives. This is at the same time both its strength and its limitation. The political can only be conceived in the long term, which itself is the movement of societies. Humanitarian action is by definition universal, or it is not. Humanitarian responsibility has no frontiers. Wherever in the world there is manifest distress, the humanitarian by vocation must respond. By contrast, the political knows borders, and where crisis occurs, political response will vary because historical relations, balance of power, and the interests of one or the other must be considered. The time and space of the humanitarian are not those of the political. These vary in opposing ways, and this is another way to locate the founding principles of humanitarian action: the refusal of all forms of problem solving through sacrifice of the weak and vulnerable. No victim can be intentionally discriminated against, OR neglected to the advantage of another. One life today cannot be measured by its value tomorrow: and the relief of suffering "here," cannot legitimize the abandoning of relief "over there." The limitation of means naturally must mean the making of choice, but the context and the constraints of action do not alter the fundamentals of this humanitarian vision. It is a vision that by definition must ignore political choices.

YITZAK RABIN AND YASSER ARAFAT

Yitzak Rabin (Israel, born in Jerusalem in 1922) and Shimon Peres (Israel, born in Poland in 1923) shared the 1994 Nobel Peace Prize with Yasser Arafat (a Palestinian born in Cairo in 1929) for their efforts to create peace in the Middle East. For years they were military commanders on opposing sides, in a protracted and bloody struggle "among the most irreconcilable and menacing in international politics," acknowledges the Nobel citation: "The parties have caused each other great suffering." For more than thirty years Arafat, in pursuit of his dream of an independent Palestinian homeland, waged war against Israel. His revolutionary leadership of the Palestine Liberation Organization (PLO)—driven out of Jordan by its violent guerrilla attacks on Israel and out of Lebanon by the Israeli army—kept him constantly on the move, always in secret. He survived a plane crash, assassination attempts by Israeli Intelligence agencies, and a stroke. In 1988 Arafat announced a major change of policy in a speech to the United Nations. The PLO renounced terrorism, he said, and supported "the right of all parties concerned in the Middle East conflict to live in peace and security, including the state of Palestine, Israel and other neighbors." This trio of military commanders brokered the Oslo Accords of 1993 which, acknowledged the Nobel citation, "called for great courage on both sides, and which opened up opportunities for a new development towards fraternity in the Middle East," including the establishment of a Palestinian state.

Peres was the Director-General of the Ministry of Defense from 1952 to 1959, and Minister of Defense from 1974 to 1977. He later served in the government as Prime Minister and a variety of other capacities. At the time of the Nobel award he was serving his second term as Israel's Minister of Foreign Affairs. Always a writer, amidst continuous public service Peres wrote hundreds of articles and essays and seven books, including *David's Sling* (1970) and *Battling for Peace* (1995). Rabin's military career began in 1940, when at eighteen he joined the "Palmach," the elite unit of the Haganah. He served for twenty-eight years in Israel's defense, commanding the Israeli Defense Forces during the Six-Day War. After serving as ambassador to the United States (1968–1973), he became simultaneously active in the Israeli government and in peace efforts in the Middle East, negotiating disengagement agreements with Egypt and Syria (1974). In 1985, as Minister of Defense (1984–1990), he presented the proposal for withdrawing IDF forces from Lebanon and establishing a security zone to guarantee peace to the settlements along Israel's northern frontier. Despite the activity of suicide bombers in July 1994, and April and October 1995, a peace treaty between Jordan and Israel was signed in October, 1995. Sadly, Rabin was assassinated shortly thereafter, on November 4, 1995. Even more sadly, the current disintegration of the Oslo Accords reveals the fragility of the hopes and dreams for permanent peace in the Middle East.

Yitzhak Rabin, The One Radical Solution Is Peace

1   . . . I wanted to be a water engineer. I studied in an agricultural school and I thought that being a water engineer was an important profession in the parched Middle East. I still think so today. However, I was compelled to resort to the gun.

2   I served in the military for decades. Under my command, young men and women who wanted to live, wanted to love, went to their deaths instead. Under my command, they killed the enemy's men who had been sent out to kill us.

3   In my current position, I have ample opportunity to fly over the state of Israel, and lately over other parts of the Middle East, as well. The view from the plane is breathtaking: deep-blue lakes, dark-green fields, dun-coloured deserts, stone-gray mountains, and the entire countryside peppered with white-washed, red-roofed houses.

4   And cemeteries. Graves as far as the eye can see. . . .

5   I was a young man who has now grown fully in years. And of all the memories I have stored up in my seventy-two years, what I shall remember most, to my last day, are the silences:

6   The heavy silence of the moment after, and the terrifying silence of the moment before.

As a military man, as a commander, I issued orders for dozens, prob- ⁷
ably hundreds of military operations. And together with the joy of victory
and grief of bereavement, I shall always remember the moment just after
taking the decision to mount an action: the hush as senior officers or cabinet ministers slowly rise from their seats; the sight of their receding backs;
the sound of the closing door; and then the silence in which I remain alone.

That is the moment you grasp that as a result of the decision just ⁸
made, people will be going to their deaths. People from my nation, people
from other nations. And they still don't know it.

At that hour, they are still laughing and weeping; still weaving plans ⁹
and dreams about love; still musing about planting a garden or building
a house—and they have no idea these are their last hours on earth. Which
of them is fated to die? Whose picture will appear in a black border in tomorrow's newspaper? Whose mother will soon be in mourning? Whose
world will crumble under the weight of the loss?

As a former military man, I will also forever remember the silence of ¹⁰
the moment before: the hush when the hands of the clock seem to be spinning forward, when time is running out and in another hour, another
minute, the inferno will erupt.

In that moment of great tension just before the finger pulls the trigger, ¹¹
just before the fuse begins to burn; in the terrible quiet of that moment,
there's still time to wonder, alone: Is it really imperative to act? Is there no
other choice? No other way?

And then the order is given, and the inferno begins. . . . ¹²

For decades God has not taken pity on the kindergarteners in the ¹³
Middle East, or the schoolchildren, or their elders. There has been no pity
in the Middle East for generations. . . .

A child is born into an utterly undemocratic world. He cannot choose his ¹⁴
father and mother. He cannot pick his sex or colour, his religion, nationality, or homeland. Whether he is born in a manor or a manger, whether
he lives under a despotic or democratic regime, is not his choice. From the
moment he comes, close-fisted, into the world, his fate lies in the hands of
his nation's leaders. It is they who will decide whether he lives in comfort
or despair, in security or in fear. His fate is given to us to resolve—to the
Presidents and Prime Ministers of countries, democratic or otherwise.

Just as no two fingerprints are identical, so no two people are alike, ¹⁵
and every country has its own laws and culture, traditions and leaders.
But there is one universal message which can embrace the entire world,
one precept which can be common to different regimes, to races which
bear no resemblance, to cultures alien to each other.

It is a message which the Jewish people has borne for thousands of ¹⁶
years, a message found in the Book of Books . . . in the words in Deuter-
onomy: "Therefore take good heed to yourselves"—or, in contemporary
terms, the message of the Sanctity of Life.

17   The leaders of nations must provide their peoples with the conditions—the "infrastructure," if you will—which enables them to enjoy life: freedom of speech and of movement; food and shelter; and most important of all: life itself. A man cannot enjoy his rights if he is not among the living. And so every country must protect and preserve the key element in its national ethos: the lives of its citizens.

18   To defend those lives, we call upon our citizens to enlist in the army. And to defend the lives of our citizens serving in the army, we invest huge sums in planes, and tanks, in armored plating and concrete fortifications. Yet despite it all, we fail to protect the lives of our citizens and soldiers. Military cemeteries in every corner of the world are silent testimony to the failure of national leaders to sanctify human life.

19   There is only one radical means of sanctifying human lives. Not armored plating, or tanks, or planes, or concrete fortifications.

The one radical solution is peace.

20   The profession of soldiering embraces a certain paradox. We take the best and bravest of our young men into the army. We supply them with equipment which costs a virtual fortune. We rigorously train them for the day when they must do their duty—and we except them to do it well. Yet we fervently pray that day will never come—that the planes will never take flight, the tanks will never move forward, the soldiers will never mount the attacks for which they have been trained so well.

21   We pray it will never happen because of the Sanctity of Life.

22   History as a whole, and modern history in particular, has known harrowing times when national leaders turned their citizens into cannon fodder in the name of wicked doctrines: vicious Fascism and fiendish Nazism. Pictures of children marching to the slaughter, photos of terrified women at the gates of crematoria must loom before the eyes of every leader in our generation, and the generations to come. They must serve as a warning to all who wield power.

23   Almost all the regimes which did not place man and the Sanctity of Life at the heart of their world view, all those regimes have collapsed and are no more. You can see it for yourselves in our own day.

24   Yet this is not the whole picture. To preserve the Sanctity of Life, we must sometimes risk it. Sometimes there is no other way to defend our citizens than to fight for their lives, for their safety and sovereignty. This is the creed of every democratic state. . . .

25   In the coming days, a special Commission of the Israel Defence Forces will finish drafting a Code of Conduct for our soldiers. The formulation regarding human life will read as follows, and I quote:

26   In recognition of its supreme importance, the soldier will preserve human life in every way possible and endanger himself, or others, only to the extent deemed necessary to fulfil this mission.

The Sanctity of Life, in the view of the soldiers of the Israel Defence 27 Forces, will find expression in all their actions; in considered and precise planning; in intelligent and safety-minded training and in judicious implementation, in accordance with their mission; in taking the professionally proper degree of risk and degree of caution; and in the constant effort to limit casualties to the scope required to achieve the objective.

For many years ahead—even if wars come to an end, after peace comes to 28 our land—these words will remain a pillar of fire which goes before our camp, a guiding light for our people. And we take pride in that. . . .

We will pursue the course of peace with determination and fortitude. 29 We will not let up.

We will not give in.

Peace will triumph over all our enemies, because the alternative is 30 grimmer for us all.

And we will prevail. 31

We will prevail because we regard the building of peace as a great 32 blessing for us, and for our children after us. We regard it as a blessing for our neighbours on all sides, and for our partners in this enterprise—the United States, Russia, Norway, and all mankind. . . .

I wish to thank our partners—the Egyptians, Jordanians, Palestinians, 33 and the Chairman of the Palestine Liberation Organization, Mr. Yasser Arafat, with whom we share this Nobel Prize—who have chosen the path of peace and are writing a new page in the annals of the Middle East. . . .

Yasser Arafat, The Crescent Moon of Peace

. . . Ever since I was entrusted by my people to undertake the arduous task 1 of seeking our lost home, I have been filled with a warm faith that all those in exile who bore the keys to their homes with them as they bore their limbs, an inseparable part of them, and those in the homeland, who bore their wounds as they bear their names . . . would, one day, for all their sacrifices, be granted the rewards of returning and freedom.

And that the difficult journey on that long pain-filled path would 2 end in their own hallways.

Now, as we celebrate together the first sighting of the crescent moon 3 of peace, I stare into the eyes of those martyrs whose look has seared into my consciousness as I stand here on this podium and who ask me about the homeland, about their vacant places. I hide my tears from them and tell them: "How right you were. Your generous sacrifice has enabled us to

behold the Holy Land, to tread our first steps on it in a difficult battle, the battle for peace, the peace of the brave."

4   Now, as we celebrate the reawakening of creative forces within us and restore the war-torn home that overlooks the neighbours' where our children shall play together and compete to pick flowers, now, I feel national and human pride in my Palestinian Arab people whose powers of patience and giving, of retaining a never-ending bond between homeland, history and people, have added a new chapter to the homeland's ancient legends, that of The Epic of Hope.

5   To them, to the sons and daughters of that kind enduring nation, that nation of yew and dew, of fire and sweat, I dedicate this Nobel Prize. I shall bear it to those children who have been promised freedom, safety and security in a homeland free of the threats of external occupation or internal exploitation.

6   I know, I know full well, Mr Chairman, that this supreme and greatly significant prize was not awarded to me and to my partners: Mr.Yitzhak Rabin, the Israeli Prime Minister, and Mr. Shimon Peres, the Foreign Minister, to crown an achievement: but as an encouragement to pursue a route with greater steps and deeper awareness, with truer intentions so that we may transform the peace option, the peace of the brave, from words into practice and reality and for us to be worthy of carrying forward the message entrusted to us by our peoples, as well as humanity and a universal moral duty. The Palestinians, whose national cause guards the gates of Arab-Israeli peace, look forward like their Arab brethren, to that comprehensive, just and lasting peace, based on "land for peace" and compliance with international legitimacy and resolutions. Peace, for us, is an asset and in our interest. It is an absolute human asset that allows an individual to freely develop his individuality unbound by any regional, religious or ethnic fetters. It restores to Arab-Israeli relations their innocent nature, and enables the Arab spirit to reflect through unrestrained human expression its profound understanding of the Jewish-European tragedy, just as it allows the tortured Jewish spirit to express its unfettered empathy for the suffering endured by the Palestinian people over their ruptured history. Only the tortured can understand those who have endured torture.

7   Peace is in our interest: as only in an atmosphere of just peace shall the Palestinian people achieve their legitimate ambition for independence and sovereignty, and be able to develop their national and cultural identity, as well as enjoy sound neighbourly relations, mutual respect and co-operation with the Israeli people. They, in return, will be able to articulate their Middle Eastern identity, and to open up economically and culturally towards their Arab neighbours. The Arabs are looking forward to developing their region which the long years of war had prevented from

finding its true place in today's world, in an atmosphere of democracy, pluralism and prosperity.

Just as war is a great adventure, peace is a challenge and wager. If we fail 8 to endow peace with the wherewithal to withstand the tempest and the storm, if we fail to nurture peace so that it may gain in strength, if we fail to give it scope to grow and gain in strength, the wager could be wasted and lost. So, from this rostrum I call upon my partners in peace to speed up the peace process, to bring about an early withdrawal, to allow elections to be held and to move on rapidly to the next stage, so that peace may become entrenched and grow, become an established reality. . . .

. . . Even though the peace process has not reached its full scope, the 9 new environment of trust as well as the modest steps implemented during the first and second years of the peace agreement are very promising and call for the lifting of reservations, for procedures to be simplified. We must fulfil what remains, especially the transfer of power and taking further steps in Israeli withdrawal from the West Bank and the settlements to achieve full withdrawal. This would provide our society with the opportunity to rebuild its infrastructure and to contribute from its location, with its own heritage, knowledge and know-how in forging our new world. . . .

Peace cannot thrive, and the peace process cannot be consolidated in 10 the absence of the necessary material conditions.

I call on my partners in peace to reinforce the peace process with the nec- 11 essary comprehensive and strategic vision.

Confidence alone does not make peace. But acknowledging rights 12 and confidence do. Failure to recognize these rights creates a sense of injustice, it keeps the embers burning under the ashes. It moves peace towards the quicksands of danger and rekindles a fuse that is ready to explode.

We view peace as an historic strategic option[,] not a tactical one di- 13 rected by current calculations of gain or loss. The peace process is not only a political process, it is an integrated operation where national awareness, economic, scientific and technological development play a major role, just as cultural, social and creative merging play essential roles that are of the very essence of the peace process and fortify it. I review all this as I recall the difficult peace journey we have travelled; we have only covered a short distance. We have to arm ourselves with courage and utmost temerity to cover the longer distance ahead, towards the homebase of just and comprehensive peace, and to be able to assimilate that creative force of the deeper meanings of peace.

As long as we have decided to coexist in peace we must do so on a 14 firm basis that will withstand time and for generations. . . .

15   Let us protect this new-born infant from the winter winds, let us nurture it with milk and honey, from the land of milk and honey, and on the land of Salem, Abraham, Ismael and Isaac, the Holy Land, the Land of Peace.

===

NELSON MANDELA AND FREDERIK WILLEM DE KLERK

Nelson Mandela and Frederik Willem de Klerk shared the Nobel Peace Prize in 1993 for "their work for the peaceful termination of the apartheid regime," the citation explains, "and for laying the foundations of a new democratic South Africa." For twenty-eight years Mandela (born in Transeki, South Africa, in 1918) was the imprisoned leader of the African National Congress and—as time went on—an internationally known symbol of determined resistance to apartheid. His autobiography, *Long Walk to Freedom* (1994), explains, in serenely charitable language, the great physical and psychological fortitude he needed to endure the hard labor (which included several oppressive years of breaking rocks), isolation, and other deprivations of this long and harsh time. De Klerk (born in Johannesburg in 1936, son of Senator Jan de Klerk), who had held a series of ministerial positions in the South African government from 1978 to 1989, "was not known to advocate reform" before his election as state president in September 1989. Nevertheless, says the Nobel Prize committee, "In his first speech after assuming the party leadership he called for a nonracist South Africa and for negotiations about the country's future. He lifted the ban on the ANC and released Nelson Mandela. He brought apartheid to an end and opened the way for the drafting of a new constitution for the country based on the principle of one person, one vote." Thus, coming from very different points of departure, Mandela and de Klerk looked "ahead to South African reconciliation instead of back at the deep wounds of the past," showing "great integrity and great political courage."

Nelson Mandela,
The End of Apartheid

1   Because of their courage and persistence for many years, we can, today, even set the dates when all humanity will join together to celebrate one of the outstanding human victories of our century.

2   When that moment comes, we shall, together, rejoice in a common victory over racism, apartheid and white minority rule.

3   That triumph will finally bring to a close a history of five hundred years of African colonisation that began with the establishment of the Portuguese empire.

Thus, it will mark a great step forward in history and also serve as a   4
common pledge of the peoples of the world to fight racism, wherever it
occurs and whatever guise it assumes.

At the southern tip of the continent of Africa, a rich reward in the   5
making, an invaluable gift is in the preparation for those who suffered in
the name of all humanity when they sacrificed everything—for liberty,
peace, human dignity and human fulfillment.

This reward will not be measured in money. Nor can it be reckoned   6
in the collective price of the rare metals and precious stones that rest in the
bowels of the African soil we tread in the footsteps of our ancestors.

It will and must be measured by the happiness and welfare of the   7
children, at once the most vulnerable citizens in any society and the greatest of our treasures.

The children must, at last, play in the open veld, no longer tortured   8
by the pangs of hunger or ravaged by disease or threatened with the
scourge of ignorance, molestation and abuse, and no longer required to
engage in deeds whose gravity exceeds the demands of their tender years.

In front of this distinguished audience, we commit the new South   9
Africa to the relentless pursuit of the purposes defined in the World Declaration on the Survival, Protection and Development of Children.

The reward of which we have spoken will and must also be meas-   10
ured by the happiness and welfare of the mothers and fathers of these
children, who must walk the earth without fear of being robbed, killed for
political or material profit, or spat upon because they are beggars.

They too must be relieved of the heavy burden of despair which they   11
carry in their hearts, born of hunger, homelessness and unemployment.

The value of that gift to all who have suffered will and must be meas-   12
ured by the happiness and welfare of all the people of our country, who
will have torn down the inhuman walls that divide them.

These great masses will have turned their backs on the grave insult   13
to human dignity which described some as masters and others as servants,
and transformed each into a predator whose survival depended on the destruction of the other.

The value of our shared reward will and must be measured by the   14
joyful peace which will triumph, because the common humanity that
bonds both black and white into one human race, will have said to each
one of us that we shall all live like the children of paradise.

Thus shall we live, because we will have created a society which rec-   15
ognises that all people are born equal, with each entitled in equal measure
to life, liberty, prosperity, human rights and good governance.

Such a society should never allow again that there should be pris-   16
oners of conscience nor that any person's human right should be violated.

Neither should it ever happen that once more the avenues to peace-   17
ful change are blocked by usurpers who seek to take power away from the
people, in pursuit of their own, ignoble purposes.

*South African President Nelson Mandela (on left) and South African
Deputy President F. W. de Klerk (on right) holding their Nobel Peace Prize
gold medals and diplomas on December 10, 1993. Interpret and comment
on the significance of this photograph—historical, ethical, political, human.*

18   In relation to these matters, we appeal to those who govern Burma
that they release our fellow Nobel Peace Prize laureate, Aung San Suu Kyi,
and engage her and those she represents in serious dialogue, for the benefit of all the people of Burma.

19   We pray that those who have the power to do so will, without further
delay, permit that she uses her talents and energies for the greater good of
the people of her country and humanity as a whole.

20   Far from the rough and tumble of the politics of our own country. I
would like to take this opportunity to join the Norwegian Nobel Committee and pay tribute to my joint laureate[,] Mr. F. W. de Klerk.

21   He had the courage to admit that a terrible wrong had been done to
our country and people through the imposition of the system of apartheid.

22   He had the foresight to understand and accept that all the people of
South Africa must through negotiations and as equal participants in the
process, together determine what they want to make of their future.

23   But there are still some within our country who wrongly believe
they can make a contribution to the cause of justice and peace by clinging
to the shibboleths that have been proved to spell nothing but disaster.

24   It remains our hope that these, too, will be blessed with sufficient
reason to realise that history will not be denied and that the new society

cannot be created by reproducing the repugnant past, however refined or enticingly repackaged.

We would also like to take advantage of this occasion to pay tribute to the many formations of the democratic movement of our country, including the members of our Patriotic Front, who have themselves played a central role in bringing our country as close to the democratic transformation as it is today. 25

We are happy that many representatives of these formations, including people who have served or are serving in the "homeland" structures, came with us to Oslo. They too must share the accolade which the Nobel Peace Prize confers. 26

We live with the hope that as she battles to remake herself, South Africa, will be like a microcosm of the new world that is striving to be born. 27

This must be a world of democracy and respect for human rights, a world freed from the horrors of poverty, hunger, deprivation and ignorance, relieved of the threat and the scourge of civil wars and external aggression and unburdened of the great tragedy of millions forced to become refugees. 28

The processes in which South Africa and Southern Africa as a whole are engaged, beckon and urge us all that we take this tide at the flood and make of this region as a living example of what all people of conscience would like the world to be. 29

We do not believe that this Nobel Peace Prize is intended as a commendation for matters that have happened and passed. 30

We hear the voices which say that it is an appeal from all those, throughout the universe, who sought an end to the system of apartheid. 31

We understand their call, that we devote what remains of our lives to the use of our country's unique and painful experience to demonstrate, in practice, that the normal condition for human existence is democracy, justice, peace, non-racism, non-sexism, prosperity for everybody, a healthy environment and equality and solidarity among the peoples. 32

Moved by that appeal and inspired by the eminence you have thrust upon us, we undertake that we too will do what we can to contribute to the renewal of our world so that none should, in future, be described as the "wretched of the earth." 33

Let it never be said by future generations that indifference, cynicism or selfishness made us fail to live up to the ideals of humanism which the Nobel Peace Prize encapsulates. 34

Let the strivings of us all, prove Martin Luther King Jr. to have been correct, when he said that humanity can no longer be tragically bound to the starless midnight of racism and war. 35

Let the efforts of us all, prove that he was not a mere dreamer when he spoke of the beauty of genuine brotherhood and peace being more precious than diamonds or silver or gold. 36

Let a new age dawn! 37

Frederik Willem de Klerk, Reformation and Reconciliation in South Africa

1   Five years ago people would have seriously questioned the sanity of anyone who would have predicted that Mr Mandela and I would be joint recipients of the 1993 Nobel Peace Prize.

2   And yet both of us are here before you today.

3   We are political opponents.

4   We disagree strongly on key issues and we will soon fight a strenuous election campaign against one another. But we will do so, I believe, in the frame of mind and within the framework of peace which has already been established.

5   We will do it—and many other leaders will do it with us—because there is no other road to peace and prosperity for the people of our country. In the conflicts of the past, there was no gain for anyone in our country. Through reconciliation all of us are now becoming winners.

6   The compromises we have reached demand sacrifices on all sides. It was not easy for the supporters of Mr Mandela or mine to relinquish the ideals they had cherished for many decades.

7   But we did it. And because we did it, there is hope.

8   The coming election will not be about the past. It will be about the future. It will not be about Blacks or Whites, or Afrikaners and Xhosas. It will be about the best solutions for the future in the interests of all our people. It will not be about apartheid or armed struggle. It will be about future peace and stability, about progress and prosperity, about nation-building.

9   In my first speech about becoming Leader of the National Party, I said on February the 8th, 1989:

10   Our goal is a new South Africa:
A totally changed South Africa;
a South Africa which has rid itself of the
antagonism of the past;
a South Africa free of domination or oppression
in whatever form;
a South Africa within which the democratic
forces—all reasonable people—align themselves
behind mutually acceptable goals and against
radicalism, irrespective of where it comes from.

11   Since then we have made impressive progress, thanks to the cooperation of political, spiritual, business and community leaders over a wide spectrum. To Mr Mandela I sincerely say: Congratulations. And in accepting

this Peace Prize today I wish to pay tribute to all who are working for peace in our land. On behalf of all South Africans who supported me, directly or indirectly, I accept it in humility, deeply aware of my own shortcomings.

I thank those who decided to make the award for the recognition 12 they have granted in doing so—recognition of a mighty deed of reformation and reconciliation that is taking place in South Africa. The road ahead is still full of obstacles and, therefore, dangerous. There is, however, no question of turning back.

AUNG SAN SUU KYI

Aung San Suu Kyi, the daughter of Burma's liberation leader Aung San, was born in Rangoon, then Burma, now Myanmar, in 1945. In 1991 she was awarded the Nobel Peace Prize, which her sons accepted on her behalf because she was under house arrest. Her father, General Aung San, then commander of the Burma Independence Army, was assassinated when Suu Kyi was two years old. Her mother, Daw Khin Kyi, continued to champion the cause, attaining prominence in social planning and social policy, and it was partly through her efforts that the Independent Union of Burma was established in 1948. In 1960 Daw Khin Kyi was appointed Burma's ambassador to India. Suu Kyi, who accompanied her mother, attended preparatory school in New Delhi, followed by a B.A. in philosophy, politics, and economics at Oxford. Her background, marriage to Michael Aris, a scholar of Tibetan civilization, and friendships with high-ranking officials in England, the United States, Bhutan, Japan, and India, led to work at the UN, study at Oxford, and international visibility as she assumed leadership of the opposition party, the National League for Democracy, in Burma as her mother was dying in 1988.

Harassment of Suu Kyi and her nonviolent party began immediately, with brutal arrests and killings. After facing down troops with rifles aimed at her in April 1989, she was placed under house arrest in July 1989. Her heroic actions had already made her an important symbol in the struggle against oppression. In May 1990, despite Suu Kyi's continued detention, her party won 82 percent of the seats in parliament, but the military state voided the results. It was in this climate that the Nobel Prize committee awarded her the Peace Prize, "to honor her nonviolent struggle for democracy and human rights" and to show "support for the many people throughout the world who are striving to attain democracy, human rights, and ethnic conciliation by peaceful means." As of 2002, Aung San Suu Kyi had spent a total of ten years under house arrest, refusing offers of freedom and reunion with her husband (who died in 1999 without being allowed to visit her) and sons if she would leave the country and withdraw from politics. Like Nelson Mandela, she chose separation from her family as one of the personal sacrifices she had to make in order to work for a larger, more humanitarian cause—in this case, a free Burma. Released in June 2002, her volatile political status offers no assurance of continued freedom.

The Revolution of Spirit

1   . . . I stand before you here today to accept on behalf of my mother, Aung San Suu Kyi, this greatest of prizes, the Nobel Prize for Peace. Because circumstances do not permit my mother to be here in person, I will do my best to convey the sentiments I believe she would express.

2   Firstly, I know that she would begin by saying that she accepts the Nobel Prize for Peace not in her own name but in the name of all the people of Burma. She would say that this prize belongs not to her but to all those men, women and children who, even as I speak, continue to sacrifice their well being, their freedom and their lives in pursuit of a democratic Burma. Theirs is the prize and theirs will be the eventual victory in Burma's long struggle for peace, freedom and democracy.

3   Speaking as her son, however, I would add that I personally believe that by her own dedication and personal sacrifice she has come to be a worthy symbol through whom the plight of all the people of Burma may be recognized.

4   And no one must underestimate that plight. The plight of those in the countryside and towns, living in poverty and destitution, those in prison, battered and tortured; the plight of the young people, the hope of Burma, dying of malaria in the jungles to which they have fled; that of the Buddhist monks, beaten and dishonoured. Nor should we forget the many senior and highly respected leaders besides my mother who are all incarcerated.

5   It is on their behalf that I thank you, from my heart, for this supreme honour. The Burmese people can today hold their heads a little higher in the knowledge that in this far distant land their suffering has been heard and heeded.

6   We must also remember that the lonely struggle taking place in a heavily guarded compound in Rangoon is part of the much larger struggle, world-wide, for the emancipation of the human spirit from political tyranny and psychological subjection. The Prize, I feel sure, is also intended to honour all those engaged in this struggle wherever they may be. It is not without reason that today's events in Oslo fall on the International Human Rights Day, celebrated throughout the world.

7   Mr Chairman, the whole international community has applauded the choice of your Committee. Just a few days ago, the United Nations passed a unanimous and historic resolution welcoming Secretary-General Javier Pérez de Cuéllar's statement on the significance of this award and

"Read" the speech that Aung San Suu Kyi is making. Who is her audience? What does she want to happen as a consequence of her speaking? How do her physical attractiveness, gender, and dress reinforce—or contradict—your interpretation?

endorsing his repeated appeals for my mother's early release from detention. Universal concern at the grave human rights situation in Burma was clearly expressed. Alone and isolated among the entire nations of the world a single dissenting voice was heard, from the military junta in Rangoon, too late and too weak.

This regime has through almost thirty years of misrule reduced the once prosperous "Golden Land" of Burma to one of the world's most economically destitute nations. In their heart of hearts even those in power now in Rangoon must know that their eventual fate will be that of all totalitarian regimes who seek to impose their authority through fear, repression, and hatred. When the present Burmese struggle for democracy erupted onto the streets in 1988 it was the first of what became an international tidal wave of such movements throughout Eastern Europe, Asia and Africa. Today, in 1991, Burma stands conspicuous in its continued suffering at the hands of a repressive, intransigent junta, the State Law and Order Restoration Council. However, the example of those nations which have successfully achieved democracy holds out an important message to the Burmese people: that, in the last resort, through the sheer economic unworkability of totalitarianism this present regime will be swept away. And today in the face of rising inflation, a mismanaged economy and near worthless Kyat, the Burmese Government is undoubtedly reaping as it has sown.

9   However, it is my deepest hope that it will not be in the face of complete economic collapse that the regime will fall, but that the ruling junta may yet heed such appeals to basic humanity as that which the Nobel Committee has expressed in its award of this year's Prize. I know that within the military government there *are* those to whom the present policies of fear and repression are abhorrent, violating as they do the most sacred principles of Burma's Buddhist heritage. This is no empty wishful thinking but a conviction my mother reached in the course of her dealings with those in positions of authority, illustrated by the election victories of her party in constituencies comprised almost exclusively of military personnel and their families. It is my profoundest wish that these elements for moderation and reconciliation among those now in authority may make their sentiments felt in Burma's hour of deepest need.

10   I know that if she were free today my mother would in thanking you also ask you to pray that the oppressors and the oppressed should thrown down their weapons and join together to build a nation founded on humanity in the spirit of peace.

11   Although my mother is often described as a political dissident who strives by peaceful means for democratic change, we should remember that her quest is basically spiritual. As she has said, "The quintessential revolution is that of the spirit," and she has written of the "essential spiritual aims" of the struggle. The realization of this depends solely on human responsibility. At the root of that responsibility lies, and I quote, "the concept of perfection, the urge to achieve it, the intelligence to find a path towards it, and the will to follow that path if not to the end, at least the distance needed to rise above individual limitation. . . ." "To live the full life," she says, "one must have the courage to bear the responsibility of the needs of others . . . one must *want* to bear this responsibility." And she links this firmly to her faith when she writes, ". . . Buddhism, the foundation of traditional Burmese culture, places the greatest value on man, who alone of all beings can achieve the supreme state of Buddhahood. Each man has in him the potential to realize the truth through his own will and endeavour and to help others to realize it." Finally she says, "The quest for democracy in Burma is the struggle of a people to live whole, meaningful lives as free and equal members of the world community. It is part of the unceasing human endeavour to prove that the spirit of man can transcend the flaws of his nature."

12   It only remains for me to thank you all from the bottom of my heart. Let us hope and pray that from today the wounds start to heal and that in the years to come the 1991 Nobel Prize for Peace will be seen as a historic step towards the achievement of true peace in Burma. The lessons of the past will not be forgotten, but it is our hope for the future that we celebrate today.

RIGOBERTA MENCHÚ

Rigoberta Menchú received the 1992 Nobel Peace Prize "in recognition of her work for social justice and ethno-cultural reconciliation based on respect for the rights of indigenous peoples." In the 1970s and 1980s Guatemala, like many other countries in South and Central America, was filled with tremendous tension between descendants of European immigrants and the native Indian peoples, who were brutally suppressed and persecuted. Menchú, a social and political activist, said the Nobel committee, "stands out as a vivid symbol of peace and reconciliation across ethnic, cultural and social dividing lines," nationwide and worldwide.

Rigoberta Menchú was born in 1959 to a poor Indian peasant family in Guatemala and raised in the Quiche branch of the Mayan culture. In childhood she helped with the family farm work, which included picking coffee on the large plantations. As a teenager she became involved in social reform activities through the Catholic Church, including becoming an advocate for women's rights—efforts that aroused opposition of those in power, especially after a guerilla organization became active in the area. The Menchú family was accused of guerilla activities; her father was imprisoned and tortured for allegedly having participated in the execution of a local plantation owner. After his release he became a member of the Committee of the Peasant Union (CUC), which Rigoberta joined in 1979—the year her brother was tortured and killed by the army. The following year her father was killed by security forces, and her mother died after being arrested, raped, and tortured. In 1980 Rigoberta, who had taught herself Spanish and a variety of Mayan languages, figured prominently in a strike organized by the CUC to improve conditions for farm workers. In 1981 her activities in educating the Indian peasant population to resist military oppression forced her to go into hiding in Guatemala and then flee to Mexico. She helped to found an opposition body, "The United Representation of the Guatemalan Opposition (RUOG)." In a week of recorded interviews with anthropologist Elisabeth Burgos-Debray, she told her life story. The book, *I, Rigoberta Menchú*, was published in 1983, translated into a dozen languages, and soon acquired incendiary international fame as the embodiment of the atrocities committed by the Guatemalan army in peasant villages during the civil war.

In 1999 David Stoll, though fully supportive of her Nobel Prize, published a critique of the book—*Menchú and the Story of All Poor Guatemalans* (1999)—demonstrating that parts of her own and her family history are in error, even when she speaks as an eyewitness. Stoll, an anthropologist who studied Mayan peasants, claims he trusted Menchú's presentation of the Guatemalan army atrocities, but he feels that "by inaccurately portraying the events in her own village as representative of what happened in all such indigenous villages in Guatemala, she gives a misleading interpretation of the relationship of the Mayan peasants to the revolutionary movement." The Nobel Prize committee defended its decision to award the prize to Menchú, saying that this "was not based exclusively or primarily on the autobiography," and dismissed any suggestion that the Committee should consider revoking the prize. *The Rigoberta Menchú Controversy*, ed. Arturo Arias (2002) is a superb collection of "primary documents—newspaper articles, interviews, and official statements" complemented by assessments by distinguished international scholars of the political, historical, and cultural implications of this debate.

Five Hundred Years of Mayan Oppression

1   Please allow me, ladies and gentlemen, to say some words about my country and the Civilization of the Mayas. The Maya people developed and spread geographically through some 300,000 square km; they occupied parts of the South of Mexico, Belize, Guatemala, as well as Honduras and El Salvador; they developed a very rich civilization in the area of political organization, as well as in social and economic fields; they were great scientists in the fields of mathematics, astronomy, agriculture, architecture and engineering; they were great artists in the fields of sculpture, painting, weaving and carving. . . .

2   Who can predict what other great scientific conquests and developments these people could have achieved, if they had not been conquered in blood and fire, and subjected to an ethnocide that affected nearly 50 million people in the course of 500 years.

3   I would describe the meaning of this Nobel Prize, in the first place as a tribute to the indian people who have been sacrificed and have disappeared because they aimed at a more dignified and just life with fraternity and understanding among the human beings. To those who are no longer alive to keep up the hope for a change in the situation in respect of poverty and marginalization of the indians, of those who have been banished, of the helpless in Guatemala as well as in the entire American Continent.

4   This growing concern is comforting, even though it comes 500 years later, to the suffering, the discrimination, the oppression and the exploitation that our people has been exposed to, but who, thanks to their own cosmovision—and concept of life, have managed to withstand and finally see some promising prospects. How those roots, that were to be eradicated, now begin to grow with strength, hopes and visions for the future!

5   It also represents a sign of the growing international interest for, and understanding of the original Rights of the People, of the future of more than 60 million indians that live in our America, and their uproar because of the 500 years of oppression that they have endured. For the genocides beyond comparison that they have had to suffer all this time, and from which other countries and the elite of the Americas have profited and taken advantage.

Let there be freedom for the indians, wherever they may be in the 6 American Continent or else in the world, because while they are alive, a glow of hope will be alive as well as the real concept of life.

The expressions of great happiness by the Indian Organizations in 7 the entire Continent and the worldwide congratulations received for the award of the Nobel Peace Prize, clearly indicate the great importance of this decision. It is the recognition of the European debt to the American indigenous people; it is an appeal to the conscience of Humanity so that those conditions of marginalization that condemned them to colonialism and exploitation may be eradicated; it is a cry for life, peace, justice, equality and fraternity between human beings.

The peculiarities of the vision of the indian people are expressed 8 according to the way in which they relate. First of all, between human being[s], through communication. Second, with the earth, as with our mother, because she gives us our lives and is not a mere merchandise. Third, with nature, because we are integral parts of it, and not its owners.

To us mother earth is not only a source of economic riches that give 9 us the maize, which is our life, but she also provides so many other things that the privileged ones of today strive after. The earth is the root and the source of our culture. She keeps our memories, she receives our ancestors and she therefore demands that we honour her and return to her, with tenderness and respect, those goods that she gives us. We have to take care of her and look after mother earth so that our children and grandchildren may continue to benefit from her. If the world does not learn now to show respect to nature, what kind of future will the new generations have?

From these basic features derive behaviour, rights and obligations in 10 the American Continent, for indians as well as for non-indians, whether they be racially mixed, blacks, whites or Asian. The whole society has the obligation to show mutual respect, to learn from each other and to share material and scientific achievements, in the most convenient way. The indians have never had, and they do not have, the place that they should have occupied in the progress and benefits of science and technology, although they have represented an important basis.

If the indian civilizations and the European civilizations could have 11 made exchanges in a peaceful and harmonious manner, without destruction, exploitation, discrimination and poverty, they could, no doubt, have achieved greater and more valuable conquests for Humanity.

Let us not forget that when the Europeans came to America, there 12 were flourishing and strong civilizations there. One cannot talk about a discovery of America, because one discovers that which one does not know about, or that which is hidden. But America and its native civilizations had discovered themselves long before the fall of the Roman Empire and the Medieval Europe. The significance of its cultures form part of the heritage of humanity and continue to astonish the learned ones. . . .

13   We the indians are willing to combine tradition with modernism, but not at all costs. We will not tolerate nor permit that our future be planned as possible guardians of ethno-touristic projects at continental level.

14   At a time when the commemoration of the Fifth Centenary of the arrival of Columbus in America has repercussions all over the world, the revival of hopes for the indian people claims that we reassert to the world our existence and the value of our cultural identity. It demands that we endeavour to actively participate in the decisions that concern our destiny, in the building-up of our countries/nations. Should we, in spite of all, not be taken into consideration, there are factors that guarantee our future: struggle and endurance; courage; the decision to maintain our traditions that have been exposed to so many perils and sufferings; solidarity towards our struggle on the part of numerous countries, governments, organizations and citizens of the world.

15   That is why I dream of the day when the relationship between the indigenous people and other people is strengthened; when they can join their potentialities and their capabilities and contribute to make life on this planet less unequal.

THE 14TH DALAI LAMA, TENZIN GYATSO

The 14th Dalai Lama, Tenzin Gyatso, born to a peasant family in Takster, Tibet in 1935, was recognized at the age of two as the reincarnation of his predecessor, the 13th Dalai Lama. Dalai Lamas (the name means "Oceans of Wisdom") are the manifestations of the Bodhisattva of Compassion, who chose to reincarnate to serve the people. His monastic education began at six and culminated in a Doctorate of Buddhist Philosophy awarded when he was twenty-five. His political education took place concurrently, for in 1950 he assumed full power as Head of State and Government when Tibet's autonomy was threatened by Communist China. His meetings with Mao Tse-Tung and Chou En-Lai were in vain, for in 1959 he was forced into exile in India by the Chinese military occupation of Tibet—events depicted in the popular film *Kundun* (meaning "The Presence").

Since then the Dalai Lama has conducted the Tibetan government-in-exile from Dharamsala, India, and—unlike many of his predecessors—traveled worldwide on diplomatic missions, in part aiming to preserve the integrity of the Tibetan national identity and cultural heritage. He proposed to the Congressional Human Rights Caucus in 1987 a Five-Point Peace Plan designed to ensure the integrity of Tibet: (1) designate Tibet as a zone of peace, (2) end the massive transfer of ethnic Chinese into Tibet, (3) restore to Tibet fundamental human rights and democratic freedoms, (4) abandon China's use of Tibet to produce nuclear weapons and as a dumping ground for nuclear waste, and (5) create a self-governing Tibet, in association with the People's Republic of China. The Tibetan people themselves, insists His Holiness, "must be the ultimate deciding authority." It was because of these "constructive and forward-looking proposals for the solution of international conflicts, human rights issues, and global environmental problems" that the 14th Dalai Lama was awarded the Nobel Peace Prize for 1989.

Inner Peace and Human Rights

P eace, in the sense of the absence of war, is of little value to someone who 1 is dying of hunger or cold. It will not remove the pain of torture inflicted on a prisoner of conscience. It does not comfort those who have lost their loved ones in floods caused by senseless deforestation in a neighbouring country. Peace can only last where human rights are respected, where the people are fed, and where individuals and nations are free. True peace with oneself and with the world around us can only be achieved through the development of mental peace. The other phenomena mentioned above are similarly interrelated. Thus, for example, we see that a clean environment, wealth or democracy mean little in the face of war, especially nuclear war, and that material development is not sufficient to ensure human happiness.

Material progress is of course important for human advancement. In 2 Tibet, we paid much too little attention to technological and economic development, and today we realise that this was a mistake. At the same time, material development without spiritual development can also cause serious problems. In some countries too much attention is paid to external things and very little importance is given to inner development. I believe both are important and must be developed side by side so as to achieve a good balance between them. Tibetans are always described by foreign visitors as being a happy, jovial people. This is part of our national character, formed by cultural and religious values that stress the importance of mental peace through the generation of love and kindness to all other living sentient beings, both human and animal. Inner peace is the key: if you have inner peace, the external problems do not affect your deep sense of peace and tranquility. In that state of mind you can deal with situations with calmness and reason, while keeping your inner happiness. That is very important. Without this inner peace, no matter how comfortable your life is materially, you may still be worried, disturbed or unhappy because of circumstances.

Clearly, it is of great importance, therefore, to understand the inter- 3 relationship among these and other phenomena, and to approach and attempt to solve problems in a balanced way that takes these different aspects into consideration. Of course it is not easy. But it is of little benefit to try to solve one problem if doing so creates an equally serious new one.

So really we have no alternative: we must develop a sense of universal responsibility not only in the geographic sense, but also in respect to the different issues that confront our planet.

4   Responsibility does not only lie with the leaders of our countries or with those who have been appointed or elected to do a particular job. It lies with each one of us individually. Peace, for example, starts with each one of us. When we have inner peace, we can be at peace with those around us. When our community is in a state of peace, it can share that peace with neighbouring communities, and so on. When we feel love and kindness towards others, it not only makes others feel loved and cared for, but it helps us also to develop inner happiness and peace. And there are ways in which we can consciously work to develop feelings of love and kindness. For some of us, the most effective way to do so is through religious practice. For others it may be non-religious practices. What is important is that we each make a sincere effort to take our responsibility for each other and for the natural environment we live in seriously.

5   I am very encouraged by the developments which are taking place around us. After the young people of many countries, particularly in northern Europe, have repeatedly called for an end to the dangerous destruction of the environment which was being conducted in the name of economic development, the world's political leaders are now starting to take meaningful steps to address this problem. The report to the United Nations Secretary-General by the World Commission on the Environment and Development (the Brundtland Report) was an important step in educating governments on the urgency of the issue. Serious efforts to bring peace to war-torn zones and to implement the right to self-determination of some people have resulted in the withdrawal of Soviet troops from Afghanistan and the establishment of independent Namibia. Through persistent nonviolent popular efforts dramatic changes, bringing many countries closer to real democracy, have occurred in many places, from Manila in the Philippines to Berlin in East Germany. With the Cold War era apparently drawing to a close, people everywhere live with renewed hope. Sadly, the courageous efforts of the Chinese people to bring similar change to their country was brutally crushed last June. But their efforts too are a source of hope. The military might has not extinguished the desire for freedom and the determination of the Chinese people to achieve it. I particularly admire the fact that these young people who have been taught that "power grows from the barrel of the gun," chose, instead, to use nonviolence as their weapon.

6   What these positive changes indicate, is that reason, courage, determination, and the inextinguishable desire for freedom can ultimately win. In the struggle between forces of war, violence and oppression on the one hand, and peace, reason and freedom on the other, the latter are gaining the upper hand. This realisation fills us Tibetans with hope that some day we too will once again be free.

The awarding of the Nobel Prize to me, a simple monk from faraway 7
Tibet, here in Norway, also fills us Tibetans with hope. It means, despite
the fact that we have not drawn attention to our plight by means of violence, we have not been forgotten. It also means that the values we cherish,
in particular our respect for all forms of life and the belief in the power of
truth, are today recognised and encouraged. It is also a tribute to my mentor, Mahatma Gandhi, whose example is an inspiration to so many of us.
This year's award is an indication that this sense of universal responsibility is developing. I am deeply touched by the sincere concern shown
by so many people in this part of the world for the suffering of the people
of Tibet. That is a source of hope not only for us Tibetans, but for all oppressed people.

As you know, Tibet has, for forty years, been under foreign occupa- 8
tion. Today, more than a quarter of a million Chinese troops are stationed
in Tibet. Some sources estimate the occupation army to be twice this
strength. During this time, Tibetans have been deprived of their most basic
human rights, including the right to life, movement, speech, worship, only
to mention a few. More than one sixth of Tibet's population of six million
died as a direct result of the Chinese invasion and occupation. Even before
the Cultural Revolution started, many of Tibet's monasteries, temples and
historic buildings were destroyed. Almost everything that remained was
destroyed during the Cultural Revolution. I do not wish to dwell on this
point, which is well documented. What is important to realise, however, is
that despite the limited freedom granted after 1979, to rebuild parts of
some monasteries and other such tokens of liberalisation, the fundamental
human rights of the Tibetan people are still today being systematically violated. In recent months this bad situation has become even worse.

If it were not for our community in exile, so generously sheltered and 9
supported by the government and people of India and helped by organisations and individuals from many parts of the world, our nation would
today be little more than a shattered remnant of a people. Our culture, religion and national identity would have been effectively eliminated. As it
is, we have built schools and monasteries in exile and have created democratic institutions to serve our people and preserve the seeds of our civili-
sation. With this experience, we intend to implement full democracy in a
future free Tibet. Thus, as we develop our community in exile on modern
lines, we also cherish and preserve our own identity and culture and bring
hope to millions of our countrymen and -women in Tibet.

The issue of most urgent concern at this time, is the massive influx 10
of Chinese settlers into Tibet. Although in the first decades of occupation
a considerable number of Chinese were transferred into the eastern parts
of Tibet—in the Tibetan provinces of Amdo (Chinghai) and Kham (most of
which has been annexed by neighboring Chinese provinces)—since 1983
an unprecedented number of Chinese have been encouraged by their government to migrate to all parts of Tibet, including central and western Tibet

(which the People's Republic of China refers to as the so-called Tibet Autonomous Region). Tibetans are rapidly being reduced to an insignificant minority in their own country. This development, which threatens the very survival of the Tibetan nation, its culture and spiritual heritage, can still be stopped and reversed. But this must be done now, before it is too late.

BETTY WILLIAMS

"The violent and intractable Irish problem," as the *Random House Encyclopedia* calls it, has dominated Irish politics, military policy, friendships, and home and civic life throughout much of modern Ireland's history, but particularly since the Easter uprising of April 24, 1916—a small armed insurrection of Catholics against British rule, with long-lasting political consequences. This led to partition of the island in 1922, establishing the largely Catholic Irish Free State in the South (capital, Dublin), while the Protestant loyalists to the British crown were to live largely in Northern Ireland, whose capital is Belfast. Yet the populations are mixed, and remain under continual tension. As in many other countries with a common culture and bitter religious divisions, the borders are porous; the inhabitants are suspicious of one another, if not possessed of downright hatred; they have enduring bitter memories and itchy trigger fingers. In the early 1970s the Catholic Provisional IRA (Irish Republican Army) began a series of guerilla terrorist attacks to prevent British troops stationed in Northern Ireland from concentrating on Catholic enclaves, with the ultimate aim of driving the British out and reunifying Ireland as a Catholic country.

The incident that provided the impetus for the formation of the movement of the Peace People, an ad hoc coalition of Catholic and Protestant women (and some men) in Northern Ireland, occurred in Belfast on August 10, 1976. In pursuit of a stolen car, driven by Danny Lennon, who may or may not have been a member of the Provisional IRA and who may or may not have fired on a patrol of the King's Own Border Regiment, the King's Own troops mortally wounded Lennon, whose runaway car killed two children on the spot, 8-year-old Joanna Maguire and her six-week-old baby brother Andrew. Their two-year-old brother died the next day.

Mairead Corrigan, their aunt, a Catholic secretary at the Guinness brewery, was interviewed on BBC-TV that evening in a widely rebroadcast commentary: "Only one percent of the people of this province want this slaughter," she said before breaking down in tears. Betty Williams, a Catholic housewife married to a Protestant, had witnessed the accident, and was moved to action by Corrigan's speech. Within forty-eight hours she had circulated a petition signed by 6,000 people, demanding that the Provisional IRA stop its military campaign. Williams and Corrigan met Ciaran McKeown, a young Catholic journalist, at the Maguire children's funeral; he provided organizational strategy to maintain the momentum of this interfaith peace movement. They effected sufficient rapprochement so that in December 1976 northern and southern Irish met on a historic bridge over the River Boyne to pledge an end to sectarian hatred at the spot where it had begun 300 years earlier.

The trio received the Nobel Peace Prize in 1976 for their grassroots efforts. Each of the recipients made an acceptance speech; space permits reprinting only part of one here. Unfortunately, the spirit of reconciliation has not prevailed. In 2001 Paul Connolly, a sociologist at the University of Ulster, commissioned by the Northern Ireland Community Relations Council, interviewed 352 Northern Irish Catholic and Protestant children between three and six years of age about their attitudes toward the political situation there. Here are their typical replies:

> Protestant children, when asked "What do you know about Catholics?"
>
> They rob.
>
> They're bad. They batter Almond drive people. Almond Drive—that's where I live.
>
> Catholics are different from ordinary human beings because they are badder.
>
> The police come after them. They make petrol bombs, get petrol at garages, throw them, and they blow up.
>
> Catholic children, when asked "What do you know about Protestants?"
>
> They want to kill all the Catholics.
>
> They're like Catholics. They do the same things only they're stronger.
>
> Protestants would take people hostage. The police give them their weapons and make a deal to get the hostages.
>
> Catholics don't like Protestants, and that's why they don't like them. They're bad.

The Movement of the Peace People

I feel humble in officially receiving the Nobel Peace Prize, because so many people have been involved in the campaign that drew such attention to our leadership that an award like this could justifiably be made. Mairead Corrigan and I may take some satisfaction with us all the days of our lives that we did make that initial call, a call which unlocked the massive desire for peace within the hearts of the Northern Irish people, and as we so soon discovered, in the hearts of people around the world. . . .

But unlocking the desire for peace would never have been enough. All the energy, all the determination to express an overwhelming demand for an end to the sickening cycle of useless violence would have reverberated briefly and despairingly among the people, as had happened so many times before . . . if we had not organized ourselves to use that energy and that determination positively, once and for all.

3   So in that first week Maircad Corrigan, Ciaran McKeown and I founded the Movement of the Peace People, in order to give real leadership and direction to the desire which we were certain was there, deep within the hearts of the vast majority of the people, . . . and even deep within the hearts of those who felt, perhaps still do, feel obliged, to oppose us in public.

4   We are for life and creation, and we are against war and destruction, and in our rage in that terrible week, we screamed that the violence had to stop.

5   But we also began to do something about it besides shouting. Ciaran McKeown wrote "The Declaration of the Peace People" which in its simple words pointed along the path of true peace, and with the publication of that Declaration, we announced the founding of the Movement of the Peace People, and we began planning a series of rallies which would last four months, and through which we would mobilize hundreds of thousands of people and challenge them to take the road of the Declaration.

6   The words are simple but the path is not easy, as all the people ever associated with the historic Nobel Peace Prize must know. It is a path on which we must not only reject the use of all the techniques of violence, but along which we must seek out the work of peace . . . and do it. It is the way of dedication, hard work and courage.

7   Hundreds of thousands of people turned out during those four months and we would not be standing here if they had not. So I feel humble that I should be receiving this award, but I am very proud to be here in the name of all the Peace People to accept it. . . .

8   And with that sense of history, we feel a special sense of honour . . . honour for women, perhaps a little specially at this time. War has traditionally been a man's work, although we know that often women were the cause of violence. But the voice of women, the voice of those most closely involved in bringing forth new life, has not always been listened to when it pleaded and implored against the waste of life in war after war. The voice of women has a special role and a special soul-force in the struggle for a non-violent world. We do not wish to replace religious sectarianism, or ideological division with sexism or any kind of militant feminism. But we do believe, as Ciaran McKeown who is with us in spirit, believes, that women have a leading role to play in this great struggle.

9   So we are honoured, in the name of all women, that women have been honoured especially for their part in leading a non-violent movement for a just and peaceful society. Compassion is more important than intellect, in calling forth the love that the work of peace needs, and intuition can often be a far more powerful searchlight than cold reason. We have to think, and think hard, but if we do not have compassion before we even start thinking, then we are quite likely to start fighting over theories. The

whole world is divided ideologically, and theologically, right and left, and men are prepared to fight over their ideological differences. Yet the whole human family can be united by compassion. And, as Ciaran said recently in Israel, "compassion recognizes human rights automatically . . . it does not need a charter."

Because of the role of women over so many centuries in so many dif- 10 ferent cultures, they have been excluded from what have been called public affairs; for that very reason they have concentrated much more on things close to home . . . and they have kept far more in touch with the true realities . . . the realities of giving birth and love. The moment has perhaps come in human history when, for very survival, those realities must be given pride of place over the vainglorious adventures that lead to war.

But we do not wish to see a division over this . . . merely a natural 11 and respectful and loving co-operation. Women and men together can make this a beautiful people's world, and that is why we called ourselves, "THE PEACE PEOPLE."

So, in humility at the efforts of so many people, I am proud to stand here on their behalf, and accept this honour on behalf of all of us.

But I am also angry. I am as angry today, in a calm and a deep sense 12 at the wastage of human life that continues each day, as I was when I saw young life squashed on a Belfast street.

I am angry, the Peace People are angry that war at home dribbles on, 13 and around the world we see the same stupidity gathering momentum for far worse wars than the little one which the little population of Northern Ireland, has had to endure. We are angry at the waste of resources that goes on every day for militarism while human beings live in misery and sometimes even live in the hope of a quick death to release them from their hopelessness. We rage as $500,000 are spent every minute of every day on war and the preparation for war; while in every one of those minutes human beings, more than 8 people, die of neglect. Every day 12,000 people die of neglect and malnutrition and misery; yet every day, $720 *million* are spent on armaments. Just think of those insane priorities. . . .

We know that this insane and immoral imbalance of priorities cannot 14 be changed overnight; we also know that it will not be changed without the greatest struggle, the incessant struggle to get the human race to stop wasting its vast resources on arms, and start investing in the people who must live out their lives on the planet we share, east and west, north and south. And that struggle must be all the greater because it has to be an unarmed, a non-violent struggle, and requires more courage and more persistence than the courage to squeeze triggers or press murderous buttons. Men must not only end war, they must begin to have the courage not even to prepare for war.

Someday we must take seriously the words of Carl Sandburg: "Some- 15 day there will be a war, and no one will come." Won't that be beautiful,

Someday there will be a "war" but no one will come. And of course, if no one comes there will be no war. And we don't have to go, we don't have to have war, but it seems to take more courage to say NO to war then to say YES, and perhaps we women have for too long encouraged the idea that it is brave and manly to go to war, often to "defend" women and children. Let women everywhere from this day on encourage men to have the courage not to turn up for war, not to work for a militarized world but a world of peace, a non-violent world.

16   To begin to have that kind of real courage, people must begin to breach the barriers which divide them. We are divided on the surface on this planet, by physical barriers, emotional barriers, ideological barriers, barriers of prejudice and hatreds of every kind. . . .

17 We as Peace People go much further: we believe in taking down the barriers, but we also believe in the most energetic reconciliation among peoples by getting them to know each other, talk each other's languages, understand each other's fears and beliefs, getting to know each other physically, philosophically and spiritually. It is much harder to kill your near neighbour than the thousands of unknown and hostile aliens at the other end of a nuclear missile. We have to create a world in which there are no unknown, hostile aliens at the other end of any missiles, and that is going to take a tremendous amount of sheer hard work.

For Discussion and Writing

Each of the following issues is complicated, for matters of war and peace are never simple, never static, particularly when negotiated in an international arena. Most can be seen not just from two points of view, but from many perspectives embedded in the political, economic, religious, ethical, and cultural values of a great variety of individuals, cultures, and countries. In discussing any of these topics, or others stimulated by your reading and thinking, you will find it helpful to talk with your peers and to consult reliable outside sources, perhaps beginning with one or two of those listed. You will be aiming to write papers informed by accurate information, terms clearly defined, that avoid blanket generalizations and simplistic conclusions.

Rather than trying to cover the gigantic issues embedded in the overall subject, pick a segment of the topic that is small enough to handle in a well-developed paper. The complex nature of the issues embedded in these subjects—terrorism, war, peace, national culture, values, justice, security, civil liberties, vengeance, social action, leadership—lends itself to group projects. Each participant could be assigned to research a specific segment of a larger issue and the results could be combined in a coauthored paper. It is advisable, even when discussing issues on which you feel strongly, to avoid either/or thinking, stereotyping, and incendiary language. It is appropriate, however, to build your case on accurate information, principle, and passion—the principles of communication—and of life—that have guided the Nobel Prize winners and established exemplary models for nations as well as individual citizens.

Because the events related to international terrorism as well as to world peace occur in a constantly changing world, you will need to update your information before discussing either the World Trade Center bombings of 1993 or 2001, or any other terroristic activities or their implications or consequences. The print sources identified in the following list are good places to start. Be aware that all of them, like any other source of information on any subject—especially one as incendiary as international terrorism—contain opinions and other interpretations of fact that support the author's point of view, just as your own writing does. As every reading in *The Essay Connection* illustrates, every author expresses biases; reliable authors also honor the obligation to be fair. Most of these sources on international terrorism, like the readings in the "Terrorism" chapter, are pro-Western, written by authors from the United States or Great Britain. The exception is *Orientalism*, Palestinian Edward Said's work that claims Western study of the Middle East is a means of reducing and dominating that culture through continuing the colonial oppression of the nineteenth and twentieth centuries. This pro-Western bias is why it is particularly necessary to balance these views with the views on peace from Nobel Prize winners throughout the world.

Atlantic Monthly continuing coverage. See July–November 2002, for example.
"The Fractured Landscape: Reflections on September 11, 2001 and Its After-
    math." *The Chronicle Review* (28 September 2001); see also "Reflections
    on Fractured Landscapes, Then and Now," *Chronicle Review* (Septem-
    ber 2002).
Gerecht, Reuel Marc. "The Gospel According to Osama Bin Laden," *Atlantic*
    (January 2002): 46–48.
Hazlitt, William. "On the Pleasure of Hating" (c. 1826). [widely reprinted
    or see **www.bluepete.com/Literature/Essays/Hazlitt/Hating.htm**]
Juergensmeyer, Mark. *Terror in the Mind of God: The Global Rise of Religious
    Violence.* Berkeley: U of California Press, 2000.
Lelyveld, Joseph. "All Suicide Bombers Are Not Alike." *New York Times
    Magazine* (28 October 2001): 49–53, 62, 78–79.
Lewis, Bernard. *The Middle East: A Brief History of the Last 2,000 Years.* New
    York: Scribner, 1996.
Lewis, Bernard. *What Went Wrong.* New York: Oxford, 2001.
Said, Edward. *Orientalism.* New York: Random House, 1979.
South Atlantic Quarterly (Spring 2002). See the entire issue.
Vollman, William T. "The Taliban," *New Yorker* (15 May 2000): 58–66.

Because much of your information will arrive via an Internet search,
it's important to conduct a search that is efficient, focused, and that yields
reliable results. The following principles should help.

How to Search for (and Recognize)
Good Sites on the Internet

1. Pick popular, reliable search engines (for example, Google, Yahoo, etc.).
2. Use terms appropriate to your search. If you want more hits, or more
    general information, use broad terms ("philosophy," "peace," "terror-
    ism"); if you want fewer hits, or more specific information, use more
    detail ("Western philosophy," "peace initiatives," "international ter-
    rorism"). Keep refining your terms: To "international terrorism" add
    a country, an event, a time span and so on, with more and more
    restrictions until your results are a manageable number and many of
    the entries are recent.
3. Be flexible: Try a couple of different search terms if you don't find
    what you're looking for the first time, or try your search in another
    search engine. Look through a couple of pages of results; don't just
    settle for the first dozen hits. Patience here will pay off in finding the
    best sites available.
4. Look for reliable sources: Anyone can put a page on the Internet, and
    sometimes bad or misleading information is not readily apparent.
    Look for organizations, companies, or names you recognize. Read
    Web addresses (URLs) carefully to ensure the accuracy of your sources

(a page might *look* like the Microsoft Web site, but check the address for **http://www.microsoft.com** to make sure). Look at the kind of information the site provides. The Web address should represent the actual source name, such as **www.nobel.se/peace/laureates** and date of the particular prizewinner. Exercise caution with an address you don't know; you may be able to check an unfamiliar name on another Internet source.

5. Use the best information you can find, and read it carefully and critically. Blatantly biased Web sites are often identifiable by their inflammatory language and distorted information. Like junk mail, such biased sources are relatively easy to identify. It's more difficult to recognize less blatant forms of bias in the guise of serious scholarship. Look for balance and fairness—in the choice of evidence and in the language in which it's presented. So in reading Internet sources, it's wise to be as skeptical as you would in reading your mail. Sources with an axe to grind send out verbal cues to the audience—weird or extreme language, unsupported claims, incendiary or insulting generalizations. Reader, beware!

These sites discuss international terrorism.

The International Policy Institute for Counter-Terrorism (Israel)
http://www.ict.org.il/
The Federation of American Scientists site
http://www.fas.org/index.html
http://www.fas.org/irp/threat/commission.html
http://www.fas.org/irp/threat/terror.htm
The Centre for Defence and International Security Studies (U.K.)
http://www.cdiss.org/terror.htm
U.S. Department of State's Response to Terrorism site
http://usinfo.state.gov/topical/pol/terror/
FEMA's Fact Sheet on terrorism
http://www.fema.gov/library/terrorf.htm
The UN page on terrorism
http://www.un.org/terrorism/

These sites discuss peace initiatives.

The UN page on peace and security
http://www.un.org/peace/
The United States Institute of Peace
http://www.usip.org/
Peace Brigades International (U.K.)
http://www.peacebrigades.org/
The Carnegie Endowment for International Peace
http://www.ceip.org/

Stockholm International Peace Research Institute
   http://www.sipri.se/
The Peace Corps
   http://www.peacecorps.gov/indexf.cfm
Volunteers for Peace
   http://www.vfp.org/

These are philosophy sites.

Western philosophy
   http://www.philosophypages.com/
Chinese philosophy
   http://uweb.superlink.net/~fsu/philo.html
This site, out of Hong Kong, deals with both Eastern and Western thought
   http://www.arts.cuhk.edu.hk/Philo.html

Ways to Think and Write About the Readings

1. Define *terrorism,* based on selected readings in the "Terrorism" and "World Peace" chapters and supplemented by your own under-standing of the term. Illustrate your definition with examples from these readings, noting where these conflict with and reinforce one an-other. Is terrorism a constant term or one that changes with changing interpretations of current events and past history? What are the major differences between *terror* and *terrorism?*

2. Provide an extended definition of *peace,* using examples from the speeches or lives of two or three of the Nobel Peace Prize recipients and supplemented by your own understanding of the term. Is *peace* a constant term or one that changes with changing interpretations of current events and past history? Why do war, imprisonment, tor-ture, genocide, segregation, and other forms of evil figure so promi-nently in the struggle to find and maintain peace?

3. Is world peace possible? Is long-term prosperity possible without peace? Will our quest involve nation with (or against) nation; culture with (or against) culture; technology, economy, or ideology with (or against) its counterpart?

4. What are—or should be—the highest priorities for our private life in the United States? Security? Freedom? Peace and prosperity? How do—or should—these coincide with our national priorities?

5. What changes will terrorist attacks, and the infinite possibilities of future terrorism—specific or vague—make in the ways we live our lives, plan for our futures, look at our neighbors, our friends, and our enemies?

6. What civil liberties are indispensable to life as guaranteed by the Constitution of the United States? What can we, as individuals and as a nation, do to balance the free and open nature of our hospitable society against needs for protection and security?

7. Is it possible for our country to act unilaterally in attaining any of its aims? To what extent do we live in a world in which the interests of all countries are intimately intertwined? Is is even possible for our country to consider autonomy, in light of its global business interests and dependence on foreign oil and a host of other products? You might pick a single area—medicine, automobiles, the Internet—and focus your answer on this.

8. How can we avoid dividing the world into "us" against "them," suspicion and paranoia, and nevertheless be on guard—but against what?

9. What qualities does it take to become a nationally or internationally distinguished leader? What can the rest of us learn from the experiences of the Nobel Peace Prize winners?

10. What would you personally be willing to sacrifice your time and freedom to attain? Would you lay down your life for a cause? If so, what is that cause, and why is it worth this degree of commitment?

11. Pick a historical document, either published (such as the Declaration of Independence) or unpublished. An unpublished document might be a photograph or letter your family may own that concerns an event that has passed into history, such as an invention (the atomic bomb, personal computers, a particular car), the Great Depression or other period of unemployment; or a war (the Civil War, World War I, World War II, the Korean War, the Vietnam War); or a major sporting or literary event; or the outcome of an election. Flesh out the meaning of the event through consulting family members involved in the document (either as its producers or subjects) and appropriate reference works and Web sites, on or off line. Then, write a paper explaining what you've come to understand about the event, using the document as the focal point of your discussion. (See Gilbert Highet's essay on the "Declaration of Independence," 486–91, for a very detailed model of this type of interpretation.)

12. Every one of us has been alive during one or more major historical events somewhere in our own state or country, as well as elsewhere in the world. These include discoveries, explorations, inventions, conflicts, and—with good fortune—resolutions of such conflicts. Perhaps you have been an eyewitness to such an event, or a participant in it, or affected by it—whether this is a manifestation of cloning, a discovery in outer space, the attack on the World Trade Center and the Pentagon of September 11, 2001, or a matter of more local concern. Sometimes the event seems highly significant when it happens; at

other times its full meaning becomes apparent only with the passage of time. In all cases, the event is subject to a myriad of interpretations, from many perspectives, which continue to change as time moves on. Either on your own, or with a partner or group, select a memorable event or phenomenon that has occurred during your lifetime and write an interpretation of its significance when it first happened, and its changing meaning(s) over time for different people (perhaps, those in your group of co-authors). If you were an eyewitness, how did you interpret the event at the time you experienced it? How has your understanding deepened and/or changed since that time?

Glossary

abstract refers to qualities, ideas, or states of being that exist but that our senses cannot perceive. What we perceive are the concrete by-products of abstract ideas. No single object or action can be labeled *love,* but a warm embrace or a passionate kiss is a visible, concrete token of the abstraction we call "love." In "Notes of a Native Speaker," Eric Liu, though Asian, characterizes his cultural self as "white" (410–20). In many instances abstract words such as *beauty, hatred, stupidity,* or *kindness* are more clearly understood if illustrated with **concrete** examples (*see* **concrete** and **general/specific**).

allusion is a writer's reference to a person, place, thing, literary character, or quotation that the reader is expected to recognize. Because the reader supplies the meaning and the original context, such references are economical; writers don't have to explain them. By alluding to a young man as a *Romeo, Don Juan,* or *Casanova,* a writer can present the subject's amorous nature without needing to say more. To make sure that references will be understood, writers have to choose what their readers can reasonably be expected to recognize.

analogy is a comparison made between two things, qualities, or ideas that have certain similarities although the items themselves may be very different. For example, Scott Russell Sanders characterizes his alcoholic father, "Like a torture victim who refuses to squeal, he would never admit that he had touched a drop, not even in his last year when he seemed to be dissolving in alcohol before our very eyes" ("Under the Influence," 274–86). The emphasis is on the similarities between Mr. Sanders, drunk or sober, and the torture victim; dissimilarities would have weakened the analogy. **Metaphors** and **similes** are two figures of speech that are based on analogies, and such comparisons are often used in argumentation (*see* **figures of speech** *and* **argumentation**).

argument, in a specialized literary sense, is a prose summary of the plot, main idea, or subject of a prose or poetic work. For *argumentation,* see introductions to the chapters "Appeal to Reason: Deductive and Inductive Arguments," "Appealing to Emotion and Ethics," and "Terrorism."

audience consists of the readers of a given writing. Writers may write some pieces solely for themselves; others for their peers, teachers, or supervisors; others for people with special interest in and knowledge of the subject. Writers aware of some of the following dimensions can adapt the level of their language and the details of their presentation to different sorts of readers. What is the age range of the intended readers? The educational level? Their national, regional, or local background? Have they relevant biases, beliefs? How much do they know about the subject? Why should they be interested in it or in the writer's views? Gertrude Stein once observed, "I write for myself and strangers." By answering some of the questions above, the writer can try to convert strangers into friends or, at least, into willing participants in the ongoing dialogue between writer and readers.

cliché is a commonplace expression that reveals the writer's lack of imagination to use fresher, more vivid language. If a person finds himself *between a rock and a hard place,* he might decide to use a cliché, *come hell or high water,* in hopes that it will hit his reader *like a ton of bricks*. Such expressions, though, *fall on deaf ears* and roll off the reader *like water off a duck's back*. A cliché is *as dead as a mackerel;* its excessive familiarity dulls the reader's responses. Avoid clichés *like the plague*.

coherence indicates an orderly relationship among the parts in a whole essay or other literary work. Writing is coherent when the interconnections among clauses, sentences, and paragraphs are clearly and logically related to the main subject under discussion. The writer may establish and maintain coherence through the use of transitional words or phrases (however; likewise), a consistent point of view, an ordered chronological or spatial presentation of information, appropriate pronoun references for nouns, or strategic repetition of important words or sentence structures.

colloquial expressions (*see* **diction**)

colloquialism (*see* **diction**)

conclusion refers to sentences, paragraphs, or longer sections of an essay that bring the work to a logical or psychologically satisfying end. Although a conclusion may (**a**) summarize or restate the essay's main point, and thereby refresh the reader's memory, it may also end with (**b**) the most important point, or (**c**) a memorable example, anecdote, or quotation, or (**d**) identify the broader implications or ultimate development of the subject, or (**e**) offer a prediction. Stylistically, it's best to end with a bang, not a whimper; Lincoln's "Gettysburg Address" (484–86) concludes with the impressive ". . . and that government of the people, by the people, for the people, shall not perish from the earth." A vigorous conclusion grows organically from the material that precedes it and is not simply tacked on to get the essay over with.

concrete terms give readers something specific to see, hear, touch, smell, or feel, while abstract terms are more general and intangible. Writers employ concrete words to show their subject or characters in action, rather than merely to tell about them. Yet a concrete word does not have to be hard, like cement; anything directly perceived by the senses is considered concrete, including an ostrich plume, the sound of a harp, a smile, or a cone of cotton candy (*see* **abstract** *and* **general/specific**).

connotation and denotation refer to two levels of interpreting the meanings of words. Denotation is the literal, explicit "core" meaning—the "dictionary" definition. Connotation refers to additional meanings implied or suggested by the word, or associated with it, depending on the user's or reader's personal experience, attitudes, and cultural conditioning. For example, the word *athlete* denotes a skilled participant in a sport. But to a sports enthusiast, *athlete* is likely to connote not just the phenomenon of one's participation in sports, but positive physical and moral qualities, such as robust physical condition, well-coordinated movements, a wholesome character, a love of the outdoors, and a concern with fair play. Those disenchanted with sports might regard an *athlete* as a marketable commodity for unscrupulous businessmen, an overpaid exploiter of the public, a drug user, or someone who has developed every part of his anatomy but his brain—a "dumb jock."

contrast (*see* **comparison/contrast**)

deduction (*see* **induction/deduction**)

deductive (*see* **induction/deduction**)

denotation (*see* **connotation/denotation**)

diction is word choice. Hemingway was talking about diction when he explained that the reason he allegedly rewrote the last page of *A Farewell to Arms* thirty-nine times was because of problems in "getting the words right." Getting the words right means choosing, arranging, and using words appropriate to the purpose, audience, and sometimes the form of a particular piece of writing. Puns are fine in limericks and shaggy-dog stories ("I wouldn't send a knight out on a dog like this"), but they're out of place in technical reports and obituaries. Diction ranges on a continuum from highly formal (a *repast*) to informal writing and conversation (a *meal*) to slang (*eats*), as illustrated below.

formal English words and grammatical constructions used by educated native speakers of English in sermons, oratory, and in many serious books, scientific reports, and lectures. *See* Abraham Lincoln, "The Gettysburg Address" (484–86).

informal (conversational or colloquial) *English* the more relaxed but still standard usage in polite (but not stuffy) conversation or writing, as in much popular newspaper writing and in many of the essays in this book. In informal writing it's all right to use contractions ("I'll go to the wedding, but I won't wear tails") and some abbreviations, but not all ("As Angela attached the IV bottle to the holder, she wondered whether the patient had OD'd on carbohydrates"). OK is generally acceptable in conversation, but it's not OK in most formal or informal writing.

slang highly informal (often figurative) word choice in speech or writing. It may be used by specialized groups (*pot, grass, uppers*) or more general speakers to add vividness and humor (often derogatory) to their language. Although some slang is old and sometimes even becomes respectable (*cab*), it often erupts quickly into the language and just as quickly disappears (*twenty-three skidoo*); it's better to avoid all slang than to use outmoded slang.

regionalisms expressions used by people of a certain region of the country, often derived from the native languages of earlier settlers, such as *arroyo* for *deep ditch* used in the Southwest.

dialect the spoken (and sometimes written) language of a group of people that reflects their social, educational, economic, and geographic status ("My mamma done tole me . . ."). Dialect may include regionalisms. In parts of the Northeast, *youse* is a dialect form of *you*, while its counterpart in the South is *y'all*. Even some educated Southerners say *ain't*, but they don't usually write it except to be humorous.

technical terms (jargon) words used by those in a particular trade, occupation, business, or specialized activity. For example, medical personnel use *stat* (immediately) and *NPO* (nothing by mouth); surfers' vocabularies include *shooting the curl, hotdogging,* and *hang ten; hardware* has different meanings for carpenters and computer users.

emphasis makes the most important ideas, characters, themes, or other elements stand out. The principal ways of achieving emphasis are through the use of the following:

proportion saying more about the major issues and less about the minor ones.

position   placing important material in the key spots, the beginning or ends of paragraphs or larger units. Arrangement in climactic order, with the main point of an argument or the funniest joke last, can be particularly effective.

repetition   of essential words, phrases, and ideas ("Ask not what your country can do for you; ask what you can do for your country.")

focus   pruning of verbal underbrush and unnecessary detail to accentuate the main features.

mechanical devices   such as capitalization, underlining (italics), and exclamation points, conveying enthusiasm, excitement, and emphasis, as advertisers and new journalists well know. Tom Wolfe's title *Las Vegas (What?) Las Vegas (Can't Hear You! Too Noisy) Las Vegas!!!!* illustrates this practice, as well as the fact that nothing exceeds like excess.

essay refers to a composition, usually or primarily nonfiction, on a central theme or subject, usually brief and written in prose. As the contents of this book reveal, essays come in varied modes—among them descriptive, narrative, analytic, argumentative—and moods, ranging from humorous to grim, whimsical to bitterly satiric. Essays are sometimes categorized as *formal* or *informal,* depending on the author's content, style, and organization. Formal essays, written in formal language, tend to focus on a single significant idea supported with evidence carefully chosen and arranged, such as Robert Reich's "The Global Elite" (461–71). Informal essays sometimes have a less obvious structure than formal essays; the subject may seem less significant, even ordinary; the manner of presentation casual, personal, or humorous. Yet these distinctions blur. Although E. B. White's "Once More to the Lake" (122–28) discusses a personal experience in conversation and humorous language, its apparently trivial subject, the vacation of a boy and his father in the Maine woods, takes on universal, existential significance.

evidence is supporting information that explains or proves a point. General comments or personal opinions that are not substantiated with evidence leave the reader wanting some proof of accuracy. Writers establish credibility by backing general statements with examples, facts, and figures that make evident their knowledge of the subject. We believe what Martin Luther King, Jr. says about racism and segregation in "Letter from Birmingham Jail" (445–61) because his specific examples show that he has experienced these events and has understood their context and implications.

exposition is a mode of discourse that, as its name indicates, exposes information, through explaining, defining, or interpreting its subject. Expository prose is to the realm of writing what the Ford automobile has been historically to the auto industry—useful, versatile, accessible to the average person, and heavy duty—for it is the mode of the most research reports, critical analyses, examination answers, case histories, reviews, and term papers. In exposition, writers employ a variety of techniques, such as definition, illustration, classification, comparison and contrast, analogy, and cause-and-effect reasoning. Exposition is not an exclusive mode; it is often blended with **argumentation, description,** and **narration** to provide a more complete or convincing discussion of a subject.

figures of speech are used by writers who want to make their subject unique or memorable through vivid language. Literal language often lacks the connotations of figurative language. Instead of merely conveying information ("The car was messy"), a writer might use a figure of speech to attract attention ("The car was a Dumpster on wheels"). Figures of speech enable the writer to play with words and with the reader's imagination. Some of the most frequently used figures of speech include the following:

metaphor   an implied comparison that equates two things or qualities. "No dictionary of synonyms for **drunk** would soften the anguish of watching our prince turn into a frog" (Scott Russell Sanders).

simile   a direct comparison; usually with the connecting word *like* or *as*. ". . . inside [the sawed board] there was this smell waiting, as of something freshly baked" (Scott Russell Sanders).

personification   humanization of inanimate or nonhuman objects or qualities, as in giving a car, a boat, or a plane a person's name.

hyperbole   an elaborate exaggeration, often intended to be humorous or ironic. "When I was younger I could remember anything, whether it had happened or not; but my faculties are decaying now, and soon I shall be so I cannot remember any but the things that never happened" (Mark Twain).

understatement   a deliberate downplaying of the seriousness of something. As with the *hyperbole*, the antithesis of understatement, this is often done for the sake of humor or irony. [My "Modest Proposal"] is "innocent, cheap, easy, effectual" (Jonathan Swift).

paradox   a contradiction that upon closer inspection is actually truthful. ("You never know what you've got until you lose it.")

rhetorical question   a question that demands no answer, asked for dramatic impact. In "Letter from Birmingham Jail" (445–61) Martin Luther King, Jr. asks, "Will we be extremists for hate or for love? Will we be extremists for the preservation of injustice or for the extension of justice?"

metonomy   the representation of an object, public office, or concept by something associated with it. ("Watergate brought down the White House, as Woodward and Bernstein explain in *All the President's Men*.")

dead metaphor   a word or phrase, originally a figure of speech, that through constant use is treated literally (the *arm* of a chair, the *leg* of a table, the *head* of a bed).

focus represents the writer's control and limitation of a subject to a specific aspect or set of features, determined in part by the subject under discussion (*what* the writer is writing about), the audience (to *whom* the writer is writing), and the purpose (*why* the writer is writing). Thus, instead of writing about food in general, someone writing for college students on limited budgets might focus on imaginative but economical meals.

general and specific are the ends of a continuum that designates the relative degree of abstractness or concreteness of a word. General terms identify the class (*house*); specific terms restrict the class by naming its members (a *Georgian* *mansion,* a *Dutch colonial,* a *brick ranch).* To clarify relationships, words may be arranged in a series from general to specific: writers, twentieth-century authors, Southern novelists, Eudora Welty (*see* **abstract** *and* **concrete**).

generalization (*see* **induction/deduction** *and* **logical fallacies**)

hyperbole (*see* **figures of speech**). *See* Judy Brady, "I Want a Wife" (361–64).

induction and deduction refer to two different methods of arriving at a conclusion. Inductive reasoning relies on examining specific instances, examples, or facts in an effort to arrive at a general conclusion. If you were to sample several cakes—chocolate, walnut, mocha, and pineapple upside-down—you might reach the general conclusion that all cakes are sweet. Conversely, deductive reasoning involves examining general principles in order to arrive at a specific conclusion. If you believe that all cakes are sweet, you would expect the next cake you encounter, say, lemon chiffon, to be sweet. Yet both of these types of reasoning can lead to erroneous generalizations if the reasoner or writer has not examined all of the relevant aspects of the issue. For instance, not all cakes are sweet—consider the biscuit cake in strawberry shortcake. Likewise, even if a writer cited five separate instances in which members of a particular ethnic group displayed criminal behavior, it would be incorrect to conclude that all members of this group are criminal. Beware, therefore, of using absolute words such as *always, never, everyone, no one, only,* and *none. See* the chapter "Appeal to Reason: Deductive and Inductive Arguments," introduction (435–40).

inductive (*see* **induction/deduction**)

introduction is the beginning of a written work that is likely to present the author's subject, focus (perhaps including the thesis), attitude toward it, and possibly the plan for organizing supporting materials. The length of the introduction is usually proportionate to the length of what follows; short essays may be introduced by a sentence or two; a book may require an entire introductory chapter. In any case, an introduction should be sufficiently forceful and interesting to let readers know what is to be discussed and entice them to continue reading. An effective introduction might do one or more of the following:

1. state the thesis or topic emphatically;
2. present a controversial or startling focus on the topic;
3. offer a witty or dramatic quotation, statement, metaphor, or analogy;
4. provide background information to help readers understand the subject, its history, or significance;
5. give a compelling anecdote or illustration from real life;
6. refer to an authority on the subject.

irony is a technique that enables the writer to say one thing while meaning another, often with critical intention. Three types of irony are frequently used by writers: *verbal, dramatic,* and *situational.* Verbal irony is expressed with tongue in cheek, often implying the opposite of what is overtly stated. The verbal ironist maintains tight control over tone, counting on the alert reader (or listener) to recognize the discrepancy between words and meaning, as does Jonathan Swift in "A Modest Proposal" (491–99), where deadpan advocacy of cannibalism is really a monstrous proposal. Dramatic irony, found in plays, novels, and other forms of fiction, allows readers to see the wisdom or folly of characters' actions in light of information they have—the ace up their sleeve—that the characters lack. For example, readers know Desdemona is innocent of cheating on her husband, Othello, but his ignorance of the truth and of the behavior of virtuous women leads him to murder her in a jealous rage. Situational irony, life's joke on life, entails opposition between what would ordinarily occur and what actually happens in a particular instance. In O. Henry's "The Gift of the Magi," the husband sells his watch to buy his wife combs for her hair, only to find out she has sold her hair to buy him a watch chain.

jargon (*see* **diction**)

logical fallacies are errors in reasoning and often occur in arguments. *See* the chapter "Appeal to Reason: Deductive and Inductive Arguments," introduction (435–40).

metaphor (*see* **figures of speech**)

metonomy (*see* **figures of speech**)

modes of discourse are traditionally identified as narration, description, argumentation, and exposition. In writing they are often intermingled. The *narration* of Frederick Douglass's "Resurrection" (133–38), for instance, involves *description of characters* and settings, an explanation (*exposition*) of their motives, while the expression of its theme serves as an *argument*, direct and indirect. Through its characters, actions, and situations it argues powerfully against slavery.

nonfiction is writing based on fact but shaped by the writer's interpretations, point of view, style, and other literary techniques. Nonfiction writings in essay or book form include interviews, portraits, biographies and autobiographies, travel writings, direct arguments, implied arguments in the form of narratives or satires, investigative reporting, reviews, literary criticism, sports articles, historical accounts, how-to instructions, and scientific and technical reports, among other types. These vary greatly in purpose (to inform, argue, entertain . . .), form, length (from a paragraph to multiple volumes), intended audience (from general readers to specialists), mood (somber to joyous, straightforward to parody), and techniques, including those of fiction—scene setting, characterization, dialogue, and so forth. *The Essay Connection* gives examples of most of these.

non sequitur a conclusion that does not follow logically from the premises. In humorous writing, the *non sequitur* conclusion is illogical, unexpected, and perhaps ridiculous: the resulting surprise startles readers into laughter—as when George Bernard Shaw's Eliza Dolittle says, upon devouring a chocolate, "I wouldn't have eaten it, but I'm too ladylike to take it out of my mouth."

objective refers to the writer's presentation of material in a personally detached, unemotional way that emphasizes the topic, rather than the author's attitudes or feelings about it as would be the case in a **subjective** presentation. Some process analyses, such as many computer instruction manuals, are written objectively. Many other process writings combine objective information with the author's personal, and somewhat subjective, views on how to do it (*see* the chapter "Process Analysis"). The more heavily emotional the writing, the more subjective it is.

oxymoron a contradiction in terms, such as "study date" or "airline food." Thus Judy Brady might consider a liberated housewife (see "I Want a Wife," 361–64) an oxymoron.

paradox (*see* **figures of speech**)

paragraph has a number of functions. Newspaper paragraphs, which are usually short and consist of a sentence or two, serve as punctuation—visual units to break up columns for ease of reading. A paragraph in most other prose is usually a single unified group of sentences that explain or illustrate a central idea, whether expressed overtly in a topic sentence, or merely implied. Paragraphs emphasize ideas; each new topic (or sometimes each important subtopic) demands a new paragraph. Short (sometimes even one-sentence) paragraphs can provide transitions from one major area of discussion to another, or indicate a change of speakers in dialogue.

parallelism is the arrangement of two or more equally important ideas in similar grammatical form ("I came, I saw, I conquered"). Not only is it an effective method of presenting more than one thought at a time, it also makes reading more understandable and memorable for the reader because of the almost rhythmic quality it produces. Within a sentence parallel structure can exist between words that are paired ("All work and no play made Jack a candidate for cardiac arrest"), items in a series ("His world revolved around debits, credits, cash flows, and profits"), phrases ("Reading books, preparing reports, and dictating interoffice memos—these were a few of his favorite things"), and clauses ("Most people work only to live; Jack lived only to work"). Parallelism can also be established between sentences in a paragraph and between paragraphs in a longer composition, often through the repetition of key words and phrases, as Lincoln does throughout the Gettysburg Address (484–86).

parallel structure (*see* **parallelism**)

paraphrase is putting someone else's ideas—usually the essential points or illustrations—into your own words, for your own purposes. Although a summary condenses the original material, a paraphrase is a restatement that may be short or as long as the original, even longer. Students writing research papers frequently find that paraphrasing information from their sources eliminates excessive lengthy quotations, and may clarify the originals. Be sure to acknowledge the source of either quoted or paraphrased material to avoid plagiarism.

parody exaggerates the subject matter, philosophy, characters, language, style, or other features of a given author or particular work. Such imitation calls attention to both versions; such scrutiny may show the original to be a masterpiece—or to be in need of improvement. Parody derives much of its humor from the double vision of the subject that writer and readers share, as in Ann Upperco Dolman's "Learning to Drive" (146–50).

person is a grammatical distinction made between the speaker (first person—*I, we*), the one spoken to (second person—*you*), and the one spoken about (third person—*he, she, it, they*). In an essay or fictional work the point of view is often identified by person. Eric Liu's "Notes of a Native Speaker" (410–20) is written in the first person, while Gilbert Highet's "The Gettysburg Address" (486–91) is a third-person work (*see* **point of view**).

persona, literally a "mask," is a fictitious mouthpiece or an alter ego character devised by a writer for the purpose of telling a story or making comments that may or may not reflect the author's feelings and attitudes. The persona may be a narrator, as in Swift's "A Modest Proposal" (491–99), whose ostensibly humanitarian perspective advocates cannibalism and regards the poor as objects to be exploited. Swift as author emphatically rejects these views. In such cases the persona functions as a disguise for the highly critical author.

personification (*see* **figures of speech**)

plot is the cause-and-effect relationship between events that tell a story. Unlike narration, which is an ordering of events as they occur, a plot is a writer's plan for showing how the occurrence of these events actually brings about a certain effect. The plot lets the reader see how actions and events are integral parts of something much larger than themselves.

point of view refers to the position—physical, mental, numerical—a writer takes when presenting information (*point*), and his attitude toward the subject (*view*). A writer sometimes adopts a point of view described as "limited," which restricts the inclusion of thoughts other than the narrator's, as Scott Russell Sanders does in "Under the Influence" (274–86). Conversely, the "omniscient" point of view allows the writer to know, see, and tell everything, not only about himself, but about others as well, as Isaac Asimov does in "Those Crazy Ideas" (158–67).

prewriting is a writer's term for thinking about and planning what to say before the pen hits the legal pad. Reading, observing, reminiscing, and fantasizing can all be prewriting activities if they lead to writing something down. The most flexible stage in the writing process, prewriting enables writers to mentally formulate, compose, edit, and discard before they begin the physical act of putting words on paper. Peter Elbow discusses this in *Writing Without Teachers*.

purpose identifies the author's reasons for writing. The purposes of a writing are many and varied. One can write to *clarify an issue for oneself*, or to *obtain self-understanding* ("Why I Like to Eat"). One can write to *tell a story*, to *narrate* ("My 1000-Pound Weight Loss"), or to *analyze a process* ("How to Make Quadruple Chocolate Cake"). Writing can explain *cause and effect* ("Obesity and Heart Attacks: The Fatal Connection"); it can *describe* ("The Perfect Meal"), *define* ("Calories"), *divide and classify* ("Fast Food, Slow Food, and Food That Just Sits There"). Writing can *illustrate* through examples ("McDonald's as a Symbol of American Culture"), and it can *compare and contrast* people, things, or ideas. Writing can *argue, deductively* or *inductively* ("Processed Foods Are Packaged Problems"), sometimes appealing more to emotions than to reason ("Anorexia! Beware!"). Writing can also provide *entertainment*, sometimes through parody or satire.

revise to revise is to make changes in focus, accommodation of audience, structure or organization, emphasis, development, style, mechanics, and spelling in order to bring the written work closer to one's ideal. For most writers, revising is the essence of writing. Donald M. Murray discusses the revising process in "The Maker's Eye" (88–97); the chapter "Writing: Re-Vision and Revision" also includes original drafts and revisions of writing by Mary Ruffin for "Mama's Smoke" (107–15).

rhetoric, the art of using language effectively to serve the writer's purpose, originally referred to speech-making. Rhetoric now encompasses composition; its expanded definition includes a host of dynamic relationships between writer (or speaker), text (or message), and readers (or hearers). The information in this book is divided into rhetorical modes, such as exposition, narration, description, and argumentation.

rhetorical question (*see* **figures of speech**)

satire is humorous, witty criticism of people's foolish, thoughtless, or evil behavior. The satirist ridicules some aspect of human nature—or life in general—that should be changed. Depending on the subject and the severity of the author's attack, a satire can be mildly abrasive or ironic, as in David Foster Wallace's "Lunchtime at the Illinois State Fair" (69–74), or viciously scathing, as is Swift in "A Modest Proposal" (491–99). Usually (although not always) the satirist seeks to bring about reform through criticism.

sentence, grammatically defined, is an independent clause containing a subject and verb, and may also include modifiers and related words. *Sentence structure* is another name for *syntax*, the arrangement of individual words in a sentence that shows their relationship to each other. Besides word choice (*diction*), writers pay special attention to the way their chosen words are arranged to form clauses, phrases, entire sentences. A *thesis sentence* (or *statement*) is the main idea in a written work that reflects the author's purpose. Some writings, notably parodies and satires, only imply a thesis; direct arguments frequently provide an explicitly stated thesis, usually near the beginning, and organize subsequent paragraphs around this central thought. A *topic sentence* clearly reflects the major idea and unifying thought of a given paragraph. When it is placed near the beginning of a paragraph, a topic sentence provides the basis for other sentences in the paragraph. When the topic sentence comes at the end of a paragraph or essay, it may function as the conclusion of a logical argument, or the climax of an escalating emotional progression.

simile (*see* **figures of speech**)

slang (*see* **diction**)

specific (*see* **general/specific**)

style, the manner in which a writer says what he wants to say, as the result of the author's *diction* (word choice) and *syntax* (sentence structure), *arrangement of ideas, emphasis,* and *focus.* It is also a reflection of the author's *voice* (personality). Although Ntozake Shange, "What Is It We Really Harvestin' Here? (184–91); Amy Jo Keifer, "The Death of a Farm" (475–77); and Matt Nocton, "Harvest of Gold, Harvest of Shame" (515–21) all describe farming, the writers' styles differ considerably.

subjective (*see* **objective**)

summary (*see* **paraphrase**)

symbol refers to a person, place, thing, idea, or action that represents something other than itself. In Maxine Hong Kingston's "On Discovery" (101–03), the man painfully transformed into a woman symbolizes the denigrated status of all Chinese women.

tone the author's attitude toward a subject being discussed can be serious (Tannen's "Technologically Enhanced Aggression" [304–14]), critical (Kozol's "The Human Cost of an Illiterate Society" [210–18]), or loving (Mary Ruffin's "Mama's Smoke" [107–15]) among many possibilities. Tone lets readers know how they are expected to react to what the writer is saying.

topic sentence (*see* **sentence**)

transition is the writer's ability to move the reader smoothly along the course of ideas. Abrupt changes in topics confuse the reader, but transitional words and phrases help tie ideas together. Stylistically, transition serves another purpose by adding fullness and body to otherwise short, choppy sentences and paragraphs. Writers use transition to show how ideas, things, and events are arranged chronologically (*first, next, after, finally*), spatially (*here, there, next to, behind*), comparatively (*like, just as, similar to*), causally (*thus, because, therefore*), and in opposition to each other (*unlike, but, contrary to*). Pronouns, connectives, repetition, and parallel sentence structure are other transitional vehicles that move the reader along.

understatement (*see* **figures of speech**)

voice refers to the extent to which the writer's personality is expressed in his or her work. In *personal voice,* the writer is on fairly intimate terms with the audience, referring to herself as "I" and the readers as "you." In *impersonal voice,* the writer may refer to himself as "one" or "we," or try to eliminate personal pronouns when possible. Formal writings, such as speeches, research papers, and sermons, are more likely to use an impersonal voice than are more informal writings, such as personal essays. In grammar, *voice* refers to the form of a verb: *active* ("I *mastered* the word processor") or *passive* ("The word processor *was mastered* by me").

Credits

Text Credits

NATALIE ANGIER, "Why Men Don't Last: Self-Destruction as a Way of Life," *New York Times*, 2/17/99. Copyright © 1999 Natalie Angier. Used by permission.

KOFI ANNAN, "The United Nations in the 21st Century" from Nobel Prize Speech 2001. Copyright © The Nobel Foundation.

YASSIR ARAFAT, "The Crescent Moon of Peace" from Nobel Prize Speech 1994. Copyright © The Nobel Foundation.

GELAREH ASAYESH, "Shrouded in Contradiction." Reprinted by permission of International Creative Management, Inc. Copyright © 2001 by Gelareh Asayesh. First appeared in the *New York Times Magazine*, 11/2/01, p. 100.

ISAAC ASIMOV, "Those Crazy Ideas," copyright © 1959 by Mercury Press from *Fact and Fancy* by Isaac Asimov. Used by permission of Doubleday, a division of Random House, Inc.

LYNDA BARRY, "The Sanctuary of School," from *New York Times*, January 5, 1992. Copyright © 1992 by Lynda Barry. Reprinted by permission of the author.

WENDELL BERRY, "Thoughts in the Presence of Fear," *South Atlantic Quarterly*, Vol. 101, No. 2, Spring 2002, pp. 279–284. Copyright © 2002 Wendell Berry. Originally appeared on OrionOnline.org as "Thoughts on America Series" and was published subsequently in the book, *In the Presence of Fear: Three Essays for a Changed World* (December 2001), The Orion Society. Reprinted by permission.

JUDY BRADY, "I Want a Wife." Originally published in *Ms.* Magazine. Copyright © 1970 by Judy Brady. Reprinted by permission of the author.

STEWART BRAND, "Written on the Wind" from *Civilization*, Oct/Nov 1998, pp. 70–72. Reprinted by permission of the author.

DAVID CARR, "The Futility of 'Homeland Defense'" from *Atlantic Monthly*, Jan 2002, pp. 53–55. Copyright © 2002 David Carr. Reprinted by permission.

JIMMY CARTER, from Nobel Prize Speech 2002. Copyright © The Nobel Foundation.

STEPHANIE COONTZ, "Blaming the Family for Economic Decline" from *The Way We Really Are*. Copyright © 1997 Basic Books, A Division of HarperCollins Publishers Inc. Reprinted by permission of Basic Books, a member of Perseus Books, L.L.C.

THE 14TH DALAI LAMA, TENZIN GYATSO, "Inner Peace and Human Rights" from Nobel Prize Speech 1989. Copyright © The Nobel Foundation.

FREDERIK WILLEM DE KLERK, "Reformation and Reconciliation in South Africa" from Nobel Prize Speech 1993. Copyright © The Nobel Foundation.

PAUL DE PALMA, "http://www.when_is_ enough_enough?.com" from *The American Scholar*, Winter 1999, pp. 61–72. Copyright © 1999 by Paul De Palma. Reprinted by permission.

LOUISE ERDRICH, "Leap Day, the Baby-sitter, Dream, Walking" from *The Blue Jay's Dance* by Louise Erdrich. Copyright © 1995 by Louise Erdrich. Reprinted by permission of HarperCollins Publishers, Inc.

ELIE WIESEL, "Why I Write: Making No Become Yes." Copyright © 1985 by Elirion Associates. Reprinted by permission Georges Borchardt, Inc. Originally appeared in *The New York Times Book Review,* 4/14/85.
BETTY WILLIAMS, "The Movement of the Peace People" from Nobel Prize Speech 1976. Copyright © The Nobel Foundation.
CHARLES M. YOUNG, "Losing: An American Tradition" from *Men's Journal,* 2000. Copyright © 2000. Reprinted by permission.
NING YU, "Red and Black or One English Major's Beginning." Reprinted by permission of the author.
ZITKALA-SA from "The School Days of an Indian Girl," *Atlantic Monthly,* February 1900. Copyright 1900 Atlantic Monthly.

Photo and Cartoon Credits

p. 1: © Royalty-Free/CORBIS.
p. 19: © Bill Ross/CORBIS.
p. 27: © Owen Franken/CORBIS.
p. 31: Drawing by Twohy © 2001 The New Yorker Magazine, Inc. Reprinted by permission of cartoonbank.com.
p. 44: © CORBIS.
p. 71: © Phil Schermeister/CORBIS.
p. 84: © Ed Bock/CORBIS.
p. 96: Reprinted by permission of United Features Syndicate, Inc.
p. 106: © George Shelley/CORBIS.
p. 117: © Randy Wells/CORBIS.
p. 129: © AP/The Wenatchee World/Wide World.
p. 135: © CORBIS.
p. 148: © Ariel Skelley/CORBIS.
p. 153: © Bojan Brecelj/CORBIS.
p. 172: © Mug Shots/CORBIS.
p. 195: © Stephanie Maze/CORBIS.
p. 205: © David Turnley/CORBIS.
p. 221: © CORBIS.
p. 228: © CORBIS.
p. 247: © CORBIS.
p. 256: © Dave G. Houser/CORBIS.
p. 269: © Derrick A. Bruce/CORBIS.
p. 281: © AP/Wide World.
p. 295: © Ted Streshinsky/CORBIS.
p. 309: © Larry Williams/CORBIS.
p. 329: © Reuters NewMedia Inc./CORBIS.
p. 337: © Michael Keller/CORBIS.
p. 346: © Peter Johnson/CORBIS.
p. 380: © ER Productions/CORBIS.
p. 386: © John Henley/CORBIS.
p. 406: © AP/Wide World.
p. 412: © Jose Luis Pelaez, Inc./CORBIS.

Index of Authors

❀ *Student writings.*